PENGUIN CLASSICS

THE HISTORY OF ENGLAND

LORD MACAULAY

Hugh Trevor-Roper has been Regius Professor of Modern History at Oxford since 1957. He published his first book, *Archbishop Laud*, in 1940; in 1947 he published *The Last Days of Hitler*, an immediate best-seller. In 1957 his *Historical Essays* were published, and in 1964 he edited a series of essays collected in honour of Sir Keith Feiling on his eightieth birthday. His more recent publications include *Religion, the Reformation and Social Change* (1967), *The Philby Affair* (1968), *The European Witch-Craze of the 16th and 17th Centuries* (1970), *The Plunder of the Arts in the Seventeenth Century* (1970), *Princes and Artists* (1976) and *Hermit of Peking: The Hidden Life of Sir Edmund Backhouse* (1976, originally published as *A Hidden Life*).

LORD MACAULAY

The History of England

EDITED AND ABRIDGED
WITH AN INTRODUCTION BY
HUGH TREVOR-ROPER

PENGUIN BOOKS

Penguin Books Ltd, Harmondsworth,
Middlesex, England
Penguin Books, 40 West 23rd Street,
New York, New York 10010, U.S.A.
Penguin Books Australia Ltd, Ringwood,
Victoria, Australia
Penguin Books Canada Limited, 2801 John Street,
Markham, Ontario, Canada L3R 1B4
Penguin Books (N.Z.) Ltd, 182–190 Wairau Road,
Auckland 10, New Zealand

First published 1848–1861
This selection first published in the United States of America
by the Washington Square Press 1968
Published in the Penguin English Library 1979
Reprinted 1980, 1982, 1983

Reprinted in Penguin Classics 1986

Printed in the United States of America by
Offset Paperback Mfrs., Inc., Dallas, Pennsylvania
Set in Monotype Ehrhardt

Contents

Lord Macaulay: Introduction

WHIG HISTORY

LORD MACAULAY is unquestionably the greatest of the 'whig historians'. By the clarifying brilliance of his style, and his compelling gift of narrative, he won an instant and apparently effortless success in the nineteenth century. The interpretation of English history which he gave became the standard interpretation for nearly a century: so universally accepted that we hardly realize the novelty which it once contained. Admittedly, that interpretation has now become unfashionable. But it can never be altogether rejected. Much of it – both in factual scholarship and in general interpretation – has become part of the permanent acquisition of historical science. The severest critics themselves are generally unaware of the extent to which they depend on the achievement of their victim. In order to appreciate that debt, it will be useful to begin by considering the interpretation of English history before Macaulay stamped it, indelibly, with his imprint.

For 'whig history' is essentially English. In its crudest form it is the interpretation imposed on the English past by an English political party in search, at the same time, of both a historical pedigree and a political justification. This is not to deny that the thesis may also be true, or that it may also be applicable to other countries. In fact, the whig theory of history has foreign as well as English origins. It owes much to the French Huguenots and even more (including the name 'whig') to the Scots. There are Continental historians – the French Protestant statesman-historian F. P. G. Guizot is an obvious example – who can be described as 'whigs'. But it is in England that the continuous 'whig' party was developed and in England that the consistent whig theory of history was elaborated. It was also to English history that it was most naturally applied. A 'whig' interpretation of Europe is conceivable; but it could never be expressed with Macaulay's brilliant clarity. The pattern would not admit the simple antitheses which are possible, and perhaps justified, in the special English circumstances. Macaulay himself was well aware of this. He was, he once wrote, 'as much puzzled as pleased' by the success of his *History* abroad, 'for the book is quite insular in spirit. There is nothing cosmopolitan about it.'

Whig history, then, is insular history. It is also Protestant history. Indeed, its Protestantism is inseparable, in origin, from its insularity: for it was the revolt from Rome, in the sixteenth century, which caused historians – not only in England or Scotland – to look for a national history, independent of that universal Roman Church which had been served and extolled by the monkish chroniclers of the past. But these earliest national, Protestant historians, if they had dissociated the history of their countries from foreign 'despotism', had not, at that time, supplied it with any secular ideology. If they were Protestant, they were not yet republican or 'whig'. In some countries they might be. In France, for instance, the Huguenot writers soon discovered that national Protestantism could only be secured in opposition to the Valois monarchy; and so, after the Massacre of St Bartholomew in 1572, they discovered that the ancient constitution of France was not monarchical but oligarchical. The same discovery was made in Scotland, after the deposition of Mary Queen of Scots. Buchanan's *History of Scotland* (1582), like Hotman's *Franco-Gallia* (1573), seeks to justify aristocratic revolt against monarchy by appeal to an ancient 'Protestant' tradition, and for this reason both would be reprinted by the English whigs of the seventeenth century. But in Elizabethan England the new national Protestant historiography had no reason to be anti-monarchical. Far from it. Since the Protestant Revolution had been made and was preserved by English sovereigns, not against them, its historians looked back and saw the national Protestant tradition maintained by the English monarchy. While Hotman and Buchanan cried up the 'whig grandees' of ancient France or legendary Scotland, the hero of their English colleagues was not the English baronage, who extorted *Magna Carta* from King John, but King John himself.

In view of the bad name which King John would acquire among the later whigs, this may seem ironical. But we must remember that King John stood up (for a time) against the most imperious of medieval Popes. He was thus a precursor of those other 'despotic' but national Protestant monarchs, Henry VIII and Queen Elizabeth.

That was all very well in Tudor times. But when the Stuarts came from Scotland to rule over England, the terms of the formula soon changed. In seventeenth-century England, as in sixteenth-century France and Scotland, the national Protestants found themselves in opposition to the Crown. So, when they looked back into history, they discovered that the English, like the French and Scottish, constitution had always been essentially aristocratic. It was a monarchy, but a 'mixed monarchy'. Sir Edward Coke, the great champion of the English common law, discovered a continuous parliamentary constitution going back to the ancient Britons. More cautious antiquaries were prepared to settle for the Anglo-Saxons. In the course of the seventeenth century, while the English parliamentary classes fought, with differing weapons, against successive Stuart kings, their antiquaries built up a historical 'myth' according to which the English monarchy had always been implicitly contractual. Even the rude fact of the Norman Conquest had not interrupted this good old Anglo-Saxon tradition, for William the Conqueror (they said) had accepted and perpetuated the existing constitution. And this constitution had been preserved intact ever since. It had been guaranteed by the Common Law, strengthened by *Magna Carta*, guarded by Parliament; and those kings who had sought to break the contract had found themselves resisted, even deposed. Such had been the fate of Edward II in 1327, of Richard II in 1399; such would be the fate of Charles I in 1649, of James II in 1688. Of the 'Tudor despotism' of the sixteenth century, these historical theorists did not find it convenient to speak.

All through the seventeenth century this 'whig' theory of the ancient contractual constitution of England was improved by antiquarian research, political struggle, and philosophical speculation. Royalists, high Anglicans, 'tories' resisted it on all fronts;

but they resisted in vain. The 'Glorious Revolution' of 1688, followed by the Hanoverian succession in 1715, inaugurated the period known in English history as 'the whig ascendancy': the triumph of the whigs in politics, in philosophy, and in historiography. In the early years of the whig ascendancy the first complete and up-to-date history of England was published. It was, and would long remain, the classic whig history. Its author, Paul Rapin de Thoyras, was a French Huguenot who had served William of Orange as a soldier in Ireland and had then been employed as a tutor in the household of William's Dutch favourite, William Bentinck, Earl of Portland. He wrote it in Wesel, in Germany, in the French language, and published it in Holland in 1723.

Rapin wrote mainly for foreigners. He set out to explain, to bewildered Europeans, how it was that England, after a century of external impotence and internal faction, had suddenly appeared, powerful and united, as the arbiter of Europe; and he explained it by accepting and expounding, with great clarity and moderation, the official whig thesis, *viz.* that England, alone in Europe, had contrived to preserve the old free constitution which had once been the common property of the 'barbarian' conquerors of Rome but which, elsewhere, had been lost. His explanation, solidly based on new documents published by the order of the English whig government and edited by the whig historiographer royal, Thomas Rymer, was widely accepted. Rapin's work was translated and continued in England, respected by tories as well as by whigs, and enthusiastically praised by Voltaire. For our purposes it is important because it is the classic expression of the pre-Macaulay 'whig' interpretation of English history, and the difference between Rapin and Macaulay is the measure of the novelty of Macaulay's 'whig' history.

Not that the innovations were entirely Macaulay's own work. The greatest innovator was a man whose name is seldom mentioned by Macaulay but whose work is always in his mind – a man whom he regarded as his greatest intellectual enemy, but to whom he was deeply, if indirectly, indebted – David Hume. For it was David Hume, the 'tory' historian of England, who, by totally destroying the 'whig' history of Rapin and advancing a completely new philosophy of history, imposed on the new generation of English whigs the need to think again.

Hume's *History of England* was published in the years 1754 to 1761, the last years, as it happened, of the 'whig ascendancy'. When he wrote, few of his readers could remember anything but whig rule and the whig Establishment was sunk in doctrinal complacency. That complacency, in the historical field, he completely shattered. He himself came to history from outside the closed whig world, first because he was a Scot (and it was difficult to find much virtue in Scottish whiggism), secondly because he had begun as a philosopher, not as a historian. Moreover, as a philosopher, he had – like Gibbon – been captivated by Montesquieu, the great transformer of historical philosophy. Thus influenced, Hume was able to look at history in a new way, and the new way in which he looked at it made the old whig thesis (and the old tory thesis, too) permanently obsolete.

Hume did not believe that sacred 'constitutions' were the guarantee of 'liberty'. To him all constitutions were relative, and effective liberty was the result not of constitutional forms but of social and economic progress and 'sophistication of manners': the same 'liberal' constitution which might guarantee 'liberty' in a mature society (like England) might merely perpetuate faction and oppression in an immature society (like seventeenth-century Scotland). In fact, Hume devalued all 'constitutional' ideas and measured the virtue of government by the extent to which the established forms permitted economic and social progress or 'utility'. By this criterion many authoritarian systems were better guarantees of 'liberty' than many ancient anarchical 'constitutions'. In his *History*, Hume expressed these ideas with exquisite wit in an irresistible style; and he deployed his wit most mercilessly at the sacred cows of the official whig faith: at the virtuous Anglo-Saxons, at the medieval barons, at the whig 'patriots' of the seventeenth century.

For half a century after the publication of Hume's work, the whig historians raged impotently at it; but they were quite unable to set up again the shattered Humpty-Dumpty of Rapin. The 'new whigs' of the end of the eighteenth century – the political party which, after a generation in the wilderness, was at last to capture power in 1830 – needed a new historical philosophy; and that historical philosophy had to incorporate the permanent content of Hume's work. That permanent quality was its dynamism. Rapin had represented liberty as an ancient inheritance of which the whigs were the hereditary guardians. Hume had represented it as a continuing capacity for social improvement. For the immutable legacy of our ancestors he had substituted the new idea of social progress.

The fusion of Hume's historical philosophy with whig politics was the work, essentially, of Scottish whig writers, who worked under the social patronage of the disconsolate English whig aristocrats, nursing their wounds and preparing their next campaign in the London home of their leader, Charles James Fox. This was Holland House, in which Fox lived as the uncle and guardian of the young Lord Holland, who afterwards continued his patronage. Intellectually the ablest of these new whig writers was John Millar, a radical disciple of Hume, who for forty years was professor of law at Glasgow University, and who dedicated his *Historical View of the English Government* to Charles James Fox. Millar had a great influence on Scottish whiggism and it was his disciples who, in 1801, founded the *Edinburgh Review*, soon to be the intellectual organ of the English whig party. Charles James Fox himself was among those who sought to re-establish whig history. In his political eclipse, he decided to write a history of the English Revolution of 1688 in order to vindicate the whig party from the aspersions of Hume. In 1800 and 1801, during the brief peace of Amiens, he carried out some research in the French archives and prepared his material; but he completed only a fragment, which was afterwards published by his nephew Lord Holland. His work was taken over by another Scottish whig, who was also a *protégé* of Holland House, and who was to have a great influence on Macaulay, Sir James Mackintosh.

Mackintosh's plan was more ambitious than that of Fox. Like Fox, he was determined to re-establish, against Hume, the historical pedigree of the whig party. He was also, like Millar, imbued with Hume's philosophy. But he proposed to go further than Fox. Having been deeply impressed by the French Revolution, which he at first welcomed for its liberal promise, then repudiated for its radical performance, he was concerned to show that true whiggism not only secured English liberty and progress in 1688 but also saved England from the bloody revolution which had overtaken France and Europe from 1789. He therefore planned to write a history of England from 1688 to 1789. In order to equip himself financially for this task, he accepted the lucrative post of Recorder of Bombay and spent the years 1804 to 1811 in India. On his return he became a member of Parliament; and when the whigs returned to office in 1830, he was appointed a member of the Board of Control for India. But although, in those years, he collected a vast mass of material (which now fills forty bound volumes in the British Museum), he wrote little; and when he died in 1832, he too left only a fragment of his History. That fragment, which began with the accession of James II in 1685 and ended with the settlement of the Crown on William III in February 1689, was published in 1834 as *History of the Revolution in England in 1688*.

Thus by 1834, although the whigs had recovered political power, English historiography was still dominated by the 'tory' Hume. And yet successive whig writers had believed that, even out of Hume's historical philosophy, a new whig interpretation of history could be constructed. The basic materials for such a history lay to hand. Vast manuscript collections – those of Fox and Mackintosh – were available to Holland House. The theory was already presented – by Mackintosh and others – in the *Edinburgh Review*. All that was needed was a historian with the energy and literary power to complete what Fox and Mackintosh had merely begun. It was this opportunity that was seized by Macaulay.

THOMAS BABINGTON MACAULAY

Macaulay was born in 1800, at Rothley Temple in Leicestershire, the home of his uncle Thomas Babington, after whom he was named. His father, Zachary Macaulay, was a Scottish Highlander by birth, who had gone to Jamaica at an early age and devoted the rest of his life to the abolition of the slave-trade. He was a pious Evangelical and one of the members of the 'Clapham Sect' – practical Evangelicals who sought to reform social abuses in general and to abolish slavery in particular. Like most other members of his group, Zachary Macaulay was a tory. Many of them were also Quakers. Macaulay's mother was the daughter of a Quaker bookseller in Bristol. These biographical details may be of some interest for Macaulay's own intellectual development, of which we know very little; for although Macaulay always respected his father and his father's philanthropic work, he emphatically rejected the political and religious world in which he had been brought up. He was educated at an Evangelical school before going to Cambridge, and we know that he arrived at Cambridge a tory; but when he first appeared as a writer, a few years later, his views were absolutely fixed, and fixed for life. He was a whig. Moreover, he not only rejected his family toryism: he also, in his writings, expressed consistent contempt for Highlanders and Quakers; he was completely without religious sense, being a conventional conformist, expressing amused disdain for all kinds of nonconformity; and if he never ceased to be liberal, and to hate the institution of slavery, he would speak with contempt of professional 'negrophils'. Nor can Zachary Macaulay have felt altogether happy at his son's later devotion to Holland House and, in particular, to Lady Holland: for Lady Holland was the daughter of a West Indian planter and brought to her husband a West Indian plantation, worked by slaves. She would refer to Macaulay's father, somewhat contemptuously, as 'a great saint, Zachariah, and the bitterest foe to all West Indian concerns'.[1]

It thus seems that Macaulay's whiggism may have been part of a general reaction against his family circle, and this, in turn, may account for its intensity. But whiggism, it seems, was not his first or direct reaction from the toryism in which he had been brought up. There had been an intermediate conversion. For a short time, while an undergraduate at Trinity College, Cambridge, Macaulay had been a radical. He was converted to radicalism by a fellow undergraduate, Charles Austin, a well-known Cambridge converter. But although he remained a life-

1. G. S. H. Fox-Strangways, 6th Earl of Ilchester (ed.), *Elizabeth Lady Holland to her son 1821–1845* (1946), p. 108.

long friend of Austin, Macaulay quickly rejected radicalism, and afterwards attacked both radicals and radicalism as violently as he would attack tories and toryism. He had settled for aristocratic, political whiggism. This he first showed in 1822, when he won an annual college prize for an essay on William III, Prince of Orange and King of England.[2] William III, the maker of the 'Glorious Revolution' of 1688, the founder (however involuntary) of the whig Establishment, was to remain Macaulay's lifelong hero. From this time on we may say that his views were fixed. Age and practice might sophisticate the expression of them, but their substance, even in detail, would never change.

However, if Macaulay became, and remained, an uncompromising whig, it was a whig of a special kind. He was a 'new whig', a whig of the party which, in his own words, had been 'purified' in the reign of George III; which had been inspired by Burke, led by Rockingham, and sustained in opposition by Fox; and which had now retreated into the aristocratic citadel of Holland House. Moreover, among those aristocratic whigs, Macaulay, who was not at all aristocratic (his 'want of pedigree', wrote Lady Holland, was a serious handicap in 'that most aristocratic assembly', the English House of Commons[3]), was distinguished by what we may call his Scottish inheritance. He had absorbed the 'utilitarian' philosophy which had made Hume a tory, which had been made whig by Adam Smith, Millar and Mackintosh, and which was now the philosophy of the *Edinburgh Review*. Macaulay's rejection of political utilitarianism – the utilitarianism of the radicals – did not entail a rejection of utilitarian ideals: indeed Macaulay, in the crude materialism of his concept of progress, is sometimes positively vulgar. What Macaulay rejected was the idea that material progress could be attained or preserved by the direct political action of a 'democratic' party, lacking political experience and relying on academic theories or paper constitutions. Entirely unphilosophical in his outlook, entirely empirical in his politics, he despised theory and theorists – even

2. This essay was published in *The Times Literary Supplement* on 1 May 1969.

3. Earl of Ilchester, op. cit., p. 184.

the great whig theorists meant little to him – and trusted implicitly in the continuing political capacity of a practised, liberal,
historically educated ruling class. Progress, defined in utilitarian
terms, would, he believed, be far more painlessly achieved, and
far more securely based, under the leadership of whig magnates
than by the direct action of political pedants. In the past, English
'whigs' – whether so named or not – had been more successful than English republicans, English 'Levellers', or French
Jacobins. In the present, and for the foreseeable future, they
would be more successful than English 'Utilitarians', French
'socialists', or American 'democrats'. This was the lesson of
history.

Once fixed in these views, Macaulay was eager to assert them,
and from the time when he left Cambridge, he proposed to himself a life of politics and literature. Success in both fields was not
long in coming: indeed, throughout his life, Macaulay suffered
from instantaneous success in every field – in politics, in oratory,
in prose, even in poetry. In 1825 he published, in the *Edinburgh
Review*, his long essay on Milton. This was a trenchant, uncompromising expression of the whig view, and at once attracted
notice. Other articles in the *Edinburgh Review* followed, including
(in 1829) a violent diatribe against the radical 'utilitarians', and
especially their prophet James Mill. By means of these two
essays, the one excoriating the tories, the other the radicals,
Macaulay recommended himself to the aristocratic whig leaders,
and, in particular, to his father's friend, Henry Petty-Fitz-
maurice, second Marquis of Lansdowne. Lord Lansdowne was
the son of a famous father, a whig Prime Minister who had been
the friend and patron of radical thinkers and who had sent his son
to study at Edinburgh University together with Brougham, Jeff-
rey, Horner, and Sydney Smith, the founders of the *Edinburgh
Review*. In 1830 Lansdowne offered Macaulay the representation
of his 'pocket' parliamentary borough of Calne, Wiltshire.
Macaulay was duly elected, and thus entered parliament at the
beginning of the long-delayed whig triumph. Next year his
speech in support of the Reform Bill made him famous. A few
weeks later he received the highest mark of social favour that any
young whig could hope for: he was invited to Holland House. In

the same year he received also a political reward. He was made Secretary of the Board of Control for India.

Macaulay joined the Board of Control just at the time when Mackintosh was vacating it by death. He already knew Mackintosh in parliament and had been noticed and befriended by him. Two years later he was to follow Mackintosh's example again. In 1833 the constitution of the East India Company was changed and a supreme council for India was set up. In 1834 Macaulay was offered a seat on this supreme council. The term was for five years; the salary £10,000 a year. Like Mackintosh, Macaulay calculated that such a post would enable him to save enough money to finance a life of literature thereafter. In fact he stayed in India for only three and a half years, but in the course of his residence there he made a permanent mark on Indian administration, for he took a prominent part in founding the educational system of India and ensured that English, not any of the Indian languages, should be the language of instruction. He also set up and presided over the Committee which devised the criminal code for India. At the same time he continued to read and write. His reading, largely in the classical languages, was immense, and thanks to his phenomenal memory, he rarely forgot anything that he had once read. His writing was still for the *Edinburgh Review*. It was in India that he wrote his famous essay on Bacon, which reveals at once the strength and the limitations of his mind. But a more important essay, at least for our purpose, is his long review of the posthumous fragment of Mackintosh's *History*.

In this essay, which appeared in the *Edinburgh Review* in July 1835, Macaulay expressed once again the new whig philosophy. He also took the opportunity to make another violent attack on radical doctrines, as expressed by Mackintosh's editor, William Wallace. The attack was so violent that Macaulay was nearly forced, on his return, to fight a duel with Wallace. But the interest of the review lies largely in its implications. In writing it, Macaulay must have been acutely aware of the void which first Fox, then Mackintosh, had sought, and failed, to fill; and this awareness happened to coincide with a great void that had suddenly opened in his own life.

At the beginning of January 1835 Macaulay received news

from England of the death of his younger sister Margaret. It was a terrible blow: 'what she was to me', he wrote at the time, 'no words can express ... That I have not utterly sunk under this blow, I owe chiefly to literature.' 'Literature', he wrote twelve months later, 'has saved my life and my reason. Even now, I dare not, in the intervals of business, remain alone for a minute without a book in my hand.' And he added that he was 'more than half determined', on his return to England, 'to abandon politics and to give myself wholly to letters: to undertake some great historical work which may be at once the business and the amusement of my life.' With Mackintosh's fragment before his eyes and this resolution in his mind, it could hardly be doubted what that great historical work would be. Macaulay would write what Mackintosh had meant to write: the whig history of England from 1688 until recent times. 'I do not believe', he would afterwards write, 'there is in our literature so great a void as that which I am trying to supply. English history from 1688 to the French Revolution is even to educated people almost a *terra incognita*.' And on another occasion he wrote that he was determined not to 'fritter away' his powers 'like poor Mackintosh'.

In order to carry out this project, Macaulay resolved to return to England at the first opportunity. In the summer of 1838 he was back in London. However, he did not at once devote all his energies to his new task. Immediately after his return, he made a tour of Italy; he continued to write essays for the *Edinburgh Review*; and he returned to the House of Commons, this time as member for Edinburgh.

All these diversions took up his time and some of them added significantly to his literary output. He was active in parliament, where he delivered some famous speeches. 'Whenever he rose to speak', Gladstone would afterwards write, 'it was a summons like a trumpet-call to fill the benches'. His speech on the proposed Copyright Act of 1841 was an oratorical triumph: Macaulay carried the majority of the Commons to his side and killed the proposal. He also held high political office as Secretary at War in Lord Melbourne's government from 1839 to 1841. The essays which he wrote between 1839 and 1842 include the two most widely published of all his essays, those on Clive and Warren

Hastings: the fruit of his Indian experience. And meanwhile, as a result of his Italian visit, he had entered – and conquered – a new field: that of poetry. In 1842 he published his *Lays of Ancient Rome*.

Macaulay's *Lays of Ancient Rome* are more important than they might seem for his historical work. The idea of writing such poems was supplied to him by the work of the German historian B. G. Niebuhr. Niebuhr's *History of Rome* began to appear in English in 1828. It was reviewed in the *Edinburgh Review*, and at once caused great interest in England. Macaulay himself, at first reading, regarded it as marking 'an era in the intellectual history of Europe'. What particularly excited historians was Niebuhr's interpretation of early Roman history, as represented by Livy. Niebuhr argued that Livy had no authentic historical sources for so remote a period, and that his formal narrative was in fact based on traditional ballads or 'lays'. Macaulay afterwards lost faith in Niebuhr – especially on discovering that he was an abject conservative in politics – but the idea of such old Roman 'lays' remained in his mind. There it was fertilized by contact with another strong interest which Macaulay shared with many other nineteenth-century historians: his interest in the writings of Sir Walter Scott.

Macaulay had always been an admirer of Scott. He knew his poems by heart and, in his historical work, consciously imitated Scott's method of writing: his use of description, of local colour, or popular tradition or ephemeral literature. A good historian, he wrote in an early essay,[4] should not confine himself to battles, sieges, negotiations, politics; he should also 'intersperse the details which are the charm of historical romances'. In this way, he added, 'Sir Walter Scott . . . has used those fragments of truth, which historians have scornfully thrown behind them, in a manner which may well excite their envy. He has constructed out of their gleanings works which, even considered as histories, are scarcely less valuable than theirs. But a truly great historian would reclaim those materials which the novelist has appropriated.' Macaulay's skill in such reclamation is obvious to all readers of his work, and the pervasive influence of Scott in

4. 'History', *Edinburgh Review*, 1828.

Macaulay's *History* was at once remarked by critics as different
as Maria Edgeworth and John Wilson Croker.[5] The theory of
Niebuhr attracted Macaulay because it suggested, once again,
the interdependence of history and ballad-literature: it gave him
the idea, of which he often spoke, of 'restoring to poetry the
legends of which poetry had been robbed by history'. So when
he travelled in Italy, the scenes of ancient Roman history had on
him the same effect which the scenes of the Scottish Border had
had upon Scott: they inspired him to re-create the ballads which
the Roman historian (according to Niebuhr) had also recognized
as the legitimate material of history.

Macaulay's *Lays of Ancient Rome*, once again, were an instant
success, and Macaulay, as always, was pleased, not to say complacent, at their success. But he did not allow this new literary
interest to distract him from his main purpose. Even while he
was in Italy, and acquiring the local colour for his poems, he was
thinking of his *History*. 'As soon as I return,' he wrote, 'I shall
seriously commence my *History*'; and he sketched its plan. By
beginning in 1688 and continuing, if possible, to 1830, he would
be able to incorporate, and to connect, the triumphs of the old
whigs, who made the Glorious Revolution and secured the Hanoverian succession, and of the new whigs who, after the loss of the
American colonies, set out on the long struggle for parliamentary
reform. Between these two revolutions, which he would portray
in detail as 'the revolution which brought the Crown into harmony with Parliament and the revolution which brought Parliament into harmony with the nation', he would dispatch 'more
concisely' the intermediate events, necessary only to prove the
essential continuity of the whig party. From 1838 onwards he
was at work on his programme, modifying it as he studied more
deeply – for instance, he soon realized that he must start before
1688 in order to 'glide imperceptibly into the full current of my

5. Maria Edgeworth lamented that in Macaulay's first volume 'there is no
mention of Sir Walter Scott throughout the work, even in places where it
seems impossible that the historian could resist paying the becoming tribute
which genius owes, and loves to pay, to genius' (letter to Dr Holland
quoted by Trevelyan, *Life and Letters of Lord Macaulay*, Ch. XI). Croker
singled out 'the example and success of the author of *Waverley*' as the 'true
source' of Macaulay's design (*Quarterly Review*, Vol. lxxxiv, March 1849).

narrative'. After 1842, when he had dispatched his *Lays of Ancient Rome* and basked, for a time, in the applause, he contracted his dispersed activities in order to concentrate exclusively on his *History*.

In 1843 he agreed to publish his collected essays. Here his hand was forced by American piracy: inaccurate versions were already circulating widely, and Macaulay agreed, somewhat reluctantly, to supply an authorized text. His essays, like everything else that he wrote, at once became a best-seller. After that, he wrote only two major essays: one on William Pitt the elder, Earl of Chatham, which summarizes, in mature form, his interpretation of eighteenth-century English history; one on the French Jacobin Bertrand Barère, which illustrates, once again, his hatred of political radicalism. Both these essays were published in 1844. Next year, Macaulay wrote to Macvey Napier, the editor of the *Edinburgh Review*, that he could undertake no more such articles. He would work exclusively on his *History*.

At the same time, he detached himself as far as possible from politics, which he now definitely subordinated to literature. He had been out of office anyway since the fall of the whig government in 1841. On the return of his party to power in 1846, he accepted the office of Paymaster-General. This was a comparative sinecure which would give him what he wanted: 'leisure and quiet more than salary and business'. He did not speak much in Parliament, and he lost the support of the electors of Edinburgh, who accused him of caring 'more for his *History* than for the jobs of his constituents'. In consequence of this apparent indifference, he lost his seat, and with it his office, in the General Election of 1847. He remained out of Parliament for the next five years, refusing all proffered seats. In 1852 the Edinburgh whigs turned back to him and invited him to stand. He refused; but they nevertheless elected him to Parliament. For the next four years he attended Parliament, but he spoke rarely. He never held political office again. In 1856 he applied for the Chiltern Hundreds – that is, retired from Parliament. During these years, and indeed for the rest of his life, he was absorbed in the *History* which he was determined to leave as his monument.

In writing his *History*, Macaulay had certain advantages over his predecessors. First of all, he had their work. Fox's fragment, indeed, did not carry him far, but Mackintosh's work, though also a fragment, was, so far as it went, a solid and original piece of historical research, and a comparison of it with Macaulay's first volumes shows Macaulay's continuous reliance on it: he often repeated Mackintosh's words, and he sometimes adopted his errors. But even more valuable to him than the finished work of Fox and Mackintosh was their raw material. The transcripts which Fox had made were supplied to Macaulay by Lord Holland; the huge manuscript collection of Mackintosh was put at his disposal by Mackintosh's son. These magnificent collections saved Macaulay a great deal of labour, especially at the beginning of his work. Thanks, in part, to them, Macaulay was able to publish the first two volumes of his *History* in November 1848. These two volumes coincided exactly, in scope, with the work of Mackintosh. They carried the story down to the deposition of James II.

As with his first essay, as with his first speech, as with his first poems, the success of these first volumes of the *History* was instantaneous. Macaulay had intended that it should be: his work was 'to have a permanent place in our literature'. And his confidence was well based. He was sure of his thesis – the whig thesis. There was merit, no doubt, he wrote in his journal, in the great 'philosophical historians' of the eighteenth century, Hume, Robertson, Voltaire, and Gibbon, 'yet it is not the thing. I have a conception of history more just, I am confident, than theirs.' He took great trouble over his style: 'how little', he exclaimed, 'the all-important art of making meaning pellucid is studied now! Hardly any popular writer except myself thinks of it.' And he was determined to be not only pellucid but also 'amusing', readable: 'I shall not be satisfied unless I produce something which shall for a few days supersede the last fashionable novel on the tables of young ladies.' But even he had hardly reckoned on the scale of his success. Thirteen thousand copies were sold in four months. 'Of such a run', he wrote in his diary, 'I had never dreamed.' It was exhilarating; but it was also sobering. It made him feel 'extremely anxious about the second part. Can it possibly come up to the first?' For now he had to deal with the un-charted field of the reign of William III.

Faced with this challenge, Macaulay made even greater efforts. Three months after the publication of the first volumes he recorded in his diary that he had decided 'to change my plan about my *History*': 'I will first set myself to know the whole subject: – to get, by reading and travelling, a full acquaintance with William's reign. I reckon that it will take me eighteen months to do this. I must visit Holland, Belgium, Scotland, Ireland, France. The Dutch archives and French archives must be ransacked. I will see whether anything is to be got from other diplomatic collections. I must see Londonderry, the Boyne, Aghrim, Limerick, Kinsale, Namur again, Landen, Steinkirk. I must turn over hundreds, thousands of pamphlets. Lambeth, the Bodleian and the other Oxford libraries, the Devonshire papers, the British Museum, must be explored, and notes made: and then I shall go to work. When the materials are ready, and the *History* mapped out in my mind, I ought easily to write on an average two of my pages daily. In two years from the time I begin writing, I shall have more than finished my second part. Then I reckon a year for polishing, retouching and printing.' On this system he worked methodically, first obtaining a general under-standing of the period – 'the reign of William III, so mysterious to me a few weeks ago,' he wrote in June 1849, 'is now beginning to take a clear form' – then studying each particular episode and sketching his first account of it, while the impressions were fresh, 'at a headlong pace'. Afterwards he wrote out the revised version in a regular 'task' of six pages a day. His aim was perfect clarity: 'the great object is that, after all this trouble, they may read as if they had been spoken off, and may seem to flow as easily as table-talk.' No one can deny that he achieved this result: for full effect, Macaulay's work ought to be read aloud.

The result was another well-deserved success. At the end of 1855, when his third and fourth volumes were published, bring-the story down to the Peace of Ryswick in 1697, they were even more successful than their predecessors. In ten weeks 26,500 copies were sold, and eleven weeks after publication Macaulay received from his publisher a record-breaking cheque for £20,000.

From then on, Macaulay's reputation was not only insular: it was world-wide. His work was translated into almost every European language, and even Persian. In America its sale – a pirate sale – was surpassed only by that of the Bible. He received numerous foreign honours. He was praised by Ranke, nominated to the Institut de France by Guizot. But his work was by no means finished; a long stretch still lay ahead of him; and his health was by now seriously impaired. In 1852 he had suffered a heart attack and, as he said, 'became twenty years older in a week'. If he were to complete, or even continue his work, he would be obliged to contract his life still further. He therefore gave up his seat in Parliament, accepted from the whig Prime Minister Lord Palmerston a peerage as Lord Macaulay of Rothley Temple and, giving up his bachelor apartments in the Albany, bought the lease of a spacious villa, Holly Lodge, in Kensington. It was in a suitably whig quarter, for his next-door neighbour was the whig Duke of Argyll and Holland House was hard by. There he settled down in comfort, with four men-servants to supply his needs, and, in the intervals of entertainment, continued to read and write. But he never completed his work. Illness diminished its tempo, and by 1857 he had contracted his original ambition. He no longer hoped to reach the American Revolution or the 'new whigs' of the late eighteenth century. 'I now look forward', he wrote, 'to the accession of the House of Hanover as my extreme goal.'[6] In fact even that goal was beyond his reach. He did not, himself, publish another volume. He died on 28 December 1859, and was buried in Westminster Abbey.

At his death, Macaulay's papers passed to his surviving sister Hannah, to whom he had always been devoted. She had accompanied him to India and had there married Charles Edward Trevelyan, who was afterwards a distinguished public servant in both England and India. She now edited and published the last chapters of his manuscript. They appeared in 1861 as the fifth

6. Macaulay to H. S. Randall, 18 January 1857; printed in H. M. Lydenberg, 'What did Macaulay say about America? Text of Four Letters to Henry S. Randall' (New York Public Library, 1925).

volume of the *History*, which they carried down to the death of William III in 1702. The rest of Macaulay's papers remained in the hands of the Trevelyan family, who, for a hundred years, have been the hereditary custodians, even high-priests (if a whig high-priest is conceivable), of Macaulay's fame.

After Hannah Lady Trevelyan's edition of Volume V of the *History* came the excellent biography of Macaulay written by her son, Macaulay's nephew, Sir George Otto Trevelyan. This was based on Macaulay's papers, which Trevelyan edited with a certain benevolent partiality towards his uncle. Afterwards Sir G. O. Trevelyan, by writing *The History of the American Revolution*, supplied, in some sense, the originally intended conclusion to Macaulay's work. The more immediate conclusion, to which Macaulay himself had afterwards restricted his ambition, was supplied by Sir G. O. Trevelyan's second son, George Macaulay Trevelyan, regius professor of history and Master of Trinity College, Cambridge, with his three-volume *History of the Reign of Queen Anne*. By his *History of England in the 18th Century*, G. M. Trevelyan may also be said to have supplied the 'more concise' connecting link which Macaulay had envisaged. In 1962, on the death of G. M. Trevelyan, Macaulay's papers passed to Trinity College, Cambridge.

THE HISTORY OF ENGLAND

Thus in the end Macaulay, like his predecessors Fox and Mackintosh, only completed a fragment of the work which he had set out to do. But, in fact, no one can regard the *History of England* as a fragment. It is a solid work filling, in the original edition, five volumes. It has a clearly defined theme: the history of the Revolution of 1688 and the reign of William III which effectively consolidated that Revolution. By its forward and backward glances – its long introductory chapter and its frequent illustrations from later periods – it gives Macaulay's interpretation of the whole course of English history. And in so doing, it expresses, with absolute clarity, the new, modernized 'whig' thesis. If Macaulay's immediate purpose was to destroy the long dominion of Hume's 'tory' history, he certainly succeeded where Fox and

Mackintosh had failed. From the moment of its publication, his *History* replaced that of Hume as the canon of historical orthodoxy in England: replaced it so completely that it is difficult now to see past its long and apparently effortless triumph. This is the measure of Macaulay's victory. It could hardly have been more complete even if he had finished his work and carried it down to the victory of the new whigs in 1830.

Today Macaulay has gone the way of Hume, into historical perspective. The whig thesis is no longer exciting, no longer irresistible. Parts of it have been accepted and are regarded as truisms; parts have been exposed, with damaging effect, to that persistent light of criticism which, in the noonday of whig triumph, was so easily outglared. Macaulay's qualities were always obvious. With his dogmatic character, his rhetorical style, his 'pellucidity', he never left his readers in doubt, never even suggested that doubt was a permissible state of mind. In his own time, he carried them with him by the obviousness of his merits. Today, it is his faults which are more obvious. If we are to assess his permanent contribution to historical study, it will therefore be best to begin by admitting his obvious faults, some of which are the inescapable by-products of his merits.

Macaulay owed his success, in part, to the absolute clarity of his views and his style. This clarity proceeded from his own conviction. From the age of twenty-two, as far as we know, his convictions were fixed: he never changed his mind. And because his convictions were strong and clear, he tended, when faced with the evidence on any subject, instantly to range it in accordance with them. He did not, of course, do this crudely. His mind was both powerful and liberal. He had a marvellous understanding of political realities, which his own political experience naturally improved. His wide reading in all kinds of literature, classical, modern, and ephemeral – ballads, plays, novels, and sheer trash – enlarged his vision. He was no doctrinaire but an exceptionally well-read man of the world. Nevertheless, whatever concessions he would make, however elevated or sophisticated his expression of it, his judgement was always influenced by his convictions; and however liberal and rational these convictions might be, they were overpowering. They caused him to make

dogmatic judgements in fields where he was unqualified to speak
and would never stoop to learn. To the modern reader, the dog-
matism of his comments, in such fields, can be even more offensive than their ignorance or insensitivity.

These fields which Macaulay so brusquely invaded include the
fields of literary criticism, art, and human psychology. In spite of
his vast reading, and his obvious pleasure in it, Macaulay's appreciation of literature was severely limited. He read the classics
voraciously, but indiscriminately, and his comments are rather
those of a schoolmaster awarding marks than of a catholic or
sensitive critic. He admired no poetry written since the early
poems of Scott and reckoned that his own *Lays of Ancient Rome*
were better than anything written in the rest of the decade: years
which (as David Knowles reminds us) saw the publication of the
early works of Tennyson, Browning, and Matthew Arnold.[7] Of
pictorial art he understood even less. In Italy he swept through
the galleries, distributing confident priorities but showing no
appreciation at all. Of music he knew nothing. Dining at Windsor
Castle, he once recorded that 'the band covered the talk with a
succession of sonorous tunes. "The Campbells Are Coming" was
one.' 'This', says his nephew, 'is the only authentic instance on
record of Macaulay's having known one tune from another.' Of
religious sense he had none, though he delighted in the worldly
details of theology. And yet on all these subjects 'cocksure Tom',
as his contemporaries called him, did not hesitate to lay down the
law. His literary essays, when they touch literature itself, are
worthless (as he himself afterwards admitted[8]). His descriptions
of art, architecture, music are of a frigid, conventional pomposity
if they are not positively absurd. Queen Mary is laboriously ridiculed for her 'frivolous and inelegant' taste in china: she admired the 'hideous' and 'grotesque baubles' of Ming porcelain.
If the English country gentry of the late seventeenth century

7. David Knowles, *Lord Macaulay 1800–1859*, a lecture (Cambridge,
1960).

8. On 26 June 1838 Macaulay wrote to Macvey Napier, the Editor of the
Edinburgh Review, that he was willing to be judged by his historical and political essays, 'but I have never written a page of criticism on poetry or the fine
arts which I would not burn if I had the power' (*Letters of T. B. Macaulay*,
ed. T. Pinney, III, 245).

attempted to decorate their houses, says Macaulay, they only achieved 'deformity'. But the suburban or seaside villas of the Victorian middle class are always given the highest marks. Whenever Macaulay wishes to emphasize the material progress which one hundred and fifty years of whiggism have brought to the English towns, he cannot forbear to mention the 'long avenues of villas, embowered in lilacs and laburnums', the 'gay villas peeping from the midst of shrubberies and flower-beds', the 'villas multiplying fast, each embosomed in its gay little paradise of lilacs and roses'.

This philistinism, which can be so infuriating to the reader of Macaulay, springs directly from his philosophy. He saw history as the history of progress, and progress as material progress. In one of his earliest essays he had looked forward to a materialist millennium in the twentieth century, when villas would crowd up to the top of Ben Nevis and Helvellyn, 'machines constructed on principles yet unknown' would be in every house, and there would be 'no highways but railroads, no travelling but steam'. This same spirit of complacent materialism runs through his whole work. It is the new content which the 'Scottish' school had injected into whiggism to excite the nineteenth-century middle classes and to depress us who face the consequences of its realization. But even if we dislike it, we have to recognize that Macaulay, in thus emphasizing it, did isolate and define an important element in historical change.

Moreover, in isolating and defining material progress, Macaulay attached it – as he attached everything – to political action. He did not, like Hume, see progress as distinct from politics. To him, progress needed a constant political motor. In his own time he saw that the whig party could be that motor; and having once seized on this formula, he generalized it. He projected it both forwards and backwards in time. He saw the whig party of the seventeenth century as the direct precursor of the whig party of the nineteenth century, constantly pursuing, under the same social leadership, the same ultimate ends. Equally, the same party, he thought, would achieve the progress of the twentieth century. That the whig party might dissolve and that material progress might be achieved through the programme of European 'socialism' or American 'democracy', or English 'toryism', seemed to him quite impossible. The very thought of such ideas provoked him to omniscient scorn.

It is easy to expose Macaulay's errors about the future – his confident predictions that 'democracy' would reduce America 'to the state of Barbary or the Morea'.[9] Historians are often wrong about the future. But what about his interpretation of the past? Here he may well have been right. His thesis is not in itself absurd. But even here he may equally have been wrong. In spite of superficial appearances, in spite of the continuity of names, it is perfectly possible that the seventeenth-century whigs and the nineteenth-century whigs were different parties, pursuing different aims, in entirely different circumstances. It is possible that the seventeenth-century whigs never thought of 'progress', even if they accidentally forwarded it. It is also possible that the circumstances of the two periods were so different as to preclude comparison: that any connection between them could only be accidental, the connection of names, not things. Such was the view of the greatest historian of Macaulay's time, Leopold von Ranke, who held that every age was 'immediate to God' and must be studied from within, on its own terms, in its own right. But Macaulay, though he reviewed Ranke's *Lives of the Popes* and once met Ranke at breakfast (it was a very unsuccessful breakfast),[10] never sought to understand either the method or the philosophy of the German school. If he had, he would no doubt have dismissed Ranke, like Niebuhr, as an abject tory.

This refusal to admit the autonomy of the past, this insistence that the past must be judged in relation to the present, and is responsible to the present, is fundamental to Macaulay's historical interpretation and is the cause of some of his historical errors. Macaulay once wrote – in his essay on Ranke, although not with reference to Ranke's ideas – that 'a Christian of the 5th century with a Bible is neither better nor worse situated than a Christian of the 19th century with a Bible ... The absurdity of literal inter-

9. See his essay, 'Mill's Essay on Government', *Edinburgh Review*, 1829; also his letters to H. S. Randall cited above, p. 24, n. 6.

10. For Macaulay and Ranke, see Sir Charles Firth, *A Commentary on Macaulay's History of England* (1938), pp. 249–56.

pretation was as great and as obvious in the 16th century as it is now.' Such a view, which implies that there is no difference in 'intellectual climate' between one age and another, may well seem grotesquely unhistorical to us who live in the post-Rankean age. In Macaulay, who looked back to the eighteenth-century Enlightenment and had never breathed the atmosphere of Göttingen, it was more venial. But it explains the summary judgements which he too easily pronounced on the statesmen and thinkers of the past, his tendency to set them in the dock and (as Ranke himself expressed it) to borrow his tone from the proceedings of the criminal courts. To Ranke, there was no dock in which the past could be put: one generation was outside the jurisdiction of another.

And once they were in the dock, how did the men of the past fare at the hands of the judge? With his clear mind, his complete understanding of his own historical law, and his absolute certainty, Macaulay never wavered in his judgement. It was not an unconsidered judgement. Macaulay would survey all the facts, take past convictions into consideration, allow extenuating circumstances, and then, in his own favourite word, 'pronounce'. But judgement, once decided, was firm. There was no qualification. Ignorance of the law – that is, of the newly enacted, retroactive whig law of history – excused no one. If a man was found to be a 'tory', however virtuous, he must be sentenced, and even his admitted virtues were somewhat suspect. On the other hand, a good whig record could excuse the same faults which, in a tory, merely aggravated his crime. And once the sentence was 'pronounced', there could be no reconsideration, no reversal, no appeal.

Macaulay's double standard of judgement is incontestable. It is entirely political. It is applied to evidence: the same sources are treated as authentic when they ascribe vices to Marlborough, 'Jacobite libels' when they ascribe other vices to William III. It is applied to persons. James II's liaison with the plain but intelligent Catherine Sedley was disreputable profligacy; William III's liaison with the plain but intelligent Elizabeth Villiers was an excusable lapse: she 'possessed talents which well fitted her to partake his cares.' When Charles II accepted money from

France, no words of condemnation are strong enough for such 'degradation', such 'complacent infamy'. When the whig hero Algernon Sidney did exactly the same, his action is described as 'indelicate', and even that adjective is quickly smothered in excuses: the censure, as J. W. Croker wrote in his review of Macaulay's first volume, is 'so light as to sound like applause'.[11]

Macaulay's injustice to persons is not solely dependent on their political choice. It may equally arise from their political doubt, from their refusal to choose. Confident himself, he had no patience with the hesitations of others. Political and unspeculative himself, he had no patience with the unpolitical and the speculative. Complex and divided personalities were ruthlessly simplified by him: caricatured as a bundle of contradictions and cast contemptuously aside. Archbishop Cranmer, hesitating in his pursuit of religious truth and the political means of ensuring it; Archbishop Sancroft, hesitating to adjust his sworn beliefs to the revolution which was necessary to preserve them – these men are castigated in outrageous terms. Even those whose convictions were clear and consistent obtained no benefit of their consistency unless its framework was obvious to Macaulay and recognized by him. Francis Bacon and William Penn were such men. They were not tories; they were not divided or hesistant personalities; but they did not fit neatly into Macaulay's categories. The whole context of their thought was different. They breathed a different 'intellectual climate'. But Macaulay did not admit such differences. Consequently, in his pages, they pay the price. Since the artist is intellectually incapable of portraying them, they are caricatured.

Moreover, these and such caricatures, in Macaulay's pages, are compounded by repetition. Once he had made up his mind about any man (and he made it up very quickly), all later evidence automatically adjusted itself in support of that conclusion, and every episode, thus interpreted, served to aggravate the original charge. Thus Macaulay very early made up his mind about John Graham of Claverhouse, Viscount Dundee, the Jacobite commander in Scotland, and about John Churchill, the great Duke of Marlborough. Already in 1838, before he had even begun to

11. *Quarterly Review*, Vol. lxxxiv (March 1849).

work on his *History*, he had – in his essay on Sir William Temple
– consigned them both to 'the deeper recesses' of Dante's Hell.
So, when he came to write his *History*, he approached every
episode in which they were concerned with an absolute certainty
that it would show them in an odious light. By the time he had
interpreted the episode, it generally did; and although his interpretation was often grossly erroneous, it served to blacken their
prospects still further when they next appeared in court.

Many are the historical characters whom Macaulay, having
once decided to condemn, pursued through his *History* (as Croker
wrote concerning his persecution of Marlborough) 'with more
than the ferocity, and much less than the sagacity, of a blood-
hound'. Perhaps the most outrageous – and also the most interesting – of such pursuits is his vendetta against William Penn,
the second founder of Quakerism. It is interesting because it
shows not only the lengths to which Macaulay would go in deni-
gration but also, by its consequences, the absolute irreversibility
both of his own judgement, even when he was demonstrably
convicted of error, and of whig opinion, so long as it was held
enthralled by the new orthodoxy which he had established.

Why did Macaulay hate Penn? Partly, no doubt, because he
hated Quakers. Quakers, by definition, were unpolitical, which to
Macaulay was a fault. But Penn aggravated this fault by nevertheless becoming involved, however accidentally, in political
action. He was thus not only wrongheaded but naïve. All this
might well have been excused had Penn been involved on the
whig side. But Penn was a personal friend of James II, and his
very refusal to become involved in politics made him in effect,
an accomplice of the King. Even if Macaulay's animosity was not
sharpened by a distaste for his parents' Quaker friends, there was
enough material here to prejudice him against Penn; his prejudice was sharpened by a gross error of identification which
Macaulay took over from Mackintosh; and thereafter every incident in which Penn appeared was misinterpreted in order to fit,
and to aggravate, the character thus ascribed to him. By the time
he had finished with him, Macaulay had represented Penn as a
man who (in Paget's words) 'prostituted himself to the meanest
wishes of a cruel and profligate court, gloated with delight on the

horrors of the scaffold and the stake, was the willing tool of a bloodthirsty and treacherous tyrant, a trafficker in simony and suborner of perjury, a conspirator seeking to deluge his country in blood, a sycophant, a traitor and a liar.' In fact, every one of Macaulay's particular charges can be proved to be false.

Two attempts were made during Macaulay's lifetime to correct his libel of Penn. The first was by the Quakers themselves. Immediately after the publication of Macaulay's first volume, a new edition of Thomas Clarkson's *Memoirs of William Penn* was published, with a new preface by W. E. Forster, factually refuting the charges. About the same time, a deputation of Quakers called on Macaulay to persuade him of his error. Macaulay looked forward to the encounter with confident glee: 'The Quakers', he recorded, 'have fixed Monday at 11.0 for my opportunity. Many a man, says Sancho, comes for wool and goes home shorn.' On Monday they duly came. Complacent as ever, Macaulay described the visit. 'Then the Quakers, five in number. Never was there such a rout. They had absolutely nothing to say . . .' As Sir Charles Firth says, if the Quakers 'had absolutely nothing to say' it was presumably because they were not allowed to speak.

In an attempt to secure a public hearing, Forster's preface was published separately, and in 1851 W. Hepworth Dixon published a new *Life of Penn* with a whole chapter refuting Macaulay's charges. Macaulay paid not the slightest attention, and in 1856 a new edition of the first volumes of his *History* confidently repeated the libels. This roused the indignation of a new critic, this time a strong whig: John Paget. In 1858 Paget published a scholarly pamphlet entitled *An Enquiry into the evidence relating to the charges brought by Lord Macaulay against William Penn.* Next year Paget similarly exposed Macaulay's no less glaring errors concerning the Duke of Marlborough, the Massacre of Glencoe, and the Scottish Highlands. All these were published in Macaulay's lifetime. In 1860, after Macaulay's death, Paget showed that Macaulay had similarly libelled Viscount Dundee. All these essays Paget collected and published in 1861 as *The New Examen.* But just as Macaulay had ignored the criticism made during his life, so the whig Establishment ignored it after his death. The *Edinburgh Review* dismissed Paget's book with con-

tempt, hardly deigning to notice 'so very inaccurate a performance'[12]; Trevelyan, in his biography, never mentioned Paget or
allowed it to appear that Macaulay was in error on any subject;
and *The New Examen*, having fallen stillborn from the press,
was never reprinted till 1936, when Sir Winston Churchill, hearing from Lord Rosebery of this rare and unknown book, stimulated a new edition in defence of his ancestor.

How could Macaulay be guilty of such gross errors, such
shocking injustices? It is clear from his own language that he
genuinely believed that he was right. And yet the evidence
against him, which was shown to him, is absolutely unanswerable. Mere prejudice is not a sufficient explanation for this psychological problem. The most natural explanation lies in the
combination of political prejudice with an extraordinary memory.

Macaulay's memory was indeed a prodigy – and a prodigy of
which he was undoubtedly vain. Numerous stories are told about
it. He knew the whole of *Paradise Lost* and the whole *Pilgrim's
Progress* by heart. He could take in at a glance, and retain in his
mind, a whole printed page; and too often he discharged it again
in his conversation. 'He should take two table-spoonfuls of the
waters of Lethe every morning', said Sydney Smith. But this
great gift had its disadvantages. Macaulay would remember the
pattern in which he had arranged the evidence, and which he had
imprinted on his mind, rather than the evidence itself; and he
would unconsciously refer back not to the evidence but only to
the pattern. As Gladstone wrote, 'the possessor of such a vehicle
as his memory could not but have had something of an over-
weening confidence in what it told him.' Macaulay's memory did
not often let him down. He seldom forgot a fact. Unfortunately
he seldom, if ever, detached a fact from the pattern in which, and
through which, his memory had preserved it.

It is impossible to ignore Macaulay's gross personal injustices.
They are the major blemish in all his work. But having made this
admission, it is important to recognize that these injustices are
limited. They damage only his treatment of persons, of human
motivation: an area in which Macaulay, with his psychological
insensitivity, was always weak. They do not affect the value of his

12. *Edinburgh Review*, October 1861.

work as narrative of events, as political analysis, as historical explanation; and it is in these fields that his greatness lies. A minor historian would have been forgotten long ago, had he committed errors as gross as those of Macaulay. Macaulay, in spite of his errors, remains one of the great historians.

In order to appreciate this, it is necessary first to consider Macaulay's originality. Macaulay may not have been the first to advance what we may call the 'whig-utilitarian' historical thesis – i.e., the thesis that the substance of history is material progress and that such progress can be attained through the application of particular political principles – for this thesis is implicit in the work of some of his Scottish predecessors, such as Millar and Mackintosh. But he was certainly the first to express this thesis in a consistent and persuasive historical form. He was able to do this not only by the clarity of his ideas and the literary force of his writing, but also by his originality as a technical historian. Hume, whom he replaced, may have been a profounder historical philosopher; but the superiority of Macaulay in mere historical scholarship – in the range of his sources and in his own mastery of them – makes Hume seem, by comparison, an amateur.

Of course there are admissions to be made. Behind Macaulay always stands Mackintosh. Macaulay's first two volumes rest heavily on Mackintosh; and even after Mackintosh's *History* had ceased, Macaulay still relied on Mackintosh's vast manuscript collections, which supplied many of his needs down to 1702. Since Macaulay himself never got beyond 1702, we may say that he never completely emancipated himself from Mackintosh, who still supplied the bulk of his foreign transcripts. But the fact remains that, for the period of the reign of William III – a particularly complicated period since William was the head, and England the principal power, of a European coalition – Macaulay was a pioneer; and he was a pioneer because he used a range of material infinitely greater than had been used by any of his predecessors. When Macaulay wrote that the reign of William III, as he approached it, was 'mysterious', he was stating a general truth. Nobody, till then, had elucidated it. Macaulay was the first to do so; and he did so from a wide range of sources, printed and manuscript, literary and historical, public and private, British and

foreign. To supplement Mackintosh's collection, he obtained
transcripts of national archives from Paris and the Hague; he
paid a personal visit to the archive of Venice; and he acquired,
through Guizot, the whig statesman-historian of France, copies
of Spanish archives from Simancas. On the other hand, he made
little use of Italian and no use of German or Austrian sources.

In this widened use of sources Macaulay was helped, of course,
by external facts. Since the French Revolution, there had been a
general opening of the archives of Europe. Macaulay profited by
that fact, just as other historians would do: indeed the historians
of the German school – in particular Ranke – would apply a far
more professional technique to a far wider range of the documents
thus made available. To historians like Lord Acton, who was himself trained in the German school, Macaulay was both amateur
and insular. Even non-historians like Gladstone recognized the
great gulf which separated Macaulay from the new German pio-
neers of historical method and source-criticism. But for all the
gaps which posterity can find in his range of sources, and in his
use of them, compared with his predecessors, Macaulay was himself a professional.

Macaulay also improved on his predecessors by the scale of his
study. He may have been (as he himself admitted) insular, in that
he saw European problems from a purely English point of view;
but at least he was the first historian to study the Revolution of
1688 and its aftermath as a British, not a purely English, revolution. Everyone knows that the Revolution of 1688, though it was
precipitated by purely English affairs, was not stabilized till it had
been extended to Ireland and Scotland; and that the result of that
extension was not merely to secure the benefits of the Revolution
in England: it was also to transform the government and society
of Ireland and to join Scotland with England in the United Kingdom. But English historians have customarily treated this extension of the Revolution as a mere military operation, as if Ireland
and Scotland were simply the theatres in which the victory of
William III over James II was completed. This, no doubt, was
William's own view, and the view of the English statesmen of the
time. But Macaulay, as a historian, looked deeper than they. Himself a Scotchman who, through the Union, had become a British

statesman, aware of the unceasing importance of Ireland in British affairs, he recognized that each country had distinct problems, which the Revolution might either settle or inflame; and his analysis of these problems is one of the most valuable parts of his work. He did for the Glorious Revolution of 1688 what nobody, even now, has done for the Puritan Revolution of 1640 to 1660: he saw it as a social and political revolution whose progress and consequences were equally important to all three kingdoms.

In the technique of presentation, too, Macaulay was an innovator. He marks an important stage in the transition from the 'philosophical' historians of the Enlightenment, whose work he continued, to the 'romantic' narrative historians of the nineteenth century, who imitated him. Like his 'philosophical' predecessors, he believed that the significance of the past lay in its relation to the present. Like them, he saw history as the record of 'progress' – progress, in his view, not towards 'freedom' but, by means of freedom, to ever greater prosperity. But equally, his view of history was coloured by the new romanticism which separated the past from the present in order to give it, in spite of its continuity, a distinctive colouring.

Macaulay's romanticism is admittedly of a very qualified kind. He openly despised those who, in his own time, affected to prefer the past to the present. He insisted that romanticism itself was a luxury, dependent on material progress: the beauty of wild scenery, as in the Scottish Highlands, could only excite pleasure when roads and inns, industry and public order, had made it safe to travel there. But however relative, his romanticism was genuine. It was not only as the incidental poet of the *Lays of Ancient Rome*: it was in his convictions as a historian, that he was deeply influenced, like so many other nineteenth-century historians, by Sir Walter Scott. Indeed, we may say that Macaulay's historical philosophy is a synthesis of the eighteenth-century idea of progress and the nineteenth-century cult of the romantic past. We may add that he was able to achieve this synthesis because English history – unlike German or French history – itself combined essential progress with the superficial forms of the romantic past. Macaulay dwells with equal emphasis, as occasion allows, on the

external pageantry of former times and the thread of progress
which makes the inner reality of the present time so much better;
and the Revolution of 1688 seemed to him particularly glorious
in that it contrived to secure them both: to preserve the antique
forms of a static, feudal, Christian monarchy around the substance of a progressive, secular, materialist state.

This 'relative romanticism', this romanticism of form combined with a materialism of substance, shows itself in Macaulay's
literary method. He was the first great historian to make use of
local and temporal 'colour'. The eighteenth-century historians
had never sought to capture the atmosphere of the past. They
had not judged it necessary to travel, except for the general purpose of broadening the mind. Robertson wrote of the European
empire of Charles V, of America and of India, without ever leaving Britain. Gibbon wrote the whole history of the Byzantine
Empire without ever visiting any part of that empire. Macaulay
was far more 'modern'. Wherever possible, he visited the sites
which he was to describe in his *History*. He followed William III's
progress through Ireland, inspected Londonderry, Limerick, the
Boyne. He went to Scotland to visit the passes of Killiecrankie
and Glencoe. He travelled abroad almost every summer to look
at cities, fortresses, battlefields. And when he looked at them, his
imagination peopled them with their historic inhabitants. He
had, as he once told his sister, a love of such 'castle-building'
whereby 'the past is in my mind soon constructed into a romance'. He even composed imaginary conversations, 'long and
sufficiently animated, in the style, if not with the merits, of Sir
Walter Scott's'. To such 'castle-building' he ascribed his 'accu-
racy as to facts'. To the same castle-building we may ascribe his
inaccuracies as to persons. There are historical dangers, as well
as literary advantages, in 'recapturing' the supposed 'atmosphere' of the past.

In order to recapture that atmosphere Macaulay relied heavily
on literature. The literary reserves on which he could draw were
formidable. Poetry, plays, pamphlets, satires, lampoons, ballads,
novelettes, farces – all the residue of his enormous, promiscuous
reading lay ready to hand, accurately labelled, in his preservative
memory and could be drawn upon at will to illustrate the social

habits and popular opinions of the time. This wide range of illustrations renders his writing direct, vivid, and cogent; but the method has its dangers, too. Literature, after all, is not life: it is a heightened version of life; life itself is duller, more prosaic. Satire and drama, particularly, are by definition a caricature of reality. It may be legitimate to use such literature as evidence of opinion – to illustrate the rivalry between the Old and New East India Companies by a quotation from Nicholas Rowe's comedy *The Biter*, and the mania for speculation by a scene in Shadwell's *Stockjobbers* – but it is not legitimate to use it, without careful reservation, as evidence of historical fact or personal character. Macaulay was never a man of careful reservations. Consequently, some of his most entertaining or most damaging passages can be discredited as resting not on historical evidence but on literary exaggerations. Just as he illustrates the character of Marlborough from Jacobite libels and that of Jeffreys from whig tirades, so he caricatures the country clergy by accepting the evidence of stage-parsons and the society of the Scottish Highlands by relying on chosen passages from exasperated or satirical foreigners. This is a danger into which other, later historians have fallen. The late R. H. Tawney, for instance – as politically committed a historian as Macaulay – tended to illustrate the 'acquisitive society' of early seventeenth-century England from Jacobean comedy. But the dangers inherent in a historical method do not invalidate the method itself, and by his command and use of literature for historical purposes Macaulay undoubtedly gave a new, if somewhat perilous, depth to the art of the historian.

In all these respects Macaulay, in his own time, was an innovator. But his most permanent contribution to the study of politics – what makes his *History*, in spite of all its blemishes, so difficult to fault – is his unerring grasp of political reality. Uninterested in abstract ideas, insensitive in his approach to persons, Macaulay had nevertheless an unfailing appreciation of political situations. Himself a politician, who had lived through the excitement of the parliamentary struggle for Reform and had enjoyed personal experience of government both in England and in India, he understood the pressures of politics, the need and the moment of action. And since, unlike Hume, he believed that material progress was essentially linked to political action, and that effective politics depended not on academic blueprints or new constitutions, but on empirical skill serving an enlightened general philosophy, this understanding of the scope and limits of political action was an essential part of his historical philosophy. That philosophy might lack depth, but it was never caught without an answer. The historian could see, at any moment, what ought to have been done; and he often said so, with irritating self-assurance.

Again and again, in his *History*, Macaulay declares his faith in political action rather than political theory, as the means of progress. The key to history is politics; and politics is not a philosophical but an empirical science. The politician is an engineer, not a mathematician. He must indeed have some knowledge of the philosophy of government, just as the engineer must be versed in the philosophy of equilibrium and motion; 'but as he who has actually to build must bear in mind many things never noticed by D'Alembert and Euler, so must he who has actually to govern be perpetually guided by considerations to which no allusion is to be found in the writings of Adam Smith or Jeremy Bentham.' Constitutions, political manifestos, are not to be admired for their philosophical profundity, for their intellectual symmetry. They are not to be examined 'as we should examine a chapter of Aristotle or of Hobbes'. They are to be considered 'not as words but as deeds. If they effect that which they are intended to effect, they are rational, though they may be contradictory. If they fail of attaining their end, they are absurd, though they carry demonstration with them.' Consistently with this doctrine, Macaulay, in his history, while describing the political conduct of Sunderland and Godolphin, Somers and Montagu, totally ignores the great work which, for all Europe, was to provide the philosophical basis of the Glorious Revolution, the two *Treatises on Government* by John Locke; and in his practical Indian statesmanship he was not inhibited by the whig doctrines which he had learned to apply to English history.

If Macaulay's key to history is politics, equally his key to politics is history. The problems of government, he insists, are not philosophical, nor can we ever explain political results by examining political motives or 'the principles of human nature'. The explanation of political action is to be sought in the history of political action. History is 'that noble science of politics which is equally removed from the barren theories of the utilitarian sophists' and from mere political expediency.[13] The best politicians are those who have studied history and the best historians are those who have taken part in politics – especially in whig politics. So Macaulay extols Fox and Mackintosh as historians because 'they had spoken history, acted history, lived history': the very fact that they had been politicians gave them, according to Macaulay, 'great advantages over almost every English historian who has written since the time of Burnet'.[14] The choice of Bishop Burnet, in this context, may seem odd to us, when Macaulay might have cited Bolingbroke or – even more aptly – Clarendon, who not only fulfilled all the necessary conditions but expressed, in his attack on Hobbes and in his essay on other historians, the very views of Macaulay. But then Burnet was a whig; Bolingbroke and Clarendon were tories.

Macaulay's acute political sense, his recognition of the scope, the limits, and the timing of political action, is indeed his greatest contribution to historical writing. It never failed him. As S. R. Gardiner, the historian of seventeenth-century England, wrote, 'his judgment of a political situation was as superb as his judgment of personal character was weak.'[15] He not only appreciated, instinctively, the exact balance of political forces at any given moment; he also saw how great political problems should be faced and solved. It might or might not be true that only the historic whig party could carry out such solutions, but the solutions which he proposed – whether as a historian, for the settlement of Ireland, or as a statesman, for the education of India – were not only based on a vast historical knowledge and inspired by a genuine belief in material progress: they were also unquestionably right. Perhaps Macaulay's greatest achievement, as a historian, was not merely his success in temporarily capturing historical interpretation for his political party, or even his in-

13. Essay, 'Mill's Essay on Government'.
14. Essay, 'Sir James Mackintosh'.
15. S. R. Gardiner, *Cromwell's Place in History* (1902), p. 17.

corporation of the utilitarian philosophy in the historical process, but his reassertion – a reassertion since made on behalf of other political parties – of the primacy of politics in that process, as the essential motor even of social change.

This is not an obvious quality. No virtue, in a historian, is obvious, except style. History is too subtle a process to be firmly seized or summarily decided. Consequently Macaulay's virtues are much less apparent than his faults, which are faults precisely for this reason: they are the result of too instant apprehension. These faults appear at their worst in Macaulay's *Essays*, where there is less room for the emergence of subtlety. But in the long haul of the *History*, although the particular judgements are identical, the deeper virtues become gradually apparent, as almost everyone who has become familiar with it agrees. It is no doubt for this reason that Lord Acton, who hated Macaulay, regarding his philosophy as 'utterly base, contemptible and odious', nevertheless made a remarkable, and otherwise unintelligible, distinction between the *Essays* and the *History*, between Macaulay in haste and Macaulay at a more reflective pace. The essays, he wrote, were 'flashy and superficial', 'only pleasant reading, and key to half the prejudices of our age. It is the *History* (with one or two speeches) that is wonderful. He knew nothing respectably before the 17th century. He knew nothing of foreign history, or religion, philosophy, science, or art. His account of debates has been thrown into the shade by Ranke, his account of diplomatic affairs by Klopp. He is, I am persuaded, grossly, basely unfair. Read him therefore to find out how it comes that the most unsympathetic of critics can think him very nearly the greatest of English writers.'[16]

16. Lord Acton, *Letters to Mary Gladstone*, ed. H. Paul (London, 1904), pp. 173, 210.

A Note on the Text

IN this selection I have sought to illustrate, as far as possible, the width of Macaulay's view of the Revolution and the historical philosophy which informs it. The introductory passages to each extract are designed to supply continuity of narrative and, incidentally, to explain Macaulay's terms and so to make the selection self-contained and reduce the footnotes to the minimum. In general, I have omitted Macaulay's own footnotes, which are largely technical, but I have retained such as seem to me to add points of substance or interest to the text. Where explanation or comment seems to me necessary, I have added notes of my own. These are always distinguishable from Macaulay's notes, being placed in brackets. I have felt free occasionally to modernize Macaulay's spelling, especially of foreign names. Otherwise the only liberty I have taken with the text is occasionally to break up Macaulay's long paragraphs; but I have done this, I hope, on rational principles of sense and euphony, which he himself would not reject.

Bibliographical Note

MACAULAY'S complete works consist of his *Lays of Ancient Rome* and other poems, his essays, his parliamentary speeches, and his *History of England*.

The *Lays of Ancient Rome* were first published in 1842. Later editions included two other poems, 'Ivry' and 'The Armada'.

Critical and Historical Essays were first published in collected form in 1843; but this collection, which has often been reprinted, omits several essays, some of which are important biographically (for example, the three essays on James Mill and utilitarianism, the essay on history, written in 1828, and the essay on Barère, written in 1844). These omitted essays, together with other writings, were collected and published in 1860 by Macaulay's friend and executor T. F. Ellis as *Lord Macaulay's Miscellaneous Writings*.

Macaulay's parliamentary speeches were first printed in an unauthorized and inaccurate edition (by Henry Vizetelly) in 1853. This caused him to publish a correct edition, entitled *Speeches of the Rt. Hon. T. B. Macaulay M.P., corrected by himself* (1854).

The *History of England* was first published as follows: Volumes I and II, 1848; Volumes III and IV, 1855; Volume V (edited by Lady Trevelyan), 1861. The best annotated edition is that of T. F. Henderson, published in the World's Classics, in five volumes (London, 1931). There is an excellent illustrated edition by Sir Charles Firth (London, 1913–15). An invaluable companion work to the *History* is Sir Charles Firth's posthumously published *A Commentary on Macaulay's History of England* (London, 1938).

Macaulay's complete works were first published by Lady Trevelyan in 1866, in eight volumes. The best edition is *The Works of Lord Macaulay*, Albany edition, twelve volumes (London, 1898).

Since then, two minor writings of Macaulay have been printed. The first is his undergraduate prize essay on William III, printed in the *Times Literary Supplement* on 1 May 1969; the other is the first eighty-eight pages of a projected *History of France* from 1814 to 1830, begun in 1831 but never completed. These printed pages were recently discovered in the archives of Longman & Co., Macaulay's publishers, and have been edited by Joseph Hamburger under the title *Napoleon and the Restoration of the Bourbons* (London, 1977).

The Life and Letters of Lord Macaulay by Sir G. O. Trevelyan (1876) is a classic biography. Although its whig assumptions and personal sympathy sometimes need correction, it defies competition and no rival biography has ever been attempted. On its publication it was the subject of a long review-essay in *The Quarterly Review* (1876) by W. E. Gladstone (reprinted in *Gladstone's Gleanings of Past Years*, 1879, II); and this essay is one of the best independent judgements on Macaulay by a contemporary. Sir G. O. Trevelyan also published *Marginal Notes by Lord Macaulay* (1907). A. N. L. Munby's David Murray lecture for 1965, *Macaulay's Library* (Glasgow, 1966), gives further evidence of Macaulay's intellectual interests.

A complete edition of the *Letters of Thomas Babington Macaulay* is in the course of publication, edited by T. Pinney (Cambridge, 1974–).

Chronological Notes

1754–61 David Hume's *History of England* published.

1800 25 October, Macaulay born at Rothley Temple, Leicestershire.

1801 *Edinburgh Review* founded.

1806 Death of Charles James Fox.

1808 Fox's *History of the Early Part of the Reign of James II* published by Lord Holland.

1812–18 Macaulay educated at the Rev. Mr Preston's Evangelical school at Little Shelford, near Cambridge.

1818 Macaulay goes to Trinity College, Cambridge.

1824 Macaulay elected Fellow of Trinity College.

1825 Macaulay begins writing for *Edinburgh Review*. Essay on Milton.

1830 Macaulay member of Parliament for Calne, Wiltshire.

1831 2 March, Macaulay's speech in House of Commons on second reading of Reform Bill. He is received at Holland House.

1832 30 May, death of Sir James Mackintosh.

1832 June, Macaulay appointed Commissioner of Board of Control for India.

1833 Macaulay appointed member of Supreme Council for India.

1834 February, Macaulay sails to Calcutta.

1834 Publication of Mackintosh's *History of the Revolution in England in 1688* (reviewed by Macaulay in *Edinburgh Review*, 1835).

1834 Hannah Macaulay marries (Sir) Charles Trevelyan in Calcutta.

1837 December, Macaulay leaves India; arrives London, June 1838.

1838 13 May, death of Zachary Macaulay.

1838   Macaulay visits Italy, begins *Lays of Ancient Rome* (published 1842).

1839   Macaulay begins *History of England*.

1839–47   Macaulay member of Parliament for Edinburgh.

1839–41   Macaulay Secretary at War with a seat in the Cabinet.

1843   Macaulay's *Critical and Historical Essays* published.

1848   November, Macaulay's *History of England*, Volumes I and II, published.

1852   Macaulay re-elected M.P. for Edinburgh (retired 1856).

1855   December, *History of England*, Volumes III and IV, published.

1856   May, Macaulay moves to Holly Lodge, Kensington.

1857   Macaulay accepts peerage.

1859   28 December, death of Macaulay.

1861   *History of England*, Volume V, published by Lady Trevelyan.

1861   John Paget's *New Examen* published.

1876   Sir G. O. Trevelyan's *Life and Letters of Lord Macaulay* published.

The History of England

I

Macaulay's Purpose

[*Macaulay begins his* History – *which was intended to be a history of England from 1688 to 1789 – with a declaration of his purpose.*]

I PURPOSE to write the history of England from the accession of King James the Second down to a time which is within the memory of men still living. I shall recount the errors which, in a few months, alienated a loyal gentry and priesthood from the House of Stuart. I shall trace the course of that revolution which terminated the long struggle between our sovereigns and their parliaments, and bound up together the rights of the people and the title of the reigning dynasty. I shall relate how the new settlement was, during many troubled years, successfully defended against foreign and domestic enemies; how, under that settlement, the authority of law and the security of property were found to be compatible with a liberty of discussion and of individual action never before known; how, from the auspicious union of order and freedom, sprang a prosperity of which the annals of human affairs had furnished no example; how our country, from a state of ignominious vassalage, rapidly rose to the place of umpire among European powers; how her opulence and her martial glory grew together; how, by wise and resolute good faith, was gradually established a public credit fruitful of marvels which to the statesmen of any former age would have seemed incredible; how a gigantic commerce gave birth to a maritime power, compared with which every other maritime power, ancient or modern, sinks into insignificance; how Scotland, after ages of enmity, was at length united to England, not merely by legal bonds, but by indissoluble ties of interest and affection; how, in America, the British colonies rapidly became mightier and wealthier than the realms which Cortes and Pizarro had added to the dominions of Charles the Fifth; how, in Asia, British adventurers

founded an empire not less splendid and more durable than that
of Alexander.

Nor will it be less my duty faithfully to record disasters ming-
gled with triumphs, and great national crimes and follies far more
humiliating than any disaster. It will be seen that even what we
justly account our chief blessings were not without alloy. It will
be seen that the system which effectually secured our liberties
against the encroachments of kingly power gave birth to a new
class of abuses from which absolute monarchies are exempt. It
will be seen that, in consequence partly of unwise interference,
and partly of unwise neglect, the increase of wealth and the extension of trade produced, together with immense good, some
evils from which poor and rude societies are free. It will be seen
how, in two important dependencies of the crown, wrong was followed by just retribution; how imprudence and obstinacy broke
the ties which bound the North American colonies to the parent
state; how Ireland, cursed by the domination of race over race,
and of religion over religion, remained indeed a member of the
empire, but a withered and distorted member, adding no strength
to the body politic, and reproachfully pointed at by all who feared
or envied the greatness of England.

Yet, unless I greatly deceive myself, the general effect of this
chequered narrative will be to excite thankfulness in all religious
minds, and hope in the breasts of all patriots. For the history of
our country during the last hundred and sixty years is eminently
the history of physical, of moral, and of intellectual improvement. Those who compare the age on which their lot has fallen
with a golden age which exists only in their imagination may talk
of degeneracy and decay: but no man who is correctly informed
as to the past will be disposed to take a morose or desponding
view of the present.

I should very imperfectly execute the task which I have undertaken if I were merely to treat of battles and sieges, of the rise and
fall of administrations, of intrigues in the palace, and of debates
in the parliament. It will be my endeavour to relate the history of
the people as well as the history of the government, to trace the
progress of useful and ornamental arts, to describe the rise of religious sects and the changes of literary taste, to portray the man-

ners of successive generations, and not to pass by with neglect even the revolutions which have taken place in dress, furniture, repasts, and public amusements. I shall cheerfully bear the reproach of having descended below the dignity of history, if I can succeed in placing before the English of the nineteenth century a true picture of the life of their ancestors.

The events which I propose to relate form only a single act of a great and eventful drama extending through ages, and must be very imperfectly understood unless the plot of the preceding acts be well known. I shall therefore introduce my narrative by a slight sketch of the history of our country from the earliest times. I shall pass very rapidly over many centuries: but I shall dwell at some length on the vicissitudes of that contest which the administration of King James the Second brought to a decisive crisis.

2

The State of England in 1685:
Squires and Parsons

[*Having stated his purpose, Macaulay, in his first chapter, gives an outline sketch of English history from its beginning to the Restoration of Charles II in 1660. In this sketch he already makes clear his own 'whig' philosophy of history. Implicitly rejecting earlier 'whig' theories, which had ascribed the English 'constitution' to the Anglo-Saxons or to Henry II, and dismissing Norman rule as a mere foreign conquest, he firmly placed the beginning of 'the history of the English nation' in the thirteenth century, which saw the dissolution of foreign, Norman tyranny and the signing of the Great Charter. By the next century, he insisted, parliamentary control of legislation and taxation and ministerial responsibility were already established, and under the protection of this 'mixed' English constitution social oppression was gradually lightened, economic prosperity increased. The Protestant Reformation, essentially a Teutonic movement, hastened this process. But in the early seventeenth century the new Stuart kings and a new party in the Church sought to put the clock back and thereby forced the champions of English progress to organize the defence of the threatened constitution – even to the extent of enlisting, against the violence and absurdity of Charles I, the opposite violence and absurdity of Puritanism. The policy which Charles I's opponents ought to have adopted, says Macaulay, with his usual confidence, 'is obvious': the dignity of the royal office should have been preserved; the person should have been discarded. 'Thus our ancestors acted in 1399 and in 1689.' But circumstances and personalities made this 'obvious' course impractical at the time. In the reign of Charles I, there was no Henry Bolingbroke, as in 1399, no William of Orange, as in 1689. So the revolution degenerated into violence, out of which emerged first a republic, then a military despotism: systems which, having no place in the continuity of English history, finally foundered. After their collapse, the monarchy and the Anglican Church were restored on the basis of the old constitu-*

tion, explicitly reaffirmed, and the Stuarts were thus given a second chance. History and experience had taught them the essential conditions of government, which were also, incidentally, conditions of economic progress. All that they had to do was to learn the lesson.

Unfortunately they did not learn. In his second chapter Macaulay describes the rule of Charles II, who, instead of adjusting himself to the constitution, merely sought to pursue the old aims of his father. His methods were indeed less rigid, for he was intelligent, indolent, and pleasure-loving, and had no desire either to be a martyr or 'to go on his travels again'. He therefore did not make a frontal attack on the English 'constitution', but sought to evade it by skilful tactics and financial dependence on Louis XIV, then dominant in Europe. In order to enjoy subsidies from France, Charles II abandoned the policy of 'collective security' against French aggression (formulated in the Triple Alliance of 1668, with Holland and Sweden) and made, behind the back of his own ministers, the Secret Treaty of Dover with Louis XIV (1670). This policy once again drove the domestic enemies of the Crown into dangerously radical courses. They organized a great public scare ('the Popish Plot') and used it in an attempt to exclude from the succession the King's brother and heir, James, Duke of York, a convert to Roman Catholicism who had given clear evidence of his aims and had none of his brother's saving graces of indolence, intelligence, and personal charm. But these radical excesses rebounded against them. Their candidate for the succession, the King's natural son, the Duke of Monmouth, then as afterwards, was unacceptable to moderate men. Legitimacy prevailed over illegitimacy; the 'Popish Plot' of 1679, after terrible excesses, ended by discrediting its authors; and Charles II skilfully exploited his advantages. After the Oxford Parliament of 1680, the 'Exclusionists' (now known as the Whigs) were demoralized and persecuted. Their leaders were punished and scattered. The ablest of them, the Earl of Shaftesbury, fled abroad and died. Others – Lord Russell, Algernon Sidney – were executed for alleged conspiracy (the so-called Rye House Plot). When he died in 1685, Charles II handed over to his brother a throne which seemed securely based on the triumph of the anti-whig, the 'tory' party.

Who were the 'tories'? In his third chapter, Macaulay describes the social condition of England in 1685: its population, its economic resources, its military and naval strength, its communications, cities, institutions, social and intellectual life – always emphasizing the material improvement which had taken place in subsequent years. In the course of this account he gives a somewhat tendentious description of the two social classes which provided the solid base of the 'tory' party: the country gentry and the Anglican clergy.]

WHILE these great changes had been in progress, the rent of land has, as might be expected, been almost constantly rising. In some districts it has multiplied more than tenfold. In some it has not more than doubled. It has probably, on the average, quadrupled.

Of the rent, a large proportion was divided among the country gentlemen, a class of persons whose position and character it is most important that we should clearly understand; for by their influence and by their passions the fate of the nation was, at several important conjunctures, determined.

We should be much mistaken if we pictured to ourselves the squires of the seventeenth century as men bearing a close resemblance to their descendants, the county members and chairmen of quarter sessions with whom we are familiar. The modern country gentleman generally receives a liberal education, passes from a distinguished school to a distinguished college, and has every opportunity to become an excellent scholar. He has generally seen something of foreign countries. A considerable part of his life has generally been passed in the capital; and the refinements of the capital follow him into the country. There is perhaps no class of dwellings so pleasing as the rural seats of the English gentry. In the parks and pleasure grounds, nature, dressed yet not disguised by art, wears her most alluring form. In the buildings, good sense and good taste combine to produce a happy union of the comfortable and the graceful. The pictures, the musical instruments, the library, would in any other country be considered as proving the owner to be an eminently polished and accomplished man. A country gentleman who witnessed the Revolution was probably in receipt of about a fourth part of the rent which his acres now yield to his posterity. He was, therefore, as compared with his posterity, a poor man, and was generally under the necessity of residing, with little interruption, on his estate. To travel on the Continent, to maintain an establishment in London, or even to visit London frequently, were pleasures in which only the great proprietors could indulge. It may be confidently affirmed that of the squires whose names were then in the Commissions of Peace and Lieutenancy not one in twenty went to town once in five years, or had ever in his life wandered so far as Paris. Many lords of manors had received an education differing little from that of their menial servants. The heir of an estate often passed his boyhood and youth at the seat of his family with no better tutors than grooms and gamekeepers, and scarce attained learning enough to sign his name to a Mittimus.

If he went to school and to college, he generally returned before he was twenty to the seclusion of the old hall, and there, unless his mind were very happily constituted by nature, soon forgot his academical pursuits in rural business and pleasures. His chief serious employment was the care of his property. He examined samples of grain, handled pigs, and, on market days, made bargains over a tankard with drovers and hop merchants. His chief pleasures were commonly derived from field sports and from an unrefined sensuality. His language and pronunciation were such as we should now expect to hear only from the most ignorant clowns. His oaths, coarse jests, and scurrilous terms of abuse, were uttered with the broadest accent of his province. It was easy to discern, from the first words which he spoke, whether he came from Somersetshire or Yorkshire. He troubled himself little about decorating his abode, and, if he attempted decoration, seldom produced anything but deformity. The litter of a farmyard gathered under the windows of his bedchamber, and the cabbages and gooseberry bushes grew close to his hall door. His table was loaded with coarse plenty; and guests were cordially welcomed to it. But, as the habit of drinking to excess was general in the class to which he belonged, and as his fortune did not enable him to intoxicate large assemblies daily with claret or canary, strong beer was the ordinary beverage. The quantity of beer consumed in those days was indeed enormous. For beer then was to the middle and lower classes, not only all that beer now is, but all that wine, tea, and ardent spirits now are. It was only at great houses, or on great occasions, that foreign drink was placed on the board. The ladies of the house, whose business it had commonly been to cook the repast, retired as soon as the dishes had been devoured, and left the gentlemen to their ale and tobacco. The coarse jollity of the afternoon was often prolonged till the revellers were laid under the table.

It was very seldom that the country gentleman caught glimpses of the great world; and what he saw of it tended rather to confuse than to enlighten his understanding. His opinions respecting religion, government, foreign countries and former times, having been derived, not from study, from observation, or from conversation with enlightened companions, but from such traditions as were current in his own small circle, were the opinions of a child. He adhered to them, however, with the obstinacy which is generally found in ignorant men accustomed to be fed with flattery. His animosities were numerous and bitter. He hated Frenchmen and Italians, Scotchmen and Irishmen, Papists and Presbyterians, Independents and Baptists, Quakers and Jews. Towards London and Londoners he felt an aversion which more than once produced important political effects. His wife and daughter were in tastes and acquirements below a housekeeper or a stillroom maid of the present day. They stitched and spun, brewed gooseberry wine, cured marigolds, and made the crust for the venison pasty.

From this description it might be supposed that the English esquire of the seventeenth century did not materially differ from a rustic miller or alehouse keeper of our time. There are, however, some important parts of his character still to be noted, which will greatly modify this estimate. Unlettered as he was and unpolished, he was still in some most important points a gentleman. He was a member of a proud and powerful aristocracy, and was distinguished by many both of the good and of the bad qualities which belong to aristocrats. His family pride was beyond that of a Talbot or a Howard. He knew the genealogies and coats of arms of all his neighbours, and could tell which of them had assumed supporters without any right, and which of them were so unfortunate as to be great grandsons of aldermen. He was a magistrate, and, as such, administered gratuitously to those who dwelt around him a rude patriarchal justice, which, in spite of innumerable blunders and of occasional acts of tyranny, was yet better than no justice at all. He was an officer of the trainbands; and his military dignity, though it might move the mirth of gallants who had served a compaign in Flanders, raised his character in his own eyes and in the eyes of his neighbours. Nor indeed was his soldiership justly a subject of derision. In every county there were elderly gentlemen who had seen service which was no child's play. One had been knighted by Charles the First after the battle of Edgehill. Another still wore a patch over the scar which he had received at Naseby. A third had defended his old house till Fairfax had blown in the door with a petard. The presence of these old Cavaliers, with their old swords and holsters, and with their old stories about Goring and Lunsford, gave to the musters of militia an earnest and warlike aspect which would otherwise have been wanting. Even those country gentlemen who were too young to have themselves exchanged blows with the cuirassiers of the Parliament had, from childhood, been surrounded by the traces of recent war, and fed with stories of the martial exploits of their fathers and uncles. Thus the character of the English esquire of the seventeenth century was compounded by two elements which we are not accustomed to find united. His ignorance and uncouthness, his low tastes and gross phrases, would, in our time, be considered as indicating a nature and a breeding thoroughly plebeian. Yet he was essentially a patrician, and had, in large measure, both the virtues and the vices which flourish among men set from their birth in high place, and accustomed to authority, to observance, and to self-respect. It is not easy for a generation which is accustomed to find chivalrous sentiments only in company with liberal studies and polished manners to image to itself a man with the deportment, the vocabulary, and the accent of a carter, yet punctilious on matters of genealogy and precedence, and ready to risk his life rather than see a stain cast on the honour of his house. It is however only by thus joining together things seldom or never found together in our own experience, that we can form a just idea of that rustic aristo-

cracy which constituted the main strength of the armies of
Charles the First, and which long supported, with strange fidelity,
the interest of his descendants.

The gross, uneducated, untravelled country gentleman was
commonly a Tory: but, though devotedly attached to hereditary
monarchy, he had no partiality for courtiers and ministers. He
thought, not without reason, that Whitehall was filled with the
most corrupt of mankind; that of the great sums which the
House of Commons had voted to the crown since the Restoration
part had been embezzled by cunning politicians, and part squandered on buffoons and foreign courtesans. His stout English
heart swelled with indignation at the thought that the government of his country should be subject to French dictation. Being
himself generally an old Cavalier, or the son of an old Cavalier,
he reflected with bitter resentment on the ingratitude with which
the Stuarts had requited their best friends. Those who heard him
grumble at the neglect with which he was treated, and at the profusion with which wealth was lavished on the bastards of Nell
Gwynn and Madam Carwell,[1] would have supposed him ripe for
rebellion. But all this ill humour lasted only till the throne was
really in danger. It was precisely when those whom the sovereign
had loaded with wealth and honours shrank from his side that
the country gentlemen, so surly and mutinous in the season of
his prosperity, rallied round him in a body. Thus, after murmuring twenty years at the misgovernment of Charles the Second,
they came to his rescue in his extremity, when his own Secretaries of State and Lords of the Treasury had deserted him, and
enabled him to gain a complete victory over the opposition; nor
can there be any doubt that they would have shown equal
loyalty to his brother James, if James would, even at the last
moment, have refrained from outraging their strongest feeling.
For there was one institution, and one only, which they prized
even more than hereditary monarchy; and that institution was
the Church of England. Their love of the Church was not, indeed, the effect of study or meditation. Few among them could
have given any reason, drawn from Scripture or ecclesiastical

[1. Louise de Kerouaille, Duchess of Portsmouth, one of Charles II's
mistresses, was commonly known as Madam Carwell.]

history, for adhering to her doctrines, her ritual, and her polity; nor were they, as a class, by any means strict observers of that code of morality which is common to all Christian sects. But the experience of many ages proves that men may be ready to fight to the death, and to persecute without pity, for a religion whose creed they do not understand, and whose precepts they habitually disobey.[2]

The rural clergy were even more vehement in Toryism than the rural gentry, and were a class scarcely less important. It is to be observed, however, that the individual clergyman, as compared with the individual gentleman, then ranked much lower than in our days. The main support of the Church was derived from the tithe; and the tithe bore to the rent a much smaller ratio than at present. King estimated the whole income of the parochial and collegiate clergy at only four hundred and eighty thousand pounds a year; Davenant at only five hundred and forty-four thousand a year.[3] It is certainly now more than seven times as great as the larger of these two sums. The average rent of the land has not, according to any estimate, increased proportionally. It follows that rectors and vicars must have been, as compared with the neighbouring knights and squires, much poorer in the seventeenth than in the nineteenth century.

The place of the clergyman in society had been completely changed by the Reformation. Before that event, ecclesiastics had formed the majority of the House of Lords, had, in wealth and splendour, equalled, and sometimes outshone, the greatest of the temporal barons, and had generally held the highest civil offices. The Lord Treasurer was often a Bishop. The Lord Chancellor was almost always so. The Lord Keeper of the Privy Seal and the Master of the Rolls were ordinarily churchmen. Churchmen transacted the most important diplomatic business. Indeed, almost all that large portion of the administration which rude and

2. My notion of the country gentleman of the seventeenth century has been derived from sources too numerous to be recapitulated. I must leave my description to the judgment of those who have studied the history and the lighter literature of that age.

[3. Gregory King (1648–1712) and Charles Davenant (1656–1714) were, after Sir William Petty, the two ablest statisticians of the time.]

warlike nobles were incompetent to conduct was considered as
especially belonging to divines. Men, therefore, who were averse
to the life of camps, and who were, at the same time, desirous to
rise in the state, ordinarily received the tonsure. Among them
were sons of all the most illustrious families, and near kinsmen
of the throne, Scropes and Nevilles, Bourchiers, Staffords, and
Poles. To the religious houses belonged the rents of immense
domains, and all that large portion of the tithe which is now in the
hands of laymen. Down to the middle of the reign of Henry the
Eighth, therefore, no line of life bore so inviting an aspect to
ambitious and covetous natures as the priesthood. Then came a
violent revolution. The abolition of the monasteries deprived the
Church at once of the greater part of her wealth, and of her predominance in the Upper House of Parliament. There was no
longer an Abbot of Glastonbury or an Abbot of Reading seated
among the peers, and possessed of revenues equal to those of a
powerful Earl. The princely splendour of William of Wykeham
and of William of Waynflete had disappeared. The scarlet hat
of the Cardinal, the silver cross of the Legate, were no more.

The clergy had also lost the ascendency which is the natural
reward of superior mental cultivation. Once the circumstance
that a man could read had raised a presumption that he was in
orders. But, in an age which produced such laymen as William
Cecil and Nicholas Bacon, Roger Ascham and Thomas Smith,
Walter Mildmay and Francis Walsingham, there was no reason
for calling away prelates from their dioceses to negotiate treaties,
to superintend the finances, or to administer justice. The spiritual character not only ceased to be a qualification for high civil
office, but began to be regarded as a disqualification. Those
worldly motives, therefore, which had formerly induced so many
able, aspiring, and high born youths to assume the ecclesiastical
habit, ceased to operate. Not one parish in two hundred then
afforded what a man of family considered as a maintenance. There
were still indeed prizes in the Church: but they were few; and
even the highest were mean, when compared with the glory
which had once surrounded the princes of the hierarchy. The
state kept by Parker and Grindal seemed beggarly to those who
remembered the imperial pomp of Wolsey, his palaces, which

had become the favourite abodes of royalty, Whitehall and Hampton Court, the three sumptuous tables daily spread in his refectory, the forty-four gorgeous copes in his chapel, his running footmen in rich liveries, and his body guards with gilded pole-axes. Thus the sacerdotal office lost its attraction for the higher classes. During the century which followed the accession of Elizabeth, scarce a single person of noble descent took orders. At the close of the reign of Charles the Second, two sons of peers were Bishops; four or five sons of peers were priests, and held valuable preferment: but these rare exceptions did not take away the reproach which lay on the body.

The clergy were regarded as, on the whole, a plebeian class. And, indeed, for one who made the figure of a gentleman, ten were mere menial servants. A large proportion of those divines who had no benefices, or whose benefices were too small to afford a comfortable revenue, lived in the houses of laymen. It had long been evident that this practice tended to degrade the priestly character. Laud had exerted himself to effect a change; and Charles the First had repeatedly issued positive orders that none but men of high rank should presume to keep domestic chaplains. But these injunctions had become obsolete. Indeed, during the domination of the Puritans, many of the ejected ministers of the Church of England could obtain bread and shelter only by attaching themselves to the households of royalist gentlemen; and the habits which had been formed in those times of trouble continued long after the re-establishment of monarchy and episcopacy. In the mansions of men of liberal sentiments and cultivated understandings, the chaplain was doubtless treated with urbanity and kindness. His conversation, his literary assistance, his spiritual advice, were considered as an ample return for his food, his lodging, and his stipend. But this was not the general feeling of the country gentlemen. The coarse and ignorant squire who thought that it belonged to his dignity to have grace said every day at his table by an ecclesiastic in full canonicals, found means to reconcile dignity with economy. A young Levite – such was the phrase then in use – might be had for his board, a small garret, and ten pounds a year, and might not only perform his own professional functions, might not only be the most patient of butts and of listeners, might not only be always ready in fine weather for bowls, and in rainy weather for shovelboard, but might also save the expense of a gardener, or of a groom. Sometimes the reverend man nailed up the apricots, and sometimes he curried the coach horses. He cast up the farrier's bills. He walked ten miles with a message or a parcel. He was permitted to dine with the family; but he was expected to content himself with the plainest fare. He might fill himself with the corned beef and the carrots: but, as soon as the tarts and the cheesecakes made their appearance, he quitted his seat, and stood aloof till he was summoned to return thanks for the repast, from a great part of which he had been excluded.

Perhaps, after some years of service, he was presented to a living sufficient to support him: but he often found it necessary to purchase his preferment by a species of simony, which furnished an inexhaustible subject of pleasantry to three or four generations of scoffers. With his cure he was expected to take a wife. The wife had ordinarily been in the patron's service; and it was well if she was not suspected of standing too high in the patron's favour. Indeed, the nature of the matrimonial connections which the clergymen of that age were in the habit of forming is the most certain indication of the place which the order held in the social system. An Oxonian, writing a few months after the death of Charles the Second, complained bitterly, not only that the country attorney and the country apothecary looked down with disdain on the country clergyman, but that one of the lessons most earnestly inculcated on every girl of honourable family was to give no encouragement to a lover in orders, and that, if any young lady forgot this precept, she was almost as much disgraced as by an illicit amour. Clarendon, who assuredly bore no ill will to the Church, mentions it as a sign of the confusion of ranks which the great rebellion had produced, that some damsels of noble families had bestowed themselves on divines. A waiting woman was generally considered as the most suitable helpmate for a parson. Queen Elizabeth, as head of the Church, had given what seemed to be a formal sanction to this prejudice, by issuing special orders that no clergyman should presume to marry a servant girl, without the consent of the master or mistress. During several generations accordingly the relation between priests and handmaidens was a theme for endless jest; nor would it be easy to find, in the comedy of the seventeenth century, a single instance of a clergyman who wins a spouse above the rank of a cook. Even so late as the time of George the Second, the keenest of all observers of life and manners, himself a priest, remarked that, in a great household, the chaplain was the resource of a lady's maid whose character had been blown upon, and who was therefore forced to give up hopes of catching the steward.[4]

In general the divine who quitted his chaplainship for a benefice and a wife found that he had only exchanged one class of vexations for another. Not one living in fifty enabled the incumbent to bring up a family comfortably. As children multiplied and grew, the household of the priest became more and more beggarly. Holes appeared more and more plainly in the thatch of his parsonage and in his single cassock. Often it was only by toiling on his glebe, by feeding swine, and by loading dungcarts, that he could obtain daily bread; nor did his utmost exertions always prevent the bailiffs from taking his concordance and his inkstand in execution. It was a white day on which he was admitted into the kitchen of a great house, and regaled by the servants with cold meat and ale. His children were brought up like the children of the neighbouring peasantry. His boys followed the plough; and his girls went out to service. Study he found impossible: for the advowson of his living would hardly have sold for a sum sufficient to purchase a good theological library; and he might be considered as unusually lucky if he had ten or twelve dog-eared volumes among the pots and pans on his shelves. Even a keen and strong intellect might be expected to rust in so unfavourable a situation.

Assuredly there was at that time no lack in the English Church of ministers distinguished by abilities and learning. But it is to be observed that these ministers were not scattered among the rural population. They were brought together at a few places where the means of acquiring knowledge were abundant, and where the opportunities of vigorous intellectual exercise were

4. Swift's *Directions to Servants*.

frequent. At such places were to be found divines qualified by parts, by eloquence, by wide knowledge of literature, of science, and of life, to defend their Church victoriously against heretics and sceptics, to command the attention of frivolous and worldly congregations, to guide the deliberations of senates, and to make religion respectable, even in the most dissolute of courts. Some laboured to fathom the abysses of metaphysical theology; some were deeply versed in biblical criticism; and some threw light on the darkest parts of ecclesiastical history. Some proved themselves consummate masters of logic. Some cultivated rhetoric with such assiduity and success that their discourses are still justly valued as models of style. These eminent men were to be found, with scarce a single exception, at the Universities, at the great Cathedrals, or in the capital. Barrow had lately died at Cambridge; and Pearson had gone thence to the episcopal bench. Cudworth and Henry More were still living there. South and Pococke, Jane and Aldrich, were at Oxford. Prideaux was in the close of Norwich, and Whitby in the close of Salisbury. But it was chiefly by the London clergy, who were always spoken of as a class apart, that the fame of their profession for learning and eloquence was upheld. The principal pulpits of the metropolis were occupied about this time by a crowd of distinguished men, from among whom was selected a large proportion of the rulers of the Church. Sherlock preached at the Temple, Tillotson at Lincoln's Inn, Wake and Jeremy Collier at Gray's Inn, Burnet at the Rolls, Stillingfleet at St Paul's Cathedral, Patrick at St Paul's, Covent Garden, Fowler at St Giles's, Cripplegate, Sharp at St Giles's in the Fields, Tenison at St Martin's, Sprat at St Margaret's, Beveridge at St Peter's in Cornhill. Of these twelve men, all of high note in ecclesiastical history, ten became Bishops, and four Archbishops. Meanwhile almost the only important theological works which came forth from a rural parsonage were those of George Bull, afterwards Bishop of St David's; and Bull never would have produced those works, had he not inherited an estate, by the sale of which he was enabled to collect a library, such as probably no other country clergyman in England possessed.

Thus the Anglican priesthood was divided into two sections,

which, in acquirements, in manners, and in social position, differed widely from each other. One section, trained for cities and
courts, comprised men familiar with all ancient and modern
learning; men able to encounter Hobbes or Bossuet at all the
weapons of controversy; men who could, in their sermons, set
forth the majesty and beauty of Christianity with such justness of
thought, and such energy of language, that the indolent Charles
roused himself to listen, and the fastidious Buckingham forgot
to sneer; men whose address, politeness, and knowledge of the
world qualified them to manage the consciences of the wealthy
and noble; men with whom Halifax loved to discuss the interests
of empires, and from whom Dryden was not ashamed to own
that he had learned to write.[5] The other section was destined to
ruder and humbler service. It was dispersed over the country,
and consisted chiefly of persons not at all wealthier, and not
much more refined, than small farmers or upper servants.

Yet it was in these rustic priests, who derived but a scanty
subsistence from their tithe sheaves and tithe pigs, and who had
not the smallest chance of ever attaining high professional honours, that the professional spirit was strongest. Among those
divines who were the boast of the Universities and the delight of
the capital, and who had attained, or might reasonably expect to
attain, opulence and lordly rank, a party, respectable in numbers,
and more respectable in character, leaned towards constitutional
principles of government, lived on friendly terms with Presbyterians, Independents, and Baptists, would gladly have seen a full
toleration granted to all Protestant sects, and would even have
consented to make alterations in the Liturgy, for the purpose of
conciliating honest and candid Nonconformists. But such latitudinarianism was held in horror by the country parson. He was,
indeed, prouder of his ragged gown than his superiors of their
lawn and of their scarlet hoods. The very consciousness that
there was little in his worldly circumstances to distinguish him
from the villagers to whom he preached led him to hold immod-

5. 'I have frequently heard him (Dryden) own with pleasure, that if he had
any talent for English prose it was owing to his having often read the writings
of the great Archbishop Tillotson'. Congreve's Dedication of Dryden's
Plays.

erately high the dignity of that sacerdotal office which was his
single title to reverence. Having lived in seclusion, and having had
little opportunity of correcting his opinions by reading or conversation, he held and taught the doctrines of indefeasible
hereditary right, of passive obedience, and of non-resistance in
all their crude absurdity. Having been long engaged in a petty war
against the neighbouring dissenters, he too often hated them for
the wrongs which he had done them, and found no fault with the
Five Mile Act and the Conventicle Act,[6] except that those odious
laws had not a sharper edge.

Whatever influence his office gave him was exerted with passionate zeal on the Tory side; and that influence was immense. It
would be a great error to imagine, because the country rector was
in general not regarded as a gentleman, because he could not
dare to aspire to the hand of one of the young ladies at the manor
house, because he was not asked into the parlours of the great,
but was left to drink and smoke with grooms and butlers, that
the power of the clerical body was smaller than at present. The
influence of a class is by no means proportioned to the consideration which the members of that class enjoy in their individual
capacity. A Cardinal is a much more exalted personage than a
begging friar: but it would be a grievous mistake to suppose that
the College of Cardinals has exercised a greater dominion over
the public mind of Europe than the Order of Saint Francis. In
Ireland, at present, a peer holds a far higher station in society
than a Roman Catholic priest: yet there are in Munster and Connaught few counties where a combination of priests would not
carry an election against a combination of peers. In the seventeenth century the pulpit was to a large portion of the population
what the periodical press now is. Scarce any of the clowns who
came to the parish church ever saw a Gazette or a political pamphlet. Ill informed as their spiritual pastor might be, he was yet
better informed than themselves: he had every week an opportunity of haranguing them; and his harangues were never answered. At every important conjuncture, invectives against the Whigs

[6. Two Acts of Parliament, forming part of the so-called 'Clarendon
Code' of 1661–5, designed to secure the predominance of the Anglican
Church and restrict the rights of Dissenters.]

and exhortations to obey the Lord's anointed resounded at once from many thousands of pulpits; and the effect was formidable indeed. Of all the causes which, after the dissolution of the Oxford Parliament, produced the violent reaction against the Exclusionists, the most potent seems to have been the oratory of the country clergy.

3

The New Reign

[*At the beginning of his reign, James II took care to reassure his subjects by stating that he would defend the Anglican Church and strictly respect the rights of the people. He allowed it to appear that he would continue his brother's policy of relying on the high Anglican tories, and that he would claim no more than equal rights for his own co-religionists, the Roman Catholics. But by his attentions to the French ambassador, Paul Barillon, who had acted as Louis XIV's paymaster in the previous reign, he also showed that he was determined to continue his brother's policy of dependence on France; and by certain ministerial changes he indicated that he was prepared to go beyond his brother both in domestic severity and in foreign dependence. The most sinister signs were two: the displacement of George Savile, Marquis of Halifax, 'the Trimmer', who had secured the defeat of the Exclusion Bill and thereby enabled James to succeed to the throne, but who was resolutely opposed to the aggrandizement of France; and the elevation of Sir George Jeffreys, who was to play a notorious part in the new reign. In his fourth chapter Macaulay describes these changes, and is enabled incidentally to introduce one of the characters whom he would consistently and unwarrantably denigrate: John Churchill, afterwards Duke of Marlborough.*]

THE great offices of state had become vacant by the demise of the crown; and it was necessary for James to determine how they should be filled. Few of the members of the late cabinet had any reason to expect his favour. Sunderland, who was Secretary of State, and Godolphin, who was First Lord of the Treasury, had supported the Exclusion Bill. Halifax, who held the Privy Seal, had opposed that bill with unrivalled powers of argument and eloquence. But Halifax was the mortal enemy of despotism and of Popery. He saw with dread the progress of the French arms on the continent, and the influence of French gold in the

counsels of England. Had his advice been followed, the laws
would have been strictly observed; clemency would have been
extended to the vanquished Whigs: the Parliament would have
been convoked in due season; an attempt would have been made
to reconcile our domestic factions; and the principles of the
Triple Alliance would again have guided our foreign policy. He
had therefore incurred the bitter animosity of James. The Lord
Keeper Guilford[1] could hardly be said to belong to either of the
parties into which the court was divided. He could by no means
be called a friend of liberty; and yet he had so great a reverence
for the letter of the law that he was not a serviceable tool of
arbitrary power. He was accordingly designated by the vehement Tories as a Trimmer, and was to James an object of aversion with which contempt was largely mingled. Ormond, who
was Lord Steward of the Household and Viceroy of Ireland, then
resided at Dublin. His claims on the royal gratitude were superior
to those of any other subject. He had fought bravely for Charles
the First; he had shared the exile of Charles the Second; and,
since the Restoration, he had, in spite of many provocations,
kept his loyalty unstained. Though he had been disgraced during
the predominance of the Cabal,[2] he had never gone into factious
opposition, and had, in the days of the Popish Plot and Exclusion
Bill, been foremost among the supporters of the throne. He was
now old, and had been recently tried by the most cruel of all calamities. He had followed to the grave a son who should have been
his own chief mourner, the gallant Ossory. The eminent services,
the venerable age, and the domestic misfortunes of Ormond
made him an object of general interest to the nation. The Cavaliers regarded him as, both by right of seniority and right of
merit, their head; and the Whigs knew that, faithful as he had
always been to the cause of monarchy, he was no friend either to
despotism or to Popery. But, high as he stood in the public estimation, he had little favour to expect from his new master.
James, indeed, while still a subject, had urged his brother to

[1. Francis North, Lord Guilford, had been Lord Keeper since December
1682.]

[2. The name given to the administration through which Charles II
governed in the years 1668–73.]

make a complete change in the Irish administration. Charles had assented; and it had been arranged that, in a few months, Rochester should be appointed Lord Lieutenant.

Rochester was the only member of the Cabinet who stood high in the favour of the new King. The general expectation was that he would be immediately placed at the head of affairs, and that all the other great officers of state would be changed. This expectation prove to be well founded in part only. Rochester was declared Lord Treasurer, and thus became prime minister. Neither a Lord High Admiral nor a Board of Admiralty was appointed. The new King, who loved the details of naval business, and would have made a respectable clerk in the dockyard at Chatham, determined to be his own minister of marine. Under him the management of that important department was confided to Samuel Pepys, whose library and diary have kept his name fresh to our time. No servant of the late sovereign was publicly disgraced. Sunderland exerted so much art and address, employed so many intercessors, and was in possession of so many secrets, that he was suffered to retain his seals. Godolphin's obsequiousness, industry, experience, and taciturnity, could ill be spared. As he was no longer wanted at the Treasury, he was made Chamberlain to the Queen. With these three Lords the King took counsel on all important questions. As to Halifax, Ormond, and Guilford, he determined not yet to dismiss them, but merely to humble and annoy them.

Halifax was told that he must give up the Privy Seal and accept the Presidency of the Council. He submitted with extreme reluctance. For, though the President of the Council had always taken precedence of the Lord Privy Seal, the Lord Privy Seal was, in that age, a much more important officer than the Lord President. Rochester had not forgotten the jest which had been made a few months before on his own removal from the Treasury, and enjoyed in his turn the pleasure of kicking his rival upstairs. The Privy Seal was delivered to Rochester's elder brother, Henry Earl of Clarendon.

To Barillon James expressed the strongest dislike of Halifax. 'I know him well, I never can trust him. He shall have no share in the management of public business. As to the place which I have given him, it will just serve to show how little influence he has.' But to Halifax it was thought convenient to hold a very different language. 'All the past is forgotten,' said the King, 'except the service which you did me in the debate on the Exclusion Bill.' This speech has often been cited to prove that James was not so vindictive as he has been called by his enemies. It seems rather to prove that he by no means deserved the praises which have been bestowed on his sincerity by his friends.

Ormond was politely informed that his services were no longer needed in Ireland, and was invited to repair to Whitehall, and to perform the functions of Lord Steward. He dutifully submitted, but did not affect to deny that the new arrangement wounded his feelings deeply. On the eve of his departure he gave a magnificent banquet at Kilmainham Hospital, then just completed, to the officers of the garrison of Dublin. After dinner he rose, filled a goblet to the brim with wine, and, holding it up, asked whether he had spilt one drop. 'No, gentlemen; whatever the courtiers may say, I am not yet sunk into dotage. My hand does not fail me yet; and my hand is not steadier than my heart. To the health of King James!' Such was the last farewell of Ormond to Ireland. He left the administration in the hands of Lord Justices, and repaired to London, where he was received with unusual marks of public respect. Many persons of rank went forth to meet him on the road. A long train of equipages followed him into Saint James's Square, where his mansion stood; and the Square was thronged by a multitude which greeted him with loud acclamations.

The Great Seal was left in Guilford's custody: but a marked indignity was at the same time offered to him. It was determined that another lawyer of more vigour and audacity should be called to assist in the administration. The person selected was Sir George Jeffreys, Chief Justice of the Court of King's Bench. The depravity of this man has passed into a proverb. Both the great English parties have attacked his memory with emulous violence: for the Whigs considered him as their most barbarous enemy; and the Tories found it convenient to throw on him the blame of all the crimes which had sullied their triumph. A diligent and candid inquiry will show that some frightful stories which have been told concerning him are false or exaggerated. Yet the dispassionate historian will be able to make very little deduction from the vast mass of infamy with which the memory of the wicked judge has been loaded.

He was a man of quick and vigorous parts, but constitutionally prone to insolence and to the angry passions. When just emerging from boyhood he had risen into practice at the Old Bailey bar, a bar where advocates have always used a licence of tongue unknown in Westminster Hall. Here, during many years, his chief business was to examine and cross-examine the most hardened miscreants of a great capital. Daily conflicts with prostitutes and thieves called out and exercised his powers so effectually that he became the most consummate bully ever known in his profession. All tenderness for the feelings of others, all self-respect, all sense of the becoming, were obliterated from his mind. He acquired a boundless command of the rhetoric in which the vulgar express hatred and contempt. The profusion of maledictions and vituperative epithets which composed his vocabulary could hardly have been rivalled in the fishmarket or the beargarden. His countenance and his voice must always have been unamiable. But these natural advantages – for such he seems to have thought them – he had improved to such a degree that there were few who, in his paroxysms of rage, could see or hear him without emotion. Impudence and ferocity sat upon his brow. The glare of his eyes had a fascination for the unhappy victim on whom they were fixed. Yet his brow and his eye were said to be less terrible than the savage lines of his mouth. His yell of fury, as was said by one who had often heard it, sounded like the thunder of the judgment day. These qualifications he carried, while still a young man, from the bar to the bench. He early became Common Serjeant and then Recorder of London. As a judge at the City sessions he exhibited the same propensities which afterwards, in a higher post, gained for him an unenviable immortality. Already might be remarked in him the most odious vice which is incident to human nature, a delight in misery merely as misery. There was a fiendish exultation in the way in which he pronounced sentence on offenders. Their weeping and imploring seemed to titillate him voluptuously; and he loved to scare them into fits by dilating with luxuriant amplification on all the details of what they were to suffer. Thus, when he had the opportunity of ordering an unlucky adventuress to be whipped at the cart's tail, 'Hangman,' he would exclaim, 'I charge you to pay particular attention to this lady! Scourge her soundly, man. Scourge her till the blood runs down! It is Christmas, a cold time for Madam to strip in! See that you warm her shoulders thoroughly!' He was hardly less facetious when he passed judgment on poor Lodowick Muggleton, the drunken tailor who fancied himself a prophet. 'Impudent rogue!' roared Jeffreys, 'thou shalt have an easy, easy, easy punishment!' One part of this easy punishment was the pillory, in which the wretched fanatic was almost killed with brickbats.

By this time the heart of Jeffreys had been hardened to that temper which tyrants require in their worst implements. He had hitherto looked for professional advancement to the corporation of London. He had therefore professed himself a Roundhead, and had always appeared to be in a higher state of exhilaration when he explained to Popish priests that they were to be cut down alive, and were to see their own bowels burned, than when he passed ordinary sentences of death. But, as soon as he had got all that the City could give, he made haste to sell his forehead of brass and his tongue of venom to the Court. Chiffinch, who was accustomed to act as broker in infamous contracts of more than one kind, lent his aid.[3] He had conducted many amorous and many political intrigues; but he assuredly never rendered a more scandalous service to his masters than when he introduced Jeffreys to Whitehall. The renegade soon found a patron in the obdurate and revengeful James, but was always regarded with scorn and disgust by Charles, whose faults, great as they were, had no affinity with insolence and cruelty. 'That man,' said the King, 'has no learning, no sense, no manners, and more impudence than ten carted streetwalkers.' Work was to be done, however, which could be trusted to no man who reverenced law or was sensible of shame, and thus Jeffreys, at an age which a barrister thinks himself fortunate if he is employed to conduct

[3. William Chiffinch, closet-keeper to Charles II, was master of the backstairs to the court.]

an important cause, was made Chief Justice of the King's Bench.

His enemies could not deny that he possessed some of the qualities of a great judge. His legal knowledge, indeed, was merely such as he had picked up in practice of no very high kind. But he had one of those happily constituted intellects which, across labyrinths of sophistry, and through masses of immaterial facts, go straight to the true point. Of his intellect, however, he seldom had the full use. Even in civil causes his malevolent and despotic temper perpetually disordered his judgment. To enter his court was to enter the den of a wild beast, which none could tame, and which was as likely to be roused to rage by caresses as by attacks. He frequently poured forth on plaintiffs and defendants, barristers and attorneys, witnesses and jurymen, torrents of frantic abuse, intermixed with oaths and curses. His looks and tones had inspired terror when he was merely a young advocate struggling into practice. Now that he was at the head of the most formidable tribunal in the realm, there were few indeed who did not tremble before him. Even when he was sober, his violence was sufficiently frightful. But in general his reason was overclouded and his evil passions stimulated by the fumes of intoxication. His evenings were ordinarily given to revelry. People who saw him only over his bottle would have supposed him to be a man gross indeed, sottish, and addicted to low company and low merriment, but social and goodhumoured. He was constantly surrounded on such occasions by buffoons selected, for the most part, from among the vilest pettifoggers who practised before him. These men bantered and abused each other for his entertainment. He joined in their ribald talk, sang catches with them, and, when his head grew hot, hugged and kissed them in an ecstasy of drunken fondness. But, though wine at first seemed to soften his heart, the effect a few hours later was very different. He often came to the judgment seat, having kept the court waiting long, and yet having but half slept off his debauch, his cheeks on fire, his eyes staring like those of a maniac. When he was in this state, his boon companions of the preceding night, if they were wise, kept out of his way: for the recollection of the familiarity to which he had admitted them inflamed his malignity; and he was sure to take every opportunity of overwhelming them with execration and invective. Not the least odious of his many odious peculiarities was the pleasure which he took in publicly browbeating and mortifying those whom, in his fits of maudlin tenderness, he had encouraged to presume on his favour.

The services which the government had expected from him were performed, not merely without flinching, but eagerly and triumphantly. His first exploit was the judicial murder of Algernon Sidney.[4] What followed was in perfect harmony with this beginning. Respectable Tories lamented the disgrace which the barbarity and indecency of so great a functionary brought upon the administration of justice. But the excesses which filled such men with horror were titles to the esteem of James. Jeffreys, therefore, after the death of Charles, obtained a seat in the cabinet and a peerage. This last honour was a signal mark of royal approbation. For, since the judicial system of the realm had been remodelled in the thirteenth century, no Chief Justice had been a Lord of Parliament.[5]

Guilford now found himself superseded in all his political functions, and restricted to his business as a judge in equity. At Council he was treated by Jeffreys with marked incivility. The whole legal patronage was in the hands of the Chief Justice; and it was well known by the bar that the surest way to propitiate the Chief Justice was to treat the Lord Keeper with disrespect.

James had not been many hours king when a dispute arose between the two heads of the law. The customs had been settled on Charles only for life, and could not therefore be legally exacted by the new sovereign. Some weeks must elapse before a House of Commons could be chosen. If, in the meantime, the duties were suspended, the revenue would suffer; the regular course to trade would be interrupted; the consumer would derive no benefit; and the only gainers would be those fortunate speculators whose cargoes might happen to arrive during the interval between the demise of the crown and the meeting of the Parliament. The

[4. Algernon Sidney, the republican, had been executed in 1683 for alleged conspiracy against Charles II.]

[5. Although attempts to whitewash Jeffreys are doomed to fail, it should be observed that Macaulay's portrait is a caricature, based on partial sources.]

Treasury was besieged by merchants whose warehouses were filled with goods on which duty had been paid, and who were in grievous apprehension of being undersold and ruined. Impartial men must admit that this was one of those cases in which a government may be justified in deviating from the strictly constitutional course. But, when it is necessary to deviate from the strictly constitutional course, the deviation clearly ought to be no greater than the necessity requires. Guilford felt this, and gave advice which did him honour. He proposed that the duties should be levied, but should be kept in the Exchequer apart from other sums till the Parliament should meet. In this way the King, while violating the letter of the laws, would show that he wished to conform to their spirit. Jeffreys gave very different counsel. He advised James to put forth an edict declaring it to be His Majesty's will and pleasure that the customs should continue to be paid. This advice was well suited to the King's temper. The judicious proposition of the Lord Keeper was rejected as worthy only of a Whig, or of what was still worse, a Trimmer. A proclamation, such as the Chief Justice had suggested, appeared. Some people expected that a violent outbreak of public indignation would be the consequence: but they were deceived. The spirit of opposition had not yet revived; and the court might safely venture to take steps which, five years before, would have produced a rebellion. In the City of London, lately so turbulent, scarcely a murmur was heard.

The proclamation, which announced that the customs would still be levied, announced also that a Parliament would shortly meet. It was not without many misgivings that James had determined to call the Estates of his realm together. The moment was, indeed, most auspicious for a general election. Never since the accession of the House of Stuart had the constituent bodies been so favourably disposed towards the court. But the new sovereign's mind was haunted by an apprehension not to be mentioned, even at this distance of time, without shame and indignation. He was afraid that by summoning his Parliament he might incur the displeasure of the King of France.

To the King of France it mattered little which of the two English parties triumphed at the elections: for all the Parliaments which had met since the Restoration, whatever might have been their temper as to domestic politics, had been jealous of the growing power of the House of Bourbon. On this subject there was little difference between the Whigs and the sturdy country gentlemen who formed the main strength of the Tory party. Lewis had therefore spared neither bribes nor menaces to prevent Charles from convoking the Houses; and James, who had from the first been in the secret of his brother's foreign politics, had now, in becoming King of England, become also a hireling and vassal of France.

Rochester, Godolphin, and Sunderland, who now formed the interior cabinet, were perfectly aware that their late master had been in the habit of receiving money from the court of Versailles. They were consulted by James as to the expediency of convoking the legislature. They owned the great importance of keeping Lewis in good humour: but it seemed to them that the calling of a Parliament was not a matter of choice. Patient as the nation appeared to be, there were limits to its patience. The principle that the money of the subject could not be lawfully taken by the King without the assent of the Commons, was firmly rooted in the public mind; and though, on an extraordinary emergency, even Whigs might be willing to pay, during a few weeks, duties not imposed by statute, it was certain that even Tories would become refractory if such irregular taxation should continue longer than the special circumstances which alone justified it. The Houses then must meet; and, since it was so, the sooner they were summoned the better. Even the short delay which would be occasioned by a reference to Versailles might produce irreparable mischief. Discontent and suspicion would spread fast through society. Halifax would complain that the fundamental principles of the constitution were violated. The Lord Keeper, like a cowardly pedantic special pleader as he was, would take the same side. What might have been done with a good grace would at last be done with a bad grace. Those very ministers whom His Majesty most wished to lower in the public estimation would gain popularity at his expense. The ill temper of the nation might seriously affect the result of the elections.

These arguments were unanswerable. The King therefore

notified to the country his intention of holding a Parliament. But he was painfully anxious to exculpate himself from the guilt of having acted undutifully and disrespectfully towards France. He led Barillon into a private room, and there apologized for having dared to take so important a step without the previous sanction of Lewis. 'Assure your master,' said James, 'of my gratitude and attachment. I know that without his protection I can do nothing. I know what troubles my brother brought on himself by not adhering steadily to France. I will take good care not to let the Houses meddle with foreign affairs. If I see in them any disposition to make mischief, I will send them about their business. Explain this to my good brother. I hope that he will not take it amiss that I have acted without consulting him. He has a right to be consulted; and it is my wish to consult him about everything. But in this case the delay even of a week might have produced serious consequences.'

These ignominious excuses were, on the following morning, repeated by Rochester. Barillon received them civilly. Rochester, grown bolder, proceeded to ask for money. 'It will be well laid out,' he said; 'your master cannot employ his revenues better. Represent to him strongly how important it is that the King of England should be dependent, not on his own people, but on the friendship of France alone.'

Barillon hastened to communicate to Lewis the wishes of the English government; but Lewis had already anticipated them. His first act, after he was apprised of the death of Charles, was to collect bills of exchange on England to the amount of five hundred thousand livres, a sum equivalent to about thirty-seven thousand five hundred pounds sterling. Such bills were not then to be easily procured in Paris at a day's notice. In a few hours, however, the purchase was effected, and a courier started for London. As soon as Barillon received the remittance, he flew to Whitehall, and communicated the welcome news. James was not ashamed to shed, or pretend to shed, tears of delight and gratitude. 'Nobody but your King,' he said, 'does such kind, such noble things. I never can be grateful enough. Assure him that my attachment will last to the end of my days.' Rochester, Sunderland, and Godolphin came, one after another, to embrace the ambassador, and to whisper to him that he had given new life to their royal master.

But though James and his three advisers were pleased with the promptitude which Lewis had shown, they were by no means satisfied with the amount of the donation. As they were afraid, however, that they might give offence by importunate mendicancy, they merely hinted their wishes. They declared that they had no intention of higgling with so generous a benefactor as the French King, and that they were willing to trust entirely to his munificence. They, at the same time, attempted to propitiate him by a large sacrifice of national honour. It was well known that one chief end of his politics was to add the Belgian provinces to his dominions. England was bound by a treaty, which had been concluded by Spain when Danby was Lord Treasurer, to resist any attempt which France might make on those provinces. The three ministers informed Barillon that their master considered that treaty as no longer obligatory. It had been made, they said, by Charles: it might, perhaps, have been binding on him; but his brother did not think himself bound by it. The most Christian King might, therefore, without any fear of opposition from England, proceed to annex Brabant and Hainault to his empire.

It was at the same time resolved that an extraordinary embassy should be sent to assure Lewis of the gratitude and affection of James. For this mission was selected a man who did not as yet occupy a very eminent position, but whose renown, strangely made up of infamy and glory, filled at a later period the whole civilised world.

Soon after the Restoration, in the gay and dissolute times celebrated by the lively pen of Hamilton, James, young and ardent in the pursuit of pleasure, had been attracted by Arabella Churchill, one of the maids of honour who waited on his first wife. The young lady was not beautiful: but the taste of James was not nice: and she became his avowed mistress. She was the daughter of a poor Cavalier knight who haunted Whitehall, and made himself ridiculous by publishing a dull and affected folio, long forgotten, in praise of monarchy and monarchs. The necessities of the

Churchills were pressing; their loyalty was ardent; and their only feeling about Arabella's seduction seems to have been joyful surprise that so plain a girl should have attained such high preferment.

Her interest was indeed of great use to her relations; but none of them was so fortunate as her eldest brother John, a fine youth, who carried a pair of colours in the foot guards. He rose fast in the court and in the army, and was early distinguished as a man of fashion and of pleasure. His stature was commanding, his face handsome, his address singularly winning, yet of such dignity that the most impertinent fops never ventured to take any liberty with him; his temper, even in the most vexatious and irritating circumstances, always under perfect command. His education had been so much neglected, that he could not spell the most common words of his own language: but his acute and vigorous understanding amply supplied the place of book learning. He was not loquacious: but, when he was forced to speak in public, his natural eloquence moved the envy of practised rhetoricians. His courage was singularly cool and imperturbable. During many years of anxiety and peril, he never, in any emergency, lost, even for a moment, the perfect use of his admirable judgment.

In his twenty-third year he was sent with his regiment to join the French forces, then engaged in operations against Holland. His serene intrepidity distinguished him among thousands of brave soldiers. His professional skill commanded the respect of veteran officers. He was publicly thanked at the head of the army, and received many marks of esteem and confidence from Turenne, who was then at the height of his military glory.

Unhappily the splendid qualities of John Churchill were mingled with alloy of the most sordid kind. Some propensities, which in youth are singularly ungraceful, began very early to show themselves in him. He was thrifty in his very vices, and levied ample contributions on ladies enriched by the spoils of more liberal lovers. He was, during a short time, the object of the violent but fickle fondness of the Duchess of Cleveland. On one occasion he was caught with her by the King, and was forced to leap out of the window. She rewarded this hazardous feat of gallantry with a present of five thousand pounds. With this sum the prudent young hero instantly bought an annuity of five hundred a year, well secured on landed property. Already his private drawers contained heaps of broad pieces which, fifty years later, when he was a Duke, a Prince of the Empire, and the richest subject in Europe, remained untouched.

After the close of the war he was attached to the household of the Duke of York, accompanied his patron to the Low Countries and to Edinburgh, and was rewarded for his services with a Scotch peerage and with the command of the only regiment of dragoons which was then on the English establishment. His wife had a post in the family of James's younger daughter, the Princess of Denmark.

Lord Churchill was now sent as ambassador extraordinary to Versailles. He had it in charge to express the warm gratitude of the English government for the money which had been so generously bestowed. It had been originally intended that he should, at the same time, ask Lewis for a much larger sum; but, on full consideration, it was apprehended that such indelicate greediness might disgust the benefactor whose spontaneous liberality had been so signally displayed. Churchill was therefore directed to confine himself to thanks for what was past, and to say nothing about the future.

But James and his ministers, even while protesting that they did not mean to be importunate, contrived to hint, very intelligibly, what they wished and expected. In the French ambassador they had a dexterous, a zealous, and, perhaps, not a disinterested intercessor. Lewis made some difficulties, probably with the design of enhancing the value of his gifts. In a very few weeks, however, Barillon received from Versailles fifteen hundred thousand livres more. This sum, equivalent to about a hundred and twelve thousand pounds sterling, he was instructed to dole out cautiously. He was authorised to furnish the English government with thirty thousand pounds, for the purpose of corrupting members of the new House of Commons. The rest he was directed to keep in reserve for some extraordinary emergency, such as a dissolution or an insurrection.

The turpitude of these transactions is universally acknowledged: but their real nature seems to be often misunderstood;

for, though the foreign policy of the two last Kings of the House of Stuart has never, since the correspondence of Barillon was exposed to the public eye, found an apologist among us, there is still a party which labours to excuse their domestic policy. Yet it is certain that between their domestic policy and their foreign policy there was a necessary and indissoluble connection. If they had upheld, during but a few months, the honour of the country abroad, they would have been compelled to change the whole system of their administration at home. To praise them for refusing to govern in conformity with the sense of Parliament, and yet to blame them for submitting to the dictation of Lewis, is inconsistent. For they had only one choice, to be dependent on Lewis, or to be dependent on Parliament.

James, to do him justice, would gladly have found out a third way: but there was none. He became the slave of France: but it would be incorrect to represent him as a contented slave. He had spirit enough to be at times angry with himself for submitting to such thraldom, and impatient to break loose from it; and this disposition was studiously encouraged by the agents of many foreign powers.

His accession had excited hopes and fears in every continental court: and the commencement of his administration was watched by strangers with interest scarcely less deep than that which was felt by his own subjects. One government alone wished that the troubles which had, during three generations, distracted England, might be eternal. All other governments, whether republican or monarchical, whether Protestant or Roman Catholic, wished to see those troubles happily terminated.

The nature of the long contest between the Stuarts and their Parliaments was indeed very imperfectly apprehended by foreign statesmen: but no statesman could fail to perceive the effect which that contest had produced on the balance of power in Europe. In ordinary circumstances, the sympathies of the courts of Vienna and Madrid would doubtless have been with a prince struggling against subjects, and especially with a Roman Catholic prince struggling against heretical subjects: but all such sympathies were now overpowered by a stronger feeling. The fear and hatred inspired by the greatness, the injustice, and the arrogance of the French King were at the height. His neighbours might well doubt whether it were more dangerous to be at war or at peace with him. For in peace he continued to plunder and to outrage them; and they had tried the chances of war against him in vain. In this perplexity they looked with intense anxiety towards England. Would she act on the principles of the Triple Alliance or on the principles of the treaty of Dover? On that issue depended the fate of all her neighbours. With her help Lewis might yet be withstood: but no help could be expected from her till she was at unity with herself. Before the strife between the throne and the Parliament began, she had been a power of the first rank: on the day on which that strife terminated she became a power of the first rank again; but while the dispute remained undecided, she was condemned to inaction and to vassalage. She had been great under the Plantagenets and Tudors: she was again great under the princes who reigned after the Revolution: but, under the Kings of the House of Stuart, she was a blank in the map of Europe. She had lost one class of energies, and had not yet acquired another. That species of force, which, in the fourteenth century, had enabled her to humble France and Spain, had ceased to exist. That species of force, which, in the eighteenth century, humbled France and Spain once more, had not yet been called into action. The government was no longer a limited monarchy after the fashion of the middle ages. It had not yet become a limited monarchy after the modern fashion. With the vices of two different systems it had the strength of neither. The elements of our polity, instead of combining in harmony, counteracted and neutralised each other. All was transition, conflict, and disorder. The chief business of the sovereign was to infringe the privileges of the legislature. The chief business of the legislature was to encroach on the prerogatives of the sovereign. The King readily accepted foreign aid, which relieved him from the misery of being dependent on a mutinous Parliament. The Parliament refused to the King the means of supporting the national honour abroad, from an apprehension, too well founded, that those means might be employed in order to establish despotism at home. The effect of these jealousies was that our country, with all her vast resources, was of as little weight in

Christendom as the duchy of Savoy or the duchy of Lorraine, and certainly of far less weight than the small province of Holland.

France was deeply interested in prolonging this state of things. All other powers were deeply interested in bringing it to a close. The general wish of Europe was that James would govern in conformity with law and with public opinion. From the Escurial itself came letters, expressing an earnest hope that the new King of England would be on good terms with his Parliament and his people. From the Vatican itself came cautions against immoderate zeal for the Roman Catholic faith.

4

James II's Dissenting Allies: the Quakers

[*Relying on the high-Anglican tories who had supported his brother
(although already beginning to affront them by his favour to Roman
Catholics), James II persecuted the religious allies of the whigs, the
Protestant Dissenters. But one group of such Dissenters escaped this
persecution: the Quakers, whose sect had been founded by George
Fox in the 1650s, and whose most distinguished leader at this time,
after Fox, was the courtly and saintly William Penn. James indulged
the Quakers partly because they were completely unpolitical (and
therefore politically naïve), partly because he was personally friendly
with Penn. For the same reasons, Macaulay hated both Penn and the
Quakers; and having once made up his mind to hate them, he pursued them in the same vindictive spirit in which he pursued Marlborough. That is, he invariably put the most hostile construction on
the evidence and sometimes, in his haste to condemn, misread the
evidence. The following two passages, though travesties of the truth,
show Macaulay's method of dealing with persons whom he had decided, on political grounds, to condemn. The first is his characteriza-
tion of William Penn, in Chapter IV; the second, which shows that
his animosity was not against Penn only but against the Quakers
generally, comes from Chapter XVII. Macaulay is there describing
– very inaccurately – an episode which occurred in 1691, when Penn
was suspected (quite wrongly) of complicity in a plot against William III. The episode enables Macaulay to advertise, somewhat ir-
relevantly, his dislike of the founder of Quakerism, George Fox.*]

A. WILLIAM PENN

ONE sect of Protestant Dissenters indeed he, even at this early
period of his reign, regarded with some tenderness, the Society
of Friends. His partiality for that singular fraternity cannot be
attributed to religious sympathy; for, of all who acknowledge the
divine mission of Jesus, the Roman Catholic and the Quaker diff-

er most widely. It may seem paradoxical to say that this very circumstance constituted a tie between the Roman Catholic and the Quaker; yet such was really the case. For they deviated in opposite directions so far from what the great body of the nation regarded as right that even liberal men generally considered them both as lying beyond the pale of the largest toleration. Thus the two extreme sects, precisely because they were extreme sects, had a common interest distinct from the interest of the intermediate sects. The Quakers were also guiltless of all offence against James and his House. They had not been in existence as a community till the war between his father and the Long Parliament was drawing towards a close. They had been cruelly persecuted by some of the revolutionary governments. They had, since the Restoration, in spite of much ill usage, submitted themselves meekly to the royal authority, for they had, though reasoning on premises which the Anglican divines regarded as heterodox, arrived, like the Anglican divines, at the conclusion, that no excess of tyranny on the part of a prince can justify active resistance on the part of a subject. No libel on the government had ever been traced to a Quaker. In no conspiracy against the government had a Quaker been implicated. The society had not joined in the clamour for the Exclusion Bill, and had solemnly condemned the Rye House Plot as a hellish design and a work of the devil. Indeed, the Friends then took very little part in civil contentions; for they were not, as now, congregated in large towns, but were generally engaged in agriculture, a pursuit from which they have been gradually driven by the vexations consequent on their strange scruple about paying tithe. They were, therefore, far removed from the scene of political strife. They also, even in domestic privacy, avoided on principle all political conversation. For such conversation was, in their opinion, unfavourable to their spirituality of mind, and tended to disturb the austere composure of their deportment. The yearly meetings of that age repeatedly admonished the brethren not to hold discourse touching affairs of state. Even within the memory of persons now living those grave elders who retained the habits of an earlier generation systematically discouraged such worldly talk. It was natural that James should make a wide distinction between this harmless race and those fierce and restless sects which considered resistance to tyranny as a Christian duty, which had, in Germany, France, and Holland, made war on legitimate princes, and which had, during four generations, borne peculiar enmity to the House of Stuart.

It happened, moreover, that it was possible to grant large relief to the Roman Catholic and to the Quaker without mitigating the sufferings of the Puritan sects. A law which was then in force imposed severe penalties on every person who refused to take the oath of supremacy when required to do so. This law did not affect Presbyterians, Independents, or Baptists; for they were all ready to call God to witness that they renounced all spiritual connection with foreign prelates and potentates. But the Roman Catholic would not swear that the Pope had no jurisdiction in England, and the Quaker would not swear to anything. On the other hand, neither the Roman Catholic nor the Quaker was touched by the Five Mile Act, which, of all the laws in the Statute Book, was perhaps the most annoying to the Puritan Nonconformists.[1]

The Quakers had a powerful and zealous advocate at court. Though, as a class, they mixed little with the world, and shunned politics as a pursuit dangerous to their spiritual interests, one of them, widely distinguished from the rest by station and fortune, lived in the highest circles, and had constant access to the royal ear. This was the celebrated William Penn. His father had held great naval commands, had been a Commissioner of the Admiralty, had sat in Parliament, had received the honour of knighthood, and had been encouraged to expect a peerage. The son had been liberally educated, and had been designed for the profession of arms, but had, while still young, injured his prospects and disgusted his friends by joining what was then generally considered as a gang of crazy heretics. He had been sent sometimes to the Tower, and sometimes to Newgate. He had been tried at the Old Bailey for preaching in defiance of the law. After a time, however, he had been reconciled to his family, and had succeeded in obtaining such powerful protection that, while all the gaols of England were filled with his brethren, he was permitted, during

[1. See above, p. 68 and fn 6.]

many years, to profess his opinions without molestation. Towards the close of the late reign he had obtained, in satisfaction of an old debt due to him from the crown, the grant of an immense region in North America. In this tract, then peopled only by Indian hunters, he had invited his persecuted friends to settle. His colony was still in its infancy when James mounted the throne.

Between James and Penn there had long been a familiar acquaintance. The Quaker now became a courtier, and almost a favourite. He was every day summoned from the gallery into the closet, and sometimes had long audiences while peers were kept waiting in the ante-chambers. It was noised abroad that he had more real power to help and hurt than many nobles who filled high offices. He was soon surrounded by flatterers and suppliants. His house at Kensington was sometimes thronged, at his hour of rising, by more than two hundred suitors. He paid dear, however, for this seeming prosperity. Even his own sect looked coldly on him, and requited his services with obloquy. He was loudly accused of being a Papist, nay, a Jesuit. Some affirmed that he had been educated at St Omers, and others, that he had been ordained at Rome. These calumnies, indeed, could find credit only with the undiscerning multitude: but with these calumnies were mingled accusations much better founded.

To speak the whole truth concerning Penn is a task which requires some courage; for he is rather a mythical than a historical person. Rival nations and hostile sects have agreed in canonizing him. England is proud of his name. A great commonwealth beyond the Atlantic regards him with a reverence similar to that which the Athenians felt for Theseus, and the Romans for Quirinus.[2] The respectable society of which he was a member honours him as an apostle. By pious men of other persuasions he is generally regarded as a bright pattern of Christian virtue. Meanwhile admirers of a very different sort have sounded his praises. The French philosophers of the eighteenth century pardoned what they regarded as his superstitious fancies in consideration of his contempt for priests, and of his cosmopolitan benevolence, im-

[2. Theseus and Quirinus (or Romulus) were the legendary founders of Athens and Rome respectively.]

partially extended to all races and to all creeds. His name has thus become, throughout all civilised countries, a synonym for probity and philanthropy.

Nor is this high reputation altogether unmerited. Penn was without doubt a man of eminent virtues. He had a strong sense of religious duty and a fervent desire to promote the happiness of mankind. On one or two points of high importance he had notions more correct than were, in his day, common even among men of enlarged minds; and, as the proprietor and legislator of a province which, being almost uninhabited when it came into his possession, afforded a clear field for moral experiments, he had the rare good fortune of being able to carry his theories into practice without any compromise, and yet without any shock to existing institutions. He will always be mentioned with honour as a founder of a colony, who did not, in his dealings with a savage people, abuse the strength derived from civilisation, and as a lawgiver who, in an age of persecution, made religious liberty the corner stone of a polity. But his writings and his life furnish abundant proofs that he was not a man of strong sense. He had no skill in reading the characters of others. His confidence in persons less virtuous than himself led him into great errors and misfortunes. His enthusiasm for one great principle sometimes impelled him to violate other great principles which he ought to have held sacred. Nor was his rectitude altogether proof against the temptations to which it was exposed in that splendid and polite, but deeply corrupted society, with which he now mingled.

The whole court was in a ferment with intrigues of gallantry and intrigues of ambition. The traffic in honours, places, and pardons was incessant. It was natural that a man who was daily seen at the palace, and who was known to have free access to majesty, should be frequently importuned to use his influence for purposes which a rigid morality must condemn. The integrity of Penn had stood firm against obloquy and persecution. But now, attacked by royal smiles, by female blandishments, by the insinuating eloquence and delicate flattery of veteran diplomatists and courtiers, his resolution began to give way. Titles and phrases against which he had often borne his testimony dropped occasionally from his lips and his pen. It would be well if he had been guilty of nothing worse than such compliances with the fashions of the world. Unhappily it cannot be concealed that he bore a chief part in some transactions condemned, not merely by the rigid code of the society to which he belonged, but by the general sense of all honest men. He afterwards solemnly protested that his hands were pure from illicit gain, and that he had never received any gratuity from those whom he had obliged, though he might easily, while his influence at court lasted, have made a hundred and twenty thousand pounds. To this assertion full credit is due. But bribes may be offered to vanity as well as to cupidity; and it is impossible to deny that Penn was cajoled into bearing a part in some unjustifiable transactions of which others enjoyed the profits.

The first use which he made of his credit was highly commendable. He strongly represented the sufferings of the Quakers to the new King, who saw with pleasure that it was possible to grant indulgence to these quiet sectaries and to the Roman Catholics, without showing similar favour to other classes which were then under persecution. A list was framed of prisoners against whom proceedings had been instituted for not taking the oaths, or for not going to church, and of whose loyalty certificates had been produced to the government. These persons were discharged, and orders were given that no similar proceeding should be instituted till the royal pleasure should be further signified. In this way about fifteen hundred Quakers, and a still greater number of Roman Catholics, regained their liberty.

B. GEORGE FOX

A warrant was issued against Penn; and he narrowly escaped the messengers. It chanced that, on the day on which they were sent in search of him, he was attending a remarkable ceremony at some distance from his home.[3] An event had taken place which a historian, whose object is to record the real life of a nation, ought not to pass unnoticed. While London was agitated by the news

[3. This is incorrect. The proclamation for the arrest of Penn was issued on 5 February 1691, three weeks after Fox's funeral.]

that a plot had been discovered, George Fox, the founder of the sect of Quakers, died.

More than forty years had elapsed since Fox had begun to see visions and to cast out devils. He was then a youth of pure morals and grave deportment, with a perverse temper, with the education of a labouring man, and with an intellect in the most unhappy of all states, that is to say, too much disordered for liberty, and not sufficiently disordered for Bedlam. The circumstances in which he was placed were such as could scarcely fail to bring out in the strongest form the constitutional diseases of his mind. At the time when his faculties were ripening, Episcopalians, Presbyterians, Independents, Baptists, were striving for mastery, and were, in every corner of the realm, refuting and reviling each other. He wandered from congregation to congregation: he heard priests harangue against Puritans: he heard Puritans harangue against priests; and he in vain applied for spiritual direction and consolation to doctors of both parties. One jolly old clergyman of the Anglican communion told him to smoke tobacco and sing psalms: another advised him to go and lose some blood. The young inquirer turned in disgust from these advisers to the Dissenters, and found them also blind guides. After some time he came to the conclusion that no human being was competent to instruct him in divine things, and that the truth had been communicated to him by direct inspiration from heaven. He argued that, as the division of languages began at Babel, and as the persecutors of Christ put on the cross an inscription in Latin, Greek and Hebrew, the knowledge of languages, and more especially of Latin, Greek and Hebrew, must be useless to a Christian minister. Indeed, he was so far from knowing many languages, that he knew none; nor can the most corrupt passage in Hebrew be more unintelligible to the unlearned than his English often is to the most acute and attentive reader. One of the precious truths which were divinely revealed to this new apostle was, that it was falsehood and adulation to use the second person plural instead of the second person singular. Another was, that to talk of the month of March was to worship the bloodthirsty god Mars, and that to talk of Monday was to pay idolatrous homage to the moon. To

say Good morning or Good evening was highly reprehensible, for
those phrases evidently imported that God had made bad days
and bad nights. A Christian was bound to face death itself rather
than touch his hat to the greatest of mankind. When Fox was
challenged to produce any Scriptural authority for this dogma,
he cited the passage in which it is written that Shadrach, Mesh-
ech and Abednego were thrown into the fiery furnace with their
hats on; and, if his own narrative may be trusted, the Chief Justice of England was altogether unable to answer this argument
except by crying out, 'Take him away, gaoler.' Fox insisted much
on the not less weighty argument that the Turks never show their
bare heads to their superiors; and he asked, with great animation,
whether those who bore the noble name of Christians ought not
to surpass Turks in virtue. Bowing he strictly prohibited, and,
indeed, seemed to consider it as the effect of Satanical influence;
for, as he observed, the woman in the Gospel, while she had a
spirit of infirmity, was bowed together, and ceased to bow as
soon as Divine power had liberated her from the tyranny of the
Evil One. His expositions of the sacred writings were of a very
peculiar kind. Passages, which had been, in the apprehension of
all the readers of the Gospels during sixteen centuries, figurative,
he construed literally. Passages, which no human being before
him had ever understood in any other than a literal sense, he construed figuratively. Thus, from those rhetorical expressions in
which the duty of patience under injuries is enjoined he deduced
the doctrine that self-defence against pirates and assassins is unlawful. On the other hand, the plain commands to baptize with
water, and to partake of bread and wine in commemoration of the
redemption of mankind, he pronounced to be allegorical. He long
wandered from place to place, teaching this strange theology,
shaking like an aspen leaf in his paroxysms of fanatical excitement, forcing his way into churches, which he nicknamed steeple
houses, interrupting prayers and sermons with clamour and
scurrility, and pestering rectors and justices with epistles much
resembling burlesques of those sublime odes in which the Hebrew
prophets foretold the calamities of Babylon and Tyre. He soon acquired great notoriety by these feats. His strange face, his strange
chant, his immovable hat and his leather breeches were known

all over the country; and he boasts that, as soon as the rumour was heard, 'The Man in Leather Breeches is coming,' terror seized hypocritical professors, and hireling priests made haste to get out of his way. He was repeatedly imprisoned and set in the stocks, sometimes justly, for disturbing the public worship of congregations, and sometimes unjustly, for merely talking nonsense. He soon gathered round him a body of disciples, some of whom went beyond himself in absurdity. He has told us that one of his friends walked naked through Skipton declaring the truth, and that another was divinely moved to go naked during several years to marketplaces, and to the houses of gentlemen and clergymen. Fox complains bitterly that these pious acts, prompted by the Holy Spirit, were requited by an untoward generation with hooting, pelting, coachwhipping and horsewhipping. But, though he applauded the zeal of the sufferers, he did not go quite to their lengths. He sometimes, indeed, was impelled to strip himself partially. Thus he pulled off his shoes and walked barefoot through Lichfield, crying, 'Woe to the bloody city.' But it does not appear that he ever thought it his duty to appear before the public without that decent garment from which his popular appellation was derived.

If we form our judgment of George Fox simply by looking at his own actions and writings, we shall see no reason for placing him, morally or intellectually, above Ludowick Muggleton or Joanna Southcote. But it would be most unjust to rank the sect which regards him as its founder with the Muggletonians or the Southcotians. It chanced that among the thousands whom his enthusiasm infected were a few persons whose abilities and attainments were of a very different order from his own. Robert Barclay was a man of considerable parts and learning. William Penn, though inferior to Barclay in both natural and acquired abilities, was a gentleman and a scholar. That such men should have become the followers of George Fox ought not to astonish any person who remembers what quick, vigorous and highly cultivated intellects were in our own times duped by the unknown tongues. The truth is that no powers of mind constitute a security against errors of this description. Touching God and His ways with man, the highest human faculties can discover little more than the meanest. In theology the interval is small indeed between Aristotle and a child, between Archimedes and a naked savage. It is not strange, therefore, that wise men, weary of investigation, tormented by uncertainty, longing to believe something, and yet seeing objections to every thing, should submit themselves absolutely to teachers who, with firm and undoubting faith, lay claim to a supernatural commission. Thus we frequently see inquisitive and restless spirits take refuge from their own scepticism in the bosom of a church which pretends to infallibility, and, after questioning the existence of a Deity, bring themselves to worship a wafer. And thus it was that Fox made some converts to whom he was immeasurably inferior in every thing except the energy of his convictions. By these converts his rude doctrines were polished into a form somewhat less shocking to good sense and good taste. No proposition which he had laid down was retracted. No indecent or ridiculous act which he had done or approved was condemned: but what was most grossly absurd in his theories and practices was softened down, or at least not obtruded on the public: whatever could be made to appear specious was set in the fairest light: his gibberish was translated into English: meanings which he would have been quite unable to comprehend were put on his phrases; and his system, so much improved that he would not have known it again, was defended by numerous citations from Pagan philosophers and Christian fathers whose names he had never heard. Still, however, those who had remodelled his theology continued to profess, and doubtless to feel, profound reverence for him; and his crazy epistles were to the last received and read with respect in Quaker meetings all over the country. His death produced a sensation which was not confined to his own disciples. On the morning of the funeral a great multitude assembled round the meeting house in Gracechurch Street. Thence the corpse was borne to the burial ground of the sect near Bunhill Fields. Several orators addressed the crowd which filled the cemetery. Penn was conspicuous among those disciples who committed the venerable corpse to the earth. The ceremony had scarcely been finished when he learned that warrants were out against him. He instantly took flight, and remained many months concealed from the public eye.

A short time after his disappearance, Sidney received from him a strange communication. Penn begged for an interview, but insisted on a promise that he should be suffered to return unmolested to his hiding place. Sidney obtained the royal permission to make an appointment on these terms. Penn came to the rendezvous, and spoke at length in his own defence. He declared that he was a faithful subject of King William and Queen Mary, and that, if he knew of any design against them, he would discover it. Departing from his Yea and Nay, he protested, as in the presence of God, that he knew of no plot, and that he did not believe that there was any plot, unless the ambitious projects of the French government might be called plots. Sidney, amazed probably by hearing a person, who had such an abhorrence of lies that he would not use the common forms of civility, and such an abhorrence of oaths that he would not kiss the book in a court of justice, tell something very like a lie, and confirm it by something very like an oath, asked how, if there were really no plot, the letters and minutes which had been found on Ashton were to be explained. This question Penn evaded. 'If,' he said, 'I could only see the King, I would confess every thing to him freely. I would tell him much that it would be important for him to know. It is only in that way that I can be of service to him. A witness for the Crown I cannot be: for my conscience will not suffer me to be sworn.' He assured Sidney that the most formidable enemies of the government were the discontented Whigs. 'The Jacobites are not dangerous. There is not a man among them who has common understanding. Some persons who came over from Holland with the King are much more to be dreaded.' It does not appear that Penn mentioned any names. He was suffered to depart in safety. No active search was made for him. He lay hid in London during some months, and then stole down to the coast of Sussex and made his escape to France. After about three years of wandering and lurking he, by the mediation of some eminent men, who overlooked his faults for the sake of his good qualities, made his peace with the government, and again ventured to resume his ministrations. The return which he made for the lenity with which he had been treated does not much raise his character. Scarcely had he begun to harangue in public about the unlawfulness of war, when he sent a message earnestly exhorting James to make an immediate descent on England with thirty thousand men.[4]

[4. Macaulay's whole account of Penn's actions is grossly inaccurate, as Paget has shown (*The New Examen*, pp. 194–293). Penn did not go into hiding or flee abroad, and the charge that he urged James to invade England with thirty thousand men is an elaboration of a worthless Jacobite speculation.]

5

The First Revolts: Argyll, Monmouth, and the Bloody Assize

[*The first attack on the government of James II came from the defeated English and Scottish whigs who, after the failure of their conspiracies against Charles II, were nursing their wounds abroad, in the Netherlands. The chief of the Scottish exiles was the Earl of Argyll, the head of clan Campbell, known in the Highlands as MacCallum More. His father had been the organizer of Scottish opposition to Charles I, and had been executed in 1661. The son had been condemned to death on a frivolous charge by James, when viceroy of Scotland under Charles II, and had escaped to Holland. The leader, or figurehead, of the English exiles was the Duke of Monmouth, the popular idol of Protestantism, whom the 'Exclusionists' had sought to substitute for James as heir to the throne and who, on their failure, had been advised to go into exile by his father Charles II. In 1685 both the Scottish and the English exiles sought to strike at James II while his power was new, and while the embers of the anti-Catholic resentment of 1679 were still warm. Argyll sailed with a party of followers to the West of Scotland, where he hoped to raise his clan, but was captured, taken to Edinburgh, condemned and executed. Monmouth, accompanied by Lord Grey of Wark and other exiled whigs (including Robert Ferguson, 'the Plotter', his 'evil angel'), landed at Lyme Regis, in the West of England. He summoned the country to revolt, gathered an army, published a defamatory declaration against James (evidently written by Ferguson), and declared himself King. But at the battle of Sedgemoor, in Somerset, his rustic army was defeated by the royal army, commanded by Louis Duras, a French Huguenot, who had been ennobled by Charles II as Earl of Feversham. The following passage, from Chapter V, describes the aftermath of the battle of Sedgemoor and the fearful revenge which James, through his agent, Lord Chief Justice Jeffreys, took not only on the rebels but on all who had aided or comforted them.*]

IT was four o'clock: the sun was rising; and the routed army
came pouring into the streets of Bridgewater. The uproar, the
blood, the gashes, the ghastly figures which sank down and never
rose again, spread horror and dismay through the town. The
pursuers, too, were close behind. Those inhabitants who had
favoured the insurrection expected sack and massacre, and implored the protection of their neighbours who professed the
Roman Catholic religion, or had made themselves conspicuous
by Tory politics; and it is acknowledged by the bitterest of Whig
historians that this protection was kindly and generously given.

During that day the conquerors continued to chase the fugitives. The neighbouring villagers long remembered with what a
clatter of horsehoofs and what a storm of curses the whirlwind of
cavalry swept by. Before evening five hundred prisoners had been
crowded into the parish church of Weston Zoyland. Eighty of
them were wounded; and five expired within the consecrated
walls. Great numbers of labourers were impressed for the purpose
of burying the slain. A few, who were notoriously partial to the
vanquished side, were set apart for the hideous office of quartering the captives. The tithing men of the neighbouring parishes
were busied in setting up gibbets and providing chains. All this
while the bells of Weston Zoyland and Chedzoy rang joyously,
and the soldiers sang and rioted on the moor amidst the corpses.
For the farmers of the neighbourhood had made haste, as soon
as the event of the fight was known, to send hogsheads of their
best cider as peace offerings to the victors.

Feversham passed for a goodnatured man; but he was a foreigner, ignorant of the laws and careless of the feelings of the
English. He was accustomed to the military licence of France,
and had learned from his great kinsman, the conqueror of the
Palatinate, not indeed how to conquer, but how to devastate.[1] A
considerable number of prisoners were immediately selected for
execution. Among them was a youth famous for his speed. Hopes
were held out to him that his life would be spared if he could run
a race with one of the colts of the marsh. The space through
which the man kept up with the horse is still marked by well

[1. Feversham was a nephew of Louis XIV's famous general, the Vicomte
de Turenne.]

known bounds on the moor, and is about three quarters of a mile. Feversham was not ashamed, after seeing the performance, to send the wretched performer to the gallows. The next day a long line of gibbets appeared on the road leading from Bridgewater to Weston Zoyland. On each gibbet a prisoner was suspended. Four of the sufferers were left to rot in irons.

Meanwhile Monmouth, accompanied by Grey, by Buyse,[2] and by a few other friends, was flying from the field of battle. At Chedzoy he stopped a moment to mount a fresh horse and to hide his blue riband and his George. He then hastened towards the Bristol Channel. From the rising ground on the north of the field of battle he saw the flash and the smoke of the last volley fired by his deserted followers. Before six o'clock he was twenty miles from Sedgemoor. Some of his companions advised him to cross the water, and to seek refuge in Wales; and this would undoubtedly have been his wisest course. He would have been in Wales long before the news of his defeat was known there; and, in a country so wild and so remote from the seat of government, he might have remained long undiscovered. He determined, however, to push for Hampshire, in the hope that he might lurk in the cabins of deer stealers among the oaks of the New Forest, till means of conveyance to the Continent could be procured. He therefore, with Grey and the German, turned to the south east. But the way was beset with dangers. The three fugitives had to traverse a country in which everyone already knew the event of the battle, and in which no traveller of suspicious appearance could escape a close scrutiny. They rode on all day, shunning towns and villages. Nor was this so difficult as it may now appear. For men then living could remember the time when the wild deer ranged freely through a succession of forests from the banks of the Avon in Wiltshire to the southern coast of Hampshire.

At length, on Cranborne Chase, the strength of the horses failed. They were therefore turned loose. The bridles and saddles were concealed. Monmouth and his friends procured rustic attire, disguised themselves, and proceeded on foot towards the New Forest. They passed the night in the open air: but before morn-

[2. Anton Buyse was a German officer who had been in the service of the Elector of Brandenburg and who accompanied Monmouth from Holland.]

ing they were surrounded on every side by toils. Lord Lumley,
who lay at Ringwood with a strong body of the Sussex militia,
had sent forth parties in every direction. Sir William Portman,
with the Somerset militia, had formed a chain of posts from the
sea to the northern extremity of Dorset. At five in the morning of
the seventh, Grey, who had wandered from his friends, was
seized by two of the Sussex scouts. He submitted to his fate with
the calmness of one to whom suspense was more intolerable than
despair. 'Since we landed,' he said, 'I have not had one comfortable meal or one quiet night.'

It could hardly be doubted that the chief rebel was not far off.
The pursuers redoubled their vigilance and activity. The cottages scattered over the heathy country on the boundaries of
Dorsetshire and Hampshire were strictly examined by Lumley;
and the clown with whom Monmouth had changed clothes was
discovered. Portman came with a strong body of horse and foot to
assist in the search. Attention was soon drawn to a place well fitted
to shelter fugitives. It was an extensive tract of land, separated
by an inclosure from the open country, and divided by numerous hedges into small fields. In some of these fields the rye, the
pease, and the oats were high enough to conceal a man. Others
were overgrown with fern and brambles. A poor woman reported
that she had seen two strangers lurking in this covert. The near
prospect of reward animated the zeal of the troops. It was agreed
that every man who did his duty in the search should have a share
of the promised five thousand pounds. The outer fence was
strictly guarded: the space within was examined with indefatigable diligence; and several dogs of quick scent were turned out
among the bushes. The day closed before the work could be completed: but careful watch was kept all night. Thirty times the
fugitives ventured to look through the outer hedge: but everywhere they found a sentinel on the alert: once they were seen and
fired at; they then separated and concealed themselves in different hiding places.

At sunrise the next morning the search recommenced, and
Buyse was found. He owned that he had parted from the Duke
only a few hours before. The corn and copsewood were now
beaten with more care than ever. At length a gaunt figure was dis-

covered hidden in a ditch. The pursuers sprang on their prey. Some of them were about to fire: but Portman forbade all violence. The prisoner's dress was that of a shepherd; his beard, prematurely grey, was of several day's growth. He trembled greatly, and was unable to speak. Even those who had often seen him were at first in doubt whether this were truly the brilliant and graceful Monmouth. His pockets were searched by Portman, and in them were found, among some raw pease gathered in the rage of hunger, a watch, a purse of gold, a small treatise on fortification, an album filled with songs, receipts, prayers, and charms, and the George with which, many years before, King Charles the Second had decorated his favourite son. Messengers were instantly despatched to Whitehall with the good news, and with the George as a token that the news was true. The prisoner was conveyed under a strong guard to Ringwood.

And all was lost; and nothing remained but that he should prepare to meet death as became one who had thought himself not unworthy to wear the crown of William the Conqueror and of Richard the Lionhearted, of the hero of Cressy and of the hero of Agincourt. The captive might easily have called to mind other domestic examples, still better suited to his condition. Within a hundred years, two sovereigns whose blood ran in his veins, one of them a delicate woman, had been placed in the same situation in which he now stood.[3] They had shown, in the prison and on the scaffold, virtue of which, in the season of prosperity, they had seemed incapable, and had half redeemed great crimes and errors by enduring with Christian meekness and princely dignity all that victorious enemies could inflict. Of cowardice Monmouth had never been accused; and, even had he been wanting in constitutional courage, it might have been expected that the defect would be supplied by pride and by despair. The eyes of the whole world were upon him. The latest generations would know how, in that extremity, he had borne himself. To the brave peasants of the West he owed it to show that they had not poured forth their blood for a leader unworthy of their attachment. To her who had sacrificed everything for his sake he owed it so to bear himself that, though she might weep for him, she should not blush for

[3. Mary Queen of Scots and Charles I.]

him.[4] It was not for him to lament and supplicate. His reason, too, should have told him that lamentation and supplication would be unavailing. He had done that which could never be forgiven. He was in the grasp of one who never forgave.

But the fortitude of Monmouth was not that highest sort of fortitude which is derived from reflection and from self-respect; nor had nature given him one of those stout hearts from which neither adversity nor peril can extort any sign of weakness. His courage rose and fell with his animal spirits. It was sustained on the field of battle by the excitement of action, by the hope of victory, by the strange influence of sympathy. All such aids were now taken away. The spoiled darling of the court and of the populace, accustomed to be loved and worshipped wherever he appeared, was now surrounded by stern gaolers in whose eyes he read his doom. Yet a few hours of gloomy seclusion, and he must die a violent and shameful death. His heart sank within him. Life seemed to be worth purchasing by any humiliation; nor could his mind, always feeble, and now distracted by terror, perceive that humiliation must degrade, but could not save him.

As soon as he reached Ringwood he wrote to the King. The letter was that of a man whom a craven fear had made insensible to shame. He professed in vehement terms his remorse for his treason. He affirmed that, when he promised his cousins at the Hague not to raise troubles in England, he had fully meant to keep his word. Unhappily he had afterwards been seduced from his allegiance by some horrid people who had heated his mind by calumnies and misled him by sophistry: but now he abhorred them: he abhorred himself. He begged in piteous terms that he might be admitted to the royal presence. There was a secret which he could not trust to paper, a secret which lay in a single word, and which, if he spoke that word, would secure the throne against all danger. On the following day he despatched letters, imploring the Queen Dowager and the Lord Treasurer to intercede in his behalf.

When it was known in London how he had abased himself the general surprise was great; and no man was more amazed than Barillon, who had resided in England during two bloody pro-

[4. The reference is to Henrietta Lady Wentworth, Monmouth's mistress.]

scriptions, and had seen numerous victims, both of the Opposition and of the Court, submit to their fate without womanish entreaties and lamentations.

Monmouth and Grey remained at Ringwood two days. They were then carried up to London, under the guard of a large body of regular troops and militia. In the coach with the Duke was an officer whose orders were to stab the prisoner if a rescue were attempted. At every town along the road the trainbands of the neighbourhood had been mustered under the command of the principal gentry. The march lasted three days, and terminated at Vauxhall, where a regiment, commanded by George Legge, Lord Dartmouth, was in readiness to receive the prisoners. They were put on board of a state barge, and carried down the river to Whitehall Stairs. Lumley and Portman had alternately watched the Duke day and night till they had brought him within the walls of the palace.

Both the demeanour of Monmouth and that of Grey, during the journey, filled all observers with surprise. Monmouth was altogether unnerved. Grey was not only calm but cheerful, talked pleasantly of horses, dogs, and field sports, and even made jocose allusions to the perilous situation in which he stood.

The King cannot be blamed for determining that Monmouth should suffer death. Every man who heads a rebellion against an established government stakes his life on the event: and rebellion was the smallest part of Monmouth's crime. He had declared against his uncle a war without quarter. In the manifesto put forth at Lyme, James had been held up to execration as an incendiary, as an assassin who had strangled one innocent man and cut the throat of another, and, lastly, as the poisoner of his own brother. To spare an enemy who had not scrupled to resort to such extremities would have been an act of rare, perhaps of blamable generosity. But to see him and not to spare him was an outrage on humanity and decency. This outrage the King resolved to commit. The arms of the prisoner were bound behind him with a silken cord; and, thus secured, he was ushered into the presence of the implacable kinsman whom he had wronged.

Then Monmouth threw himself on the ground, and crawled to the King's feet. He wept. He tried to embrace his uncle's knees with his pinioned arms. He begged for life, only life, life at any price. He owned that he had been guilty of a great crime, but tried to throw the blame on others, particularly on Argyll, who would rather have put his legs into the boots[5] than have saved his own life by such baseness. By the ties of kindred, by the memory of the late King, who had been the best and truest of brothers, the unhappy man adjured James to show some mercy. James gravely replied that this repentance was of the latest, that he was sorry for the misery which the prisoner had brought on himself, but that the case was not one for lenity. A Declaration, filled with atrocious calumnies, had been put forth. The regal title had been assumed. For treasons so aggravated there could be no pardon on this side of the grave. The poor terrified Duke vowed that he had never wished to take the crown, but had been led into that fatal error by others. As to the Declaration, he had not written it: he had not read it: he had signed it without looking at it: it was all the work of Ferguson, that bloody villain Ferguson. 'Do you expect me to believe,' said James, with contempt but too well merited, 'that you set your hand to a paper of such moment without knowing what it contained?' One depth of infamy only remained; and even to that the prisoner descended. He was pre-eminently the champion of the Protestant religion. The interest of that religion had been his plea for conspiring against the government of his father, and for bringing on his country the miseries of civil war: yet he was not ashamed to hint that he was inclined to be reconciled to the Church of Rome. The King eagerly offered him spiritual assistance, but said nothing of pardon or respite. 'Is there then no hope?' asked Monmouth. James turned away in silence. Then Monmouth strove to rally his courage, rose from his knees, and retired with a firmness which he had not shown since his overthrow.

Grey was introduced next. He behaved with a propriety and fortitude which moved even the stern and resentful King, frankly owned himself guilty, made no excuses, and did not once stoop to ask his life. Both the prisoners were sent to the Tower by water. There was no tumult; but many thousands of people,

[5. 'The boots' were a particularly painful form of torture used in Scotland.]

with anxiety and sorrow in their faces, tried to catch a glimpse of the captives. The Duke's resolution failed as soon as he had left the royal presence. On his way to his prison he bemoaned himself, accused his followers, and abjectly implored the intercession of Dartmouth. 'I know, my Lord, that you loved my father. For his sake, for God's sake, try if there be any room for mercy.' Dartmouth replied that the King had spoken the truth, and that a subject who assumed the regal title excluded himself from all hope of pardon.

Soon after Monmouth had been lodged in the Tower, he was informed that his wife had, by the royal command, been sent to see him. She was accompanied by the Earl of Clarendon, Keeper of the Privy Seal. Her husband received her very coldly, and addressed almost all his discourse to Clarendon, whose intercession he earnestly implored. Clarendon held out no hopes; and that same evening two prelates, Turner, Bishop of Ely, and Ken, Bishop of Bath and Wells, arrived at the Tower with a solemn message from the King. It was Monday night. On Wednesday morning Monmouth was to die.

He was greatly agitated. The blood left his cheeks; and it was some time before he could speak. Most of the short time which remained to him he wasted in vain attempts to obtain, if not a pardon, at least a respite. He wrote piteous letters to the King and to several courtiers, but in vain. Some Catholic divines were sent to him from court. But they soon discovered that, though he would gladly have purchased his life by renouncing the religion of which he had professed himself in an especial manner the defender, yet, if he was to die, he would as soon die without their absolution as with it.

Nor were Ken and Turner much better pleased with his frame of mind. The doctrine of non-resistance was, in their view, as in the view of most of their brethren, the distinguishing badge of the Anglican Church. The two Bishops insisted on Monmouth's owning that, in drawing the sword against the government, he had committed a great sin; and, on this point, they found him obstinately heterodox. Nor was this his only heresy. He maintained that his connection with Lady Wentworth was blameless in the sight of God. He had been married, he said, when a child. He

had never cared for his duchess. The happiness which he had
not found at home he had sought in a round of loose amours,
condemned by religion and morality. Henrietta had reclaimed
him from a life of vice. To her he had been strictly constant. They
had, by common consent, offered up fervent prayers for the
divine guidance. After those prayers they had found their affection for each other strengthened; and they could then no longer
doubt that, in the sight of God, they were a wedded pair. The
Bishops were so much scandalized by this view of the conjugal
relation that they refused to administer the sacrament to the prisoner. All that they could obtain from him was a promise that,
during the single night which still remained to him, he would
pray to be enlightened if he were in error.

On the Wednesday morning, at his particular request, Doctor
Thomas Tenison, who then held the vicarage of St Martin's,
and, in that important cure, had obtained the high esteem of the
public, came to the Tower. From Tenison, whose opinions were
known to be moderate, the Duke expected more indulgence than
Ken and Turner were disposed to show. But Tenison, whatever might be his views concerning non-resistance in the abstract,
thought the late rebellion rash and wicked, and considered Monmouth's notion respecting marriage as a most dangerous delusion.
Monmouth was obstinate. He had prayed, he said, for the divine
direction. His sentiments remained unchanged; and he could not
doubt that they were correct. Tenison's exhortations were in a
milder tone than those of the Bishops. But he, like them, thought
that he should not be justified in administering the Eucharist to
one whose penitence was of so unsatisfactory a nature.

The hour drew near: all hope was over; and Monmouth had
passed from pusillanimous fear to the apathy of despair. His
children were brought to his room that he might take leave of
them, and were followed by his wife. He spoke to her kindly, but
without emotion. Though she was a woman of great strength of
mind, and had little cause to love him, her misery was such that
none of the bystanders could refrain from weeping. He alone was
unmoved.

It was ten o'clock. The coach of the Lieutenant of the Tower
was ready. Monmouth requested his spiritual advisers to accom-

pany him to the place of execution; and they consented: but they told him that, in their judgment, he was about to die in a perilous state of mind, and that, if they attended him, it would be their duty to exhort him to the last. As he passed along the ranks of the guards he saluted them with a smile, and mounted the scaffold with a firm tread. Tower Hill was covered up to the chimney tops with an innumerable multitude of gazers, who, in awful silence, broken only by sighs and the noise of weeping, listened for the last accents of the darling of the people. 'I shall say little,' he began. 'I come here, not to speak, but to die. I die a Protestant of the Church of England.' The Bishops interrupted him, and told him that, unless he acknowledged resistance to be sinful, he was no member of their church. He went on to speak of his Henrietta. She was, he said, a young lady of virtue and honour. He loved her to the last, and he could not die without giving utterance to his feelings. The Bishops again interfered and begged him not to use such language. Some altercation followed. The divines have been accused of dealing harshly with the dying man. But they appear to have only discharged what, in their view, was a sacred duty. Monmouth knew their principles, and, if he wished to avoid their importunity, should have dispensed with their attendance.

Their general arguments against resistance had no effect on him. But when they reminded him of the ruin which he had brought on his brave and loving followers, of the blood which had been shed, of the souls which had been sent unprepared to the great account, he was touched, and said, in a softened voice, 'I do own that. I am sorry that it ever happened.' They prayed with him long and fervently; and he joined in their petitions till they invoked a blessing on the King. He remained silent. 'Sir,' said one of the assistants, 'do you not pray for the King with us?' Monmouth paused some time, and, after an internal struggle, exclaimed 'Amen.' But it was in vain that the prelates implored him to address to the soldiers and to the people a few words on the duty of obedience to the government. 'I will make no speeches,' he exclaimed. 'Only ten words, my Lord.' He turned away, called his servant, and put into the man's hand a toothpick case, the last token of ill starred love. 'Give it,' he said, 'to that person.' He

then accosted John Ketch the executioner, a wretch who had butchered many brave and noble victims, and whose name has,
during a century and a half, been vulgarly given to all who have
succeeded him in his odious office. 'Here,' said the Duke, 'are
six guineas for you. Do not hack me as you did my Lord Russell.
I have heard that you struck him three or four times. My servant
will give you some more gold if you do the work well.' He then
undressed, felt the edge of the axe, expressed some fear that it
was not sharp enough, and laid his head on the block. The
divines in the meantime continued to ejaculate with great energy,
'God accept your repentance; God accept your imperfect repentance.'

The hangman addressed himself to his office. But he had been
disconcerted by what the Duke had said. The first blow inflicted
only a slight wound. The Duke struggled, rose from the block,
and looked reproachfully at the executioner. The head sank down
once more. The stroke was repeated again and again; but still the
neck was not severed, and the body continued to move. Yells
of rage and horror rose from the crowd. Ketch flung down the
axe with a curse. 'I cannot do it,' he said; 'my heart fails me.'
'Take up the axe, man,' cried the sheriff. 'Fling him over the
rails,' roared the mob. At length the axe was taken up. Two
more blows extinguished the last remains of life; but a knife was
used to separate the head from the shoulders. The crowd was
wrought up to such an ecstasy of rage that the executioner was
in danger of being torn in pieces, and was conveyed away under a
strong guard.

In the meantime many handkerchiefs were dipped in the
Duke's blood; for, by a large part of the multitude he was regarded as a martyr who had died for the Protestant religion. The head
and body were placed in a coffin covered with black velvet, and
were laid privately under the communion table of St Peter's
Chapel in the Tower. Within four years the pavement of the
chancel was again disturbed, and hard by the remains of Monmouth were laid the remains of Jeffreys. In truth there is no sadder spot on the earth than that little cemetery. Death is there
associated, not, as in Westminster Abbey and Saint Paul's, with
genius and virtue, with public veneration and with imperishable

renown; not, as in our humblest churches and churchyards, with everything that is most endearing in social and domestic charities; but with whatever is darkest in human nature and in human destiny, with the savage triumph of implacable enemies, with the inconstancy, the ingratitude, the cowardice of friends, with all the miseries of fallen greatness and of blighted fame. Thither have been carried, through successive ages, by the rude hands of gaolers, without one mourner following, the bleeding relics of men who had been the captains of armies, the leaders of parties, the oracles of senates, and the ornaments of courts. Thither was borne, before the window where Jane Grey was praying, the mangled corpse of Guilford Dudley. Edward Seymour, Duke of Somerset, and Protector of the realm, reposes there by the brother whom he murdered. There has mouldered away the headless trunk of John Fisher, Bishop of Rochester and Cardinal of Saint Vitalis, a man worthy to have lived in a better age, and to have died in a better cause. There are laid John Dudley, Duke of Northumberland, Lord High Admiral, and Thomas Cromwell, Earl of Essex, Lord High Treasurer. There, too, is another Essex, on whom nature and fortune have lavished all their bounties in vain, and whom valour, grace, genius, royal favour, popular applause, conducted to an early and ignominious doom. Not far off sleep two chiefs of the great house of Howard, Thomas, fourth Duke of Norfolk, and Philip, eleventh Earl of Arundel. Here and there, among the thick graves of unquiet and aspiring statesmen, lie more delicate sufferers; Margaret of Salisbury, the last of the proud name of Plantagenet, and those two fair Queens who perished by the jealous rage of Henry. Such was the dust with which the dust of Monmouth mingled.[6]

Yet a few months, and the quiet village of Toddington, in Bedfordshire, witnessed a still sadder funeral. Near that village stood an ancient and stately hall, the seat of the Wentworths. The transept of the parish church had long been their burial place. To that burial place, in the spring which followed the death of Monmouth, was borne the coffin of the young Baroness Wentworth of

6. I cannot refrain from expressing my disgust at the barbarous stupidity which has transformed this most interesting little church into the likeness of a meetinghouse in a manufacturing town.

Nettlestede. Her family reared a sumptuous mausoleum over her remains: but a less costly memorial of her was long contemplated with far deeper interest. Her name, carved by the hand of him whom she loved too well, was, a few years ago, still discernible on a tree in the adjoining park.

It was not by Lady Wentworth alone that the memory of Monmouth was cherished with idolatrous fondness. His hold on the hearts of the people lasted till the generation which had seen him had passed away. Ribands, buckles, and other trifling articles of apparel which he had worn, were treasured up as precious relics by those who had fought under him at Sedgemoor. Old men who long survived him desired, when they were dying, that these trinkets might be buried with them. One button of gold thread which narrowly escaped this fate may still be seen at a house which overlooks the field of battle. Nay, such was the devotion of the people to their unhappy favourite that, in the face of the strongest evidence by which the fact of a death was ever verified, many continued to cherish a hope that he was still living, and that he would again appear in arms. A person, it was said, who was remarkably like Monmouth had sacrificed himself to save the Protestant hero. The vulgar long continued, at every important crisis, to whisper that the time was at hand, and that King Monmouth would soon show himself. In 1686, a knave who had pretended to be the Duke, and had levied contributions in several villages of Wiltshire, was apprehended, and whipped from Newgate to Tyburn. In 1698, when England had long enjoyed constitutional freedom under a new dynasty, the son of an innkeeper passed himself on the yeomanry of Sussex as their beloved Monmouth, and defrauded many who were by no means of the lowest class. Five hundred pounds were collected for him. The farmers provided him with a horse. Their wives sent him baskets of chickens and ducks, and were lavish, it was said, of favours of a more tender kind; for, in gallantry at least, the counterfeit was a not unworthy representative of the original. When this impostor was thrown into prison for his fraud, his followers maintained him in luxury. Several of them appeared at the bar to countenance him when he was tried at the Horsham assizes. So long did this delusion last that, when George the Third had been some years on the English throne, Voltaire thought it necessary gravely to confute the hypothesis that the man in the iron mask was the Duke of Monmouth.

It is, perhaps, a fact scarcely less remarkable that, to this day, the inhabitants of some parts of the west of England, when any bill affecting their interests is before the House of Lords, think themselves entitled to claim the help of the Duke of Buccleuch, the descendant of the unfortunate leader for whom their ancestors bled.

The history of Monmouth would alone suffice to refute the imputation of inconstancy which is so frequently thrown on the common people. The common people are sometimes inconstant; for they are human beings. But that they are inconstant as compared with the educated classes, with aristocracies, or with princes, may be confidently denied. It would be easy to name demagogues whose popularity has remained undiminished while sovereigns and parliaments have withdrawn their confidence from a long succession of statesmen. When Swift had survived his faculties many years, the Irish populace still continued to light bonfires on his birthday, in commemoration of the services which they fancied that he had rendered to his country when his mind was in full vigour. While seven administrations were raised to power and hurled from it in consequence of court intrigues or of changes in the sentiments of the higher classes of society, the profligate Wilkes retained his hold on the affections of a rabble whom he pillaged and ridiculed. Politicians, who, in 1807, had sought to curry favour with George the Third by defending Caroline of Brunswick, were not ashamed, in 1820, to curry favour with George the Fourth by persecuting her. But in 1820, as in 1807, the whole body of working men was fanatically devoted to her cause. So it was with Monmouth. In 1680 he had been adored alike by the gentry and by the peasantry of the west. In 1685 he came again. To the gentry he had become an object of aversion: but by the peasantry he was still loved with a love strong as death, with a love not to be extinguished by misfortunes or faults, by the flight from Sedgemoor, by the letter from Ringwood, or by the tears and abject supplications at Whitehall. The charge which may with justice be brought against the common

people is, not that they are inconstant, but that they almost invariably choose their favourite so ill that their constancy is a
vice and not a virtue.

While the execution of Monmouth occupied the thoughts of
the Londoners, the counties which had risen against the government were enduring all that a ferocious soldiery could inflict.
Feversham had been summoned to the court, where honours and
rewards which he little deserved awaited him. He was made a
knight of the Garter and Captain of the first and most lucrative
troop of Life Guards: but Court and City laughed at his military
exploits; and the wit of Buckingham gave forth its last feeble
flash at the expense of the general who had won a battle in bed.[7]
Feversham left in command at Bridgewater Colonel Percy Kirke,
a military adventurer whose vices had been developed by the
worst of all schools, Tangier.[8]

Kirke had during some years commanded the garrison of that
town, and had been constantly employed in hostilities against
tribes of foreign barbarians, ignorant of the laws which regulate
the warfare of civilised and Christian nations. Within the ramparts of his fortress he was a despotic prince. The only check on
his tyranny was the fear of being called to account by a distant
and a careless government. He might therefore safely proceed to
the most audacious excesses of rapacity, licentiousness and cruelty. He lived with boundless dissoluteness, and procured by extortion the means of indulgence. No goods could be sold till
Kirke had had the refusal of them. No question of right could be
decided till Kirke had been bribed. Once, merely from a malignant whim, he staved all the wine in a vintner's cellar. On another
occasion he drove all the Jews from Tangier. Two of them he
sent to the Spanish Inquisition, which forthwith burned them.
Under this iron domination scarce a complaint was heard; for

[7. George Villiers, second Duke of Buckingham, *The Battle of Sedgemoor*,
a Farce (first printed 1704). Macaulay dwells heavily on the fact that Feversham was in bed when Monmouth attacked; but the time was one a.m.; and
he got up.]

[8. Tangier had been an English possession from 1662 to 1684, having
been ceded by Portugal as part of the dowry of Catherine of Braganza, on her
marriage to Charles II.]

hatred was effectually kept down by terror. Two persons who had been refractory were found murdered; and it was universally believed that they had been slain by Kirke's order. When his soldiers displeased him he flogged them with merciless severity; but he indemnified them by permitting them to sleep on watch, to reel drunk about the streets, to rob, beat, and insult the merchants and the labourers.

When Tangier was abandoned, Kirke returned to England. He still continued to command his old soldiers, who were designated sometimes as the First Tangier Regiment, and sometimes as Queen Catherine's Regiment. As they had been levied for the purpose of waging war on an infidel nation, they bore on their flag a Christian emblem, the Paschal Lamb. In allusion to this device, and with a bitterly ironical meaning, these men, the rudest and most ferocious in the English army, were called Kirke's Lambs. The regiment, now the second of the line, still retains this ancient badge, which is however thrown into the shade by decorations honourably earned in Egypt, in Spain, and in the heart of Asia.

Such was the captain and such the soldiers who were now let loose on the people of Somersetshire. From Bridgewater Kirke marched to Taunton. He was accompanied by two carts filled with wounded rebels whose gashes had not been dressed, and by a long drove of prisoners on foot, who were chained two and two. Several of these he hanged as soon as he reached Taunton, without the form of a trial. They were not suffered even to take leave of their nearest relations. The sign post of the White Hart Inn served for a gallows. It is said that the work of death went on in sight of the windows where the officers of the Tangier regiment were carousing, and that at every health a wretch was turned off. When the legs of the dying men quivered in the last agony, the colonel ordered the drums to strike up. He would give the rebels, he said, music to their dancing. The tradition runs that one of the captives was not even allowed the indulgence of a speedy death. Twice he was suspended from the sign post, and twice cut down. Twice he was asked if he repented of his treason; and twice he replied that, if the thing were to do again, he would do it. Then he was tied up for the last time. So many dead bodies were quartered that the executioner stood ankle deep in blood. He was assisted by a poor man whose loyalty was suspected, and who was compelled to ransom his own life by seething the remains of his friends in pitch. The peasant who had consented to perform this hideous office afterwards returned to his plough. But a mark like that of Cain was upon him. He was known through his village by the horrible name of Tom Boilman. The rustics long continued to relate that, though he had, by his sinful and shameful deed, saved himself from the vengeance of the Lambs, he had not escaped the vengeance of a higher power. In a great storm he fled for shelter under an oak, and was there struck dead by lightning.

The number of those who were thus butchered cannot now be ascertained. Nine were entered in the parish registers of Taunton: but those registers contain the names of such only as had Christian burial. Those who were hanged in chains, and those whose heads and limbs were sent to the neighbouring villages, must have been much more numerous. It was believed in London, at the time, that Kirke put a hundred captives to death during the week which followed the battle.[9]

Cruelty, however, was not this man's only passion. He loved money; and was no novice in the arts of extortion. A safe conduct might be bought of him for thirty or forty pounds; and such a safe conduct, though of no value in law, enabled the purchaser to pass the posts of the Lambs without molestation, to reach a seaport, and to fly to a foreign country. The ships which were bound for New England were crowded at this juncture with so many fugitives from Sedgemoor that there was great danger lest the water and provisions should fail.

*

The government was dissatisfied with Kirke, not on account of the barbarity with which he had treated his needy prisoners, but on account of the interested lenity which he had shown to rich delinquents. He was soon recalled from the west. A less irregular

[9. Macaulay's account both of the character and of the actions of Kirke is unfair. He was a coarse but efficient officer and his acts of cruelty were all performed in execution of explicit orders from his commander, Lord Feversham.]

and at the same time a more cruel massacre was about to be perpetrated. The vengeance was deferred during some weeks. It was thought desirable that the Western Circuit should not begin till the other circuits had terminated. In the meantime the gaols of Somersetshire and Dorsetshire were filled with thousands of captives. The chief friend and protector of these unhappy men in their extremity was one who abhorred their religious and political opinions, one whose order they hated, and to whom they had done unprovoked wrong, Bishop Ken. That good prelate used all his influence to soften the gaolers, and retrenched from his own episcopal state that he might be able to make some addition to the coarse and scanty fare of those who had defaced his beloved Cathedral. His conduct on this occasion was of a piece with his whole life. His intellect was indeed darkened by many superstitions and prejudices: but his moral character, when impartially reviewed, sustains a comparison with any in ecclesiastical history, and seems to approach, as near as human infirmity permits, to the ideal perfection of Christian virtue.

His labour of love was of no long duration. A rapid and effectual gaol delivery was at hand. Early in September, Jeffreys, accompanied by four other judges, set out on that circuit of which the memory will last as long as our race and language. The officers who commanded the troops in the districts through which his course lay had orders to furnish him with whatever military aid he might require. His ferocious temper needed no spur; yet a spur was applied. The health and spirits of the Lord Keeper[10] had given way. He had been deeply mortified by the coldness of the King and by the insolence of the Chief Justice, and could find little consolation on looking back on a life, not indeed blackened by any atrocious crime, but sullied by cowardice, selfishness, and servility. So deeply was the unhappy man humbled that, when he appeared for the last time in Westminster Hall, he took with him a nosegay to hide his face, because, as he afterwards owned, he could not bear the eyes of the bar and of the audience. The prospect of his approaching end seems to have inspired him with unwonted courage. He determined to discharge his conscience, requested an audience of the King, spoke earnestly of the

[10. Francis North, Lord Guilford. See above, pp. 71, 73-4.]

dangers inseparable from violent and arbitrary counsels, and condemned the lawless cruelties which the soldiers had committed in Somersetshire. He soon after retired from London to die. He breathed his last a few days after the Judges set out for the West. It was immediately notified to Jeffreys that he might expect the Great Seal as the reward of faithful and vigorous service.

At Winchester the Chief Justice first opened his commission. Hampshire had not been the theatre of war; but many of the vanquished rebels had, like their leader, fled thither. Two of them, John Hickes, a Nonconformist divine, and Richard Nel-thorpe, a lawyer who had been outlawed for his share in the Rye House Plot, had sought refuge at the house of Alice, widow of John Lisle. John Lisle had sat in the Long Parliament and in the High Court of Justice, had been a Commissioner of the Great Seal in the days of the Commonwealth, and had been created a lord by Cromwell. The titles given by the Protector had not been recognised by any government which had ruled England since the downfall of his house; but they appear to have been often used in conversation even by Royalists. John Lisle's widow was therefore commonly known as the Lady Alice. She was related to many respectable, and to some noble, families; and she was generally esteemed even by the Tory gentlemen of her county. For it was well known to them that she had deeply re-gretted some violent acts in which her husband had borne a part, that she had shed bitter tears for Charles the First, and that she had protected and relieved many Cavaliers in their distress. The same womanly kindness, which had led her to befriend the Royalists in their time of trouble, would not suffer her to refuse a meal and a hiding place to the wretched men who now intreated her to protect them. She took them into her house, set meat and drink before them, and showed them where they might take rest. The next morning her dwelling was surrounded by soldiers. Strict search was made. Hickes was found concealed in the malt-house, and Nelthorpe in the chimney.

If Lady Alice knew her guests to have been concerned in the insurrection, she was undoubtedly guilty of what in strictness is a capital crime. For the law of principal and accessory, as res-pects high treason, then was, and is to this day, in a state disgraceful to English jurisprudence. In cases of felony, a distinction, founded on justice and reason, is made between the principal and the accessory after the fact. He who conceals from justice one whom he knows to be a murderer, though liable to punishment, is not liable to the punishment of murder; but he who shelters one whom he knows to be a traitor is, according to all our jurists, guilty of high treason. It is unnecessary to point out the absurdity and cruelty of a law which includes under the same definition, and visits with the same penalty, offences lying at the opposite extremes of the scale of guilt. The feeling which makes the most loyal subject shrink from the thought of giving up to a shameful death the rebel who, vanquished, hunted down, and in mortal agony, begs for a morsel of bread and a cup of water, may be a weakness: but it is surely a weakness very nearly allied to virtue, a weakness which, constituted as human beings are, we can hardly eradicate from the mind without eradicating many noble and benevolent sentiments. A wise and good ruler may not think it right to sanction this weakness; but he will generally connive at it, or punish it very tenderly. In no case will he treat it as a crime of the blackest dye. Whether Flora Macdonald was justified in concealing the attainted heir of the Stuarts, whether a brave soldier of our own time was justified in assisting the escape of Lavalette, are questions on which casuists may differ: but to class such actions with the crimes of Guy Fawkes and Fieschi is an outrage to humanity and common sense. Such, however, is the classification of our law. It is evident that nothing but a lenient administration could make such a state of the law endurable. And it is just to say that, during many generations, no English government, save one, has treated with rigour persons guilty of harbouring defeated and flying insurgents. To women especially has been granted, by a kind of tacit prescription, the right of indulging, in the midst of havoc and vengeance, that compassion which is the most endearing of all their charms. Since the beginning of the great civil war, numerous rebels, some of them far more important than Hickes or Nelthorpe, have been protected against the severity of victorious governments by female adroitness and generosity. But no English ruler who has been thus baffled, the savage and implacable James alone excepted, has had the barbarity even to think of putting a lady to a cruel and shameful death for so venial and amiable a transgression.

Odious as the law was, it was strained for the purpose of destroying Alice Lisle. She could not, according to the doctrine laid down by the highest authority, be convicted till after the conviction of the rebels whom she had harboured. She was, however, sent to the bar before either Hickes or Nelthorpe had been tried. It was no easy matter in such a case to obtain a verdict for the crown. The witnesses prevaricated. The jury, consisting of the principal gentlemen of Hampshire, shrank from the thought of sending a fellow creature to the stake for conduct which seemed deserving rather of praise than of blame. Jeffreys was beside himself with fury. This was the first case of treason on the circuit; and there seemed to be a strong probability that his prey would escape him. He stormed, cursed, and swore in language which no well-bred man would have used at a race or a cockfight. One witness named Dunne, partly from concern for Lady Alice, and partly from fright at the threats and maledictions of the Chief Justice, entirely lost his head, and at last stood silent. 'Oh how hard the truth is,' said Jeffreys, 'to come out of a lying Presbyterian knave.' The witness, after a pause of some minutes, stammered a few unmeaning words. 'Was there ever,' exclaimed the judge, with an oath, 'was there ever such a villain on the face of the earth? Dost thou believe that there is a God? Dost thou believe in Hell fire? Of all the witnesses that I ever met with I never saw thy fellow.' Still the poor man, scared out of his senses, remained mute; and again Jeffreys burst forth. 'I hope, gentlemen of the jury, that you take notice of the horrible carriage of this fellow. How can one help abhorring both these men and their religion? A Turk is a saint to such a fellow as this. A Pagan would be ashamed of such villainy. Oh blessed Jesus! What a generation of vipers do we live among!' 'I cannot tell what to say, my Lord,' faltered Dunne. The judge again broke forth into a volley of oaths. 'Was there ever,' he cried, 'such an impudent rascal? Hold the candle to him that we may see his brazen face. You, gentlemen, that are of counsel for the crown, see that an information for perjury be preferred against this fellow.'

After the witness had been thus handled, the Lady Alice was called on for her defence. She began by saying, what may possibly have been true, that, though she knew Hickes to be in trouble when she took him in, she did not know or suspect that he had been concerned in the rebellion. He was a divine, a man of peace. It had, therefore, never occurred to her that he could have borne arms against the government; and she had supposed that he wished to conceal himself because warrants were out against him for field preaching. The Chief Justice began to storm. 'But I will tell you. There is not one of those lying, snivelling, canting Presbyterians but, one way or another, had a hand in the rebellion. Presbytery has all manner of villainy in it. Nothing but Presbytery could have made Dunne such a rogue. Show me a Presbyterian; and I'll show thee a lying knave.' He summed up in the same style, declaimed during an hour against Whigs and Dissenters, and reminded the jury that the prisoner's husband had borne a part in the death of Charles the First, a fact which was not proved by any testimony, and which, if it had been proved, would have been utterly irrelevant to the issue. The jury retired, and remained long in consultation. The judge grew impatient. He could not conceive, he said, how, in so plain a case, they should even have left the box. He sent a messenger to tell them that, if they did not instantly return, he would adjourn the court and lock them up all night. Thus put to the torture, they came, but came to say that they doubted whether the charge had been made out. Jeffreys expostulated with them vehemently, and, after another consultation, they gave a reluctant verdict of Guilty.

On the following morning sentence was pronounced. Jeffreys gave direction that Alice Lisle should be burned alive that very afternoon. This excess of barbarity moved the pity and indignation even of the class which was most devoted to the crown. The clergy of Winchester Cathedral remonstrated with the Chief Justice, who, brutal as he was, was not mad enough to risk a quarrel on such a subject with a body so much respected by the Tory party. He consented to put off the execution five days. During that time the friends of the prisoner besought James to show her mercy. Ladies of high rank interceded for her. Feversham, whose recent victory had increased his influence at court, and who, it is said, had been bribed to take the compassionate side, spoke in her favour. Clarendon, the King's brother-in-law, pleaded her cause. But all was vain. The utmost that could be obtained was that her sentence should be commuted from burning to beheading. She was put to death on a scaffold in the market-place of Winchester, and underwent her fate with serene courage.

In Hampshire Alice Lisle was the only victim: but, on the day following her execution, Jeffreys reached Dorchester, the principal town of the county in which Monmouth had landed, and the judicial massacre began.

The court was hung, by order of the Chief Justice, with scarlet; and this innovation seemed to the multitude to indicate a bloody purpose. It was also rumoured that, when the clergyman who preached the assize sermon inforced the duty of mercy, the ferocious mouth of the Judge was distorted by an ominous grin. These things made men augur ill of what was to follow.

More than three hundred prisoners were to be tried. The work seemed heavy; but Jeffreys had a contrivance for making it light. He let it be understood that the only chance of obtaining pardon or respite was to plead guilty. Twenty-nine persons, who put themselves on their country and were convicted, were ordered to be tied up without delay. The remaining prisoners pleaded guilty by scores. Two hundred and ninety-two received sentence of death. The whole number hanged in Dorchester amounted to seventy-four.

From Dorchester Jeffreys proceeded to Exeter. The civil war had barely grazed the frontier of Devonshire. Here, therefore, comparatively few persons were capitally punished. Somersetshire, the chief seat of the rebellion, had been reserved for the last and most fearful vengeance. In this county two hundred and thirty-three prisoners were in a few days hanged, drawn, and quartered. At every spot where two roads met, on every market-place, on the green of every large village which had furnished Monmouth with soldiers, ironed corpses clattering in the wind, or heads and quarters stuck on poles, poisoned the air, and made the traveller sick with horror. In many parishes the peasantry could not assemble in the house of God without seeing the ghastly face of a neighbour grinning at them over the porch. The Chief Justice was all himself. His spirits rose higher and higher as the work went on. He laughed, shouted, joked, and swore in such a way that many thought him drunk from morning to night. But in him it was not easy to distinguish the madness produced by evil passions from the madness produced by brandy. A prisoner affirmed that the witnesses who appeared against him were not entitled to credit. One of them, he said, was a Papist, and another a prostitute. 'Thou impudent rebel,' exclaimed the judge, 'to reflect on the King's evidence! I see thee, villain, I see thee already with the halter round thy neck.' Another produced testimony that he was a good Protestant. 'Protestant!' said Jeffreys; 'you mean Presbyterian. I'll hold you a wager of it. I can smell a Presbyterian forty miles.' One wretched man moved the pity even of bitter Tories. 'My Lord,' they said, 'this poor creature is on the parish.' 'Do not trouble yourselves,' said the Judge. 'I will ease the parish of the burden.' It was not only on the prisoners that his fury broke forth. Gentlemen and noblemen of high consideration and stainless loyalty, who ventured to bring to his notice any extenuating circumstance, were almost sure to receive what he called, in the coarse dialect which he had learned in the pothouses of Whitechapel, a lick with the rough side of his tongue. Lord Stawell, a Tory peer, who could not conceal his horror at the remorseless manner in which his poor neighbours were butchered, was punished by having a corpse suspended in chains at his park gate. In such spectacles originated many tales of terror, which were long told over the cider by the Christmas fires of the farmers of Somersetshire. Within the last forty years peasants, in some districts, well knew the accursed spots, and passed them unwillingly after sunset.[11]

Jeffreys boasted that he had hanged more traitors than all his predecessors together since the Conquest. It is certain that the number of persons whom he executed in one month, and in one shire, very much exceeded the number of all the political offenders who have been executed in our island since the Revolution. The rebellions of 1715 and 1745 were of longer duration, of wider extent, and of more formidable aspect than that which was put

11. This I can attest from my own childish recollections.

down at Sedgemoor. It has not been generally thought that, either after the rebellion of 1715, or after the rebellion of 1745, the House of Hanover erred on the side of clemency. Yet all the executions of 1715 and 1745 added together will appear to have been few indeed when compared with those which disgraced the Bloody Assizes. The number of the rebels whom Jeffreys hanged on this circuit was three hundred and twenty.

Such havoc must have excited disgust even if the sufferers had been generally odious. But they were, for the most part, men of blameless life, and of high religious profession. They were regarded by themselves, and by a large proportion of their neighbours, not as wrongdoers, but as martyrs who sealed with blood the truth of the Protestant religion. Very few of the convicts professed any repentance for what they had done. Many, animated by the old Puritan spirit, met death, not merely with fortitude, but with exultation. It was in vain that the ministers of the Established Church lectured them on the guilt of rebellion and on the importance of priestly absolution. The claim of the King to unbounded authority in things temporal, and the claim of the clergy to the spiritual power of binding and loosing, moved the bitter scorn of the intrepid sectaries. Some of them composed hymns in the dungeon, and chanted them on the fatal sledge. Christ, they sang while they were undressing for the butchery, would soon come to rescue Zion and to make war on Babylon, would set up his standard, would blow his trumpet, and would requite his foes tenfold for all the evil which had been inflicted on his servants. The dying words of these men were noted down; their farewell letters were kept as treasures; and, in this way, with the help of some invention and exaggeration, was formed a copious supplement to the Marian martyrology.[12]

*

The number of prisoners whom Jeffreys transported was eight hundred and forty-one. These men, more wretched than their associates who suffered death, were distributed into gangs, and bestowed on persons who enjoyed favour at court. The conditions

[12. That is, to John Foxe's 'Book of Martyrs', the record of the persecution under Mary Tudor.]

of the gift were that the convicts should be carried beyond sea as
slaves, that they should not be emancipated for ten years, and
that the place of their banishment should be some West Indian
island. This last article was studiously framed for the purpose of
aggravating the misery of the exiles. In New England or New
Jersey they would have found a population kindly disposed to
them and a climate not unfavourable to their health and vigour.
It was therefore determined that they should be sent to colonies
where a Puritan could hope to inspire little sympathy, and where
a labourer born in the temperate zone could hope to enjoy little
health. Such was the state of the slave market that these bond-
men, long as was the passage, and sickly as they were likely to
prove, were still very valuable. It was estimated by Jeffreys that,
on an average, each of them, after all charges were paid, would be
worth from ten to fifteen pounds. There was therefore much
angry competition for grants. Some Tories in the West conceived
that they had, by their exertions and sufferings during the insurrection, earned a right to share in the profits which had been
eagerly snatched up by the sycophants of Whitehall. The courtiers, however, were victorious.

The misery of the exiles fully equalled that of the negroes who
are now carried from Congo to Brazil. It appears from the best
information which is at present accessible that more than one fifth
of those who were shipped were flung to the sharks before the
end of the voyage. The human cargoes were stowed close in the
holds of small vessels. So little space was allowed that the wretches, many of whom were still tormented by unhealed wounds,
could not all lie down at once without lying on one another. They
were never suffered to go on deck. The hatchway was constantly
watched by sentinels armed with hangers and blunderbusses. In
the dungeon below all was darkness, stench, lamentation, disease and death. Of ninety-nine convicts who were carried out in
one vessel, twenty-two died before they reached Jamaica, although the voyage was performed with unusual speed. The survivors when they arrived at their house of bondage were mere
skeletons. During some weeks coarse biscuit and fetid water had
been doled out to them in such scanty measure that any one of
them could easily have consumed the ration which was assigned

to five. They were, therefore, in such a state that the merchant to whom they had been consigned found it expedient to fatten them before selling them.

Meanwhile the property both of the rebels who had suffered death, and of those more unfortunate men who were withering under the tropical sun, was fought for and torn in pieces by a crowd of greedy informers. By law a subject attainted of treason forfeits all his substance; and this law was enforced after the Bloody Assizes with a rigour at once cruel and ludicrous. The brokenhearted widows and destitute orphans of the labouring men whose corpses hung at the cross roads were called upon by the agents of the Treasury to explain what had become of a basket, of a goose, of a flitch of bacon, of a keg of cider, of a sack of beans, of a truss of hay. While the humbler retainers of the government were pillaging the families of the slaughtered peasants, the Chief Justice was fast accumulating a fortune out of the plunder of a higher class of Whigs. He traded largely in pardons. His most lucrative transaction of this kind was with a gentleman named Edmund Prideaux. It is certain that Prideaux had not been in arms against the government; and it is probable that his only crime was the wealth which he had inherited from his father, an eminent lawyer who had been high in office under the Protector. No exertions were spared to make out a case for the crown. Mercy was offered to some prisoners on condition that they would bear evidence against Prideaux. The unfortunate man lay long in gaol, and at length, overcome by fear of the gallows, consented to pay fifteen thousand pounds for his liberation. This great sum was received by Jeffreys. He bought with it an estate, to which the people gave the name of Aceldama, from that accursed field which was purchased with the price of innocent blood.

He was ably assisted in the work of extortion by the crew of parasites who were in the habit of drinking and laughing with him. The office of these men was to drive hard bargains with convicts under the strong terrors of death, and with parents trembling for the lives of children. A portion of the spoil was abandoned by Jeffreys to his agents. To one of his boon companions, it is said, he tossed a pardon for a rich traitor across the

table during a revel. It was not safe to have recourse to any intercession except that of his creatures; for he guarded his profitable
monopoly of mercy with jealous care. It was even suspected that
he sent some persons to the gibbet solely because they had
applied for the royal clemency through channels independent of
him.

Some courtiers nevertheless contrived to obtain a small share
of this traffic. The ladies of the Queen's household distinguished
themselves pre-eminently by rapacity and hardheartedness. Part
of the disgrace which they incurred falls on their mistress: for it
was solely on account of the relation in which they stood to her
that they were able to enrich themselves by so odious a trade;
and there can be no question that she might with a word or a look
have restrained them. But in truth she encouraged them by her
evil example, if not by her express approbation. She seems to
have been one of that large class of persons who bear adversity
better than prosperity. While her husband was a subject and an
exile, shut out from public employment, and in imminent danger
of being deprived of his birthright, the suavity and humility of
her manners conciliated the kindness even of those who most
abhorred her religion. But when her good fortune came her good
nature disappeared. The meek and affable Duchess turned out
an ungracious and haughty Queen.[13] The misfortunes which she
subsequently endured have made her an object of some interest;
but that interest would be not a little heightened if it could be
shown that, in the season of her greatness, she saved, or even
tried to save, one single victim from the most frightful proscription that England has ever seen. Unhappily the only request that
she is known to have referred touching the rebels was that a
hundred of those who were sentenced to transportation might be
given to her. The profit which she cleared on the cargo, after
making large allowance for those who died of hunger and fever
during the passage, cannot be estimated at less than a thousand
guineas. We cannot wonder that her attendants should have imitated her unprincely greediness and her unwomanly cruelty. They
exacted a thousand pounds from Roger Hoare, a merchant of

[13. James II's queen was his second wife, Mary, Duchess of Modena,
whom he had married in 1673.]

Bridgewater, who had contributed to the military chest of the rebel army. But the prey on which they pounced most eagerly was one which it might have been thought that even the most un-gentle natures would have spared.

Already some of the girls who had presented the standard to Monmouth at Taunton had cruelly expiated their offence. One of them had been thrown into a prison where an infectious malady was raging. She had sickened and died there. Another had presen-ted herself at the bar before Jeffreys to beg for mercy. 'Take her, gaoler,' vociferated the judge, with one of those frowns which had often struck terror into stouter hearts than hers. She burst into tears, drew her hood over her face, followed the gaoler out of court, fell ill of fright, and in a few hours was a corpse. Most of the young ladies, however, who had walked in the procession, were still alive. Some of them were under ten years of age. All had acted under the orders of their schoolmistress, without know-ing that they were committing a crime. The Queen's maids of honour asked the royal permission to wring money out of the parents of the poor children; and the permission was granted. An order was sent down to Taunton that all these little girls should be seized and imprisoned. Sir Francis Warre, of Hester-combe, the Tory member of Bridgewater, was requested to under-take the office of exacting the ransom. He was charged to declare in strong language that the maids of honour would not endure delay, that they were determined to prosecute to outlawry, un-less a reasonable sum were forthcoming, and that by a reasonable sum was meant seven thousand pounds. Warre excused himself from taking any part in a transaction so scandalous. The maids of honour then requested William Penn to act for them; and Penn accepted the commission. Yet it should seem that a little of the pertinacious scrupulosity which he had often shown about taking off his hat would not have been altogether out of place on this occasion. He probably silenced the remonstrances of his conscience by repeating to himself that none of the money which he extorted would go into his own pocket; that if he refused to be the agent of the ladies they would find agents less humane; that by complying he should increase his influence at the court, and that his influence at the court had already enabled him, and might still enable him, to render great services to his oppressed brethren. The maids of honour were at last forced to content themselves with less than a third part of what they had demanded.[14]

No English sovereign has ever given stronger proofs of a cruel nature than James the Second. Yet his cruelty was not more odious than his mercy. Or perhaps it may be more correct to say that his mercy and his cruelty were such that each reflects infamy on the other. Our horror at the fate of the simple clowns, the young lads, the delicate women, to whom he was inexorably severe, is increased when we find to whom and for what considerations he granted his pardon.

The rule by which a prince ought, after a rebellion, to be guided in selecting rebels for punishment is perfectly obvious. The ringleaders, the men of rank, fortune and education, whose power and whose artifices have led the multitude into error, are the proper objects of severity. The deluded populace, when once the slaughter on the field of battle is over, can scarcely be treated too leniently. This rule, so evidently agreeable to justice and humanity, was not only not observed, it was inverted. While those who ought to have been spared were slaughtered by hundreds, the few who might with propriety have been left to the utmost rigour of the law were spared. This eccentric clemency has perplexed some writers, and has drawn forth ludicrous eulogies from others. It was neither at all mysterious nor at all praiseworthy. It may be distinctly traced in every case either to a sordid or to a malignant motive, either to thirst for money or to thirst for blood.

In the case of Grey there was no mitigating circumstance. His parts and knowledge, the rank which he had inherited in the state, and the high command which he had borne in the rebel army, would have pointed him out to a just government as a much fitter object of punishment than Alice Lisle, than William

[14. This is one of the many occasions on which Macaulay's hatred of Penn has blinded him to evidence. The agent of the maids of honour in this transaction was not William Penn but one George Penne, an obscure person used in other similar transactions. Macaulay's error was copied from Sir James Mackintosh; but he refused to correct it even when the full evidence was shown to him.]

Hewling, than any of the hundreds of ignorant peasants whose skulls and quarters were exposed in Somersetshire. But Grey's estate was large and was strictly entailed. He had only a life interest in his property; and he could forfeit no more interest than he had. If he died, his lands at once devolved on the next heir. If he were pardoned, he would be able to pay a large ransom. He was therefore suffered to redeem himself by giving a bond for forty thousand pounds to the Lord Treasurer, and smaller sums to other courtiers.

*

And now Jeffreys had done his work, and returned to claim his reward. He arrived at Windsor from the West, leaving carnage, mourning, and terror behind him. The hatred with which he was regarded by the people of Somersetshire has no parallel in our history. It was not to be quenched by time or by political changes, was long transmitted from generation to generation, and raged fiercely against his innocent progeny. When he had been many years dead, when his name and title were extinct, his grand-daughter the Countess of Pomfret, travelling along the western road, was insulted by the populace, and found that she could not safely venture herself among the descendants of those who had witnessed the Bloody Assizes.

But at the court Jeffreys was cordially welcomed. He was a judge after his master's own heart. James had watched the circuit with interest and delight. In his drawing room and at his table he had frequently talked of the havoc which was making among his disaffected subjects with a glee at which the foreign ministers stood aghast. With his own hand he had penned accounts of what he facetiously called his Lord Chief Justice's campaign in the West. Some hundreds of rebels, His Majesty wrote to the Hague, had been condemned. Some of them had been hanged: more should be so: and the rest should be sent to the plantations. It was to no purpose that Ken wrote to implore mercy for the mis-guided people, and described with pathetic eloquence the fright-ful state of his diocese. He complained that it was impossible to walk along the highways without seeing some terrible spectacle, and that the whole air of Somersetshire was tainted with death.

The King read, and remained, according to the saying of Church-ill, hard as the marble chimney pieces of Whitehall. At Windsor the great seal of England was put into the hands of Jeffreys, and in the next London Gazette it was solemnly notified that this honour was the reward of the many eminent and faithful ser-vices which he had rendered to the crown.

6

James II and the Catholic Parties

[*James II owed his accession and his survival to the support of the tories who, since the collapse of the whigs in 1680, had built up a solid party in the country on behalf of the Crown and the Anglican Church. But he was himself a Catholic convert, and he was determined to use the power of the Crown in order to undermine the Anglican Church. The failure of Argyll and Monmouth encouraged him in this resolve: he now thought that the authority of the Crown was complete. So did certain ambitious politicians, who adjusted their policy accordingly: in particular, the Secretary of State, who would soon become the most powerful of James's ministers, Robert Spencer, Earl of Sunderland.*

However, this Catholic policy was very dangerous. Not only did it risk the loss of tory support: it was not even approved by all Roman Catholics. At home the hereditary English Catholics held back, and James gave his confidence to converts, who were soon reinforced by his disreputable Irish general, Richard Talbot, newly created Earl of Tyrconnel. Abroad, the Catholics were equally divided by international tensions.

The aggressive policy of Louis XIV in Europe had driven the Pope into alliance with the enemies of France. Consequently, the Pope was opposed to the policy of James which placed England at the disposal of France. He was more concerned to see a stable, independent Protestant England, opposed to France, than a Catholic England controlled by France or an England divided by religious faction, unable to support the enemies of France. On the other hand the Jesuits at this time – largely in consequence of their struggle with the French Jansenists – supported the policy of Louis XIV, even against the Pope. They therefore became the chief agents and supporters of James's policy. But the Jesuits, as the aggressive, political agents of the Counter-Reformation, had always been particularly detested in Protestant England, even by the secular clergy and old Catholic laity. James thus found himself relying not on the united Catholic

Church, nor on the main body of the English Catholics, but on a party within that Church and that body. In the first of the two following passages (from Chapter VI) Macaulay describes the situation and politics of the Jesuits. In the second (from Chapter VIII) he describes the feeling of the old English Catholic gentry on whom James mistakenly thought that he could rely.]

A. THE JESUITS

As each of the two parties at the Court of James had the support of foreign princes, so each had also the support of an ecclesiastical authority to which the King paid great deference. The Supreme Pontiff was for legal and moderate courses; and his sentiments were expressed by the Nuncio and by the Vicar Apostolic. On the other side was a body of which the weight balanced even the weight of the Papacy, the mighty Order of Jesus.

That at this conjuncture these two great spiritual powers, once, as it seemed, inseparably allied, should have been opposed to each other, is a most important and remarkable circumstance. During a period of little less than a thousand years the regular clergy had been the chief support of the Holy See. By that See they had been protected from episcopal interference; and the protection which they had received had been amply repaid. But for their exertions it is probable that the Bishop of Rome would have been merely the honorary president of a vast aristocracy of prelates. It was by the aid of the Benedictines that Gregory the Seventh was enabled to contend at once against the Franconian Caesars and against the secular priesthood. It was by the aid of the Dominicans and Franciscans that Innocent the Third crushed the Albigensian sectaries. In the sixteenth century the Pontificate, exposed to new dangers more formidable than had ever before threatened it, was saved by a new religious order, which was animated by intense enthusiasm and organized with exquisite skill. When the Jesuits came to the rescue of the Papacy, they found it in extreme peril: but from that moment the tide of battle turned. Protestantism, which had, during a whole generation, carried all before it, was stopped in its progress, and rapidly beaten back from the foot of the Alps to the shores of the Baltic.

Before the Order had existed a hundred years, it had filled the whole world with memorials of great things done and suffered for the faith. No religious community could produce a list of men so variously distinguished: none had extended its operations over so vast a space; yet in none had there ever been such perfect unity of feeling and action. There was no region of the globe, no walk of speculative or of active life, in which Jesuits were not to be found. They guided the counsels of Kings. They deciphered Latin inscriptions. They observed the motions of Jupiter's satellites. They published whole libraries: controversy, casuistry, history, treatises on optics, Alcaic odes, editions of the fathers, madrigals, catechisms, and lampoons. The liberal education of youth passed almost entirely into their hands, and was conducted by them with conspicuous ability. They appear to have discovered the precise point to which intellectual culture can be carried without risk of intellectual emancipation. Enmity itself was compelled to own that, in the art of managing and forming the tender mind, they had no equals. Meanwhile they assiduously and successfully cultivated the eloquence of the pulpit. With still greater assiduity and still greater success they applied themselves to the ministry of the confessional. Throughout Catholic Europe the secrets of every government and of almost every family of note were in their keeping. They glided from one Protestant country to another under innumerable disguises, as gay Cavaliers, as simple rustics, as Puritan preachers. They wandered to countries which neither mercantile avidity nor liberal curiosity had ever impelled any stranger to explore. They were to be found in the garb of Mandarins, superintending the observatory at Pekin. They were to be found, spade in hand, teaching the rudiments of agriculture to the savages of Paraguay. Yet, whatever might be their residence, whatever might be their employment, their spirit was the same, entire devotion to the common cause, implicit obedience to the central authority. None of them had chosen his dwelling place or his vocation for himself. Whether the Jesuit should live under the arctic circle or under the equator, whether he should pass his life in arranging gems and collating manuscripts at the Vatican or in persuading naked barbarians in the southern hemisphere not to eat each other, were matters which he left with profound submission to the decision of others. If he was wanted at Lima, he was on the Atlantic in the next fleet. If he was wanted at Bagdad, he was toiling through the desert with the next caravan. If his ministry was needed in some country where his life was more insecure than that of a wolf, where it was a crime to harbour him, where the heads and quarters of his brethren, fixed in the public places, showed him what he had to expect, he went without remonstrance or hesitation to his doom. Nor is this heroic spirit yet extinct. When, in our own time, a new and terrible pestilence passed round the globe,[1] when, in some great cities, fear had dissolved all the ties which hold society together, when the secular clergy had deserted their flocks, when medical succour was not to be purchased by gold, when the strongest natural affections had yielded to the love of life, even then the Jesuit was found by the pallet which bishop and curate, physician and nurse, father and mother, had deserted, bending over infected lips to catch the faint accents of confession, and holding up to the last, before the expiring penitent, the image of the expiring Redeemer.

But with the admirable energy, disinterestedness, and self-devotion which were characteristic of the Society, great vices were mingled. It was alleged, and not without foundation, that the ardent public spirit which made the Jesuit regardless of his ease, of his liberty, and of his life, made him also regardless of truth and of mercy; that no means which could promote the interest of his religion seemed to him unlawful, and that by the interest of his religion he too often meant the interest of his Society. It was alleged that, in the most atrocious plots recorded in history, his agency could be distinctly traced; that, constant only in attachment to the fraternity to which he belonged, he was in some countries the most dangerous enemy of freedom, and in others the most dangerous enemy of order. The mighty victories which he boasted that he had achieved in the cause of the Church were, in the judgment of many illustrious members of that Church, rather apparent than real. He had indeed laboured with a wonderful show of success to reduce the world under her laws; but he had done so by relaxing her laws to suit the temper of the

[1. The reference is to the cholera epidemic of 1831–3.]

world. Instead of toiling to elevate human nature to the noble
standard fixed by divine precept and example, he had lowered
the standard till it was beneath the average level of human
nature. He gloried in multitudes of converts who had been baptized in the remote regions of the East: but it was reported that
from some of those converts the facts on which the whole theology
of the Gospel depends had been cunningly concealed, and that
others were permitted to avoid persecution by bowing down before the images of false gods, while internally repeating Paters
and Aves. Nor was it only in heathen countries that such arts
were said to be practised. It was not strange that people of all
ranks, and especially of the highest ranks, crowded to the confessionals in the Jesuit temples; for from those confessionals
none went discontented away. There the priest was all things to
all men. He showed just so much rigour as might not drive those
who knelt at his spiritual tribunal to the Dominican or the
Franciscan church. If he had to deal with a mind truly devout,
he spoke in the saintly tones of the primitive fathers: but with
that very large part of mankind who have religion enough to
make them uneasy when they do wrong, and not religion enough
to keep them from doing wrong, he followed a very different system. Since he could not reclaim from them guilt, it was his business to save them from remorse. He had at his command an immense dispensary of anodynes for wounded consciences. In the
books of casuistry which had been written by his brethren, and
printed with the approbation of his superiors, were to be found
doctrines consolatory to transgressors of every class. There the
bankrupt was taught how he might, without sin, secrete his goods
from his creditors. The servant was taught how he might, without sin, run off with his master's plate. The pandar was assured
that a Christian man might innocently earn his living by carrying
letters and messages between married women and their gallants.
The high-spirited and punctilious gentlemen of France were
gratified by a decision in favour of duelling. The Italians, accustomed to darker and baser modes of vengeance, were glad to learn
that they might, without any crime, shoot at their enemies from
behind hedges. To deceit was given a licence sufficient to destroy
the whole value of human contracts and of human testimony. In

truth, if society continued to hold together, if life and property enjoyed any security, it was because common sense and common humanity restrained men from doing what the Society of Jesus assured them that they might with a safe conscience do.

So strangely were good and evil intermixed in the character of these celebrated brethren; and the intermixture was the secret of their gigantic power. That power could never have belonged to mere hypocrites. It could never have belonged to rigid moralists. It was to be attained only by men sincerely enthusiastic in the pursuit of a great end, and at the same time unscrupulous as to the choice of means.

From the first the Jesuits had been bound by a peculiar allegiance to the Pope. Their mission had been not less to quell all mutiny within the Church than to repel the hostility of her avowed enemies. Their doctrine was in the highest degree what has been called on our side of the Alps Ultramontane, and differed almost as much from the doctrine of Bossuet as from that of Luther. They condemned the Gallican liberties, the claim of oecumenical councils to control the Holy See, and the claim of Bishops to an independent commission from heaven. Lainez, in the name of the whole fraternity, proclaimed at Trent, amidst the applause of the creatures of Pius the Fourth, and the murmurs of French and Spanish prelates, that the government of the faithful had been committed by Christ to the Pope alone, that in the Pope alone all sacerdotal authority was concentrated, and that through the Pope alone priests and bishops derived whatever divine authority they possessed. During many years the union between the Supreme Pontiffs and the Order had continued unbroken. Had that union been still unbroken when James the Second ascended the English throne, had the influence of the Jesuits as well as the influence of the Pope been exerted in favour of a moderate and constitutional policy, it is probable that the great revolution which in a short time changed the whole state of European affairs would never have taken place. But, even before the middle of the seventeenth century, the Society, proud of its services and confident in its strength, had become impatient of the yoke. A generation of Jesuits sprang up, who looked for protection and guidance rather to the court of France than to the

court of Rome; and this disposition was not a little strengthened when Innocent the Eleventh was raised to the papal
throne.

The Jesuits were, at that time, engaged in a war to the death
against an enemy whom they had at first disdained but whom
they had at length been forced to regard with respect and fear.
Just when their prosperity was at the height, they were braved by
a handful of opponents, who had indeed no influence with the
rulers of this world, but who were strong in religious faith and
intellectual energy.[2] Then followed a long, a strange, a glorious
conflict of genius against power. The Jesuit called cabinets, tribunals, universities to his aid; and they responded to the call.
Port Royal appealed, not in vain, to the hearts and to the understandings of millions. The dictators of Christendom found
themselves, on a sudden, in the position of culprits. They were
arraigned on the charge of having systematically debased the
standard of evangelical morality, for the purpose of increasing
their own influence; and the charge was enforced in a manner
which at once arrested the attention of the whole world: for the
chief accuser was Blaise Pascal. His intellectual powers were such
as have rarely been bestowed on any of the children of men; and
the vehemence of the zeal which animated him was but too well
proved by the cruel penances and vigils under which his macer-
ated frame sank into an early grave. His spirit was the spirit of
Saint Bernard: but the delicacy of his wit, the purity, the energy,
the simplicity of his rhetoric, had never been equalled, except by
the great masters of Attic eloquence.[3] All Europe read and admired, laughed and wept. The Jesuits attempted to reply, but
their feeble answers were received by the public with shouts of
mockery. They wanted, it is true, no talent or accomplishment
into which men can be drilled by elaborate discipline; but such
discipline, though it may bring out the powers of ordinary minds,
has a tendency to suffocate, rather than to develop, original
genius. It was universally acknowledged that, in the literary contest, the Jansenists were completely victorious.

[2. The reference is to the Jansenists, whose intellectual centre was the
abbey of Port-Royal, near Paris.]

[3. The reference is to Blaise Pascal's *Lettres Provinciales* (1657).]

To the Jesuits nothing was left but to oppress the sect which they could not confute. Lewis the Fourteenth was now their chief support. His conscience had, from boyhood, been in their keeping; and he had learned from them to abhor Jansenism quite as much as he abhorred Protestantism, and very much more than he abhorred Atheism. Innocent the Eleventh, on the other hand, leaned to the Jansenist opinions. The consequence was, that the Society found itself in a situation never contemplated by its founder. The Jesuits were estranged from the Supreme Pontiff; and they were closely allied with a prince who proclaimed himself the champion of the Gallican liberties and the enemy of Ultra-montane pretensions. Thus the Order became in England an instrument of the designs of Lewis, and laboured, with a success which the Roman Catholics afterwards long and bitterly deplored, to widen the breach between the King and the Parliament, to thwart the Nuncio, to undermine the power of the Lord Treasurer, and to support the most desperate schemes of Tyrconnel.

Thus on one side were the Hydes and the whole body of Tory churchmen, Powis and all the most respectable noblemen and gentlemen of the King's own faith, the States General, the House of Austria, and the Pope. On the other side were a few Roman Catholic adventurers, of broken fortune and tainted reputation, backed by France and by the Jesuits.

The chief representative of the Jesuits at Whitehall was an English brother of the Order, who had, during some time, acted as Vice-provincial, who had been long regarded by James with peculiar favour, and who had lately been made Clerk of the Closet. This man, named Edward Petre, was descended from an honourable family. His manners were courtly: his speech was flowing and plausible; but he was weak and vain, covetous and ambitious. Of all the evil counsellors who had access to the royal ear, he bore, perhaps, the largest part in the ruin of the House of Stuart.

B. THE ENGLISH CATHOLIC GENTRY

['*A general cry of alarm and indignation*' greeted the discovery that *James II, at the end of 1687, had appointed a number of Roman*

Catholics as sheriffs in the counties, and therefore arbiters of the imminent parliamentary elections.]

For a time the most gloomy apprehensions prevailed: but soon they began to subside. There was good reason to believe that there was a point beyond which the King could not reckon on the support even of those Sheriffs who were members of his own Church. Between the Roman Catholic courtier and the Roman Catholic country gentleman there was very little sympathy. That cabal which domineered at Whitehall consisted partly of fanatics, who were ready to break through all rules of morality and to throw the world into confusion for the purpose of propagating their religion, and partly of hypocrites, who, for lucre, had apostatized from the faith in which they had been brought up, and who now overacted the zeal characteristic of neophytes. Both the fanatical and the hypocritical courtiers were generally destitute of all English feeling. In some of them devotion to their Church had extinguished every national sentiment. Some were Irishmen, whose patriotism consisted in mortal hatred of the Saxon conquerors of Ireland. Some, again, were traitors, who received regular hire from a foreign power. Some had passed a great part of their lives abroad, and either were mere cosmopolites, or felt a positive distaste for the manners and institutions of the country which was now subjected to their rule. Between such men and the lord of a Cheshire or Staffordshire manor who adhered to the old Church there was scarcely anything in common. He was neither a fanatic nor a hypocrite. He was a Roman Catholic because his father and grandfather had been so; and he held his hereditary faith, as men generally hold a hereditary faith, sincerely, but with little enthusiasm. In all other points he was a mere English squire, and, if he differed from the neighbouring squires, differed from them by being somewhat more simple and clownish than they. The disabilities under which he lay had prevented his mind from expanding to the standard, moderate as that standard was, which the minds of Protestant country gentlemen then ordinarily attained. Excluded, when a boy, from Eton and Westminster, when a youth, from Oxford and Cambridge, when a man, from Parliament and from the bench of justice, he generally

vegetated as quietly as the elms of the avenue which led to his
ancestral grange. His cornfields, his dairy and his cider press, his
greyhounds, his fishing rod and his gun, his ale and his tobacco,
occupied almost all his thoughts. With his neighbours, in spite of
his religion, he was generally on good terms. They knew him to
be unambitious and inoffensive. He was almost always of a good
old family. He was always a Cavalier. His peculiar notions were
not obtruded, and caused no annoyance. He did not, like a Puritan, torment himself and others with scruples about everything
that was pleasant. On the contrary, he was as keen a sportsman,
and as jolly a boon companion, as any man who had taken the
oath of supremacy and the declaration against transsubstantiation. He met his brother squires at the cover, was in with them
at the death, and, when the sport was over, took them home with
him to a venison pasty and to October four years in bottle. The
oppressions which he had undergone had not been such as to
impel him to any desperate resolution. Even when his Church
was barbarously persecuted, his life and property were in little
danger. The most impudent false witnesses could hardly venture
to shock the common sense of mankind by accusing him of being
a conspirator. The Papists whom Oates selected for attack were
peers, prelates, Jesuits, Benedictines, a busy political agent, a
lawyer in high practice, a court physician. The Roman Catholic
country gentleman, protected by his obscurity, by his peaceable
demeanour, and by the good will of those among whom he lived,
carted his hay or filled his bag with game unmolested, while
Coleman and Langhorne, Whitbread and Pickering, Archbishop
Plunkett and Lord Stafford, died by the halter or the axe. An
attempt was indeed made by a knot of villains to bring home a
charge of treason to Sir Thomas Gascoigne, an aged Roman
Catholic baronet of Yorkshire: but twelve of the best gentlemen
of the West Riding, who knew his way of life, could not be convinced that their honest old acquaintance had hired cut-throats
to murder the King, and, in spite of charges which did very little
honour to the bench, found a verdict of Not Guilty. Sometimes,
indeed, the head of an old and respectable provincial family might
reflect with bitterness that he was excluded, on account of his
religion, from places of honour and authority which men of hum-

bler descent and less ample estate were thought competent to fill: but he was little disposed to risk land and life in a struggle against overwhelming odds; and his honest English spirit would have shrunk with horror from means such as were contemplated by the Petres and Tyrconnels. Indeed he would have been as ready as any of his Protestant neighbours to gird on his sword, and to put pistols in his holsters, for the defence of his native land against an invasion of French or Irish Papists. Such was the general character of the men to whom James now looked as to his most trustworthy instruments for the conduct of county elections. He soon found that they were not inclined to throw away the esteem of their neighbours, and to endanger their heads and their estates, by rendering him an infamous and criminal service. Several of them refused to be Sheriffs. Of those who accepted the shrievalty many declared that they would discharge their duty as fairly as if they were members of the Established Church, and would return no candidate who had not a real majority.

7

James II Looks to Ireland

[*In spite of the narrow base on which it rested, James continued his Catholic policy. He advertised his preference for Catholic servants, encouraged conversions to Catholicism, and promoted converts to office in church and state, including the deanery of Christ Church, Oxford. He set up a Court of High Commission, composed of his own creatures, to regulate – that is, to catholicize – the Established Church. By a collusive action at law, he obtained a legal judgement that the Crown could, in particular cases, dispense with the anti-Catholic laws, and he resolved to make use of this right on an extensive scale. In all these actions he was abetted by Sunderland, who was determined, by such compliance, to achieve the highest office. James also gave authority to Catholic converts in Scotland. There the two Drummond brothers, the Earl of Perth and Lord Melfort, displaced the Protestant and tory Duke of Queensberry. But in Scotland, as in England, these measures hardened opposition against the King and forced him to seek new allies and a wider base. These he found in Ireland, among the subject Celts whose Catholicism was, in part, the expression of their national hatred for their English conquerors.*

In order to mobilize the Catholicism of the Irish, James resolved to change the government of Ireland. During most of the reign of Charles II, the Lord Lieutenant of Ireland had been James Butler, Duke of Ormond, whose great services in the civil war gave him unchallenged authority. Ormond was the head of an old Anglo-Norman family ; but he was also a Protestant, of independent mind, the enlightened champion of the English interest. At his accession, when he was still relying on tory support, James had dismissed Ormond and had replaced him, after some delay, by one whom he supposed to be more docile : his own brother-in-law, Henry Hyde, Earl of Clarendon. However, Clarendon, like his brother Rochester and indeed all his family, was a staunch Anglican, and as such could not be trusted to forward in Ireland an anti-English Catholic policy. James therefore decided to advance, at his expense, the disreputable Catholic

*Irishman who had become one of his trusted allies, Richard Talbot,
Earl of Tyrconnel.*

*In the following passage (from Chapter VI) Macaulay describes
the social and political structure of Ireland, and the methods by which
James sought to transfer power from the English Protestants to the
Irish Catholics. The culmination of this process was the formal re-
placement of Clarendon, as Lord Lieutenant, by Tyrconnel. At the
same time, in England, the Lord Treasurer, Rochester, was being replaced by Sunderland, who offered hopes (soon to be fulfilled) of his
conversion. Thus the Anglican tory Hydes, whose father, the first
Earl of Clarendon, had secured the Restoration of the monarchy and
the Church, were both discarded. In all three Kingdoms the Catholic
or catholicizing party was in power.]*

WHEN the historian of this troubled reign turns to Ireland, his
task becomes peculiarly difficult and delicate. His steps – to borrow the fine image used on a similar occasion by a Roman poet –
are on the thin crust of ashes, beneath which the lava is still glow-
ing. The seventeenth century has, in that unhappy country, left
to the nineteenth a fatal heritage of malignant passions. No amnesty for the mutual wrongs inflicted by the Saxon defenders of
Londonderry, and by the Celtic defenders of Limerick, has ever
been granted from the heart by either race. To this day a more
than Spartan haughtiness alloys the many noble qualities which
characterize the children of the victors, while a Helot feeling,
compounded of awe and hatred, is but too often discernible in
the children of the vanquished. Neither of the hostile castes can
justly be absolved from blame; but the chief blame is due to that
short-sighted and headstrong prince who, placed in a situation in
which he might have reconciled them, employed all his power to
inflame their animosity, and at length forced them to close in a
grapple for life and death.

The grievances under which the members of his Church
laboured in Ireland differed widely from those which he was attempting to remove in England and Scotland. The Irish Statute
Book, afterwards polluted by intolerance as barbarous as that of
the dark ages, then contained scarce a single enactment, and not
a single stringent enactment, imposing any penalty on Papists as

such. On our side of Saint George's Channel every priest who received a neophyte into the bosom of the Church of Rome was liable to be hanged, drawn, and quartered. On the other side he incurred no such danger. A Jesuit who landed at Dover took his life in his hand; but he walked the streets of Dublin in security. Here no man could hold office, or even earn his livelihood as a barrister or a schoolmaster, without previously taking the oath of supremacy: but in Ireland a public functionary was not held to be under the necessity of taking that oath unless it were formally tendered to him. It therefore did not exclude from employment any person whom the government wished to promote. The sacramental test and the declaration against transsubstantiation were unknown; nor was either House of Parliament closed against any religious sect.

It might seem, therefore, that the Irish Roman Catholic was in a situation which his English and Scottish brethren in the faith might well envy. In fact, however, his condition was more pitiable and irritating than theirs. For, though not persecuted as a Roman Catholic, he was oppressed as an Irishman. In his country the same line of demarcation which separated religions separated races; and he was of the conquered, the subjugated, the degraded race. On the same soil dwelt two populations, locally intermixed, and politically sundered. The difference of religion was by no means the only difference, and was perhaps not even the chief difference, which existed between them. They sprang from different stocks. They spoke different languages. They had different national characters as strongly opposed as any two national characters in Europe. They were in widely different stages of civilisation. Between two such populations there could be little sympathy; and centuries of calamities and wrongs had generated a strong antipathy. The relation in which the minority stood to the majority resembled the relation in which the followers of William the Conqueror stood to the Saxon churls, or the relation in which the followers of Cortes stood to the Indians of Mexico.

The appellation of Irish was then given exclusively to the Celts and to those families which, though not of Celtic origin, had in the course of ages degenerated into Celtic manners. These people, probably somewhat under a million in number, had, with few exceptions, adhered to the Church of Rome. Among them resided about two hundred thousand colonists, proud of their Saxon blood and of their Protestant faith.

The great preponderance of numbers on one side was more than compensated by a great superiority of intelligence, vigour, and organization on the other. The English settlers seem to have been, in knowledge, energy, and perseverance, rather above than below the average level of the population of the mother country. The aboriginal peasantry, on the contrary, were in an almost savage state. They never worked till they felt the sting of hunger. They were content with accommodation inferior to that which, in happier countries, was provided for domestic cattle. Already the potato, a root which can be cultivated with scarcely any art, industry, or capital, and which cannot be long stored, had become the food of the common people. From a people so fed diligence and forethought were not to be expected. Even within a few miles of Dublin, the traveller, on a soil the richest and most verdant in the world, saw with disgust the miserable burrows out of which squalid and half naked barbarians stared wildly at him as he passed.

The aboriginal aristocracy retained in no common measure the pride of birth, but had lost the influence which is derived from wealth and power. Their lands had been divided by Cromwell among his followers. A portion, indeed, of the vast territory which he had confiscated had, after the restoration of the House of Stuart, been given back to the ancient proprietors. But much the greater part was still held by English emigrants under the guarantee of an Act of Parliament.[1] This act had been in force a quarter of a century; and under it mortgages, settlements, sales, and leases without number had been made. The old Irish gentry were scattered over the whole world. Descendants of Milesian[2] chieftains swarmed in all the courts and camps of the Continent. Those despoiled proprietors who still remained in their native land, brooded gloomily over their losses, pined for the opulence and dignity of which they had been deprived, and cherished wild

[1. The Act of Settlement, 1662.]
[2. Milesian – Irish; the Irish claiming political descent from a fabulous Spanish King Milesius.]

hopes of another revolution. A person of this class was described by his countrymen as a gentleman who would be rich if justice were done, as a gentleman who had a fine estate if he could only get it. He seldom betook himself to any peaceful calling. Trade, indeed, he thought a far more disgraceful resource than marauding. Sometimes he turned freebooter. Sometimes he contrived, in defiance of the law, to live by coshering, that is to say, by quartering himself on the old tenants of his family, who, wretched as was their own condition, could not refuse a portion of their pittance to one whom they still regarded as their rightful lord. The native gentleman who had been so fortunate as to keep or to regain some of his land too often lived like the petty prince of a savage tribe, and indemnified himself for the humiliations which the dominant race made him suffer by governing his vassals despotically, by keeping a rude harem, and by maddening or stupefying himself daily with strong drink.[3] Politically he was insignificant. No statute, indeed, excluded him from the House of Commons: but he had almost as little chance of obtaining a seat there as a man of colour has of being chosen a Senator of the United States. In fact only one Papist had been returned to the Irish Parliament since the Restoration. The whole legislative and executive power was in the hands of the colonists; and the ascendancy of the ruling caste was upheld by a standing army of seven thousand men, on whose zeal for what was called the English interest full reliance could be placed.

On a close scrutiny it would have been found that neither the Irishry nor the Englishry formed a perfectly homogeneous body. The distinction between those Irish who were of Celtic blood, and those Irish who sprang from the followers of Strongbow and De Burgh,[4] was not altogether effaced. The Fitzes sometimes permitted themselves to speak with scorn of the Os and Macs; and the Os and Macs sometimes repaid that scorn with aversion. In the preceding generation one of the most powerful of the O'Neills refused to pay any mark of respect to a Roman Catholic

3. Miss Edgeworth's King Corny belongs to a later and much more civilised generation; but whoever has studied that admirable portrait can form some notion of what King Corny's great grandfather must have been.

[4. The twelfth-century 'Anglo-Norman' conquerors of Ireland.]

gentleman of old Norman descent. 'They say that the family has
been here four hundred years. No matter. I hate the clown as if
he had come yesterday.' It seems, however, that such feelings
were rare, and that the feud which had long raged between the
aboriginal Celts and the degenerate English had nearly given place
to the fiercer feud which separated both races from the modern
and Protestant colony.

The colony had its own internal disputes, both national and
religious. The majority was English; but a large minority came
from the south of Scotland. One half of the settlers belonged to
the Established Church; the other half were Dissenters. But in
Ireland Scot and Southron were strongly bound together by their
common Saxon origin. Churchman and Presbyterian were strongly bound together by their common Protestantism. All the colonists had a common language and a common pecuniary interest.
They were surrounded by common enemies, and could be safe
only by means of common precautions and exertions. The few
penal laws, therefore, which had been made in Ireland against
Protestant Nonconformists, were a dead letter. The bigotry of
the most sturdy churchman would not bear exportation across
St George's Channel. As soon as the Cavalier arrived in Ireland,
and found that, without the hearty and courageous assistance of
his Puritan neighbours, he and all his family would run imminent
risk of being murdered by Popish marauders, his hatred of Puritanism, in spite of himself, began to languish and die away. It was
remarked by eminent men of both parties that a Protestant who,
in Ireland, was called a high Tory would in England have been
considered as a moderate Whig.

The Protestant Nonconformists, on their side, endured, with
more patience than could have been expected, the sight of the
most absurd ecclesiastical establishment that the world has ever
seen. Four Archbishops and eighteen Bishops were employed in
looking after about a fifth part of the number of churchmen who
inhabited the single diocese of London. Of the parochial clergy a
large proportion were pluralists and resided at a distance from
their cures. There were some who drew from their benefices incomes of little less than a thousand a year, without ever performing any spiritual function. Yet this monstrous institution was

much less disliked by the Puritans settled in Ireland than the Church of England by the English sectaries. For in Ireland religious divisions were subordinate to national divisions; and the Presbyterian, while, as a theologian, he could not but condemn the established hierarchy, yet looked on that hierarchy with a sort of complacency when he considered it as a sumptuous and ostentatious trophy of the victory achieved by the great race from which he sprang.

Thus the grievances of the Irish Roman Catholic had hardly anything in common with the grievances of the English Roman Catholic. The Roman Catholic of Lancashire or Staffordshire had only to turn Protestant; and he was at once, in all respects, on a level with his neighbours: but, if the Roman Catholics of Munster and Connaught had turned Protestants, they would still have continued to be a subject people. Whatever evils the Roman Catholic suffered in England were the effects of harsh legislation, and might have been remedied by a more liberal legislation. But between the two populations which inhabited Ireland there was an inequality which legislation had not caused and could not remove. The dominion which one of those populations exercised over the other was the dominion of wealth over poverty, of knowledge over ignorance, of civilised over uncivilised man.

James himself seemed, at the commencement of his reign, to be perfectly aware of these truths. The distractions of Ireland, he said, arose, not from the differences between the Catholics and the Protestants, but from the differences between the Irish and the English. The consequences which he should have drawn from this just proposition were sufficiently obvious; but unhappily for himself and for Ireland he failed to perceive them.

If only national animosity could be allayed, there could be little doubt that religious animosity, not being kept alive, as in England, by cruel penal acts and stringent test acts, would of itself fade away. To allay a national animosity such as that which the two races inhabiting Ireland felt for each other could not be the work of a few years. Yet it was a work to which a wise and good prince might have contributed much; and James would have undertaken that work with advantages such as none of his predecessors or successors possessed. At once an Englishman and a

Roman Catholic, he belonged half to the ruling and half to the subject caste, and was therefore peculiarly qualified to be a mediator between them. Nor is it difficult to trace the course which he ought to have pursued. He ought to have determined that the existing settlement of landed property should be inviolable; and he ought to have announced that determination in such a manner as effectually to quiet the anxiety of the new proprietors, and to extinguish any wild hopes which the old proprietors might entertain. Whether, in the great transfer of estates, injustice had or had not been committed, was immaterial. That transfer, just or unjust, had taken place so long ago, that to reverse it would be to unfix the foundations of society. There must be a time of limitation to all rights. After thirty-five years of actual possession, after twenty-five years of possession solemnly guaranteed by statute, after innumerable leases and releases, mortgages and devises, it was too late to search for flaws in titles. Nevertheless something might have been done to heal the lacerated feelings and to raise the fallen fortunes of the Irish gentry. The colonists were in a thriving condition. They had greatly improved their property by building, planting, and fencing. The rents had almost doubled within a few years; trade was brisk; and the revenue, amounting to about three hundred thousand pounds a year, more than defrayed all the charges of the local government, and afforded a surplus which was remitted to England. There was no doubt that the next Parliament which should meet at Dublin, though representing almost exclusively the English interest, would, in return for the King's promise to maintain that interest in all its legal rights, willingly grant to him a very considerable sum for the purpose of indemnifying, at least in part, such native families as had been wrongfully despoiled. It was thus that in our own time the French government put an end to the disputes engendered by the most extensive confiscation that ever took place in Europe. And thus, if James had been guided by the advice of his most loyal Protestant counsellors, he would have at least greatly mitigated one of the chief evils which afflicted Ireland.

Having done this, he should have laboured to reconcile the hostile races to each other by impartially protecting the rights and restraining the excesses of both. He should have punished with equal severity the native who indulged in the licence of barbarism, and the colonist who abused the strength of civilisation. As far as the legitimate authority of the crown extended – and in Ireland it extended far – no man who was qualified for office by integrity and ability should have been considered as disqualified by extraction or by creed for any public trust. It is probable that a Roman Catholic King, with an ample revenue absolutely at his disposal, would, without much difficulty, have secured the cooperation of the Roman Catholic prelates and priests in the great work of reconciliation. Much, however, must still have been left to the healing influence of time. The native race would still have had to learn from the colonists industry and forethought, the arts of life, and the language of England. There could not be equality between men who lived in houses and men who lived in sties, between men who were fed on bread and men who were fed on potatoes, between men who spoke the noble tongue of great philosophers and poets and men who, with a perverted pride, boasted that they could not writhe their mouths into chattering such a jargon as that in which the Advancement of Learning and the Paradise Lost were written.[5] Yet it is not unreasonable to believe that, if the gentle policy which has been described had been steadily followed by the government, all distinctions would gradually have been effaced, and that there would now have been no more trace of the hostility which has been the curse of Ireland than there is of the equally deadly hostility which once raged between the Saxons and the Normans in England.

Unhappily James, instead of becoming a mediator became the fiercest and most reckless of partisans. Instead of allaying the animosity of the two populations, he inflamed it to a height before unknown. He determined to reverse their relative position, and to put the Protestant colonists under the feet of the Popish Celts. To be of the established religion, to be of the English blood, was, in his view, a disqualification for civil and military employment. He meditated the design of again confiscating and again portioning out the soil of half the island, and showed his inclination so

5. It was an O'Neill of great eminence who said that it did not become him to writhe his mouth to chatter English. Preface to the first volume of the *Hibernia Anglicana*.

clearly that one class was soon agitated by terrors which he afterwards vainly wished to soothe, and the other by hopes which he
afterwards vainly wished to restrain. But this was the smallest
part of his guilt and madness. He deliberately resolved, not
merely to give to the aboriginal inhabitants of Ireland the entire
possession of their own country, but also to use them as his
instruments for setting up arbitrary government in England.

The event was such as might have been foreseen. The colonists
turned to bay with the stubborn hardihood of their race. The
mother country justly regarded their cause as her own. Then
came a desperate struggle for a tremendous stake. Everything
dear to nations was wagered on both sides: nor can we justly
blame either the Irishman or the Englishman for obeying, in that
extremity, the law of self-preservation. The contest was terrible,
but short. The weaker went down. His fate was cruel; and yet for
the cruelty with which he was treated there was, not indeed a
defence, but an excuse: for, though he suffered all that tyranny
could inflict, he suffered nothing that he would not himself have
inflicted. The effect of the insane attempt to subjugate England
by means of Ireland was that the Irish became hewers of wood
and drawers of water to the English. The old proprietors, by their
effort to recover what they had lost, lost the greater part of what
they had retained. The momentary ascendancy of Popery produced such a series of barbarous laws against Popery as made the
statute book of Ireland a proverb of infamy throughout Christendom. Such were the bitter fruits of the policy of James.

We have seen that one of his first acts, after he became King,
was to recall Ormond from Ireland. Ormond was the head of the
English interest in that kingdom: he was firmly attached to the
Protestant religion; and his power far exceeded that of an ordinary Lord Lieutenant, first, because he was in rank and wealth
the greatest of the colonists, and, secondly, because he was not
only the chief of the civil administration, but also commander of
the forces. The King was not at that time disposed to commit the
government wholly to Irish hands. He had indeed been heard to
say that a native viceroy would soon become an independent sovereign. For the present, therefore, he determined to divide the

power which Ormond had possessed, to entrust the civil administration to an English and Protestant Lord Lieutenant, and to give the command of the army to an Irish and Roman Catholic General. The Lord Lieutenant was Clarendon; the General was Tyrconnel.

Tyrconnel sprang, as has already been said, from one of those degenerate families of the Pale which were popularly classed with the aboriginal population of Ireland. He sometimes, indeed, in his rants, talked with Norman haughtiness of the Celtic barbarians: but all his sympathies were really with the natives. The Protestant colonists he hated; and they returned his hatred. Clarendon's inclinations were very different: but he was, from temper, interest, and principle, an obsequious courtier. His spirit was mean; his circumstances were embarrassed; and his mind had been deeply imbued with the political doctrines which the Church of England had in that age too assiduously taught. His abilities, however, were not contemptible; and, under a good King, he would probably have been a respectable viceroy.

About three quarters of a year elapsed between the recall of Ormond and the arrival of Clarendon at Dublin. During that interval the King was represented by a board of Lords Justices: but the military administration was in Tyrconnel's hands. Already the designs of the court began gradually to unfold themselves. A royal order came from Whitehall for disarming the population. This order Tyrconnel strictly executed as respected the English. Though the country was infested by predatory bands, a Protestant gentleman could scarcely obtain permission to keep a brace of pistols. The native peasantry, on the other hand, were suffered to retain their weapons. The joy of the colonists was therefore great, when at length, in December 1685, Tyrconnel was summoned to London and Clarendon set out for Dublin. But it soon appeared that the government was really directed, not at Dublin, but in London. Every mail that crossed St George's Channel brought tidings of the boundless influence which Tyrconnel exercised on Irish affairs. It was said that he was to be a Marquess, that he was to be a Duke, that he was to have the command of the forces, that he was to be entrusted with the task of remodelling the army and the courts of justice. Clarendon was bitterly mortified at finding himself a subordinate member of that administration of which he had expected to be the head. He complained that whatever he did was misrepresented by his detractors, and that the gravest resolutions touching the country which he governed were adopted at Westminster, made known to the public, discussed at coffee houses, communicated in hundreds of private letters, some weeks before one hint had been given to the Lord Lieutenant. His own personal dignity, he said, mattered little: but it was no light thing that the representative of the majesty of the throne should be made an object of contempt to the people. Panic spread fast among the English when they found that the viceroy, their fellow countryman and fellow Protestant, was unable to extend to them the protection which they had expected from him. They began to know by bitter experience what it is to be a subject caste. They were harassed by the natives with accusations of treason and sedition. This Protestant had corresponded with Monmouth: that Protestant had said something disrespectful of the King four or five years ago, when the Exclusion Bill was under discussion; and the evidence of the most infamous of mankind was ready to substantiate every charge. The Lord Lieutenant expressed his apprehension that, if these practices were not stopped, there would soon be at Dublin a reign of terror similar to that which he had seen in London, when every man held his life and honour at the mercy of Oates and Bedloe.[6]

Clarendon was soon informed, by a concise despatch from Sunderland, that it had been resolved to make without delay a complete change in both the civil and the military government of Ireland, and to bring a large number of Roman Catholics instantly into office. His Majesty, it was most ungraciously added, had taken counsel on these matters with persons more competent to advise him than his inexperienced Lord Lieutenant could possibly be.

Before this letter reached the viceroy the intelligence which it contained had, through many channels, arrived in Ireland. The terror of the colonists was extreme. Outnumbered as they were by the native population, their condition would be pitiable indeed if the native population were to be armed against them with the

[6. That is, during the scare of the 'Popish Plot' in 1679–80.]

whole power of the state; and nothing less than this was threatened. The English inhabitants of Dublin passed each other in the streets with dejected looks. On the Exchange business was suspended. Landowners hastened to sell their estates for whatever could be got, and to remit the purchase money to England. Traders began to call in their debts and to make preparations for retiring from business. The alarm soon affected the revenue. Clarendon attempted to inspire the dismayed settlers with a confidence which he was himself far from feeling. He assured them that their property would be held sacred, and that, to his certain knowledge, the King was fully determined to maintain the Act of Settlement which guaranteed their right to the soil. But his letters to England were in a very different strain. He ventured even to expostulate with the King, and, without blaming His Majesty's intention of employing Roman Catholics, expressed a strong opinion that the Roman Catholics who might be employed should be Englishmen.

The reply of James was dry and cold. He declared that he had no intention of depriving the English colonists of their land, but that he regarded a large portion of them as his enemies, and that, since he consented to leave so much property in the hands of his enemies, it was the more necessary that the civil and military administration should be in the hands of his friends.

Accordingly several Roman Catholics were sworn of the Privy Council; and orders were sent to corporations to admit Roman Catholics to municipal advantages. Many officers of the army were arbitrarily deprived of their commissions and of their bread. It was to no purpose that the Lord Lieutenant pleaded the cause of some whom he knew to be good soldiers and loyal subjects. Among them were old Cavaliers, who had fought bravely for monarchy, and who bore the marks of honourable wounds. Their places were supplied by men who had no recommendation but their religion. Of the new Captains and Lieutenants, it was said, some had been cowherds, some footmen, some noted marauders; some had been so used to wear brogues that they stumbled and shuffled about strangely in their military jack boots. Not a few of the officers who were discarded took refuge in the Dutch service, and enjoyed, four years later, the pleasure of driving their successors before them in ignominious rout through the waters of the Boyne.

The distress and alarm of Clarendon were increased by news which reached him through private channels. Without his approbation, without his knowledge, preparations were making for arming and drilling the whole Celtic population of the country of which he was the nominal governor. Tyrconnel from London directed the design; and the prelates of his Church were his agents. Every priest had been instructed to prepare an exact list of all his male parishioners capable of bearing arms, and to forward it to his Bishop.

It had already been rumoured that Tyrconnel would soon return to Dublin armed with extraordinary and independent powers; and the rumour gathered strength daily. The Lord Lieutenant, whom no insult could drive to resign the pomp and emoluments of his place, declared that he should submit cheerfully to the royal pleasure, and approve himself in all things a faithful and obedient subject. He had never, he said, in his life, had any difference with Tyrconnel, and he trusted that no difference would now arise. Clarendon appears not to have recollected that there had once been a plot to ruin the fame of his innocent sister, and that in that plot Tyrconnel had borne a chief part. This is not exactly one of the injuries which high-spirited men most readily pardon. But, in the wicked court where the Hydes had long been pushing their fortunes, such injuries were easily forgiven and forgotten, not from magnanimity or Christian charity, but from mere baseness and want of moral sensibility.

In June 1686, Tyrconnel came. His commission authorised him only to command the troops: but he brought with him royal instructions touching all parts of the administration, and at once took the real government of the island into his own hands. On the day after his arrival he explicitly said that commissions must be largely given to Roman Catholic officers, and that room must be made for them by dismissing more Protestants. He pushed on the remodelling of the army eagerly and indefatigably. It was indeed the only part of the functions of a Commander in Chief which he was competent to perform; for, though courageous in brawls and duels, he knew nothing of military duty. At the very first review which he held, it was evident to all who were near to him that he did not know how to draw up a regiment. To turn Englishmen out and to put Irishmen in was, in his view, the beginning and the end of the administration of war. He had the insolence to cashier the Captain of the Lord Lieutenant's own bodyguard: nor was Clarendon aware of what had happened till he saw a Roman Catholic, whose face was quite unknown to him, escorting the state coach. The change was not confined to the officers alone. The ranks were completely broken up and recomposed. Four or five hundred soldiers were turned out of a single regiment chiefly on the ground that they were below the proper stature. Yet the most unpractised eye at once perceived that they were taller and better made men than their successors, whose wild and squalid appearance disgusted the beholders. Orders were given to the new officers that no man of the Protestant religion was to be suffered to enlist. The recruiting parties, instead of beating their drums for volunteers at fairs and markets, as had been the old practice, repaired to places to which the Roman Catholics were in the habit of making pilgrimages for purposes of devotion. In a few weeks the General had introduced more than two thousand natives into the ranks; and the people about him confidently affirmed that by Christmas day not a man of English race would be left in the whole army.

On all questions which arose in the Privy Council, Tyrconnel showed similar violence and partiality. John Keating, Chief Justice of the Common Pleas, a man distinguished by ability, integrity, and loyalty, represented with great mildness that perfect equality was all that the General could reasonably ask for his own Church. The King, he said, evidently meant that no man fit for public trust should be excluded because he was a Roman Catholic, and that no man unfit for public trust should be admitted because he was a Protestant. Tyrconnel immediately began to curse and swear. 'I do not know what to say to that; I would have all Catholics in.' The most judicious Irishmen of his own religious persuasion were dismayed at his rashness, and ventured to remonstrate with him; but he drove them from him with imprecations. His brutality was such that many thought him mad. Yet it was less strange than the shameless volubility with which he uttered falsehoods. He had long before earned the nickname of Lying Dick Talbot; and, at Whitehall, any wild fiction was commonly designated as one of Dick Talbot's truths. He now daily proved that he was well entitled to his unenviable reputation. Indeed in him mendacity was almost a disease. He would, after giving orders for the dismission of English officers, take them into his closet, assure them of his confidence and friendship, and implore heaven to confound him, sink him, blast him, if he did not take good care of their interests. Sometimes those to whom he had thus perjured himself learned, before the day closed, that he had cashiered them.

On his arrival, though he swore savagely at the Act of Settlement, and called the English interest a foul thing, a roguish thing, and a damned thing, he yet pretended to be convinced that the distribution of property could not, after the lapse of so many years, be altered. But, when he had been a few weeks at Dublin, his language changed. He began to harangue vehemently at the Council board on the necessity of giving back the land to the old owners. He had not, however, as yet, obtained his master's sanction to this fatal project. National feeling still struggled feebly against superstition in the mind of James. He was an Englishman: he was an English King; and he could not, without some misgivings, consent to the destruction of the greatest colony that England had ever planted. The English Roman Catholics with whom he was in the habit of taking counsel were almost unanimous in favour of the Act of Settlement. Not only the honest and moderate Powis, but the dissolute and headstrong Dover, gave judicious and patriotic advice. Tyrconnel could hardly hope to counteract at a distance the effect which such advice must produce on the royal mind. He determined to plead the cause of his caste in person; and accordingly he set out, at the end of August, for England.

His presence and his absence were equally dreaded by the Lord Lieutenant. It was, indeed, painful to be daily browbeaten by an enemy: but it was not less painful to know that an enemy was daily breathing calumny and evil counsel in the royal ear. Clarendon was overwhelmed by manifold vexations. He made a progress through the country, and found that he was everywhere treated by the Irish population with contempt. The Roman Catholic priests exhorted their congregations to withhold from him all marks of honour. The native gentry, instead of coming to pay their respects to him, remained at their houses. The native peasantry everywhere sang Erse songs in praise of Tyrconnel, who would, they doubted not, soon reappear to complete the humiliation of their oppressors. The viceroy had scarcely returned to Dublin, from his unsatisfactory tour, when he received letters which informed him that he had incurred the King's serious displeasure. His Majesty – so these letters ran – expected his servants not only to do what he commanded, but to do it from the heart, and with a cheerful countenance. The Lord Lieutenant had not, indeed, refused to cooperate in the reform of the army and of the civil administration; but his cooperation had been reluctant and perfunctory: his looks had betrayed his feelings; and everybody saw that he disapproved of the policy which he was employed to carry into effect. In great anguish of mind he wrote to defend himself; but he was sternly told that his defence was not satisfactory. He then, in the most abject terms, declared that he would not attempt to justify himself, that he acquiesced in the royal judgment, be it what it might, that he prostrated himself in the dust, that he implored pardon, that of all penitents he was the most sincere, that he should think it glorious to die in his Sovereign's cause, but found it impossible to live under his Sovereign's displeasure. Nor was this mere interested hypocrisy, but, at least in part, unaffected slavishness and poverty of spirit; for in confidential letters, not meant for the royal eye, he bemoaned himself to his family in the same strain. He was miserable; he was crushed; the wrath of the King was insupportable; if that wrath could not be mitigated, life would not be worth having. The poor man's terror increased when he learned that it had been determined at Whitehall to recall him, and to appoint, as his successor, his rival and calumniator, Tyrconnel. Then for a time the prospect seemed to clear; the King was in better humour; and during a few days Clarendon flattered himself that his brother's intercession had prevailed, and that the crisis was passed.

In truth the crisis was only beginning. While Clarendon was

trying to lean on Rochester, Rochester was unable longer to support himself. As in Ireland the elder brother, though retaining the guard of honour, the sword of state, and the title of Excellency, had really been superseded by the Commander of the Forces, so in England, the younger brother, though holding the white staff, and walking, by virtue of his high office, before the great hereditary nobles, was fast sinking into a mere financial clerk. The Parliament was again prorogued to a distant day, in opposition to the Treasurer's known wishes. He was not even told that there was to be another prorogation, but was left to learn the news from the Gazette. The real direction of affairs had passed to the cabal which dined with Sunderland on Fridays. The cabinet met only to hear the despatches from foreign courts read: nor did those despatches contain anything which was not known on the Royal Exchange; for all the English Envoys had received orders to put into the official letters only the common talk of antechambers, and to reserve important secrets for private communications which were addressed to James himself, to Sunderland, or to Petre. Yet the victorious faction was not content. The King was assured by those whom he most trusted that the obstinacy with which the nation opposed his designs was really to be imputed to Rochester. How could the people believe that their Sovereign was unalterably resolved to persevere in the course on which he had entered, when they saw at his right hand, ostensibly first in power and trust among his counsellors, a man who notoriously regarded that course with strong disapprobation? Every step which had been taken with the object of humbling the Church of England, and of elevating the Church of Rome, had been opposed by the Treasurer. True it was that, when he had found opposition vain, he had gloomily submitted, nay, that he had sometimes even assisted in carrying into effect the very plans against which he had most earnestly contended. True it was that, though he disliked the Ecclesiastical Commission, he had consented to be a Commissioner. True it was that he had, while declaring that he could see nothing blamable in the conduct of the Bishop of London, voted sullenly and reluctantly for the sentence of deprivation. But this was not enough. A prince, engaged in an enterprise so important and arduous as that on which James was bent, had a right to expect from his first minister, not unwilling and ungracious acquiescence, but zealous and strenuous cooperation. While such advice was daily given to James by those in whom he reposed confidence, he received, by the penny post, many anonymous letters filled with calumnies against the Lord Treasurer. This mode of attack had been contrived by Tyrconnel, and was in perfect harmony with every part of his infamous life.

The King hesitated. He seems, indeed, to have really regarded his brother-in-law with personal kindness: the effect of near affinity, of long and familiar intercourse, and of many mutual good offices. It seemed probable that, as long as Rochester continued to submit himself, though tardily and with murmurs, to the royal pleasure, he would continue to be in name prime minister. Sunderland, therefore, with exquisite cunning, suggested to his master the propriety of asking the only proof of obedience which it was quite certain that Rochester never would give. At present – such was the language of the artful Secretary – it was impossible to consult with the first of the King's servants respecting the object nearest to the King's heart. It was lamentable to think that religious prejudices should, at such a conjuncture, deprive the government of such valuable assistance. Perhaps those prejudices might not prove insurmountable. Then the deceiver whispered that, to his knowledge, Rochester had of late had some misgivings about the points in dispute between the Protestants and Catholics.

This was enough. The King eagerly caught at the hint. He began to flatter himself that he might at once escape from the disagreeable necessity of removing a friend, and secure an able coadjutor for the great work which was in progress. He was also elated by the hope that he might have the merit and the glory of saving a fellow creature from perdition. He seems, indeed, about this time, to have been seized with an unusually violent fit of zeal for his religion; and this is the more remarkable, because he had just relapsed, after a short interval of self-restraint, into debauchery which all Christian divines condemn as sinful, and which, in an elderly man married to an agreeable young wife, is regarded even by people of the world as disreputable. Lady Dorchester had returned from Dublin, and was again the King's mistress. Her return was politically of no importance. She had learned by experience the folly of attempting to save her lover from the destruction to which he was running headlong. She therefore suffered the Jesuits to guide his political conduct; and they, in return, suffered her to wheedle him out of money. She was, however, only one of several abandoned women who at this time shared, with his beloved Church, the dominion over his mind. He seems to have determined to make some amends for neglecting the welfare of his own soul by taking care of the souls of others. He set himself, therefore, to labour, with real good will, but with the good will of a coarse, stern, and arbitrary mind, for the conversion of his kinsman.

Every audience which the Treasurer obtained was spent in arguments about the authority of the Church and the worship of images. Rochester was firmly resolved not to abjure his religion; but he had no scruple about employing in self-defence artifices as discreditable as those which had been used against him. He affected to speak like a man whose mind was not made up, professed himself desirous to be enlightened if he was in error, borrowed Popish books, and listened with civility to Popish divines.

*

[*After a long drawn-out comedy in the course of which Rochester pretended that he was convertible in the hope of keeping his post, James finally put the matter clearly; either he must become a Catholic or give up the white staff.*]

Rochester saw that all was over, and that the wisest course left to him was to make his retreat with as much money and as much credit as possible. He succeeded in both objects. He obtained a pension of four thousand pounds a year for two lives on the post office. He had made great sums out of the estates of traitors, and carried with him in particular Grey's bond for forty thousand pounds, and a grant of all the estate which the crown had in Grey's extensive property. No person had ever quitted office on terms so advantageous.

To the applause of the sincere friends of the Established

Church Rochester had, indeed, very slender claims. To save his place he had sat in that tribunal which had been illegally created for the purpose of persecuting her.[7] To save his place he had given a dishonest vote for degrading one of her most eminent ministers, had affected to doubt her orthodoxy, had listened with the outward show of docility to teachers who called her schismatical and heretical, and had offered to cooperate strenuously with her deadliest enemies in their designs against her. The highest praise to which he was entitled was this, that he had shrunk from the exceeding wickedness and baseness of publicly abjuring, for lucre, the religion in which he had been brought up, which he believed to be true, and of which he had long made an ostentatious profession. Yet he was extolled by the great body of Churchmen as if he had been the bravest and purest of martyrs. The Old and New Testaments, the Martyrologies of Eusebius and of Foxe, were ransacked to find parallels for his heroic piety. He was Daniel in the den of lions, Shadrach in the fiery furnace, Peter in the dungeon of Herod, Paul at the bar of Nero, Ignatius in the amphitheatre, Latimer at the stake. Among the many facts which prove that the standard of honour and virtue among the public men of that age was low, the admiration excited by Rochester's constancy is, perhaps, the most decisive.

In his fall he dragged down Clarendon. On the seventh of January 1687, the Gazette announced to the people of London that the Treasury was put into commission. On the eighth arrived at Dublin a despatch formally signifying that in a month Tyrconnel would assume the government of Ireland. It was not without great difficulty that this man had surmounted the numerous impediments which stood in the way of his ambition. It was well known that the extermination of the English colony in Ireland was the object on which his heart was set. He had, therefore, to overcome some scruples in the royal mind. He had to surmount the opposition, not merely of all the Protestant members of the government, not merely of the moderate and respectable heads of the Roman Catholic body, but even of several members of the Jesuitical cabal. Sunderland shrank from the thought of an Irish revolution, religious, political, and social. To the Queen Tyrcon-

[7. That is, James's new Court of High Commission.]

nel was personally an object of aversion. Powis was therefore
suggested as the man best qualified for the viceroyalty. He was of
illustrious birth: he was a sincere Roman Catholic: and yet he
was generally allowed by candid Protestants to be an honest man
and a good Englishman. All opposition, however, yielded to Tyrconnel's energy and cunning. He fawned, bullied, and bribed indefatigably. Petre's help was secured by flattery. Sunderland was
plied at once with promises and menaces. An immense price was
offered for his support, no less than an annuity of five thousand
pounds a year from Ireland, redeemable by payment of fifty
thousand pounds down. If this proposal were rejected, Tyrconnel threatened to let the King know that the Lord President had,
at the Friday dinners, described His Majesty as a fool who must
be governed either by a woman or by a priest. Sunderland, pale
and trembling, offered to procure for Tyrconnel supreme military
command, enormous appointments, anything but the viceroyalty: but all compromise was rejected; and it was necessary to
yield. Mary of Modena herself was not free from suspicion of
corruption. There was in London a renowned chain of pearls
which was valued at ten thousand pounds. It had belonged to
Prince Rupert; and by him it had been left to Margaret Hughes,
a courtesan who, towards the close of his life, had exercised a
boundless empire over him. Tyrconnel loudly boasted that with
this chain he had purchased the support of the Queen. There
were those, however, who suspected that this story was one of
Dick Talbot's truths, and that it had no more foundation than
the calumnies which, twenty-six years before, he had invented to
blacken the fame of Anne Hyde. To the Roman Catholic courtiers
generally he spoke of the uncertain tenure by which they held
offices, honours, and emoluments. The King might die tomorrow, and might leave them at the mercy of a hostile government
and a hostile rabble. But, if the old faith could be made dominant
in Ireland, if the Protestant interest in that country could be destroyed, there would still be, in the worst event, an asylum at
hand to which they might retreat, and where they might either
negotiate or defend themselves with advantage. A Popish priest
was hired with the promise of the mitre of Waterford to preach
at Saint James's against the Act of Settlement; and his sermon,

though heard with deep disgust by the English part of the auditory, was not without its effect. The struggle which patriotism had for a time maintained against bigotry in the royal mind was at an end. 'There is work to be done in Ireland,' said James, 'which no Englishman will do.'

All obstacles were at length removed; and in February 1687, Tyrconnel began to rule his native country with the power and appointments of Lord Lieutenant, but with the humbler title of Lord Deputy.

His arrival spread dismay through the whole English population. Clarendon was accompanied, or speedily followed, across St George's Channel, by a large proportion of the most respectable inhabitants of Dublin, gentlemen, tradesmen, and artificers. It was said that fifteen hundred families emigrated in a few days. The panic was not unreasonable. The work of putting the colonists down under the feet of the natives went rapidly on. In a short time almost every Privy Councillor, Judge, Sheriff, Mayor, Alderman, and Justice of the Peace was a Celt and a Roman Catholic. It seemed that things would soon be ripe for a general election, and that a House of Commons bent on abrogating the Act of Settlement would easily be assembled. Those who had lately been the lords of the island now cried out, in the bitterness of their souls, that they had become a prey and a laughing-stock to their own serfs and menials; that houses were burnt and cattle stolen with impunity; that the new soldiers roamed the country, pillaging, insulting, ravishing, maiming, tossing one Protestant in a blanket, tying up another by the hair and scourging him; that to appeal to the law was vain; that Irish Judges, Sheriffs, juries, and witnesses were all in a league to save Irish criminals; and that, even without an Act of Parliament, the whole soil would soon change hands; for that, in every action of ejectment tried under the administration of Tyrconnel, judgment had been given for the native against the Englishman.

While Clarendon was at Dublin the Privy Seal had been in the hands of Commissioners. His friends hoped that it would, on his return to London, be again delivered to him. But the King and the Jesuitical cabal had determined that the disgrace of the Hydes should be complete. Lord Arundell of Wardour, a Roman Catholic, received the Privy Seal. Bellasyse, a Roman Catholic, was made First Lord of the Treasury; and Dover, another Roman Catholic, had a seat at the board. The appointment of a ruined gambler to such a trust would alone have sufficed to disgust the public. The dissolute Etherege, who then resided at Ratisbon as English envoy, could not refrain from expressing, with a sneer, his hope that his old boon companion, Dover, would keep the King's money better than his own. In order that the finances might not be ruined by incapable and inexperienced Papists, the obsequious, diligent and silent Godolphin was named a Commissioner of the Treasury, but continued to be Chamberlain to the Queen.

The dismission of the two brothers is a great epoch in the reign of James. From that time it was clear that what he really wanted was not liberty of conscience for the members of his own church, but liberty to persecute the members of other churches. Pretending to abhor tests, he had himself imposed a test. He thought it hard, he thought it monstrous, that able and loyal men should be excluded from the public service solely for being Roman Catholics. Yet he had himself turned out of office a Treasurer, whom he admitted to be both loyal and able, solely for being a Protestant. The cry was that a general proscription was at hand, and that every public functionary must make up his mind to lose his soul or to lose his place. Who indeed could hope to stand where the Hydes had fallen? They were the brothers-in-law of the King, the uncles and natural guardians of his children, his friends from early youth, his steady adherents in adversity and peril, his obsequious servants since he had been on the throne. Their sole crime was their religion; and for this crime they had been discarded. In great perturbation men began to look round for help; and soon all eyes were fixed on one whom a rare concurrence both of personal qualities and of fortuitous circumstances pointed out as the deliverer.

8

William of Orange

[*The deliverer was William of Orange, the Stadholder of Holland, who for fifteen years had been the soul and the organizer of European opposition to Louis XIV, and who was also, as both nephew and son-in-law of James II, in the line of succession to the English throne. As such, he was a familiar figure in English politics and his court at the Hague had become the refuge of many Englishmen who, since 1680, had found life under Charles II and James II uncomfortable. To him, as the next male heir (James II having no son), the eyes of disappointed English tories, as well as disaffected English whigs, now began to turn.*

William was Macaulay's hero. This was not because he was himself a 'whig' (he was not) but because he played an essential part in ensuring that the Revolution of 1688 followed a 'whig' and not a radical course. Without him either James II would have succeeded in his designs (or at least would have been forced to revert to a 'tory' course and stabilize the monarchy on an Anglican, tory base), or the revolution would have become violent and radical, as in the 1640s. Monmouth had not been able to play this essential role. He was illegitimate; he was no statesman; he relied on radical political adventurers and the deluded common people. But Orange was a legitimate claimant to the throne and an able statesman. He might be less interested in the liberties of England than in mobilizing English resources against Louis XIV in Europe, but he saw that, in order to mobilize those resources, he must unite the English opposition to James II and, while conserving the royal power for his own purposes, base it on the common interest of the English Protestant parties. Because he was able to do this, Macaulay – as always, moralizing and personalizing political attitudes – sang his praises and put the most favourable construction on all the evidence concerning him. In his narrative William benefited from the same historiographical methods of which Penn and Churchill were the victims.

The following passage comes from Macaulay's Chapter VII.]

THE place which William Henry, Prince of Orange Nassau, occupies in the history of England and of mankind is so great that it
may be desirable to portray with some minuteness the strong
lineaments of his character.

He was now in his thirty-seventh year. But both in body and
in mind he was older than other men of the same age. Indeed it
might be said that he had never been young. His external appearance is almost as well known to us as to his own captains and
counsellors. Sculptors, painters, and medallists exerted their utmost skill in the work of transmitting his features to posterity;
and his features were such as no artist could fail to seize, and such
as, once seen, could never be forgotten. His name at once calls
up before us a slender and feeble frame, a lofty and ample forehead, a nose curved like the beak of an eagle, an eye rivalling that
of an eagle in brightness and keenness, a thoughtful and somewhat sullen brow, a firm and somewhat peevish mouth, a cheek
pale, thin, and deeply furrowed by sickness and by care. That
pensive, severe, and solemn aspect could scarcely have belonged
to a happy or a good-humoured man. But it indicates in a manner not to be mistaken capacity equal to the most arduous enterprises, and fortitude not to be shaken by reverses or dangers.

Nature had largely endowed William with the qualities of a
great ruler; and education had developed those qualities in no
common degree. With strong natural sense, and rare force of will,
he found himself, when first his mind began to open, a fatherless
and motherless child, the chief of a great but depressed and disheartened party, and the heir to vast and indefinite pretensions,
which excited the dread and aversion of the oligarchy then supreme in the United Provinces. The common people, fondly attached during a century to his house, indicated, whenever they
saw him, in a manner not to be mistaken, that they regarded him
as their rightful head. The able and experienced ministers of the
republic, mortal enemies of his name, came every day to pay their
feigned civilities to him, and to observe the progress of his mind.
The first movements of his ambition were carefully watched:
every unguarded word uttered by him was noted down; nor had
he near him any adviser on whose judgment reliance could be
placed. He was scarcely fifteen years old when all the domestics

who were attached to his interest, or who enjoyed any share of his confidence, were removed from under his roof by the jealous government. He remonstrated with energy beyond his years, but in vain. Vigilant observers saw the tears more than once rise in the eyes of the young state prisoner. His health, naturally delicate, sank for a time under the emotions which his desolate situation had produced. Such situations bewilder and unnerve the weak, but call forth all the strength of the strong. Surrounded by snares in which an ordinary youth would have perished, William learned to tread at once warily and firmly. Long before he reached manhood he knew how to keep secrets, how to baffle curiosity by dry and guarded answers, how to conceal all passions under the same show of grave tranquillity.

Meanwhile he made little proficiency in fashionable or literary accomplishments. The manners of the Dutch nobility of that age wanted the grace which was found in the highest perfection among the gentlemen of France, and which, in an inferior degree, embellished the Court of England; and his manners were altogether Dutch. Even his countrymen thought him blunt. To foreigners he often seemed churlish. In his intercourse with the world in general he appeared ignorant or negligent of those arts which double the value of a favour and take away the sting of a refusal. He was little interested in letters or science. The discoveries of Newton and Leibnitz, the poems of Dryden and Boileau, were unknown to him. Dramatic performances tired him; and he was glad to turn away from the stage and to talk about public affairs, while Orestes was raving, or while Tartuffe was pressing Elmira's hand. He had indeed some talent for sarcasm, and not seldom employed, quite unconsciously, a natural rhetoric, quaint, indeed, but vigorous and original. He did not, however, in the least affect the character of a wit or of an orator. His attention had been confined to those studies which form strenuous and sagacious men of business. From a child he listened with interest when high questions of alliance, finance, and war were discussed. Of geometry he learned as much as was necessary for the construction of a ravelin or a hornwork. Of languages, by the help of a memory singularly powerful, he learned as much as was necessary to enable him to comprehend and answer without assistance everything that was said to him, and every letter which he received. The Dutch was his own tongue. He understood Latin, Italian, and Spanish. He spoke and wrote French, English, and German, inelegantly, it is true, and inexactly, but fluently and intelligibly. No qualification could be more important to a man whose life was to be passed in organizing great alliances, and in commanding armies assembled from different countries.

One class of philosophical questions had been forced on his attention by circumstances, and seems to have interested him more than might have been expected from his general character. Among the Protestants of the United Provinces, as among the Protestants of our island, there were two great religious parties which almost exactly coincided with two great political parties. The chiefs of the municipal oligarchy were Arminians, and were commonly regarded by the multitude as little better than Papists. The princes of Orange had generally been the patrons of the Calvinistic divinity, and owed no small part of their popularity to their zeal for the doctrines of election and final perseverance, a zeal not always enlightened by knowledge or tempered by humanity. William had been carefully instructed from a child in the theological system to which his family was attached, and regarded that system with even more than the partiality which men generally feel for a hereditary faith. He had ruminated on the great enigmas which had been discussed in the Synod of Dort,[1] and had found in the austere and inflexible logic of the Genevese school something which suited his intellect and his temper. That example of intolerance indeed which some of his predecessors had set he never imitated. For all persecution he felt a fixed aversion, which he avowed, not only where the avowal was obviously politic, but on occasions where it seemed that his interest would have been promoted by dissimulation or by silence. His theological opinions, however, were even more decided than those of his ancestors. The tenet of predestination was the keystone of his religion. He often declared that, if he were to abandon that tenet, he must abandon with it all belief in a superintending Providence, and must become a mere Epicurean.

[1. The Synod of Dort, in 1618, established the basic tenets of the Calvinist Churches of Europe and condemned the more liberal 'Arminian' views.]

Except in this single instance, all the sap of his vigorous mind was early drawn away from the speculative to the practical. The faculties which are necessary for the conduct of important business ripened in him at a time of life when they have scarcely begun to blossom in ordinary men. Since Octavius[2] the world had seen no such instance of precocious statesmanship. Skilful diplomatists were surprised to hear the weighty observations which at seventeen the Prince made on public affairs, and still more surprised to see a lad, in situations in which he might have been expected to betray strong passion, preserve a composure as imperturbable as their own. At eighteen he sat among the fathers of the commonwealth, grave, discreet, and judicious as the oldest among them. At twenty-one, in a day of gloom and terror, he was placed at the head of the administration. At twenty-three he was renowned throughout Europe as a soldier and a politician. He had put domestic factions under his feet: he was the soul of a mighty coalition; and he had contended with honour in the field against some of the greatest generals of the age.

His personal tastes were those rather of a warrior than of a statesman: but he, like his great-grandfather, the silent prince who founded the Batavian commonwealth, occupies a far higher place among statesmen than among warriors. The event of battles, indeed, is not an unfailing test of the abilities of a commander; and it would be peculiarly unjust to apply this test to William: for it was his fortune to be almost always opposed to captains who were consummate masters of their art, and to troops far superior in discipline to his own. Yet there is reason to believe that he was by no means equal, as a general in the field, to some who ranked far below him in intellectual powers. To those whom he trusted he spoke on this subject with the magnanimous frankness of a man who had done great things, and who could well afford to acknowledge some deficiencies. He had never, he said, served an apprenticeship to the military profession. He had been placed, while still a boy, at the head of an army. Among his officers there had been none competent to instruct him. His own blunders and their consequences had been his only lessons. 'I

[2. That is, the Emperor Augustus, whose original name was Caius Octavius.]

would give,' he once exclaimed, 'a good part of my estates to have served a few campaigns under the Prince of Condé before I had to command against him.' It is not improbable that the circumstance which prevented William from attaining any eminent dexterity in strategy may have been favourable to the general vigour of his intellect. If his battles were not those of a great tactician, they entitled him to be called a great man. No disaster could for one moment deprive him of his firmness or of the entire possession of all his faculties. His defeats were repaired with such marvellous celerity that, before his enemies had sung the Te Deum, he was again ready for conflict; nor did his adverse fortune ever deprive him of the respect and confidence of his soldiers.

That respect and confidence he owed in no small measure to his personal courage. Courage, in the degree which is necessary to carry a soldier without disgrace through a campaign, is possessed, or might, under proper training, be acquired, by the great majority of men. But courage like that of William is rare indeed. He was proved by every test: by war, by wounds, by painful and depressing maladies, by raging seas, by the imminent and constant risk of assassination – a risk which has shaken very strong nerves, a risk which severely tried even the adamantine fortitude of Cromwell. Yet none could ever discover what that thing was which the Prince of Orange feared. His advisers could with difficulty induce him to take any precaution against the pistols and daggers of conspirators. Old sailors were amazed at the composure which he preserved amidst roaring breakers on a perilous coast. In battle his bravery made him conspicuous even among tens of thousands of brave warriors, drew forth the generous applause of hostile armies, and was never questioned even by the injustice of hostile factions. During his first campaigns he exposed himself like a man who sought for death, was always foremost in the charge and last in the retreat, fought, sword in hand, in the thickest press, and, with a musket ball in his arm and the blood streaming over his cuirass, still stood his ground and waved his hat under the hottest fire. His friends adjured him to take more care of a life invaluable to his country; and his most illustrious antagonist, the great Condé, remarked, after the bloody day of Seneff, that the Prince of Orange had in all things borne himself like an old general, except in exposing himself like a young soldier. William denied that he was guilty of temerity. It was, he said, from a sense of duty and on a cool calculation of what the public interest required that he was always at the post of danger. The troops which he commanded had been little used to war, and shrank from a close encounter with the veteran soldiery of France. It was necessary that their leader should show them how battles were to be won. And in truth more than one day which had seemed hopelessly lost was retrieved by the hardihood with which he rallied his broken battalions and cut down with his own hand the cowards who set the example of flight. Sometimes, however, it seemed that he had a strange pleasure in venturing his person. It was remarked that his spirits were never so high and his manners never so gracious and easy as amidst the tumult and carnage of a battle. Even in his pastimes he liked the excitement of danger. Cards, chess, and billiards gave him no pleasure. The chase was his favourite recreation; and he loved it most when it was most hazardous. His leaps were sometimes such that his boldest companions did not like to follow him. He seems even to have thought the most hardy field sports of England effeminate, and to have pined in the Great Park of Windsor for the game which he had been used to drive to bay in the forests of Guelders, wolves, and wild boars, and huge stags with sixteen antlers.

The audacity of his spirit was the more remarkable because his physical organization was unusually delicate. From a child he had been weak and sickly. In the prime of manhood his complaints had been aggravated by a severe attack of smallpox. He was asthmatic and consumptive. His slender frame was shaken by a constant hoarse cough. He could not sleep unless his head was propped by several pillows, and could scarcely draw his breath in any but the purest air. Cruel headaches frequently tortured him. Exertion soon fatigued him. The physicians constantly kept up the hopes of his enemies by fixing some date beyond which, if there were anything certain in medical science, it was impossible that his broken constitution could hold out. Yet, through a life which was one long disease, the force of his mind never failed, on any great occasion, to bear up his suffering and languid body.

He was born with violent passions and quick sensibilities: but the strength of his emotions was not suspected by the world. From the multitude his joy and his grief, his affection and his resentment, were hidden by a phlegmatic serenity, which made him pass for the most cold-blooded of mankind. Those who brought him good news could seldom detect any sign of pleasure. Those who saw him after a defeat looked in vain for any trace of vexation. He praised and reprimanded, rewarded and punished, with the stern tranquillity of a Mohawk chief: but those who knew him well and saw him near were aware that under all this ice a fierce fire was constantly burning. It was seldom that anger deprived him of power over himself. But when he was really enraged the first outbreak of his passion was terrible. It was indeed scarcely safe to approach him. On these rare occasions, however, as soon as he regained his self-command, he made such ample reparation to those whom he had wronged as tempted them to wish that he would go into a fury again. His affection was as impetuous as his wrath. Where he loved, he loved with the whole energy of his strong mind. When death separated him from what he loved, the few who witnessed his agonies trembled for his reason and his life. To a very small circle of intimate friends, on whose fidelity and secrecy he could absolutely depend, he was a different man from the reserved and stoical William whom the multitude supposed to be destitute of human feelings. He was kind, cordial, open, even convivial and jocose, would sit at table many hours, and would bear his full share in festive conversation.

Highest in his favour stood a gentleman of his household named Bentinck, sprung from a noble Batavian race, and destined to be the founder of one of the great patrician houses of England. The fidelity of Bentinck had been tried by no common test. It was while the United Provinces were struggling for existence against the French power that the young Prince on whom all their hopes were fixed was seized by the smallpox. That disease had been fatal to many members of his family, and at first wore, in his case, a peculiarly malignant aspect. The public consternation was great. The streets of the Hague were crowded from daybreak to sunset by persons anxiously asking how his Highness was. At length his complaint took a favourable turn. His escape was attributed partly to his own singular equanimity, and partly to the intrepid and indefatigable friendship of Bentinck. From the hands of Bentinck alone William took food and medicine. By Bentinck alone William was lifted from his bed and laid down in it. 'Whether Bentinck slept or not while I was ill,' said William to Temple, with great tenderness, 'I know not. But this I know, that, through sixteen days and nights, I never once called for anything but that Bentinck was instantly at my side.' Before the faithful servant had entirely performed his task, he had himself caught the contagion. Still, however, he bore up against drowsiness and fever till his master was pronounced convalescent. Then, at length, Bentinck asked leave to go home. It was time: for his limbs would no longer support him. He was in great danger, but recovered, and, as soon as he left his bed, hastened to the army, where, during many sharp campaigns, he was ever found, as he had been in peril of a different kind, close to William's side.

Such was the origin of a friendship as warm and pure as any that ancient or modern history records. The descendants of Bentinck still preserve many letters written by William to their ancestor: and it is not too much to say that no person who has not studied those letters can form a correct notion of the Prince's character. He whom even his admirers generally accounted the most distant and frigid of men here forgets all distinctions of rank, and pours out all his thoughts with the ingenuousness of a schoolboy. He imparts without reserve secrets of the highest moment. He explains with perfect simplicity vast designs affecting all the governments of Europe. Mingled with his communications on such subjects are other communications of a very different, but perhaps not of a less interesting kind. All his adventures, all his personal feelings, his long runs after enormous stags, his carousals on St Hubert's day, the growth of his plantations, the failure of his melons, the state of his stud, his wish to procure an easy pad nag for his wife, his vexation at learning that one of his household, after ruining a girl of good family, refused to marry her, his fits of seasickness, his coughs, his head-

aches, his devotional moods, his gratitude for the divine protection after a great escape, his struggles to submit himself to the
divine will after a disaster, are described with an amiable gar-
rulity hardly to have been expected from the most discreet and
sedate statesman of the age. Still more remarkable is the careless
effusion of his tenderness, and the brotherly interest which he
takes in his friend's domestic felicity. When an heir is born to
Bentinck, 'he will live, I hope,' says William, 'to be as good a
fellow as you are; and, if I should have a son, our children will
love each other, I hope, as we have done.' Through life he continues to regard the little Bentincks with paternal kindness. He
calls them by endearing diminutives: he takes charge of them in
their father's absence, and, though vexed at being forced to refuse
them any pleasure, will not suffer them to go on a hunting party,
where there would be risk of a push from a stag's horn, or to sit
up late at a riotous supper. When their mother is taken ill during
her husband's absence, William, in the midst of business of the
highest moment, finds time to send off several expresses in one
day with short notes containing intelligence of her state. On one
occasion, when she is pronounced out of danger after a severe
attack, the Prince breaks forth into fervent expressions of gratitude to God. 'I write,' he says, 'with tears of joy in my eyes.'
There is a singular charm in such letters, penned by a man whose
irresistible energy and inflexible firmness extorted the respect of
his enemies, whose cold and ungracious demeanour repelled the
attachment of almost all his partisans, and whose mind was occupied by gigantic schemes which have changed the face of the
world.

His kindness was not misplaced. Bentinck was early pronounced by Temple to be the best and truest servant that ever
prince had the good fortune to possess, and continued through life
to merit that honourable character. The friends were indeed made
for each other. William wanted neither a guide nor a flatterer.
Having a firm and just reliance on his own judgment, he was not
partial to counsellors who dealt much in suggestions and objections. At the same time he had too much discernment, and too
much elevation of mind, to be gratified by sycophancy. The confidant of such a prince ought to be a man, not of inventive genius

or commanding spirit, but brave and faithful, capable of executing orders punctually, of keeping secrets inviolably, of observing facts vigilantly, and of reporting them truly; and such a man was Bentinck.

William was not less fortunate in marriage than in friendship. Yet his marriage had not at first promised much domestic happiness. His choice had been determined chiefly by political considerations: nor did it seem likely that any strong affection would grow up between a handsome girl of sixteen, well disposed indeed, and naturally intelligent, but ignorant and simple, and a bridegroom who, though he had not completed his twenty-eighth year, was in constitution older than her father, whose manner was chilling, and whose head was constantly occupied by public business or by field sports. For a time William was a negligent husband. He was indeed drawn away from his wife by other women, particularly by one of her ladies, Elizabeth Villiers, who, though destitute of personal attractions, and disfigured by a hideous squint, possessed talents which well fitted her to partake his cares. He was indeed ashamed of his errors, and spared no pains to conceal them: but, in spite of all his precautions, Mary well knew that he was not strictly faithful to her. Spies and talebearers, encouraged by her father, did their best to inflame her resentment. A man of a very different character, the excellent Ken, who was her chaplain at the Hague during some months, was so much incensed by her wrongs that he, with more zeal than discretion, threatened to reprimand her husband severely. She, however, bore her injuries with a meekness and patience which deserved, and gradually obtained, William's esteem and gratitude.

Yet there still remained one cause of estrangement. A time would probably come when the Princess, who had been educated only to work embroidery, to play on the spinet, and to read the Bible and the *Whole Duty of Man*,[3] would be the chief of a great monarchy, and would hold the balance of Europe, while her lord, ambitious, versed in affairs, and bent on great enterprises, would find in the British government no place marked out for him, and would hold power only from her bounty and during her pleasure.

[3. A famous work of Anglican piety, first published anonymously in 1658. It was probably by Richard Allestree.]

It is not strange that a man so fond of authority as William, and so conscious of a genius for command, should have strongly felt that jealousy which, during a few hours of royalty, put dissension between Guilford Dudley and the Lady Jane, and which produced a rupture still more tragical between Darnley and the Queen of Scots. The Princess of Orange had not the faintest suspicion of her husband's feelings. Her preceptor, Bishop Compton, had instructed her carefully in religion, and had especially guarded her mind against the arts of Roman Catholic divines, but had left her profoundly ignorant of the English constitution and of her own position. She knew that her marriage vow bound her to obey her husband; and it had never occurred to her that the relation in which they stood to each other might one day be inverted. She had been nine years married before she discovered the cause of William's discontent; nor would she ever have learned it from himself. In general his temper inclined him rather to brood over his griefs than to give utterance to them; and in this particular case his lips were sealed by a very natural delicacy. At length a complete explanation and reconciliation were brought by the agency of Gilbert Burnet.[4]

[4. Burnet, whom William afterwards made Bishop of Salisbury, was at his time a whig *émigré* at the Hague, intimate with both William and Mary.]

9

The Attack on the Universities

[*With the fall of the Hydes and the elevation, in all three kingdoms, of Catholic factions, the leaders of English society, tory as well as whig, turned towards William of Orange. Meanwhile James pursued his chosen course. He now felt strong enough to declare open war on the established Church of England. In order to isolate the Church, he issued, on 4 April 1687, a skilfully phrased but illegal Declaration of Indulgence, granting complete freedom of public worship to all Dissenters, whether Protestant or Catholic. He thus sought to weaken the Anglican Church by abolishing its monopoly and, at the same t`me, to enlist the Protestant Dissenters as allies in a process which would end in the re-establishment of a Catholic monopoly. By a timely pamphlet, his anonymous* Letter to a Dissenter, Halifax *warned Protestant Dissenters not to fall into the trap, and the Anglican Church sought to outbid the King by offering the Dissenters a more legal security. At this point James directly challenged the Anglican Church by making, at Oxford and Cambridge, a spectacular public attack on its property-rights. He thus impressed ' on every Anglican priest and prelate the conviction that, if he refused to lend his aid for the purpose of destroying the Church of which he was a minister, he would in an hour be reduced to beggary.'*

Macaulay describes the attack on the universities in his Chapter VIII.]

IT would have been prudent to try the first experiment on some obscure individual. But the government was under an infatuation such as, in a more simple age, would have been called judicial. War was therefore at once declared against the two most venerable corporations of the realm, the Universities of Oxford and Cambridge.

The power of those bodies has during many ages been great; but it was at the height during the latter part of the seventeenth century. None of the neighbouring countries could boast of such splendid and opulent seats of learning. The schools of Edinburgh and Glasgow, of Leyden and Utrecht, of Louvain and Leipzig, of Padua and Bologna, seemed mean to scholars who had been educated in the magnificent foundations of Wykeham and Wolsey, of Henry the Sixth and Henry the Eighth. Literature and science were, in the academical system of England, surrounded with pomp, armed with magistracy, and closely allied with all the most august institutions of the state. To be the Chancellor of an University was a distinction eagerly sought by the magnates of the realm. To represent an University in Parliament was a favourite object of the ambition of statesmen. Nobles and even princes were proud to receive from an University the privilege of wearing the doctoral scarlet. The curious were attracted to the Universities by ancient buildings rich with the tracery of the middle ages, by modern buildings which exhibited the highest skill of Jones and Wren, by noble halls and chapels, by museums, by botanical gardens, and by the only great public libraries which the kingdom then contained. The state which Oxford especially displayed on solemn occasions rivalled that of sovereign princes. When her Chancellor, the venerable Duke of Ormond, sat in his embroidered mantle on his throne under the painted ceiling of the Sheldonian theatre, surrounded by hundreds of graduates robed according to their rank, while the noblest youths of England were solemnly presented to him as candidates for academical honours, he made an appearance scarcely less regal than that which his master made in the Banqueting House of Whitehall. At the Universities had been formed the minds of almost all the eminent clergymen, lawyers, physicians, wits, poets, and orators of the land, and of a large proportion of the nobility and of the opulent gentry. It is also to be observed that the connection between the scholar and the school did not terminate with his residence. He often continued to be through life a member of the academical body, and to vote as such at all important elections. He therefore regarded his old haunts by the Cam and the Isis with even more than the affection which educated men ordinarily feel for the place of their education. There was no corner of England in which both Universities had not grateful and zealous sons. Any attack on the honour or interests of either Cambridge or Oxford was certain to excite the resentment of a powerful, active, and intelligent class scattered over every county from Northumberland to Cornwall.

The resident graduates, as a body, were perhaps not superior positively to the resident graduates of our time: but they occupied a far higher position as compared with the rest of the community. For Cambridge and Oxford were then the only two provincial towns in the kingdom in which could be found a large number of men whose understandings had been highly cultivated. Even the capital felt great respect for the authority of the Universities, not only on questions of divinity, of natural philosophy, and of classical antiquity, but also on points on which capitals generally claim the right of deciding in the last resort. From Will's coffeehouse, and from the pit of the theatre royal in Drury Lane, an appeal lay to the two great national seats of taste and learning. Plays which had been enthusiastically applauded in London were not thought out of danger till they had undergone the more severe judgment of audiences familiar with Sophocles and Terence.

The great moral and intellectual influence of the English Universities had been strenuously exerted on the side of the crown. The headquarters of Charles the First had been at Oxford; and the silver tankards and salvers of all the colleges had been melted down to supply his military chest. Cambridge was not less loyally disposed. She had sent a large part of her plate to the royal camp; and the rest would have followed had not the town been seized by the troops of the Parliament. Both Universities had been treated with extreme severity by the victorious Puritans. Both had hailed the restoration with delight. Both had steadily opposed the Exclusion Bill. Both had expressed the deepest horror at the Rye House Plot. Cambridge had not only deposed her Chancellor Monmouth, but had marked her abhorrence of his treason in a manner unworthy of a seat of learning, by committing to the flames the canvas on which his pleasing face and figure had been portrayed by the utmost skill of Kneller. Oxford, which lay nearer to the Western insurgents, had given still stronger proofs of loyalty. The students, under the sanction of their preceptors, had taken arms by hundreds in defence of hereditary right. Such were the bodies which James now determined to insult and plunder in direct defiance of the laws and of his plighted faith.

Several Acts of Parliament, as clear as any that were to be found in the statute book, had provided that no person should be admitted to any degree in either University without taking the oath of supremacy, and another oath of similar character called the oath of obedience. Nevertheless, in February 1687, a royal letter was sent to Cambridge directing that a Benedictine monk, named Alban Francis, should be admitted a Master of Arts.

The academical functionaries, divided between reverence for the King and reverence for the law, were in great distress. Messengers were despatched in all haste to the Duke of Albemarle, who had succeeded Monmouth as Chancellor of the University. He was requested to represent the matter properly to the King. Meanwhile the Registrar and Bedells waited on Francis, and informed him that, if he would take the oaths according to law, he should be instantly admitted. He refused to be sworn, remonstrated with the officers of the University on their disregard of the royal mandate, and, finding them resolute, took horse, and hastened to relate his grievances at Whitehall.

The heads of the colleges now assembled in council. The best legal opinions were taken, and were decidedly in favour of the course which had been pursued. But a second letter from Sunderland, in high and menacing terms, was already on the road. Albemarle informed the University, with many expressions of concern, that he had done his best, but that he had been coldly and ungraciously received by the King. The academical body, alarmed by the royal displeasure, and conscientiously desirous to meet the royal wishes, but determined not to violate the clear law of the land, submitted the humblest and most respectful explanations, but to no purpose. In a short time came down a summons citing the Vice-chancellor and the Senate to appear before the new High Commission at Westminster on the twenty-first of April. The Vice-Chancellor was to attend in person; the Senate, which consists of all the Doctors and Masters of the University, was to send deputies.

When the appointed day arrived, a great concourse filled the

Council chamber. Jeffreys sat at the head of the board. Rochester, since the white staff had been taken from him, was no longer a member. In his stead appeared the Lord Chamberlain, John Sheffield, Earl of Mulgrave. The fate of this nobleman has, in one respect, resembled the fate of his colleague Sprat. Mulgrave wrote verses which scarcely ever rose above absolute mediocrity: but, as he was a man of high note in the political and fashionable world, these verses found admirers. Time dissolved the charm, but, unfortunately for him, not until his lines had acquired a prescriptive right to a place in all collections of the works of English poets. To this day accordingly his insipid essays in rhyme and his paltry songs to Amoretta and Gloriana are reprinted in company with Comus and Alexander's Feast. The consequence is that our generation knows Mulgrave chiefly as a poetaster, and despises him as such. In truth however he was, by the acknowledgment of those who neither loved nor esteemed him, a man distinguished by fine parts, and in parliamentary eloquence inferior to scarcely any orator of his time. His moral character was entitled to no respect. He was a libertine without that openness of heart and hand which sometimes makes libertinism amiable, and a haughty aristocrat without that elevation of sentiment which sometimes makes aristocratical haughtiness respectable. The satirists of the age nicknamed him Lord Allpride. Yet was his pride compatible with all ignoble vices. Many wondered that a man who had so exalted a sense of his dignity could be so hard and niggardly in all pecuniary dealings. He had given deep offence to the royal family by venturing to entertain the hope that he might win the heart and hand of the Princess Anne. Disappointed in this attempt, he had exerted himself to regain by meanness the favour which he had forfeited by presumption. His epitaph, written by himself, still informs all who pass through Westminster Abbey that he lived and died a sceptic in religion; and we learn from the memoirs which he wrote that one of his favourite subjects of mirth was the Romish superstition. Yet he began, as soon as James was on the throne, to express a strong inclination towards Popery, and at length in private affected to be a convert. This abject hypocrisy had been rewarded by a place in the Ecclesiastical Commission.

Before that formidable tribunal now appeared the Vice-Chancellor of the University of Cambridge, Doctor John Pechell. He was a man of no great ability or vigour; but he was accompanied by eight distinguished academicians, elected by the Senate. One of these was Isaac Newton, Fellow of Trinity College, and Professor of mathematics. His genius was then in the fullest vigour. The great work, which entitles him to the highest place among the geometricians and natural philosophers of all ages and of all nations, had been some time printing under the sanction of the Royal Society, and was almost ready for publication. He was the steady friend of civil liberty and of the Protestant religion: but his habits by no means fitted him for the conflicts of active life. He therefore stood modestly silent among the delegates, and left to men more versed in practical business the task of pleading the cause of his beloved University.

Never was there a clearer case. The law was express. The practice had been almost invariably in conformity with the law. It might perhaps have happened that, on a day of great solemnity, when many honorary degrees were conferred, a person who had not taken the oaths might have passed in the crowd. But such an irregularity, the effect of mere haste and inadvertence, could not be cited as a precedent. Foreign ambassadors of various religions, and in particular one Mussulman, had been admitted without the oaths. But it might well be doubted whether such cases fell within the reason and spirit of the Acts of Parliament. It was not even pretended that any person to whom the oaths had been tendered and who had refused them had ever taken a degree: and this was the situation in which Francis stood. The delegate offered to prove that, in the late reign, several royal mandates had been treated as nullities because the persons recommended had not chosen to qualify according to law, and that, on such occasions, the government had always acquiesced in the propriety of the course taken by the University.

But Jeffreys would hear nothing. He soon found out that the Vice-Chancellor was weak, ignorant, and timid, and therefore gave a loose to all that insolence which had long been the terror of the Old Bailey. The unfortunate Doctor, unaccustomed to such a presence and to such treatment, was soon harassed and scared into helpless agitation. When other academicians who were more capable of defending their cause attempted to speak they were rudely silenced. 'You are not Vice-Chancellor. When you are, you may talk. Till then it will become you to hold your peace.' The defendants were thrust out of the court without a hearing. In a short time they were called in again, and informed that the Commissioners had determined to deprive Pechell of the Vice-Chancellorship, and to suspend him from all the emoluments to which he was entitled as Master of a college, emoluments which were strictly of the nature of freehold property. 'As for you,' said Jeffreys to the delegates, 'most of you are divines. I will therefore send you home with a text of scripture, "Go your way and sin no more, lest a worse thing happen to you."'

These proceedings might seem sufficiently unjust and violent. But the King had already begun to treat Oxford with such rigour that the rigour shown towards Cambridge might, by comparison, be called lenity. Already University College had been turned by Obadiah Walker into a Roman Catholic seminary. Already Christ Church was governed by a Roman Catholic Dean. Mass was already said daily in both those colleges. The tranquil and majestic city, so long the stronghold of monarchical principles, was agitated by passions which it had never before known. The undergraduates, with the connivance of those who were in authority over them, hooted the members of Walker's congregation, and chanted satirical ditties under his windows. Some fragments of the serenades which then disturbed the High Street have been preserved. The burden of one ballad was this:

> Old Obadiah
> Sings Ave Maria.

When the actors came down to Oxford, the public feeling was expressed still more strongly. Howard's *Committee* was performed. This play, written soon after the Restoration, exhibited the Puritans in an odious and contemptible light, and had therefore been, during a quarter of a century, a favourite with Oxonian audiences. It was now a greater favourite than ever; for, by a lucky coincidence, one of the most conspicuous characters was an old hypocrite named Obadiah. The audience shouted with delight when, in the last scene, Obadiah was dragged in with a halter round his neck; and the acclamations redoubled when one of the players, departing from the written text of the comedy, proclaimed that Obadiah should be hanged because he had changed his religion. The King was much provoked by this insult. So mutinous indeed was the temper of the University that one of the newly raised regiments, the same which is now called the Second Dragoon Guards, was quartered at Oxford for the purpose of preventing an outbreak.

These events ought to have convinced James that he had entered on a course which must lead him to his ruin. To the clamours of London he had been long accustomed. They had been raised against him, sometimes unjustly, and sometimes vainly. He had repeatedly braved them, and might brave them still. But that Oxford, the seat of loyalty, the headquarters of the Cavalier army, the place where his father and brother had held their court when they thought themselves insecure in their stormy capital, the place where the writings of the great republican teachers had recently been committed to the flames, should now be in a ferment of discontent, that those high-spirited youths who a few months before had eagerly volunteered to march against the Western insurgents should now be with difficulty kept down by sword and carbine, these were signs full of evil omen to the House of Stuart. The warning, however, was lost on the dull, stubborn, self-willed tyrant. He was resolved to transfer to his own Church all the wealthiest and most splendid foundations of England. It was to no purpose that the best and wisest of his Roman Catholic counsellors remonstrated. They represented to him that he had it in his power to render a great service to the cause of his religion without violating the rights of property. A grant of two thousand pounds a year from his privy purse would support a Jesuit college at Oxford. Such a sum he might easily spare. Such a college, provided with able, learned, and zealous teachers, would be a formidable rival to the old academical institutions, which exhibited but too many symptoms of the languor almost inseparable from opulence and security. King James's College would soon be, by the confession even of Protestants, the first place of education in the island, as respected both science and moral discipline. This would be the most effectual and the least invidious method by which the Church of England could be humbled and the Church of Rome exalted. The Earl of Ailesbury, one of the most devoted servants of the royal family, declared that, though a Protestant, and by no means rich, he would himself contribute a thousand pounds towards this design, rather than that his master should violate the rights of property, and break faith with the Established Church. The scheme, however, found no favour in the sight of the King. It was indeed ill suited, in more ways than one, to his ungentle nature. For to bend and break the spirits of men gave him pleasure; and to part with his money gave him pain. What he had not the generosity to do at his own expense he determined to do at the expense of others. When once he was engaged, pride and obstinacy prevented him from receding; and he was at length led, step by step, to acts of Turkish tyranny, to acts which impressed the nation with a conviction that the estate of a Protestant English freeholder under a Roman Catholic King must be as insecure as that of a Greek under Moslem domination.

Magdalen College at Oxford, founded in the fifteenth century by William of Waynflete, Bishop of Winchester and Lord High Chancellor, was one of the most remarkable of our academical institutions. A graceful tower, on the summit of which a Latin hymn was annually chanted by choristers at the dawn of May day, caught far off the eye of the traveller who came from London. As he approached he found that this tower rose from an embattled pile, low and irregular, yet singularly venerable, which, embowered in verdure, overhung the sluggish waters of the Cherwell. He passed through a gateway beneath a noble oriel, and found himself in a spacious cloister adorned with emblems of virtues and vices, rudely carved in grey stone by the masons of the fifteenth century. The table of the society was plentifully spread in a stately refectory hung with paintings, and rich with fantastic carving. The service of the Church was performed morning and evening in a chapel which had suffered much violence from the Reformers, and much from the Puritans, but which was, under every disadvantage, a building of eminent beauty, and which has, in our own time, been restored with rare taste and skill. The spacious gardens along the river side were remarkable for the size of the trees, among which towered conspicuous one of the vegetable wonders of the island, a gigantic oak, older by a century, men said, than the oldest college in the University.

The statutes of the society ordained that the Kings of England and Princes of Wales should be lodged in Magdalen. Edward the Fourth had inhabited the building while it was still unfinished. Richard the Third had held his court there, had heard disputations in the hall, had feasted there royally, and had mended the cheer of his hosts by a present of fat bucks from his forests. Two heirs apparent of the crown who had been prematurely snatched away, Arthur the elder brother of Henry the Eighth, and Henry the elder brother of Charles the First, had been members of the college. Another prince of the blood, the last and best of the Roman Catholic Archbishops of Canterbury, the gentle Reginald Pole, had studied there. In the time of the civil war Magdalen had been true to the cause of the crown. There Rupert had fixed his quarters; and, before some of his most daring enterprises, his trumpets had been heard sounding to horse through those quiet cloisters. Most of the Fellows were divines, and could aid the King only by their prayers and their pecuniary contributions. But one member of the body, a Doctor of Civil Law, raised a troop of undergraduates, and fell fighting bravely at their head against the soldiers of Essex. When hostilities had terminated, and the Roundheads were masters of England, six sevenths of the members of the foundation refused to make any submission to usurped authority. They were consequently ejected from their dwellings and deprived of their revenues. After the Restoration the survivors returned to their pleasant abode. They had now been succeeded by a new generation which inherited their opinions and their spirit. During the Western rebellion such Magdalen men as were not disqualified by their age or profession for the use of arms had eagerly volunteered to fight for the crown. It would be difficult to name any corporation in the kingdom which had higher claims to the gratitude of the House of Stuart.

The society consisted of a President, of forty Fellows, of thirty scholars called Demies, and of a train of chaplains, clerks, and choristers. At the time of the general visitation in the reign of Henry the Eighth the revenues were far greater than those of any similar institution in the realm, greater by nearly one half than those of the magnificent foundation of Henry the Sixth at Cambridge, and considerably more than double those which William of Wykeham had settled on his college at Oxford. In the days of James the Second the riches of Magdalen were immense, and were exaggerated by report. The college was popularly said to be wealthier than the wealthiest abbeys of the Continent. When the leases fell in – so ran the vulgar rumour – the rents would be raised to the prodigious sum of forty thousand pounds a year.

The Fellows were, by the statutes which their founder had drawn up, empowered to select their own President from among persons who were, or had been, Fellows either of their society or of New College. This power had generally been exercised with freedom. But in some instances royal letters had been received recommending to the choice of the corporation qualified persons who were in favour at court; and on such occasions it had been the practice to show respect to the wishes of the sovereign.

In March 1687, the President of the college died. One of the Fellows, Doctor Thomas Smith, popularly nicknamed Rabbi Smith, a distinguished traveller, book-collector, antiquary, and orientalist, who had been chaplain to the embassy at Constantinople, and had been employed to collate the Alexandrian manuscript, aspired to the vacant post. He conceived that he had some claims on the favour of the government as a man of learning and as a zealous Tory. His loyalty was in truth as fervent and steadfast as was to be found in the whole Church of England. He had long been intimately acquainted with Parker, Bishop of Oxford, and hoped to obtain by the interest of that prelate a royal letter to the college. Parker promised to do his best, but soon reported that he had found difficulties. 'The King,' he said, 'will recommend no person who is not a friend to His Majesty's religion. What can you do to pleasure him as to that matter?' Smith answered that, if he became President, he would exert himself to promote learning, true Christianity, and loyalty. 'That will not do,' said the Bishop. 'If so,' said Smith manfully, 'let who will be President: I can promise nothing more.'

The election had been fixed for the thirteenth of April, and the Fellows were summoned to attend. It was rumoured that a royal letter would come down recommending one Anthony Farmer to the vacant place. This man's life had been a series of shameful acts. He had been a member of the University of Cambridge, and had escaped expulsion only by a timely retreat. He had then joined the Dissenters. Then he had gone to Oxford, had entered himself at Magdalen, and had soon become notorious there for every kind of vice. He generally reeled into his college at night speechless with liquor. He was celebrated for having headed a disgraceful riot at Abingdon. He had been a constant frequenter of noted haunts of libertines. At length he had turned pander, had exceeded even the ordinary vileness of his vile calling, and had received money from dissolute young gentlemen commoners for services such as it is not good that history should record. This wretch, however, had pretended to turn Papist. His apostasy atoned for all his vices; and, though still a youth, he was selected to rule a grave and religious society in which the scandal given by his depravity was still fresh.

As a Roman Catholic he was disqualified for academical office by the general law of the land. Never having been a Fellow of Magdalen College or of New College, he was disqualified for the vacant presidency by a special ordinance of William of Waynflete. William of Waynflete had also enjoined those who partook of his bounty to have a particular regard to moral character in choosing their head; and, even if he had left no such injunction, a body chiefly composed of divines could not with decency entrust such a man as Farmer with the government of a place of education.

The Fellows respectfully represented to the King the difficulty in which they should be placed, if, as was rumoured, Farmer should be recommended to them, and begged that, if it were His Majesty's pleasure to interfere in the election, some person for whom they could legally and conscientiously vote might be proposed. Of this dutiful request no notice was taken. The royal letter arrived. It was brought down by one of the Fellows who had lately turned Papist, Robert Charnock, a man of parts and spirit, but of a violent and restless temper, which impelled him a few years later to an atrocious crime and to a terrible fate. On the thirteenth of April the society met in the chapel. Some hope was still entertained that the King might be moved by the remonstrance which had been addressed to him. The assembly therefore adjourned till the fifteenth, which was the last day on which, by the constitution of the college, the election could take place.

The fifteenth of April came. Again the Fellows repaired to their chapel. No answer had arrived from Whitehall. Two or three of the Seniors, among whom was Smith, were inclined to postpone the election once more rather than take a step which might give offence to the King. But the language of the statutes was clear. Those statutes the members of the foundation had sworn to observe. The general opinion was that there ought to be no further delay. A hot debate followed. The electors were too much excited to take their seats; and the whole choir was in a tumult. Those who were for proceeding appealed to their oaths and to the rules laid down by the founder whose bread they had eaten. The King, they truly said, had no right to force on them even a qualified candidate. Some expressions unpleasing to Tory ears were dropped in the course of the dispute; and Smith was provoked into exclaiming that the spirit of Ferguson had possessed his brethren. It was at length resolved by a great majority that it was necessary to proceed immediately to the election. Charnock left the chapel. The other Fellows, having first received the sacrament, proceeded to give their voices. The choice fell on John Hough, a man of eminent virtue and prudence, who, having borne persecution with fortitude and prosperity with meekness, having risen to high honours and having modestly declined honours higher still, died in extreme old age, yet in full vigour of mind, more than fifty-six years after this eventful day.

The society hastened to acquaint the King with the circumstances which had made it necessary to elect a President without further delay, and requested the Duke of Ormond, as patron of the whole University, and the Bishop of Winchester, as visitor of Magdalen College, to undertake the office of intercessors: but the King was far too angry and too dull to listen to explanations.

Early in June the Fellows were cited to appear before the High Commission at Whitehall. Five of them, deputed by the rest, obeyed the summons. Jeffreys treated them after his usual fashion. When one of them, a grave Doctor named Fairfax, hinted some doubt as to the validity of the Commission, the

Chancellor began to roar like a wild beast. 'Who is this man? What commission has he to be impudent here? Seize him. Put him into a dark room. What does he do without a keeper? He is under my care as a lunatic. I wonder that nobody has applied to me for the custody of him.' But when this storm had spent its force, and the depositions concerning the moral character of the King's nominee had been read, none of the Commissioners had the front to pronounce that such a man could properly be made the head of a great college. Obadiah Walker and the other Oxonian Papists who were in attendance to support their proselyte were utterly confounded. The Commission pronounced Hough's election void, and suspended Fairfax from his fellowship: but about Farmer no more was said; and, in the month of August, arrived a royal letter recommending Parker, Bishop of Oxford, to the Fellows.

Parker was not an avowed Papist. Still there was an objection to him which, even if the presidency had been vacant, would have been decisive: for he had never been a Fellow of either New College or Magdalen. But the presidency was not vacant: Hough had been duly elected; and all the members of the college were bound by oath to support him in his office. They therefore, with many expressions of loyalty and concern, excused themselves from complying with the King's mandate.

While Oxford was thus opposing a firm resistance to tyranny, a stand not less resolute was made in another quarter. James had, some time before, commanded the trustees of the Charterhouse,[1] men of the first rank and consideration in the kingdom, to admit a Roman Catholic named Popham into the hospital which was under their care. The Master of the house, Thomas Burnet, a clergyman of distinguished genius, learning, and virtue, had the courage to represent to them, though the ferocious Jeffreys sat at the board, that what was required of them was contrary both to the will of the founder and to an Act of Parliament. 'What is that to the purpose?' said a courtier who was one of the governors. 'It is very much to the purpose, I think,' answered a voice, feeble with age and sorrow, yet not to be heard without respect by any

[1. An exceptionally rich 'Hospital' – i.e. Almshouse – combined with a school, founded in London in 1611 and governed by highly-placed trustees.]

assembly, the voice of the venerable Ormond. 'An Act of Parliament,' continued the patriarch of the Cavalier party, 'is, in my judgment, no light thing.' The question was put whether Popham should be admitted, and it was determined to reject him. The Chancellor, who could not well ease himself by cursing and swearing at Ormond, flung away in a rage, and was followed by some of the minority. The consequence was that there was not a quorum left, and that no formal reply could be made to the royal mandate.

The next meeting took place only two days after the High Commission had pronounced sentence of deprivation against Hough, and of suspension against Fairfax. A second mandate under the Great Seal was laid before the trustees: but the tyrannical manner in which Magdalen College had been treated had roused instead of subduing their spirit. They drew up a letter to Sunderland in which they requested him to inform the King that they could not, in this matter, obey His Majesty without breaking the law and betraying their trust.

There can be little doubt that, had ordinary signatures been appended to this document, the King would have taken some violent course. But even he was daunted by the great names of Ormond, Halifax, Danby, and Nottingham, the chiefs of all the sections of that great party to which he owed his crown. He therefore contented himself with directing Jeffreys to consider what course ought to be taken. It was announced at one time that a proceeding would be instituted in the King's Bench, at another that the Ecclesiastical Commission would take up the case: but these threats gradually died away.

The summer was now far advanced; and the King set out on a progress, the longest and the most splendid that had been known for many years. From Windsor he went on the sixteenth of August to Portsmouth, walked round the fortifications, touched some scrofulous people,[2] and then proceeded in one of his yachts to Southampton. From Southampton he travelled to Bath, where he

[2. The touch of a true king was said to cure 'the King's evil' or scrofula. The Stuarts, even in exile, continued to prove their divine right by 'touching for the King's evil'; but William III and the Hanoverians discarded the practice as superstitious.]

remained a few days, and where he left the Queen. When he departed, he was attended by the High Sheriff of Somersetshire and by a large body of gentlemen to the frontier of the county, where the High Sheriff of Gloucestershire, with a not less splendid retinue, was in attendance. The Duke of Beaufort soon met the royal coaches, and conducted them to Badminton, where a banquet worthy of the fame which his splendid housekeeping had won for him was prepared. In the afternoon the cavalcade proceeded to Gloucester. It was greeted two miles from the city by the Bishop and clergy. At the South Gate the Mayor waited with the keys. The bells rang and the conduits flowed with wine as the King passed through the streets to the close which encircles the venerable Cathedral. He lay that night at the deanery, and on the following morning set out for Worcester. From Worcester he went to Ludlow, Shrewsbury, and Chester, and was everywhere received with outward signs of joy and respect, which he was weak enough to consider as proofs that the discontent excited by his measures had subsided, and that an easy victory was before him. Barillon, more sagacious, informed Lewis that the King of England was under a delusion, that the progress had done no real good, and that those very gentlemen of Worcestershire and Shropshire who had thought it their duty to receive their Sovereign and their guest with every mark of honour would be found as refractory as ever when the question of the test should come on.

On the road the royal train was joined by two courtiers who in temper and opinions differed widely from each other. Penn was at Chester on a pastoral tour. His popularity and authority among his brethren had greatly declined since he had become a tool of the King and of the Jesuits. He was, however, most graciously received by James, and, on the Sunday, was permitted to harangue in the tennis court, while Cartwright preached in the Cathedral, and while the King heard mass at an altar which had been decked in the Shire Hall. It is said, indeed, that His Majesty deigned to look into the tennis court and to listen with decency to his friend's melodious eloquence.

The furious Tyrconnel had crossed the sea from Dublin to give an account of his administration. All the most respectable

English Catholics looked coldly on him as on an enemy of their race and a scandal to their religion. But he was cordially welcomed by his master, and dismissed with assurances of undiminished confidence and steady support. James expressed his delight at learning that in a short time the whole government of Ireland would be in Roman Catholic hands. The English colonists had already been stripped of all political power. Nothing remained but to strip them of their property; and this last outrage was deferred only till the cooperation of an Irish Parliament should have been secured.

From Cheshire the King turned southward, and, in the full belief that the Fellows of Magdalen College, however mutinous they might be, would not dare to disobey a command uttered by his own lips, directed his course towards Oxford. By the way he made some little excursions to places which peculiarly interested him, as a King, a brother, and a son. He visited the hospitable roof of Boscobel and the remains of the oak so conspicuous in the history of his house.[3] He rode over the field of Edgehill, where the Cavaliers first crossed swords with the soldiers of the Parliament. On the third of September he dined in great state at the palace of Woodstock, an ancient and renowned mansion, of which not a stone is now to be seen, but of which the site is still marked on the turf of Blenheim Park by two sycamores which grow near the stately bridge. In the evening he reached Oxford. He was received there with the wonted honours. The students in their academical garb were ranged to welcome him on the right hand and on the left, from the entrance of the city to the great gate of Christ Church. He lodged at the deanery, where, among other accommodations, he found a chapel fitted up for the celebration of the mass. On the day after his arrival, the Fellows of Magdalen College were ordered to attend him. When they appeared before him he treated them with an insolence such as had never been shown to their predecessors by the Puritan visitors. 'You have not dealt with me like gentlemen,' he exclaimed. 'You have been unmannerly as well as undutiful.' They fell on their knees and tendered a petition. He would not look at it. 'Is this your Church

[3. It was in the oak-tree of Boscobel that Charles II had hidden from his pursuers after his defeat by Cromwell at Worcester in September 1651.]

of England loyalty? I could not have believed that so many
clergymen of the Church of England would have been concerned
in such a business. Go home. Get you gone. I am King. I will be
obeyed. Go to your chapel this instant; and admit the Bishop of
Oxford. Let those who refuse look to it. They shall feel the whole
weight of my hand. They shall know what it is to incur the displeasure of their Sovereign.' The Fellows, still kneeling before
him, again offered him their petition. He angrily flung it down.
'Get you gone, I tell you. I will receive nothing from you till you
have admitted the Bishop.'

They retired and instantly assembled in their chapel. The
question was propounded whether they would comply with His
Majesty's command. Smith was absent. Charnock alone answered in the affirmative. The other Fellows who were at the meeting
declared that in all things lawful they were ready to obey the
King, but that they would not violate their statutes and their oaths.

The King, greatly incensed and mortified by his defeat,
quitted Oxford and rejoined the Queen at Bath. His obstinacy
and violence had brought him into an embarrassing position. He
had trusted too much to the effect of his frowns and angry tones,
and had rashly staked, not merely the credit of his administration,
but his personal dignity, on the issue of the contest. Could he
yield to subjects whom he had menaced with raised voice and
furious gestures? Yet could he venture to eject in one day a
crowd of respectable clergymen from their homes, because they
had discharged what the whole nation regarded as a sacred duty?
Perhaps there might be an escape from this dilemma. Perhaps
the college might still be terrified, caressed, or bribed into submission.

The agency of Penn was employed. He had too much good
feeling to approve of the violent and unjust proceedings of the
government, and even ventured to express part of what he
thought. James was, as usual, obstinate in the wrong. The courtly
Quaker, therefore, did his best to seduce the college from the
path of right. He first tried intimidation. Ruin, he said, im-
pended over the society. The King was highly incensed. The
case might be a hard one. Most people thought it so. But every
child knew that His Majesty loved to have his own way and

could not bear to be thwarted. Penn, therefore, exhorted the Fellows not to rely on the goodness of their cause, but to submit, or at least to temporise. Such counsel came strangely from one who had himself been expelled from the University for raising a riot about the surplice, who had run the risk of being disinherited rather than take off his hat to the princes of the blood, and who had been more than once sent to prison for haranguing in conventicles. He did not succeed in frightening the Magdalen men. In answer to his alarming hints he was reminded that in the last generation thirty-four out of the forty Fellows had cheerfully left their beloved cloisters and gardens, their hall and their chapel, and had gone forth not knowing where they should find a meal or a bed, rather than violate the oath of allegiance. The King now wished them to violate another oath. He should find that the old spirit was not extinct.

Then Penn tried a gentler tone. He had an interview with Hough and with some of the Fellows, and, after many professions of sympathy and friendship, began to hint at a compromise. The King could not bear to be crossed. The college must give way. Parker must be admitted. But he was in very bad health. All his preferments would soon be vacant. 'Doctor Hough,' said Penn, 'may then be Bishop of Oxford. How should you like that, gentlemen?' Penn had passed his life in declaiming against hireling ministry. He held that he was bound to refuse the payment of tithes, and this even when he had bought land chargeable with tithes, and had been allowed the value of the tithes in the purchase money. According to his own principles, he would have committed a great sin if he had interfered for the purpose of obtaining a benefice on the most honourable terms for the most pious divine. Yet to such a degree had his manners been corrupted by evil communications, and his understanding obscured by inordinate zeal for a single object, that he did not scruple to become a broker in simony of a peculiarly discreditable kind, and to use a bishopric as a bait to tempt a divine to perjury. Hough replied with civil contempt that he wanted nothing from the crown but common justice. 'We stand,' he said, 'on our statutes and our oaths: but, even setting aside our statutes and oaths, we feel that we have our religion to defend. The Papists have robbed us of University College. They have robbed us of Christ Church. The fight is now for Magdalen. They will soon have all the rest.'

Penn was foolish enough to answer that he really believed that the Papists would now be content. 'University,' he said, 'is a pleasant college. Christ Church is a noble place. Magdalen is a fine building. The situation is convenient. The walks by the river are delightful. If the Roman Catholics are reasonable they will be satisfied with these.' This absurd avowal would alone have made it impossible for Hough and his brethren to yield. The negotiation was broken off; and the King hastened to make the disobedient know, as he had threatened, what it was to incur his displeasure.[4]

A special commission was directed to Cartwright, Bishop of Chester, to Wright, Chief Justice of the King's Bench, and to Sir Thomas Jenner, a Baron of the Exchequer, appointing them to exercise visitatorial jurisdiction over the college. On the twentieth of October they arrived at Oxford, escorted by three troops of cavalry with drawn swords. On the following morning the Commissioners took their seats in the hall of Magdalen. Cartwright pronounced a loyal oration which, a few years before, would have called forth the acclamations of an Oxonian audience, but which was now heard with sullen indignation. A long dispute followed. The President defended his rights with skill, temper, and resolution. He professed great respect for the royal authority. But he steadily maintained that he had by the laws of England a freehold interest in the house and revenues annexed to the presidency. Of that interest he could not be deprived by an arbitrary mandate of the Sovereign. 'Will you submit,' said the Bishop, 'to our visitation?' 'I submit to it,' said Hough with great dexterity, 'so far as it is consistent with the laws, and no farther.' 'Will you deliver up the key of your lodgings?' said Cartwright. Hough remained silent. The question was repeated; and Hough returned a mild but resolute refusal. The Commissioners pronounced him an in-

[4. As usual when he touches William Penn, Macaulay here travesties the evidence. Penn was not employed by the King 'to seduce the college from the path of right': he was employed by the college to represent its case to the King; which he did. Having made his initial error, Macaulay has interpreted and twisted the other evidence in order to sustain it.]

truder, and charged the Fellows no longer to recognise his authority, and to assist at the admission of the Bishop of Oxford. Charnock eagerly promised obedience; Smith returned an evasive answer: but the great body of the members of the college firmly declared that they still regarded Hough as their rightful head.

And now Hough himself craved permission to address a few words to the Commissioners. They consented with much civility, perhaps expecting from the calmness and suavity of his manner that he would make some concession. 'My Lords,' said he, 'you have this day deprived me of my freehold: I hereby protest against all your proceedings as illegal, unjust, and null; and I appeal from you to our sovereign Lord the King in his courts of justice.' A loud murmur of applause arose from the gownsmen who filled the hall. The Commissioners were furious. Search was made for the offenders, but in vain. Then the rage of the whole board was turned against Hough. 'Do not think to huff us, sir,' cried Jenner, punning on the President's name. 'I will uphold His Majesty's authority,' said Wright, 'while I have breath in my body. All this comes of your popular protest. You have broken the peace. You shall answer it in the King's Bench. I bind you over in one thousand pounds to appear there next term. I will see whether the civil power cannot manage you. If that is not enough, you shall have the military too.' In truth Oxford was in a state which made the Commissioners not a little uneasy. The soldiers were ordered to have their carbines loaded. It was said that an express was sent to London for the purpose of hastening the arrival of more troops. No disturbance however took place. The Bishop of Oxford was quietly installed by proxy: but only two members of Magdalen College attended the ceremony. Many signs showed that the spirit of resistance had spread to the common people. The porter of the college threw down his keys. The butler refused to scratch Hough's name out of the buttery book, and was instantly dismissed. No blacksmith could be found in the whole city who would force the lock of the President's lodgings. It was necessary for the Commissioners to employ their own servants, who broke open the door with iron bars. The sermons which on the following Sunday were preached in the Uni-

versity church were full of reflections such as stung Cartwright
to the quick, though such as he could not discreetly resent.

And here, if James had not been infatuated, the matter might
have stopped. The Fellows in general were not inclined to carry
their resistance further. They were of opinion that, by refusing
to assist in the admission of the intruder, they had sufficiently
proved their respect for their statutes and oaths, and that, since he
was now in actual possession, they might justifiably submit to
him as their head, till he should be removed by sentence of a
competent court. Only one Fellow, Doctor Fairfax, refused to
yield even to this extent. The Commissioners would gladly have
compromised the dispute on these terms; and during a few hours
there was a truce which many thought likely to end in an amic-
able arrangement: but soon all was again in confusion. The
Fellows found that the popular voice loudly accused them of pusillanimity. The townsmen already talked ironically of a Magdalen
conscience, and exclaimed that the brave Hough and the honest
Fairfax had been betrayed and abandoned. Still more annoying
were the sneers of Obadiah Walker and his brother renegades.
This then, said those apostates, was the end of all the big words
in which the society had declared itself resolved to stand by its
lawful President and by its Protestant faith. While the Fellows,
bitterly annoyed by the public censure, were regretting the
modified submission which they had consented to make, they
learned that this submission was by no means satisfactory to the
King. It was not enough, he said, that they offered to obey the
Bishop of Oxford as President in fact. They must distinctly admit the Commission and all that had been done under it to be
legal. They must acknowledge that they had acted undutifully;
they must declare themselves penitent; they must promise to be-
have better in future, must implore His Majesty's pardon, and
lay themselves at his feet. Two Fellows of whom the King had
no complaint to make, Charnock and Smith, were excused from
the obligation of making these degrading apologies.

Even James never committed a grosser error. The Fellows, already angry with themselves for having conceded so much, and
galled by the censure of the world, eagerly caught at the opportunity which was now offered them of regaining the public es-

teem. With one voice they declared that they would never ask pardon for being in the right, or admit that the visitation of their college and the deprivation of their President had been legal.

Then the King, as he had threatened, laid on them the whole weight of his hand. They were by one sweeping edict condemned to expulsion. Yet this punishment was not deemed sufficient. It was known that many noblemen and gentlemen who possessed church patronage would be disposed to provide for men who had suffered so much for the laws of England and for the Protestant religion. The High Commission therefore pronounced the ejected Fellows incapable of ever holding any church preferment. Such of them as were not yet in holy orders were pronounced incapable of receiving the clerical character. James might enjoy the thought that he had reduced many of them from a situation in which they were surrounded by comforts, and had before them the fairest professional prospects, to hopeless indigence.

But all these severities produced an effect directly the opposite of that which he had anticipated. The spirit of Englishmen, that sturdy spirit which no King of the House of Stuart could ever be taught by experience to understand, swelled up high and strong against injustice. Oxford, the quiet seat of learning and loyalty, was in a state resembling that of the City of London on the morning after the attempt of Charles the First to seize the five members. The Vice-Chancellor had been asked to dine with the Commissioners on the day of the expulsion. He refused. 'My taste,' he said, 'differs from that of Colonel Kirke. I cannot eat my meals with appetite under a gallows.' The scholars refused to pull off their caps to the new rulers of Magdalen College. Smith was nicknamed Doctor Roguery, and was publicly insulted in a coffeehouse. When Charnock summoned the Demies to perform their academical exercises before him, they answered that they were deprived of their lawful governors and would submit to no usurped authority. They assembled apart both for study and for divine service. Attempts were made to corrupt them by offers of the lucrative fellowships which had just been declared vacant: but one undergraduate after another manfully answered that his conscience would not suffer him to profit by injustice. One lad who was induced to take a fellowship was turned out of the hall by the rest. Youths were invited from other colleges, but with small success. The richest foundation in the kingdom seemed to have lost all attractions for needy students. Meanwhile, in London and all over the country, money was collected for the support of the ejected Fellows. The Princess of Orange, to the great joy of all Protestants, subscribed two hundred pounds. Still, however, the King held on his course. The expulsion of the Fellows was soon followed by the expulsion of a crowd of Demies. All this time the new President was fast sinking under bodily and mental disease. He had made a last feeble effort to serve the government by publishing, at the very time when the college was in a state of open rebellion against his authority, a defence of the Declaration of Indulgence, or rather a defence of the doctrine of transubstantiation. This piece called forth many answers, and particularly one from Burnet, written with extraordinary vigour and acrimony. A few weeks after the expulsion of the Demies, Parker died in the house of which he had violently taken possession. Men said that his heart was broken by remorse and shame. He lies in the beautiful antechapel of the college: but no monument marks his grave.

Then the King's whole plan was carried into full effect. The college was turned into a Popish seminary. Bonaventure Giffard, the Roman Catholic Bishop of Madura, was appointed President. The Roman Catholic service was performed in the chapel. In one day twelve Roman Catholics were admitted Fellows. Some servile Protestants applied for fellowships, but met with refusals. Smith, an enthusiast in loyalty, but still a sincere member of the Anglican Church, could not bear to see the altered aspect of the house. He absented himself; he was ordered to return into residence: he disobeyed: he was expelled; and the work of spoliation was complete.

The nature of the academical system of England is such that no event which seriously affects the interests and honour of either University can fail to excite a strong feeling throughout the country. Every successive blow, therefore, which fell on Magdalen College, was felt to the extremities of the kingdom. In the coffeehouses of London, in the Inns of Court, in the closes of all the Cathedral towns, in parsonages and manor houses scattered over the remotest shires, pity for the sufferers and indignation against the government went on growing. The protest of Hough was everywhere applauded: the forcing of his door was everywhere mentioned with abhorrence: and at length the sentence of deprivation fulminated against the Fellows dissolved those ties, once so close and dear, which had bound the Church of England to the House of Stuart. Bitter resentment and cruel apprehension took the place of love and confidence. There was no prebendary, no rector, no vicar, whose mind was not haunted by the thought that, however quiet his temper, however obscure his situation, he might, in a few months, be driven from his dwelling by an arbitrary edict to beg in a ragged cassock with his wife and children, while his freehold, secured to him by laws of immemorial antiquity and by the royal word, was occupied by some apostate. This then was the reward of that heroic loyalty never once found wanting through the vicissitudes of fifty tempestuous years. It was for this that the clergy had endured spoliation and persecution in the cause of Charles the First. It was for this that they had supported Charles the Second in his hard contest with the Whig opposition. It was for this that they had stood in the front of the battle against those who sought to despoil James of his birthright. To their fidelity alone their oppressor owed the power which he was now employing to their ruin. They had long been in the habit of recounting in acrimonious language all that they had suffered at the hand of the Puritan in the day of his power. Yet for the Puritan there was some excuse. He was an avowed enemy: he had wrongs to avenge; and even he, while remodelling the ecclesiastical constitution of the country, and ejecting all who would not subscribe his Covenant, had not been altogether without compassion. He had at least granted to those whose benefices he seized a pittance sufficient to support life. But the hatred felt by the King towards that Church which had saved him from exile and placed him on a throne was not to be so easily satiated. Nothing but the utter ruin of his victims would content him. It was not enough that they were expelled from their homes and stripped of their revenues. They found every walk of life towards which men of their habits could look for a subsistence closed against them with malignant care, and nothing left to them but the precarious and degrading resource of alms.

The Anglican clergy therefore, and that portion of the laity which was strongly attached to Protestant episcopacy, now regarded the King with those feelings which injustice aggravated by ingratitude naturally excites. Yet had the Churchman still many scruples of conscience and honour to surmount before he could bring himself to oppose the government by force. He had been taught that passive obedience was enjoined without restriction or exception by the divine law. He had professed this opinion ostentatiously. He had treated with contempt the suggestion that an extreme case might possibly arise which would justify a people in drawing the sword against regal tyranny. Both principle and shame therefore restrained him from imitating the example of the rebellious Roundheads, while any hope of a peaceful and legal deliverance remained; and such a hope might reasonably be cherished as long as the Princess of Orange stood next in succession to the crown. If he would but endure with patience this trial of his faith, the laws of nature would soon do for him what he could not, without sin and dishonour, do for himself. The wrongs of the Church would be redressed; her property and dignity would be fenced by new guarantees; and those wicked ministers who had injured and insulted her in the day of her adversity would be signally punished.

10

The Seven Bishops

[*Having shown the strength of his purpose in the universities, James set out to realize it in the country. He appointed Catholics as sheriffs, in the hope that they would secure the return of an obedient Parliament. Then, on 28 April 1688, he issued a second Declaration of Indulgence, which he afterwards commanded to be publicly read, at time of divine service, on successive Sundays, first in all the London churches, afterwards in all the churches through England. The Church of England clergy were thus ordered to act as the agents of their own ruin.*

Faced by this threat, the Archbishop of Canterbury, William Sancroft, summoned several bishops to London, and six of them, with him, signed a petition to the King respectfully stating that they held the Declaration to be illegal, and that therefore they could not be parties to its publication in church. These recalcitrant bishops, who became famous as 'the Seven Bishops', were Sancroft himself; William Lloyd, Bishop of St Asaph; Francis Turner, Bishop of Ely; John Lake, Bishop of Chichester; Thomas Ken, Bishop of Bath and Wells; Thomas White, Bishop of Peterborough; and Sir John Trelawney, Bishop of Bristol.

This passage is also from Macaulay's Chapter VIII.]

IT was now late on Friday evening: and on Sunday morning the Declaration was to be read in the churches of London. It was necessary to put the paper into the King's hands without delay. The six Bishops set off for Whitehall. The Archbishop, who had long been forbidden the court, did not accompany them. Lloyd, leaving his five brethren at the house of Lord Dartmouth in the vicinity of the palace, went to Sunderland, and begged that minister to read the petition, and to ascertain when the King would be willing to receive it. Sunderland, afraid of compromising himself, refused to look at the paper, but went immediately to the royal closet. James directed that the Bishops should be admitted. He had heard from his tool Cartwright[1] that they were disposed to obey the royal mandate, but that they wished for some little modifications in form, and that they meant to present a humble request to that effect. His Majesty was therefore in very good humour. When they knelt before him, he graciously told them to rise, took the paper from Lloyd, and said, 'This is my Lord of Canterbury's hand.' 'Yes, sir, his own hand,' was the answer. James read the petition; he folded it up; and his countenance grew dark. 'This,' he said, 'is a great surprise to me. I did not expect this from your Church, especially from some of you. This is a standard of rebellion.' The Bishops broke out into passionate professions of loyalty: but the King, as usual, repeated the same words over and over. 'I tell you, this is a standard of rebellion.' 'Rebellion!' cried Trelawney, falling on his knees. 'For God's sake, sir, do not say so hard a thing of us. No Trelawney can be a rebel. Remember that my family has fought for the crown. Remember how I served your Majesty when Monmouth was in the West.' 'We put down the last rebellion,' said Lake: 'we shall not raise another.' 'We rebel!' exclaimed Turner; 'we are ready to die at your Majesty's feet.' 'Sir,' said Ken, in a more manly tone, 'I hope that you will grant to us that liberty of conscience which you grant to all mankind.' Still James went on. 'This is rebellion. This is a standard of rebellion. Did ever a good Churchman question the dispensing power before? Have not some of you preached for it and written for it? It is a standard of rebellion. I will have my Declaration published.' 'We have two duties to perform,' answered Ken, 'our duty to God, and our duty to your Majesty. We honour you: but we fear God.' 'Have I deserved this?' said the King, more and more angry, 'I who have been such a friend to your Church! I did not expect this from some of you. I will be obeyed. My Declaration shall be published. You are trumpeters of sedition. What do you do here? Go to your dioceses and see that I am obeyed. I will keep this paper. I will not part with it. I will remember you that have signed it.' 'God's will be done,' said Ken. 'God has given me the dispensing power,' said the King, 'and I will maintain it. I tell

[1. Thomas Cartwright, whom James had made Bishop of Chester.]

you that there are still seven thousand of your Church who have not bowed the knee to Baal.'

The Bishops respectfully retired. That very evening the document which they had put into the hands of the King appeared word for word in print, was laid on the tables of all the coffee-houses, and was cried about the streets. Everywhere the people rose from their beds, and came out to stop the hawkers. It was said that the printer cleared a thousand pounds in a few hours by this penny broadside. This is probably an exaggeration; but it is an exaggeration which proves that the sale was enormous. How the petition got abroad is still a mystery. Sancroft declared that he had taken every precaution against publication, and that he knew of no copy except that which he had himself written, and which James had taken out of Lloyd's hand. The veracity of the Archbishop is beyond all suspicion. It is, however, by no means improbable that some of the divines who assisted in framing the petition may have remembered so short a composition accurately, and may have sent it to the press. The prevailing opinion, however, was that some person about the King had been indiscreet or treacherous. Scarcely less sensation was produced by a short letter which was written with great power of argument and language, printed secretly, and largely circulated on the same day by the post and by the common carriers. A copy was sent to every clergyman in the kingdom. The writer did not attempt to disguise the danger which those who disobeyed the royal mandate would incur: but he set forth in a lively manner the still greater danger of submission. 'If we read the Declaration,' said he, 'we fall to rise no more. We fall unpitied and despised. We fall amidst the curses of a nation whom our compliance will have ruined.' Some thought that this paper came from Holland. Others attributed it to Sherlock. But Prideaux, Dean of Norwich, who was a principal agent in distributing it, believed it to be the work of Halifax.

The conduct of the prelates was rapturously extolled by the general voice: but some murmurs were heard. It was said that such grave men, if they thought themselves bound in conscience to remonstrate with the King, ought to have remonstrated earlier. Was it fair to him to leave him in the dark till within thirty-six hours of the time fixed for the reading of the Declaration? Even if he wished to revoke the Order in Council, it was too late to do so. The inference seemed to be that the petition was intended, not to move the royal mind, but merely to inflame the discontents of the people. These complaints were utterly groundless. The King had laid on the Bishops a command new, surprising, and embarrassing. It was their duty to communicate with each other, and to ascertain as far as possible the sense of the profession of which they were the heads before they took any step. They were dispersed over the whole kingdom. Some of them were distant from others a full week's journey. James allowed them only a fortnight to inform themselves, to meet, to deliberate, and to decide; and he surely had no right to think himself aggrieved because that fortnight was drawing to a close before he learned their decision. Nor is it true that they did not leave him time to revoke his order if he had been wise enough to do so. He might have called together his Council on Saturday morning, and before night it might have been known throughout London and the suburbs that he had yielded to the intreaties of the fathers of the Church. The Saturday, however, passed over without any sign of relenting on the part of the government; and the Sunday arrived, a day long remembered.

In the City and Liberties of London were about a hundred parish churches. In only four of these was the Order in Council obeyed. At Saint Gregory's the Declaration was read by a divine of the name of Martin. As soon as he uttered the first words, the whole congregation rose and withdrew. At Saint Matthew's, in Friday Street, a wretch named Timothy Hall, who had disgraced his gown by acting as broker for the Duchess of Portsmouth in the sale of pardons, and who now had hopes of obtaining the vacant bishopric of Oxford, was in like manner left alone in his church. At Serjeant's Inn, in Chancery Lane, the clerk pretended that he had forgotten to bring a copy; and the Chief Justice of the King's Bench, who had attended in order to see that the royal mandate was obeyed, was forced to content himself with this excuse. Samuel Wesley, the father of John and Charles Wesley, a curate in London, took for his text that day the noble answer of the three Jews to the Chaldean tyrant: 'Be it known unto Thee, O King, that we will not serve thy gods, nor worship the golden image which thou hast set up.' Even in the chapel of Saint James's Palace the officiating minister had the courage to disobey the order. The Westminster boys long remembered what took place that day in the Abbey. Sprat, Bishop of Rochester, officiated there as Dean. As soon as he began to read the Declaration, murmurs and the noise of people crowding out of the choir drowned his voice. He trembled so violently that men saw the paper shake in his hand. Long before he had finished, the place was deserted by all but those whose situation made it necessary for them to remain.

Never had the Church been so dear to the nation as on the afternoon of that day. The spirit of dissent seemed to be extinct. Baxter from his pulpit pronounced an eulogium on the Bishops and parochial clergy. The Dutch minister, a few hours later, wrote to inform the States General that the Anglican priesthood had risen in the estimation of the public to an incredible degree. The universal cry of the Nonconformists, he said, was that they would rather continue to lie under the penal statutes than separate their cause from that of the prelates.

Another week of anxiety and agitation passed away. Sunday came again. Again the churches of the capital were thronged by hundreds of thousands. The Declaration was read nowhere except at the very few places where it had been read the week before. The minister who had officiated at the chapel in Saint James's Palace had been turned out of his situation, and a more obsequious divine appeared with the paper in his hand: but his agitation was so great that he could not articulate. In truth the feeling of the whole nation had now become such as none but the very best and noblest, or the very worst and basest, of mankind could without much discomposure encounter.

Even the King stood aghast for a moment at the violence of the tempest which he had raised. What step was he next to take? He must either advance or recede: and it was impossible to advance without peril, or to recede without humiliation. At one moment he determined to put forth a second order enjoining the clergy in high and angry terms to publish his Declaration, and menacing every one who should be refractory with instant suspension. This order was drawn up and sent to the press, then recalled, then a second time sent to the press, then recalled a second time. A different plan was suggested by some of those who were for rigorous measures. The prelates who had signed the petition might be cited before the Ecclesiastical Commission and deprived of their sees. But to this course strong objections were urged in Council. It had been announced that the Houses would be convoked before the end of the year. The Lords would assuredly treat the sentence of deprivation as a nullity, would insist that Sancroft and his fellow petitioners should be summoned to Parliament, and would refuse to acknowledge a new Archbishop of Canterbury or a new Bishop of Bath and Wells. Thus the session, which at best was likely to be sufficiently stormy, would commence with a deadly quarrel between the crown and the peers. If therefore it were thought necessary to punish the Bishops, the punishment ought to be inflicted according to the known course of English law. Sunderland had from the beginning objected, as far as he dared, to the Order in Council. He now suggested a course which, though not free from inconveniences, was the most prudent and the most dignified that a series of errors had left open to the government. The King might with grace and majesty announce to the world that he was deeply hurt by the undutiful conduct of the Church of England; but that he could not forget all the services rendered by that Church, in trying times, to his father, to his brother, and to himself; that, as a friend to the liberty of conscience, he was unwilling to deal severely by men whom conscience, ill informed indeed, and unreasonably scrupulous, might have prevented from obeying his commands; and that he would therefore leave the offenders to that punishment which their own reflections would inflict whenever they should calmly compare their recent acts with the loyal doctrines of which they had so loudly boasted. Not only Powis and Bellasyse, who had always been for moderate counsels, but even Dover and Arundell, leaned towards this proposition. Jeffreys, on the other hand, maintained that the government would be disgraced if such transgressors as the seven Bishops were suffered to escape with a mere reprimand. He did not, however, wish them to be cited before the Ecclesiastical Commission, in which he sat as chief or rather as sole Judge. For the load of public hatred under which he already lay was too much even for his shameless forehead and obdurate heart; and he shrank from the responsibility which he would have incurred by pronouncing an illegal sentence on the rulers of the Church and the favourites of the nation. He therefore recommended a criminal information. It was accordingly resolved that the Archbishop and the six other petitioners should be brought before the Court of King's Bench on a charge of seditious libel. That they would be convicted it was scarcely possible to doubt. The Judges and their officers were tools of the court. Since the old charter of the City of London had been forfeited, scarcely one prisoner whom the government was bent on bringing to punishment had been absolved by a jury. The refractory prelates would probably be condemned to ruinous fines and to long imprisonment, and would be glad to ransom themselves by serving, both in and out of Parliament, the designs of the Sovereign.

On the twenty-seventh of May it was notified to the Bishops that on the eighth of June they must appear before the King in Council. Why so long an interval was allowed we are not informed. Perhaps James hoped that some of the offenders, terrified by his displeasure, might submit before the day fixed for the reading of the Declaration in their dioceses, and might, in order to make their peace with him, persuade their clergy to obey his order. If such was his hope it was signally disappointed. Sunday the third of June came; and all parts of England followed the example of the capital. Already the Bishops of Norwich, Gloucester, Salisbury, Winchester, and Exeter, had signed copies of the petition in token of their approbation. The Bishop of Worcester had refused to distribute the Declaration among his clergy. The Bishop of Hereford had distributed it: but it was generally understood that he was overwhelmed by remorse and shame for having done so. Not one parish priest in fifty complied with the Order in Council. In the great diocese of Chester, including the county of Lancaster, only three clergymen could be prevailed on by Cartwright to obey the King. In the diocese of Norwich are many hundreds of parishes. In only four of these was the Declaration read. The courtly Bishop of Rochester[2] could not overcome the scruples of the minister of the ordinary of Chatham, who depended on the government for bread. There is still extant a pathetic letter which this honest priest sent to the Secretary of the Admiralty. 'I cannot,' he wrote, 'reasonably expect your Honour's protection. God's will be done. I must choose suffering rather than sin.'

On the evening of the eighth of June the seven prelates, furnished by the ablest lawyers in England with full advice, repaired to the palace, and were called into the Council chamber. Their petition was lying on the table. The Chancellor took the paper up, showed it to the Archbishop, and said, 'Is this the paper which your Grace wrote, and which the six Bishops present delivered to his Majesty?' Sancroft looked at the paper, turned to the King, and spoke thus: 'Sir, I stand here a culprit. I never was so before. Once I little thought that I ever should be so. Least of all could I think that I should be charged with any offence against my King: but, since I am so unhappy as to be in this situation, your Majesty will not be offended if I avail myself of my lawful right to decline saying anything which may criminate me.' 'This is mere chicanery,' said the King. 'I hope that your Grace will not do so ill a thing as to deny your own hand.' 'Sir,' said Lloyd, whose studies had been much among the casuists, 'all divines agree that a person situated as we are may refuse to answer such a question.' The King, as slow of understanding as quick of temper, could not comprehend what the prelates meant. He persisted, and was evidently becoming very angry. 'Sir,' said the Archbishop, 'I am not bound to accuse myself. Nevertheless, if your Majesty positively commands me to answer, I will do so in the confidence that a just and generous prince will not suffer what I say in obedience to his orders to be brought in evidence against me.' 'You must not capitulate with your Sovereign,' said the Chancellor. 'No,' said the King: 'I will not give any such command. If you choose to deny your own hands, I have nothing more to say to you.'

The Bishops were repeatedly sent out into the ante-chamber,

[2. Thomas Sprat. He had sat on the Court of High Commission and generally complied with the court.]

and repeatedly called back into the Council room. At length James positively commanded them to answer the question. He did not expressly engage that their confession should not be used against them. But they, not unnaturally, supposed that, after what had passed, such an engagement was implied in his command. Sancroft acknowledged his handwriting; and his brethren followed his example. They were then interrogated about the meaning of some words in the petition, and about the letter which had been circulated with so much effect all over the kingdom: but their language was so guarded that nothing was gained by the examination. The Chancellor then told them that a criminal information would be exhibited against them in the Court of King's Bench, and called upon them to enter into recognisances. They refused. They were peers of the realm, they said. They were advised by the best lawyers in Westminster Hall that no peer could be required to enter into a recognisance in a case of libel; and they should not think themselves justified in relinquishing the privilege of their order. The King was so absurd as to think himself personally affronted because they chose, on a legal question, to be guided by legal advice. 'You believe everybody,' he said, 'rather than me.' He was indeed mortified and alarmed. For he had gone so far that, if they persisted, he had no choice left but to send them to prison; and, though he by no means foresaw all the consequences of such a step, he foresaw probably enough to disturb him. They were resolute. A warrant was therefo e made out directing the Lieutenant of the Tower to keep them in safe custody, and a barge was manned to convey them down the river.

It was known all over London that the Bishops were before the Council. The public anxiety was intense. A great multitude filled the courts of Whitehall and all the neighbouring streets. Many people were in the habit of refreshing themselves at the close of a summer day with the cool air of the Thames. But on this evening the whole river was alive with wherries. When the Seven came forth under a guard, the emotions of the people broke through all restraint. Thousands fell on their knees and prayed aloud for the men who had, with the Christian courage of Ridley and Latimer, confronted a tyrant inflamed by all the bigotry of Mary. Many dashed into the stream, and, up to their waists in ooze and water, cried to the holy fathers to bless them. All down the river, from Whitehall to London Bridge, the royal barge passed between lines of boats, from which arose a shout of 'God bless your Lordships.' The King, in great alarm, gave orders that the garrison of the Tower should be doubled, that the Guards should be held ready for action, and that two companies should be detached from every regiment in the kingdom, and sent up instantly to London. But the force on which he relied as the means of coercing the people shared all the feelings of the people. The very sentinels who were under arms at the Traitors' Gate reverently asked for a blessing from the martyrs whom they were to guard. Sir Edward Hales was Lieutenant of the Tower. He was little inclined to treat his prisoners with kindness. For he was an apostate from that Church for which they suffered; and he held several lucrative posts by virtue of that dispensing power against which they had protested. He learned with indignation that his soldiers were drinking the health of the Bishops. He ordered his officers to see that it was done no more. But the officers came back with a report that the thing could not be prevented, and that no other health was drunk in the garrison. Nor was it only by carousing that the troops showed their reverence for the fathers of the Church. There was such a show of devotion throughout the Tower that pious divines thanked God for bringing good out of evil, and for making the persecution of His faithful servants the means of saving many souls. All day the coaches and liveries of the first nobles of England were seen round the prison gates. Thousands of humbler spectators constantly covered Tower Hill. But among the marks of public respect and sympathy which the prelates received there was one which more than all the rest enraged and alarmed the King. He learned that a deputation of ten Nonconformist ministers had visited the Tower. He sent for four of these persons, and himself upbraided them. They courageously answered that they thought it their duty to forget past quarrels, and to stand by the men who stood by the Protestant religion.

Scarcely had the gates of the Tower been closed on the prisoners when an event took place which increased the public excitement. It had been announced that the Queen did not expect to be delivered till July. But, on the day after the Bishops had appeared before the Council, it was observed that the King seemed to be anxious about her state. In the evening, however, she sat playing cards at Whitehall till near midnight. Then she was carried in a sedan to Saint James's Palace, where apartments had been very hastily fitted up for her reception. Soon messengers were running about in all directions to summon physicians and priests, Lords of the Council, and Ladies of the Bedchamber. In a few hours many public functionaries and women of rank were assembled in the Queen's room. There, on the morning of Sunday, the tenth of June, a day long kept sacred by the too faithful adherents of a bad cause, was born the most unfortunate of princes, destined to seventy-seven years of exile and wandering, of vain projects, of honours more galling than insults, and of hopes such as make the heart sick.

The calamities of the poor child had begun before his birth. The nation over which, according to the ordinary course of succession, he would have reigned, was fully persuaded that his mother was not really pregnant. By whatever evidence the fact of his birth had been proved, a considerable number of people would probably have persisted in maintaining that the Jesuits had practised some skilful sleight of hand: and the evidence, partly from accident, partly from gross mismanagement, was open to some objections. Many persons of both sexes were in the royal bedchamber when the child first saw the light; but none of them enjoyed any large measure of public confidence. Of the Privy Councillors present half were Roman Catholics; and those who called themselves Protestants were generally regarded as traitors to their country and their God. Many of the women in attendance were French, Italian, and Portuguese. Of the English ladies some were Papists, and some were the wives of Papists. Some persons who were peculiarly entitled to be present, and whose testimony would have satisfied all minds accessible to reason, were absent; and for their absence the King was held responsible. The Princess Anne was, of all the inhabitants of the island, the most deeply interested in the event. Her sex and her experience qualified her to act as the guardian of her sister's birthright and her own. She had conceived strong suspicions which were daily confirmed by circumstances trifling or imaginary. She fancied that the Queen carefully shunned her scrutiny, and ascribed to guilt a reserve which was perhaps the effect of delicacy. In this temper Anne had determined to be present and vigilant when the critical day should arrive. But she had not thought it necessary to be at her post a month before that day, and had, in compliance, it was said, with her father's advice, gone to drink the Bath waters. Sancroft, whose great place made it his duty to attend, and on whose probity the nation placed entire reliance, had a few hours before been sent to the Tower by James. The Hydes were the proper protectors of the rights of the two Princesses. The Dutch Ambassador might be regarded as the representative of William, who, as first prince of the blood and consort of the King's eldest daughter, had a deep interest in what was passing. James never thought of summoning any member, male or female, of the family of Hyde; nor was the Dutch Ambassador invited to be present.

Posterity has fully acquitted the King of the fraud which his people imputed to him. But it is impossible to acquit him of folly and perverseness such as explain and excuse the error of his contemporaries. He was perfectly aware of the suspicions which were abroad. He ought to have known that those suspicions would not be dispelled by the evidence of members of the Church of Rome, or of persons who, though they might call themselves members of the Church of England, had shown themselves ready to sacrifice the interests of the Church of England in order to obtain his favour. That he was taken by surprise is true. But he had twelve hours to make his arrangements. He found no difficulty in crowding St James's Palace with bigots and sycophants on whose word the nation placed no reliance. It would have been quite as easy to procure the attendance of some eminent persons whose attachment to the Princesses and to the established religion was unquestionable.

At a later period, when he had paid dearly for his foolhardy contempt of public opinion, it was the fashion at Saint Germains to excuse him by throwing the blame on others. Some Jacobites charged Anne with having purposely kept out of the way. Nay, they were not ashamed to say that Sancroft had provoked the King to send him to the Tower, in order that the evidence which was to confound the calumnies of the malcontents might be defective. The absurdity of these imputations is palpable. Could Anne or Sancroft possibly have foreseen that the Queen's calculations would turn out to be erroneous by a whole month? Had those calculations been correct, Anne would have been back from Bath, and Sancroft would have been out of the Tower, in ample time for the birth. At all events the maternal uncles of the King's daughters were neither at a distance nor in a prison. The same messenger who summoned the whole bevy of renegades, Dover, Peterborough, Murray, Sunderland, and Mulgrave, could just as easily have summoned Clarendon. If they were Privy Councillors, so was he. His house was in Jermyn Street, not two hundred yards from the chamber of the Queen. Yet he was left to learn at St James's Church, from the agitation and whispers of the congregation, that his niece had ceased to be heiress presumptive of the crown. Was it a disqualification that he was the near kinsman of the Princesses of Orange and Denmark? Or was it a disqualification that he was unalterably attached to the Church of England?

The cry of the whole nation was that an imposture had been practised. Papists had, during some months, been predicting, from the pulpit and through the press, in prose and verse, in English and Latin, that a Prince of Wales would be given to the prayers of the Church; and they had now accomplished their own prophecy. Every witness who could not be corrupted or deceived had been studiously excluded. Anne had been tricked into visiting Bath. The Primate had, on the very day preceding that which had been fixed for the villainy, been sent to prison in defiance of the rules of law and of the privileges of peerage. Not a single man or woman who had the smallest interest in detecting the fraud had been suffered to be present. The Queen had been removed suddenly and at the dead of night to St James's Palace, because that building, less commodious for honest purposes than Whitehall, had some rooms and passages well suited for the purpose of the Jesuits. There, amidst a circle of zealots who thought nothing a crime that tended to promote the interests of their

Church, and of courtiers who thought nothing a crime that
tended to enrich and aggrandise themselves, a new-born child
had been introduced into the royal bed,[3] and then handed round
in triumph, as heir of the three kingdoms. Heated by such suspicions, suspicions unjust, it is true, but not altogether unnatural, men thronged more eagerly than ever to pay their homage to the saintly victims of the tyrant who, having long foully
injured his people, had now filled up the measure of his iniqui-
ties by more foully injuring his children.

The Prince of Orange, not himself suspecting any trick, and
not aware of the state of public feeling in England, ordered
prayers to be said under his own roof for his little brother-in-law,
and sent Zuylestein[4] to London with a formal message of congratulation. Zuylestein, to his amazement, found all the people
whom he met open-mouthed about the infamous fraud just committed by the Jesuits, and saw every hour some fresh pasquinade
on the pregnancy and the delivery. He soon wrote to the Hague
that not one person in ten believed the child to have been born of
the Queen.

The demeanour of the seven prelates meanwhile strengthened
the interest which their situation excited. On the evening of the
Black Friday, as it was called, on which they were committed,
they reached their prison just at the hour of divine service. They
instantly hastened to the chapel. It chanced that in the second
lesson were these words: 'In all things approving ourselves as the
ministers of God, in much patience, in afflictions, in distresses, in
stripes, in imprisonments.' All zealous Churchmen were delighted by this coincidence, and remembered how much comfort a similar coincidence had given, near forty years before, to
Charles the First at the time of his death.

On the evening of the next day, Saturday, the ninth, a letter
came from Sunderland enjoining the chaplain of the Tower to

[3. The child was said to have been introduced in a warming-pan; hence
'the Warming-Pan' became an article of faith to good whigs.]

[4. Willem Hendrik Zuylestein, afterwards created Earl of Rochford, a
Dutchman, was an illegitimate cousin of William of Orange and at this time
acted as his personal agent in England.]

read the Declaration during divine service on the following morning. As the time fixed by the Order in Council for the reading in London had long expired, this proceeding of the government could be considered only as a personal insult of the meanest and most childish kind to the venerable prisoners. The chaplain refused to comply: he was dismissed from his situation; and the chapel was shut up.

The Bishops edified all who approached them by the firmness and cheerfulness with which they endured confinement, by the modesty and meekness with which they received the applauses and blessings of the whole nation, and by the loyal attachment which they professed for the persecutor who sought their destruction. They remained only a week in custody. On Friday the fifteenth of June, the first day of term, they were brought before the King's Bench. An immense throng awaited their coming. From the landing-place to the Court of Requests they passed through a lane of spectators who blessed and applauded them. 'Friends,' said the prisoners as they passed, 'honour the King; and remember us in your prayers.' These humble and pious expressions moved the hearers, even to tears. When at length the procession had made its way through the crowd into the presence of the Judges, the Attorney General exhibited the information which he had been commanded to prepare, and moved that the defendants might be ordered to plead. The counsel on the other side objected that the Bishops had been unlawfully committed, and were therefore not regularly before the Court. The question whether a peer could be required to enter into recognisances on a charge of libel was argued at great length, and decided by a majority of Judges in favour of the crown. The prisoners then pleaded Not Guilty. That day fortnight, the twenty-ninth of June, was fixed for their trial. In the meantime they were allowed to be at large on their own recognisances. The crown lawyers acted prudently in not requiring sureties. For Halifax had arranged that twenty-one temporal peers of the highest consideration should be ready to put in bail, three for each defendant; and such a manifestation of the feeling of the nobility would have been no slight blow to the government. It was also known that one of the most opulent Dissenters of the City had begged that he might have the honour of giving security for Ken.

The Bishops were now permitted to depart to their own homes. The common people, who did not understand the nature of the legal proceedings which had taken place in the King's Bench, and who saw that their favourites had been brought to Westminster Hall in custody and were suffered to go away in freedom, imagined that the good cause was prospering. Loud acclamations were raised. The steeples of the churches sent forth joyous peals. Sprat was amazed to hear the bells of his own Abbey ringing merrily. He promptly silenced them: but his interference caused much angry muttering. The Bishops found it difficult to escape from the importunate crowd of their wellwishers. Lloyd was detained in Palace Yard by admirers who struggled to touch his hands and to kiss the skirt of his robe, till Clarendon, with some difficulty, rescued him and conveyed him home by a by-path. Cartwright, it is said, was so unwise as to mingle with the crowd. Some person who saw his episcopal habit asked and received his blessing. A bystander cried out, 'Do you know who blessed you?' 'Surely,' said he who had just been honoured by the benediction, 'it was one of the Seven.' 'No,' said the other; 'it is the Popish Bishop of Chester.' 'Popish dog,' cried the enraged Protestant; 'take your blessing back again.'

Such was the concourse, and such the agitation, that the Dutch Ambassador was surprised to see the day close without an insurrection. The King had been by no means at ease. In order that he might be ready to suppress any disturbance, he had passed the morning in reviewing several battalions of infantry in Hyde Park. It is, however, by no means certain that his troops would have stood by him if he had needed their services. When Sancroft reached Lambeth, in the afternoon, he found the grenadier guards, who were quartered in that suburb, assembled before the gate of his palace. They formed in two lines on his right and left, and asked his benediction as he went through them. He with difficulty prevented them from lighting a bonfire in honour of his return to his dwelling. There were, however, many bonfires that evening in the City. Two Roman Catholics who were so indiscreet as to beat some boys for joining in these rejoicings were seized by the mob, stripped naked, and ignominiously branded.

Sir Edward Hales now came to demand fees from those who had lately been his prisoners. They refused to pay anything for the detention which they regarded as illegal to an officer whose commission was, on their principles, a nullity. The Lieutenant hinted very intelligibly that, if they came into his hands again, they should be put into heavy irons and should lie on bare stones. 'We are under our King's displeasure,' was the answer; 'and most deeply do we feel it: but a fellow subject who threatens us does but lose his breath.' It is easy to imagine with what indignation the people, excited as they were, must have learned that a renegade from the Protestant faith, who held a command in defiance of the fundamental laws of England, had dared to menace divines of venerable age and dignity with all the barbarities of Lollard's Tower.

Before the day of trial the agitation had spread to the farthest corners of the island. From Scotland the Bishops received letters assuring them of the sympathy of the Presbyterians of that country, so long and so bitterly hostile to prelacy. The people of Cornwall, a fierce, bold, and athletic race, among whom there was a stronger provincial feeling than in any other part of the realm, were greatly moved by the danger of Trelawney, whom they reverenced less as a ruler of the Church than as the head of an honourable house, and the heir through twenty descents of ancestors who had been of great note before the Normans had set foot on English ground. All over the county the peasants chanted a ballad of which the burden is still remembered:

> And shall Trelawney die, and shall Trelawney die?
> Then thirty thousand Cornish boys will know the reason why.

The miners from their caverns reechoed the song with a variation:

> Then twenty thousand under ground will know the reason why.[5]

5. This fact was communicated to me in the most obliging manner by the

The rustics in many parts of the country loudly expressed a strange hope which had never ceased to live in their hearts. Their Protestant Duke, their beloved Monmouth, would suddenly appear, would lead them to victory, and would tread down the King and the Jesuits under his feet.

The ministers were appalled. Even Jeffreys would gladly have retraced his steps. He charged Clarendon with friendly messages to the Bishops, and threw on others the blame of the prosecution which he had himself recommended. Sunderland again ventured to recommend concession. The late auspicious birth, he said, had furnished the King with an excellent opportunity of withdrawing from a position full of danger and inconvenience without incurring the reproach of timidity or of caprice. On such happy occasions it had been usual for sovereigns to make the hearts of subjects glad by acts of clemency; and nothing could be more advantageous to the Prince of Wales than that he should, while still in his cradle, be the peacemaker between his father and the agitated nation. But the King's resolution was fixed. 'I will go on,' he said. 'I have been only too indulgent. Indulgence ruined my father.' The artful minister found that his advice had been formerly taken only because it had been shaped to suit the royal temper, and that, from the moment at which he began to counsel well, he began to counsel in vain. He had shown some signs of slackness in the proceeding against Magdalen College. He had recently attempted to convince the King that Tyrconnel's scheme of confiscating the property of the English colonists in Ireland was full of danger, and had, with the help of Powis and Bellasyse, so far succeeded that the execution of the design had been postponed for another year. But this timidity and scrupulosity had excited disgust and suspicion in the royal mind. The day of retribution had arrived.

Sunderland was in the same situation in which his rival Rochester had been some months before. Each of the two statesmen in turn experienced the misery of clutching, with an agonizing grasp, power which was perceptibly slipping away. Each in turn

---

Reverend R. S. Hawker of Morwenstow in Cornwall. [In reality, the 'fact' seems to have been invented by Hawker, whose 'ancient ballad' on Trelawney deceived Scott and Dickens, as well as Macaulay. *Ed.*]

saw his suggestions scornfully rejected. Both endured the pain of reading displeasure and distrust in the countenance and demeanour of their master; yet both were by their country held responsible for those crimes and errors from which they had vainly endeavoured to dissuade him. While he suspected them of trying to win popularity at the expense of his authority and dignity, the public voice loudly accused them of trying to win his favour at the expense of their own honour and of the general weal. Yet, in spite of mortifications and humiliations, they both clung to office with the gripe of drowning men. Both attempted to propitiate the King by affecting a willingness to be reconciled to his Church. But there was a point at which Rochester was determined to stop. He went to the verge of apostasy: but there he recoiled: and the world, in consideration of the firmness with which he refused to take the final step, granted him a liberal amnesty for all former compliances. Sunderland, less scrupulous and less sensible of shame, resolved to atone for his late moderation, and to recover the royal confidence, by an act which, to a mind impressed with the importance of religious truth, must have appeared to be one of the most flagitious of crimes, and which even men of the world regard as the last excess of baseness. About a week before the day fixed for the great trial, it was publicly announced that he was a Papist. The King talked with delight of this triumph of divine grace. Courtiers and envoys kept their countenances as well as they could while the renegade protested that he had been long convinced of the impossibility of finding salvation out of the communion of Rome, and that his conscience would not let him rest till he had renounced the heresies in which he had been brought up. The news spread fast. At all the coffeehouses it was told how the prime minister of England, his feet bare, and a taper in his hand, had repaired to the royal chapel and knocked humbly for admittance; how a priestly voice from within had demanded who was there; how Sunderland had made answer that a poor sinner who had long wandered from the true Church implored her to receive and to absolve him; how the doors were opened; and how the neophyte partook of the holy mysteries.

This scandalous apostasy could not but heighten the interest with which the nation looked forward to the day when the fate of the seven brave confessors of the English Church was to be decided. To pack a jury was now the great object of the King. The crown lawyers were ordered to make strict inquiry as to the sentiments of the persons who were registered in the freeholders' book. Sir Samuel Astry, Clerk of the Crown, whose duty it was, in cases of this description, to select the names, was summoned to the palace, and had an interview with James in the presence of the Chancellor. Sir Samuel seems to have done his best. For, among the forty-eight persons whom he nominated, were said to be several servants of the King, and several Roman Catholics. But as the counsel for the Bishops had a right to strike off twelve, these persons were removed. The crown lawyers also struck off twelve. The list was thus reduced to twenty-four. The first twelve who answered to their names were to try the issue.

On the twenty-ninth of June, Westminster Hall, Old and New Palace Yard, and all the neighbouring streets to a great distance were thronged with people. Such an auditory had never before and has never since been assembled in the Court of King's Bench. Thirty-five temporal peers of the realm were counted in the crowd.

All the four Judges of the Court were on the bench. Wright, who presided, had been raised to his high place over the heads of many abler and more learned men solely on account of his unscrupulous servility. Allibone was a Papist, and owed his situation to that dispensing power, the legality of which was now in question. Holloway had hitherto been a serviceable tool of the government. Even Powell, whose character for honesty stood high, had borne a part in some proceedings which it is impossible to defend. He had, in the great case of Sir Edward Hales,[6] with some hesitation, it is true, and after some delay, concurred with the majority of the bench, and had thus brought on his character a stain which his honourable conduct on this day completely effaced.

[6. The action *Godden* v. *Hales*, in 1686, was the collusive action by which James II had secured a judicial ruling that the Crown could dispense with the penal statutes in particular cases and so promote Roman Catholics to posts from which those statutes debarred them.]

The counsel were by no means fairly matched. The government had required from its law officers services so odious and disgraceful that all the ablest jurists and advocates of the Tory party had, one after another, refused to comply, and had been dismissed from their employments. Sir Thomas Powis, the Attorney General, was scarcely of the third rank in his profession. Sir William Williams, the Solicitor General, had quick parts and dauntless courage: but he wanted discretion; he loved wrangling; he had no command over his temper; and he was hated and despised by all political parties. The most conspicuous assistants of the Attorney and Solicitor were Serjeant Trinder, a Roman Catholic, and Sir Bartholomew Shower, Recorder of London, who had some legal learning, but whose fulsome apologies and endless repetitions were the jest of Westminster Hall. The government had wished to secure the services of Maynard: but he had plainly declared that he could not in conscience do what was asked of him.

On the other side were arrayed almost all the eminent forensic talents of the age. Sawyer and Finch, who, at the time of the accession of James, had been Attorney and Solicitor General, and who, during the persecution of the Whigs in the late reign, had served the crown with but too much vehemence and success, were of counsel for the defendants. With them were joined two persons who, since age had diminished the activity of Maynard, were reputed the two best lawyers that could be found in the Inns of Court: Pemberton, who had, in the time of Charles the Second, been Chief Justice of the King's Bench, who had been removed from his high place on account of his humanity and moderation, and who had resumed his practice at the bar; and Pollexfen, who had long been at the head of the Western circuit, and who, though he had incurred much unpopularity by holding briefs for the crown at the Bloody Assizes, and particularly by appearing against Alice Lisle, was known to be at heart a Whig, if not a republican. Sir Creswell Levinz was also there, a man of great knowledge and experience, but of singularly timid nature. He had been removed from the bench some years before, because he was afraid to serve the purposes of the government. He was now afraid to appear as the advocate of the Bishops, and had at first refused to receive their retainer: but it had been intimated to him by the whole body of attorneys who employed him that, if he declined this brief, he should never have another.

Sir George Treby, an able and zealous Whig, who had been Recorder of London under the old charter, was on the same side. Sir John Holt, a still more eminent Whig lawyer, was not retained for the defence, in consequence, it should seem, of some prejudice conceived against him by Sancroft, but was privately consulted on the case by the Bishop of London. The junior counsel for the Bishops was a young barrister named John Somers. He had no advantages of birth or fortune; nor had he yet had any opportunity of distinguishing himself before the eyes of the public: but his genius, his industry, his great and various accomplishments, were well known to a small circle of friends; and, in spite of his Whig opinions, his pertinent and lucid mode of arguing and the constant propriety of his demeanour had already secured to him the ear of the Court of King's Bench. The importance of obtaining his services had been strongly represented to the Bishops by Johnstone; and Pollexfen, it is said, had declared that no man in Westminster Hall was so well qualified to treat a historical and constitutional question as Somers.

The jury was sworn; it consisted of persons of highly respectable station. The foreman was Sir Roger Langley, a baronet of old and honourable family. With him were joined a knight and ten esquires, several of whom are known to have been men of large possessions. There were some Nonconformists in the number; for the Bishops had wisely resolved not to show any distrust of the Protestant Dissenters. One name excited considerable alarm, that of Michael Arnold. He was brewer to the palace; and it was apprehended that the government counted on his voice. The story goes that he complained bitterly of the position in which he found himself. 'Whatever I do,' he said, 'I am sure to be half ruined. If I say Not Guilty, I shall brew no more for the King; and if I say Guilty, I shall brew no more for anybody else.'

The trial then commenced, a trial which, even when coolly perused after the lapse of more than a century and a half, has all the interest of a drama. The advocates contended on both sides with far more than professional keenness and vehemence: the audience listened with as much anxiety as if the fate of every one of them was to be decided by the verdict; and the turns of fortune were so sudden and amazing that the multitude repeatedly passed in a single minute from anxiety to exultation and back again from exultation to still deeper anxiety.

The information charged the Bishops with having written or published, in the county of Middlesex, a false, malicious, and seditious libel. The Attorney and Solicitor first tried to prove the writing. For this purpose several persons were called to speak to the hands of the Bishops. But the witnesses were so unwilling that hardly a single plain answer could be extracted from any of them. Pemberton, Pollexfen, and Levinz contended that there was no evidence to go to the jury. Two of the Judges, Holloway and Powell, declared themselves of the same opinion; and the hopes of the spectators rose high. All at once the crown lawyers announced their intention to take another line. Powis, with shame and reluctance which he could not dissemble, put into the witness box Blathwayt, a Clerk of the Privy Council, who had been present when the King interrogated the Bishops. Blathwayt swore that he had heard them own their signatures. His testimony was decisive. 'Why,' said Judge Holloway to the Attorney, 'when you had such evidence, did you not produce it at first, without all this waste of time?' It soon appeared why the counsel for the crown had been unwilling, without absolute necessity, to resort to this mode of proof. Pemberton stopped Blathwayt, subjected him to a searching cross examination, and insisted upon having all that had passed between the King and the defendants fully related. 'That is a pretty thing indeed,' cried Williams. 'Do you think,' said Powis, 'that you are at liberty to ask our witnesses any impertinent question that comes into your heads?' The advocates of the Bishops were not men to be so put down. 'He is sworn,' said Pollexfen, 'to tell the truth and the whole truth: and an answer we must and will have.' The witness shuffled, equivocated, pretended to misunderstand the questions, implored the protection of the Court. But he was in hands from which it was not easy to escape. At length the Attorney again interposed. 'If,' he said, 'you persist in asking such a question, tell us, at least, what use you mean to make of it.' Pemberton, who, through the whole trial, did his duty manfully and ably, replied without hesitation; 'My Lords, I will answer Mr Attorney. I will deal plainly with the Court. If the Bishops owned this paper under a promise from His Majesty that their confession should not be used against them, I hope that no unfair advantage will be taken of them.' 'You put on His Majesty what I dare hardly name,' said Williams: 'since you will be so pressing, I demand, for the King, that the question may be recorded.' 'What do you mean, Mr Solicitor?' said Sawyer, interposing. 'I know what I mean,' said the apostate: 'I desire that the question may be recorded in Court.' 'Record what you will, I am not afraid of you, Mr Solicitor,' said Pemberton. Then came a loud and fierce altercation, which the Chief Justice could with difficulty quiet. In other circumstances, he would probably have ordered the question to be recorded and Pemberton to be committed. But on this great day he was overawed. He often cast a side glance towards the thick rows of Earls and Barons by whom he was watched, and who in the next Parliament might be his judges. He looked, a bystander said, as if all the peers present had halters in their pockets. At length Blathwayt was forced to give a full account of what had passed. It appeared that the King had entered into no express covenant with the Bishops. But it appeared also that the Bishops might not unreasonably think that there was an implied engagement. Indeed, from the unwillingness of the crown lawyers to put the Clerk of the Council into the witness box, and from the vehemence with which they objected to Pemberton's cross examination, it is plain that they were themselves of this opinion.

However, the handwriting was now proved. But a new and serious objection was raised. It was not sufficient to prove that the Bishops had written the alleged libel. It was necessary to prove also that they had written it in the county of Middlesex. And not only was it out of the power of the Attorney and Solicitor to prove this; but it was in the power of the defendants to prove the contrary. For it so happened that Sancroft had never once left the palace at Lambeth from the time when the Order in Council appeared till after the petition was in the King's hands.

The whole case for the prosecution had therefore completely broken down; and the audience, with great glee, expected a speedy acquittal.

The crown lawyers then changed their ground again, abandoned altogether the charge of writing a libel, and undertook to prove that the Bishops had published a libel in the county of Middlesex. The difficulties were great. The delivery of the petition to the King was undoubtedly, in the eye of the law, a publication. But how was this delivery to be proved? No person had been present at the audience in the royal closet, except the King and the defendants. The King could not well be sworn. It was therefore only by the admissions of the defendants that the fact of publication could be established. Blathwayt was again examined, but in vain. He well remembered, he said, that the Bishops owned their hands; but he did not remember that they owned the paper which lay on the table of the Privy Council to be the same paper which they had delivered to the King, or that they were even interrogated on that point. Several other official men who had been in attendance on the Council were called, and among them Samuel Pepys, Secretary of the Admiralty; but none of them could remember that anything was said about the delivery. It was to no purpose that Williams put leading questions till the counsel on the other side declared that such twisting, such wiredrawing, was never seen in a court of justice, and till Wright himself was forced to admit that the Solicitor's mode of examination was contrary to all rule. As witness after witness answered in the negative, roars of laughter and shouts of triumph, which the Judges did not even attempt to silence, shook the hall.

It seemed that at length this hard fight had been won. The case for the crown was closed. Had the counsel for the Bishops remained silent, an acquittal was certain; for nothing which the most corrupt and shameless Judge could venture to call legal evidence of publication had been given. The Chief Justice was beginning to charge the jury, and would undoubtedly have directed them to acquit the defendants; but Finch, too anxious to be perfectly discreet, interfered, and begged to be heard. 'If you will be heard,' said Wright, 'you shall be heard; but you do not understand your own interests.' The other counsel for the defence made Finch sit down, and begged the Chief Justice to proceed. He was about to do so when a messenger came to the Solicitor General with news that Lord Sunderland could prove the publication, and would come down to the court immediately. Wright maliciously told the counsel for the defence that they had only themselves to thank for the turn which things had taken. The countenances of the great multitude fell. Finch was, during some hours, the most unpopular man in the country. Why could he not sit still as his betters, Sawyer, Pemberton, and Pollexfen, had done? His love of meddling, his ambition to make a fine speech, had ruined everything.

Meanwhile the Lord President was brought in a sedan chair through the hall. Not a hat moved as he passed; and many voices cried out 'Popish dog.' He came into Court pale and trembling, with eyes fixed on the ground, and gave his evidence in a faltering voice. He swore that the Bishops had informed him of their intention to present a petition to the King, and that they had been admitted into the royal closet for that purpose. This circumstance, coupled with the circumstance that, after they left the closet, there was in the King's hands a petition signed by them, was such proof as might reasonably satisfy a jury of the fact of the publication.

Publication in Middlesex was then proved. But was the paper thus published a false, malicious, and seditious libel? Hitherto the matter in dispute had been whether a fact which everybody well knew to be true could be proved according to technical rules of evidence; but now the contest became one of deeper interest. It was necessary to inquire into the limits of prerogative and liberty, into the right of the King to dispense with statutes, into the right of the subject to petition for the redress of grievances. During three hours the counsel for the petitioners argued with great force in defence of the fundamental principles of the constitution, and proved from the journals of the House of Commons that the Bishops had affirmed no more than the truth when they represented to the King that the dispensing power which he claimed had been repeatedly declared illegal by Parliament. Somers rose last. He spoke little more than five minutes; but every word was full of weighty matter; and when he sat down his reputation as an orator and a constitutional lawyer was established. He went through the expressions which were used in the information to describe the offence imputed to the Bishops, and showed that every word, whether adjective or substantive, was altogether inappropriate. The offence imputed was a false, a malicious, a seditious libel. False the paper was not; for every fact which it set forth had been proved from the journals of Parliament to be true. Malicious the paper was not; for the defendants had not sought an occasion of strife, but had been placed by the government in such a situation that they must either oppose themselves to the royal will, or violate the most sacred obligations of conscience and honour. Seditious the paper was not; for it had not been scattered by the writers among the rabble, but delivered privately into the hands of the King alone: and a libel it was not, but a decent petition such as, by the laws of England, nay, by the laws of imperial Rome, by the laws of all civilised states, a subject who thinks himself aggrieved may with propriety present to the sovereign.

The Attorney replied shortly and feebly. The Solicitor spoke at great length and with great acrimony, and was often interrupted by the clamours and hisses of the audience. He went so far as to lay it down that no subject or body of subjects, except the Houses of Parliament, had a right to petition the King. The galleries were furious; and the Chief Justice himself stood aghast at the effrontery of this venal turncoat.

At length Wright proceeded to sum up the evidence. His language showed that the awe in which he stood of the government was tempered by the awe with which the audience, so numerous, so splendid, and so strongly excited, had impressed him. He said that he would give no opinion on the question of the dispensing power, that it was not necessary for him to do so, that he could not agree with much of the Solicitor's speech, that it was the right of the subject to petition, but that the particular petition before the Court was improperly worded, and was, in the contemplation of law, a libel. Allibone was of the same mind, but, in giving his opinion, showed such gross ignorance of law and history as brought on him the contempt of all who heard him. Holloway evaded the question of the dispensing power, but said that the petition seemed to him to be such as subjects who think themselves aggrieved are entitled to present, and therefore no libel. Powell took a bolder course. He avowed that, in his judgment, the Declaration of Indulgence was a nullity, and that the dispensing power, as lately exercised, was utterly inconsistent with all law. If these encroachments of prerogative were allowed, there was an end of Parliaments. The whole legislative authority would be in the King. 'That issue, gentlemen,' he said, 'I leave to God and to your consciences.'

It was dark before the jury retired to consider of their verdict. The night was a night of intense anxiety. Some letters are extant which were despatched during that period of suspense, and which have therefore an interest of a peculiar kind. 'It is very late,' wrote the Papal Nuncio; 'and the decision is not yet known. The Judges and the culprits have gone to their own homes. The jury remain together. Tomorrow we shall learn the event of this great struggle.'

The solicitor for the Bishops sat up all night with a body of servants on the stairs leading to the room where the jury was consulting. It was absolutely necessary to watch the officers who watched the doors; for those officers were supposed to be in the interest of the crown, and might, if not carefully observed, have furnished a courtly juryman with food, which would have enabled him to starve out the other eleven. Strict guard was therefore kept. Not even a candle to light a pipe was permitted to enter. Some basins of water for washing were suffered to pass at about four in the morning. The jurymen, raging with thirst, soon lapped up the whole. Great numbers of people walked the neighbouring streets till dawn. Every hour a messenger came from Whitehall to know what was passing. Voices, high in altercation, were repeatedly heard within the room: but nothing certain was known.

At first nine were for acquitting and three for convicting. Two of the minority soon gave way; but Arnold was obstinate. Thomas Austin, a country gentleman of great estate, who had paid close attention to the evidence and speeches, and had taken full notes, wished to argue the question. Arnold declined. He was not used, he doggedly said, to reasoning and debating. His conscience was not satisfied; and he should not acquit the Bishops. 'If you come to that,' said Austin, 'look at me. I am the largest and strongest of the twelve; and before I find such a petition as this a libel, here I will stay till I am no bigger than a tobacco pipe.' It was six in the morning before Arnold yielded. It was soon known that the jury were agreed: but what the verdict would be was still a secret.

At ten the Court again met. The crowd was greater than ever. The jury appeared in their box; and there was a breathless stillness.

Sir Samuel Astry spoke. 'Do you find the defendants, or any of them, guilty of the misdemeanour whereof they are impeached, or not guilty?' Sir Roger Langley answered, 'Not guilty.' As the words passed his lips, Halifax sprang up and waved his hat. At that signal, benches and galleries raised a shout. In a moment ten thousand persons, who crowded the great hall, replied with a still louder shout, which made the old oaken roof crack; and in another moment the innumerable throng without set up a third huzza, which was heard at Temple Bar. The boats which covered the Thames gave an answering cheer. A peal of gunpowder was heard on the water, and another, and another; and so, in a few moments, the glad tidings went flying past the Savoy and the Friars to London Bridge, and to the forest of masts below. As the news spread, streets and squares, marketplaces and coffeehouses, broke forth into acclamations. Yet were the acclamations less strange than the weeping. For the feelings of men had been wound up to such a point that at length the stern English nature, so little used to outward signs of emotion, gave way, and thousands sobbed aloud for very joy. Meanwhile, from the outskirts of the multitude, horsemen were spurring off to bear along all the great roads intelligence of the victory of our Church and nation. Yet not even that astounding explosion could awe the bitter and intrepid spirit of the Solicitor. Striving to make himself heard above the din, he called on the Judges to commit those who had violated, by clamour, the dignity of a court of justice. One of the rejoicing populace was seized. But the tribunal felt that it would be absurd to punish a single individual for an offence common to hundreds of thousands, and dismissed him with a gentle reprimand.

It was vain to think of passing at that moment to any other business. Indeed the roar of the multitude was such that, for half an hour, scarcely a word could be heard in court. Williams got to his coach amidst a tempest of hisses and curses. Cartwright, whose curiosity was ungovernable, had been guilty of the folly and indecency of coming to Westminster in order to hear the decision. He was recognised by his sacerdotal garb and by his corpulent figure, and was hooted through the hall. 'Take care,' said one, 'of the wolf in sheep's clothing.' 'Make room,' cried another, 'for the man with the Pope in his belly.'

The acquitted prelates took refuge from the crowd which implored their blessing in the nearest chapel where divine service was performing. Many churches were open on that morning throughout the capital; and many pious persons repaired thither. The bells of all the parishes of the City and Liberties were ringing. The jury meanwhile could scarcely make their way out of the hall. They were forced to shake hands with hundreds. 'God bless you,' cried the people; 'God prosper your families; you have done like honest good-natured gentlemen; you have saved us all today.' As the noblemen who had appeared to support the good cause drove off, they flung from their carriage windows handfuls of money, and bade the crowd drink to the health of the King, the Bishops, and the jury.

The Attorney went with the tidings to Sunderland, who happened to be conversing with the Nuncio. 'Never,' said Powis, 'within man's memory, have there been such shouts and such tears of joy as today.' The King had that morning visited the camp on Hounslow Heath. Sunderland instantly sent a courier thither with the news. James was in Lord Feversham's tent when the express arrived. He was greatly disturbed, and exclaimed in French, 'So much the worse for them.' He soon set out for London. While he was present, respect prevented the soldiers from giving a loose to their feelings; but he had scarcely quitted the camp when he heard a great shouting behind him. He was surprised, and asked what that uproar meant. 'Nothing,' was the answer: 'the soldiers are glad that the Bishops are acquitted.'

'Do you call that nothing?' said James. And then he repeated, 'So much the worse for them.'

He might well be out of temper. His defeat had been complete and most humiliating. Had the prelates escaped on account of some technical defect in the case for the crown, had they escaped because they had not written the petition in Middlesex, or because it was impossible to prove, according to the strict rules of law, that they had delivered to the King the paper for which they were called in question, the prerogative would have suffered no shock. Happily for the country, the fact of publication had been fully established. The counsel for the defence had therefore been forced to attack the dispensing power. They had attacked it with great learning, eloquence, and boldness. The advocates of the government had been by universal acknowledgment overmatched in the contest. Not a single Judge had ventured to declare that the Declaration of Indulgence was legal. One Judge had in the strongest terms pronounced it illegal. The language of the whole town was that the dispensing power had received a fatal blow. Finch, who had the day before been universally reviled, was now universally applauded. He had been unwilling, it was said, to let the case be decided in a way which would have left the great constitutional question still doubtful. He had felt that a verdict which should acquit his clients, without condemning the Declaration of Indulgence, would be but half a victory. It is certain that Finch deserved neither the reproaches which had been cast on him while the event was doubtful, nor the praises which he received when it had proved happy. It was absurd to blame him because, during the short delay which he occasioned, the crown lawyers unexpectedly discovered new evidence. It was equally absurd to suppose that he deliberately exposed his clients to risk, in order to establish a general principle: and still more absurd was it to praise him for what would have been a gross violation of professional duty.

That joyful day was followed by a not less joyful night. The Bishops, and some of their most respectable friends, in vain exerted themselves to prevent tumultuous demonstrations of joy. Never within the memory of the oldest, not even on that evening on which it was known through London that the army of Scotland had declared for a free Parliament,[7] had the streets been in such a glare with bonfires. Round every bonfire crowds were drinking good health to the Bishops and confusion to the Papists. The windows were lighted with rows of candles. Each row consisted of seven; and the taper in the centre, which was taller than the rest, represented the Primate. The noise of rockets, squibs, and firearms was incessant. One huge pile of faggots blazed right in front of the great gate of Whitehall. Others were lighted before the doors of Roman Catholic Peers. Lord Arundell of Wardour wisely quieted the mob with a little money: but at Salisbury House in the Strand an attempt at resistance was made. Lord Salisbury's servants sallied out and fired: but they killed only the unfortunate beadle of the parish, who had come thither to put out the fire; and they were soon routed and driven back into the house.[8]

None of the spectacles of that night interested the common people so much as one with which they had, a few years before, been familiar, and which they now, after a long interval, enjoyed once more, the burning of the Pope. This once familiar pageant is known to our generation only by descriptions and engravings. A figure, by no means resembling those rude representations of Guy Fawkes which are still paraded on the fifth of November, but made of wax with some skill, and adorned at no small expense with robes and a tiara, was mounted on a chair resembling that in which the Bishops of Rome are still, on some great festivals, borne through Saint Peter's Church to the high altar. His Holiness was generally accompanied by a train of Cardinals and Jesuits. At his ear stood a buffoon disguised as a devil with horns and tail. No rich and zealous Protestant grudged his guinea on such an occasion, and, if rumour could be trusted, the cost of the procession was sometimes not less than a thousand pounds. After the Pope had been borne some time in state over the heads of the multitude, he was committed to the flames with loud acclama-

[7. 'The army of Scotland' is General Monck's English army, brought to London from Scotland in 1659. Monck's declaration for 'a free Parliament' ensured the Restoration of Charles II.]

[8. James Cecil, fourth Earl of Salisbury, had recently become a convert to Catholicism.]

tions. In the time of the popularity of Oates and Shaftesbury this show was exhibited annually in Fleet Street before the windows of the Whig Club on the anniversary of the birth of Queen Elizabeth. Such was the celebrity of these grotesque rites, that Barillon once risked his life in order to peep at them from a hiding place. But, from the day when the Rye House Plot was discovered, till the day of the acquittal of the Bishops, the ceremony had been disused. Now, however, several Popes made their appearance in different parts of London. The Nuncio was much shocked; and the King was more hurt by this insult to his Church than by all the other affronts which he had received. The magistrates, however, could do nothing. The Sunday had dawned, and the bells of the parish churches were ringing for early prayers, before the fires began to languish and the crowds to disperse. A proclamation was speedily put forth against the rioters. Many of them, mostly young apprentices, were apprehended; but the bills were thrown out at the Middlesex sessions. The magistrates, many of whom were Roman Catholics, expostulated with the grand jury and sent them three or four times back, but to no purpose.

Meanwhile the glad tidings were flying to every part of the kingdom, and were everywhere received with rapture. Gloucester, Bedford, and Lichfield were among the places which were distinguished by peculiar zeal: but Bristol and Norwich, which stood nearest to London in population and wealth, approached nearest to London in enthusiasm on this joyful occasion.

The prosecution of the Bishops is an event which stands by itself in our history. It was the first and the last occasion on which two feelings of tremendous potency, two feelings which have generally been opposed to each other, and either of which, when strongly excited, has sufficed to convulse the state, were united in perfect harmony. Those feelings were love of the Church and love of freedom. During many generations every violent outbreak of High Church feeling, with one exception, has been unfavourable to civil liberty; every violent outbreak of zeal for liberty, with one exception, has been unfavourable to the authority and influence of the prelacy and the priesthood. In 1688 the cause of the hierarchy was for a moment that of the popular party. More than nine thousand clergymen, with the Primate and his most re-

spectable suffragans at their head, offered themselves to endure
bonds and the spoiling of their goods for the great fundamental
principle of our free constitution. The effect was a coalition
which included the most zealous Cavaliers, the most zealous
Republicans, and all the intermediate sections of the community.
The spirit which had supported Hampden in the preceding generation, the spirit which, in the succeeding generation, supported
Sacheverell, combined to support the Archbishop who was
Hampden and Sacheverell in one. Those classes of society which
are most deeply interested in the preservation of order, which in
troubled times are generally most ready to strengthen the hands
of government, and which have a natural antipathy to agitators,
followed, without scruple, the guidance of a venerable man, the
first peer of the realm, the first minister of the Church, a Tory in
politics, a saint in manners, whom tyranny had in his own des-
pite turned into a demagogue. Those, on the other hand, who
had always abhorred episcopacy, as a relic of Popery, and as an
instrument of arbitrary power, now asked on bended knees the
blessing of a prelate who was ready to wear fetters and to lay his
aged limbs on bare stones rather than betray the interests of the
Protestant religion and set the prerogative above the laws. With
love of the Church and with love of freedom was mingled, at this
great crisis, a third feeling which is among the most honourable
peculiarities of our national character. An individual oppressed
by power, even when destitute of all claim to public respect and
gratitude, generally finds strong sympathy among us. Thus, in
the time of our grandfathers, society was thrown into confusion
by the persecution of Wilkes. We have ourselves seen the nation
roused almost to madness by the wrongs of Queen Caroline. It is
probable, therefore, that, even if no great political and religious
interests had been staked on the event of the proceeding against
the Bishops, England would not have seen, without strong emotions of pity and anger, old men of stainless virtue pursued by the
vengeance of a harsh and inexorable prince who owed to their
fidelity the crown which he wore.

Actuated by these sentiments our ancestors arrayed themselves
against the government in one huge and compact mass. All ranks,
all parties, all Protestant sects, made up that vast phalanx. In the

van were the Lords Spiritual and Temporal. Then came the landed gentry and the clergy, both the Universities, all the Inns of Court, merchants, shopkeepers, farmers, the porters who plied in the streets of the great towns, the peasants who ploughed the fields. The league against the King included the very foremast men who manned his ships, the very sentinels who guarded his palace. The names of Whig and Tory were for a moment forgotten. The old Exclusionist took the old Abhorrer[9] by the hand. Episcopalians, Presbyterians, Independents, Baptists, forgot their long feuds, and remembered only their common Protestantism and their common danger. Divines bred in the school of Laud talked loudly, not only of toleration, but of comprehension. The Archbishop soon after his acquittal put forth a pastoral letter which is one of the most remarkable compositions of that age. He had, from his youth up, been at war with the Nonconformists, and had repeatedly assailed them with unjust and unchristian asperity. His principal work was a hideous caricature of the Calvinistic theology.[10] He had drawn up for the thirtieth of January and for the twenty-ninth of May forms of prayer which reflected on the Puritans in language so strong that the government had thought fit to soften it down. But now his heart was melted and opened. He solemnly enjoined the Bishops and clergy to have a very tender regard to their brethren the Protestant Dissenters, to visit them often, to entertain them hospitably, to discourse with them civilly, to persuade them, if it might be, to conform to the Church, but, if that were found impossible, to join them heartily and affectionately in exertions for the blessed cause of the Reformation.

Many pious persons in subsequent years remembered that time with bitter regret. They described it as a short glimpse of a golden age between two iron ages. Such lamentation, though natural, was not reasonable. The coalition of 1688 was produced, and could be produced, only by tyranny which approached to insanity, and by danger which threatened at once all the great institutions of the country. If there has never since been similar

[9. The 'Abhorrers' were the supporters of the Court who, in 1679, had declared their 'abhorrence' of the extreme whig faction, the 'Petitioners'.]

10. *Fur Praedestinatus* [1651; but almost certainly not by Sancroft.]

union, the reason is that there has never since been similar mis-government. It must be remembered that, though concord is in itself better than discord, discord may indicate a better state of things than is indicated by concord. Calamity and peril often force men to combine. Prosperity and security often encourage them to separate.

II

James II's Irish Army

[*With the acquittal of the Seven Bishops it was clear that James II could not rely on any party in England. The whigs had always been his enemies. He had now alienated the tories. He had lost the Church without gaining the Dissenters. Meanwhile the opposition was being organized. On the very day on which the bishops were acquitted, seven English magnates – including both whigs and tories – had explicitly but secretly invited William of Orange to follow Monmouth's example and invade England with an army. Although James did not yet know this, he felt the insecurity of his position. If he was to defend it, he needed a reserve force. It is true, he had already supplied himself with such a reserve: in 1686 he had formed a camp on Hounslow Heath and had stationed there an army of thirteen thousand men: horse, foot, and artillery. But, in the two years which followed, this army had gradually lost its usefulness. It became, says Macaulay, 'merely a gay suburb of London. The King, as was amply proved two years later, had gravely miscalculated. He had forgotten that vicinity operates in more ways than one. He had hoped that his army would overawe London; but the result of his policy was that the feelings and opinions of London took complete possession of his army.' When this became clear, James decided, once again, to appeal from Protestant England to Catholic Ireland. In Chapter IX, Macaulay describes the effects of this decision.*]

THE army was scarcely less disaffected than the clergy or the gentry. The garrison of the Tower had drunk the health of the imprisoned Bishops. The footguards stationed at Lambeth had, with every mark of reverence, welcomed the Primate back to his palace. Nowhere had the news of the acquittal been received with more clamorous delight than at Hounslow Heath. In truth, the great force which the King had assembled for the purpose of overawing his mutinous capital had become more mutinous than the capital itself, and was more dreaded by the court than by the citizens. Early in August, therefore, the camp was broken up, and the troops were sent to quarters in different parts of the country.

James flattered himself that it would be easier to deal with separate battalions than with many thousands of men collected in one mass. The first experiment was tried on Lord Lichfield's regiment of infantry, now called the Twelfth of the Line. That regiment was probably selected because it had been raised, at the time of the Western insurrection, in Staffordshire, a province where the Roman Catholics were more numerous and powerful than in almost any other part of England. The men were drawn up in the King's presence. Their major informed them that His Majesty wished them to subscribe an engagement, binding them to assist in carrying into effect his intentions concerning the test, and that all who did not choose to comply must quit the service on the spot. To the King's great astonishment, whole ranks instantly laid down their pikes and muskets. Only two officers and a few privates, all Roman Catholics, obeyed his command. He remained silent for a short time. Then he bade the men take up their arms. 'Another time,' he said, with a gloomy look, 'I shall not do you the honour to consult you.'

It was plain that, if he determined to persist in his designs, he must remodel his army. Yet materials for that purpose he could not find in our island. The members of his Church, even in the districts where they were most numerous, were a small minority of the people. Hatred of Popery had spread through all classes of his Protestant subjects, and had become the ruling passion even of ploughmen and artisans. But there was another part of his dominions where a very different spirit animated the great body of the population. There was no limit to the number of Roman Catholic soldiers whom the good pay and quarters of England would attract across St George's Channel. Tyrconnel had been, during some time, employed in forming out of the peasantry of his country a military force on which his master might depend. Already Papists, of Celtic blood and speech, composed almost the whole army of Ireland. Barillon earnestly and repeatedly advised James to bring over that army for the purpose of coercing the English.

James wavered. He wished to be surrounded by troops on whom he could rely: but he dreaded the explosion of national feeling which the appearance of a great Irish force on English ground must produce. At last, as usually happens when a weak man tries to avoid opposite inconveniences, he took a course which united them all. He brought over Irishmen, not indeed enough to hold down the single city of London, or the single county of York, but more than enough to excite the alarm and rage of the whole kingdom, from Northumberland to Cornwall. Battalion after battalion, raised and trained by Tyrconnel, landed on the western coast and moved towards the capital; and Irish recruits were imported in considerable numbers, to fill up vacancies in the English regiments.

Of the many errors which James committed, none was more fatal than this. Already he had alienated the hearts of his people by violating their laws, confiscating their estates, and persecuting their religion. Of those who had once been most zealous for monarchy, he had already made many rebels in heart. Yet he might still, with some chance of success, have appealed to the patriotic spirit of his subjects against an invader. For they were a race insular in temper as well as in geographical position. Their national antipathies were, indeed, in that age, unreasonably and unamiably strong. Never had the English been accustomed to the control or interference of any stranger. The appearance of a foreign army on their soil might impel them to rally even round a King whom they had no reason to love. William might perhaps have been unable to overcome this difficulty; but James removed it. Not even the arrival of a brigade of Lewis's musketeers would have excited such resentment and shame as our ancestors felt when they saw armed columns of Papists, just arrived from Dublin, moving in military pomp along the high roads.

No man of English blood then regarded the aboriginal Irish as his countrymen. They did not belong to our branch of the great human family. They were distinguished from us by more than one moral and intellectual peculiarity, which the difference of situation and of education, great as that difference was, did not seem altogether to explain. They had an aspect of their own, a mother tongue of their own. When they talked English their pro-

nunciation was ludicrous; their phraseology was grotesque, as is
always the phraseology of those who think in one language and
express their thoughts in another. They were therefore foreigners; and of all foreigners they were the most hated and despised:
the most hated, for they had, during five centuries, always been
our enemies; the most despised, for they were our vanquished,
enslaved, and despoiled enemies. The Englishman compared
with pride his own fields with the desolate bogs whence the Rapparees issued forth to rob and murder, and his own dwelling
with the hovels where the peasants and the hogs of the Shannon
wallowed in filth together. He was a member of a society far inferior, indeed, in wealth and civilisation, to the society in which
we live, but still one of the wealthiest and most highly civilised
societies that the world had then seen: the Irish were almost as
rude as the savages of Labrador. He was a freeman: the Irish
were the hereditary serfs of his race. He worshipped God after a
pure and rational fashion: the Irish were sunk in idolatry and
superstition. He knew that great numbers of Irish had repeatedly
fled before a small English force, and that the whole Irish population had been held down by a small English colony; and he very
complacently inferred that he was naturally a being of a higher
order than the Irishman: for it is thus that a dominant race always explains its ascendency and excuses its tyranny. That in
vivacity, humour, and eloquence, the Irish stand high among the
nations of the world is now universally acknowledged. That,
when well disciplined, they are excellent soldiers has been proved
on a hundred fields of battle. Yet it is certain that, a century and
a half ago, they were generally despised in our island as both a
stupid and a cowardly people. And these were the men who were
to hold England down by main force while her civil and ecclesiastical constitution was destroyed. The blood of the whole nation
boiled at the thought. To be conquered by Frenchmen or by
Spaniards would have seemed comparatively a tolerable fate.
With Frenchmen and Spaniards we had been accustomed to
treat on equal terms. We had sometimes envied their prosperity,
sometimes dreaded their power, sometimes congratulated ourselves on their friendship. In spite of our unsocial pride, we admitted that they were great nations, and that they could boast of

men eminent in the arts of war and peace. But to be subjugated by an inferior caste was a degradation beyond all other degradation. The English felt as the white inhabitants of Charleston and New Orleans would feel if those towns were occupied by negro garrisons.

The real facts would have been sufficient to excite uneasiness and indignation: but the real facts were lost amidst a crowd of wild rumours which flew without ceasing from coffeehouse to coffeehouse and from ale-bench to ale-bench, and became more wonderful and terrible at every stage of the progress. The number of the Irish troops who had landed on our shores might justly excite serious apprehensions as to the King's ulterior designs; but it was magnified tenfold by the public apprehensions. It may well be supposed that the rude kerne of Connaught, placed, with arms in his hands, among a foreign people whom he hated, and by whom he was hated in turn, was guilty of some excesses. These excesses were exaggerated by report; and, in addition to the outrages which the stranger had really committed, all the offences of his English comrades were set down to his account. From every corner of the kingdom a cry arose against the foreign barbarians who forced themselves into private houses, seized horses and waggons, extorted money and insulted women. These men, it was said, were the sons of those who, forty-seven years before, had massacred Protestants by tens of thousands. The history of the rebellion of 1641, a history which, even when soberly related, might well move pity and horror, and which had been frightfully distorted by national and religious antipathies, was now the favourite topic of conversation. Hideous stories of houses burned with all the inmates, of women and young children butchered, of near relations compelled by torture to be the murderers of each other, of corpses outraged and mutilated, were told and heard with full belief and intense interest. Then it was added that the dastardly savages who had by surprise committed all these cruelties on an unsuspecting and defenceless colony had, as soon as Oliver came among them on his great mission of vengeance, flung down their arms in panic terror, and had sunk, without trying the chances of a single pitched field, into that slavery which was their fit portion. Many signs indicated that another great spoliation and slaughter of the Saxon settlers was meditated by the Lord Lieutenant. Already thousands of Protestant colonists, flying from the injustice and insolence of Tyrconnel, had raised the indignation of the mother country by describing all that they had suffered, and all that they had, with too much reason, feared. How much the public mind had been excited by the complaints of these fugitives had recently been shown in a manner not to be mistaken. Tyrconnel had transmitted for the royal approbation the heads of a bill repealing the law by which half the soil of Ireland was held, and he had sent to Westminster, as his agents, two of his Roman Catholic countrymen who had lately been raised to high judicial office; Nugent, Chief Justice of the Irish Court of King's Bench, a personification of all the vices and weaknesses which the English then imagined to be characteristic of the Popish Celt, and Rice, a Baron of the Irish Exchequer, who, in abilities and attainments, was perhaps the foremost man of his race and religion. The object of the mission was well known; and the two Judges could not venture to show themselves in the streets. If ever they were recognised, the rabble shouted, 'Room for the Irish Ambassadors;' and their coach was escorted with mock solemnity by a train of ushers and harbingers bearing sticks with potatoes stuck on the points.

So strong and general, indeed, was at that time the aversion of the English to the Irish that the most distinguished Roman Catholics partook of it. Powis and Bellasyse expressed, in coarse and acrimonious language, even at the Council board, their antipathy to the aliens. Among English Protestants that antipathy was still stronger: and perhaps it was strongest in the army. Neither officers nor soldiers were disposed to bear patiently the preference shown by their master to a foreign and a subject race. The Duke of Berwick, who was Colonel of the Eighth Regiment of the Line, then quartered at Portsmouth, gave orders that thirty men just arrived from Ireland should be enlisted. The English soldiers declared that they would not serve with these intruders. John Beaumont, the Lieutenant Colonel, in his own name and in the name of five of the Captains, protested to the Duke's face against this insult to the English army and nation. 'We raised the regiment,' he said, 'at our own charges to defend His Majesty's crown in a time of danger. We had then no difficulty in procuring hundreds of English recruits. We can easily keep every company up to its full complement without admitting Irishmen. We therefore do not think it consistent with our honour to have these strangers forced on us; and we beg that we may either be permitted to command men of our own nation or to lay down our commissions.' Berwick sent to Windsor for directions. The King, greatly exasperated, instantly despatched a troop of horse to Portsmouth with orders to bring the six refractory officers before him. A council of war sat on them. They refused to make any submission; and they were sentenced to be cashiered, the highest punishment which a court martial was then competent to inflict. The whole nation applauded the disgraced officers; and the prevailing sentiment was stimulated by an unfounded rumour that, while under arrest, they had been treated with cruelty.

Public feeling did not then manifest itself by those signs with which we are familiar, by large meetings, and by vehement harangues. Nevertheless it found a vent. Thomas Wharton, who, in the last Parliament, had represented Buckinghamshire, and who was already conspicuous both as a libertine and as a Whig, had written a satirical ballad on the administration of Tyrconnel. In this little poem an Irishman congratulates a brother Irishman, in a barbarous jargon, on the approaching triumph of Popery and of the Milesian race. The Protestant heir will be excluded. The Protestant officers will be broken. The Great Charter and the praters who appeal to it will be hanged in one rope. The good Talbot will shower commissions on his countrymen, and will cut the throats of the English. These verses, which were in no respect above the ordinary standard of street poetry, had for burden some gibberish which was said to have been used as a watchword by the insurgents of Ulster in 1641. The verses and the tune caught the fancy of the nation. From one end of England to the other all classes were constantly singing this idle rhyme. It was especially the delight of the English army. More than seventy years after the Revolution, a great writer delineated, with exquisite skill, a veteran who had fought at the Boyne and at Namur. One of the characteristics of the good old soldier is his trick of whistling 'Lillibullero.'

Wharton afterwards boasted that he had sung a King out of three kingdoms. But in truth the success of 'Lillibullero' was the effect, and not the cause, of that excited state of public feeling which produced the Revolution.

12

The Arrival of the Prince of Orange

[*Meanwhile William was preparing the invasion to which he had been invited by the English malcontents, and which, to him, was part of the European war against France. The enterprise was of great difficulty. The fiasco of Monmouth's expedition had shown that it was unsafe to rely merely on English exiles and an English army to be raised on landing. A professional army was needed. But a Dutch army might be difficult to raise and impossible to transport, since the form of government in the United Provinces of the Netherlands gave any province the right of veto. Such a veto might be used either by the powerful city of Amsterdam, which was traditionally opposed both to the House of Orange and to the war with France, or by other Dutch cities, unwilling to denude Holland of troops and so to expose it to French attack. Moreover, a foreign army, even if it could be brought to England, might well rouse English nationalism against it. However, these difficulties were partly removed by Louis XIV himself, whose religious and economic policy alienated the city of Amsterdam and whose sudden invasion of the Palatinate, in the Rhineland, removed the threat from the Netherlands. Thereupon the States-General of the Netherlands, in secret session, approved William's expedition. In England, too, the supporters of William increased. Even Sunderland reinsured himself by a message of support. Churchill, whose help could be invaluable since he controlled both the English army and the mind of James's daughter, the Princess Anne, promised his help. (But even on this occasion, Macaulay refuses him any credit: Churchill's letter, he says, was written 'with a certain elevation of language, which was the sure mark that he was going to commit a baseness', etc., etc.)*

Thus encouraged, William raised his army. As his second-in-command he appointed a famous Protestant soldier, the septuagenarian Frederick Count Schomberg, who had been a Marshal of France under Louis XIV till forced by his religion to give up his command. The command of the English and Scottish forces was

*given to Hugh Mackay, general of the Scottish brigade in the Dutch
service. He was afterwards to be William's commander in Scotland.
An Englishman, Arthur Herbert, afterwards Earl of Torrington,
commanded the invading fleet. William also took with him two
Scottish émigré clergymen: the Episcopalian Gilbert Burnet and the
Presbyterian William Carstares, who were to be his advisers on the
ecclesiastical affairs of England and Scotland respectively. Burnet
also assisted him in drawing up a Declaration, in English, to justify
his invasion. Thus equipped, he prepared his descent upon England.
He intended to land in Yorkshire, where his English allies had prepared for his reception.*

*James, in apprehension, now offered belated concessions to the
tories, whom he had affronted, and dismissed Sunderland, whom he
could no longer trust. He appointed Lord Preston to succeed Sunderland as Lord President of the Council, and collected a fleet, under
Lord Dartmouth, in the Thames estuary, in order to stop William's
passage.*

*The following passage, from Chapter IX, describes William's
journey and arrival in England.*]

ON the sixteenth of October, according to the English reckoning,
was held a solemn sitting of the States of Holland. The Prince
came to bid them farewell. He thanked them for the kindness
with which they had watched over him when he was left an
orphan child, for the confidence which they had reposed in him
during his administration, and for the assistance which they had
granted to him at this momentous crisis. He entreated them to
believe that he had always meant and endeavoured to promote
the interest of his country. He was now quitting them, perhaps
never to return. If he should fall in defence of the reformed
religion and of the independence of Europe, he commended his
beloved wife to their care. The Grand Pensionary answered in a
faltering voice; and in all that grave senate there was none who
could refrain from shedding tears. But the iron stoicism of William never gave way; and he stood among his weeping friends
calm and austere as if he had been about to leave them only for a
short visit to his hunting grounds at Loo.

The deputies of the principal towns accompanied him to his

yacht. Even the representatives of Amsterdam, so long the chief seat of opposition to his administration, joined in paying him this compliment. Public prayers were offered for him on that day in all the churches of the Hague.

In the evening he arrived at Helvoetsluys and went on board of a frigate called the *Brill*. His flag was immediately hoisted. It displayed the arms of Nassau quartered with those of England. The motto, embroidered in letters three feet long, was happily chosen. The House of Orange had long used the elliptical device, 'I will maintain.' The ellipsis was now filled up with words of high import: 'the liberties of England and the Protestant religion.'

The Prince had not been many hours on board when the wind became fair. On the nineteenth the armament put to sea, and traversed, before a strong breeze, about half the distance between the Dutch and English coasts. Then the wind changed, blew hard from the west, and swelled into a violent tempest. The ships, scattered and in great distress, regained the shore of Holland as they best might. The *Brill* reached Helvoetsluys on the twenty-first. The Prince's fellow passengers had observed with admiration that neither peril nor mortification had for one moment disturbed his composure. He now, though suffering from seasickness, refused to go on shore: for he conceived that, by remaining on board, he should in the most effectual manner notify to Europe that the late misfortune had only delayed for a very short time the execution of his purpose. In two or three days the fleet reassembled. One vessel only had been cast away. Not a single soldier or sailor was missing. Some horses had perished: but this loss the Prince with great expedition repaired; and, before the *London Gazette* had spread the news of his mishap, he was again ready to sail.

His Declaration preceded him only by a few hours. On the first of November it began to be mentioned in mysterious whispers by the politicians of London, was passed secretly from man to man, and was slipped into the boxes of the post office. One of the agents was arrested, and the packets of which he was in charge were carried to Whitehall. The King read, and was greatly troubled. His first impulse was to hide the paper from all human

eyes. He threw into the fire every copy which had been brought
to him, except one; and that one he would scarcely trust out of
his own hands.

The paragraph in the manifesto which disturbed him most was
that in which it was said that some of the Peers, Spiritual and
Temporal, had invited the Prince of Orange to invade England.
Halifax, Clarendon, and Nottingham were then in London. They
were immediately summoned to the palace and interrogated.
Halifax, though conscious of innocence, refused at first to make
any answer. 'Your Majesty asks me,' said he, 'whether I have
committed high treason. If I am suspected, let me be brought
before my peers. And how can your Majesty place any dependence on the answer of a culprit whose life is at stake? Even if I
had invited His Highness over, I should without scruple plead
Not Guilty.' The King declared that he did not at all consider
Halifax as a culprit, and that he had asked the question as one
gentleman asks another who has been calumniated whether there
be the least foundation for the calumny. 'In that case,' said
Halifax, 'I have no objection to aver, as a gentleman speaking to
a gentleman, on my honour, which is as sacred as my oath, that I
have not invited the Prince of Orange over.' Clarendon and Nottingham said the same.

The King was still more anxious to ascertain the temper of the
prelates. If they were hostile to him, his throne was indeed in
danger. But it could not be. There was something monstrous in
the supposition that any Bishop of the Church of England could
rebel against his Sovereign. Compton[1] was called into the royal
closet, and was asked whether he believed that there was the
slightest ground for the Prince's assertion. The Bishop was in a
strait; for he was himself one of the seven who had signed the invitation; and his conscience, not a very enlightened conscience,

[1. Henry Compton, son of the Earl of Northampton, was Bishop of
London, and a strong Protestant. He had been tutor to James II's daughters,
Mary and Anne, and it was largely through his influence that they both
resisted their father's Catholic policy. For his own opposition to that policy,
Compton had been suspended from his episcopal functions by the Court of
High Commission in 1686. He was thus not one of the Seven Bishops; but
he was one of the seven magnates who issued the first formal invitation to
William.]

would not suffer him, it seems, to utter a direct falsehood. 'Sir,' he said, 'I am quite confident that there is not one of my brethren who is not as guiltless as myself in this matter.' The equivocation was ingenious: but whether the difference between the sin of such an equivocation and the sin of a lie be worth any expense of ingenuity may perhaps be doubted. The King was satisfied. 'I fully acquit you all,' he said. 'But I think it necessary that you should publicly contradict the slanderous charge brought against you in the Prince's declaration.' The Bishop very naturally begged that he might be allowed to read the paper which he was required to contradict; but the King would not suffer him to look at it.

On the following day appeared a proclamation threatening with the severest punishment all who should circulate, or who should even dare to read, William's manifesto. The Primate and the few Spiritual Peers who happened to be then in London had orders to wait upon the King. Preston was in attendance with the Prince's Declaration in his hand. 'My Lords,' said James, 'listen to this passage. It concerns you.' Preston then read the sentence in which the Spiritual Peers were mentioned. The King proceeded: 'I do not believe one word of this: I am satisfied of your innocence; but I think it fit to let you know of what you are accused.'

The Primate, with many dutiful expressions, protested that the King did him no more than justice. 'I was born in your Majesty's allegiance. I have repeatedly confirmed that allegiance by my oath. I can have but one King at one time. I have not invited the Prince over; and I do not believe that a single one of my brethren has done so.' 'I am sure I have not,' said Crewe of Durham. 'Nor I,' said Cartwright of Chester. Crewe and Cartwright might well be believed; for both had sat in the Ecclesiastical Commission. When Compton's turn came, he parried the question with an adroitness which a Jesuit might have envied. 'I gave your Majesty my answer yesterday.'

James repeated again and again that he fully acquitted them all. Nevertheless it would, in his judgment, be for his service and for their own honour that they should publicly vindicate themselves. He therefore required them to draw up a paper setting forth their abhorrence of the Prince's design. They remained silent: their silence was supposed to imply consent; and they were suffered to withdraw.

Meanwhile the fleet of William was on the German Ocean. It was on the evening of Thursday the first of November that he put to sea the second time. The wind blew fresh from the east. The armament, during twelve hours, held a course towards the north west. The light vessels sent out by the English Admiral for the purpose of obtaining intelligence brought back news which confirmed the prevailing opinion that the enemy would try to land in Yorkshire. All at once, on a signal from the Prince's ship, the whole fleet tacked, and made sail for the British Channel. The same breeze which favoured the voyage of the invaders prevented Dartmouth from coming out of the Thames. His ships were forced to strike yards and topmasts; and two of his frigates, which had gained the open sea, were shattered by the violence of the weather and driven back into the river.

The Dutch fleet ran fast before the gale, and reached the Straits at about ten in the morning of Saturday the third of November. William himself, in the *Brill*, led the way. More than six hundred vessels, with canvas spread to a favourable wind, followed in his train. The transports were in the centre. The men of war, more than fifty in number, formed an outer rampart. Herbert, with the title of Lieutenant Admiral General, commanded the whole fleet. His post was in the rear, and many English sailors, inflamed against Popery, and attracted by high pay, served under him. It was not without great difficulty that the Prince had prevailed on some Dutch officers of high reputation to submit to the authority of a stranger. But the arrangement was eminently judicious. There was, in the King's fleet, much discontent and an ardent zeal for the Protestant faith. But within the memory of old mariners the Dutch and English navies had thrice, with heroic spirit and various fortune, contended for the empire of the sea. Our sailors had not forgotten the broom with which Tromp had threatened to sweep the Channel, or the fire which De Ruyter had lighted in the dockyards of the Medway. Had the rival nations been once more brought face to face on the element of which both claimed the sovereignty, all other thoughts might have given place to mutual animosity. A bloody and obstinate battle might have been fought. Defeat would have been fatal to William's enterprise. Even victory would have deranged all his deeply meditated schemes of policy. He therefore wisely determined that the pursuers, if they overtook him, should be hailed in their own mother tongue, and adjured, by an admiral under whom they had served, and whom they esteemed, not to fight against old messmates for Popish tyranny. Such an appeal might possibly avert a conflict. If a conflict took place, one English commander would be opposed to another; nor would the pride of the islanders be wounded by learning that Dartmouth had been compelled to strike to Herbert.

Happily William's precautions were not necessary. Soon after midday he passed the Straits. His fleet spread to within a league of Dover on the north and of Calais on the south. The men of war on the extreme right and left saluted both fortresses at once. The troops appeared under arms on the decks. The flourish of trumpets, the clash of cymbals, and the rolling of drums were distinctly heard at once on the English and French shores. An innumerable company of gazers blackened the white beach of Kent. Another mighty multitude covered the coast of Picardy. Rapin de Thoyras,[2] who, driven by persecution from his country, had taken service in the Dutch army and accompanied the Prince to England, described the spectacle, many years later, as the most magnificent and affecting that was ever seen by human eyes. At sunset the armament was off Beachy Head. Then the lights were kindled. The sea was in a blaze for many miles. But the eyes of all the steersmen were fixed throughout the night on three huge lanterns which flamed on the stern of the *Brill*.

Meanwhile a courier had been riding post from Dover Castle to Whitehall with news that the Dutch had passed the Straits and were steering westward. It was necessary to make an immediate change in all the military arrangements. Messengers were despatched in every direction. Officers were roused from their beds at dead of night. At three on the Sunday morning there was a great muster by torchlight in Hyde Park. The King had sent

[2. Paul de Rapin Thoyras, a Huguenot, afterwards wrote, in French, the first complete history of England. See Introduction, p. 10.]

several regiments northward in the expectation that William would land in Yorkshire. Expresses were despatched to recall them. All the forces except those which were necessary to keep the peace of the capital were ordered to move to the west. Salisbury was appointed as the place of rendezvous: but, as it was thought possible that Portsmouth might be the first point of attack, three battalions of guards and a strong body of cavalry set out for that fortress. In a few hours it was known that Portsmouth was safe; and those troops received orders to change their route and to hasten to Salisbury.

When Sunday the fourth of November dawned, the cliffs of the Isle of Wight were full in view of the Dutch armament. That day was the anniversary both of William's birth and of his marriage. Sail was slackened during part of the morning; and divine service was performed on board of the ships. In the afternoon and through the night the fleet held on its course. Torbay was the place where the Prince intended to land. But the morning of Monday the fifth of November was hazy. The pilot of the *Brill* could not discern the sea marks, and carried the fleet too far to the west. The danger was great. To return in the face of the wind was impossible. Plymouth was the next port. But at Plymouth a garrison had been posted under the command of Lord Bath. The landing might be opposed; and a check might produce serious consequences. There could be little doubt, moreover, that by this time the royal fleet had got out of the Thames and was hastening full sail down the Channel. Russell saw the whole extent of the peril, and exclaimed to Burnet, 'You may go to prayers, Doctor. All is over.' At that moment the wind changed: a soft breeze sprang up from the south: the mist dispersed; the sun shone forth; and, under the mild light of an autumnal noon, the fleet turned back, passed round the lofty cape of Berry Head, and rode safe in the harbour of Torbay.

Since William looked on that harbour its aspect has greatly changed. The amphitheatre which surrounds the spacious basin now exhibits everywhere the signs of prosperity and civilisation. At the northeastern extremity has sprung up a great watering place, to which strangers are attracted from the most remote parts of our island by the Italian softness of the air; for in that climate the myrtle flourishes unsheltered; and even the winter is milder than the Northumbrian April. The inhabitants are about ten thousand in number. The newly built churches and chapels, the baths and libraries, the hotels and public gardens, the infirmary and the museum, the white streets, rising terrace above terrace, the gay villas peeping from the midst of shrubberies and flower beds, present a spectacle widely different from any that in the seventeenth century England could show. At the opposite end of the bay lies, sheltered by Berry Head, the stirring market town of Brixham, the wealthiest seat of our fishing trade. A pier and a haven were formed there at the beginning of the present century, but have been found insufficient for the increasing traffic. The population is about six thousand souls. The shipping amounts to more than two hundred sails. The tonnage exceeds many times the tonnage of the port of Liverpool under the Kings of the House of Stuart. But Torbay, when the Dutch fleet cast anchor there, was known only as a haven where ships sometimes took refuge from the tempests of the Atlantic. Its quiet shores were undisturbed by the bustle either of commerce or of pleasure; and the huts of ploughmen and fishermen were thinly scattered over what is now the site of crowded marts and of luxurious pavilions.

The peasantry of the coast of Devonshire remembered the name of Monmouth with affection, and held Popery in detestation. They therefore crowded down to the seaside with provisions and offers of service. The disembarkation instantly commenced. Sixty boats conveyed the troops to the coast. Mackay was sent on shore first with the British regiments. The Prince soon followed. He landed where the quay of Brixham now stands. The whole aspect of the place has been altered. Where we now see a port crowded with shipping, and a marketplace swarming with buyers and sellers, the waves then broke on a desolate beach: but a fragment of the rock on which the deliverer stepped from his boat has been carefully preserved, and is set up as an object of public veneration in the centre of that busy wharf.

As soon as the Prince had planted his foot on dry ground he called for horses. Two beasts, such as the small yeomen of that time were in the habit of riding, were procured from the neighbouring village. William and Schomberg mounted and proceeded to examine the country.

As soon as Burnet was on shore he hastened to the Prince. An amusing dialogue took place between them. Burnet poured forth his congratulations with genuine delight, and then eagerly asked what were His Highness's plans. Military men are seldom disposed to take counsel with gownsmen on military matters; and William regarded the interference of unprofessional advisers, in questions relating to war, with even more than the disgust ordinarily felt by soldiers on such occasions. But he was at that moment in an excellent humour, and, instead of signifying his displeasure by a short and cutting reprimand, graciously extended his hand, and answered his chaplain's question by another question: 'Well, Doctor, what do you think of predestination now?' The reproof was so delicate that Burnet, whose perceptions were not very fine, did not perceive it. He answered with great fervour that he should never forget the signal manner in which Providence had favoured their undertaking.

During the first day the troops who had gone on shore had many discomforts to endure. The earth was soaked with rain. The baggage was still on board of the ships. Officers of high rank were compelled to sleep in wet clothes on the wet ground: the Prince himself had no better quarters than a hut afforded. His banner was displayed on the thatched roof; and some bedding brought from his ship was spread for him on the floor. There was some difficulty about landing the horses; and it seemed probable that this operation would occupy several days. But on the following morning the prospect cleared. The wind was gentle. The water in the bay was as even as glass. Some fishermen pointed out a place where the ships could be brought within sixty feet of the beach. This was done; and in three hours many hundreds of horses swam safely to shore.

The disembarkation had hardly been effected when the wind rose again, and swelled into a fierce gale from the west. The enemy coming in pursuit down the Channel had been stopped by the same change of weather which enabled William to land. During two days the King's fleet lay on an unruffled sea in sight of Beachy Head. At length Dartmouth was able to proceed. He passed the Isle of Wight, and one of his ships came in sight of the Dutch topmasts in Torbay. Just at this moment he was encountered by the tempest, and compelled to take shelter in the harbour of Portsmouth. At that time James, who was not incompetent to form a judgment on a question of seamanship, declared himself perfectly satisfied that his Admiral had done all that man could do, and had yielded only to the irresistible hostility of the winds and waves. At a later period the unfortunate prince began, with little reason, to suspect Dartmouth of treachery, or at least of slackness.

The weather had indeed served the Protestant cause so well that some men of more piety than judgment fully believed the ordinary laws of nature to have been suspended for the preservation of the liberty and religion of England. Exactly a hundred years before, they said, the Armada, invincible by man, had been scattered by the wrath of God. Civil freedom and divine truth were again in jeopardy; and again the obedient elements had fought for the good cause. The wind had blown strong from the east while the Prince wished to sail down the Channel, had turned to the south when he wished to enter Torbay, had sunk to a calm during the disembarkation, and, as soon as the disembarkation was completed, had risen to a storm, and had met the pursuers in the face. Nor did men omit to remark that, by an extraordinary coincidence, the Prince had reached our shores on a day on which the Church of England commemorated, by prayer and thanksgiving, the wonderful escape of the royal House and of the three Estates from the blackest plot ever devised by Papists.[3] Carstares, whose suggestions were sure to meet with attention from the Prince, recommended that, as soon as the landing had been effected, public thanks should be offered to God for the protection so conspicuously accorded to the great enterprise. This advice was taken, and with excellent effect. The troops, taught to regard themselves as favourites of heaven, were inspired with new courage; and the English people formed the most favourable opinion of a general and an army so attentive to the duties of religion.

On Tuesday, the sixth of November, William's army began to

[3. That is, the Gunpowder Plot of 5 November 1605.]

march up the country. Some regiments advanced as far as New-ton Abbot. A stone, set up in the midst of that little town, still marks the spot where the Prince's Declaration was solemnly read to the people. The movements of the troops were slow: for the rain fell in torrents; and the roads of England were then in a state which seemed frightful to persons accustomed to the excellent communications of Holland. William took up his quarters, during two days, at Ford, a seat of the ancient and illustrious family of Courtenay, in the neighbourhood of Newton Abbot. He was magnificently lodged and feasted there; but it is remarkable that the owner of the house, though a strong Whig, did not choose to be the first to put life and fortune in peril, and cautiously abstained from doing anything which, if the King should prevail, could be treated as a crime.

Exeter, in the meantime, was greatly agitated. Lamplugh, the bishop, as soon as he heard that the Dutch were at Torbay, set off in terror for London. The Dean fled from the deanery. The magistrates were for the King, the body of the inhabitants for the Prince. Everything was in confusion when, on the morning of Thursday, the eighth of November, a body of troops, under the command of Mordaunt,[4] appeared before the city. With Mordaunt came Burnet, to whom William had entrusted the duty of protecting the clergy of the Cathedral from injury and insult. The Mayor and Aldermen had ordered the gates to be closed, but yielded on the first summons. The deanery was prepared for the reception of the Prince. On the following day, Friday the ninth, he arrived. The magistrates had been pressed to receive him in state at the entrance of the city, but had steadfastly refused. The pomp of that day, however, could well spare them. Such a sight had never been seen in Devonshire. Many went forth half a day's journey to meet the champion of their religion. All the neighbouring villages poured forth their inhabitants. A great crowd, consisting chiefly of young peasants, brandishing their cudgels, had assembled on the top of Haldon Hill, whence the army, marching from Chudleigh, first descried the rich valley of the

[4. Charles Mordaunt, afterwards Earl of Peterborough, one of the most active of whig *émigrés*. He had been the first to advise William to invade England.]

Exe, and the two massive towers rising from the cloud of smoke which overhung the capital of the West. The road, all down the long descent, and through the plain to the banks of the river, was lined, mile after mile, with spectators. From the West Gate to the Cathedral Close, the pressing and shouting on each side was such as reminded Londoners of the crowds on the Lord Mayor's day. The houses were gaily decorated. Doors, windows, balconies, and roofs were thronged with gazers. An eye accustomed to the pomp of war would have found much to criticize in the spectacle. For several toilsome marches in the rain, through roads where one who travelled on foot sank at every step up to the ankles in clay, had not improved the appearance either of the men or of their accoutrements. But the people of Devonshire, altogether unused to the splendour of well ordered camps, were overwhelmed with delight and awe. Descriptions of the martial pageant were circulated all over the kingdom. They contained much that was well fitted to gratify the vulgar appetite for the marvellous. For the Dutch army, composed of men who had been born in various climates, and had served under various standards, presented an aspect at once grotesque, gorgeous, and terrible to islanders who had, in general, a very indistinct notion of foreign countries.

First rode Macclesfield at the head of two hundred gentlemen, mostly of English blood, glittering in helmets and cuirasses, and mounted on Flemish war horses. Each was attended by a negro, brought from the sugar plantations on the coast of Guiana. The citizens of Exeter, who had never seen so many specimens of the African race, gazed with wonder on those black faces set off by embroidered turbans and white feathers. Then with drawn broadswords came a squadron of Swedish horsemen in black armour and fur cloaks. They were regarded with a strange interest; for it was rumoured that they were natives of a land where the ocean was frozen and where the night lasted through half the year, and that they had themselves slain the huge bears whose skins they wore. Next, surrounded by a goodly company of gentlemen and pages, was borne aloft the Prince's banner. On its broad folds the crowd which covered the roofs and filled the windows read with delight that memorable inscription, 'The

Protestant religion and the liberties of England.' But the acclamations redoubled when, attended by forty running footmen,
the Prince himself appeared, armed on back and breast, wearing
a white plume and mounted on a white charger. With how martial an air he curbed his horse, how thoughtful and commanding
was the expression of his ample forehead and falcon eye, may still
be seen on the canvas of Kneller. Once those grave features re-
laxed into a smile. It was when an ancient woman, perhaps one of
the zealous Puritans who through twenty-eight years of persecution had waited with firm faith for the consolation of Israel, perhaps the mother of some rebel who had perished in the carnage
of Sedgemoor, or in the more fearful carnage of the Bloody Circuit, broke from the crowd, rushed through the drawn swords
and curvetting horses, touched the hand of the deliverer, and
cried out that now she was happy.

Near to the Prince was one who divided with him the gaze of
the multitude. That, men said, was the great Count Schomberg,
the first soldier in Europe, since Turenne and Condé were gone,
the man whose genius and valour had saved the Portuguese
monarchy on the field of Montes Claros, the man who had
earned a still higher glory by resigning the truncheon of a Marshal of France for the sake of the true religion. It was not forgotten that the two heroes who, indissolubly united by their common Protestantism, were entering Exeter together, had twelve
years before been opposed to each other under the walls of Mae-
stricht, and that the energy of the young Prince had not then
been found a match for the cool science of the veteran who now
rode in friendship by his side. Then came a long column of the
whiskered infantry of Switzerland, distinguished in all the continental wars of two centuries by pre-eminent valour and discipline, but never till that week seen on English ground. And then
marched a succession of bands designated, as was the fashion of
that age, after their leaders, Bentinck, Solmes and Ginkel, Talmash and Mackay. With peculiar pleasure Englishmen might
look on one gallant regiment which still bore the name of the
honoured and lamented Ossory. The effect of the spectacle was
heightened by the recollection of the renowned events in which
many of the warriors now pouring through the West Gate had

borne a share. For they had seen service very different from that of the Devonshire militia or of the camp at Hounslow. Some of them had repelled the fiery onset of the French on the field of Seneff; and others had crossed swords with the infidels in the cause of Christendom on that great day when the siege of Vienna was raised.

The very senses of the multitude were fooled by imagination. Newsletters conveyed to every part of the kingdom fabulous accounts of the size and strength of the invaders. It was affirmed that they were, with scarcely an exception, above six feet high, and that they wielded such huge pikes, swords, and muskets, as had never before been seen in England. Nor did the wonder of the population diminish when the artillery arrived, twenty-one huge pieces of brass cannon, which were with difficulty tugged along by sixteen cart-horses to each. Much curiosity was excited by a strange structure mounted on wheels. It proved to be a moveable smithy, furnished with all tools and materials necessary for repairing arms and carriages. But nothing raised so much admiration as the bridge of boats, which was laid with great speed on the Exe for the conveyance of waggons, and afterwards as speedily taken to pieces and carried away. It was made, if report said true, after a pattern contrived by the Christians who were warring against the Great Turk on the Danube. The foreigners inspired as much good will as admiration. Their politic leader took care to distribute the quarters in such a manner as to cause the smallest possible inconvenience to the inhabitants of Exeter and of the neighbouring villages. The most rigid discipline was maintained. Not only were pillage and outrage effectually prevented, but the troops were required to demean themselves with civility towards all classes. Those who had formed their notions of an army from the conduct of Kirke and his Lambs were amazed to see soldiers who never swore at a landlady or took an egg without paying for it. In return for this moderation the people furnished the troops with provisions in great abundance and at reasonable prices.

Much depended on the course which, at this great crisis, the clergy of the Church of England might take; and the members of the Chapter of Exeter were the first who were called upon to de-

clare their sentiments. Burnet informed the Canons, now left
without a head by the flight of the Dean, that they could not be
permitted to use the prayer for the Prince of Wales, and that a
solemn service must be performed in honour of the safe arrival
of the Prince. The Canons did not choose to appear in their
stalls; but some of the choristers and prebendaries attended.
William repaired in military state to the Cathedral. As he passed
under the gorgeous screen, that renowned organ, scarcely surpassed by any of those which are the boast of his native Holland,
gave out a peal of triumph. He mounted the Bishop's seat, a
stately throne rich with the carving of the fifteenth century.
Burnet stood below; and a crowd of warriors and nobles appeared on the right hand and on the left. The singers, robed in
white, sang the Te Deum. When the chant was over, Burnet
read the Prince's Declaration: but as soon as the first words were
uttered, prebendaries and singers crowded in all haste out of the
choir. At the close Burnet cried in a loud voice, 'God save the
Prince of Orange!' and many fervent voices answered, 'Amen.'

On Sunday, the eleventh of November, Burnet preached before the Prince in the Cathedral, and dilated on the signal mercy
vouchsafed by God to the English Church and nation. At the
same time a singular event happened in a humbler place of worship. Ferguson resolved to preach at the Presbyterian meeting
house. The minister and elders would not consent: but the turbulent and half-witted knave, fancying that the times of Fleet-
wood and Harrison were come again, forced the door, went
through the congregation sword in hand, mounted the pulpit,
and there poured forth a fiery invective against the King. The
time for such follies had gone by; and this exhibition excited
nothing but derision and disgust.

While these things were passing in Devonshire the ferment
was greater in London. The Prince's Declaration, in spite of all
precautions, was now in every man's hands. On the sixth of
November James, still uncertain on what part of the coast the
invaders had landed, summoned the Primate and three other
Bishops, Compton of London, White of Peterborough, and Sprat
of Rochester, to a conference in the closet. The King listened graciously while the prelates made warm professions of loyalty, and

assured them that he did not suspect them. 'But where,' said he, 'is the paper that you were to bring me?' 'Sir,' answered Sancroft, 'we have brought no paper. We are not solicitous to clear our fame to the world. It is no new thing to us to be reviled and falsely accused. Our consciences acquit us: your Majesty acquits us: and we are satisfied.' 'Yes,' said the King; 'but a declaration from you is necessary to my service.' He then produced a copy of the Prince's manifesto. 'See,' he said, 'how you are mentioned here.' 'Sir,' answered one of the Bishops, 'not one person in five hundred believes this manifesto to be genuine.' 'No!' cried the King fiercely; 'then those five hundred would bring the Prince of Orange to cut my throat.' 'God forbid,' exclaimed the prelates in concert. But the King's understanding, never very clear, was now quite bewildered. One of his peculiarities was that, whenever his opinion was not adopted, he fancied that his veracity was questioned. 'This paper not genuine!' he exclaimed, turning over the leaves with his hands. 'Am I not worthy to be believed? Is my word not to be taken?' 'At all events, sir,' said one of the Bishops, 'this is not an ecclesiastical matter. It lies within the sphere of the civil power. God has entrusted your Majesty with the sword: and it is not for us to invade your functions.' Then the Archbishop, with that gentle and temperate malice which inflicts the deepest wounds, declared that he must be excused from setting his hand to any political document. 'I and my brethren, sir,' he said, 'have already smarted severely for meddling with affairs of state; and we shall be very cautious how we do so again. We once subscribed a petition of the most harmless kind: we presented it in the most respectful manner; and we found that we had committed a high offence. We were saved from ruin only by the merciful protection of God. And, sir, the ground then taken by your Majesty's Attorney and Solicitor was that, out of Parliament, we were private men, and that it was criminal presumption in private men to meddle with politics. They attacked us so fiercely that for my part I gave myself over for lost.' 'I thank you for that, my Lord of Canterbury,' said the King; 'I should have hoped that you would not have thought yourself lost by falling into my hands.'

Such a speech might have become the mouth of a merciful

sovereign, but it came with a bad grace from a prince who had burned a woman alive for harbouring one of his flying enemies, from a prince round whose knees his own nephew had clung in vain agonies of supplication. The Archbishop was not to be so silenced. He resumed his story, and recounted the insults which the creatures of the court had offered to the Church of England, among which some ridicule thrown on his own style occupied a conspicuous place. The King had nothing to say but that there was no use in repeating old grievances, and that he had hoped that these things had been quite forgotten. He, who never forgot the smallest injury that he had suffered, could not understand how others should remember for a few weeks the most deadly injuries that he had inflicted.

At length the conversation came back to the point from which it had wandered. The King insisted on having from the Bishops a paper declaring their abhorrence of the Prince's enterprise. They, with many professions of the most submissive loyalty, pertinaciously refused. The Prince, they said, asserted that he had been invited by temporal as well as by spiritual peers. The imputation was common. Why should not the purgation be common also? 'I see how it is,' said the King. 'Some of the temporal peers have been with you, and have persuaded you to cross me in this matter.' The Bishops solemnly averred that it was not so. But it would, they said, seem strange that, on a question involving grave political and military considerations, the temporal peers should be entirely passed over, and the prelates alone should be required to take a prominent part. 'But this,' said James, 'is my method. I am your King. It is for me to judge what is best. I will go my own way; and I call on you to assist me.' The Bishops assured him that they would assist him in their proper department, as Christian ministers with their prayers, and as peers of the realm with their advice in his Parliament. James, who wanted neither the prayers of heretics nor the advice of Parliaments, was bitterly disappointed. After a long altercation, 'I have done,' he said, 'I will urge you no further. Since you will not help me, I trust to myself and to my own arms.'

The Bishops had hardly left the royal presence, when a courier arrived with the news that on the preceding day the Prince of

Orange had landed in Devonshire. During the following week London was violently agitated. On Sunday, the eleventh of November, a rumour was circulated that knives, gridirons, and cauldrons, intended for the torturing of heretics, were concealed in the monastery which had been established under the King's protection at Clerkenwell. Great multitudes assembled round the building, and were about to demolish it, when a military force arrived. The crowd was dispersed, and several of the rioters were slain. An inquest sat on the bodies, and came to a decision which strongly indicated the temper of the public mind. The jury found that certain loyal and well disposed persons, who had gone to put down the meetings of traitors and public enemies at a mass-house, had been wilfully murdered by the soldiers; and this strange verdict was signed by all the jurors. The ecclesiastics at Clerkenwell, naturally alarmed by these symptoms of popular feeling, were desirous to place their property in safety. They succeeded in removing most of their furniture before any report of their intentions got abroad. But at length the suspicions of the rabble were excited. The two last carts were stopped in Holborn, and all that they contained was publicly burned in the middle of the street. So great was the alarm among the Catholics that all their places of worship were closed, except those which belonged to the royal family and to foreign Ambassadors.

On the whole, however, things as yet looked not unfavourably for James. The invaders had been more than a week on English ground. Yet no man of note had joined them. No rebellion had broken out in the north or the east. No servant of the crown appeared to have betrayed his trust. The royal army was assembling fast at Salisbury, and, though inferior in discipline to that of William, was superior in numbers.

The Prince was undoubtedly surprised and mortified by the slackness of those who had invited him to England. By the common people of Devonshire, indeed, he had been received with every sign of good will: but no nobleman, no gentleman of high consideration, had yet repaired to his quarters. The explanation of this singular fact is probably to be found in the circumstance that he had landed in a part of the island where he had not been expected. His friends in the north had made their arrangements for a rising, on the supposition that he would be among them with an army. His friends in the west had made no arrangements at all, and were naturally disconcerted at finding themselves suddenly called upon to take the lead in a movement so important and perilous. They had also fresh in their recollection, and indeed full in their sight, the disastrous consequences of rebellion, gibbets, heads, mangled quarters, families still in deep mourning for brave sufferers who had loved their country well but not wisely. After a warning so terrible and so recent, some hesitation was natural, It was equally natural, however, that William, who, trusting to promises from England, had put to hazard, not only his own fame and fortunes, but also the prosperity and independence of his native land, should feel deeply mortified. He was, indeed, so indignant, that he talked of falling back to Torbay, re-embarking his troops, returning to Holland, and leaving those who had betrayed him to the fate which they deserved. At length, on Monday, the twelfth of November, a gentleman named Burrington, who resided in the neighbourhood of Crediton, joined the Prince's standard, and his example was followed by several of his neighbours.

Men of higher consequence had already set out from different parts of the country for Exeter. The first of these was John Lord Lovelace, distinguished by his taste, by his magnificence, and by the audacious and intemperate vehemence of his Whiggism. He had been five or six times arrested for political offences. The last crime laid to his charge was, that he had contemptuously denied the validity of a warrant, signed by a Roman Catholic Justice of the Peace. He had been brought before the Privy Council and strictly examined, but to little purpose. He resolutely refused to criminate himself; and the evidence against him was insufficient. He was dismissed; but, before he retired, James exclaimed in great heat, 'My Lord, this is not the first trick that you have played me.' 'Sir,' answered Lovelace, with undaunted spirit, 'I never played any trick to your Majesty, or to any other person. Whoever has accused me to your Majesty of playing tricks is a liar.' Lovelace had subsequently been admitted into the confidence of those who planned the Revolution. His mansion, built by his ancestors out of the spoils of Spanish galleons from the

Indies, rose on the ruins of a house of Our Lady in that beautiful valley through which the Thames, not yet defiled by the precincts of a great capital, nor rising and falling with the flow and ebb of the sea, rolls under woods of beech round the gentle hills of Berkshire. Beneath the stately saloon, adorned by Italian pencils, was a subterraneous vault, in which the bones of ancient monks had sometimes been found. In this dark chamber some zealous and daring opponents of the government had held many midnight conferences during that anxious time when England was impatiently expecting the Protestant wind. The season for action had now arrived. Lovelace, with seventy followers, well armed and mounted, quitted his dwelling, and directed his course westward. He reached Gloucestershire without difficulty. But Beaufort, who governed that county, was exerting all his great authority and influence in support of the crown. The militia had been called out. A strong party had been posted at Cirencester. When Lovelace arrived there he was informed that he could not be suffered to pass. It was necessary for him either to relinquish his undertaking or to fight his way through. He resolved to force a passage; and his friends and tenants stood gallantly by him. A sharp conflict took place. The militia lost an officer and six or seven men; but at length the followers of Lovelace were overpowered: he was made a prisoner, and sent to Gloucester Castle.

Others were more fortunate. On the day on which the skirmish took place at Cirencester, Richard Savage, Lord Colchester, son and heir of the Earl Rivers, and father, by a lawless amour, of that unhappy poet whose misdeeds and misfortunes form one of the darkest portions of literary history,[5] came with between sixty and seventy horse to Exeter. With him arrived the bold and turbulent Thomas Wharton. A few hours later came Edward Russell, son of the Earl of Bedford, and brother of the virtuous nobleman whose blood had been shed on the scaffold. Another arrival still more important was speedily announced. Colchester, Wharton, and Russell belonged to that party which had been constantly opposed to the court. James Bertie, Earl of

[5. Richard Savage, the poet, claimed to be the illegitimate son of Lord Rivers; but the claim rests on his assertion alone.]

Abingdon, had, on the contrary, been regarded as a supporter of arbitrary government. He had been true to James in the days of the Exclusion Bill. He had, as Lord Lieutenant of Oxfordshire, acted with vigour and severity against the adherents of Monmouth, and had lighted bonfires to celebrate the defeat of Argyll. But dread of Popery had driven him into opposition and rebellion. He was the first peer of the realm who made his appearance at the quarters of the Prince of Orange.

But the King had less to fear from those who openly arrayed themselves against his authority, than from the dark conspiracy which had spread its ramifications through his army and his family. Of that conspiracy Churchill, unrivalled in sagacity and address, endowed by nature with a certain cool intrepidity which never failed him either in fighting or lying, high in military rank, and high in the favour of the Princess Anne, must be regarded as the soul. It was not yet time for him to strike the decisive blow. But even thus early he inflicted, by the instrumentality of a subordinate agent, a wound, serious if not deadly on the royal cause.

Edward Viscount Cornbury, eldest son of the Earl of Clarendon, was a young man of slender abilities, loose principles, and violent temper. He had been early taught to consider his relationship to the Princess Anne as the groundwork of his fortunes, and had been exhorted to pay her assiduous court. It had never occurred to his father that the hereditary loyalty of the Hydes could run any risk of contamination in the household of the King's favourite daughter: but in that household the Churchills held absolute sway; and Cornbury became their tool. He commanded one of the regiments of dragoons which had been sent westward. Such dispositions had been made that, on the fourteenth of November, he was, during a few hours, the senior officer at Salisbury, and all the troops assembled there were subject to his authority. It seems extraordinary that, at such a crisis, the army on which every thing depended should have been left, even for a moment, under the command of a young Colonel who had neither abilities nor experience. There can be little doubt that so strange an arrangement was the result of deep design, and as little doubt to what head and to what heart the design is to be imputed.

Suddenly three of the regiments of cavalry which had assembled at Salisbury were ordered to march westward. Cornbury put himself at their head, and conducted them first to Blandford and thence to Dorchester. From Dorchester, after a halt of an hour or two, they set out for Axminster. Some of the officers began to be uneasy, and demanded an explanation of these strange movements. Cornbury replied that he had instructions to make a night attack on some troops which the Prince of Orange had posted at Honiton. But suspicion was awake. Searching questions were put, and were evasively answered. At last Cornbury was pressed to produce his orders. He perceived, not only that it would be impossible for him to carry over all the three regiments, as he had hoped, but that he was himself in a situation of considerable peril. He accordingly stole away with a few followers to the Dutch quarters. Most of his troops returned to Salisbury: but some who had been detached from the main body, and who had no suspicion of the designs of their commander, proceeded to Honiton. There they found themselves in the midst of a large force which was fully prepared to receive them. Resistance was impossible. Their leader pressed them to take service under William. A gratuity of a month's pay was offered to them, and was by most of them accepted.

The news of these events reached London on the fifteenth. James had been on the morning of that day in high good humour. Bishop Lamplugh had just presented himself at court on his arrival from Exeter, and had been most graciously received. 'My Lord,' said the King, 'you are a genuine old Cavalier.' The archbishopric of York, which had now been vacant more than two years and a half, was immediately bestowed on Lamplugh as the reward of loyalty. That afternoon, just as the King was sitting down to dinner, arrived an express with the tidings of Cornbury's defection. James turned away from his untasted meal, swallowed a crust of bread and a glass of wine, and retired to his closet. He afterwards learned that, as he was rising from table, several of the Lords in whom he reposed the greatest confidence were shaking hands and congratulating each other in the adjoining gallery. When the news was carried to the Queen's apartments she and her ladies broke out into tears and loud cries of sorrow.

The blow was indeed a heavy one. It was true that the direct loss to the crown and the direct gain to the invaders hardly amounted to two hundred men and as many horses. But where could the King henceforth expect to find those sentiments in which consists the strength of states and of armies? Cornbury was the heir of a house conspicuous for its attachment to monarchy. His father Clarendon, his uncle Rochester, were men whose loyalty was supposed to be proof to all temptation. What must be the strength of that feeling against which the most deeply rooted hereditary prejudices were of no avail, of that feeling which could reconcile a young officer of high birth to desertion, aggravated by breach of trust and by gross falsehood? That Cornbury was not a man of brilliant parts or enterprising temper made the event more alarming. It was impossible to doubt that he had in some quarter a powerful and artful prompter. Who that prompter was soon became evident. In the meantime no man in the royal camp could feel assured that he was not surrounded by traitors. Political rank, military rank, the honour of a nobleman, the honour of a soldier, the strongest professions, the purest Cavalier blood, could no longer afford security. Every man might reasonably doubt whether every order which he received from his superior was not meant to serve the purposes of the enemy. That prompt obedience without which an army is merely a rabble was necessarily at an end. What discipline could there be among soldiers who had just been saved from a snare by refusing to follow their commanding officer on a secret expedition, and by insisting on a sight of his orders?

Cornbury was soon kept in countenance by a crowd of deserters superior to him in rank and capacity: but during a few days he stood alone in his shame, and was bitterly reviled by many who afterwards imitated his example and envied his dishonourable precedence. Among these was his own father. The first outbreak of Clarendon's rage and sorrow was highly pathetic. 'Oh God!' he ejaculated, 'that a son of mine should be a rebel!' A fortnight later he made up his mind to be a rebel himself. Yet it would be unjust to pronounce him a mere hypocrite. In revolutions men live fast: the experience of years is crowded into hours: old habits of thought and action are violently broken; novelties, which at first sight inspire dread and disgust, become in a few days familiar, endurable, attractive. Many men of far purer virtue and higher spirit than Clarendon were prepared, before that memorable year ended, to do what they would have pronounced wicked and infamous when it began.

The unhappy father composed himself as well as he could, and sent to ask a private audience of the King. It was granted. James said, with more than his usual graciousness, that he from his heart pitied Cornbury's relations, and should not hold them at all accountable for the crime of their unworthy kinsman. Clarendon went home, scarcely daring to look his friends in the face. Soon, however, he learned with surprise that the act, which had, as he at first thought, for ever dishonoured his family, was applauded by some persons of high station. His niece, the Princess of Denmark, asked him why he shut himself up. He answered that he had been overwhelmed with confusion by his son's villainy. Anne seemed not at all to understand this feeling. 'People,' she said, 'are very uneasy about Popery. I believe that many of the army will do the same.'

And now the King, greatly disturbed, called together the principal officers who were still in London. Churchill, who was about this time promoted to the rank of Lieutenant General, made his appearance with that bland serenity which neither peril nor infamy could ever disturb. The meeting was attended by Henry Fitzroy, Duke of Grafton, whose audacity and activity made him conspicuous among the natural children of Charles the Second. Grafton was colonel of the first regiment of Foot Guards. He seems to have been at this time completely under Churchill's influence, and was prepared to desert the royal standard as soon as the favourable moment should arrive. Two other traitors were in the circle, Kirke and Trelawney, who commanded those two fierce and lawless bands then known as the Tangier regiments. Both of them had, like the other Protestant officers of the army, long seen with extreme displeasure the partiality which the King had shown to members of his own Church; and Trelawney re-

membered with bitter resentment the persecution of his brother
the Bishop of Bristol. James addressed the assembly in terms
worthy of a better man and of a better cause. It might be, he
said, that some of the officers had conscientious scruples about
fighting for him. If so he was willing to receive back their commissions. But he adjured them as gentlemen and soldiers not to
imitate the shameful example of Cornbury. All seemed moved
and none more than Churchill. He was the first to vow with well
feigned enthusiasm that he would shed the last drop of his blood
in the service of his gracious master: Grafton was loud and forward in similar protestations; and the example was followed by
Kirke and Trelawney.

Deceived by these professions, the King prepared to set out for
Salisbury.

✳

His last act before his departure was to appoint a Council of
five Lords to represent him in London during his absence. Of
the five, two were Papists, and by law incapable of office. Joined
with them was Jeffreys, a Protestant indeed, but more detested
by the nation than any Papist. To the other two members of this
board, Preston and Godolphin, no serious objection could be
made. On the day on which the King left London the Prince of
Wales was sent to Portsmouth. That fortress was strongly garrisoned, and was under the government of Berwick. The fleet
commanded by Dartmouth lay close at hand: and it was supposed that, if things went ill, the royal infant would, without
difficulty, be conveyed from Portsmouth to France.

13

The Vacancy of Government

[*With the threat of civil war, defection became general throughout the country. A decisive desertion was that of Churchill, who abandoned the royal camp at Salisbury on 24 November. While applauding the patriotism of all other deserters, Macaulay of course castigates that of Churchill, who left behind him, he says, 'a letter written with that decorum which he never failed to preserve in the midst of guilt and dishonour.' Churchill acknowledged that he owed all to royal favour, but refused to fight against the Protestant cause. His desertion was immediately followed by that of the Princess Anne, who was personally dominated by the Churchills. She fled by night, under the protection of her former tutor, Bishop Compton, and arrived ultimately at Nottingham where the Earl of Devonshire headed the revolt. Under the impact of these events, James gave up the idea of battle and returned to London. The desertion of both his daughters shattered him, and he resolved to gain time by offering to call a free parliament and to negotiate with William. His plan was to send his wife and infant son to France, and then himself to leave England and plan a reconquest of his kingdom from Ireland or France. This plan was at first blocked by Lord Dartmouth who positively refused to put the Prince of Wales in the hands of Louis XIV. However, James afterwards found a Frenchman, the Comte de Lauzun, to carry out this part of his programme, and once he had learned that his wife and son were safely abroad, he carried out the rest of it. Leaving his commissioners in unreal negotiation with William at Hungerford, he ordered his commander-in-chief, Lord Feversham, to disband his army, destroyed the writs summoning a new parliament, threw the Great Seal into the Thames to prevent the use of the royal authority against him, and fled secretly to Sheerness where a boat was waiting to take him to France.*

Next morning the King's flight was discovered. There was a factual vacancy of government. Macaulay detested radicalism of any kind, and in his tenth chapter he makes the most of the anarchy thus

created: an anarchy which could be terminated only if William, cut-
ting through the debates on legitimacy which divided his whig and tory
supporters, advanced on London and boldly assumed the govern-
ment.]

IT was a terrible moment. The King was gone. The Prince had
not arrived. No Regency had been appointed. The Great Seal,
essential to the administration of ordinary justice, had disappeared. It was soon known that Feversham had, on the receipt
of the royal order, instantly disbanded his forces. What respect
for law or property was likely to be found among soldiers, armed
and congregated, emancipated from the restraints of discipline,
and destitute of the necessaries of life? On the other hand, the
populace of London had, during some weeks, shown a strong disposition to turbulence and rapine. The urgency of the crisis
united for a short time all who had any interest in the peace of
society. Rochester had till that day adhered firmly to the royal
cause. He now saw that there was only one way of averting general confusion. 'Call your troop of Guards together,' he said to
Northumberland, 'and declare for the Prince of Orange.' The
advice was promptly followed. The principal officers of the army
who were then in London held a meeting at Whitehall, and resolved that they would submit to William's authority, and would,
till his pleasure should be known, keep their men together and
assist the civil power to preserve order. The Peers repaired to
Guildhall, and were received there with all honour by the magistracy of the city. In strictness of law they were no better entitled
than any other set of persons to assume the executive administration. But it was necessary to the public safety that there should be
a provisional government; and the eyes of men naturally turned
to the hereditary magnates of the realm. The extremity of the
danger drew Sancroft forth from his palace. He took the chair;
and, under his presidency, the new Archbishop of York, five
Bishops, and twenty-two temporal Lords, determined to draw
up, subscribe, and publish a Declaration.

By this instrument they declared that they were firmly attached to the religion and constitution of their country, and that
they had cherished the hope of seeing grievances redressed and

tranquillity restored by the Parliament which the King had lately summoned, but that this hope had been extinguished by his flight. They had therefore determined to join with the Prince of Orange, in order that the freedom of the nation might be vindicated, that the rights of the Church might be secured, that a just liberty of conscience might be given to Dissenters, and that the Protestant interest throughout the world might be strengthened. Till His Highness should arrive, they were prepared to take on themselves the responsibility of giving such directions as might be necessary for the preservation of order. A deputation was instantly sent to lay this Declaration before the Prince, and to inform him that he was impatiently expected in London.

The Lords then proceeded to deliberate on the course which it was necessary to take for the prevention of tumult. They sent for the two Secretaries of State. Middleton refused to submit to what he regarded as an usurped authority: but Preston, astounded by his master's flight, and not knowing what to expect, or whither to turn, obeyed the summons. A message was sent to Skelton, who was Lieutenant of the Tower, requesting his attendance at Guildhall. He came, and was told that his services were no longer wanted, and that he must instantly deliver up his keys. He was succeeded by Lord Lucas. At the same time the Peers ordered a letter to be written to Dartmouth, enjoining him to refrain from all hostile operations against the Dutch fleet, and to displace all the Popish officers who held commands under him.

The part taken in these proceedings by Sancroft, and by some other persons who had, up to that day, been strictly faithful to the principle of passive obedience, deserves especial notice. To usurp the command of the military and naval forces of the state, to remove the officers whom the King had set over his castles and his ships, and to prohibit his Admiral from giving battle to his enemies, was surely nothing less than rebellion. Yet several honest and able Tories of the school of Filmer persuaded themselves that they could do all these things without incurring the guilt of resisting their Sovereign. The distinction which they took was, at least, ingenious.

Government, they said, is the ordinance of God. Hereditary

monarchical government is eminently the ordinance of God. While the King commands what is lawful we must obey him actively. When he commands what is unlawful we must obey him passively. In no extremity are we justified in withstanding him by force. But, if he chooses to resign his office, his rights over us are at an end. While he governs us, though he may govern us ill, we are bound to submit: but, if he refuses to govern us at all, we are not bound to remain for ever without a government. Anarchy is not the ordinance of God; nor will he impute it to us as a sin that, when a prince, whom, in spite of extreme provocations, we have never ceased to honour and obey, has departed we know not whither, leaving no vicegerent, we take the only course which can prevent the entire dissolution of society. Had our Sovereign remained among us, we were ready, little as he deserved our love, to die at his feet. Had he, when he quitted us, appointed a regency to govern us with vicarious authority during his absence, to that regency alone should we have looked for direction. But he has disappeared, having made no provision for the preservation of order or the administration of justice. With him, and with his Great Seal, has vanished the whole machinery by which a murderer can be punished, by which the right to an estate can be decided, by which the effects of a bankrupt can be distributed. His last act has been to free thousands of armed men from the restraints of military discipline, and to place them in such a situation that they must plunder or starve. Yet a few hours, and every man's hand will be against his neighbour. Life, property, female honour, will be at the mercy of every lawless spirit. We are at this moment actually in that state of nature about which theorists have written so much; and in that state we have been placed, not by our fault, but by the voluntary defection of him who ought to have been our protector. His defection may be justly called voluntary: for neither his life nor his liberty was in danger. His enemies had just consented to treat with him on a basis proposed by himself, and had offered immediately to suspend all hostile operations, on conditions which he could not deny to be liberal. In such circumstances it is that he has abandoned his trust. We retract nothing. We are in nothing inconsistent. We still assert our old doctrines without qualification. We still hold that it is in all cases sinful to resist the magistrate: but we say that there is no longer any magistrate to resist. He who was the magistrate, after long abusing his powers, has at last abdicated them. The abuse did not give us a right to depose him: but the abdication gives us a right to consider how we may best supply his place.

It was on these grounds that the Prince's party was now swollen by many adherents who had previously stood aloof from it. Never, within the memory of man, had there been so near an approach to entire concord among all intelligent Englishmen as at this conjuncture: and never had concord been more needed. Legitimate authority there was none. All those evil passions which it is the office of government to restrain, and which the best governments restrain but imperfectly, were on a sudden emancipated from control; avarice, licentiousness, revenge, the hatred of sect to sect, the hatred of nation to nation. On such occasions it will ever be found that the human vermin which, neglected by ministers of state and ministers of religion, barbarous in the midst of civilisation, heathen in the midst of Christianity, burrows among all physical and all moral pollution, in the cellars and garrets of great cities, will at once rise into a terrible importance.

So it was now in London. When the night, the longest night, as it chanced, of the year, approached, forth came from every den of vice, from the bear garden of Hockley, and from the labyrinth of tippling houses and brothels in the Friars, thousands of housebreakers and highwaymen, cutpurses and ringdroppers. With these were mingled thousands of idle apprentices, who wished merely for the excitement of a riot. Even men of peaceable and honest habits were impelled by religious animosity to join the lawless part of the population. For the cry of No Popery, a cry which has more than once endangered the existence of London, was the signal for outrage and rapine. First the rabble fell on the Roman Catholic places of worship. The buildings were demolished. Benches, pulpits, confessionals, breviaries were heaped up and set on fire. A great mountain of books and furniture blazed on the site of the convent at Clerkenwell. Another pile was kindled before the ruins of the Franciscan house in Lincoln's Inn Fields. The chapel in Lime Street, the chapel in Bucklersbury, were pulled down. The pictures, images and crucifixes were carried along the streets in triumph, amidst lighted tapers torn from the altars. The procession bristled thick with swords and staves, and on the point of every sword and on every staff was an orange. The King's printing house, whence had issued, during the preceding three years, innumerable tracts in defence of Papal supremacy, image worship, and monastic vows, was, to use a coarse metaphor which then, for the first time, came into use, completely gutted. The vast stock of paper, much of which was still unpolluted by types, furnished an immense bonfire. From monasteries, temples, and public offices, the fury of the multitude turned to private dwellings. Several houses were pillaged and destroyed: but the smallness of the booty disappointed the plunderers; and soon a rumour was spread that the most valuable effects of the Papists had been placed under the care of the foreign Ambassadors.

To the savage and ignorant populace the law of nations and the risk of bringing on their country the just vengeance of all Europe were as nothing. The houses of the Ambassadors were besieged. A great crowd assembled before Barillon's door in St James's Square. He, however, fared better than might have been expected. For, though the government which he represented was held in abhorrence, his liberal housekeeping and exact payments had made him personally popular. Moreover he had taken the precaution of asking for a guard of soldiers; and, as several men of rank, who lived near him, had done the same, a considerable force was collected in the Square. The rioters, therefore, when they were assured that no arms or priests were concealed under his roof, left him unmolested. The Venetian Envoy was protected by a detachment of troops: but the mansions occupied by the ministers of the Elector Palatine and of the Grand Duke of Tuscany were destroyed. One precious box the Tuscan minister was able to save from the marauders. It contained nine volumes of memoirs, written in the hand of James himself. These volumes reached France in safety, and, after the lapse of more than a century, perished there in the havoc of a revolution far more terrible than that from which they had escaped. But some fragments still remain, and, though grievously mutilated, and imbedded in great masses of childish fiction, well deserve to be attentively studied.

The rich plate of the Chapel Royal had been deposited at Wild House, near Lincoln's Inn Fields, the residence of the Spanish ambassador Ronquillo. Ronquillo, conscious that he and his court had not deserved ill of the English nation, had thought it unnecessary to ask for soldiers: but the mob was not in a mood to make nice distinctions. The name of Spain had long been associated in the public mind with the Inquisition and the Armada, with the cruelties of Mary and the plots against Elizabeth. Ronquillo had also made himself many enemies among the common people by availing himself of his privilege to avoid the necessity of paying his debts. His house was therefore sacked without mercy; and a noble library, which he had collected, perished in the flames. His only comfort was that the host in his chapel was rescued from the same fate.

The morning of the twelfth of December rose on a ghastly sight. The capital in many places presented the aspect of a city taken by storm. The Lords met at Whitehall, and exerted themselves to restore tranquillity. The trainbands were ordered under arms. A body of cavalry was kept in readiness to disperse tumultuous assemblages. Such atonement as was at that moment possible was made for the gross insults which had been offered to foreign governments. A reward was promised for the discovery of the property taken from Wild House; and Ronquillo, who had not a bed or an ounce of plate left, was splendidly lodged in the deserted palace of the Kings of England. A sumptuous table was kept for him; and the yeomen of the guard were ordered to wait in his antechamber with the same observance which they were in the habit of paying to the Sovereign. These marks of respect soothed even the punctilious pride of the Spanish court, and averted all danger of a rupture.

In spite, however, of the well meant efforts of the provisional government, the agitation grew hourly more formidable. It was heightened by an event which, even at this distance of time, can hardly be related without a feeling of vindictive pleasure. A scrivener who lived at Wapping, and whose trade was to furnish the seafaring men there with money at high interest, had some time before lent a sum on bottomry. The debtor applied to equity for relief against his own bond; and the case came before Jeffreys. The counsel for the borrower, having little else to say, said that the lender was a Trimmer. The Chancellor instantly fired. 'A Trimmer! where is he? Let me see him. I have heard of that kind of monster. What is it made like?' The unfortunate creditor was forced to stand forth. The Chancellor glared fiercely on him, stormed at him, and sent him away half dead with fright. 'While I live,' the poor man said, as he tottered out of the court, 'I shall never forget that terrible countenance.' And now the day of retribution had arrived. The Trimmer was walking through Wapping, when he saw a well known face looking out of the window of an alehouse. He could not be deceived. The eyebrows, indeed, had been shaved away. The dress was that of a common sailor from Newcastle, and was black with coal dust: but there was no mistaking the savage eye and mouth of Jeffreys.

The alarm was given. In a moment the house was surrounded by hundreds of people shaking bludgeons and bellowing curses. The fugitive's life was saved by a company of the trainbands; and he was carried before the Lord Mayor. The Mayor was a simple man who had passed his whole life in obscurity, and was bewildered by finding himself an important actor in a mighty revolution. The events of the last twenty-four hours, and the perilous state of the city which was under his charge, had disordered his mind and his body. When the great man, at whose frown, a few days before, the whole kingdom had trembled, was dragged into the justice room begrimed with ashes, half dead with fright, and followed by a raging multitude, the agitation of the unfortunate Mayor rose to the height. He fell into fits, and was carried to his bed, whence he never rose. Meanwhile the throng without was constantly becoming more numerous and more savage. Jeffreys begged to be sent to prison. An order to that effect was procured from the Lords who were sitting at Whitehall; and he was conveyed in a carriage to the Tower. Two regiments of militia were drawn out to escort him, and found the duty a difficult one. It was repeatedly necessary for them to form, as if for the purpose of repelling a charge of cavalry, and to present a forest of pikes to the mob. The thousands who were disappointed of their revenge pursued the coach, with howls of rage, to the gate of the Tower, brandishing cudgels, and holding up halters full in the prisoner's view. The wretched man meantime was in convulsions of terror. He wrung his hands; he looked wildly out, sometimes at one window, sometimes at the other, and was heard even above the tumult, crying 'Keep them off, gentlemen! For God's sake keep them off!' At length, having suffered far more than the bitterness of death, he was safely lodged in the fortress where some of his most illustrious victims had passed their last days, and where his own life was destined to close in unspeakable ignominy and horror.[1]

All this time an active search was making after Roman Catholic priests. Many were arrested. Two Bishops, Ellis and Leyburn, were sent to Newgate. The Nuncio, who had little reason to expect that either his spiritual or his political character would be respected by the multitude, made his escape disguised as a lackey in the train of the minister of the Duke of Savoy.

Another day of agitation and terror closed, and was followed by a night the strangest and most terrible that England had ever seen. Early in the evening an attack was made by the rabble on a stately house which had been built a few months before for Lord Powis, which in the reign of George the Second was the residence of the Duke of Newcastle, and which is still conspicuous at the northwestern angle of Lincoln's Inn Fields. Some troops were sent thither: the mob was dispersed, tranquillity seemed to be restored, and the citizens were retiring quietly to their beds. Just at this time arose a whisper which swelled fast into a fearful clamour, passed in an hour from Piccadilly to Whitechapel, and spread into every street and alley of the capital. It was said that the Irish whom Feversham had let loose were marching on London and massacring every man, woman, and child on the road. At one in the morning the drums of the militia beat to arms. Everywhere terrified women were weeping and wringing their hands, while their fathers and husbands were equipping themselves for fight. Before two the capital wore a face of stern preparedness which might well have daunted a real enemy, if such an enemy had been approaching. Candles were blazing at all the windows. The public places were as bright as at noonday. All the

[1. Jeffreys died in the Tower, four months later, aged forty-one.]

great avenues were barricaded. More than twenty thousand pikes and muskets lined the streets. The late daybreak of the winter solstice found the whole City still in arms. During many years the Londoners retained a vivid recollection of what they called the Irish Night.

When it was known that there had been no cause of alarm, attempts were made to discover the origin of the rumour which had produced so much agitation. It appeared that some persons who had the look and dress of clowns just arrived from the country had first spread the report in the suburbs a little before midnight: but whence these men came, and by whom they were employed, remained a mystery. And soon news arrived from many quarters which bewildered the public mind still more. The panic had not been confined to London. The cry that disbanded Irish soldiers were coming to murder the Protestants had, with malignant ingenuity, been raised at once in many places widely distant from each other. Great numbers of letters, skilfully framed for the purpose of frightening ignorant people, had been sent by stage coaches, by waggons, and by the post, to various parts of England. All these letters came to hand almost at the same time. In a hundred towns at once the populace was possessed with the belief that armed barbarians were at hand, bent on perpetrating crimes as foul as those which had disgraced the rebellion of Ulster. No Protestant would find mercy. Children would be compelled by torture to murder their parents. Babes would be stuck on pikes, or flung into the blazing ruins of what had lately been happy dwellings. Great multitudes assembled with weapons: the people in some places began to pull down bridges, and to throw up barricades: but soon the excitement went down. In many districts those who had been so foully imposed upon learned with delight, alloyed by shame, that there was not a single Popish soldier within a week's march. There were places, indeed, where some straggling bands of Irish made their appearance and demanded food: but it can scarcely be imputed to them as a crime that they did not choose to die of hunger; and there is no evidence that they committed any wanton outrage. In truth they were much less numerous than was commonly supposed;

and their spirit was cowed by finding themselves left on a sudden without leaders or provisions, in the midst of a mighty population which felt towards them as men feel towards a drove of wolves. Of all the subjects of James none had more reason to execrate him than these unfortunate members of his church and defenders of his throne.

It is honourable to the English character that, notwithstanding the aversion with which the Roman Catholic religion and the Irish race were then regarded, notwithstanding the anarchy which was the effect of the flight of James, notwithstanding the artful machinations which were employed to scare the multitude into cruelty, no atrocious crime was perpetrated at this conjuncture. Much property, indeed, was destroyed and carried away. The houses of many Roman Catholic gentlemen were attacked. Parks were ravaged. Deer were slain and stolen. Some venerable specimens of the domestic architecture of the middle ages bear to this day the marks of popular violence. The roads were in many places made impassable by a self-appointed police, which stopped every traveller till he proved that he was not a Papist. The Thames was infested by a set of pirates who, under pretence of searching for arms or delinquents, rummaged every boat that passed. Obnoxious persons were insulted and hustled. Many persons who were not obnoxious were glad to ransom their persons and effects by bestowing some guineas on the zealous Protestants who had, without any legal authority, assumed the office of inquisitors. But in all this confusion, which lasted several days and extended over many counties, not a single Roman Catholic lost his life. The mob showed no inclination to blood, except in the case of Jeffreys; and the hatred which that bad man inspired had more affinity with humanity than with cruelty.

Many years later Hugh Speke affirmed that the Irish Night was his work, that he had prompted the rustics who raised London, and that he was the author of the letters which had spread dismay through the country. His assertion is not intrinsically improbable: but it rests on no evidence except his own word. He was a man quite capable of committing such a villainy, and quite capable also of falsely boasting that he had committed it.

14

William of Orange Becomes
King of England

[*Before William could reach London, the peaceful transfer of royal power was held up by an accident. Some fishermen at Sheerness, suspecting James to be a fugitive from authority, caused him to be arrested. He was identified, released, and returned to London, where a Council of Peers had formed a provisional government until the question of the Crown should be settled. The reappearance of James in London caused general embarrassment; but he found himself unable to make a party there and ultimately accepted orders from William to retire to Rochester, from which he soon afterwards made his escape to France. After the King's second withdrawal from London, William entered the city. Refusing to claim the Crown by conquest, he appointed a body, consisting of those peers and those members of Charles II's House of Commons who were available, together with the City magistrates, and invited them to consider the state of the country. The initiative was taken by the Lords, under the presidency of Halifax, whose authority, thanks to his majestic 'trimming', was recognized by all. He had held the balance to the end, but was now convinced that William must rule. This body requested William to assume the government of the country and summon a 'convention' or unofficial parliament. At the same time the two Drummonds were driven from power in Scotland, and an assembly of Scottish lords, under the chairmanship of the Duke of Hamilton, invited William to assume the government and to summon a similar Convention of the Estates of Scotland. Thus William found himself invested with authority over both kingdoms.*

Authority, but not yet kingship. The question of a transfer of the Crown raised theoretical issues which divided the Convention. While the whigs were prepared to declare James deposed and the throne vacant, tories were unwilling to admit that any subordinate power could alter the line of succession. At most they would accept William as regent. However, under the pressure of events, a compromise was

reached. It was assumed that James had 'abdicated' the government
and thereby left the throne vacant, and on this assumption the
Crown was settled equally on William and Mary, for their joint and
separate lives. During their joint lives, William was to be sole ruler:
he had made it clear that he would accept nothing less than effective
royal power, limited only by the constitutional liberties of England as
now set out in the 'Declaration of Right'; and Mary supported him
in his demand.

At the close of his tenth chapter, Macaulay describes the tender of
the Crown to William and Mary and summarizes the peculiar
character of the English 'Glorious Revolution'.]

ON the morning of Wednesday, the thirteenth of February, the
court of Whitehall and all the neighbouring streets were filled
with gazers. The magnificent Banqueting House, the masterpiece of Inigo, embellished by masterpieces of Rubens, had been
prepared for a great ceremony. The walls were lined by the Yeomen of the Guard. Near the northern door, on the right hand, a
large number of Peers had assembled. On the left were the Commons with their Speaker, attended by the mace. The southern
door opened: and the Prince and Princess of Orange, side by side,
entered, and took their place under the canopy of state.

Both Houses approached bowing low. William and Mary advanced a few steps. Halifax on the right, and Powle on the left,
stood forth; and Halifax spoke. The Convention, he said, had
agreed to a resolution which he prayed their Highnesses to hear.
They signified their assent; and the clerk of the House of Lords
read, in a loud voice, the Declaration of Right. When he had
concluded, Halifax, in the name of all the Estates of the Realm,
requested the Prince and Princess to accept the crown.

William, in his own name and in that of his wife, answered
that the crown was, in their estimation, the more valuable because
it was presented to them as a token of the confidence of the nation. 'We thankfully accept,' he said, 'what you have offered us.'
Then, for himself, he assured them that the laws of England,
which he had once already vindicated, should be the rules of his
conduct, that it should be his study to promote the welfare of the
kingdom, and that, as to the means of doing so, he should con-

stantly recur to the advice of the Houses, and should be disposed to trust their judgment rather than his own. These words were received with a shout of joy which was heard in the streets below, and was instantly answered by huzzas from many thousands of voices. The Lords and Commons then reverently retired from the Banqueting House and went in procession to the great gate of Whitehall, where the heralds and pursuivants were waiting in their gorgeous tabards. All the space as far as Charing Cross was one sea of heads. The kettle drums struck up; the trumpets pealed: and Garter King at Arms, in a loud voice, proclaimed the Prince and Princess of Orange King and Queen of England, charged all Englishmen to pay, from that moment, faith and true allegiance to the new sovereigns, and besought God, who had already wrought so signal a deliverance for our Church and nation, to bless William and Mary with a long and happy reign.

Thus was consummated the English Revolution. When we compare it with those revolutions which have, during the last sixty years, overthrown so many ancient governments, we cannot but be struck by its peculiar character. Why that character was so peculiar is sufficiently obvious, and yet seems not to have been always understood either by eulogists or by censors.

The continental revolutions of the eighteenth and nineteenth centuries took place in countries where all trace of the limited monarchy of the middle ages had long been effaced. The right of the prince to make laws and to levy money had, during many generations, been undisputed. His throne was guarded by a great regular army. His administration could not, without extreme peril, be blamed even in the mildest terms. His subjects held their personal liberty by no other tenure than his pleasure. Not a single institution was left which had, within the memory of the oldest man, afforded efficient protection to the subject against the utmost excess of tyranny. Those great councils which had once curbed the regal power had sunk into oblivion. Their composition and their privileges were known only to antiquaries. We cannot wonder, therefore, that, when men who had been thus ruled succeeded in wresting supreme power from a government which they had long in secret hated, they should have been impatient to demolish and unable to construct, that they should have been

fascinated by every specious novelty, that they should have proscribed every title, ceremony, and phrase associated with the old
system, and that, turning away with disgust from their own
national precedents and traditions, they should have sought for
principles of government in the writings of theorists, or aped,
with ignorant and ungraceful affectation, the patriots of Athens
and Rome. As little can we wonder that the violent action of the
revolutionary spirit should have been followed by reaction
equally violent, and that confusion should speedily have engendered despotism sterner than that from which it had sprung.

Had we been in the same situation; had Strafford succeeded in
his favourite scheme of Thorough; had he formed an army as
numerous and as well disciplined as that which, a few years later,
was formed by Cromwell; had a series of judicial decisions, similar to that which was pronounced by the Exchequer Chamber in
the case of shipmoney, transferred to the Crown the right of tax-
ing the people; had the Star Chamber and the High Commission
continued to fine, mutilate, and imprison every man who dared
to raise his voice against the government; had the press been as
completely enslaved here as at Vienna or at Naples; had our
Kings gradually drawn to themselves the whole legislative
power; had six generations of Englishmen passed away without a
single session of Parliament; and had we then at length risen up
in some moment of wild excitement against our masters, what an
outbreak would that have been! With what a crash, heard and
felt to the farthest ends of the world, would the whole vast fabric
of society have fallen! How many thousands of exiles, once the
most prosperous and the most refined members of this great
community, would have begged their bread in continental cities,
or have sheltered their heads under huts of bark in the uncleared
forests of America! How often should we have seen the pavement
of London piled up in barricades, the houses dinted with bullets,
the gutters foaming with blood! How many times should we have
rushed wildly from extreme to extreme, sought refuge from
anarchy in despotism, and been again driven by despotism into
anarchy! How many years of blood and confusion would it have
cost us to learn the very rudiments of political science! How
many childish theories would have duped us! How many rude

and ill poised constitutions should we have set up, only to see them tumble down! Happy would it have been for us if a sharp discipline of half a century had sufficed to educate us into a capacity of enjoying true freedom.

These calamities our Revolution averted. It was a revolution strictly defensive, and had prescription and legitimacy on its side. Here, and here only, a limited monarchy of the thirteenth century had come down unimpaired to the seventeenth century. Our parliamentary institutions were in full vigour. The main principles of our government were excellent. They were not, indeed, formally and exactly set forth in a single written instrument; but they were to be found scattered over our ancient and noble statutes; and, what was of far greater moment, they had been engraven on the hearts of Englishmen during four hundred years. That, without the consent of the representatives of the nation, no legislative act could be passed, no tax imposed, no regular soldiery kept up, that no man could be imprisoned, even for a day, by the arbitrary will of the sovereign, that no tool of power could plead the royal command as a justification for violating any right of the humblest subject, were held, both by Whigs and Tories, to be fundamental laws of the realm. A realm of which these were the fundamental laws stood in no need of a new constitution.

But, though a new constitution was not needed, it was plain that changes were required. The misgovernment of the Stuarts, and the troubles which that misgovernment had produced, sufficiently proved that there was somewhere a defect in our polity; and that defect it was the duty of the Convention to discover and to supply.

Some questions of great moment were still open to dispute. Our constitution had begun to exist in times when statesmen were not much accustomed to frame exact definitions. Anomalies, therefore, inconsistent with its principles and dangerous to its very existence, had sprung up almost imperceptibly, and, not having, during many years, caused any serious inconvenience, had gradually acquired the force of prescription. The remedy for these evils was to assert the rights of the people in such language

as should terminate all controversy, and to declare that no precedent could justify any violation of those rights.

When this had been done it would be impossible for our rulers
to misunderstand the law: but, unless something more were
done, it was by no means improbable that they might violate it.
Unhappily the Church had long taught the nation that hereditary monarchy, alone among our institutions, was divine and inviolable; that the right of the House of Commons to a share in the
legislative power was a right merely human, but that the right of
the King to the obedience of his people was from above; that the
Great Charter was a statute which might be repealed by those
who had made it, but that the rule which called the princes of the
blood royal to the throne in order of succession was of celestial
origin, and that any Act of Parliament inconsistent with that rule
was a nullity. It is evident that, in a society in which such superstitions prevail, constitutional freedom must ever be insecure. A
power which is regarded merely as the ordinance of man cannot
be an efficient check on a power which is regarded as the ordinance of God. It is vain to hope that laws, however excellent, will
permanently restrain a King who, in his own opinion, and in that
of a great part of his people, has an authority infinitely higher in
kind than the authority which belongs to those laws. To deprive
royalty of these mysterious attributes, and to establish the principle that Kings reigned by a right in no respect differing from
the right by which freeholders chose knights of the shire, or from
the right by which Judges granted writs of Habeas Corpus, was
absolutely necessary to the security of our liberties.

Thus the Convention had two great duties to perform. The
first was to clear the fundamental laws of the realm from ambiguity. The second was to eradicate from the minds, both of the
governors and of the governed, the false and pernicious notion
that the royal prerogative was something more sublime and holy
than those fundamental laws. The former object was attained by
the solemn recital and claim with which the Declaration of Right
commences; the latter by the resolution which pronounced the
throne vacant, and invited William and Mary to fill it.

The change seems small. Not a single flower of the crown was touched. Not a single new right was given to the people. The whole English law, substantive and adjective, was, in the judgment of all the greatest lawyers, of Holt and Treby, of Maynard and Somers, exactly the same after the Revolution as before it. Some controverted points had been decided according to the sense of the best jurists; and there had been a slight deviation from the ordinary course of succession. This was all; and this was enough.

As our Revolution was a vindication of ancient rights, so it was conducted with strict attention to ancient formalities. In almost every word and act may be discerned a profound reverence for the past. The Estates of the Realm deliberated in the old halls and according to the old rules. Powle was conducted to his chair between his mover and his seconder with the accustomed forms. The Serjeant with his mace brought up the messengers of the Lords to the table of the Commons; and the three obeisances were duly made. The conference was held with all the antique ceremonial. On one side of the table, in the Painted Chamber, the managers of the Lords sat covered and robed in ermine and gold. The managers of the Commons stood bareheaded on the other side. The speeches present an almost ludicrous contrast to the revolutionary oratory of every other country. Both the English parties agreed in treating with solemn respect the ancient constitutional traditions of the state. The only question was, in what sense those traditions were to be understood. The assertors of liberty said not a word about the natural equality of men and the inalienable sovereignty of the people, about Harmodius or Timoleon, Brutus the elder or Brutus the younger. When they were told that, by the English law, the crown, at the moment of a demise, must descend to the next heir, they answered that, by the English law, a living man could have no heir. When they were told that there was no precedent for declaring the throne vacant, they produced from among the records in the Tower a roll of parchment, near three hundred years old, on which, in quaint characters and barbarous Latin, it was recorded that the Estates of the Realm had declared vacant the throne of a perfidious and tyrannical Plantagenet. When at length the dispute had been accommodated, the new sovereigns were proclaimed with the old pageantry. All the fantastic pomp of heraldry was there, Clarencieux and Norroy, Portcullis and Rouge Dragon, the trumpets, the banners, the grotesque coats embroidered with lions and lilies. The title of King of France, assumed by the conqueror of Cressy, was not omitted in the royal style. To us, who have lived in the year 1848, it may seem almost an abuse of terms to call a proceeding, conducted with so much deliberation, with so much sobriety, and with such minute attention to prescriptive etiquette, by the terrible name of Revolution.

And yet this revolution, of all revolutions the least violent, has been of all revolutions the most beneficent. It finally decided the great question whether the popular element which had, ever since the age of Fitzwalter and De Montfort, been found in the English polity, should be destroyed by the monarchical element, or should be suffered to develop itself freely, and to become dominant. The strife between the two principles had been long, fierce, and doubtful. It had lasted through four reigns. It had produced seditions, impeachments, rebellions, battles, sieges, proscriptions, judicial massacres. Sometimes liberty, sometimes royalty, had seemed to be on the point of perishing. During many years one half of the energy of England had been employed in counteracting the other half. The executive power and the legislative power had so effectually impeded each other that the state had been of no account in Europe. The King at Arms, who proclaimed William and Mary before Whitehall Gate, did in truth announce that this great struggle was over; that there was entire union between the throne and the Parliament; that England, long dependent and degraded, was again a power of the first rank; that the ancient laws by which the prerogative was bounded would henceforth be held as sacred as the prerogative itself, and would be followed out to all their consequences; that the executive administration would be conducted in conformity with the sense of the representatives of the nation; and that no reform, which the two Houses should, after mature deliberation, propose, would be obstinately withstood by the sovereign. The Declaration of Right, though it made nothing law which had not been law before, contained the germ of the law which gave religious freedom to the Dissenter, of the law which secured the independence of the

Judges, of the law which limited the duration of Parliaments, of the law which placed the liberty of the press under the protection of juries, of the law which prohibited the slave trade, of the law which abolished the sacramental test, of the law which relieved the Roman Catholics from civil disabilities, of the law which reformed the representative system, of every good law which has been passed during a hundred and sixty years, of every good law which may hereafter, in the course of ages, be found necessary to promote the public weal, and to satisfy the demands of public opinion.

The highest eulogy which can be pronounced on the revolution of 1688 is this, that it was our last revolution. Several generations have now passed away since any wise and patriotic Englishman has meditated resistance to the established government. In all honest and reflecting minds there is a conviction, daily strengthened by experience, that the means of effecting every improvement which the constitution requires may be found within the constitution itself.

Now, if ever,[1] we ought to be able to appreciate the whole importance of the stand which was made by our forefathers against the House of Stuart. All around us the world is convulsed by the agonies of great nations. Governments which lately seemed likely to stand during ages have been on a sudden shaken and overthrown. The proudest capitals of Western Europe have streamed with civil blood. All evil passions, the thirst of gain and the thirst of vengeance, the antipathy of class to class, the antipathy of race to race, have broken loose from the control of divine and human laws. Fear and anxiety have clouded the faces and depressed the hearts of millions. Trade has been suspended, and industry paralysed. The rich have become poor; and the poor have become poorer. Doctrines hostile to all sciences, to all arts, to all industry, to all domestic charities, doctrines which, if carried into effect, would, in thirty years, undo all that thirty centuries have done for mankind, and would make the fairest provinces of France and Germany as savage as Congo or Patagonia, have been avowed from the tribune and defended by the sword. Europe has been threatened with subjugation by barbarians, compared with whom

[1. That is, in 1848, when revolution broke out over most of Europe.]

the barbarians who marched under Attila and Alboin were enlightened and humane. The truest friends of the people have
with deep sorrow owned that interests more precious than any
political privileges were in jeopardy, and that it might be necessary to sacrifice even liberty in order to save civilisation. Meanwhile in our island the regular course of government has never
been for a day interrupted. The few bad men who longed for
license and plunder have not had the courage to confront for one
moment the strength of a loyal nation, rallied in firm array round
a parental throne. And, if it be asked what has made us to differ
from others, the answer is that we never lost what others are
wildly and blindly seeking to regain. It is because we had a pre-
serving revolution in the seventeenth century that we have not
had a destroying revolution in the nineteenth. It is because we
had freedom in the midst of servitude that we have order in the
midst of anarchy. For the authority of law, for the security of
property, for the peace of our streets, for the happiness of our
homes, our gratitude is due, under Him who raises and pulls
down nations at his pleasure, to the Long Parliament, to the Convention, and to William of Orange.

15

The Revolution in Ireland

A. THE SIEGE OF LONDONDERRY, APRIL–JULY 1689

[*The Revolution in England had been swift, bloodless, and complete;
but it could not be regarded as irreversible as long as James II retained a base in the British Isles and was supported by the militant
enemies of William in Europe. In fact he had such a base and such
support. If the Protestant party had triumphed in the Saxon lands –
in England and in Lowland Scotland – James II, like his father before him, could appeal to the 'Celtic fringe' – to Catholic Ireland
and the untamed Highlands of Scotland where social, tribal, and
racial tensions were polarized around this new struggle. Further, unlike his father, James could rely on strong foreign support. Louis
XIV, now at the height of his power, welcomed his fugitive client
with magnanimous courtesy, installed him as his pensioner in St Germain-en-Laye near Paris, and promised to secure his restoration. It
was to his own interest to do so. In leaving open William's way to
England, he had supposed that he was diverting his greatest enemy
into a blind alley: that England would be effectively neutralized, as
it had been during the Thirty Years War, by prolonged internal convulsions; that the Netherlands would similarly be neutralized by
their involvement in those convulsions; and that he would be left free
to impose his will in Europe. The rapidity of events in England
totally destroyed these hopes, and Louis now saw his enemies not
weakened but immensely strengthened as the resources of England
were drawn into the war against him. In these circumstances it was
essential to him to undermine the power of William in his new kingdom. Policy, as well as gratitude and chivalry, obliged him to give
active support to the Stuart cause.*

*The immediate theatre for such action was Ireland. James had already taken the administration, the courts, and the army of Ireland
away from the Protestant English settlers and placed them in the
hands of Tyrconnel and the Catholic Irish. With his Irish army, he*

proposed to invade Scotland and rally the Highland clans in support of the Scottish Jacobites. In order to cross these designs, it was essential for William to intervene at once in Ireland. The Protestants still had a narrow base in Ireland, Ulster, where the Anglo-Saxon settlement (largely from Scotland) was deepest. For James, it was essential to overrun this base and use it for the reconquest of Scotland. For William it was essential to preserve the same base for the reconquest of Ireland. Thus the initial struggle centred on the two positions still held and defended by the Protestants of Ulster: the fort of Enniskillen, on an island in Lough Erne, in county Fermanagh, and the city of Londonderry, commanding the great natural harbour of Lough Foyle.

In order to establish his power in Ireland, James sailed from Brest. He was accompanied by a few English and Scottish Jacobites, including Lord Melfort, the fugitive Scottish Secretary of State; but the expedition was French. James sailed in a French fleet, with French advisers and experts, including Louis's ablest diplomatist, the Comte d'Avaux, and an experienced general, the Comte de Rosen, a Livonian soldier of fortune, who was to be Marshal of France. He landed at Kinsale and arrived in Dublin on 24 March 1689. He then summoned an Irish parliament to meet on 7 May, and himself marched to Ulster where the fall of Londonderry was supposed to be imminent. The following passages from Chapter XII describe the famous siege of Londonderry by James and its relief by the forces of William.]

IN the camp it was generally expected that Londonderry would fall without a blow. Rosen confidently predicted that the mere sight of the Irish army would terrify the garrison into submission. But Richard Hamilton, who knew the temper of the colonists better, had misgivings. The assailants were sure of one important ally within the walls. Lundy, the Governor, professed the Protestant religion, and had joined in proclaiming William and Mary; but he was in secret communication with the enemies of his Church and of the Sovereigns to whom he had sworn fealty. Some have suspected that he was a concealed Jacobite, and that he had affected to acquiesce in the Revolution only in order that he might be better able to assist in bringing about a Restoration: but it is probable that his conduct is rather to be attributed to faintheartedness and poverty of spirit than to zeal for any public cause. He seems to have thought resistance hopeless; and in truth, to a military eye, the defences of Londonderry appeared contemptible. The fortifications consisted of a simple wall overgrown with grass and weeds: there was no ditch even before the gates: the drawbridges had long been neglected: the chains were rusty and could scarcely be used: the parapets and towers were built after a fashion which might well move disciples of Vauban[1] to laughter; and these feeble defences were on almost every side commanded by heights. Indeed those who laid out the city had never meant that it should be able to stand a regular siege, and had contented themselves with throwing up works sufficient to protect the inhabitants against a tumultuary attack of the Celtic peasantry. Avaux assured Louvois[2] that a single French battalion would easily storm such defences. Even if the place should, notwithstanding all disadvantages, be able to repel a large army directed by the science and experience of generals who had served under Condé and Turenne, hunger must soon bring the contest to an end. The stock of provisions was small; and the population had been swollen to seven or eight times the ordinary number by a multitude of colonists flying from the rage of the natives.

Lundy, therefore, from the time when the Irish army entered Ulster, seems to have given up all thought of serious resistance. He talked so despondingly that the citizens and his own soldiers murmured against him. He seemed, they said, to be bent on discouraging them. Meanwhile the enemy drew daily nearer and nearer; and it was known that James himself was coming to take the command of his forces.

Just at this moment a glimpse of hope appeared. On the fourteenth of April ships from England anchored in the bay. They had on board two regiments which had been sent, under the command of a Colonel named Cunningham, to reinforce the

[1. Sebastian de Vauban, the greatest of military engineers, the architect of Louis XIV's fortresses.]

[2. François Michel Le Tellier, Marquis de Louvois, Louis XIV's Minister of War.]

garrison. Cunningham and several of his officers went on shore and conferred with Lundy. Lundy dissuaded them from landing their men. The place, he said, could not hold out. To throw more troops into it would therefore be worse than useless: for the more numerous the garrison, the more prisoners would fall into the hands of the enemy. The best thing that the two regiments could do would be to sail back to England. He meant, he said, to withdraw himself privately; and the inhabitants must then try to make good terms for themselves.

He went through the form of holding a council of war; but from this council he excluded all those officers of the garrison whose sentiments he knew to be different from his own. Some, who had ordinarily been summoned on such occasions, and who now came uninvited, were thrust out of the room. Whatever the Governor said was echoed by his creatures. Cunningham and Cunningham's companions could scarcely venture to oppose their opinion to that of a person whose local knowledge was necessarily far superior to theirs, and whom they were by their instructions directed to obey. One brave soldier murmured. 'Understand this,' he said, 'to give up Londonderry is to give up Ireland.' But his objections were contemptuously overruled. The meeting broke up. Cunningham and his officers returned to the ships, and made preparations for departing. Meanwhile Lundy privately sent a messenger to the headquarters of the enemy, with assurances that the city should be peaceably surrendered on the first summons.

But as soon as what had passed in the council of war was whispered about the streets, the spirit of the soldiers and citizens swelled up high and fierce against the dastardly and perfidious chief who had betrayed them. Many of his own officers declared that they no longer thought themselves bound to obey him. Voices were heard threatening, some that his brains should be blown out, some that he should be hanged on the walls. A deputation was sent to Cunningham imploring him to assume the command. He excused himself on the plausible ground that his orders were to take directions in all things from the Governor. Meanwhile it was rumoured that the persons most in Lundy's confidence were stealing out of the town one by one. Long after dusk on the evening of the seventeenth it was found that the gates were open and that the keys had disappeared. The officers who made the discovery took on themselves to change the passwords and to double the guards. The night, however, passed over without any assault.

After some anxious hours the day broke. The Irish, with James at their head, were now within four miles of the city. A tumultuous council of the chief inhabitants was called. Some of them vehemently reproached the Governor to his face with his treachery. He had sold them, they cried, to their deadliest enemy: he had refused admission to the force which good King William had sent to defend them. While the altercation was at the height, the sentinels who paced the ramparts announced that the vanguard of the hostile army was in sight. Lundy had given orders that there should be no firing; but his authority was at an end. Two gallant soldiers, Major Henry Baker and Captain Adam Murray, called the people to arms. They were assisted by the eloquence of an aged clergyman, George Walker, rector of the parish of Donaghmore, who had, with many of his neighbours, taken refuge in Londonderry. The whole of the crowded city was moved by one impulse. Soldiers, gentlemen, yeomen, artisans, rushed to the walls and manned the guns. James, who, confident of success, had approached within a hundred yards of the southern gate, was received with a shout of 'No surrender,' and with a fire from the nearest bastion. An officer of his staff fell dead by his side. The King and his attendants made all haste to get out of reach of the cannon balls. Lundy, who was now in imminent danger of being torn limb from limb by those whom he had betrayed, hid himself in an inner chamber. There he lay during the day, and at night, with the generous and politic connivance of Murray and Walker, made his escape in the disguise of a porter. The part of the wall from which he let himself down is still pointed out; and people still living talk of having tasted the fruit of a pear tree which assisted him in his descent. His name is, to this day, held in execration by the Protestants of the North of Ireland; and his effigy was long, and perhaps still is, annually hung and burned by them with marks of abhorrence similar to those which in England are appropriated to Guy Fawkes.

And now Londonderry was left destitute of all military and of all civil government. No man in the town had a right to command any other: the defences were weak: the provisions were scanty: an incensed tyrant and a great army were at the gates. But within was that which has often, in desperate extremities, retrieved the fallen fortunes of nations. Betrayed, deserted, disorganized, unprovided with resources, begirt with enemies, the noble city was still no easy conquest. Whatever an engineer might think of the strength of the ramparts, all that was most intelligent, most courageous, most high-spirited among the Englishry of Leinster and of Northern Ulster was crowded behind them. The number of men capable of bearing arms within the walls was seven thousand; and the whole world could not have furnished seven thousand men better qualified to meet a terrible emergency with clear judgment, dauntless valour, and stubborn patience. They were all zealous Protestants; and the Protestantism of the majority was tinged with Puritanism. They had much in common with that sober, resolute, and godfearing class out of which Cromwell had formed his unconquerable army. But the peculiar situation in which they had been placed had developed in them some qualities which, in the mother country, might possibly have remained latent. The English inhabitants of Ireland were an aristocratic caste, which had been enabled, by superior civilisation, by close union, by sleepless vigilance, by cool intrepidity, to keep in subjection a numerous and hostile population. Almost every one of them had been in some measure trained both to military and to political functions. Almost everyone was familiar with the use of arms, and was accustomed to bear a part in the administration of justice. It was remarked by contemporary writers that the colonists had something of the Castilian haughtiness of manner, though none of the Castilian indolence, that they spoke English with remarkable purity and correctness, and that they were, both as militiamen and as jurymen, superior to their kindred in the mother country.

In all ages, men situated as the Anglo-Saxons in Ireland were situated have had peculiar vices and peculiar virtues, the vices and virtues of masters, as opposed to the vices and virtues of slaves. The member of a dominant race is, in his dealings with the subject race, seldom indeed fraudulent – for fraud is the resource of the weak – but imperious, insolent, and cruel. Towards his brethren, on the other hand, his conduct is generally just, kind, and even noble. His self-respect leads him to respect all who belong to his own order. His interest impels him to cultivate a good understanding with those whose prompt, strenuous, and courageous assistance may at any moment be necessary to preserve his property and life. It is a truth ever present to his mind that his own wellbeing depends on the ascendency of the class to which he belongs. His very selfishness therefore is sublimed into public spirit: and this public spirit is stimulated to fierce enthusiasm by sympathy, by the desire of applause, and by the dread of infamy. For the only opinion which he values is the opinion of his fellows; and in their opinion devotion to the common cause is the most sacred of duties. The character, thus formed, has two aspects. Seen on one side, it must be regarded by every well constituted mind with disapprobation. Seen on the other, it irresistibly extorts applause. The Spartan, smiting and spurning the wretched Helot, moves our disgust. But the same Spartan, calmly dressing his hair, and uttering his concise jests, on what he well knows to be his last day, in the pass of Thermopylæ, is not to be contemplated without admiration. To a superficial observer it may seem strange that so much evil and so much good should be found together. But in truth the good and the evil, which at first sight appear almost incompatible, are closely connected, and have a common origin. It was because the Spartan had been taught to revere himself as one of a race of sovereigns, and to look down on all that was not Spartan as of an inferior species, that he had no fellow feeling for the miserable serfs who crouched before him, and that the thought of submitting to a foreign master, or of turning his back before an enemy, never, even in the last extremity, crossed his mind. Something of the same character, compounded of tyrant and hero, has been found in all nations which have domineered over more numerous nations. But it has nowhere in modern Europe shown itself so conspicuously as in Ireland. With what contempt, with what antipathy, the ruling minority in that country long regarded the subject majority may be best learned from the hateful laws which, within the memory of men still living, disgraced the Irish statute book. Those laws were at length annulled: but the spirit which had dictated them survived them, and even at this day sometimes breaks out in excesses pernicious to the commonwealth and dishonourable to the Protestant religion. Nevertheless it is impossible to deny that the English colonists have had, with too many of the faults, all the noblest virtues of a sovereign caste. The faults have, as was natural, been most offensively exhibited in times of prosperity and security: the virtues have been most resplendent in times of distress and peril; and never were those virtues more signally displayed than by the defenders of Londonderry, when their Governor had abandoned them, and when the camp of their mortal enemy was pitched before their walls.

No sooner had the first burst of the rage excited by the perfidy of Lundy spent itself than those whom he had betrayed proceeded, with a gravity and prudence worthy of the most renowned senates, to provide for the order and defence of the city. Two governors were elected, Baker and Walker. Baker took the chief military command. Walker's especial business was to preserve internal tranquillity, and to dole out supplies from the magazines. The inhabitants capable of bearing arms were distributed into eight regiments. Colonels, captains, and subordinate officers were appointed. In a few hours every man knew his post, and was ready to repair to it as soon as the beat of the drum was heard. That machinery, by which Oliver had, in the preceding generation, kept up among his soldiers so stern and so pertinacious an enthusiasm, was again employed with not less complete success. Preaching and praying occupied a large part of every day. Eighteen clergymen of the Established Church and seven or eight nonconformist ministers were within the walls. They all exerted themselves indefatigably to rouse and sustain the spirit of the people. Among themselves there was for the time entire harmony. All disputes about church government, postures, ceremonies, were forgotten. The Bishop, having found that his lectures on passive obedience were derided even by the Episcopalians, had withdrawn himself, first to Raphoe, and then to England, and was preaching in a chapel in London. On the other hand, a Scotch fanatic named Hewson, who had exhorted the

Presbyterians not to ally themselves with such as refused to subscribe the Covenant, had sunk under the well merited disgust
and scorn of the whole Protestant community. The aspect of the
Cathedral was remarkable. Cannon were planted on the summit
of the broad tower which has since given place to a tower of different proportions. Ammunition was stored in the vaults. In the
choir the liturgy of the Anglican Church was read every morning. Every afternoon the Dissenters crowded to a simpler worship.

James had waited twenty-four hours, expecting, as it should
seem, the performance of Lundy's promises; and in twenty-four
hours the arrangements for the defence of Londonderry were
complete. On the evening of the nineteenth of April, a trumpeter
came to the southern gate, and asked whether the engagements
into which the Governor had entered would be fulfilled. The
answer was that the men who guarded these walls had nothing to
do with the Governor's engagements, and were determined to
resist to the last.

On the following day a messenger of higher rank was sent,
Claude Hamilton, Lord Strabane, one of the few Roman Catholic peers of Ireland. Murray, who had been appointed to the
command of one of the eight regiments into which the garrison
was distributed, advanced from the gate to meet the flag of truce;
and a short conference was held. Strabane had been authorised to
make large promises. The citizens should have a free pardon for
all that was past if they would submit to their lawful Sovereign.
Murray himself should have a colonel's commission, and a thousand pounds in money. 'The men of Londonderry,' answered
Murray, 'have done nothing that requires a pardon, and own no
Sovereign but King William and Queen Mary. It will not be safe
for your Lordship to stay longer, or to return on the same errand.
Let me have the honour of seeing you through the lines.'

James had been assured, and had fully expected, that the city
would yield as soon as it was known that he was before the walls.
Finding himself mistaken, he broke loose from the control of
Melfort, and determined to return instantly to Dublin. Rosen
accompanied the King. The direction of the siege was intrusted

to Maumont.[3] Richard Hamilton was second, and Pusignan third, in command.

The operations now commenced in earnest. The besiegers began by battering the town. It was soon on fire in several places. Roofs and upper stories of houses fell in, and crushed the inmates. During a short time the garrison, many of whom had never before seen the effect of a cannonade, seemed to be discomposed by the crash of chimneys, and by the heaps of ruin mingled with disfigured corpses. But familiarity with danger and horror produced in a few hours the natural effect. The spirit of the people rose so high that their chiefs thought it safe to act on the offensive. On the twenty-first of April a sally was made under the command of Murray. The Irish stood their ground resolutely; and a furious and bloody contest took place. Maumont, at the head of a body of cavalry, flew to the place where the fight was raging. He was struck in the head by a musket ball, and fell a corpse. The besiegers lost several other officers, and about two hundred men, before the colonists could be driven in. Murray escaped with difficulty. His horse was killed under him; and he was beset by enemies: but he was able to defend himself till some of his friends made a rush from the gate to his rescue, with old Walker at their head.

In consequence of the death of Maumont, Hamilton was once more commander of the Irish army.[4] His exploits in that post did not raise his reputation. He was a fine gentleman and a brave soldier; but he had no pretensions to the character of a great general, and had never, in his life, seen a siege. Pusignan had more science and energy. But Pusignan survived Maumont little more than a fortnight. At four in the morning of the sixth of May, the garrison made another sally, took several flags, and killed many of the besiegers. Pusignan, fighting gallantly, was shot through the body. The wound was one which a skilful surgeon might have cured: but there was no such surgeon in the Irish camp; and the communication with Dublin was slow and

[3. The French Lieutenant-General under Rosen.]

[4. Richard Hamilton had commanded the force sent to Ulster by Tyrconnel before the arrival of James with his French officers.]

irregular. The poor Frenchman died, complaining bitterly of the barbarous ignorance and negligence which had shortened his days. A medical man, who had been sent down express from the capital, arrived after the funeral. James, in consequence, as it should seem, of this disaster, established a daily post between Dublin Castle and Hamilton's headquarters. Even by this conveyance letters did not travel very expeditiously: for the couriers went on foot; and, from fear probably of the Enniskilleners, took a circuitous route from military post to military post.

May passed away: June arrived; and still Londonderry held out. There had been many sallies and skirmishes with various success: but, on the whole, the advantage had been with the garrison. Several officers of note had been carried prisoners into the city; and two French banners, torn after hard fighting from the besiegers, had been hung as trophies in the chancel of the Cathedral. It seemed that the siege must be turned into a blockade. But before the hope of reducing the town by main force was relinquished, it was determined to make a great effort. The point selected for assault was an outwork called Windmill Hill, which was not far from the southern gate. Religious stimulants were employed to animate the courage of the forlorn hope. Many volunteers bound themselves by oath to make their way into the works or to perish in the attempt. Captain Butler, son of the Lord Mountgarret, undertook to lead the sworn men to the attack. On the walls the colonists were drawn up in three ranks. The office of those who were behind was to load the muskets of those who were in front. The Irish came on boldly and with a fearful uproar, but after long and hard fighting were driven back. The women of Londonderry were seen amidst the thickest fire serving out water and ammunition to their husbands and brothers. In one place, where the wall was only seven feet high, Butler and some of his sworn men succeeded in reaching the top; but they were all killed or made prisoners. At length, after four hundred of the Irish had fallen, their chiefs ordered a retreat to be sounded.

Nothing was left but to try the effect of hunger. It was known that the stock of food in the city was but slender. Indeed it was thought strange that the supplies should have held out so long.

Every precaution was now taken against the introduction of provisions. All the avenues leading to the city by land were closely guarded. On the south were encamped, along the left bank of the Foyle, the horsemen who had followed Lord Galmoy from the valley of the Barrow. Their chief was of all the Irish captains the most dreaded and the most abhorred by the Protestants. For he had disciplined his men with rare skill and care; and many frightful stories were told of his barbarity and perfidy. Long lines of tents, occupied by the infantry of Butler and O'Neil, of Lord Slane and Lord Gormanstown, by Nugent's Westmeath men, by Eustace's Kildare men, and by Cavanagh's Kerry men, extended northward till they again approached the water side. The river was fringed with forts and batteries which no vessel could pass without great peril. After some time it was determined to make the security still more complete by throwing a barricade across the stream, about a mile and a half below the city. Several boats full of stones were sunk. A row of stakes was driven into the bottom of the river. Large pieces of fir wood, strongly bound together, formed a boom which was more than a quarter of a mile in length, and which was firmly fastened to both shores, by cables a foot thick. A huge stone, to which the cable on the left bank was attached, was removed many years later, for the purpose of being polished and shaped into a column. But the intention was abandoned, and the rugged mass still lies, not many yards from its original site, amidst the shades which surround a pleasant country house named Boom Hall. Hard by is the well from which the besiegers drank. A little further off is the burial ground where they laid their slain, and where even in our own time the spade of the gardener has struck upon many skulls and thighbones at a short distance beneath the turf and flowers.

*

[*Meanwhile, in Dublin, James's Irish Parliament was passing acts of indiscriminate confiscation and attainder against English settlers and Protestants. In consequence of these acts, which revealed James as the tool of an Irish faction, and so further reduced his chances of support in England, evicted English settlers arrived as refugees in England.*]

The fugitive Englishry found in England warm sympathy and munificent relief. Many were received into the houses of friends and kinsmen. Many were indebted for the means of subsistence to the liberality of strangers. Among those who bore a part in this work of mercy, none contributed more largely or less ostentatiously than the Queen. The House of Commons placed at the King's disposal fifteen thousand pounds for the relief of those refugees whose wants were most pressing, and requested him to give commissions in the army to those who were qualified for military employment. An Act was also passed enabling beneficed clergymen who had fled from Ireland to hold preferment in England.

Yet the interest which the nation felt in these unfortunate guests was languid when compared with the interest excited by that portion of the Saxon colony which still maintained in Ulster a desperate conflict against overwhelming odds. On this subject scarcely one dissentient voice was to be heard in our island. Whigs, Tories, nay even those Jacobites in whom Jacobitism had not extinguished every patriotic sentiment, gloried in the glory of Enniskillen and Londonderry. The House of Commons was all of one mind. 'This is no time to be counting cost,' said honest Birch, who well remembered the way in which Oliver had made war on the Irish. 'Are those brave fellows in Londonderry to be deserted? If we lose them will not all the world cry shame upon us? A boom across the river! Why have we not cut the boom in pieces? Are our brethren to perish almost in sight of England, within a few hours' voyage of our shores?' Howe, the most vehement man of one party, declared that the hearts of the people were set on Ireland. Seymour, the leader of the other party, declared that, though he had not taken part in setting up the new government, he should cordially support it in all that might be necessary for the preservation of Ireland. The Commons appointed a committee to enquire into the cause of the delays and miscarriages which had been all but fatal to the Englishry of Ulster. The officers to whose treachery or cowardice the public ascribed the calamities of Londonderry were put under arrest. Lundy was sent to the Tower, Cunningham to the Gate House. The agitation of the public mind was in some degree calmed by the announcement that, before the end of the summer, an army powerful enough to re-establish the English ascendency in Ireland would be sent across Saint George's Channel, and that Schomberg would be the General. In the meantime an expedition which was thought to be sufficient for the relief of Londonderry was despatched from Liverpool under the command of Kirke. The dogged obstinacy with which this man had, in spite of royal solicitations, adhered to his religion, and the part which he had taken in the Revolution, had perhaps entitled him to an amnesty for past crimes. But it is difficult to understand why the Government should have selected for a post of the highest importance an officer who was generally and justly hated, who had never shown eminent talents for war, and who, both in Africa and in England, had notoriously tolerated among his soldiers a licentiousness, not only shocking to humanity, but also incompatible with discipline.

On the sixteenth of May, Kirke's troops embarked: on the twenty-second they sailed: but contrary winds made the passage slow, and forced the armament to stop long at the Isle of Man. Meanwhile the Protestants of Ulster were defending themselves with stubborn courage against a great superiority of force. The Enniskilleners had never ceased to wage a vigorous partisan war against the native population. Early in May they marched to encounter a large body of troops from Connaught, who had made an inroad into Donegal. The Irish were speedily routed, and fled to Sligo with the loss of a hundred and twenty men killed and sixty taken. Two small pieces of artillery and several horses fell into the hands of the conquerors. Elated by this success, the Enniskilleners soon invaded the county of Cavan, drove before them fifteen hundred of James's troops, took and destroyed the castle of Ballincarrig, reputed the strongest in that part of the kingdom, and carried off the pikes and muskets of the garrison. The next incursion was into Meath. Three thousand oxen and two thousand sheep were swept away and brought safe to the little island in Lough Erne. These daring exploits spread terror even to the gates of Dublin. Colonel Hugh Sutherland was ordered to march against Enniskillen with a regiment of dragoons and two regiments of foot. He carried with him arms for the native peasantry; and many repaired to his standard. The Enniskilleners did not wait till he came into their neighbourhood, but advanced to encounter him. He declined an action, and retreated, leaving his stores at Belturbet under the care of a detachment of three hundred soldiers. The Protestants attacked Belturbet with vigour, made their way into a lofty house which overlooked the town, and thence opened such a fire that in two hours the garrison surrendered. Seven hundred muskets, a great quantity of powder, many horses, many sacks of biscuits, many barrels of meal, were taken, and were sent to Enniskillen. The boats which brought these precious spoils were joyfully welcomed. The fear of hunger was removed. While the aboriginal population had, in many counties, altogether neglected the cultivation of the earth, in the expectation, it should seem, that marauding would prove an inexhaustible resource, the colonists, true to the provident and industrious character of their race, had, in the midst of war, not omitted carefully to till the soil in the neighbourhood of their strongholds. The harvest was now not far remote; and, till the harvest, the food taken from the enemy would be amply sufficient.

Yet, in the midst of success and plenty, the Enniskilleners were tortured by a cruel anxiety for Londonderry. They were bound to the defenders of that city, not only by religious and national sympathy, but by common interest. For there could be no doubt that, if Londonderry fell, the whole Irish army would instantly march in irresistible force upon Lough Erne. Yet what could be done? Some brave men were for making a desperate attempt to relieve the besieged city; but the odds were too great. Detachments however were sent which infested the rear of the blockading army, cut off supplies, and, on one occasion, carried away the horses of three entire troops of cavalry. Still the line of posts which surrounded Londonderry by land remained unbroken. The river was still strictly closed and guarded. Within the walls the distress had become extreme. So early as the eighth of June horseflesh was almost the only meat which could be purchased; and of horseflesh the supply was scanty. It was necessary to make up the deficiency with tallow; and even tallow was doled out with a parsimonious hand.

On the fifteenth of June a gleam of hope appeared. The sentinels on the top of the Cathedral saw sails nine miles off in the bay of Lough Foyle. Thirty vessels of different sizes were counted. Signals were made from the steeples and returned from the mast heads, but were imperfectly understood on both sides. At last a messenger from the fleet eluded the Irish sentinels, dived under the boom, and informed the garrison that Kirke had arrived from England with troops, arms, ammunition, and provisions, to relieve the city.

In Londonderry expectation was at the height: but a few hours of feverish joy were followed by weeks of misery. Kirke thought it unsafe to make any attempt, either by land or by water, on the lines of the besiegers, and retired to the entrance of Lough Foyle, where, during several weeks, he lay inactive.

And now the pressure of famine became every day more severe. A strict search was made in all the recesses of all the houses of the city; and some provisions, which had been concealed in cellars by people who had since died or made their escape, were discovered and carried to the magazines. The stock of cannon balls was almost exhausted; and their place was supplied by brickbats coated with lead. Pestilence began, as usual, to make its appearance in the train of hunger. Fifteen officers died of fever in one day. The Governor Baker was among those who sank under the disease. His place was supplied by Colonel John Mitchelburne.

Meanwhile it was known at Dublin that Kirke and his squadron were on the coast of Ulster. The alarm was great at the Castle. Even before this news arrived, Avaux had given it as his opinion that Richard Hamilton was unequal to the difficulties of the situation. It had therefore been resolved that Rosen should take the chief command. He was now sent down with all speed.

On the nineteenth of June he arrived at the headquarters of the besieging army. At first he attempted to undermine the walls; but his plan was discovered; and he was compelled to abandon it after a sharp fight, in which more than a hundred of his men were slain. Then his fury rose to a strange pitch. He, an old soldier, a Marshal of France in expectancy, trained in the school of the greatest generals, accustomed, during many years, to scientific war, to be baffled by a mob of country gentlemen, farmers, shopkeepers, who were protected only by a wall which any good engineer would at once have pronounced untenable! He raved, he blasphemed, in a language of his own, made up of all the dialects spoken from the Baltic to the Atlantic. He would raze the city to the ground: he would spare no living thing; no, not the young girls; not the babies at the breast. As to the leaders, death was too light a punishment for them: he would rack them: he would roast them alive. In his rage he ordered a shell to be flung into the town with a letter containing a horrible menace. He would, he said, gather into one body all the Protestants who had remained at their homes between Charlemont and the sea, old men, women, children, many of them near in blood and affection to the defenders of Londonderry. No protection, whatever might be the authority by which it had been given, should be respected. The multitude thus brought together should be driven under the walls of Londonderry, and should there be starved to death in the sight of their countrymen, their friends, their kinsmen.

This was no idle threat. Parties were instantly sent out in all directions to collect victims. At dawn, on the morning of the second of July, hundreds of Protestants, who were charged with no crime, who were incapable of bearing arms, and many of whom had protections granted by James, were dragged to the gates of the city. It was imagined that the piteous sight would quell the spirit of the colonists. But the only effect was to rouse that spirit to still greater energy. An order was immediately put forth that no man should utter the word Surrender on pain of death; and no man uttered that word. Several prisoners of high rank were in the town. Hitherto they had been well treated, and had received as good rations as were measured out to the garrison. They were now closely confined. A gallows was erected on one of the bastions; and a message was conveyed to Rosen, requesting him to send a confessor instantly to prepare his friends for death. The prisoners in great dismay wrote to the savage Livonian, but received no answer. They then addressed themselves to their countryman, Richard Hamilton. They were willing, they said, to shed their blood for their King; but they thought it hard to die the ignominious death of thieves in consequence of the barbarity of their own companions in arms. Hamilton, though a man of lax principles, was not cruel. He had been disgusted by the inhumanity of Rosen, but, being only second in command, could not venture to express publicly all that he thought. He however remonstrated strongly. Some Irish officers felt on this occasion as it was natural that brave men should feel, and declared, weeping with pity and indignation, that they should never cease to have in their ears the cries of the poor women and children who had been driven at the point of the pike to die of famine between the camp and the city. Rosen persisted during forty-eight hours. In that time many unhappy creatures perished: but Londonderry held out as resolutely as ever; and he saw that his crime was likely to produce nothing but hatred and obloquy. He at length gave way, and suffered the survivors to withdraw. The garrison then took down the gallows which had been erected on the bastion.

When the tidings of these events reached Dublin, James, though by no means prone to compassion, was startled by an atrocity of which the civil wars of England had furnished no example, and was displeased by learning that protections, given by his authority, and guaranteed by his honour, had been publicly declared to be nullities. He complained to the French ambassador, and said, with a warmth which the occasion fully justified, that Rosen was a barbarous Muscovite. Melfort could not refrain from adding that, if Rosen had been an Englishman, he would have been hanged. Avaux was utterly unable to understand this effeminate sensibility. In his opinion, nothing had been done that was at all reprehensible; and he had some difficulty in commanding himself when he heard the King and the secretary blame, in strong language, an act of wholesome severity. In truth the French ambassador and the French general were well paired. There was a great difference doubtless, in appearance and manner, between the handsome, graceful, and refined diplomatist, whose dexterity and suavity had been renowned at the most polite courts of Europe, and the military adventurer, whose look and voice reminded all who came near him that he had been born in a half savage country, that he had risen from the ranks, and that he had once been sentenced to death for marauding. But the heart of the courtier was really even more callous than that of the soldier.

Rosen was recalled to Dublin; and Richard Hamilton was again left in the chief command. He tried gentler means than those which had brought so much reproach on his predecessor. No trick, no lie, which was thought likely to discourage the starving garrison was spared. One day a great shout was raised by the whole Irish camp. The defenders of Londonderry were soon informed that the army of James was rejoicing on account of the fall of Enniskillen. They were told that they had now no chance of being relieved, and were exhorted to save their lives by capitulating. They consented to negotiate. But what they asked was, that they should be permitted to depart armed and in military array, by land or by water at their choice. They demanded hostages for the exact fulfilment of these conditions, and insisted that the hostages should be sent on board of the fleet which lay in Lough Foyle. Such terms Hamilton durst not grant: the Governors would abate nothing: the treaty was broken off; and the conflict recommenced.

By this time July was far advanced; and the state of the city was, hour by hour, becoming more frightful. The number of the inhabitants had been thinned more by famine and disease than by the fire of the enemy. Yet that fire was sharper and more constant than ever. One of the gates was beaten in: one of the bastions was laid in ruins: but the breaches made by day were repaired by night with indefatigable activity. Every attack was still repelled. But the fighting men of the garrison were so much exhausted that they could scarcely keep their legs. Several of them, in the act of striking at the enemy, fell down from mere weakness. A very small quantity of grain remained, and was doled out by mouthfuls. The stock of salted hides was considerable, and by gnawing them the garrison appeased the rage of hunger. Dogs, fattened on the blood of the slain who lay unburied round the town, were luxuries which few could afford to purchase. The price of a whelp's paw was five shillings and sixpence. Nine horses were still alive, and but barely alive. They were so lean that little meat was likely to be found upon them. It was, however, determined to slaughter them for food. The people perished so fast that it was impossible for the survivors to perform the rites of sepulture. There was scarcely a cellar in which some corpse was not decaying. Such was the extremity of distress, that the rats who came to feast in those hideous dens were eagerly hunted and greedily devoured. A small fish, caught in the river, was not to be purchased with money. The only price for which such a treasure could be obtained was some handfuls of oatmeal. Leprosies, such as strange and unwholesome diet engenders, made existence a constant torment. The whole city was poisoned by the stench exhaled from the bodies of the dead and of the half dead.

That there should be fits of discontent and insubordination among men enduring such misery was inevitable. At one moment it was suspected that Walker had laid up somewhere a secret store of food, and was revelling in private, while he exhorted others to suffer resolutely for the good cause. His house was strictly examined: his innocence was fully proved: he regained his popularity; and the garrison, with death in near prospect, thronged to the Cathedral to hear him preach, drank in his earnest eloquence with delight, and went forth from the house of God with haggard faces and tottering steps, but with spirit still unsubdued. There were, indeed, some secret plottings. A very few obscure traitors opened communications with the enemy. But it was necessary that all such dealings should be carefully concealed. None dared to utter publicly any words save words of defiance and stubborn resolution. Even in that extremity the general cry was 'No surrender.' And there were not wanting voices which, in low tones, added, 'First the horses and hides; and then the prisoners; and then each other.' It was afterwards related, half in jest, yet not without a horrible mixture of earnest, that a corpulent citizen, whose bulk presented a strange contrast to the skeletons which surrounded him, thought it expedient to conceal himself from the numerous eyes which followed him with cannibal looks whenever he appeared in the streets.

It was no slight aggravation of the sufferings of the garrison that all this time the English ships were seen far off in Lough Foyle. Communication between the fleet and the city was almost impossible. One diver who had attempted to pass the boom was drowned. Another was hanged. The language of signals was hardly intelligible. On the thirteenth of July, however, a piece of paper sewed up in a cloth button came to Walker's hands. It was a letter from Kirke, and contained assurances of speedy relief. But more than a fortnight of intense misery had since elapsed; and the hearts of the most sanguine were sick with deferred hope. By no art could the provisions which were left be made to hold out two days more.

Just at this time Kirke received a despatch from England, which contained positive orders that Londonderry should be relieved. He accordingly determined to make an attempt which, as far as appears, he might have made, with at least an equally fair prospect of success, six weeks earlier.[5]

Among the merchant ships which had come to Lough Foyle under his convoy was one called the *Mountjoy*. The master, Micaiah Browning, a native of Londonderry, had brought from England a large cargo of provisions. He had, it is said, repeatedly remonstrated against the inaction of the armament. He now eagerly volunteered to take the first risk of succouring his fellow citizens; and his offer was accepted. Andrew Douglas, master of the *Phœnix*, who had on board a great quantity of meal from Scotland, was willing to share the danger and the honour. The two merchantmen were to be escorted by the *Dartmouth* frigate of thirty-six guns, commanded by Captain John Leake, afterwards an admiral of great fame.

It was the thirtieth of July. The sun had just set: the evening sermon in the Cathedral was over; and the heartbroken congregation had separated, when the sentinels on the tower saw the sails of three vessels coming up the Foyle. Soon there was a stir in the Irish camp. The besiegers were on the alert for miles along both shores. The ships were in extreme peril: for the river was

5. The despatch, which positively commanded Kirke to attack the boom, was signed by Schomberg, who had already been appointed commander in chief of all the English forces in Ireland. Wodrow, on no better authority than the gossip of a country parish in Dumbartonshire, attributes the relief of Londonderry to the exhortations of a heroic Scotch preacher named Gordon. I am inclined to think that Kirke was more likely to be influenced by a peremptory order from Schomberg, than by the united eloquence of a whole synod of presbyterian divines.

low; and the only navigable channel ran very near to the left bank, where the headquarters of the enemy had been fixed, and where the batteries were most numerous. Leake performed his duty with a skill and spirit worthy of his noble profession, exposed his frigate to cover the merchantmen, and used his guns with great effect. At length the little squadron came to the place of peril. Then the *Mountjoy* took the lead, and went right at the boom. The huge barricade cracked and gave way: but the shock was such that the *Mountjoy* rebounded, and stuck in the mud. A yell of triumph rose from the banks: the Irish rushed to their boats, and were preparing to board; but the *Dartmouth* poured on them a well directed broadside, which threw them into disorder. Just then the *Phœnix* dashed at the breach which the *Mountjoy* had made, and was in a moment within the fence. Meantime the tide was rising fast. The *Mountjoy* began to move, and soon passed safe through the broken stakes and floating spars. But her brave master was no more. A shot from one of the batteries had struck him; and he died by the most enviable of all deaths, in sight of the city which was his birthplace, which was his home, and which had just been saved by his courage and self-devotion from the most frightful form of destruction.

The night had closed in before the conflict at the boom began; but the flash of the guns was seen, and the noise heard, by the lean and ghastly multitude which covered the walls of the city. When the *Mountjoy* grounded, and when the shout of triumph rose from the Irish on both sides of the river, the hearts of the besieged died within them. One who endured the unutterable anguish of that moment has told us that they looked fearfully livid in each other's eyes. Even after the barricade had been passed, there was a terrible half hour of suspense. It was ten o'clock before the ships arrived at the quay. The whole population was there to welcome them. A screen made of casks filled with earth was hastily thrown up to protect the landing place from the batteries on the other side of the river; and then the work of unloading began. First were rolled on shore barrels containing six thousand bushels of meal. Then came great cheeses, casks of beef, flitches of bacon, kegs of butter, sacks of pease and biscuit, ankers of brandy. Not many hours before, half a pound of

tallow and three quarters of a pound of salted hide had been
weighed out with niggardly care to every fighting man. The ration which each now received was three pounds of flour, two
pounds of beef, and a pint of pease. It is easy to imagine with
what tears grace was said over the suppers of that evening. There
was little sleep on either side of the wall. The bonfires shone
bright along the whole circuit of the ramparts. The Irish guns
continued to roar all night; and all night the bells of the rescued
city made answer to the Irish guns with a peal of joyous defiance.
Through the whole of the thirty-first of July the batteries of the
enemy continued to play. But, soon after the sun had again gone
down, flames were seen arising from the camp; and, when the
first of August dawned, a line of smoking ruins marked the site
lately occupied by the huts of the besiegers; and the citizens saw
far off the long column of pikes and standards retreating up the
left bank of the Foyle towards Strabane.

So ended this great siege, the most memorable in the annals of
the British isles. It had lasted a hundred and five days. The garrison had been reduced from about seven thousand effective men
to about three thousand. The loss of the besiegers cannot be precisely ascertained. Walker estimated it at eight thousand men. It
is certain from the despatches of Avaux that the regiments which
returned from the blockade had been so much thinned that many
of them were not more than two hundred strong. Of thirty-six
French gunners who had superintended the cannonading, thirty-
one had been killed or disabled. The means both of attack and of
defence had undoubtedly been such as would have moved the
great warriors of the Continent to laughter; and this is the very
circumstance which gives so peculiar an interest to the history of
the contest. It was a contest, not between engineers, but between
nations; and the victory remained with the nation which, though
inferior in number, was superior in civilisation, in capacity for
self-government, and in stubbornness of resolution.

As soon as it was known that the Irish army had retired, a
deputation from the city hastened to Lough Foyle, and invited
Kirke to take the command. He came accompanied by a long
train of officers, and was received in state by the two Governors,

who delivered up to him the authority which, under the pressure of necessity, they had assumed. He remained only a few days; but he had time to show enough of the incurable vices of his character to disgust a population distinguished by austere morals and ardent public spirit. There was, however, no outbreak. The city was in the highest good humour. Such quantities of provisions had been landed from the fleet, that there was in every house a plenty never before known. A few days earlier a man had been glad to obtain for twenty pence a mouthful of carrion scraped from the bones of a starved horse. A pound of good beef was now sold for three halfpence. Meanwhile all hands were busied in removing corpses which had been thinly covered with earth, in filling up the holes which the shells had ploughed in the ground, and in repairing the battered roofs of the houses. The recollection of past dangers and privations, and the consciousness of having deserved well of the English nation and of all Protestant Churches, swelled the hearts of the townspeople with honest pride. That pride grew stronger when they received from William a letter acknowledging, in the most affectionate language, the debt which he owed to the brave and trusty citizens of his good city. The whole population crowded to the Diamond to hear the royal epistle read. At the close all the guns on the ramparts sent forth a voice of joy: all the ships in the river made answer: barrels of ale were broken up; and the health of their Majesties was drunk with shouts and volleys of musketry.

Five generations have since passed away; and still the wall of Londonderry is to the Protestants of Ulster what the trophy of Marathon was to the Athenians. A lofty pillar, rising from a bastion which bore during many weeks the heaviest fire of the enemy, is seen far up and far down the Foyle. On the summit is the statue of Walker, such as when, in the last and most terrible emergency, his eloquence roused the fainting courage of his brethren. In one hand he grasps a Bible. The other, pointing down the river, seems to direct the eyes of his famished audience to the English topmasts in the distant bay. Such a monument was well deserved: yet it was scarcely needed: for in truth the whole city is to this day a monument of the great deliverance. The wall

is carefully preserved; nor would any plea of health or conveni-
ence be held by the inhabitants sufficient to justify the demolition
of that sacred enclosure which, in the evil time, gave shelter to
their race and their religion. The summit of the ramparts forms a
pleasant walk. The bastions have been turned into little gardens.
Here and there, among the shrubs and flowers, may be seen the
old culverins which scattered bricks, cased with lead, among the
Irish ranks. One antique gun, the gift of the Fishmongers of London, was distinguished, during the hundred and five memorable
days, by the loudness of its report, and still bears the name of
Roaring Meg. The Cathedral is filled with relics and trophies. In
the vestibule is a huge shell, one of many hundreds of shells
which were thrown into the city. Over the altar are still seen the
French flagstaves, taken by the garrison in a desperate sally. The
white ensigns of the House of Bourbon have long been dust: but
their place has been supplied by new banners, the work of the
fairest hands of Ulster. The anniversary of the day on which the
gates were closed, and the anniversary of the day on which the
siege was raised, have been down to our own time celebrated by
salutes, processions, banquets, and sermons: Lundy has been
executed in effigy; and the sword, said by tradition to be that of
Maumont, has, on great occasions, been carried in triumph.
There is still a Walker Club and a Murray Club. The humble
tombs of the Protestant captains have been carefully sought out,
repaired, and embellished. It is impossible not to respect the sentiment which indicates itself by these tokens. It is a sentiment
which belongs to the higher and purer part of human nature, and
which adds not a little to the strength of states. A people which
takes no pride in the noble achievements of remote ancestors will
never achieve any thing worthy to be remembered with pride by
remote descendants. Yet it is impossible for the moralist or the
statesman to look with unmixed complacency on the solemnities
with which Londonderry commemorates her deliverance, and on
the honours which she pays to those who saved her. Unhappily
the animosities of her brave champions have descended with
their glory. The faults which are ordinarily found in dominant
castes and dominant sects have not seldom shown themselves

without disguise at her festivities; and even with the expressions of pious gratitude which have resounded from her pulpits have too often been mingled words of wrath and defiance.

*

[*On the same day on which the boom of Lough Foyle was broken (30 July 1689), the tide turned also at Enniskillen, whose defenders had appealed to Kirke for assistance. Kirke could spare no men but sent arms, ammunition, and experienced officers, under whose command the defenders marched out and at Newton Butler totally routed the Irish army, under Lord Mountcashel, which had been sent to annihilate them. By this double victory, at Londonderry and at Newton Butler, the Protestant base in Ireland was saved from destruction and could be used to reconquer the island.*]

B. THE BATTLE OF THE BOYNE, 30 JUNE 1690

[*The victory in Ulster was the turning-point in the battle for Ireland. It remained to exploit it. William immediately sent his trusted lieutenant, Schomberg, to Ulster, but Schomberg was unable to achieve victory before the winter of 1689. Next year, having settled his affairs in England, William himself landed at Carrickfergus and joined Schomberg on the road to Belfast. Together they moved south to challenge the Irish army which James had led from Dublin. The decisive battle was fought on 30 June 1690, at the river Boyne. William, though wounded, rode with his army through the river and decisively routed the Irish army. But for the death of Schomberg, killed in the battle, the victory would have been even more complete. The road to Dublin was now open. James, seeing his army scattered, fled first to Dublin, then back to France. On 6 July 1690, William entered Dublin and celebrated his victory, with the crown on his head, in St Patrick's Cathedral.*

The victory was needed to compensate for an almost simultaneous defeat. While William was in Ireland, Louis XIV sought to strike him in another element. He sent a strong fleet under the Comte de Tourville into the English Channel. On 29 June – the day before the battle of the Boyne – Tourville defeated the weaker Anglo-Dutch

*navy under the Earl of Torrington off Beachy Head; after which
his ships scoured the Channel and he was even able to land troops and
sack Teignmouth in Devonshire.*

*The following passage, from Chapter XVI, describes the immedi-
ate reactions to the victory of the Boyne.*]

The fame of these great events flew fast, and excited strong emotions all over Europe. The news of William's wound everywhere
preceded by a few hours the news of his victory. Paris was roused
at dead of night by the arrival of a courier who brought the joyful
intelligence that the heretic, the parricide, the mortal enemy of
the greatness of France, had been struck dead by a cannon ball in
the sight of the two armies. The commissaries of police ran about
the city, knocked at the doors, and called the people up to illumi-
nate. In an hour streets, quays and bridges were in a blaze: drums
were beating and trumpets sounding: the bells of Notre Dame
were ringing: peals of cannon were resounding from the batteries
of the Bastille. Tables were set out in the streets; and wine was
served to all who passed. A Prince of Orange, made of straw, was
trailed through the mud, and at last committed to the flames. He
was attended by a hideous effigy of the devil, carrying a scroll, on
which was written, 'I have been waiting for thee these two
years.' The shops of several Huguenots who had been dragooned
into calling themselves Catholics, but were suspected of being
still heretics at heart, were sacked by the rabble. It was hardly
safe to question the truth of the report which had been so eagerly
welcomed by the multitude. Soon, however, some cool-headed
people ventured to remark that the fact of the tyrant's death was
not quite so certain as might be wished. Then arose a vehement
controversy about the effect of such wounds: for the vulgar notion was that no person struck by a cannon ball on the shoulder
could recover. The disputants appealed to medical authority; and
the doors of the great surgeons and physicians were thronged, it
was jocosely said, as if there had been a pestilence in Paris. The
question was soon settled by a letter from James, which announced his defeat and his arrival at Brest.

At Rome the news from Ireland produced a sensation of a very
different kind. There too the report of William's death was, dur-

ing a short time, credited. At the French embassy all was joy and triumph: but the Ambassadors of the House of Austria were in despair; and the aspect of the Pontifical Court by no means indicated exultation. Melfort, in a transport of joy, sat down to write a letter of congratulation to Mary of Modena. That letter is still extant, and would alone suffice to explain why he was the favourite of James. Herod – so William was designated – was gone. There must be a restoration; and that restoration ought to be followed by a terrible revenge and by the establishment of despotism. The power of the purse must be taken away from the Commons. Political offenders must be tried, not by juries, but by judges on whom the Crown could depend. The Habeas Corpus Act must be rescinded. The authors of the Revolution must be punished with merciless severity. 'If,' the cruel apostate wrote, 'if the King is forced to pardon, let it be as few rogues as he can.' After the lapse of some anxious hours, a messenger bearing later and more authentic intelligence alighted at the palace occupied by the representative of the Catholic King. In a moment all was changed. The enemies of France – and all the population, except Frenchmen and British Jacobites, were her enemies – eagerly felicitated one another. All the clerks of the Spanish legation were too few to make transcripts of the despatches for the Cardinals and Bishops who were impatient to know the details of the victory. The first copy was sent to the Pope, and was doubtless welcome to him.

The good news from Ireland reached London at a moment when good news was needed. The English flag had been disgraced in the English seas. A foreign enemy threatened the coast. Traitors were at work within the realm. Mary had exerted herself beyond her strength. Her gentle nature was unequal to the cruel anxieties of her position; and she complained that she could scarcely snatch a moment from business to calm herself by prayer. Her distress rose to the highest point when she learned that the camps of her father and her husband were pitched near to each other, and that tidings of a battle might be hourly expected. She stole time for a visit to Kensington, and had three hours of quiet in the garden, then a rural solitude. But the recollection of days passed there with him whom she might never see again overpowered her. 'The place,' she wrote to him, 'made me think how happy I was there when I had your dear company. But now I will say no more; for I shall hurt my own eyes, which I want now more than ever. Adieu. Think of me, and love me as much as I shall you, whom I love more than my life.'

Early on the morning after these tender lines had been despatched, Whitehall was roused by the arrival of a post from Ireland. Nottingham was called out of bed. The Queen, who was just going to the chapel where she daily attended divine service, was informed that William had been wounded. She had wept much: but till that moment she had wept alone, and had constrained herself to show a cheerful countenance to her Court and Council. But when Nottingham put her husband's letter into her hands, she burst into tears. She was still trembling with the violence of her emotions, and had scarcely finished a letter to William in which she poured out her love, her fears and her thankfulness, with the sweet natural eloquence of her sex, when another messenger arrived with the news that the English army had forced a passage across the Boyne, that the Irish were flying in confusion, and that the King was well. Yet she was visibly uneasy till Nottingham had assured her that James was safe. The grave Secretary, who seems to have really esteemed and loved her, afterwards described with much feeling that struggle of filial duty with conjugal affection. On the same day she wrote to adjure her husband to see that no harm befell her father. 'I know,' she said, 'I need not beg you to let him be taken care of: for I am confident you will for your own sake: yet add that to all your kindness; and, for my sake, let people know you would have no hurt happen to his person.' This solicitude, though amiable, was superfluous. Her father was perfectly competent to take care of himself. He had never, during the battle, run the smallest risk of hurt; and, while his daughter was shuddering at the dangers to which she fancied that he was exposed in Ireland, he was half way on his voyage to France.

It chanced that the glad tidings arrived at Whitehall on the day to which the Parliament stood prorogued. The Speaker and several members of the House of Commons who were in London met, according to form, at ten in the morning, and were sum-

moned by Black Rod to the bar of the Peers. The Parliament was
then again prorogued by commission. As soon as this ceremony
had been performed, the Chancellor of the Exchequer put into
the hands of the Clerk the despatch which had arrived from Ireland, and the Clerk read it with a loud voice to the lords and
gentlemen present. The good news spread rapidly from Westminster Hall to all the coffeehouses, and was received with transports of joy. For those Englishmen who wished to see an English
army beaten and an English colony extirpated by the French and
Irish were a minority even of the Jacobite party.

On the ninth day after the battle of the Boyne James landed at
Brest, with an excellent appetite, in high spirits, and in a talkative
humour. He told the history of his defeat to everybody who
would listen to him. But French officers who understood war,
and who compared his story with other accounts, pronounced
that, though His Majesty had witnessed the battle, he knew nothing about it, except that his army had been routed. From Brest
he proceeded to Saint Germains, where, a few hours after his arrival, he was visited by Lewis. The French King had too much
delicacy and generosity to utter a word which could sound like
reproach. Nothing, he declared, that could conduce to the comfort of the royal family of England should be wanting, as far as
his power extended. But he was by no means disposed to listen to
the political and military projects of his unlucky guest. James
recommended an immediate descent on England. That kingdom,
he said, had been drained of troops by the demands of Ireland.
The seven or eight thousand regular soldiers who were left
would be unable to withstand a great French army. The people
were ashamed of their error and impatient to repair it. As soon as
their rightful King showed himself, they would rally round him
in multitudes. Lewis was too polite and goodnatured to express
what he must have felt. He contented himself with answering
coldly that he could not decide upon any plan about the British
islands till he had heard from his generals in Ireland. James was
importunate, and seemed to think himself ill used, because, a
fortnight after he had run away from one army, he was not entrusted with another. Lewis was not to be provoked into uttering
an unkind or uncourteous word: but he was resolute; and, in

order to avoid solicitation which gave him pain, he pretended to be unwell. During some time, whenever James came to Versailles, he was respectfully informed that His Most Christian Majesty was not equal to the transaction of business. The high-spirited and quick-witted nobles who daily crowded the ante-chambers could not help sneering while they bowed low to the royal visitor, whose poltroonery and stupidity had a second time made him an exile and a mendicant. They even whispered their sarcasms loud enough to call up the haughty blood of the Guelphs in the cheeks of Mary of Modena. But the insensibility of James was of no common kind. It had long been found proof against reason and against pity. It now sustained a still harder trial, and was found proof even against contempt.

*

C. THE SIEGES OF LIMERICK, 1690, 1691

[*The battle of the Boyne had completely reversed the position of the parties in Ireland. In 1689 the English had been reduced to a narrow base in Ulster, while the rest of Ireland acknowledged James as king of Celtic Ireland. In 1690 William had replaced James in Dublin; the cities of Ireland yielded to him one after another; and the Irish found themselves falling back on a narrow base in Connaught. For them, Limerick, twice besieged by the English, acquired the same significance as Londonderry had done for their enemies. These two sieges, the first ending in victory for the Irish, the second in defeat, are described by Macaulay in Chapters XVI and XVII. The hero of them both was Patrick Sarsfield, a member of an old Anglo-Norman family, who had assisted Tyrconnel to remodel the Irish army and had commanded the Irish troops brought to England by James.*]

William meanwhile was advancing towards Limerick. In that city the army which he had put to rout at the Boyne had taken refuge, discomfited, indeed, and disgraced, but very little diminished. He would not have had the trouble of besieging the place, if the advice of Lauzun and of Lauzun's countrymen had been followed. They laughed at the thought of defending such fortifications, and indeed would not admit that the name of fortifications could properly be given to heaps of dirt, which certainly bore little resemblance to the works of Valenciennes and Philipsburg. 'It is unnecessary,' said Lauzun, with an oath, 'for the English to bring cannon against such a place as this. What you call your ramparts might be battered down with roasted apples.' He therefore gave his voice for evacuating Limerick, and declared that, at all events, he was determined not to throw away in a hopeless resistance the lives of the brave men who had been entrusted to his care by his master. The truth is, that the judgment of the brilliant and adventurous Frenchman was biased by his inclinations. He and his companions were sick of Ireland. They were ready to face death with courage, nay, with gaiety, on a field of battle. But the dull, squalid, barbarous life, which they had now been leading during several months, was more than they could bear. They were as much out of the pale of the civilised world as if they had been banished to Dahomey or Spitzbergen. The climate affected their health and spirits. In that unhappy country, wasted by years of predatory war, hospitality could offer little more than a couch of straw, a trencher of meat half raw and half burned, and a draught of sour milk. A crust of bread, a pint of wine, could hardly be purchased for money. A year of such hardships seemed a century to men who had always been accustomed to carry with them to the camp the luxuries of Paris, soft bedding, rich tapestry, sideboards of plate, hampers of Champagne, opera dancers, cooks and musicians. Better to be a prisoner in the Bastille, better to be a recluse at La Trappe, than to be generalissimo of the half naked savages who burrowed in the dreary swamps of Munster. Any plea was welcome which would serve as an excuse for returning from that miserable exile to the land of cornfields and vineyards, of gilded coaches and laced cravats, of ballrooms and theatres.

Very different was the feeling of the children of the soil. The island, which to French courtiers was a disconsolate place of banishment, was the Irishman's home. There were collected all the objects of his love and of his ambition; and there he hoped that his dust would one day mingle with the dust of his fathers. To him even the heaven dark with the vapours of the ocean, the wildernesses of black rushes and stagnant water, the mud cabins where the peasants and the swine shared their meal of roots, had a charm which was wanting to the sunny skies, the cultured fields and the stately mansions of the Seine. He could imagine no fairer spot than his country, if only his country could be freed from the tyranny of the Saxons; and all hope that his country would be freed from the tyranny of the Saxons must be abandoned if Limerick were surrendered.

The conduct of the Irish during the last two months had sunk their military reputation to the lowest point. They had, with the exception of some gallant regiments of cavalry, fled disgracefully at the Boyne, and had thus incurred the bitter contempt both of their enemies and of their allies. The English who were at Saint Germains never spoke of the Irish but as a people of dastards and traitors. The French were so much exasperated against the unfortunate nation, that Irish merchants, who had been many years settled at Paris, durst not walk the streets for fear of being insulted by the populace. So strong was the prejudice, that absurd stories were invented to explain the intrepidity with which the horse had fought. It was said that the troopers were not men of Celtic blood, but descendants of the old English of the Pale. It was also said that they had been intoxicated with brandy just before the battle. Yet nothing can be more certain than that they must have been generally of Irish race; nor did the steady valour which they displayed in a long and almost hopeless conflict against great odds bear any resemblance to the fury of a coward maddened by strong drink into momentary hardihood. Even in the infantry, undisciplined and disorganised as it was, there was much spirit, though little firmness. Fits of enthusiasm and fits of faintheartedness succeeded each other. The same battalion, which at one time threw away its arms in a panic and shrieked for quarter, would on another occasion fight valiantly. On the day of the Boyne the courage of the ill trained and ill commanded kernes had ebbed to the lowest point. When they had rallied at Limerick, their blood was up. Patriotism, fanaticism, shame, revenge, despair, had raised them above themselves. With one voice officers and men insisted that the city should be defended to the last. At the head of those who were for resisting was the brave Sarsfield; and his exhortations diffused through all ranks a spirit resembling his own. To save his country was beyond his power. All that he could do was to prolong her last agony through one bloody and disastrous year.

Tyrconnel was altogether incompetent to decide the question on which the French and the Irish differed. The only military qualities that he had ever possessed were personal bravery and skill in the use of the sword. These qualities had once enabled him to frighten away rivals from the doors of his mistresses, and to play the Hector at cockpits and hazard tables. But more was necessary to enable him to form an opinion as to the possibility of defending Limerick. He would probably, had his temper been as hot as in the days when he diced with Grammont and threatened to cut the old Duke of Ormond's throat, have voted for running any risk however desperate. But age, pain and sickness had left little of the canting, bullying, fighting Dick Talbot of the Restoration. He had sunk into deep despondency. He was incapable of strenuous exertion. The French officers pronounced him utterly ignorant of the art of war. They had observed that at the Boyne he had seemed to be stupefied, unable to give directions himself, unable even to make up his mind about the suggestions which were offered by others. The disasters which had since followed one another in rapid succession were not likely to restore the tone of a mind so pitiably unnerved. His wife was already in France with the little which remained of his once ample fortune: his own wish was to follow her thither: his voice was therefore given for abandoning the city.

At last a compromise was made. Lauzun and Tyrconnel, with the French troops, retired to Galway. The great body of the native army, about twenty thousand strong, remained at Limerick. The chief command there was entrusted to Boisseleau, who understood the character of the Irish better, and consequently judged them more favourably, than any of his countrymen. In general, the French captains spoke of their unfortunate allies with boundless contempt and abhorrence, and thus made themselves as hateful as the English.

Lauzun and Tyrconnel had scarcely departed when the advanced guard of William's army came in sight. Soon the King himself, accompanied by Auverquerque and Ginkel, and escorted by three hundred horse, rode forward to examine the fortifications. The city, then the second in Ireland, though less altered since that time than most large cities in the British isles, has undergone a great change. The new town did not then exist. The ground now covered by those smooth and broad pavements, those neat gardens, those stately shops flaming with red brick, and gay with shawls and china, was then an open meadow lying without the walls. The city consisted of two parts, which had been designated during several centuries as the English and the Irish town. The English town stands on an island surrounded by the Shannon, and consists of a knot of antique houses with gable ends, crowding thick round a venerable cathedral. The aspect of the streets is such that a traveller who wanders through them may easily fancy himself in Normandy or Flanders. Not far from the cathedral, an ancient castle overgrown with weeds and ivy looks down on the river. A narrow and rapid stream, over which, in 1690, there was only a single bridge, divides the English town from the quarter anciently occupied by the hovels of the native population. The view from the top of the cathedral now extends many miles over a level expanse of rich mould, through which the greatest of Irish rivers winds between artificial banks. But in the seventeenth century those banks had not been constructed; and that wide plain, of which the grass, verdant even beyond the verdure of Munster, now feeds some of the finest cattle in Europe, was then almost always a marsh and often a lake.

When it was known that the French troops had quitted Limerick, and that the Irish only remained, the general expectation in the English camp was that the city would be an easy conquest. Nor was that expectation unreasonable: for even Sarsfield desponded. One chance, in his opinion, there still was. William had brought with him none but small guns. Several large pieces of ordnance, a great quantity of provisions and ammunition, and a bridge of tin boats, which in the watery plain of the Shannon was frequently needed, were slowly following from Cashel. If the guns and gunpowder could be intercepted and destroyed, there might be some hope. If not, all was lost; and the best thing that a brave and high-spirited Irish gentleman could do was to forget the country which he had in vain tried to defend, and to seek in some foreign land a home or a grave.

A few hours, therefore, after the English tents had been pitched before Limerick, Sarsfield set forth, under cover of the night, with a strong body of horse and dragoons. He took the road to Killaloe, and crossed the Shannon there. During the day he lurked with his band in a wild mountain tract named from the silver mines which it contains. Those mines had many years before been worked by English proprietors, with the help of engineers and labourers imported from the Continent. But, in the rebellion of 1641, the aboriginal population had destroyed the works and massacred the workmen; nor had the devastation then committed been since repaired. In this desolate region Sarsfield found no lack of scouts or of guides: for all the peasantry of Munster were zealous on his side. He learned in the evening that the detachment which guarded the English artillery had halted for the night about seven miles from William's camp, on a pleasant carpet of green turf under the ruined walls of an old castle; that officers and men seemed to think themselves perfectly secure; that the beasts had been turned loose to graze, and that even the sentinels were dozing. When it was dark the Irish horsemen quitted their hiding place, and were conducted by the people of the country to the place where the escort lay sleeping round the guns. The surprise was complete. Some of the English sprang to their arms and made an attempt to resist, but in vain. About sixty fell. One only was taken alive. The rest fled. The victorious Irish made a huge pile of waggons and pieces of cannon. Every gun was stuffed with powder, and fixed with its mouth in the ground; and the whole mass was blown up. The solitary prisoner, a lieutenant, was treated with great civility by Sarsfield. 'If I had failed in this attempt,' said the gallant Irishman, 'I should have been off to France.'

Intelligence had been carried to William's headquarters that Sarsfield had stolen out of Limerick and was ranging the country. The King guessed the design of his brave enemy, and sent five hundred horse to protect the guns. Unhappily there was some delay, which the English, always disposed to believe the worst of the Dutch courtiers, attributed to the negligence or perverseness of Portland. At one in the morning the detachment set out, but had scarcely left the camp when a blaze like lightning and a crash like thunder announced to the wide plain of the Shannon that all was over.

Sarsfield had long been the favourite of his countrymen; and this most seasonable exploit, judiciously planned and vigorously executed, raised him still higher in their estimation. Their spirits rose; and the besiegers began to lose heart. William did his best to repair his loss. Two of the guns which had been blown up were found to be still serviceable. Two more were sent for from Waterford. Batteries were constructed of small field pieces, which, though they might have been useless against one of the fortresses of Hainault or Brabant, made some impression on the feeble defences of Limerick. Several outworks were carried by storm; and a breach in the rampart of the city began to appear.

During these operations, the English army was astonished and amused by an incident, which produced indeed no very important consequences, but which illustrates in the most striking manner the real nature of Irish Jacobitism. In the first rank of those great Celtic houses, which, down to the close of the reign of Elizabeth, bore rule in Ulster, were the O'Donnels. The head of that house had yielded to the skill and energy of Mountjoy, had kissed the hand of James the First, and had consented to exchange the rude independence of a petty prince for an eminently honourable place among British subjects. During a short time the vanquished chief held the rank of an Earl, and was the landlord of an immense domain of which he had once been the sovereign. But soon he began to suspect the government of plotting against him, and, in revenge or in self-defence, plotted against the government. His schemes failed: he fled to the Continent: his title and his estates were forfeited; and an Anglo-Saxon colony was planted in the territory which he had governed. He meanwhile took refuge at the Court of Spain. Between that court and the aboriginal Irish there had, during the long contest between Philip and Elizabeth, been a close connection. The exiled chieftain was welcomed at Madrid as a good Catholic flying from heretical persecutors. His illustrious descent and princely dignity, which to the English were subjects of ridicule, secured to him the respect of the Castilian grandees. His honours were inherited by a succession of banished men who lived and died far from the land where the memory of their family was fondly cherished by a rude peasantry, and was kept fresh by the songs of minstrels and the tales of begging friars.

At length, in the eighty-third year of the exile of this ancient dynasty, it was known over all Europe that the Irish were again in arms for their independence. Baldearg O'Donnel, who called himself the O'Donnel, a title far prouder, in the estimation of his race, than any marquisate or dukedom, had been bred in Spain, and was in the service of the Spanish government. He requested the permission of that government to repair to Ireland. But the House of Austria was now closely leagued with England; and the permission was refused. The O'Donnel made his escape, and by a circuitous route, in the course of which he visited Turkey, arrived at Kinsale a few days after James had sailed thence for France. The effect produced on the native population by the arrival of this solitary wanderer was marvellous. Since Ulster had been reconquered by the Englishry, great multitudes of the Irish inhabitants of that province had migrated southward, and were now leading a vagrant life in Connaught and Munster. These men, accustomed from their infancy to hear of the good old times, when the O'Donnel, solemnly inaugurated on the rock of Kilmacrenan by the successor of Saint Columb, governed the mountains of Donegal in defiance of the strangers of the Pale, flocked to the standard of the restored exile. He was soon at the head of seven or eight thousand Rapparees, or, to use the name peculiar to Ulster, Creaghts; and his followers adhered to him with a loyalty very different from the languid sentiment which the Saxon James had been able to inspire. Priests and even Bishops swelled the train of the adventurer. He was so much elated by his reception that he sent agents to France, who assured the ministers of Lewis that the O'Donnel would, if furnished with arms and ammunition, bring into the field thirty thousand Celts from Ulster, and that the Celts of Ulster would be found far superior in every military quality to those of Leinster, Munster and Connaught. No expression used by Baldearg indicated that he considered himself as a subject. His notion evidently was that the House of O'Donnel was as truly and as indefeasibly royal as the House of Stuart; and not a few of his countrymen were of the same mind. He made a pompous entrance into Limerick; and his appearance there raised the hopes of the garrison to a strange pitch. Numerous prophecies were recollected or invented. An O'Donnel with a red mark was to be the deliverer of his country; and Baldearg meant a red mark. An O'Donnel was to gain a great battle over the English near Limerick; and at Limerick the O'Donnel and the English were now brought face to face.

While these predictions were eagerly repeated by the defenders of the city, evil presages, grounded not on barbarous oracles, but on grave military reasons, began to disturb William and his most experienced officers. The blow struck by Sarsfield had told: the artillery had been long in doing its work: that work was even now very imperfectly done: the stock of powder had begun to run low: the autumnal rain had begun to fall. The soldiers in the trenches were up to their knees in mire. No precaution was neglected: but, though drains were dug to carry off the water, and though pewter basins of usquebaugh and brandy blazed all night in the tents, cases of fever had already occurred; and it might well be apprehended that, if the army remained but a few days longer on that swampy soil, there would be a pestilence more terrible than that which had raged twelve months before under the walls of Dundalk. A council of war was held. It was determined to make one great effort, and, if that effort failed, to raise the siege.

On the twenty-seventh of August, at three in the afternoon, the signal was given. Five hundred grenadiers rushed from the English trenches to the counterscarp, fired their pieces, and threw their grenades. The Irish fled into the town, and were followed by the assailants, who, in the excitement of victory, did not wait for orders. Then began a terrible street fight. The Irish, as soon as they had recovered from their surprise, stood resolutely to their arms; and the English grenadiers, overwhelmed by numbers, were, with great loss, driven back to the counterscarp. There the struggle was long and desperate. When indeed was the Roman Catholic Celt to fight if he did not fight on that day? The very women of Limerick mingled in the combat, stood firmly under the hottest fire, and flung stones and broken bottles at the enemy. In the moment when the conflict was fiercest a mine exploded, and hurled a fine German battalion into the air. During four hours the carnage and uproar continued. The thick cloud which rose from the breach streamed out on the wind for many miles, and disappeared behind the hills of Clare. Late in the evening the besiegers retired slowly and sullenly to their camp. Their hope was that a second attack would be made on the morrow; and the soldiers vowed to have the town or die. But the powder was now almost exhausted: the rain fell in torrents: the gloomy masses of cloud which came up from the south west threatened a havoc more terrible than that of the sword; and there was reason to fear that the roads, which were already deep in mud, would soon be in such a state that no wheeled carriage could be dragged through them. The King determined to raise the siege, and to move his troops to a healthier region. He had in truth stayed long enough: for it was with great difficulty that his guns and waggons were tugged away by long teams of oxen.

The history of the first siege of Limerick bears, in some respects, a remarkable analogy to the history of the siege of Londonderry. The southern city was, like the northern city, the last asylum of a Church and of a nation. Both places were crowded by fugitives from all parts of Ireland. Both places appeared to men who had made a regular study of the art of war incapable of resisting an enemy. Both were, in the moment of extreme danger, abandoned by those commanders who should have defended them. Lauzun and Tyrconnel deserted Limerick as Cunningham and Lundy had deserted Londonderry. In both cases, religious and patriotic enthusiasm struggled unassisted against great odds; and, in both cases, religious and patriotic enthusiasm did what veteran warriors had pronounced it absurd to attempt.

It was with no pleasurable emotions that Lauzun and Tyrconnel learned at Galway the fortunate issue of the conflict in which they had refused to take a part. They were weary of Ireland: they were apprehensive that their conduct might be unfavourably represented in France: they therefore determined to be beforehand with their accusers, and took ship together for the Continent.

Tyrconnel, before he departed, delegated his civil authority to one council, and his military authority to another. The young Duke of Berwick was declared Commander in Chief; but this dignity was merely nominal. Sarsfield, undoubtedly the first of Irish soldiers, was placed last in the list of the councillors to whom the conduct of the war was entrusted; and some believed that he would not have been in the list at all, had not the Viceroy feared that the omission of so popular a name might produce a mutiny.

*

[*After his failure before Limerick, William returned to England and thence to the major theatre of the war against Louis XIV, on the Continent. He left to Churchill, now Earl of Marlborough, the task of completing his campaign in Ireland. By his capture of Cork and Kinsale, Marlborough soon recovered control of Munster, but the Irish were left in control in Connaught, and in May 1691 they still had an army based in Limerick. In consequence of internal dissensions among its commanders, James sent his Lord Lieutenant, Tyrconnel, back from France to Ireland to exercise personal command. He was accompanied by the French General St Ruth and his subordinate D'Usson. William's army was commanded by the Dutch Baron Godard van Reede Ginkel. Another army, under the Duke of Württemberg, joined it for the campaign. Prince George of Hesse-Darmstadt and the French Huguenot, the Marquis de Ruvigny, the Englishman Talmash and the Scot Mackay held other commands. Thus the last struggle for Ireland was a cosmopolitan battle, a remote but important episode in the great continental struggle between Louis XIV and his enemies.*

The turning-point in the campaign was Ginkel's capture, on 30 June 1691, of Athlone. This city had been thought impregnable. Its fall opened the way over the Shannon into Connaught and increased the dissensions in the Irish camp. But these dissensions were suspended when the retreat of Tyrconnel into Galway and the enforced absence of D'Usson, who had been wounded at Athlone, gave sole command to St Ruth. The problem before St Ruth was to prevent Ginkel from exploiting his victory at Athlone and conquering the last Irish redoubt: Connaught.]

Saint Ruth, now left in undisputed possession of the supreme command, was bent on trying the chances of a battle. Most of the Irish officers, with Sarsfield at their head, were of a very different mind. It was, they said, not to be dissembled that, in discipline, the army of Ginkel was far superior to theirs. The wise course, therefore, evidently was to carry on the war in such a manner that the difference between the disciplined and the undisciplined soldier might be as small as possible. It was well known that raw recruits often played their part well in a foray, in a street fight or in the defence of a rampart; but that, on a pitched field, they had little chance against veterans. 'Let most of our foot be collected behind the walls of Limerick and Galway. Let the rest, together with our horse, get in the rear of the enemy, and cut off his supplies. If he advances into Connaught, let us overrun Leinster. If he sits down before Galway, which may well be defended, let us make a push for Dublin, which is altogether defenceless.' Saint Ruth might, perhaps, have thought this advice good, if his judgment had not been biased by his passions. But he was smarting from the pain of a humiliating defeat. In sight of his tent, the English had passed a rapid river, and had stormed a strong town. He could not but feel that, though others might have been to blame, he was not himself blameless. He had, to say the least, taken things too easily. Lewis, accustomed to be served during many years by commanders who were not in the habit of leaving to chance any thing which could be made secure by wisdom, would hardly think it a sufficient excuse that his general had not expected the enemy to make so bold and sudden an attack. The Lord Lieutenant would, of course, represent what had passed in the most unfavourable manner; and whatever the Lord Lieutenant said James would echo. A sharp reprimand, a letter of recall, might be expected. To return to Versailles a culprit; to approach the great King in an agony of distress; to see him shrug his shoulders, knit his brow and turn his back; to be sent, far from courts and camps, to languish at some dull country seat; this was too much to be borne; and yet this might well be apprehended. There was one escape; to fight, and to conquer or to perish.

In such a temper Saint Ruth pitched his camp about thirty

miles from Athlone on the road to Galway, near the ruined castle of Aghrim, and determined to await the approach of the English army.

His whole deportment was changed. He had hitherto treated the Irish soldiers with contemptuous severity. But now that he had resolved to stake life and fame on the valour of the despised race, he became another man. During the few days which remained to him he exerted himself to win by indulgence and caresses the hearts of all who were under his command. He, at the same time, administered to his troops moral stimulants of the most potent kind. He was a zealous Roman Catholic; and it is probable that the severity with which he had treated the Protestants of his own country ought to be partly ascribed to the hatred which he felt for their doctrines. He now tried to give the war the character of a crusade. The clergy were the agents whom he employed to sustain the courage of his soldiers. The whole camp was in a ferment with religious excitement. In every regiment priests were praying, preaching, shriving, holding up the host and the cup. While the soldiers swore on the sacramental bread not to abandon their colours, the general addressed to the officers an appeal which might have moved the most languid and effeminate natures to heroic exertion. They were fighting, he said, for their religion, their liberty and their honour. Unhappy events, too widely celebrated, had brought a reproach on the national character. Irish soldiership was everywhere mentioned with a sneer. If they wished to retrieve the fame of their country, this was the time and this the place.

The spot on which he had determined to bring the fate of Ireland to issue seems to have been chosen with great judgment. His army was drawn up on the slope of a hill, which was almost surrounded by red bog. In front, near the edge of the morass, were some fences out of which a breastwork was without difficulty constructed.

On the eleventh of July, Ginkel, having repaired the fortifications of Athlone and left a garrison there, fixed his headquarters at Ballinasloe, about four miles from Aghrim, and rode forward to take a view of the Irish position. On his return he gave orders that ammunition should be got ready for action, and that early on the morrow every man should be under arms without beat of drum. Two regiments were to remain in charge of the camp: the rest, unencumbered by baggage, were to march against the enemy.

Soon after six, the next morning, the English were on the way to Aghrim. But some delay was occasioned by a thick fog which hung till noon over the moist valley of the Suck: a further delay was caused by the necessity of dislodging the Irish from some outposts; and the afternoon was far advanced when the two armies at length confronted each other with nothing but the bog and the breastwork between them. The English and their allies were under twenty thousand; the Irish above twenty-five thousand.

Ginkel held a short consultation with his principal officers. Should he attack instantly, or wait till the next morning? Mackay was for attacking instantly; and his opinion prevailed. At five the battle began. The English foot, in such order as they could keep on treacherous and uneven ground, made their way, sinking deep in mud at every step, to the Irish works. But those works were defended with a resolution such as extorted some words of ungracious eulogy even from men who entertained the strongest prejudices against the Celtic race. Again and again the assailants were driven back. Again and again they returned to the struggle. Once they were broken, and chased across the morass: but Talmash rallied them, and forced the pursuers to retire. The fight had lasted two hours: the evening was closing in; and still the advantage was on the side of the Irish. Ginkel began to meditate a retreat. The hopes of Saint Ruth rose high. 'The day is ours, my boys,' he cried, waving his hat in the air. 'We will drive them before us to the walls of Dublin.'

But fortune was already on the turn. Mackay and Ruvigny, with the English and Huguenot cavalry, had succeeded in passing the bog at a place where two horsemen could scarcely ride abreast. Saint Ruth at first laughed when he saw the Blues, in single file, struggling through the morass under a fire which every moment laid some gallant hat and feather on the earth. 'What do they mean?' he asked; and then he swore that it was pity to see such fine fellows rushing to certain destruction. 'Let them cross, however,' he said. 'The more they are, the more we shall kill.' But soon he saw them laying hurdles on the quagmire. A broader and safer path was formed; squadron after squadron reached firm ground: the flank of the Irish army was speedily turned. The French general was hastening to the rescue when a cannon ball carried off his head. Those who were about him thought that it would be dangerous to make his fate known. His corpse was wrapped in a cloak, carried from the field, and laid, with all secrecy, in the sacred ground among the ruins of the ancient monastery of Loughrea. Till the fight was over neither army was aware that he was no more. To conceal his death from the private soldiers might perhaps have been prudent. To conceal it from his lieutenants was madness. The crisis of the battle had arrived; and there was none to give direction. Sarsfield was in command of the reserve. But he had been strictly enjoined by Saint Ruth not to stir without orders; and no orders came. Mackay and Ruvigny with their horse charged the Irish in flank. Talmash and his foot returned to the attack in front with dogged determination. The breastwork was carried. The Irish, still fighting, retreated from inclosure to inclosure. But, as inclosure after inclosure was forced, their efforts became fainter and fainter. At length they broke and fled. Then followed a horrible carnage. The conquerors were in a savage mood. For a report had been spread among them that, during the early part of the battle, some English captives who had been admitted to quarter had been put to the sword. Only four hundred prisoners were taken. The number of the slain was, in proportion to the number engaged, greater than in any other battle of that age. But for the coming on of a moonless night, made darker by a misty rain, scarcely a man would have escaped. The obscurity enabled Sarsfield, with a few squadrons which still remained unbroken, to cover the retreat. Of the conquerors six hundred were killed, and about a thousand wounded.

The English slept that night on the field of battle. On the following day they buried their companions in arms, and then marched westward. The vanquished were left unburied, a strange and ghastly spectacle. Four thousand Irish corpses were counted on the field of battle. A hundred and fifty lay in one small inclosure, a hundred and twenty in another. But the slaughter had not been confined to the field of battle. One who was there tells us that, from the top of the hill on which the Celtic camp had been pitched, he saw the country, to the distance of near four miles, white with the naked bodies of the slain. The plain looked, he said, like an immense pasture covered by flocks of sheep. As usual, different estimates were formed even by eye-witnesses. But it seems probable that the number of the Irish who fell was not less than seven thousand. Soon a multitude of dogs came to feast on the carnage. These beasts became so fierce, and acquired such a taste for human flesh, that it was long dangerous for men to travel this road otherwise than in companies.

The beaten army had now lost all the appearance of an army, and resembled a rabble crowding home from a fair after a faction fight. One great stream of fugitives ran towards Galway, another towards Limerick. The roads to both cities were covered with weapons which had been flung away. Ginkel offered sixpence for every musket. In a short time so many waggon loads were collected that he reduced the price to twopence; and still great numbers of muskets came in.

The conquerors marched first against Galway. D'Usson was there, and had under him seven regiments, thinned by the slaughter of Aghrim and utterly disorganized and disheartened. The last hope of the garrison and of the Roman Catholic inhabitants was that Baldearg O'Donnel, the promised deliverer of their race, would come to the rescue.[6] But Baldearg O'Donnel was not duped by the superstitious veneration of which he was the object. While there remained any doubt about the issue of the conflict between the Englishry and the Irishry, he had stood aloof. On the day of the battle he had remained at a safe distance with his tumultuary army; and, as soon as he had learned that his countrymen had been put to rout, he fled, plundering and burning all the way, to the mountains of Mayo. Thence he sent to Ginkel offers of submission and service. Ginkel gladly seized the opportunity of breaking up a formidable band of marauders, and of turning to good account the influence which the name of a Celtic dynasty still exercised over the Celtic race. The negotia-

[6. See above, pp. 332-4.]

tion, however, was not without difficulties. The wandering adventurer at first demanded nothing less than an earldom. After some haggling he consented to sell the love of a whole people, and his pretensions to regal dignity, for a pension of five hundred pounds a year. Yet the spell which bound his followers to him was not altogether broken. Some enthusiasts from Ulster were willing to fight under the O'Donnel against their own language and their own religion. With a small body of these devoted adherents, he joined a division of the English army, and on several occasions did useful service to William.

When it was known that no succour was to be expected from the hero whose advent had been foretold by so many seers, the Irish who were shut up in Galway lost all heart. D'Usson had returned a stout answer to the first summons of the besiegers: but he soon saw that resistance was impossible, and made haste to capitulate. The garrison was suffered to retire to Limerick with the honours of war. A full amnesty for past offences was granted to the citizens; and it was stipulated that, within the walls, the Roman Catholic priests should be allowed to perform in private the rites of their religion. On these terms the gates were thrown open. Ginkel was received with profound respect by the Mayor and Aldermen, and was complimented in a set speech by the Recorder. D'Usson, with about two thousand three hundred men, marched unmolested to Limerick.

At Limerick, the last asylum of the vanquished race, the authority of Tyrconnel was supreme. There was now no general who could pretend that his commission made him independent of the Lord Lieutenant; nor was the Lord Lieutenant now so unpopular as he had been a fortnight earlier. Since the battle there had been a reflux of public feeling. No part of that great disaster could be imputed to the Viceroy. His opinion indeed had been against trying the chances of a pitched field, and he could with some plausibility assert that the neglect of his counsels had caused the ruin of Ireland.

He made some preparations for defending Limerick, repaired the fortifications, and sent out parties to bring in provisions. The country, many miles round, was swept bare by these detachments, and a considerable quantity of cattle and fodder was collected within the walls. There was also a large stock of biscuit imported from France. The infantry assembled at Limerick were about fifteen thousand men. The Irish horse and dragoons, three or four thousand in number, were encamped on the Clare side of the Shannon. The communication between their camp and the city was maintained by means of a bridge called the Thomond Bridge, which was protected by a fort. These means of defence were not contemptible. But the fall of Athlone and the slaughter of Aghrim had broken the spirit of the army. A small party, at the head of which were Sarsfield and a brave Scotch officer named Wauchop, cherished a hope that the triumphant progress of Ginkel might be stopped by those walls from which William had, in the preceding year, been forced to retreat. But many of the Irish chiefs loudly declared that it was time to think of capitulating. Henry Luttrell, always fond of dark and crooked politics, opened a secret negotiation with the English. One of his letters was intercepted; and he was put under arrest: but many who blamed his perfidy agreed with him in thinking that it was idle to prolong the contest. Tyrconnel himself was convinced that all was lost. His only hope was that he might be able to prolong the struggle till he could receive from Saint Germains permission to treat. He wrote to request that permission, and prevailed, with some difficulty, on his desponding countrymen to bind themselves by an oath not to capitulate till an answer from James should arrive.

A few days after the oath had been administered, Tyrconnel was no more. On the eleventh of August he dined with D'Usson. The party was gay. The Lord Lieutenant seemed to have thrown off the load which had bowed down his body and mind: he drank: he jested: he was again the Dick Talbot who had diced and revelled with Grammont. Soon after he had risen from table, an apoplectic stroke deprived him of speech and sensation. On the fourteenth he breathed his last. The wasted remains of that form which had once been a model for statuaries were laid under the pavement of the Cathedral: but no inscription, no tradition, preserves the memory of the spot.

As soon as the Lord Lieutenant was no more, Plowden, who had superintended the Irish finances while there were any Irish

finances to superintend, produced a commission under the great
seal of James. This commission appointed Plowden himself,
Fitton and Nagle, Lords Justices in the event of Tyrconnel's
death. There was much murmuring when the names were made
known. For both Plowden and Fitton were Saxons. The commission, however, proved to be a mere nullity. For it was accompanied by instructions which forbade the Lords Justices to
interfere in the conduct of the war; and, within the narrow space
to which the dominions of James were now reduced, war was the
only business. The government was, therefore, really in the
hands of D'Usson and Sarsfield.

On the day on which Tyrconnel died, the advanced guard of
the English army came within sight of Limerick. Ginkel encamped on the same ground which William had occupied twelve
months before. The batteries, on which were planted guns and
bombs, very different from those which William had been forced
to use, played day and night; and soon roofs were blazing and
walls crashing in every corner of the city. Whole streets were
reduced to ashes. Meanwhile several English ships of war came
up the Shannon and anchored about a mile below the city.

Still the place held out; the garrison was, in numerical
strength, little inferior to the besieging army; and it seemed not
impossible that the defence might be prolonged till the equinoctial rains should a second time compel the English to retire. Ginkel determined on striking a bold stroke. No point in the whole
circle of the fortifications was more important, and no point
seemed to be more secure, than the Thomond Bridge, which
joined the city to the camp of the Irish horse on the Clare bank
of the Shannon. The Dutch general's plan was to separate the infantry within the ramparts from the cavalry without; and this
plan he executed with great skill, vigour and success. He laid a
bridge of tin boats on the river, crossed it with a strong body of
troops, drove before him in confusion fifteen hundred dragoons
who made a faint show of resistance, and marched towards the
quarters of the Irish horse. The Irish horse sustained but ill on
this day the reputation which they had gained at the Boyne. Indeed, that reputation had been purchased by the almost entire
destruction of the best regiments. Recruits had been without

much difficulty found. But the loss of fifteen hundred excellent soldiers was not to be repaired. The camp was abandoned without a blow. Some of the cavalry fled into the city. The rest, driving before them as many cattle as could be collected in that moment of panic, retired to the hills. Much beef, brandy and harness was found in the magazines; and the marshy plain of the Shannon was covered with firelocks and grenades which the fugitives had thrown away.

The conquerors returned in triumph to their camp. But Ginkel was not content with the advantage which he had gained. He was bent on cutting off all communication between Limerick and the county of Clare. In a few days, therefore, he again crossed the river at the head of several regiments, and attacked the fort which protected the Thomond Bridge. In a short time the fort was stormed. The soldiers who had garrisoned it fled in confusion to the city. The Town Major, a French officer, who commanded at the Thomond Gate, afraid that the pursuers would enter with the fugitives, ordered that part of the bridge which was nearest to the city to be drawn up. Many of the Irish went headlong into the stream and perished there. Others cried for quarter, and held up handkerchiefs in token of submission. But the conquerors were mad with rage: their cruelty could not be immediately restrained; and no prisoners were made till the heaps of corpses rose above the parapets. The garrison of the fort had consisted of about eight hundred men. Of these only a hundred and twenty escaped into Limerick.

This disaster seemed likely to produce a general mutiny in the besieged city. The Irish clamoured for the blood of the Town Major who had ordered the bridge to be drawn up in the face of their flying countrymen. His superiors were forced to promise that he should be brought before a court martial. Happily for him, he had received a mortal wound, in the act of closing the Thomond Gate, and was saved by a soldier's death from the fury of the multitude. The cry for capitulation became so loud and importunate that the generals could not resist it. D'Usson informed his government that the fight at the bridge had so effectually cowed the spirit of the garrison that it was impossible to continue the struggle. Some exception may perhaps be taken to the evidence of D'Usson: for undoubtedly he, like every French-man who had held any command in the Irish army, was weary of his banishment, and impatient to see Paris again. But it is certain that even Sarsfield had lost heart. Up to this time his voice had been for stubborn resistance. He was now not only willing, but impatient to treat. It seemed to him that the city was doomed. There was no hope of succour, domestic or foreign. In every part of Ireland the Saxons had set their feet on the necks of the na-tives. Sligo had fallen. Even those wild islands which intercept the huge waves of the Atlantic from the bay of Galway had ack-nowledged the authority of William. The men of Kerry, reputed the fiercest and most ungovernable part of the aboriginal popula-tion, had held out long, but had at length been routed, and chased to their woods and mountains. A French fleet, if a French fleet were now to arrive on the coast of Munster, would find the mouth of the Shannon guarded by English men of war. The stock of provisions within Limerick was already running low. If the siege were prolonged, the town would, in all human proba-bility, be reduced either by force or by blockade. And, if Ginkel should enter through the breach, or should be implored by a multitude perishing with hunger to dictate his own terms, what could be expected but a tyranny more inexorably severe than that of Cromwell? Would it not then be wise to try what conditions could be obtained while the victors had still something to fear from the rage and despair of the vanquished; while the last Irish army could still make some show of resistance behind the walls of the last Irish fortress?

On the evening of the day which followed the fight at the Thomond Gate, the drums of Limerick beat a parley; and Wau-chop, from one of the towers, hailed the besiegers, and requested Ruvigny to grant Sarsfield an interview. The brave Frenchman who was an exile on account of his attachment to one religion, and the brave Irishman who was about to become an exile on ac-count of his attachment to another, met and conferred, doubtless with mutual sympathy and respect. Ginkel, to whom Ruvigny reported what had passed, willingly consented to an armistice. For, constant as his success had been, it had not made him secure. The chances were greatly on his side. Yet it was possible that an attempt to storm the city might fail, as a similar attempt had failed twelve months before. If the siege should be turned into a blockade, it was probable that the pestilence which had been fatal to the army of Schomberg, which had compelled William to retreat, and which had all but prevailed even against the genius and energy of Marlborough, might soon avenge the carnage of Aghrim. The rains had lately been heavy. The whole plain might shortly be an immense pool of stagnant water. It might be necessary to move the troops to a healthier situation than the bank of the Shannon, and to provide for them a warmer shelter than that of tents. The enemy would be safe till the spring. In the spring a French army might land in Ireland: the natives might again rise in arms from Donegal to Kerry; and the war, which was now all but extinguished, might blaze forth fiercer than ever.

A negotiation was therefore opened with a sincere desire on both sides to put an end to the contest. The chiefs of the Irish army held several consultations at which some Roman Catholic prelates and some eminent lawyers were invited to assist. A preliminary question, which perplexed tender consciences, was submitted by the Bishops. The late Lord Lieutenant had persuaded the officers of the garrison to swear that they would not surrender Limerick till they should receive an answer to the letter in which their situation had been explained to James. The Bishops thought that the oath was no longer binding. It had been taken at a time when the communications with France were open, and in the full belief that the answer of James would arrive within three weeks. More than twice that time had elapsed. Every avenue leading to the city was strictly guarded by the enemy. His Majesty's faithful subjects, by holding out till it had become impossible for him to signify his pleasure to them, had acted up to the spirit of their promise.

The next question was what terms should be demanded. A paper, containing propositions which statesmen of our age will think reasonable, but which to the most humane and liberal English Protestants of the seventeenth century appeared extravagant, was sent to the camp of the besiegers. What was asked was that all offences should be covered with oblivion, that perfect freedom of worship should be allowed to the native population, that every parish should have its priest, and that Irish Roman Catholics should be capable of holding all offices, civil and military, and of enjoying all municipal privileges.

Ginkel knew little of the laws and feelings of the English; but he had about him persons who were competent to direct him. They had a week before prevented him from breaking a Rapparee on the wheel; and they now suggested an answer to the propositions of the enemy. 'I am a stranger here,' said Ginkel: 'I am ignorant of the constitution of these kingdoms: but I am assured that what you ask is inconsistent with that constitution; and therefore I cannot with honour consent.' He immediately ordered a new battery to be thrown up, and guns and mortars to be planted on it. But his preparations were speedily interrupted by another message from the city. The Irish begged that, since he could not grant what they had demanded, he would tell them what he was willing to grant. He called his advisers round him, and, after some consultation, sent back a paper containing the heads of a treaty, such as he had reason to believe that the government which he served would approve. What he offered was indeed much less than what the Irish desired, but was quite as much as, when they considered their situation and the temper of the English nation, they could expect. They speedily notified their assent. It was agreed that there should be a cessation of arms, not only by land, but in the ports and bays of Munster, and that a fleet of French transports should be suffered to come up the Shannon in peace and to depart in peace. The signing of the treaty was deferred till the Lords Justices, who represented William at Dublin, should arrive at Ginkel's quarters. But there was during some days a relaxation of military vigilance on both sides. Prisoners were set at liberty. The outposts of the two armies chatted and messed together. The English officers rambled into the town. The Irish officers dined in the camp. Anecdotes of what passed at the friendly meetings of these men, who had so lately been mortal enemies, were widely circulated. One story, in particular, was repeated in every part of Europe. 'Has not this last campaign,' said Sarsfield to some English officers, 'raised your opinion of Irish soldiers?' 'To tell you the truth,' answered an Englishman, 'we think of them much as we

always did.' 'However meanly you may think of us,' replied Sarsfield, 'change Kings with us, and we will willingly try our luck
with you again.' He was doubtless thinking of the day on which
he had seen the two Sovereigns at the head of two great armies,
William foremost in the charge, and James foremost in the
flight.[7]

On the first of October, Coningsby and Porter arrived at the
English headquarters. On the second the articles of capitulation
were discussed at great length and definitely settled. On the
third they were signed. They were divided into two parts, a
military treaty and a civil treaty. The former was subscribed only
by the generals on both sides. The Lords Justices set their names
to the latter.

By the military treaty it was agreed that such Irish officers and
soldiers as should declare that they wished to go to France should
be conveyed thither, and should, in the meantime, remain under
the command of their own generals. Ginkel undertook to furnish
a considerable number of transports. French vessels were also to
be permitted to pass and repass freely between Brittany and
Munster. Part of Limerick was to be immediately delivered up to
the English. But the island on which the Cathedral and the
Castle stand was to remain, for the present, in the keeping of the
Irish.

The terms of the civil treaty were very different from those
which Ginkel had sternly refused to grant. It was not stipulated
that the Roman Catholics of Ireland should be competent to hold
any political or military office, or that they should be admitted
into any corporation. But they obtained a promise that they
should enjoy such privileges in the exercise of their religion as
were consistent with the law, or as they had enjoyed in the reign
of Charles the Second.

To all inhabitants of Limerick, and to all officers and soldiers
in the Jacobite army, who should submit to the government and
notify their submission by taking the oath of allegiance, an entire
amnesty was promised. They were to retain their property: they
were to be allowed to exercise any profession which they had
exercised before the troubles: they were not to be punished for

[7. That is, at the battle of the Boyne.]

any treason, felony, or misdemeanour committed since the accession of the late King: nay, they were not to be sued for damages on account of any act of spoliation or outrage which they might have committed during the three years of confusion. This was more than the Lords Justices were constitutionally competent to grant. It was therefore added that the government would use its utmost endeavours to obtain a Parliamentary ratification of the treaty.

As soon as the two instruments had been signed, the English entered the city, and occupied one quarter of it. A narrow, but deep branch of the Shannon separated them from the quarter which was still in the possession of the Irish.

In a few hours a dispute arose which seemed likely to produce a renewal of hostilities. Sarsfield had resolved to seek his fortune in the service of France, and was naturally desirous to carry with him to the Continent such a body of troops as would be an important addition to the army of Lewis. Ginkel was as naturally unwilling to send thousands of men to swell the forces of the enemy. Both generals appealed to the treaty. Each construed it as suited his purpose, and each complained that the other had violated it. Sarsfield was accused of putting one of his officers under arrest for refusing to go to the Continent. Ginkel, greatly excited, declared that he would teach the Irish to play tricks with him, and began to make preparations for a cannonade. Sarsfield came to the English camp, and tried to justify what he had done. The altercation was sharp. 'I submit,' said Sarsfield, at last: 'I am in your power.' 'Not at all in my power,' said Ginkel; 'go back and do your worst.' The imprisoned officer was liberated: a sanguinary contest was averted; and the two commanders contented themselves with a war of words. Ginkel put forth proclamations assuring the Irish that, if they would live quietly in their own land, they should be protected and favoured, and that if they preferred a military life, they should be admitted into the service of King William. It was added that no man, who chose to reject this gracious invitation and to become a soldier of Lewis, must expect ever again to set foot on the island. Sarsfield and Wauchop exerted their eloquence on the other side. The present aspect of affairs, they said, was doubtless gloomy; but there was bright sky beyond the cloud. The banishment would be short. The return would be triumphant. Within a year the French would invade England. In such an invasion the Irish troops, if only they remained unbroken, would assuredly bear a chief part. In the meantime it was far better for them to live in a neighbouring and friendly country, under the parental care of their own rightful King, than to trust the Prince of Orange, who would probably send them to the other end of the world to fight for his ally the Emperor against the Janissaries.

The help of the Roman Catholic clergy was called in. On the day on which those who had made up their minds to go to France were required to announce their determination, the priests were indefatigable in exhorting. At the head of every regiment a sermon was preached on the duty of adhering to the cause of the Church, and on the sin and danger of consorting with unbelievers. Whoever, it was said, should enter the service of the usurpers would do so at the peril of his soul. The heretics affirmed that, after the peroration, a plentiful allowance of brandy was served out to the audience, and that, when the brandy had been swallowed, a Bishop pronounced a benediction. Thus duly prepared by physical and moral stimulants, the garrison, consisting of about fourteen thousand infantry, was drawn up in the vast meadow which lay on the Clare bank of the Shannon. Here copies of Ginkel's proclamation were profusely scattered about; and English officers went through the ranks imploring the men not to ruin themselves, and explaining to them the advantages which the soldiers of King William enjoyed. At length the decisive moment came. The troops were ordered to pass in review. Those who wished to remain in Ireland were directed to file off at a particular spot. All who passed that spot were to be considered as having made their choice for France. Sarsfield and Wauchop on one side, Porter, Coningsby and Ginkel on the other, looked on with painful anxiety. D'Usson and his countrymen, though not uninterested in the spectacle, found it hard to preserve their gravity. The confusion, the clamour, the grotesque appearance of an army in which there could scarcely be seen a shirt or a pair of pantaloons, a shoe or a stocking, presented so ludicrous a contrast to the orderly and brilliant appearance of their master's troops, that they amused themselves by wondering what the Parisians would say to see such a force mustered on the plain of Grenelle.

First marched what was called the Royal regiment, fourteen hundred strong. All but seven went beyond the fatal point. Ginkel's countenance showed that he was deeply mortified. He was consoled, however, by seeing the next regiment, which consisted of natives of Ulster, turn off to a man. There had arisen, notwithstanding the community of blood, language and religion, an antipathy between the Celts of Ulster and those of the other three provinces; nor is it improbable that the example and influence of Baldearg O'Donnel may have had some effect on the people of the land which his forefathers had ruled. In most of the regiments there was a division of opinion; but a great majority declared for France. Henry Luttrell was one of those who turned off. He was rewarded for his desertion, and perhaps for other services, with a grant of the large estate of his elder brother Simon, who firmly adhered to the cause of James, with a pension of five hundred pounds a year from the Crown, and with the abhorrence of the Roman Catholic population. After living in wealth, luxury and infamy, during a quarter of a century, Henry Luttrell was murdered while going through Dublin in his sedan chair; and the Irish House of Commons declared that there was reason to suspect that he had fallen by the revenge of the Papists. Eighty years after his death his grave near Luttrellstown was violated by the descendants of those whom he had betrayed, and his skull was broken to pieces with a pickaxe. The deadly hatred of which he was the object descended to his son and to his grandson; and, unhappily, nothing in the character either of his son or of his grandson tended to mitigate the feeling which the name of Luttrell excited.

When the long procession had closed, it was found that about a thousand men had agreed to enter into William's service. About two thousand accepted passes from Ginkel, and went quietly home. About eleven thousand returned with Sarsfield to the city.

A few hours after the garrison had passed in review, the horse, who were encamped some miles from the town, were required to make their choice; and most of them volunteered for France.

*

In Ireland there was peace. The domination of the colonists was absolute. The native population was tranquil with the ghastly tranquillity of exhaustion and of despair. There were indeed outrages, robberies, fire-raisings, assassinations. But more than a century passed away without one general insurrection. During that century, two rebellions were raised in Great Britain by the adherents of the House of Stuart. But neither when the elder Pretender was crowned at Scone, nor when the younger held his court at Holyrood, was the standard of that House set up in Connaught or Munster. In 1745, indeed, when the Highlanders were marching towards London, the Roman Catholics of Ireland were so quiet that the Lord Lieutenant could, without the smallest risk, send several regiments across Saint George's Channel to recruit the army of the Duke of Cumberland. Nor was this submission the effect of content, but of mere stupefaction and brokenness of heart. The iron had entered into the soul. The memory of past defeats, the habit of daily enduring insult and oppression, had cowed the spirit of the unhappy nation. There were indeed Irish Roman Catholics of great ability, energy and ambition: but they were to be found everywhere except in Ireland: at Versailles and at Saint Ildefonso, in the armies of Frederic and in the armies of Maria Theresa. One exile became a Marshal of France.[8] Another became Prime Minister of Spain.[9] If he had stayed in his native land he would have been regarded as an inferior by all the ignorant and worthless squireens who drank the glorious and immortal memory. In his palace at Madrid he had the pleasure of being assiduously courted by the ambassador of George the Second, and of bidding defiance in high terms to the ambassador of George the Third. Scattered over all

[8. Macaulay is presumably referring to Charles O'Brien, sixth Viscount Clare (1699–1761), who was made a Marshal of France in 1757.]

[9. Richard Wall (1694–1778), first minister of Spain, 1754 to 1764.]

Europe were to be found brave Irish generals, dexterous Irish diplomatists, Irish Counts, Irish Barons, Irish Knights of Saint Lewis and of Saint Leopold, of the White Eagle and of the Golden Fleece, who, if they had remained in the house of bondage, could not have been ensigns of marching regiments or freemen of petty corporations. These men, the natural chiefs of their race, having been withdrawn, what remained was utterly helpless and passive. A rising of the Irishry against the Englishry was no more to be apprehended than a rising of the women and children against the men.

There were indeed, in those days, fierce disputes between the mother country and the colony: but in those disputes the aboriginal population had no more interest than the Red Indians in the dispute between Old England and New England about the Stamp Act. The ruling few, even when in mutiny against the government, had no mercy for any thing that looked like mutiny on the part of the subject many. None of those Roman patriots, who poniarded Julius Caesar for aspiring to be a king, would have had the smallest scruple about crucifying a whole school of gladiators for attempting to escape from the most odious and degrading of all kinds of servitude. None of those Virginian patriots, who vindicated their separation from the British empire by proclaiming it to be a self-evident truth that all men were endowed by the Creator with an unalienable right to liberty, would have had the smallest scruple about shooting any negro slave who had laid claim to that unalienable right. And, in the same manner, the Protestant masters of Ireland, while ostentatiously professing the political doctrines of Locke and Sidney, held that a people who spoke the Celtic tongue and heard mass could have no concern in those doctrines. Molyneux questioned the supremacy of the English legislature. Swift assailed, with the keenest ridicule and invective, every part of the system of government. Lucas disquieted the administration of Lord Harrington. Boyle overthrew the administration of the Duke of Dorset. But neither Molyneux nor Swift, neither Lucas nor Boyle, ever thought of appealing to the native population. They would as soon have thought of appealing to the swine.[10]

10. In 1749 Lucas was the idol of the democracy of his own caste. It is

At a later period Henry Flood excited the dominant class to demand a Parliamentary reform, and to use even revolutionary means for the purpose of obtaining that reform. But neither he, nor those who looked up to him as their chief, and who went close to the verge of treason at his bidding, would consent to admit the subject class to the smallest share of political power. The virtuous and accomplished Charlemont, a Whig of the Whigs, passed a long life in contending for what he called the freedom of his country. But he voted against the law which gave the elective franchise to Roman Catholic freeholders; and he died fixed in the opinion that the Parliament House ought to be kept pure from Roman Catholic members. Indeed, during the century which followed the Revolution, the inclination of an English Protestant to trample on the Irishry was generally proportioned to the zeal which he professed for political liberty in the abstract. If he uttered any expression of compassion for the majority oppressed by the minority, he might be safely set down as a bigoted Tory and High Churchman.[11]

All this time hatred, kept down by fear, festered in the hearts of the children of the soil. They were still the same people that had sprung to arms in 1641 at the call of O'Neill, and in 1689 at the call of Tyrconnel. To them every festival instituted by the State was a day of mourning, and every public trophy set up by the State was a memorial of shame. We have never known, and can but faintly conceive, the feelings of a nation doomed to see constantly in all its public places the monuments of its subjuga-

curious to see what was thought of him by those who were not of his own caste. One of the chief Pariahs, Charles O'Connor, wrote thus: 'I am by no means interested, nor is any of our unfortunate population, in this affair of Lucas. A true patriot would not have betrayed such malice to such unfortunate slaves as we.' He adds, with too much truth, that those boasters the Whigs wished to have liberty all to themselves.

11. On this subject Johnson was the most liberal politician of his time. 'The Irish,' he said with great warmth, 'are in a most unnatural state: for we see there the minority prevailing over the majority.' I suspect that Alderman Beckford and Alderman Sawbridge would have been far from sympathizing with him. Charles O'Connor, whose unfavourable opinion of the Whig Lucas I have quoted, pays, in the Preface to the Dissertations on Irish History, a high compliment to the liberality of the Tory Johnson.

tion. Such monuments everywhere met the eye of the Irish Roman Catholics. In front of the Senate House of their country, they saw the statue of their conqueror. If they entered, they saw the walls tapestried with the defeats of their fathers. At length, after a hundred years of servitude, endured without one vigorous or combined struggle for emancipation, the French revolution awakened a wild hope in the bosoms of the oppressed. Men who had inherited all the pretensions and all the passions of the Parliament which James had held at the King's Inns could not hear unmoved of the downfall of a wealthy established Church, of the flight of a splendid aristocracy, of the confiscation of an immense territory. Old antipathies, which had never slumbered, were excited to new and terrible energy by the combination of stimulants which, in any other society, would have counteracted each other. The spirit of Popery and the spirit of Jacobinism, irreconcilable antagonists everywhere else, were for once mingled in an unnatural and portentous union. Their joint influence produced the third and last rising up of the aboriginal population against the colony. The great-grandsons of the soldiers of Galmoy and Sarsfield were opposed to the great-grandsons of the soldiers of Wolseley and Mitchelburne. The Celt again looked impatiently for the sails which were to bring succour from Brest; and the Saxon was again backed by the whole power of England.

Again the victory remained with the well educated and well organised minority. But, happily, the vanquished people found protection in a quarter from which they would once have had to expect nothing but implacable severity. By this time the philosophy of the eighteenth century had purified English Whiggism from that deep taint of intolerance which had been contracted during a long and close alliance with the Puritanism of the seventeenth century. Enlightened men had begun to feel that the arguments by which Milton and Locke, Tillotson and Burnet, had vindicated the rights of conscience might be urged with not less force in favour of the Roman Catholic than in favour of the Independent or the Baptist. The great party which traces its descent through the Exclusionists up to the Roundheads continued during thirty years, in spite of royal frowns and popular clamours, to demand a share in all the benefits of our free constitution for those Irish Papists whom the Roundheads and the Exclusionists had considered merely as beasts of chase or as beasts of burden. But it will be for some other historian to relate the vicissitudes of that great conflict, and the late triumph of reason and humanity. Unhappily such a historian will have to relate that the triumph won by such exertions and by such sacrifices was immediately followed by disappointment; that it proved far less easy to eradicate evil passions than to repeal evil laws; and that, long after every trace of national and religious animosity had been obliterated from the Statute Book, national and religious animosities continued to rankle in the bosoms of millions. May he be able also to relate that wisdom, justice and time gradually did in Ireland what they had done in Scotland, and that all the races which inhabit the British isles were at length indissolubly blended into one people.

16

The Revolution in Scotland

A. THE STATE OF THE HIGHLANDS

[*Meanwhile William was establishing his rule in Scotland. The Scottish Convention, like the English, had offered him the Crown, and had, at the same time, drawn up a document, 'the Claim of Right', comparable with the English 'Declaration of Right'. By this document, episcopacy was declared to be an insupportable grievance which must be abolished in Scotland, and the new King was invited to rule with the concurrence of Parliament and the Kirk. But between the English and the Scottish situation there was an important difference. The English tories had supported and by their support restrained the Revolution. In Scotland the Jacobites, through fear and discouragement, soon deserted the Convention and left it under the control of the extreme whigs. These were further supported by Scottish regiments sent by William from the South and by the Presbyterian mob, especially in the South West of Scotland, where the bigoted 'Cameronians', long persecuted by the Stuarts, had risen up to 'rabble', or extrude by force, the Episcopalian clergy. Thus the ruling Protestant party in Scotland was an exclusively 'whig' party: its whiggism would give William himself considerable trouble.*

In opposition to these Lowland whigs, the Jacobites fell back on the support of the Highlands. Thus in Scotland as in Ireland, the struggle between Protestant and Catholic, William and James, was transformed into a struggle between Saxon and Celt. But in Scotland the opposition was not national, for there was no Highland nation. It was tribal. The Highlanders were united, if at all, not so much on behalf of the Stuarts as against the most powerful of Highland clans, the Campbells, whose successive chiefs, the Earls of Argyll, known as MacCallum More, had since 1638 risen to dominance by allying themselves with the 'whigs' and the Kirk. In the 1640s other Highlanders had been temporarily united by James Graham, Earl of

*Montrose, the general of Charles I who had deserted the Covenant
when he saw that it had become the instrument of the 'whig' Marquess of Argyll; in the 1680s they were similarly united by John
Graham of Claverhouse, Viscount Dundee, the general of James II
who had fled from the Edinburgh Convention when he saw that it
had become the tool of the 'whig' Earl of Argyll.*

*Thus in Scotland, as in Ireland, the Jacobite cause was distorted
by local pressures: there by Celtic nationalism, here by tribal feuds.
In his thirteenth chapter, Macaulay describes – some would say
caricatures – the tribal society of the Highlands, and shows how
Dundee (whom he invariably and unjustly maligns) sought to
mobilize it for James and against William.]*

IT is not easy for a modern Englishman, who can pass in a day
from his club in St James's Street to his shooting box among the
Grampians, and who finds in his shooting box all the comforts
and luxuries of his club, to believe that, in the time of his great-
grandfathers, St James's Street had as little connection with the
Grampians as with the Andes. Yet so it was. In the south of our
island scarcely any thing was known about the Celtic part of
Scotland; and what was known excited no feeling but contempt
and loathing. The crags and the glens, the woods and the waters,
were indeed the same that now swarm every autumn with ad-
miring gazers and sketchers. The Trossachs wound as now between gigantic walls of rock tapestried with broom and wild
roses: Foyers came headlong down through the birchwood with
the same leap and the same roar with which he still rushes to
Loch Ness; and, in defiance of the sun of June, the snowy scalp
of Ben Cruachan rose, as it still rises, over the willowy islets of
Loch Awe. Yet none of these sights had power, till a recent
period, to attract a single poet or painter from more opulent and
more tranquil regions. Indeed, law and police, trade and industry, have done far more than people of romantic dispositions will
readily admit, to develop in our minds a sense of the wilder
beauties of nature. A traveller must be freed from all apprehension of being murdered or starved before he can be charmed by
the bold outlines and rich tints of the hills. He is not likely to be
thrown into ecstasies by the abruptness of a precipice from which

he is in imminent danger of falling two thousand feet perpendicular; by the boiling waves of a torrent which suddenly whirls away his baggage and forces him to run for his life; by the gloomy grandeur of a pass where he finds a corpse which marauders have just stripped and mangled; or by the screams of those eagles whose next meal may probably be on his own eyes.

About the year 1730, Captain Burt, one of the first Englishmen who caught a glimpse of the spots which now allure tourists from every part of the civilised world, wrote an account of his wanderings. He was evidently a man of a quick, an observant, and a cultivated mind, and would doubtless, had he lived in our age, have looked with mingled awe and delight on the mountains of Invernessshire. But, writing with the feeling which was universal in his own age, he pronounced those mountains monstrous excrescences. Their deformity, he said, was such that the most sterile plains seemed lovely by comparison. Fine weather, he complained, only made bad worse; for, the clearer the day, the more disagreeably did those misshapen masses of gloomy brown and dirty purple affect the eye. What a contrast, he exclaimed, between these horrible prospects and the beauties of Richmond Hill! Some persons may think that Burt was a man of vulgar and prosaical mind: but they will scarcely venture to pass a similar judgment on Oliver Goldsmith. Goldsmith was one of the very few Saxons who, more than a century ago, ventured to explore the Highlands. He was disgusted by the hideous wilderness, and declared that he greatly preferred the charming country round Leyden, the vast expanse of verdant meadow, and the villas with their statues and grottoes, trim flower beds, and rectilinear avenues. Yet it is difficult to believe that the author of *The Traveller* and of *The Deserted Village* was naturally inferior in taste and sensibility to the thousands of clerks and milliners who are now thrown into raptures by the sight of Loch Katrine and Loch Lomond. His feelings may easily be explained. It was not till roads had been cut out of the rocks, till bridges had been flung over the courses of the rivulets, till inns had succeeded to dens of robbers, till there was as little danger of being slain or plundered in the wildest defile of Badenoch or Lochaber as in Cornhill, that strangers could be enchanted by the blue dimples of the lakes and by the rainbows which overhung the waterfalls, and could derive a solemn pleasure even from the clouds and tempests which lowered on the mountain tops.

The change in the feeling with which the Lowlanders regarded the Highland scenery was closely connected with a change not less remarkable in the feeling with which they regarded the Highland race. It is not strange that the Wild Scotch, as they were sometimes called, should, in the seventeenth century, have been considered by the Saxons as mere savages. But it is surely strange that, considered as savages, they should not have been objects of interest and curiosity. The English were then abundantly inquisitive about the manners of rude nations separated from our island by great continents and oceans. Numerous books were printed describing the laws, the superstitions, the cabins, the repasts, the dresses, the marriages, the funerals of Laplanders and Hottentots, Mohawks and Malays. The plays and poems of that age are full of allusions to the usages of the black men of Africa and of the red men of America. The only barbarian about whom there was no wish to have any information was the Highlander. Five or six years after the Revolution, an indefatigable angler published an account of Scotland.[1] He boasted that, in the course of his rambles from lake to lake, and from brook to brook, he had left scarcely a nook of the kingdom unexplored. But, when we examine his narrative, we find that he had never ventured beyond the extreme skirts of the Celtic region. He tells us that even from the people who lived close to the passes he could learn little or nothing about the Gaelic population. Few Englishmen, he says, had ever seen Inveraray. All beyond Inveraray was chaos. In the reign of George the First, a work was published which professed to give a most exact account of Scotland; and in this work, consisting of more than three hundred pages, two contemptuous paragraphs were thought sufficient for the Highlands and the Highlanders. We may well doubt whether, in 1689, one in twenty of the well read gentlemen who assembled at Will's coffeehouse knew that, within the four seas, and at the distance of less than five hundred miles from London, were many miniature courts,

[1. This is misleading. The account used by Macaulay – R. Franck's *Northern Memoirs* – was written in 1658, although not published till 1694.]

in each of which a petty prince, attended by guards, by armour-bearers, by musicians, by a hereditary orator, by a hereditary poet laureate, kept a rude state, dispensed a rude justice, waged wars, and concluded treaties.

While the old Gaelic institutions were in full vigour, no account of them was given by any observer, qualified to judge of them fairly. Had such an observer studied the character of the Highlanders, he would doubtless have found in it closely intermingled the good and the bad qualities of an uncivilised nation. He would have found that the people had no love for their country or for their king; that they had no attachment to any commonwealth larger than the clan, or to any magistrate superior to the chief. He would have found that life was governed by a code of morality and honour widely different from that which is established in peaceful and prosperous societies. He would have learned that a stab in the back, or a shot from behind a fragment of rock, were approved modes of taking satisfaction for insults. He would have heard men relate boastfully how they or their fathers had wreaked on hereditary enemies in a neighbouring valley such vengeance as would have made old soldiers of the Thirty Years' War shudder. He would have found that robbery was held to be a calling, not merely innocent, but honourable. He would have seen, wherever he turned, that dislike of steady industry, and that disposition to throw on the weaker sex the heaviest part of manual labour, which are characteristic of savages. He would have been struck by the spectacle of athletic men basking in the sun, angling for salmon, or taking aim at grouse, while their aged mothers, their pregnant wives, their tender daughters, were reaping the scanty harvest of oats. Nor did the women repine at their hard lot. In their view it was quite fit that a man, especially if he assumed the aristocratic title of Duinhe Wassel and adorned his bonnet with the eagle's feather, should take his ease, except when he was fighting, hunting, or marauding. To mention the name of such a man in connection with commerce or with any mechanical art was an insult. Agriculture was indeed less despised. Yet a highborn warrior was much more becomingly employed in plundering the land of others than in tilling his own.

The religion of the greater part of the Highlands was a rude mixture of Popery and Paganism. The symbol of redemption was associated with heathen sacrifices and incantations. Baptized men poured libations of ale to one demon, and set out drink offerings of milk for another. Seers wrapped themselves up in bulls' hides, and awaited, in that vesture, the inspiration which was to reveal the future. Even among those minstrels and genealogists whose hereditary vocation was to preserve the memory of past events, an enquirer would have found very few who could read. In truth, he might easily have journeyed from sea to sea without discovering a page of Gaelic, printed or written. The price which he would have had to pay for his knowledge of the country would have been heavy. He would have had to endure hardships as great as if he had sojourned among the Esquimaux or the Samoyeds. Here and there, indeed, at the castle of some great lord who had a seat in the Parliament and Privy Council, and who was accustomed to pass a large part of his life in the cities of the South, might have been found wigs and embroidered coats, plate and fine linen, lace and jewels, French dishes and French wines. But, in general, the traveller would have been forced to content himself with very different quarters. In many dwellings the furniture, the food, the clothing, nay the very hair and skin of his hosts, would have put his philosophy to the proof. His lodging would sometimes have been in a hut of which every nook would have swarmed with vermin. He would have inhaled an atmosphere thick with peat smoke, and foul with a hundred noisome exhalations. At supper grain fit only for horses would have been set before him, accompanied by a cake of blood drawn from living cows. Some of the company with which he would have feasted would have been covered with cutaneous eruptions, and others would have been smeared with tar like sheep. His couch would have been the bare earth, dry or wet as the weather might be; and from that couch he would have risen half poisoned with stench, half blind with the reek of turf, and half mad with the itch.

This is not an attractive picture. And yet an enlightened and dispassionate observer would have found in the character and manners of this rude people something which might well excite admiration and a good hope. Their courage was what great exploits achieved in all the four quarters of the globe have since proved it to be. Their intense attachment to their own tribe and to their own patriarch, though politically a great evil, partook of the nature of virtue. The sentiment was misdirected and ill regulated; but still it was heroic. There must be some elevation of soul in a man who loves the society of which he is a member and the leader whom he follows with a love stronger than the love of life. It was true that the Highlander had few scruples about shedding the blood of an enemy: but it was not less true that he had high notions of the duty of observing faith to allies and hospitality to guests. It was true that his predatory habits were most pernicious to the commonwealth. Yet those erred greatly who imagined that he bore any resemblance to villains who, in rich and well governed communities, live by stealing. When he drove before him the herds of Lowland farmers up the pass which led to his native glen, he no more considered himself as a thief than the Raleighs and Drakes considered themselves as thieves when they divided the cargoes of Spanish galleons. He was a warrior seizing lawful prize of war, of war never once intermitted during the thirty-five generations which had passed away since the Teutonic invaders had driven the children of the soil to the mountains. That, if he was caught robbing on such principles, he should, for the protection of peaceful industry, be punished with the utmost rigour of the law was perfectly just. But it was not just to class him morally with the pickpockets who infested Drury Lane Theatre, or the highwaymen who stopped coaches on Blackheath. His inordinate pride of birth and his contempt for labour and trade were indeed great weaknesses, and had done far more than the inclemency of the air and the sterility of the soil to keep his country poor and rude. Yet even here there was some compensation. It must in fairness be acknowledged that the patrician virtues were not less widely diffused among the population of the Highlands than the patrician vices. As there was no other part of the island where men, sordidly clothed, lodged, and fed, indulged themselves to such a degree in the idle sauntering habits of an aristocracy, so there was no other part of the island where such men had in such a degree the better qualities of an aristocracy, grace and dignity of manner, self-respect, and that noble sensibility which makes dishonour more terrible than death. A gentleman of this sort, whose clothes were begrimed with the accumulated filth of years, and whose hovel smelt worse than an English hogstye, would often do the honours of that hovel with a lofty courtesy worthy of the splendid circle of Versailles. Though he had as little book-learning as the most stupid ploughboys of England, it would have been a great error to put him in the same intellectual rank with such ploughboys. It is indeed only by reading that men can become profoundly acquainted with any science. But the arts of poetry and rhetoric may be carried near to absolute perfection, and may exercise a mighty influence on the public mind, in an age in which books are wholly or almost wholly unknown. The first great painter of life and manners has described, with a vivacity which makes it impossible to doubt that he was copying from nature, the effect produced by eloquence and song on audiences ignorant of the alphabet. It is probable that, in the Highland councils, men who would not have been qualified for the duty of parish clerks sometimes argued questions of peace and war, of tribute and homage, with ability worthy of Halifax and Caermarthen, and that, at the Highland banquets, minstrels who did not know their letters sometimes poured forth rhapsodies in which a discerning critic might have found passages which would have reminded him of the tenderness of Otway or of the vigour of Dryden.

There was therefore even then evidence sufficient to justify the belief that no natural inferiority had kept the Celt far behind the Saxon. It might safely have been predicted that, if ever an efficient police should make it impossible for the Highlander to avenge his wrongs by violence and to supply his wants by rapine, if ever his faculties should be developed by the civilising influence of the Protestant religion and of the English language, if ever he should transfer to his country and to her lawful magistrates the affection and respect with which he had been taught to regard his own petty community and his own petty prince, the kingdom would obtain an immense accession of strength for all the purposes both of peace and of war.

Such would doubtless have been the decision of a well informed and impartial judge. But no such judge was then to be found. The Saxons who dwelt far from the Gaelic provinces could not be well informed. The Saxons who dwelt near those provinces could not be impartial. National enmities have always been fiercest among borderers; and the enmity between the Highland borderer and the Lowland borderer along the whole frontier was the growth of ages, and was kept fresh by constant injuries. One day many square miles of pasture land were swept bare by armed plunderers from the hills. Another day a score of plaids dangled in a row on the gallows of Crieff or Stirling. Fairs were indeed held on the debatable land for the necessary interchange of commodities. But to those fairs both parties came prepared for battle; and the day often ended in bloodshed. Thus the Highlander was an object of hatred to his Saxon neighbours; and from his Saxon neighbours those Saxons who dwelt far from him learned the very little that they cared to know about his habits. When the English condescended to think of him at all – and it was seldom that they did so – they considered him as a filthy abject savage, a slave, a Papist, a cutthroat, and a thief.

This contemptuous loathing lasted till the year 1745,[2] and was then for a moment succeeded by intense fear and rage. England, thoroughly alarmed, put forth her whole strength. The Highlands were subjugated rapidly, completely, and for ever. During a short time the English nation, still heated by the recent conflict, breathed nothing but vengeance. The slaughter on the field of battle and on the scaffold was not sufficient to slake the public thirst for blood. The sight of the tartan inflamed the populace of London with hatred, which showed itself by unmanly outrages to defenceless captives. A political and social revolution took place through the whole Celtic region. The power of the chiefs was destroyed: the people were disarmed: the use of the old national garb was interdicted: the old predatory habits were effectually broken; and scarcely had this change been accomplished when a strange reflux of public feeling began. Pity succeeded to aversion. The nation execrated the cruelties which had

[2. After the suppression of the last Jacobite Rebellion, in 1745, when the army of Highlanders supporting the Young Pretender reached Derby, the British government passed a series of acts to modernize the Highlands, to destroy the power of the chiefs, and to break up the tribal organization.]

been committed on the Highlanders, and forgot that for those cruelties it was itself answerable. Those very Londoners, who, while the memory of the march to Derby was still fresh, had thronged to hoot and pelt the rebel prisoners, now fastened on the prince who had put down the rebellion the nickname of Butcher. Those barbarous institutions and usages, which, while they were in full force, no Saxon had thought worthy of serious examination, or had mentioned except with contempt, had no sooner ceased to exist than they became objects of curiosity, of interest, even of admiration. Scarcely had the chiefs been turned into mere landlords, when it became the fashion to draw invidious comparisons between the rapacity of the landlord and the indulgence of the chief.

Men seemed to have forgotten that the ancient Gaelic polity had been found to be incompatible with the authority of law, had obstructed the progress of civilisation, had more than once brought on the empire the curse of civil war. As they had formerly seen only the odious side of that polity, they could now see only the pleasing side. The old tie, they said, had been parental: the new tie was purely commercial. What could be more lamentable than that the head of a tribe should eject, for a paltry arrear of rent, tenants who were his own flesh and blood, tenants whose forefathers had often with their bodies covered his forefathers on the field of battle? As long as there were Celtic marauders, they had been regarded by the Saxon population as hateful vermin who ought to be exterminated without mercy. As soon as the extermination had been accomplished, as soon as cattle were as safe in the Perthshire passes as in Smithfield market, the freebooter was exalted into a hero of romance. As long as the Gaelic dress was worn, the Saxons had pronounced it hideous, ridiculous, nay, grossly indecent. Soon after it had been prohibited, they discovered that it was the most graceful drapery in Europe. The Gaelic monuments, the Gaelic usages, the Gaelic superstitions, the Gaelic verses, disdainfully neglected during many ages, began to attract the attention of the learned from the moment at which the peculiarities of the Gaelic race began to disappear. So strong was this impulse that, where the Highlands were concerned, men of sense gave ready credence to stories without evidence, and men of taste gave rapturous applause to compositions without merit. Epic poems, which any skilful and dispassionate critic would at a glance have perceived to be almost entirely modern, and which, if they had been published as modern, would have instantly found their proper place in company with Blackmore's *Alfred* and Wilkie's *Epigoniad*, were pronounced to be fifteen hundred years old, and were gravely classed with the *Iliad*.[3] Writers of a very different order from the impostor who fabricated these forgeries saw how striking an effect might be produced by skilful pictures of the old Highland life. Whatever was repulsive was softened down: whatever was graceful and noble was brought prominently forward. Some of these works were executed with such admirable art that, like the historical plays of Shakespeare, they superseded history. The visions of the poet were realities to his readers. The places which he described became holy ground, and were visited by thousands of pilgrims.[4] Soon the vulgar imagination was so completely occupied by plaids, targets, and claymores, that, by most Englishmen, Scotchman and Highlander were regarded as synonymous words. Few people seemed to be aware that, at no remote period, a Macdonald or a Macgregor in his tartan was to a citizen of Edinburgh or Glasgow what an Indian hunter in his war paint is to an inhabitant of Philadelphia or Boston. Artists and actors represented Bruce and Douglas in striped petticoats. They might as well have represented Washington brandishing a tomahawk, and girt with a string of scalps. At length this fashion reached a point beyond which it was not easy to proceed. The last British King who held a court in Holyrood thought that he could not give a more striking proof of his respect for the usages which had prevailed in Scotland before the Union, than by disguising himself in what, before the Union, was considered by nine Scotchmen out of ten as the dress of a thief.[5]

Thus it has chanced that the old Gaelic institutions and man-

[3. The reference is to the poems of 'Ossian', first published by James Macpherson in 1760.]

[4. 'The poet' is, of course, Sir Walter Scott.]

[5. George IV visited Edinburgh in 1822 and sought to humour the natives by wearing a kilt.]

ners have never been exhibited in the simple light of truth. Up to the middle of the last century, they were seen through one false medium: they have since been seen through another. Once they loomed dimly through an obscuring and distorting haze of prejudice; and no sooner had that fog dispersed than they appeared bright with all the richest tints of poetry. The time when a perfectly fair picture could have been painted has now passed away. The original has long disappeared: no authentic effigy exists; and all that is possible is to produce an imperfect likeness by the help of two portraits, of which one is a coarse caricature and the other a masterpiece of flattery.

Among the erroneous notions which have been commonly received concerning the history and character of the Highlanders is one which it is especially necessary to correct. During the century which commenced with the campaign of Montrose, and terminated with the campaign of the young Pretender, every great military exploit which was achieved on British ground in the cause of the House of Stuart was achieved by the valour of Gaelic tribes. The English have therefore very naturally ascribed to those tribes the feelings of English cavaliers: profound reverence for the royal office, and enthusiastic attachment to the royal family. A close inquiry however will show that the strength of these feelings among the Celtic clans has been greatly exaggerated.

In studying the history of our civil contentions, we must never forget that the same names, badges, and war-cries had very different meanings in different parts of the British isles. We have already seen how little there was in common between the Jacobitism of Ireland and the Jacobitism of England. The Jacobitism of the Scotch Highlander was, at least in the seventeenth century, a third variety, quite distinct from the other two. The Gaelic population was far indeed from holding the doctrines of passive obedience and non-resistance. In fact disobedience and resistance made up the ordinary life of that population. Some of those very clans which it has been the fashion to describe as so enthusiastically loyal that they were prepared to stand by James to the death, even when he was in the wrong, had never, while he was on the throne, paid the smallest respect to his authority, even when he was clearly in the right. Their practice, their calling, had been to disobey and to defy him. Some of them had actually been proscribed by sound of horn for the crime of withstanding his lawful commands, and would have torn to pieces without scruple any of his officers who had dared to venture beyond the passes for the purpose of executing his warrant. The English Whigs were accused by their opponents of holding doctrines dangerously lax touching the obedience due to the chief magistrate. Yet no respectable English Whig ever defended rebellion, except as a rare and extreme remedy for rare and extreme evils. But among those Celtic chiefs whose loyalty has been the theme of so much warm eulogy were some whose whole existence from boyhood upwards had been one long rebellion. Such men, it is evident, were not likely to see the Revolution in the light in which it appeared to an Oxonian non-juror. On the other hand they were not, like the aboriginal Irish, urged to take arms by impatience of Saxon domination. To such domination the Scottish Celt had never been subjected. He occupied his own wild and sterile region and followed his own national usages. In his dealings with the Saxons, he was rather the oppressor than the oppressed. He exacted blackmail from them; he drove away their flocks and herds; and they seldom dared to pursue him to his native wilderness. They had never portioned out among themselves his dreary region of moor and shingle. He had never seen the tower of his hereditary chieftains occupied by an usurper who could not speak Gaelic, and who looked on all who spoke it as brutes and slaves; nor had his national and religious feelings ever been outraged by the power and splendour of a church which he regarded as at once foreign and heretical.

The real explanation of the readiness with which a large part of the population of the Highlands, twice in the seventeenth century, drew the sword for the Stuarts is to be found in the internal quarrels which divided the commonwealth of clans. For there was a commonwealth of clans, the image, on a reduced scale, of the great commonwealth of European nations. In the smaller of these two commonwealths, as in the larger, there were wars, treaties, alliances, disputes about territory and precedence, a system of public law, a balance of power. There was one inexhaustible source of discontents and disputes. The feudal system had, some centuries before, been introduced into the hill country, but had neither destroyed the patriarchal system nor amalgamated completely with it. In general he who was lord in the Norman polity was also chief in the Celtic polity; and, when this was the case, there was no conflict. But, when the two characters were separated, all the willing and loyal obedience was reserved for the chief. The lord had only what he could get and hold by force. If he was able, by the help of his own tribe, to keep in subjection tenants who were not of his own tribe, there was a tyranny of clan over clan, the most galling, perhaps, of all forms of tyranny. At different times different races had risen to an authority which had produced general fear and envy. The Macdonalds had once possessed in the Hebrides and throughout the mountain country of Argyllshire and Invernessshire, an ascendency similar to that which the House of Austria had once possessed in Christendom. But the ascendency of the Macdonalds had, like the ascendency of the House of Austria, passed away; and the Campbells, the children of Diarmid, had become in the Highlands what the Bourbons had become in Europe.

The parallel might be carried far. Imputations similar to those which it was the fashion to throw on the French government were thrown on the Campbells. A peculiar dexterity, a peculiar plausibility of address, a peculiar contempt for all the obligations of good faith, were ascribed, with or without reason, to the dreaded race. 'Fair and false like a Campbell' became a proverb. It was said that MacCallum More after MacCallum More had, with unwearied, unscrupulous, and unrelenting ambition, annexed mountain after mountain and island after island to the original domains of his House. Some tribes had been expelled from their territory, some compelled to pay tribute, some incorporated with the conquerors. At length the number of fighting men who bore the name of Campbell was sufficient to meet in the field of battle the combined forces of all the other western clans.[6]

6. Since this passage was written I was much pleased by finding that Lord Fountainhall used, in July 1676, exactly the same illustration which had occurred to me. He says that 'Argyll's ambitious grasping at the mastery of the Highlands and Western Islands of Mull, Ila, &c., stirred up other clans to enter into a combination for bearing him downe, like the confederat forces of Germanie, Spain, Holland, &c., against the growth of the French.'

It was during those civil troubles which commenced in 1638 that the power of this aspiring family reached the zenith. The Marquess of Argyll was the head of a party as well as the head of a tribe. Possessed of two different kinds of authority, he used each of them in such a way as to extend and fortify the other. The knowledge that he could bring into the field the claymores of five thousand half heathen mountaineers added to his influence among the austere Presbyterians who filled the Privy Council and the General Assembly at Edinburgh. His influence at Edinburgh added to the terror which he inspired among the mountains. Of all the Highland princes whose history is well known to us he was the greatest and most dreaded. It was while his neighbours were watching the increase of his power with hatred which fear could scarcely keep down that Montrose called them to arms. The call was promptly obeyed. A powerful coalition of clans waged war, nominally for King Charles, but really against MacCallum More. It is not easy for any person who has studied the history of that contest to doubt that, if Argyll had supported the cause of monarchy, his neighbours would have declared against it. Grave writers tell of the victory gained at Inverlochy by the royalists over the rebels. But the peasants who dwell near the spot speak more accurately. They talk of the great battle won there by the Macdonalds over the Campbells.

The feelings which had produced the coalition against the Marquess of Argyll retained their force long after his death. His son, Earl Archibald, though a man of many eminent virtues, inherited, with the ascendency of his ancestors, the unpopularity which such ascendency could scarcely fail to produce. In 1675, several warlike tribes formed a confederacy against him, but were compelled to submit to the superior force which was at his command. There was therefore great joy from sea to sea when, in 1681, he was arraigned on a futile charge, condemned to death, driven into exile, and deprived of his dignities. There was great alarm when, in 1685, he returned from banishment, and sent forth the fiery cross to summon his kinsmen to his standard; and there was again great joy when his enterprise had failed, when his army had melted away, when his head had been fixed on the Tolbooth of Edinburgh, and when those chiefs who had regarded him as an oppressor had obtained from the Crown, on easy terms, remissions of old debts and grants of new titles. While England and Scotland generally were execrating the tyranny of James, he was honoured as a deliverer in Appin and Lochaber, in Glenroy and Glenmore. The hatred excited by the power and ambition of the House of Argyll was not satisfied even when the head of that House had perished, when his children were fugitives, when strangers garrisoned the Castle of Inveraray, and when the whole shore of Loch Fyne was laid waste by fire and sword. It was said that the terrible precedent which had been set in the case of the Macgregors ought to be followed, and that it ought to be made a crime to bear the odious name of Campbell.

On a sudden all was changed. The Revolution came. The heir of Argyll returned in triumph. He was, as his predecessors had been, the head, not only of a tribe, but of a party. The sentence which had deprived him of his estate and of his honours was treated by the majority of the Convention as a nullity. The doors of the Parliament House were thrown open to him: he was selected from the whole body of Scottish nobles to administer the oath of office to the new Sovereigns; and he was authorised to raise an army on his domains for the service of the Crown. He would now, doubtless, be as powerful as the most powerful of his ancestors. Backed by the strength of the Government, he would demand all the long and heavy arrears of rent and tribute which were due to him from his neighbours, and would exact revenge for all the injuries and insults which his family had suffered. There was terror and agitation in the castles of twenty petty kings. The uneasiness was great among the Stewarts of Appin, whose territory was close pressed by the sea on one side, and by the race of Diarmid on the other. The Macnaghtens were still more alarmed. Once they had been the masters of those beautiful valleys through which the Ara and the Shira flow into Loch Fyne. But the Campbells had prevailed. The Macnaghtens had been reduced to subjection, and had, generation after generation, looked up with awe and detestation to the neighbouring Castle of Inveraray. They had recently been promised a complete emancipation. A grant, by virtue of which their chief would have held his estate immediately from the Crown, had been prepared, and was about to pass the seals, when the Revolution suddenly extinguished a hope which amounted almost to certainty.

The Macleans remembered that, only fourteen years before, their lands had been invaded and the seat of their chief taken and garrisoned by the Campbells. Even before William and Mary had been proclaimed at Edinburgh, a Maclean, deputed doubtless by the head of his tribe, had crossed the sea to Dublin, and had assured James that, if two or three battalions from Ireland were landed in Argyllshire, they would be immediately joined by four thousand four hundred claymores.

A similar spirit animated the Camerons. Their ruler, Sir Ewan Cameron, of Lochiel, surnamed the Black, was in personal qualities unrivalled among the Celtic princes. He was a gracious master, a trusty ally, a terrible enemy. His countenance and bearing were singularly noble. Some persons who had been at Versailles, and among them the shrewd and observant Simon Lord Lovat, said that there was, in person and manner, a most striking resemblance between Lewis the Fourteenth and Lochiel; and whoever compares the portraits of the two will perceive that there really was some likeness. In stature the difference was great. Lewis, in spite of high-heeled shoes and a towering wig, hardly reached the middle size. Lochiel was tall and strongly built. In agility and skill at his weapons he had few equals among the inhabitants of the hills. He had repeatedly been victorious in single combat. He was a hunter of great fame. He made vigorous war on the wolves which, down to his time, preyed on the red deer of the Grampians; and by his hand perished the last of the ferocious breed which is known to have wandered at large in our island. Nor was Lochiel less distinguished by intellectual than by bodily vigour. He might indeed have seemed ignorant to educated and travelled Englishmen, who had studied the classics under Busby at Westminster and under Aldrich at Oxford, who had learned something about the sciences among Fellows of the Royal Society, and something about the fine arts in the galleries of Florence and Rome. But though Lochiel had very little knowledge of books, he was eminently wise in council, eloquent in debate, ready in devising expedients, and skilful in managing the minds of men. His understanding preserved him from those follies into which pride and anger frequently hurried his brother chieftains. Many, therefore, who regarded his brother chieftains as mere barbarians, mentioned him with respect. Even at the Dutch Embassy in St James's Square he was spoken of as a man of such capacity and courage that it would not be easy to find his equal. As a patron of literature he ranks with the magnificent Dorset. If Dorset out of his own purse allowed Dryden a pension equal to the profits of the Laureateship, Lochiel is said to have bestowed on a celebrated bard, who had been plundered by marauders, and who implored alms in a pathetic Gaelic ode, three cows and the almost incredible sum of fifteen pounds sterling. In truth, the character of this great chief was depicted two thousand five hundred years before his birth, and depicted – such is the power of genius – in colours which will be fresh as many years after his death. He was the Ulysses of the Highlands.

*

But of all those Highlanders who looked on the recent turn of fortune with painful apprehension the fiercest and the most powerful were the Macdonalds. More than one of the magnates who bore that widespread name laid claim to the honour of being the rightful successor of those Lords of the Isles, who, as late as the fifteenth century, disputed the pre-eminence of the Kings of Scotland. This genealogical controversy, which has lasted down to our own time, caused much bickering among the competitors. But they all agreed in regretting the past splendour of their dynasty, and in detesting the upstart race of Campbell. The old feud had never slumbered. It was still constantly repeated, in verse and prose, that the finest part of the domain belonging to the ancient heads of the Gaelic nation – Islay, where they had lived with the pomp of royalty, Iona, where they had been interred with the pomp of religion, the paps of Jura, the rich peninsula of Kintyre – had been transferred from the legitimate possessors to the insatiable MacCallum More. Since the downfall of the House of Argyll, the Macdonalds, if they had not regained their ancient superiority, might at least boast that they had now no superior.

Relieved from the fear of their mighty enemy in the West, they had turned their arms against weaker enemies in the East, against the clan of Mackintosh and against the town of Inverness.

The clan of Mackintosh, a branch of an ancient and renowned tribe which took its name and badge from the wild cat of the forests, had a dispute with the Macdonalds, which originated, if tradition may be believed, in those dark times when the Danish pirates wasted the coasts of Scotland. Inverness was a Saxon colony among the Celts, a hive of traders and artisans in the midst of a population of loungers and plunderers, a solitary outpost of civilisation in a region of barbarians. Though the buildings covered but a small part of the space over which they now extend; though the arrival of a brig in the port was a rare event; though the Exchange was the middle of a miry street, in which stood a market cross much resembling a broken milestone; though the sittings of the municipal council were held in a filthy den with a roughcast wall; though the best houses were such as would now be called hovels; though the best roofs were of thatch; though the best ceilings were of bare rafters; though the best windows were, in bad weather, closed with shutters for want of glass; though the humbler dwellings were mere heaps of turf, in which barrels with the bottoms knocked out served the purpose of chimneys; yet to the mountaineer of the Grampians this city was as Babylon or as Tyre. Nowhere else had he seen four or five hundred houses, two churches, twelve malt-kilns, crowded close together. Nowhere else had he been dazzled by the splendour of rows of booths, where knives, horn spoons, tin kettles, and gaudy ribands were exposed to sale. Nowhere else had he been on board of one of those huge ships which brought sugar and wine over the sea from countries far beyond the limits of his geography. It is not strange that the haughty and warlike Macdonalds, despising peaceful industry, yet envying the fruits of that industry, should have fastened a succession of quarrels on the people of Inverness. In the reign of Charles the Second, it had been apprehended that the town would be stormed and plundered by those rude neighbours. The terms of peace which they offered showed how little they regarded the authority of the prince and of the law. Their demand was that a heavy tribute should be paid to them, that the municipal magistrates should bind themselves by an oath to deliver up to the vengeance of the clan every burgher who should shed the blood of a Macdonald, and that every burgher who should anywhere meet a person wearing the Macdonald tartan should ground arms in token of submission. Never did Lewis the Fourteenth, not even when he was encamped between Utrecht and Amsterdam, treat the States General with such despotic insolence. By the intervention of the Privy Council of Scotland a compromise was effected: but the old animosity was undiminished.

Common enmities and common apprehensions produced a good understanding between the town and the clan of Mackintosh. The foe most hated and dreaded by both was Colin Macdonald of Keppoch, an excellent specimen of the genuine Highland Jacobite. Keppoch's whole life had been passed in insulting and resisting the authority of the Crown. He had been repeatedly charged on his allegiance to desist from his lawless practices, but had treated every admonition with contempt. The government, however, was not willing to resort to extremities against him; and he long continued to rule undisturbed the stormy peaks of Cory-arrick, and the gigantic terraces which still mark the limits of what was once the Lake of Glenroy. He was famed for his knowledge of all the ravines and caverns of that dreary region; and such was the skill with which he could track a herd of cattle to the most secret hiding-place that he was known by the nickname of Coll of the Cows. At length his outrageous violations of all law compelled the Privy Council to take decided steps. He was proclaimed a rebel: letters of fire and sword were issued against him under the seal of James; and, a few weeks before the Revolution, a body of royal troops, supported by the whole strength of the Mackintoshes, marched into Keppoch's territories. He gave battle to the invaders, and was victorious. The King's forces were put to flight; the King's captain was slain; and this by a hero whose loyalty to the King many writers have very complacently contrasted with the factious turbulence of the Whigs.

If Keppoch had ever stood in any awe of the government, he was completely relieved from that feeling by the general anarchy which followed the Revolution. He wasted the lands of the

Mackintoshes, advanced to Inverness, and threatened the town with destruction. The danger was extreme. The houses were surrounded only by a wall which time and weather had so loosened that it shook in every storm. Yet the inhabitants showed a bold front; and their courage was stimulated by their preachers. Sunday the twenty-eighth of April was a day of alarm and confusion. The savages went round and round the small colony of Saxons like a troop of famished wolves round a sheepfold. Keppoch threatened and blustered. He would come in with all his men. He would sack the place. The burghers meanwhile mustered in arms round the market cross to listen to the oratory of their ministers. The day closed without an assault; the Monday and the Tuesday passed away in intense anxiety; and then an unexpected mediator made his appearance.

Dundee, after his flight from Edinburgh, had retired to his country seat in that valley through which the Glamis descends to the ancient castle of Macbeth. Here he remained quiet during some time. He protested that he had no intention of opposing the new government. He declared himself ready to return to Edinburgh, if only he could be assured that he should be protected against lawless violence; and he offered to give his word of honour, or, if that were not sufficient, to give bail, that he would keep the peace. Some of his old soldiers had accompanied him, and formed a garrison sufficient to protect his house against the Presbyterians of the neighbourhood. Here he might possibly have remained unharmed and harmless, had not an event for which he was not answerable made his enemies implacable, and made him desperate.

An emissary of James had crossed from Ireland to Scotland with letters addressed to Dundee and Balcarres.[7] Suspicion was excited. The messenger was arrested, interrogated, and searched; and the letters were found. Some of them proved to be from Melfort, and were worthy of him. Every line indicated those qualities which had made him the abhorrence of his country and the

[7. Colin Lindsay, third Earl of Balcarres, had been empowered by James to manage the civil affairs of the Jacobite cause in Scotland, while Dundee managed its military affairs.]

favourite of his master. He announced with delight the near approach of the day of vengeance and rapine, of the day when the estates of the seditious would be divided among the loyal, and when many who had been great and prosperous would be exiles and beggars. The King, Melfort said, was determined to be severe. Experience had at length convinced his Majesty that mercy would be weakness. Even the Jacobites were disgusted by learning that a Restoration would be immediately followed by a confiscation and a proscription. Some of them did not hesitate to say that Melfort was a villain, that he hated Dundee and Balcarres, that he wished to ruin them, and that, for that end, he had written these odious despatches, and had employed a messenger who had very dexterously managed to be caught. It is however quite certain that Melfort, after the publication of these papers, continued to stand as high as ever in the favour of James. It can therefore hardly be doubted that, in those passages which shocked even the zealous supporters of hereditary right, the Secretary merely expressed with fidelity the feelings and intentions of his master. Hamilton, by virtue of the powers which the Estates had, before their adjournment, confided to him, ordered Balcarres and Dundee to be arrested. Balcarres was taken and confined, first in his own house, and then in the Tolbooth of Edinburgh. But to seize Dundee was not so easy an enterprise. As soon as he heard that warrants were out against him, he crossed the Dee with his followers, and remained a short time in the wild domains of the House of Gordon. There he held some communications with the Macdonalds and Camerons about a rising. But he seems at this time to have known little and cared little about the Highlanders. For their national character he probably felt the dislike of a Saxon, for their military character the contempt of a professional soldier. He soon returned to the Lowlands, and stayed there till he learned that a considerable body of troops had been sent to apprehend him. He then betook himself to the hill country as his last refuge, pushed northward through Strathdon and Strathbogie, crossed the Spey, and, on the morning of the first of May, arrived with a small band of horsemen at the camp of Keppoch before Inverness.

The new situation in which Dundee was now placed, the new view of society which was presented to him, naturally suggested new projects to his inventive and enterprising spirit. The hundreds of athletic Celts whom he saw in their national order of battle were evidently not allies to be despised. If he could form a great coalition of clans, if he could muster under one banner ten or twelve thousand of those hardy warriors, if he could induce them to submit to the restraints of discipline, what a career might be before him!

A commission from King James, even when King James was securely seated on the throne, had never been regarded with much respect by Coll of the Cows. That chief, however, hated the Campbells with all the hatred of a Macdonald, and promptly gave in his adhesion to the cause of the House of Stuart. Dundee undertook to settle the dispute between Keppoch and Inverness. The town agreed to pay two thousand dollars, a sum which, small as it might be in the estimation of the goldsmiths of Lombard Street, probably exceeded any treasure that had ever been carried into the wilds of Coryarrick. Half the sum was raised, not without difficulty, by the inhabitants; and Dundee is said to have passed his word for the remainder.

He next tried to reconcile the Macdonalds with the Mackintoshes, and flattered himself that the two warlike tribes, lately arrayed against each other, might be willing to fight side by side under his command. But he soon found that it was no light matter to take up a Highland feud. About the rights of the contending Kings neither clan knew any thing or cared any thing. The conduct of both is to be ascribed to local passions and interests. What Argyll was to Keppoch, Keppoch was to the Mackintoshes. The Mackintoshes therefore remained neutral; and their example was followed by the Macphersons, another branch of the race of the wild cat. This was not Dundee's only disappointment. The Mackenzies, the Frasers, the Grants, the Munros, the Mackays, the Macleods, dwelt at a great distance from the territory of MacCallum More. They had no dispute with him; they owed no debt to him; and they had no reason to dread the increase of his power. They therefore did not sympathize with his alarmed and exasperated neighbours, and could not be induced to join the confederacy against him. Those chiefs, on the other hand, who lived nearer to Inveraray, and to whom the name of Campbell had long been terrible and hateful, greeted Dundee eagerly, and promised to meet him at the head of their followers on the eighteenth of May. During the fortnight which preceded that day, he traversed Badenoch and Athol, and exhorted the inhabitants of those districts to rise in arms. He dashed into the Lowlands with his horsemen, surprised Perth, and carried off some Whig gentlemen prisoners to the mountains.

Meanwhile the fiery crosses had been wandering from hamlet to hamlet over all the heaths and mountains thirty miles round Ben Nevis; and when he reached the trysting place in Lochaber he found that the gathering had begun. The headquarters were fixed close to Lochiel's house, a large pile built entirely of fir wood, and considered in the Highlands as a superb palace. Lochiel, surrounded by more than six hundred broadswords, was there to receive his guests. Macnaghten of Macnaghten and Stewart of Appin were at the muster with their little clans. Macdonald of Keppoch led the warriors who had, a few months before, under his command, put to flight the musketeers of King James. Macdonald of Clanronald was of tender years: but he was brought to the camp by his uncle, who acted as Regent during the minority. The youth was attended by a picked bodyguard composed of his own cousins, all comely in appearance, and good men of their hands. Macdonald of Glengarry, conspicuous by his dark brow and his lofty stature, came from that great valley where a chain of lakes, then unknown to fame, and scarcely set down in maps, is now the daily highway of steam vessels passing and repassing between the Atlantic and the German Ocean. None of the rulers of the mountains had a higher sense of his personal dignity, or was more frequently engaged in disputes with other chiefs. He generally affected in his manners and in his housekeeping a rudeness beyond that of his rude neighbours, and professed to regard the very few luxuries which had then found their way from the civilised parts of the world into the Highlands as signs of the effeminacy and degeneracy of the Gaelic race. But on this occasion he chose to imitate the splendour of Saxon warriors, and rode on horseback before his four

hundred plaided clansmen in a steel cuirass and a coat embroidered with gold lace. Another Macdonald, destined to a
lamentable and horrible end, led a band of hardy freebooters
from the dreary pass of Glencoe.[8] Somewhat later came the great
Hebridean potentates. Macdonald of Sleat, the most opulent and
powerful of all the grandees who laid claim to the lofty title of
Lord of the Isles, arrived at the head of seven hundred fighting
men from Skye. A fleet of long boats brought five hundred Macleans from Mull under the command of their chief, Sir John of
Duart. A far more formidable array had in old times followed his
forefathers to battle. But the power, though not the spirit, of the
clan had been broken by the arts and arms of the Campbells.
Another band of Macleans arrived under a valiant leader, who
took his title from Lochbuy, which is, being interpreted, the
Yellow Lake.

It does not appear that a single chief who had not some special
cause to dread and detest the House of Argyll obeyed Dundee's
summons. There is indeed strong reason to believe that the
chiefs who came would have remained quietly at home if the
government had understood the politics of the Highlands. Those
politics were thoroughly understood by one able and experienced
statesman, sprung from the great Highland family of Mackenzie,
the Viscount Tarbet. He at this conjuncture pointed out to Melville by letter, and to Mackay in conversation, both the cause and
the remedy of the distempers which seemed likely to bring on
Scotland the calamities of civil war. There was, Tarbet said, no
general disposition to insurrection among the Gael. Little was to
be apprehended even from those popish clans which were under
no apprehension of being subjected to the yoke of the Campbells.
It was notorious that the ablest and most active of the discontented chiefs troubled themselves not at all about the questions
which were in dispute between the Whigs and the Tories. Lochiel in particular, whose eminent personal qualities made him the
most important man among the mountaineers, cared no more for
James than for William. If the Camerons, the Macdonalds, and
the Macleans could be convinced that, under the new government, their estates and their dignities would be safe, if Mac-

[8. See below, pp. 406–32.]

Callum More would make some concessions, if their Majesties would take on themselves the payment of some arrears of rent, Dundee might call the clans to arms; but he would call to little purpose. Five thousand pounds, Tarbet thought, would be sufficient to quiet all the Celtic magnates; and in truth, though that sum might seem ludicrously small to the politicians of Westminster, though it was not larger than the annual gains of the Groom of the Stole or of the Paymaster of the Forces, it might well be thought immense by a barbarous potentate who, while he ruled hundreds of square miles, and could bring hundreds of warriors into the field, had perhaps never had fifty guineas at once in his coffers.

*

B. THE BATTLE OF KILLIECRANKIE, 27 JULY 1689

[*Dundee struggled to hold his army together in Lochaber, awaiting the reinforcements from Ireland which James promised but never sent. Meanwhile Hugh Mackay, William's general in Scotland, was no less hampered by his allies. On the one hand the 'Cameronian' bigots – like the 'Protesters' of the previous generation – scrupled to serve an 'uncovenanted', 'Erastian' ruler, who would not concede the power of persecution and revenge to the Kirk. On the other hand the whig politicians of Edinburgh, dominated by the disgruntled Sir James Montgomery and his party, 'the Club', sought to make supplies dependent on further political concessions by the King. But ultimately the uncertain situation in Perthshire drew the two armies together and led, on 27 July 1689, to the battle of Killiecrankie. This was a great victory for the Highlanders; but it was a victory whose fruits were quickly lost since Dundee – who alone, as a Saxon, could hold the various clans together – perished on the field. Macaulay's account of the battle, which follows, is also from his thirteenth chapter.*]

While these things were passing in the Parliament House, the civil war in the Highlands, having been during a few weeks suspended, broke forth again more violently than before. Since the splendour of the House of Argyll had been eclipsed, no Gaelic chief could vie in power with the Marquess of Atholl. The district from which he took his title, and of which he might almost be called the sovereign, was in extent larger than an ordinary county, and was more fertile, more diligently cultivated, and more thickly peopled than the greater part of the Highlands. The men who followed his banner were supposed to be not less numerous than all the Macdonalds and Macleans united, and were, in strength and courage, inferior to no tribe in the mountains. But the clan had been made insignificant by the insignificance of the chief. The Marquess was the falsest, the most fickle, the most pusillanimous, of mankind. Already, in the short space of six months, he had been several times a Jacobite, and several times a Williamite. Both Jacobites and Williamites regarded him with contempt and distrust, which respect for his immense power prevented them from fully expressing. After repeatedly vowing fidelity to both parties, and repeatedly betraying both, he began to think that he should best provide for his safety by abdicating the functions both of a peer and of a chieftain, by absenting himself both from the Parliament House at Edinburgh and from his castle in the mountains, and by quitting the country to which he was bound by every tie of duty and honour at the very crisis of her fate. While all Scotland was waiting with impatience and anxiety to see in which army his numerous retainers would be arrayed, he stole away to England, settled himself at Bath, and pretended to drink the waters. His principality, left without a head, was divided against itself. The general leaning of the Atholl men was towards King James. For they had been employed by him, only four years before, as the ministers of his vengeance against the House of Argyll. They had garrisoned Inveraray: they had ravaged Lorne: they had demolished houses, cut down fruit trees, burned fishing boats, broken millstones, hanged Campbells, and were therefore not likely to be pleased by the prospect of MacCallum More's restoration. One word from the Marquess would have sent two thousand claymores to the Jacobite side. But that word he would not speak; and the consequence was, that the conduct of his followers was as irresolute and inconsistent as his own.

While they were waiting for some indication of his wishes, they were called to arms at once by two leaders, either of whom might, with some show of reason, claim to be considered as the representative of the absent chief. Lord Murray, the Marquess's eldest son, who was married to a daughter of the Duke of Hamilton, declared for King William. Stewart of Ballenach, the Marquess's confidential agent, declared for King James. The people knew not which summons to obey. He whose authority would have been held in profound reverence, had plighted faith to both sides, and had then run away for fear of being under the necessity of joining either; nor was it very easy to say whether the place which he had left vacant belonged to his steward or to his heir apparent.

The most important military post in Atholl was Blair Castle. The house which now bears that name is not distinguished by any striking peculiarity from other country seats of the aristocracy. The old building was a lofty tower of rude architecture which commanded a vale watered by the Garry. The walls would have offered very little resistance to a battering train, but were quite strong enough to keep the herdsmen of the Grampians in awe. About five miles south of this stronghold, the valley of the Garry contracts itself into the celebrated glen of Killiecrankie. At present a highway as smooth as any road in Middlesex ascends gently from the low country to the summit of the defile. White villas peep from the birch forest; and, on a fine summer day, there is scarcely a turn of the pass at which may not be seen some angler casting his fly on the foam of the river, some artist sketching a pinnacle of rock, or some party of pleasure banqueting on the turf in the fretwork of shade and sunshine. But, in the days of William the Third, Killiecrankie was mentioned with horror by the peaceful and industrious inhabitants of the Perthshire Lowlands. It was deemed the most perilous of all those dark ravines through which the marauders of the hills were wont to sally forth. The sound, so musical to modern ears, of the river brawling round the mossy rocks and among the smooth pebbles, the dark masses of crag and verdure worthy of the pencil of Wilson, the fantastic peaks bathed, at sunrise and sunset, with light rich as that which glows on the canvas of Claude, suggested to our ancestors thoughts of murderous ambuscades and of bodies stripped, gashed, and abandoned to the birds of prey. The only path was narrow and rugged: a horse could with difficulty be led up: two men could hardly walk abreast; and, in some places, the way ran so close by the precipice that the traveller had great need of a steady eye and foot. Many years later, the first Duke of Atholl constructed a road up which it was just possible to drag his coach. But even that road was so steep and so strait that a handful of resolute men might have defended it against an army; nor did any Saxon consider a visit to Killiecrankie as a pleasure, till experience had taught the English Government that the weapons by which the Highlanders could be most effectually subdued were the pickaxe and the spade.

The country which lay just above this pass was now the theatre of a war such as the Highlands had not often witnessed. Men wearing the same tartan, and attached to the same lord, were arrayed against each other. The name of the absent chief was used, with some show of reason, on both sides. Ballenach, at the head of a body of vassals who considered him as the representative of the Marquess, occupied Blair Castle. Murray, with twelve hundred followers, appeared before the walls and demanded to be admitted into the mansion of his family, the mansion which would one day be his own. The garrison refused to open the gates. Messages were sent off by the besiegers to Edinburgh, and by the besieged to Lochaber. In both places the tidings produced great agitation. Mackay and Dundee agreed in thinking that the crisis required prompt and strenuous exertion. On the fate of Blair Castle probably depended the fate of all Atholl. On the fate of Atholl might depend the fate of Scotland. Mackay hastened northward, and ordered his troops to assemble in the low country of Perthshire. Some of them were quartered at such a distance that they did not arrive in time. He soon, however, had with him the three Scotch regiments which had served in Holland, and which bore the names of their Colonels: Mackay himself, Balfour, and Ramsay. There was also a gallant regiment of infantry from England, then called Hastings's, but now known as the thirteenth of the line. With these old troops were joined two regiments newly levied in the Lowlands. One of them was commanded by Lord Kenmure; the other, which had been raised on the Border, and which is still styled the King's own Borderers, by Lord Leven. Two troops of horse, Lord Annandale's and Lord Belhaven's, probably made up the army to the number of above three thousand men. Belhaven rode at the head of his troop: but Annandale, the most factious of all Montgomery's followers, preferred the Club and the Parliament House to the field.

Dundee, meanwhile, had summoned all the clans which acknowledged his commission to assemble for an expedition into Atholl. His exertions were strenuously seconded by Lochiel. The fiery crosses were sent again in all haste through Appin and Ardnamurchan, up Glenmore, and along Loch Leven. But the call was so unexpected, and the time allowed was so short, that the muster was not a very full one. The whole number of broadswords seems to have been under three thousand. With this force, such as it was, Dundee set forth. On his march he was joined by succours which had just arrived from Ulster. They consisted of little more than three hundred Irish foot, ill armed, ill clothed, and ill disciplined. Their commander was an officer named Cannon, who had seen service in the Netherlands, and who might perhaps have acquitted himself well in a subordinate post and in a regular army, but who was altogether unequal to the part now assigned to him. He had already loitered among the Hebrides so long that some ships which had been sent with him, and which were laden with stores, had been taken by English cruisers. He and his soldiers had with difficulty escaped the same fate. Incompetent as he was, he bore a commission which gave him military rank in Scotland next to Dundee.

The disappointment was severe. In truth James would have done better to withhold all assistance from the Highlanders than to mock them by sending them, instead of the well appointed army which they had asked and expected, a rabble contemptible in numbers and appearance. It was now evident that whatever was done for his cause in Scotland must be done by Scottish hands.

While Mackay from one side, and Dundee from the other, were advancing towards Blair Castle, important events had taken place there. Murray's adherents soon began to waver in their fidelity to him. They had an old antipathy to Whigs; for they considered the name of Whig as synonymous with the name of Campbell. They saw arrayed against them a large number of their kinsmen, commanded by a gentleman who was supposed to possess the confidence of the Marquess. The besieging army therefore melted rapidly away. Many returned home on the plea that, as their neighbourhood was about to be the seat of war, they must place their families and cattle in security. Others more ingenuously declared that they would not fight in such a quarrel. One large body went to a brook, filled their bonnets with water, drank a health to King James, and then dispersed. Their zeal for King James, however, did not induce them to join the standard of his general. They lurked among the rocks and thickets which overhang the Garry, in the hope that there would soon be a battle, and that, whatever might be the event, there would be fugitives and corpses to plunder.

Murray was in a strait. His force had dwindled to three or four hundred men: even in those men he could put little trust; and the Macdonalds and Camerons were advancing fast. He therefore raised the siege of Blair Castle, and retired with a few followers into the defile of Killiecrankie. There he was soon joined by a detachment of two hundred fusiliers whom Mackay had sent forward to secure the pass. The main body of the Lowland army speedily followed.

Early in the morning of Saturday the twenty-seventh of July, Dundee arrived at Blair Castle. There he learned that Mackay's troops were already in the ravine of Killiecrankie. It was necessary to come to a prompt decision. A council of war was held. The Saxon officers were generally against hazarding a battle. The Celtic chiefs were of a different opinion. Glengarry and Lochiel were now both of a mind. 'Fight, my Lord,' said Lochiel with his usual energy; 'fight immediately: fight, if you have only one to three. Our men are in heart. Their only fear is that the enemy should escape. Give them their way; and be assured that they will either perish or gain a complete victory. But if you restrain them, if you force them to remain on the defensive, I answer for nothing. If we do not fight, we had better break up and retire to our mountains.'

Dundee's countenance brightened. 'You hear, gentlemen,' he said to his Lowland officers; 'you hear the opinion of one who understands Highland war better than any of us.' No voice was raised on the other side. It was determined to fight; and the confederated clans in high spirits set forward to encounter the enemy.

The enemy meanwhile had made his way up the pass. The ascent had been long and toilsome: for even the foot had to climb by twos and threes; and the baggage horses, twelve hundred in number, could mount only one at a time. No wheeled carriage had ever been tugged up that arduous path. The head of the column had emerged and was on the table land, while the rearguard was still in the plain below. At length the passage was effected; and the troops found themselves in a valley of no great extent. Their right was flanked by a rising ground, their left by the Garry. Wearied with the morning's work, they threw themselves on the grass to take some rest and refreshment.

Early in the afternoon, they were roused by an alarm that the Highlanders were approaching. Regiment after regiment started up and got into order. In a little while the summit of an ascent which was about a musket shot before them was covered with bonnets and plaids. Dundee rode forward for the purpose of surveying the force with which he was to contend, and then drew up his own men with as much skill as their peculiar character permitted him to exert. It was desirable to keep the clans distinct. Each tribe, large or small, formed a column separated from the next column by a wide interval. One of these battalions might contain seven hundred men, while another consisted of only a hundred and twenty. Lochiel had represented that it was impossible to mix men of different tribes without destroying all that constituted the peculiar strength of a Highland army.

On the right, close to the Garry, were the Macleans. Next to them were Cannon and his Irish foot. Then came the Macdonalds of Clanronald, commanded by the guardian of their young prince. On the left were other bands of Macdonalds. At the head of one large battalion towered the stately form of Glengarry, who bore in his hand the royal standard of King James the Seventh. Still further to the left were the cavalry, a small squadron consisting of some Jacobite gentlemen who had fled from the Lowlands to the mountains and of about forty of Dundee's old troopers. The horses had been ill fed and ill tended among the Grampians, and looked miserably lean and feeble. Beyond them was Lochiel with his Camerons. On the extreme left, the men of Skye were marshalled by Macdonald of Sleat.

In the Highlands, as in all countries where war has not become a science, men thought it the most important duty of a commander to set an example of personal courage and of bodily exertion. Lochiel was especially renowned for his physical prowess. His clansmen looked big with pride when they related how he had himself broken hostile ranks and hewn down tall warriors. He probably owed quite as much of his influence to these achievements as to the high qualities which, if fortune had placed him in the English Parliament or at the French court, would have made him one of the foremost men of his age. He had the sense however to perceive how erroneous was the notion which his countrymen had formed. He knew that to give and to take blows was not the business of a general. He knew with how much difficulty Dundee had been able to keep together, during a few days, an army composed of several clans; and he knew that what Dundee had effected with difficulty Cannon would not be able to effect at all. The life on which so much depended must not be sacrificed to a barbarous prejudice. Lochiel therefore adjured Dundee not to run into any unnecessary danger. 'Your Lordship's business,' he said, 'is to overlook every thing, and to issue your commands. Our business is to execute those commands bravely and promptly.' Dundee answered with calm magnanimity that there was much weight in what his friend Sir Ewan had urged, but that no general could effect any thing great without possessing the confidence of his men. 'I must establish my character for courage. Your people expect to see their leaders in the thickest of the battle; and today they shall see me there. I promise you, on my honour, that in future fights I will take more care of myself.'

Meanwhile a fire of musketry was kept up on both sides, but more skilfully and more steadily by the regular soldiers than by the mountaineers. The space between the armies was one cloud of smoke. Not a few Highlanders dropped; and the clans grew impatient. The sun however was low in the west before Dundee gave the order to prepare for action. His men raised a great shout. The enemy, probably exhausted by the toil of the day, returned a feeble and wavering cheer. 'We shall do it now,' said Lochiel: 'that is not the cry of men who are going to win.' He had walked through all his ranks, had addressed a few words to every Cameron, and had taken from every Cameron a promise to conquer or die.

It was past seven o'clock. Dundee gave the word. The Highlanders dropped their plaids. The few who were so luxurious as to wear rude socks of untanned hide spurned them away. It was long remembered in Lochaber that Lochiel took off what probably was the only pair of shoes in his clan, and charged barefoot at the head of his men. The whole line advanced firing. The enemy returned the fire and did much execution. When only a small space was left between the armies, the Highlanders suddenly flung away their firelocks, drew their broadswords, and rushed forward with a fearful yell. The Lowlanders prepared to receive the shock; but this was then a long and awkward process; and the soldiers were still fumbling with the muzzles of their guns and the handles of their bayonets when the whole flood of Macleans, Macdonalds, and Camerons came down. In two minutes the battle was lost and won. The ranks of Balfour's regiment broke. He was cloven down while struggling in the press. Ramsay's men turned their backs and dropped their arms. Mackay's own foot were swept away by the furious onset of the Camerons. His brother and nephew exerted themselves in vain to rally the men. The former was laid dead on the ground by a stroke from a claymore. The latter, with eight wounds on his body, made his way through the tumult and carnage to his uncle's side. Even in that extremity Mackay retained all his self-possession. He had still one hope. A charge of horse might recover the day; for of horse the bravest Highlanders were supposed to stand in awe. But he called on the horse in vain. Belhaven indeed behaved like a gallant gentleman: but his troopers, appalled by the rout of the infantry, galloped off in disorder: Annandale's men followed: all was over; and the mingled torrent of redcoats and tartans went raving down the valley to the gorge of Killiecrankie.

Mackay, accompanied by one trusty servant, spurred bravely through the thickest of the claymores and targets, and reached a point from which he had a view of the field. His whole army had disappeared, with the exception of some Borderers whom Leven had kept together, and of Hastings's regiment, which had poured a murderous fire into the Celtic ranks, and which still kept unbroken order. All the men that could be collected were only a few hundreds. The general made haste to lead them across the Garry, and, having put the river between them and the enemy, paused for a moment to meditate on his situation.

He could hardly understand how the conquerors could be so unwise as to allow him even that moment for deliberation. They might with ease have killed or taken all who were with him before the night closed in. But the energy of the Celtic warriors had spent itself in one furious rush and one short struggle. The pass was choked by the twelve hundred beasts of burden which carried the provisions and baggage of the vanquished army. Such a booty was irresistibly tempting to men who were impelled to war quite as much by the desire of rapine as by the desire of glory. It is probable that few even of the chiefs were disposed to leave so rich a prize for the sake of King James. Dundee himself might at that moment have been unable to persuade his followers to quit the heaps of spoil, and to complete the great work of the day; and Dundee was no more.

At the beginning of the action he had taken his place in front of his little band of cavalry. He bade them follow him, and rode forward. But it seemed to be decreed that, on that day, the Lowland Scotch should in both armies appear to disadvantage. The horse hesitated. Dundee turned round, and stood up in his stirrups, and, waving his hat, invited them to come on. As he lifted his arm, his cuirass rose, and exposed the lower part of his left side. A musket ball struck him; his horse sprang forward and plunged into a cloud of smoke and dust, which hid from both armies the fall of the victorious general. A person named Johnstone was near him and caught him as he sank down from the saddle. 'How goes the day?' said Dundee. 'Well for King

James,' answered Johnstone: 'but I am sorry for Your Lordship.' 'If it is well for him,' answered the dying man, 'it matters the less for me.' He never spoke again; but when, half an hour later, Lord Dunfermline and some other friends came to the spot, they thought that they could still discern some faint remains of life. The body, wrapped in two plaids, was carried to the Castle of Blair.

Mackay, who was ignorant of Dundee's fate, and well acquainted with Dundee's skill and activity, expected to be instantly and hotly pursued, and had very little expectation of being able to save even the scanty remains of the vanquished army. He could not retreat by the pass: for the Highlanders were already there. He therefore resolved to push across the mountains towards the valley of the Tay. He soon overtook two or three hundred of his runaways who had taken the same road. Most of them belonged to Ramsay's regiment, and must have seen service. But they were unarmed: they were utterly bewildered by the recent disaster; and the general could find among them no remains either of martial discipline or of martial spirit. His situation was one which must have severely tried the firmest nerves. Night had set in: he was in a desert: he had no guide: a victorious enemy was, in all human probability, on his track; and he had to provide for the safety of a crowd of men who had lost both head and heart. He had just suffered a defeat of all defeats the most painful and humiliating. His domestic feelings had been not less severely wounded than his professional feelings. One dear kinsman had just been struck dead before his eyes. Another, bleeding from many wounds, moved feebly at his side. But the unfortunate general's courage was sustained by a firm faith in God, and a high sense of duty to the state. In the midst of misery and disgrace, he still held his head nobly erect, and found fortitude, not only for himself, but for all around him.

His first care was to be sure of his road. A solitary light which twinkled through the darkness guided him to a small hovel. The inmates spoke no tongue but the Gaelic, and were at first scared by the appearance of uniforms and arms. But Mackay's gentle manner removed their apprehension: their language had been familiar to him in childhood; and he retained enough of it to

communicate with them. By their directions, and by the help of a
pocket map, in which the routes through that wild country were
roughly laid down, he was able to find his way. He marched all
night. When day broke his task was more difficult than ever.
Light increased the terror of his companions. Hastings's men
and Leven's men indeed still behaved themselves like soldiers.
But the fugitives from Ramsay's were a mere rabble. They had
flung away their muskets. The broadswords from which they had
fled were ever in their eyes. Every fresh object caused a fresh
panic. A company of herdsmen in plaids driving cattle was magnified by imagination into a host of Celtic warriors. Some of the
runaways left the main body and fled to the hills, where their
cowardice met with a proper punishment. They were killed for
their coats and shoes; and their naked carcasses were left for a
prey to the eagles of Ben Lawers. The desertion would have been
much greater, had not Mackay and his officers, pistol in hand
threatened to blow out the brains of any man whom they caught
attempting to steal off.

At length the weary fugitives came in sight of Weem Castle.
The proprietor of the mansion was a friend to the new government, and extended to them such hospitality as was in his power.
His stores of oatmeal were brought out: kine were slaughtered;
and a rude and hasty meal was set before the numerous guests.
Thus refreshed, they again set forth, and marched all day over
bog, moor, and mountain. Thinly inhabited as the country was,
they could plainly see that the report of their disaster had already
spread far, and that the population was everywhere in a state of
great excitement. Late at night they reached Castle Drummond,
which was held for King William by a small garrison; and, on the
following day, they proceeded with less difficulty to Stirling.

The tidings of their defeat had outrun them. All Scotland was
in a ferment. The disaster had indeed been great: but it was
exaggerated by the wild hopes of one party and by the wild fears
of the other. It was at first believed that the whole army of King
William had perished; that Mackay himself had fallen; that Dundee, at the head of a great host of barbarians, flushed with victory
and impatient for spoil, had already descended from the hills;
that he was master of the whole country beyond the Forth; that

Fife was up to join him; that in three days he would be at Stirling; that in a week he would be at Holyrood. Messengers were sent to urge a regiment which lay in Northumberland to hasten across the border. Others carried to London earnest entreaties that His Majesty would instantly send every soldier that could be spared, nay, that he would come himself to save his northern kingdom. The factions of the Parliament House, awestruck by the common danger, forgot to wrangle. Courtiers and malcontents with one voice implored the Lord High Commissioner to close the session, and to dismiss them from a place where their deliberations might soon be interrupted by the mountaineers. It was seriously considered whether it might not be expedient to abandon Edinburgh, to send the numerous state prisoners who were in the Castle and the Tolbooth on board of a man of war which lay off Leith, and to transfer the seat of government to Glasgow.

The news of Dundee's victory was everywhere speedily followed by the news of his death; and it is a strong proof of the extent and vigour of his faculties, that his death seems everywhere to have been regarded as a complete set-off against his victory. Hamilton, before he adjourned the Estates, informed them that he had good tidings for them; that Dundee was certainly dead; and that therefore the rebels had on the whole sustained a defeat. In several letters written at that conjuncture by able and experienced politicians a similar opinion is expressed. The messenger who rode with the news of the battle to the English Court was fast followed by another who carried a despatch for the King, and, not finding His Majesty at Saint James's, galloped to Hampton Court. Nobody in the capital ventured to break the seal; but fortunately, after the letter had been closed, some friendly hand had hastily written on the outside a few words of comfort: 'Dundee is killed. Mackay has got to Stirling': and these words quieted the minds of the Londoners.

From the pass of Killiecrankie the Highlanders had retired, proud of their victory, and laden with spoil, to the Castle of Blair. They boasted that the field of battle was covered with heaps of the Saxon soldiers, and that the appearance of the corpses bore ample testimony to the power of a good Gaelic broadsword in a good Gaelic right hand. Heads were found cloven down to the throat, and skulls struck clean off just above the ears. The conquerors however had bought their victory dear. While they were advancing, they had been much galled by the musketry of the enemy; and, even after the decisive charge, Hastings's Englishmen and some of Leven's Borderers had continued to keep up a steady fire. A hundred and twenty Camerons had been slain: the loss of the Macdonalds had been still greater; and several gentlemen of birth and note had fallen.

Dundee was buried in the church of Blair Atholl: but no monument was erected over his grave; and the church itself has long disappeared. A rude stone on the field of battle marks, if local tradition can be trusted, the place where he fell. During the last three months of his life he had approved himself a great warrior and politician; and his name is therefore mentioned with respect by that large class of persons who think that there is no excess of wickedness for which courage and ability do not atone.

It is curious that the two most remarkable battles that perhaps were ever gained by irregular over regular troops should have been fought in the same week; the battle of Killiecrankie, and the battle of Newton Butler. In both battles the success of the irregular troops was singularly rapid and complete. In both battles the panic of the regular troops, in spite of the conspicuous example of courage set by their generals, was singularly disgraceful. It ought also to be noted that, of these extraordinary victories, one was gained by Celts over Saxons, and the other by Saxons over Celts. The victory of Killiecrankie indeed, though neither more splendid nor more important than the victory of Newton Butler, is far more widely renowned; and the reason is evident. The Anglo-Saxon and the Celt have been reconciled in Scotland, and have never been reconciled in Ireland. In Scotland all the great actions of both races are thrown into a common stock, and are considered as making up the glory which belongs to the whole country. So completely has the old antipathy been extinguished that nothing is more usual than to hear a Lowlander talk with complacency and even with pride of the most humiliating defeat that his ancestors ever underwent. It would be difficult to name any eminent man in whom national feeling and clannish feeling were stronger than in Sir Walter Scott. Yet when Sir Walter Scott mentioned Killiecrankie he seemed utterly to forget that he was a Saxon, that he was of the same blood and of the same speech with Ramsay's foot and Annandale's horse. His heart swelled with triumph when he related how his own kindred had fled like hares before a smaller number of warriors of a different breed and of a different tongue.

In Ireland the feud remains unhealed. The name of Newton Butler, insultingly repeated by a minority, is hateful to the great majority of the population. If a monument were set up on the field of battle, it would probably be defaced: if a festival were held in Cork or Waterford on the anniversary of the battle, it would probably be interrupted by violence. The most illustrious Irish poet of our time would have thought it treason to his country to sing the praises of the conquerors. One of the most learned and diligent Irish archæologists of our time has laboured, not indeed very successfully, to prove that the event of the day was decided by a mere accident from which the Englishry could derive no glory. We cannot wonder that the victory of the Highlanders should be more celebrated than the victory of the Enniskilleners, when we consider that the victory of the Highlanders is matter of boast to all Scotland, and that the victory of the Enniskilleners is matter of shame to three fourths of Ireland.

*

C. THE CHURCH SETTLEMENT OF SCOTLAND, 1690–91

[*The Highland victory of Killiecrankie proved a flash in the pan. Deprived of its commander, the Highland army disintegrated in victory, whereas Mackay quickly reformed his forces. On 21 August – less than a month after Killiecrankie – the Highlanders were repulsed at Dunkeld. Next year, James sent a new general from Ireland to renew the war; but a Jacobite army had barely been assembled before it was routed, at the Haughs of Cromdale, by William's commander at Inverness, Sir Thomas Livingstone. This event put an*

end to all further thoughts of war and enabled William to turn to the
ecclesiastical settlement of Scotland. Hitherto he had found himself
obstructed by the Scottish Parliament ; but Sir James Montgomery,
the leader of whig opposition, had now discredited himself with his
former allies by his new association with the Jacobites, and William
was able to exploit the advantage. His settlement, largely the work of
Carstares, was both liberal and effective. Thanks to it the inflamed
bigotries of the seventeenth century would gradually die out and a
union with England would become possible. The following passage,
describing the settlement, comes from Chapter XVI.]

So effectually had the spirit of the disaffected clans been cowed
that Mackay marched unresisted from Perth into Lochaber,
fixed his headquarters at Inverlochy, and proceeded to execute
his favourite design of erecting at that place a fortress which
might overawe the mutinous Camerons and Macdonalds. In a
few days the walls were raised: the ditches were sunk: the pallis-
ades were fixed: demiculverins from a ship of war were ranged
along the parapets; and the general departed, leaving an officer
named Hill in command of a sufficient garrison. Within the defences there was no want of oatmeal, red herrings, and beef; and
there was rather a superabundance of brandy. The new stronghold, which, hastily and rudely as it had been constructed,
seemed doubtless to the people of the neighbourhood the most
stupendous work that power and science united had ever produced, was named Fort William in honour of the King.

By this time the Scottish Parliament had reassembled at Edinburgh. William had found it no easy matter to decide what
course should be taken with that capricious and unruly body.
The English Commons had sometimes put him out of temper.
Yet they had granted him millions, and had never asked from
him such concessions as had been imperiously demanded by the
Scottish legislature, which could give him little and had given
him nothing. The English statesmen with whom he had to deal
did not generally stand or deserve to stand high in his esteem.
Yet few of them were so utterly false and shameless as the leading Scottish politicians. Hamilton was, in morality and honour,
rather above than below his fellows; and even Hamilton was

fickle, false and greedy. 'I wish to heaven,' William was once provoked into exclaiming, 'that Scotland were a thousand miles off, and that the Duke of Hamilton were King of it. Then I should be rid of them both.'

After much deliberation William determined to send Melville[9] down to Edinburgh as Lord High Commissioner. Melville was not a great statesman: he was not a great orator: he did not look or move like the representative of royalty: his character was not of more than standard purity; and the standard of purity among Scottish senators was not high: but he was by no means deficient in prudence or temper; and he succeeded, on the whole, better than a man of much higher qualities might have done.

During the first days of the Session, the friends of the government desponded, and the chiefs of the opposition were sanguine. Montgomery's head, though by no means a weak one, had been turned by the triumphs of the preceding year. He believed that his intrigues and his rhetoric had completely subjugated the Estates. It seemed to him impossible that, having exercised a boundless empire in the Parliament House when the Jacobites were absent, he should be defeated when they were present, and ready to support whatever he proposed. He had not indeed found it easy to prevail on them to attend: for they could not take their seats without taking the oaths. A few of them had some slight scruple of conscience about forswearing themselves; and many, who did not know what a scruple of conscience meant, were apprehensive that they might offend the rightful King by vowing fealty to the actual King. Some Lords, however, who were supposed to be in the confidence of James, asserted that, to their knowledge, he wished his friends to perjure themselves; and this assertion induced most of the Jacobites, with Balcarres at their head, to be guilty of perfidy aggravated by impiety.

It soon appeared, however, that Montgomery's faction, even with this reinforcement, was no longer a majority of the legislature. For every supporter that he had gained he had lost two. He had committed an error which has more than once, in British history, been fatal to great parliamentary leaders. He had ima-

[9. George, Lord Melville, William's principal agent for Scottish affairs. A moderate whig, he had been a former exile in the Netherlands.]

gined that, as soon as he chose to coalesce with those to whom he had recently been opposed, all his followers would imitate his example. He soon found that it was much easier to inflame animosities than to appease them. The great body of Whigs and Presbyterians shrank from the fellowship of the Jacobites. Some waverers were purchased by the government; nor was the purchase expensive; for a sum which would hardly be missed in the English Treasury was immense in the estimation of the needy barons of the North. Thus the scale was turned; and, in the Scottish Parliaments of that age, the turn of the scale was every thing: the tendency of majorities was always to increase, the tendency of minorities to diminish.

The first question on which a vote was taken related to the election for a borough. The ministers carried their point by six voices. In an instant every thing was changed: the spell was broken: the Club, from being a bugbear, became a laughingstock: the timid and the venal passed over in crowds from the weaker to the stronger side. It was in vain that the opposition attempted to revive the disputes of the preceding year. The King had wisely authorised Melville to give up the Committee of Articles.[10] The Estates, on the other hand, showed no disposition to pass another Act of Incapacitation, to censure the government for opening the Courts of Justice, or to question the right of the Sovereign to name the Judges.[11] An extraordinary supply was voted, small, according to the notions of English financiers, but large for the means of Scotland. The sum granted was a hundred and sixty-two thousand pounds sterling, to be raised in the course of four years.

The Jacobites, who found that they had forsworn themselves to no purpose, sat, bowed down by shame and writhing with vexation, while Montgomery, who had deceived himself and them, and who, in his rage, had utterly lost, not indeed his parts and his fluency, but all decorum and self-command, scolded like

[10. A nominated Committee which, under the Stuarts, had effectively controlled the Scottish Parliament. After the Revolution, the Parliament had pressed for its abolition. William sought to preserve it, but ultimately yielded.]

[11. These had all been whig demands made, as conditions of supply, in the previous session.]

a waterman on the Thames, and was answered with equal asperity and even more than equal ability by Sir John Dalrymple.

The most important acts of this Session were those which fixed the ecclesiastical constitution of Scotland. By the Claim of Right it had been declared that the authority of Bishops was an insupportable grievance; and William, by accepting the Crown, had bound himself not to uphold an institution condemned by the very instrument on which his title to the Crown depended. But the Claim of Right had not defined the form of Church government which was to be substituted for episcopacy; and, during the stormy Session held in the summer of 1689, the violence of the Club had made legislation impossible. During many months therefore every thing had been in confusion. One polity had been pulled down; and no other polity had been set up. In the Western Lowlands, the beneficed clergy had been so effectually rabbled, that scarcely one of them had remained at his post. In Berwickshire, the three Lothians and Stirlingshire, most of the curates had been removed by the Privy Council for not obeying that vote of the Convention which had directed all ministers of parishes, on pain of deprivation, to proclaim William and Mary King and Queen of Scotland. Thus, throughout a great part of the realm, there was no public worship except what was performed by Presbyterian divines, who sometimes officiated in tents, and sometimes, without any legal right, took possession of the churches. But there were large districts, especially on the north of the Tay, where the people had no strong feeling against episcopacy; and there were many priests who were not disposed to lose their manses and stipends for the sake of King James. Hundreds of the old curates, therefore, having been neither hunted by the populace nor deposed by the Council, still performed their spiritual functions. Every minister was, during this time of transition, free to conduct the service and to administer the sacraments as he thought fit. There was no controlling authority. The legislature had taken away the jurisdiction of Bishops, and had not established the jurisdiction of Synods.

To put an end to this anarchy was one of the first duties of the Parliament. Melville had, with the powerful assistance of Carstares, obtained, in spite of the remonstrances of English Tories, authority to assent to such ecclesiastical arrangements as might satisfy the Scottish nation. One of the first laws which the Lord Commissioner touched with the sceptre repealed the Act of Supremacy. He next gave the royal assent to a law enacting that those Presbyterian divines who had been pastors of parishes in the days of the Covenant, and had, after the Restoration, been ejected for refusing to acknowledge episcopal authority, should be restored. The number of those pastors had originally been about three hundred and fifty: but not more than sixty were still living.

The Estates then proceeded to fix the national creed. The Confession of Faith drawn up by the Assembly of Divines at Westminster, the Longer and Shorter Catechism, and the Directory, were considered by every good Presbyterian as the standards of orthodoxy; and it was hoped that the legislature would recognise them as such. This hope, however, was in part disappointed. The Confession was read at length, amidst much yawning, and adopted without alteration. But, when it was proposed that the Catechisms and the Directory should be taken into consideration, the ill humour of the audience broke forth into murmurs. For that love of long sermons which was strong in the Scottish commonalty was not shared by the Scottish aristocracy. The Parliament had already been listening during three hours to dry theology, and was not inclined to hear any thing more about original sin and election. The Duke of Hamilton said that the Estates had already done all that was essential. They had given their sanction to a digest of the great principles of Christianity. The rest might well be left to the Church. The weary majority eagerly assented, in spite of the muttering of some zealous Presbyterian ministers who had been admitted to hear the debate, and who could sometimes hardly restrain themselves from taking part in it.

The memorable law which fixed the ecclesiastical constitution of Scotland was brought in by the Earl of Sutherland. By this law the synodical polity was re-established. The rule of the Church was entrusted to the sixty ejected ministers who had just been restored, and to such other persons, whether ministers or elders, as the Sixty should think fit to admit to a participation of power. The Sixty and their nominees were authorised to visit all the parishes in the kingdom, and to turn out all ministers who were deficient in abilities, scandalous in morals, or unsound in faith. Those parishes which had, during the interregnum,[12] been deserted by their pastors, or, in plain words, those parishes of which the pastors had been rabbled, were declared vacant.

To the clause which reestablished synodical government no serious opposition appears to have been made. But three days were spent in discussing the question whether the Sovereign should have power to convoke and to dissolve ecclesiastical assemblies; and the point was at last left in dangerous ambiguity. Some other clauses were long and vehemently debated. It was said that the immense power given to the Sixty was incompatible with the fundamental principle of the polity which the Estates were about to set up. That principle was that all presbyters were equal, and that there ought to be no order of ministers of religion superior to the order of presbyters. What did it matter whether the Sixty were called prelates or not, if they were to lord it with more than prelatical authority over God's heritage? To the argument that the proposed arrangement was, in the very peculiar circumstances of the Church, the most convenient that could be made, the objectors replied that such reasoning might suit the mouth of an Erastian, but that all orthodox Presbyterians held the parity of ministers to be ordained by Christ, and that, where Christ had spoken, Christians were not at liberty to consider what was convenient.

With much greater warmth and much stronger reason the minority attacked the clause which sanctioned the lawless acts of the Western fanatics. Surely, it was said, a rabbled curate might well be left to the severe scrutiny of the sixty Inquisitors. If he was deficient in parts of learning, if he was loose in life, if he was heterodox in doctrine, those stern judges would not fail to detect and to depose him. They would probably think a game at bowls, a prayer borrowed from the English Liturgy, or a sermon in which the slightest taint of Arminianism could be discovered, a sufficient reason for pronouncing his benefice vacant. Was it not

[12. That is, between the flight of James and the tender of the Crown to William.]

monstrous, after constituting a tribunal from which he could scarcely hope for bare justice, to condemn him without allowing him to appear even before that tribunal, to condemn him without a trial, to condemn him without an accusation? Did ever any grave senate, since the beginning of the world, treat a man as a criminal merely because he had been robbed, pelted, hustled, dragged through snow and mire, and threatened with death if he returned to the house which was his by law? The Duke of Hamilton, glad to have so good an opportunity of attacking the new Lord Commissioner, spoke with great vehemence against this odious clause. We are told that no attempt was made to answer him; and, though those who tell us so were zealous Episcopalians, we may easily believe their report: for what answer was it possible to return?

Melville, on whom the chief responsibility lay, sat on the throne in profound silence through the whole of this tempestuous debate. It is probable that his conduct was determined by considerations which prudence and shame prevented him from explaining. The state of the south-western shires was such that it would have been impossible to put the rabbled ministers in possession of their dwellings and churches without employing a military force, without garrisoning every manse, without placing guards round every pulpit, and without handing over some ferocious enthusiasts to the Provost Marshal; and it would be no easy task for the government to keep down by the sword at once the Jacobites of the Highlands and the Covenanters of the Lowlands. The majority, having made up their minds for reasons which could not well be produced, became clamorous for the question. 'No more debate,' was the cry: 'We have heard enough: a vote! a vote!' The question was put according to the Scottish form, 'Approve or not approve the article?' Hamilton insisted that the question should be, 'Approve or not approve the rabbling?' After much altercation, he was overruled, and the clause passed. Only fifteen or sixteen members voted with him. He warmly and loudly exclaimed, amidst much angry interruption, that he was sorry to see a Scottish Parliament disgrace itself by such iniquity. He then left the house with several of his friends. It is impossible not to sympathize with the indignation which he expressed. Yet we ought to remember that it is the nature of injustice to generate injustice. There are wrongs which it is almost impossible to repair without committing other wrongs; and such a wrong had been done to the people of Scotland in the preceding generation. It was because the Parliament of the Restoration had legislated in insolent defiance of the sense of the nation that the Parliament of the Revolution had to abase itself before the mob.

When Hamilton and his adherents had retired, one of the preachers who had been admitted to the hall called out to the members who were near him; 'Fie! Fie! Do not lose time. Make haste, and get all over before he comes back.' This advice was taken. Four or five sturdy Prelatists stayed to give a last vote against Presbytery. Four or five equally sturdy Covenanters stayed to mark their dislike of what seemed to them a compromise between the Lord and Baal. But the Act was passed by an overwhelming majority.

Two supplementary Acts speedily followed. One of them, now happily repealed, required every office-bearer in every University of Scotland to sign the Confession of Faith and to give in his adhesion to the new form of Church government. The other settled the important and delicate question of patronage.[13] Knox had, in the First Book of Discipline, asserted the right of every Christian congregation to choose its own pastor. Melville[14] had not, in the Second Book of Discipline, gone quite so far: but he had declared that no pastor could lawfully be forced on an unwilling congregation. Patronage had been abolished by a Covenanted Parliament in 1649, and restored by a Royalist Parliament in 1661. What ought to be done in 1690 it was no easy matter to decide. Scarcely any question seems to have caused so much anxiety to William. He had, in his private instructions, given the Lord Commissioner authority to assent to the abolition of patronage, if nothing else would satisfy the Estates. But this authority

[13. That is, lay-patronage over Church livings.]

[14. Andrew Melville, the successor of Knox as leader of the Scottish Reformation. Knox's First Book of Discipline had been submitted to the General Assembly of the Kirk in 1560; Melville's Second Book was accepted by it in 1581. Macaulay has exaggerated the difference between the two Books in this respect.]

was most unwillingly given; and the King hoped that it would not be used. 'It is', he said, 'the taking of men's property.'

Melville succeeded in effecting a compromise. Patronage was abolished; but it was enacted that every patron should receive six hundred marks Scots, equivalent to about thirty-five pounds sterling, as a compensation for his rights. The sum seems ludicrously small. Yet, when the nature of the property and the poverty of the country are considered, it may be doubted whether a patron would have made much more by going into the market. The largest sum that any member ventured to propose was nine hundred marks, little more than fifty pounds sterling. The right of proposing a minister was given to a parochial council consisting of the Protestant landowners and the elders. The congregation might object to the person proposed; and the Presbytery was to judge of the objections. This arrangement did not give to the people all the power to which even the Second Book of Discipline had declared that they were entitled. But the odious name of patronage was taken away: it was probably thought that the elders and landowners of a parish would seldom persist in nominating a person to whom the majority of the congregation had strong objections; and indeed it does not appear that, while the Act of 1690 continued in force, the peace of the Church was ever broken by disputes such as produced the schisms of 1732, of 1756, and of 1843.

*

D. THE MASSACRE OF GLENCOE, 13 FEBRUARY 1692

[*After 1690 Scotland was at peace. The Jacobite cause, lacking sustenance from abroad, seemed dead; and in August 1691 the government issued a proclamation offering a free pardon to all Highlanders who had been in arms against it, provided they came in and took the oath of allegiance before 1 January 1692. The Highlanders generally complied. But one small clan paid a terrible penalty for the technical offence of its chief in coming in a few days late. This was the clan of Macdonald of Glencoe, massacred in circumstances of revolting treachery on 13 February 1692.*

The authority for this massacre came from William III and is a

*permanent stain on his memory. It seems probable that the original
plan came from the hereditary enemies of the clan, the Campbells,
and particularly from the Earl of Breadalbane, and that Breadalbane was supported by Sir John Dalrymple, Master of Stair, the
Secretary of State. But however this may be, it is clear that William
(who kept a close watch on Scottish affairs) knew what he was doing when he issued an order, on 16 January 1692, to Sir Thomas
Livingstone, the commander of his forces in Scotland, stating that 'if
MacIan of Glencoe and that tribe can be well separated from the
rest, it will be a proper vindication of the public justice to extirpate
that sect of thieves.' William evidently gave equally clear instructions to Stair, who also wrote to Livingstone, urging that 'the
thieving tribe of Glencoe may be rooted out in earnest', and suggest-
ing that Livingstone's 'further advancement' depended on it. Livingstone accordingly issued orders to chosen officers to carry out the
work. The order from the Court, he said, was 'positive not to spare
any of them' nor to 'trouble the government with prisoners'. All
orders made it clear that it was 'by the King's special command, for
the good and safety of the country, that these miscreants be cut off,
root and branch.' It thus seems perfectly clear that while the policy
may have originated with Stair and Breadalbane, the King accepted
the policy and consciously authorized the massacre, though not, of
course, any more than Stair or Breadalbane, the treacherous circumstances in which it was carried out. He intended that the clan be
destroyed as an example to the rest.*

*When the massacre had been carried out, and bungled – for a
number of clansmen escaped to tell the tale – the news excited horror.
Suppressed at home, it was published by Jacobites in France, and
the political rivals of Stair in Scotland saw in it a weapon to be exploited against him. At first they found such exploitation difficult
because of the King's part in the affair; but finally, in 1695, an
attack was prepared in the Scottish Parliament. To forestall it, William set up a Commission of Enquiry which found that Stair had exceeded his instructions. Stair thereupon resigned his office and was
rewarded by the King with a 'scroll of discharge', completely exon-
erating him. In this document the King implicitly condoned the
massacre, deploring only 'the barbarous manner of execution . . .
contrary to the laws of humanity and hospitality'; but this, as he*

*rightly said, was not ordered by Stair. So the responsibility was
transferred to Stair's subordinates. However, there is no evidence
that any of these subordinates was punished, and some of them were
promoted. Livingstone, for instance, duly received 'further advancement', becoming a peer.*

*This being so, we are naturally interested in Macaulay's treat-
ment of the subject. In fact, Macaulay's account of it, in his eighteenth chapter, is one of his most brilliant pieces of sophistry and
special pleading. All those arts of suggestion and suppression which
are used elsewhere to blacken his villains, Penn or Dundee or Marlborough, are here employed to whitewash his hero, William. Glencoe
is portrayed as a desolate region, whose human inhabitants can only
be criminals and robbers (though no direct evidence is given to prove
that they actually were). The very name of the place is mistrans-
lated for this purpose: Glencoe, the Glen of the river Coe, becomes
the 'Glen of Weeping'. The meaning of plain English words is
changed: the word 'extirpate', is, we are told, 'universally understood' to mean no more than 'disarm'. Documents are discreetly
glossed and paraphrased. By these means William is entirely cleared
and all the blame is heaped on Stair, who is accused of having mis-
used the authority of the King to perpetrate, in his name, a monstrous crime. The fact that the King himself never expressed a syl-
lable of disapproval either of Stair or of the massacre (as distinct
from the 'barbarous manner' of it), and afterwards completely
exonerated Stair, is not mentioned. And yet how well we can imagine the scalding rhetoric in which Macaulay would have indulged if
the King had been James II, not William III, and if the victims had
been not a clan of Highland Jacobites but a congregation of Cameronian Dissenters!*]

While these arrangements[15] were in progress, events had taken
place in a distant part of the island which were not, till after the
lapse of many months, known in the best informed circles of
London, but which gradually obtained a fearful notoriety, and
which, after the lapse of more than a hundred and sixty years, are
never mentioned without horror.

Soon after the Estates of Scotland had separated in the autumn

[15. Ministerial changes in England, March 1692.]

of 1690, a change was made in the administration of that kingdom. William was not satisfied with the way in which he had been represented in the Parliament House. He thought that the rabbled curates had been hardly treated. He had very reluctantly suffered the law which abolished patronage to be touched with his sceptre. But what especially displeased him was that the Acts which established a new ecclesiastical polity had not been accompanied by an Act granting liberty of conscience to those who were attached to the old ecclesiastical polity. He had directed his Commissioner Melville to obtain for the Episcopalians of Scotland an indulgence similar to that which Dissenters enjoyed in England. But the Presbyterian preachers were loud and vehement against lenity to Amalekites. Melville, with useful talents, and perhaps with fair intentions, had neither large views nor an intrepid spirit. He shrank from uttering a word so hateful to the theological demagogues of his country as Toleration. By obsequiously humouring their prejudices he quelled the clamour which was rising at Edinburgh; but the effect of his timid caution was that a far more formidable clamour soon rose in the south of the island against the bigotry of the schismatics who domineered in the north, and against the pusillanimity of the government which had not dared to withstand that bigotry. On this subject the High Churchman and the Low Churchman were of one mind ... There was, therefore, at the English Court nobody to speak a good word for Melville. It was impossible that in such circumstances he should remain at the head of the Scottish·administration. He was, however, gently let down from his high position. He continued during more than a year to be Secretary of State: but another Secretary was appointed, who was to reside near the King, and to have the chief direction of affairs. The new Prime Minister for Scotland was the able, eloquent and accomplished Sir John Dalrymple. His father, the Lord President of the Court of Session, had lately been raised to the peerage by the title of Viscount Stair; and Sir John Dalrymple was consequently, according to the ancient usage of Scotland, designated as the Master of Stair. In a few months Melville resigned his secretaryship, and accepted an office of some dignity and emolument, but of no political importance.

The Lowlands of Scotland were, during the year which followed the parliamentary session of 1690, as quiet as they had ever been within the memory of man: but the state of the Highlands caused much anxiety to the government. The civil war in that wild region, after it had ceased to flame, had continued during some time to smoulder. At length, early in the year 1691, the rebel chiefs informed the Court of Saint Germains that, pressed as they were on every side, they could hold out no longer without succour from France. James had sent them a small quantity of meal, brandy and tobacco, and had frankly told them that he could do nothing more. Money was so scarce among them that six hundred pounds sterling would have been a most acceptable addition to their funds: but even such a sum he was unable to spare. He could scarcely, in such circumstances, expect them to defend his cause against a government which had a regular army and a large revenue. He therefore informed them that he should not take it ill of them if they made their peace with the new dynasty, provided always that they were prepared to rise in insurrection as soon as he should call on them to do so.

Meanwhile it had been determined at Kensington, in spite of the opposition of the Master of Stair, to try the plan which Tarbet had recommended two years before,[16] and which, if it had been tried when he recommended it, would probably have prevented much bloodshed and confusion. It was resolved that twelve or fifteen thousand pounds should be laid out in quieting the Highlands. This was a mass of treasure which to an inhabitant of Appin or Lochaber seemed almost fabulous, and which indeed bore a greater proportion to the income of Keppoch or Glengarry than fifteen hundred thousand pounds bore to the income of Lord Bedford or Lord Devonshire. The sum was ample: but the King was not fortunate in the choice of an agent.

John Earl of Breadalbane, the head of a younger branch of the great House of Campbell, ranked high among the petty princes of the mountains. He could bring seventeen hundred claymores into the field; and, ten years before the Revolution, he had actually marched into the Lowlands with this great force for the purpose of supporting the prelatical tyranny. In those days he had

[16. See above, pp. 382–3.]

affected zeal for monarchy and episcopacy: but in truth he cared for no government and no religion. He seems to have united two different sets of vices, the growth of two different regions, and of two different stages in the progress of society. In his castle among the hills he had learned the barbarian pride and ferocity of a Highland chief. In the Council Chamber at Edinburgh he had contracted the deep taint of treachery and corruption. After the Revolution he had, like too many of his fellow nobles, joined and betrayed every party in turn, had sworn fealty to William and Mary, and had plotted against them. To trace all the turns and doublings of his course, during the year 1689 and the earlier part of 1690, would be wearisome. That course became somewhat less tortuous when the battle of the Boyne had cowed the spirit of the Jacobites. It now seemed probable that the Earl would be a loyal subject of their Majesties, till some great disaster should befall them. Nobody who knew him could trust him: but few Scottish statesmen could then be trusted; and yet Scottish statesmen must be employed. His position and connections marked him out as a man who might, if he would, do much towards the work of quieting the Highlands; and his interest seemed to be a guarantee for his zeal. He had, as he declared with every appearance of truth, strong personal reasons for wishing to see tranquillity restored. His domains were so situated that, while the civil war lasted, his vassals could not tend their herds or sow their oats in peace. His lands were daily ravaged: his cattle were daily driven away: one of his houses had been burned down. It was probable, therefore, that he would do his best to put an end to hostilities.

He was accordingly commissioned to treat with the Jacobite chiefs, and was entrusted with the money which was to be distributed among them. He invited them to a conference at his residence in Glenorchy. They came: but the treaty went on very slowly. Every head of a tribe asked for a larger share of the English gold than was to be obtained. Breadalbane was suspected of intending to cheat both the clans and the King. The dispute between the rebels and the government was complicated with another dispute still more embarrassing. The Camerons and Macdonalds were really at war, not with William, but with MacCallum More; and no arrangement to which MacCallum

More was not a party could really produce tranquillity. A grave question therefore arose, whether the money entrusted to Bread-albane should be paid directly to the discontented chiefs, or should be employed to satisfy the claims which Argyll had upon them. The shrewdness of Lochiel and the arrogant pretensions of Glengarry contributed to protract the discussions. But no Celtic potentate was so impracticable as Macdonald of Glencoe, known among the mountains by the hereditary appellation of MacIan.

MacIan dwelt in the mouth of a ravine situated not far from the southern shore of Lochleven, an arm of the sea which deeply indents the western coast of Scotland, and separates Argyllshire from Invernessshire. Near his house were two or three small hamlets inhabited by his tribe. The whole population which he governed was not supposed to exceed two hundred souls. In the neighbourhood of the little cluster of villages was some copse-wood and some pasture land: but a little further up the defile no sign of population or of fruitfulness was to be seen. In the Gaelic tongue Glencoe signifies the Glen of Weeping; and in truth that pass is the most dreary and melancholy of all the Scottish passes, the very Valley of the Shadow of Death. Mists and storms brood over it through the greater part of the finest summer; and even on those rare days when the sun is bright, and when there is no cloud in the sky, the impression made by the landscape is sad and awful. The path lies along a stream which issues from the most sullen and gloomy of mountain pools. Huge precipices of naked stone frown on both sides. Even in July the streaks of snow may often be discerned in the rifts near the summits. All down the sides of the crags heaps of ruin mark the headlong paths of the torrents. Mile after mile the traveller looks in vain for the smoke of one hut, for one human form wrapped in a plaid, and listens in vain for the bark of a shepherd's dog or the bleat of a lamb. Mile after mile the only sound that indicates life is the faint cry of a bird of prey from some stormbeaten pinnacle of rock. The pro-gress of civilisation, which has turned so many wastes into fields yellow with harvests or gay with apple blossoms, has only made Glencoe more desolate. All the science and industry of a peaceful age can extract nothing valuable from that wilderness: but, in an age of violence and rapine, the wilderness itself was valued on account of the shelter which it afforded to the plunderer and his plunder. Nothing could be more natural than that the clan to which this rugged desert belonged should have been noted for predatory habits. For, among the Highlanders generally, to rob was thought at least as honourable an employment as to cultivate the soil; and, of all the Highlanders, the Macdonalds of Glencoe had the least productive soil, and the most convenient and secure den of robbers.

Successive governments had tried to punish this wild race: but no large force had ever been employed for that purpose; and a small force was easily resisted or eluded by men familiar with every recess and every outlet of the natural fortress in which they had been born and bred. The people of Glencoe would probably have been less troublesome neighbours if they had lived among their own kindred. But they were an outpost of the Clan Donald, separated from every other branch of their own family, and almost surrounded by the domains of the hostile race of Diarmid. They were impelled by hereditary enmity, as well as by want, to live at the expense of the tribe of Campbell. Breadalbane's property had suffered greatly from their depredations; and he was not of a temper to forgive such injuries. When, therefore, the Chief of Glencoe made his appearance at the congress in Glenorchy, he was ungraciously received. The Earl, who ordinarily bore himself with the solemn dignity of a Castilian grandee, forgot, in his resentment, his wonted gravity, forgot his public character, forgot the laws of hospitality, and, with angry reproaches and menaces, demanded reparation for the herds which had been driven from his lands by MacIan's followers. MacIan was seriously apprehensive of some personal outrage, and was glad to get safe back to his own glen. His pride had been wounded; and the promptings of interest concurred with those of pride. As the head of a people who lived by pillage, he had strong reasons for wishing that the country might continue to be in a perturbed state. He had little chance of receiving one guinea of the money which was to be distributed among the malcontents. For his share of that money would scarcely meet Breadalbane's demands for compensation; and there could be little doubt that, whoever might be unpaid, Breadalbane would take care to pay himself.

MacIan therefore did his best to dissuade his allies from accepting terms from which he could himself expect no benefit; and his influence was not small. His own vassals, indeed, were few in number: but he came of the best blood of the Highlands: he had kept up a close connection with his more powerful kinsmen; nor did they like him the less because he was a robber; for he never robbed them; and that robbery, merely as robbery, was a wicked and disgraceful act, had never entered into the mind of any Celtic chief. MacIan was therefore held in high esteem by the confederates. His age was venerable: his aspect was majestic; and he possessed in large measure those intellectual qualities which, in rude societies, give men an ascendency over their fellows. Breadalbane found himself, at every step of the negotiation, thwarted by the arts of his old enemy, and abhorred the name of Glencoe more and more every day.

But the government did not trust solely to Breadalbane's diplomatic skill. The authorities at Edinburgh put forth a proclamation exhorting the clans to submit to King William and Queen Mary, and offering pardon to every rebel who, on or before the thirty-first of December 1691, should swear to live peaceably under the government of their Majesties. It was announced that those who should hold out after that day would be treated as enemies and traitors. Warlike preparations were made, which showed that the threat was meant in earnest. The Highlanders were alarmed, and, though the pecuniary terms had not been satisfactorily settled, thought it prudent to give the pledge which was demanded of them. No chief, indeed, was willing to set the example of submission. Glengarry blustered, and pretended to fortify his house. 'I will not,' said Lochiel, 'break the ice. That is a point of honour with me. But my tacksmen and people may use their freedom.' His tacksmen and people understood him, and repaired by hundreds to the Sheriff to take the oaths. The Macdonalds of Sleat, Clanronald, Keppoch, and even Glengarry, imitated the Camerons; and the chiefs, after trying to outstay each other as long as they durst, imitated their vassals.

The thirty-first of December arrived; and still the Macdonalds of Glencoe had not come in. The punctilious pride of MacIan was doubtless gratified by the thought that he had continued to defy the government after the boastful Glengarry, the ferocious Keppoch, the magnanimous Lochiel had yielded: but he bought his gratification dear.

At length, on the thirty-first of December, he repaired to Fort William, accompanied by his principal vassals, and offered to take the oaths. To his dismay he found that there was in the fort no person competent to administer them. Colonel Hill, the Governor, was not a magistrate; nor was there any magistrate nearer than Inveraray. MacIan, now fully sensible of the folly of which he had been guilty in postponing to the very last moment an act on which his life and his estate depended, set off for Inveraray in great distress. He carried with him a letter from Hill to the Sheriff of Argyllshire, Sir Colin Campbell of Ardkinglass, a respectable gentleman, who, in the late reign, had suffered severely for his Whig principles. In this letter the Colonel expressed a goodnatured hope that, even out of season, a lost sheep, and so fine a lost sheep, would be gladly received. MacIan made all the haste in his power, and did not stop even at his own house, though it lay nigh to the road. But at that time a journey through Argyllshire in the depth of winter was necessarily slow. The old man's progress up steep mountains and along boggy valleys was obstructed by snowstorms; and it was not till the sixth of January that he presented himself before the Sheriff at Inveraray. The Sheriff hesitated. His power, he said, was limited by the terms of the proclamation, and he did not see how he could swear a rebel who had not submitted within the prescribed time. MacIan begged earnestly and with tears that he might be sworn. His people, he said, would follow his example. If any of them proved refractory, he would himself send the recusant to prison, or ship him off for Flanders. His entreaties and Hill's letter overcame Sir Colin's scruples. The oath was administered; and a certificate was transmitted to the Council at Edinburgh, setting forth the special circumstances which had induced the Sheriff to do what he knew not to be strictly regular.

The news that MacIan had not submitted within the prescribed time was received with cruel joy by three powerful Scotchmen who were then at the English Court. Breadalbane had gone up to London at Christmas in order to give an account of his stewardship. There he met his kinsman Argyll. Argyll was, in personal qualities, one of the most insignificant of the long line of nobles who have borne that great name. He was the descendant of eminent men, and the parent of eminent politicians; the son of one of the bravest and most true-hearted of Scottish patriots; the father of one MacCallum More renowned as a warrior and as an orator, as the model of every courtly grace, and as the judicious patron of arts and letters, and of another MacCallum More distinguished by talents for business and command, and by skill in the exact sciences. Both of such an ancestry and of such a progeny Argyll was unworthy. He had even been guilty of the crime, common enough among Scottish politicians, but in him singularly disgraceful, of tampering with the agents of James while professing loyalty to William.[17] Still Argyll had the importance inseparable from high rank, vast domains, extensive feudal rights, and almost boundless patriarchal authority. To him, as to his cousin Breadalbane, the intelligence that the tribe of Glencoe was out of the protection of the law was most gratifying; and the Master of Stair more than sympathized with them both.

The feeling of Argyll and Breadalbane is perfectly intelligible. They were the heads of a great clan; and they had an opportunity of destroying a neighbouring clan with which they were at deadly feud. Breadalbane had received peculiar provocation. His estate had been repeatedly devastated; and he had just been thwarted in a negotiation of high moment. Unhappily there was scarcely any excess of ferocity for which a precedent could not be found in Celtic tradition. Among all warlike barbarians revenge is esteemed the most sacred of duties and the most exquisite of pleasures; and so it had long been esteemed among the Highlanders. The history of the clans abounds with frightful tales, some perhaps fabulous or exaggerated, some certainly true, of vindictive massacres and assassinations. The Macdonalds of Glengarry, for example, having been affronted by the people of Culloden, surrounded Culloden church on a Sunday, shut the doors, and burned the whole congregation alive. While the flames were

[17. This is incorrect. From 1688 onwards, Argyll remained faithful to William.]

raging, the hereditary musician of the murderers mocked the shrieks of the perishing crowd with the notes of his bagpipe. A band of Macgregors, having cut off the head of an enemy, laid it, mouth filled with bread and cheese, on his sister's table, and had the satisfaction of seeing her go mad with horror at the sight. They then carried the ghastly trophy in triumph to their chief. The whole clan met under the roof of an ancient church. Every one in turn laid his hand on the dead man's scalp, and vowed to defend the slayers. The inhabitants of Eigg seized some Macleods, bound them hand and foot, and turned them adrift in a boat to be swallowed up by the waves or to perish of hunger. The Macleods retaliated by driving the population of Eigg into a cavern, lighting a fire at the entrance, and suffocating the whole race, men, women and children.[18] It is much less strange that the two great Earls of the house of Campbell, animated by the passions of Highland chieftains, should have planned a Highland revenge, than that they should have found an accomplice, and something more than an accomplice, in the Master of Stair.

The Master of Stair was one of the first men of his time, a jurist, a statesman, a fine scholar, an eloquent orator. His polished manners and lively conversation were the delight of aristocratical societies; and none who met him in such societies would have thought it possible that he could bear the chief part in any atrocious crime. His political principles were lax, yet not more lax than those of most Scotch politicians of that age. Cruelty had never been imputed to him. Those who most disliked him did him the justice to own that, where his schemes of policy were not concerned, he was a very goodnatured man. There is not the slightest reason to believe that he gained a single pound Scots by the act which has covered his name with infamy. He had no personal reason to wish the Glencoe men ill. There had been no feud between them and his family. His property lay in a district where

[18. These illustrations are not very exact or relevant. Two of them are oral traditions taken from Dr Johnson's *Journey to the Western Islands of Scotland* and the third dates from 1589, a hundred years before the Revolution. The islanders of Eigg differed from the Highlanders of Glencoe: as James VI wrote in his *Basilikon Doron* in 1599, there was a distinction between Highlanders and islanders: the Highlanders were 'barbarous', the islanders 'utterly barbarous'.]

their tartan was never seen. Yet he hated them with a hatred as fierce and implacable as if they had laid waste his fields, burned his mansion, murdered his child in the cradle.

To what cause are we to ascribe so strange an antipathy? This question perplexed the Master's contemporaries; and any answer which may now be offered ought to be offered with diffidence. The most probable conjecture is that he was actuated by an inordinate, an unscrupulous, a remorseless zeal for what seemed to him to be the interest of the state. This explanation may startle those who have not considered how large a proportion of the blackest crimes recorded in history is to be ascribed to ill regulated public spirit. We daily see men do for their party, for their sect, for their country, for their favourite schemes of political and social reform, what they would not do to enrich or to avenge themselves. At a temptation directly addressed to our private cupidity or to our private animosity, whatever virtue we have takes the alarm. But virtue itself may contribute to the fall of him who imagines that it is in his power, by violating some general rule of morality, to confer an important benefit on a church, on a commonwealth, on mankind. He silences the remonstrances of conscience, and hardens his heart against the most touching spectacles of misery, by repeating to himself that his intentions are pure, that his objects are noble, that he is doing a little evil for the sake of a great good. By degrees he comes altogether to forget the turpitude of the means in the excellence of the end, and at length perpetrates without one internal twinge acts which would shock a buccaneer. There is no reason to believe that Dominic would, for the best archbishopric in Christendom, have incited ferocious marauders to plunder and slaughter a peaceful and industrious population, that Everard Digby would for a dukedom have blown a large assembly of people into the air, or that Robespierre would have murdered for hire one of the thousands whom he murdered from philanthropy.

The Master of Stair seems to have proposed to himself a truly great and good end, the pacification and civilisation of the Highlands. He was, by the acknowledgment of those who most hated him, a man of large views. He justly thought it monstrous that a third part of Scotland should be in a state scarcely less savage than New Guinea, that letters of fire, and sword should, through a third part of Scotland, be, century after century, a species of legal process, and that no attempt should be made to apply a radical remedy to such evils. The independence affected by a crowd of petty sovereigns, the contumacious resistance which they were in the habit of offering to the authority of the Crown and of the Court of Session, their wars, their robberies, their fire-raisings, their practice of exacting blackmail from people more peaceable and more useful than themselves, naturally excited the disgust and indignation of an enlightened and politic gownsman, who was, both by the constitution of his mind and by the habits of his profession, a lover of law and order. His object was no less than a complete dissolution and reconstruction of society in the Highlands, such a dissolution and reconstruction as, two generations later, followed the battle of Culloden. In his view the clans, as they existed, were the plagues of the kingdom; and of all the clans, the worst was that which inhabited Glencoe.

He had, it is said, been particularly struck by a frightful instance of the lawlessness and ferocity of those marauders. One of them, who had been concerned in some act of violence or rapine, had given information against his companions. He had been bound to a tree and murdered. The old chief had given the first stab; and scores of dirks had then been plunged into the wretch's body. By the mountaineers such an act was probably regarded as a legitimate exercise of patriarchal jurisdiction. To the Master of Stair it seemed that people among whom such things were done and were approved ought to be treated like a pack of wolves, snared by any device, and slaughtered without mercy. He was well read in history, and doubtless knew how great rulers had, in his own and other countries, dealt with such banditti. He doubtless knew with what energy and what severity James the Fifth had put down the moss-troopers of the border, how the chief of Henderland had been hung over the gate of the castle in which he had prepared a banquet for the King; how John Armstrong and his thirty-six horsemen, when they came forth to welcome their sovereign, had scarcely been allowed time to say a single prayer before they were all tied up and turned off. Nor probably was the Secretary ignorant of the means by which Sixtus the

Fifth had cleared the ecclesiastical state of outlaws. The eulogists of that great pontiff tell us that there was one formidable gang which could not be dislodged from a stronghold among the Apennines. Beasts of burden were therefore loaded with poisoned food and wine, and sent by a road which ran close to the fastness. The robbers sallied forth, seized the prey, feasted and died; and the pious old Pope exulted greatly when he heard that the corpses of thirty ruffians, who had been the terror of many peaceful villages, had been found lying among the mules and packages. The plans of the Master of Stair were conceived in the spirit of James and of Sixtus; and the rebellion of the mountaineers furnished what seemed to be an excellent opportunity for carrying those plans into effect.

Mere rebellion, indeed, he could have easily pardoned. On Jacobites, as Jacobites, he never showed any inclination to bear hard. He hated the Highlanders, not as enemies of this or that dynasty, but as enemies of law, of industry and of trade. In his private correspondence he applied to them the short and terrible form of words in which the implacable Roman pronounced the doom of Carthage. His project was no less than this, that the whole hill country from sea to sea, and the neighbouring islands, should be wasted with fire and sword, that the Camerons, the Macleans, and all the branches of the race of Macdonald, should be rooted out. He therefore looked with no friendly eye on schemes of reconciliation, and, while others were hoping that a little money would set everything right, hinted very intelligibly his opinion that whatever money was to be laid out on the clans would be best laid out in the form of bullets and bayonets. To the last moment he continued to flatter himself that the rebels would be obstinate, and would thus furnish him with a plea for accomplishing that great social revolution on which his heart was set. The letter is still extant in which he directed the commander of the forces in Scotland how to act if the Jacobite chiefs should not come in before the end of December. There is something strangely terrible in the calmness and conciseness with which the instructions are given. 'Your troops will destroy entirely the country of Lochaber, Lochiel's lands, Keppoch's, Glengarry's and Glencoe's. Your power shall be large enough. I hope the soldiers will not trouble the government with prisoners.'[19]

This despatch had scarcely been sent off when news arrived in London that the rebel chiefs, after holding out long, had at last appeared before the Sheriffs and taken the oaths. Lochiel, the most eminent man among them, had not only declared that he would live and die a true subject to King William, but had announced his intention of visiting England, in the hope of being permitted to kiss His Majesty's hand. In London it was announced exultingly that every clan, without exception, had submitted in time; and the announcement was generally thought most satisfactory. But the Master of Stair was bitterly disappointed. The Highlands were then to continue to be what they had been, the shame and curse of Scotland. A golden opportunity of subjecting them to the law had been suffered to escape, and might never return. If only the Macdonalds would have stood out, nay, if an example could but have been made of the two worst Macdonalds, Keppoch and Glencoe, it would have been something. But it seemed that even Keppoch and Glencoe, marauders who in any well governed country would have been hanged thirty years before, were safe. While the Master was brooding over thoughts like these, Argyll brought him some comfort. The report that MacIan had taken the oaths within the prescribed time was erroneous. The Secretary was consoled. One clan, then, was at the mercy of the government, and that clan the most lawless of all. One great act of justice, nay of charity, might be performed. One terrible and memorable example might be given.

Yet there was a difficulty. MacIan had taken the oaths. He had taken them, indeed, too late to be entitled to plead the letter of the royal promise: but the fact that he had taken them was one

[19. Macaulay represents Stair's views in too extreme a form. Stair's correspondence shows that, at least until December 1691, he desired a bloodless pacification of the Highlands: force was to be kept in reserve only. The full sentence in which Stair used 'the short and terrible form of words in which the implacable Roman pronounced the doom of Carthage' – *delenda est Carthago* – is conditional and qualified.]

which evidently ought not to have been concealed from those who were to decide his fate. By a dark intrigue, of which the history is but imperfectly known, but which was, in all probability, directed by the Master of Stair, the evidence of MacIan's tardy submission was suppressed.[20] The certificate which the Sheriff of Argyllshire had transmitted to the Council at Edinburgh was never laid before the board, but was privately submitted to some persons high in office, and particularly to Lord President Stair, the father of the Secretary. These persons pronounced the certificate irregular, and, indeed, absolutely null; and it was cancelled.

Meanwhile the Master of Stair was forming, in concert with Breadalbane and Argyll, a plan for the destruction of the people of Glencoe. It was necessary to take the King's pleasure, not, indeed, as to the details of what was to be done, but as to the question whether MacIan and his people should or should not be treated as rebels out of the pale of the ordinary law. The Master of Stair found no difficulty in the royal closet. William had, in all probability, never heard the Glencoe men mentioned except as banditti. He knew that they had not come in by the prescribed day. That they had come in after that day he did not know. If he paid any attention to the matter, he must have thought that so fair an opportunity of putting an end to the devastations and depredations from which a quiet and industrious population had suffered so much ought not to be lost.

An order was laid before him for signature. He signed it, but, if Burnet may be trusted, did not read it.[21] Whoever has seen anything of public business knows that princes and ministers daily sign, and indeed must sign, documents which they have not read: and of all documents a document relating to a small tribe of mountaineers, living in a wilderness not set down in any map, was least likely to interest a Sovereign whose mind was full of schemes on which the fate of Europe might depend. But, even on the supposition that he read the order to which he affixed his

[20. Rather, by a bureaucratic doubt in Edinburgh, of which Stair (who was in London) was probably unaware.]

[21. What Burnet says is that William signed the order 'without any enquiry about it'; which is different.]

name, there seems to be no reason for blaming him. That order, directed to the Commander of the Forces in Scotland, runs thus: 'As for MacIan of Glencoe and that tribe, if they can be well distinguished from the other Highlanders, it will be proper, for the vindication of public justice, to extirpate that set of thieves.'

These words naturally bear a sense perfectly innocent, and would, but for the horrible event which followed, have been universally understood in that sense. It is undoubtedly one of the first duties of every government to extirpate gangs of thieves. This does not mean that every thief ought to be treacherously assassinated in his sleep, or even that every thief ought to be publicly executed after a fair trial, but that every gang, as a gang, ought to be completely broken up, and that whatever severity is indispensably necessary for that end ought to be used. If William had read and weighed the words which were submitted to him by his Secretary, he would probably have understood them to mean that Glencoe was to be occupied by troops, that resistance, if resistance were attempted, was to be put down with a strong hand, that severe punishment was to be inflicted on those leading members of the clan who could be proved to have been guilty of great crimes, that some active young freebooters, who were more used to handle the broadsword than the plough, and who did not seem likely to settle down into quiet labourers, were to be sent to the army in the Low Countries, that others were to be transported to the American plantations, and that those Macdonalds who were suffered to remain in their native valley were to be disarmed and required to give hostages for good behaviour. A plan very nearly resembling this had, we know, actually been the subject of much discussion in the political circles of Edinburgh. There can be little doubt that William would have deserved well of his people if he had, in this manner, extirpated not only the tribe of MacIan, but every Highland tribe whose calling was to steal cattle and burn houses.

The extirpation planned by the Master of Stair was of a different kind. His design was to butcher the whole race of thieves, the whole damnable race. Such was the language in which his hatred vented itself. He studied the geography of the wild country which surrounded Glencoe, and made his arrangements with infernal skill. If possible, the blow must be quick, and crushing, and altogether unexpected. But if MacIan should apprehend danger and should attempt to take refuge in the territories of his neighbours, he must find every road barred. The pass of Rannoch must be secured. The Laird of Weem, who was powerful in Strath Tay, must be told that, if he harbours the outlaws, he does so at his peril. Breadalbane promised to cut off the retreat of the fugitives on one side, MacCallum More on another. It was fortunate, the Secretary wrote, that it was winter. This was the time to maul the wretches. The nights were so long, the mountain tops so cold and stormy, that even the hardiest men could not long bear exposure to the open air without a roof or a spark of fire. That the women and the children could find shelter in the desert was quite impossible. While he wrote thus, no thought that he was committing a great wickedness crossed his mind. He was happy in the approbation of his own conscience. Duty, justice, nay charity and mercy, were the names under which he disguised his cruelty; nor is it by any means improbable that the disguise imposed upon himself.

Hill, who commanded the forces assembled at Fort William, was not entrusted with the execution of the design. He seems to have been a humane man; he was much distressed when he learned that the government was determined on severity; and it was probably thought that his heart might fail him in the most critical moment. He was directed to put a strong detachment under the orders of his second in command, Lieutenant Colonel Hamilton. To Hamilton a significant hint was conveyed that he had now an excellent opportunity of establishing his character in the estimation of those who were at the head of affairs. Of the troops entrusted to him a large proportion were Campbells, and belonged to a regiment lately raised by Argyll, and called by Argyll's name. It was probably thought that, on such an occasion, humanity might prove too strong for the mere habit of military obedience, and that little reliance could be placed on hearts which had not been ulcerated by a feud such as had long raged between the people of MacIan and the people of MacCallum More.

Had Hamilton marched openly against the Glencoe men and

put them to the edge of the sword, the act would probably not have wanted apologists, and most certainly would not have wanted precedents. But the Master of Stair had strongly recommended a different mode of proceeding. If the least alarm were given, the nest of robbers would be found empty; and to hunt them down in so wild a region would, even with all the help that Breadalbane and Argyll could give, be a long and difficult business. 'Better,' he wrote, 'not meddle with them than meddle to no purpose. When the thing is resolved, let it be secret and sudden.' He was obeyed; and it was determined that the Glencoe men should perish, not by military execution, but by the most dastardly and perfidious form of assassination.

On the first of February a hundred and twenty soldiers of Argyll's regiment, commanded by a captain named Campbell and a lieutenant named Lindsay, marched to Glencoe. Captain Campbell was commonly called in Scotland Glenlyon, from the pass in which his property lay. He had every qualification for the service on which he was employed, an unblushing forehead, a smooth lying tongue, and a heart of adamant. He was also one of the few Campbells who were likely to be trusted and welcomed by the Macdonalds: for his niece was married to Alexander, the second son of MacIan.

The sight of the red coats approaching caused some anxiety among the population of the valley. John, the eldest son of the Chief, came, accompanied by twenty clansmen, to meet the strangers, and asked what this visit meant. Lieutenant Lindsay answered that the soldiers came as friends, and wanted nothing but quarters. They were kindly received, and were lodged under the thatched roofs of the little community. Glenlyon and several of his men were taken into the house of a tacksman who was named, from the cluster of cabins over which he exercised authority, Inverriggen. Lindsay was accommodated nearer to the abode of the old chief. Auchintriater, one of the principal men of the clan, who governed the small hamlet of Auchnaion, found room there for a party commanded by a serjeant named Barbour. Provisions were liberally supplied. There was no want of beef, which had probably fattened in distant pastures; nor was any payment demanded: for in hospitality, as in thievery, the Gaelic marauders rivalled the Bedouins. During twelve days the soldiers lived familiarly with the people of the glen. Old MacIan, who had before felt many misgivings as to the relation in which he stood to the government, seems to have been pleased with the visit. The officers passed much of their time with him and his family. The long evenings were cheerfully spent by the peat fire with the help of some packs of cards which had found their way to that remote corner of the world, and some French brandy which was probably part of James's farewell gift to his Highland supporters. Glenlyon appeared to be warmly attached to his niece and her husband Alexander. Every day he came to their house to take his morning draught. Meanwhile he observed with minute attention all the avenues by which, when the signal for the slaughter should be given, the Macdonalds might attempt to escape to the hills; and he reported the result of his observations to Hamilton.

Hamilton fixed five o'clock in the morning of the thirteenth of February for the deed. He hoped that, before that time, he should reach Glencoe with four hundred men, and should have stopped all the earths in which the old fox and his two cubs – so MacIan and his sons were nicknamed by the murderers – could take refuge. But, at five precisely, whether Hamilton had arrived or not, Glenlyon was to fall on, and to slay every Macdonald under seventy.

The night was rough. Hamilton and his troops made slow progress, and were long after their time. While they were contending with the wind and snow, Glenlyon was supping and playing at cards with those whom he meant to butcher before daybreak. He and Lieutenant Lindsay had engaged themselves to dine with the old Chief on the morrow.

Late in the evening a vague suspicion that some evil was intended crossed the mind of the Chief's eldest son. The soldiers were evidently in a restless state; and some of them uttered strange cries. Two men, it is said, were overheard whispering. 'I do not like this job,' one of them muttered; 'I should be glad to fight the Macdonalds. But to kill men in their beds –' 'We must do as we are bid,' answered another voice. 'If there is any thing wrong, our officers must answer for it.' John Macdonald was so uneasy that, soon after midnight, he went to Glenlyon's quarters. Glenlyon and his men were all up, and seemed to be getting their arms ready for action. John, much alarmed, asked what these preparations meant. Glenlyon was profuse of friendly assurances. 'Some of Glengarry's people have been harrying the country. We are getting ready to march against them. You are quite safe. Do you think that, if you were in any danger, I should not have given a hint to your brother Sandy and his wife?' John's suspicions were quieted. He returned to his house, and lay down to rest.

It was five in the morning, Hamilton and his men were still some miles off; and the avenues which they were to have secured were open. But the orders which Glenlyon had received were precise; and he began to execute them at the little village where he was himself quartered. His host Inverriggen and nine other Macdonalds were dragged out of their beds, bound hand and foot, and murdered. A boy twelve years old clung round the Captain's legs, and begged hard for life. He would do any thing: he would go any where: he would follow Glenlyon round the world. Even Glenlyon, it is said, showed signs of relenting: but a ruffian named Drummond shot the child dead.

At Auchnaion the tacksman Auchintriater was up early that morning, and was sitting with eight of his family round the fire, when a volley of musketry laid him and seven of his companions dead or dying on the floor. His brother, who alone had escaped unhurt, called to Serjeant Barbour, who commanded the slayers, and asked as a favour to be allowed to die in the open air. 'Well,' said the Serjeant, 'I will do you that favour for the sake of your meat which I have eaten.' The mountaineer, bold, athletic, and favoured by the darkness, came forth, rushed on the soldiers who were about to level their pieces at him, flung his plaid over their faces, and was gone in a moment.

Meanwhile Lindsay had knocked at the door of the old Chief and had asked for admission in friendly language. The door was opened. MacIan, while putting on his clothes and calling to his servants to bring some refreshment for his visitors, was shot through the head. Two of his attendants were slain with him. His wife was already up and dressed in such finery as the princesses of the rude Highland glens were accustomed to wear. The assassins pulled off her clothes and trinkets. The rings were not easily taken from her fingers: but a soldier tore them away with his teeth. She died on the following day.

The statesman, to whom chiefly this great crime is to be ascribed, had planned it with consummate ability: but the execution was complete in nothing but in guilt and infamy. A succession of blunders saved three fourths of the Glencoe men from the fate of their chief. All the moral qualities which fit men to bear a part in a massacre Hamilton and Glenlyon possessed in perfection. But neither seems to have had much professional skill. Hamilton had arranged his plan without making allowance for bad weather, and this in a country and at a season when the weather was very likely to be bad. The consequence was that the fox earths, as he called them, were not stopped in time. Glenlyon and his men committed the error of despatching their hosts with firearms instead of using the cold steel. The peal and flash of gun after gun gave notice, from three different parts of the valley at once, that murder was doing. From fifty cottages the half naked peasantry fled under cover of the night to the recesses of their pathless glen. Even the sons of MacIan, who had been especially marked out for destruction, contrived to escape. They were roused from sleep by faithful servants. John, who, by the death of his father, had become the patriarch of the tribe, quitted his dwelling just as twenty soldiers with fixed bayonets marched up to it. It was broad day long before Hamilton arrived. He found the work not even half performed. About thirty corpses lay wallowing in blood on the dunghills before the doors. One or two women were seen among the number, and, a yet more fearful and piteous sight, a little hand, which had been lopped in the tumult of the butchery from some infant. One aged Macdonald was found alive. He was probably too infirm to fly, and, as he was above seventy, was not included in the orders under which Glenlyon had acted. Hamilton murdered the old man in cold blood. The deserted hamlets were then set on fire; and the troops departed, driving away with them many sheep and goats, nine hundred kine, and two hundred of the small shaggy ponies of the Highlands.

It is said, and may but too easily be believed, that the sufferings of the fugitives were terrible. How many old men, how many women with babes in their arms, sank down and slept their last sleep in the snow; how many, having crawled, spent with toil and hunger, into nooks among the precipices, died in those dark holes, and were picked to the bone by the mountain ravens, can never be known. But it is probable that those who perished by cold, weariness and want were not less numerous than those who were slain by the assassins. When the troops had retired, the Macdonalds crept out of the caverns of Glencoe, ventured back to the spot where the huts had formerly stood, collected the scorched corpses from among the smoking ruins, and performed some rude rites of sepulture. The tradition runs that the hereditary bard of the tribe took his seat on a rock which overhung the place of slaughter, and poured forth a long lament over his murdered brethren, and his desolate home. Eighty years later that sad dirge was still repeated by the population of the valley.

The survivors might well apprehend that they had escaped the shot and the sword only to perish by famine. The whole domain was a waste. Houses, barns, furniture, implements of husbandry, herds, flocks, horses, were gone. Many months must elapse before the clan would be able to raise on its own ground the means of supporting even the most miserable existence.

It may be thought strange that these events should not have been instantly followed by a burst of execration from every part of the civilised world. The fact, however, is that years elapsed before the public indignation was thoroughly awakened, and that months elapsed before the blackest part of the story found credit even among the enemies of the government. That the massacre should not have been mentioned in the London Gazettes, in the Monthly Mercuries which were scarcely less courtly than the Gazettes, or in pamphlets licensed by official censors, is perfectly intelligible. But that no allusion to it should be found in private journals and letters, written by persons free from all restraint, may seem extraordinary. There is not a word on the subject in Evelyn's Diary. In Narcissus Luttrell's Diary is a remarkable entry made five weeks after the butchery. The letters from Scotland, he says, described that kingdom as perfectly tranquil, except that there was still some grumbling about ecclesiastical questions.

The Dutch ministers regularly reported all the Scotch news to their government. They thought it worth while, about this time, to mention that a collier had been taken by a privateer near Berwick, that the Edinburgh mail had been robbed, that a whale, with a tongue seventeen feet long and seven feet broad, had been stranded near Aberdeen. But it is not hinted in any of their despatches that there was any rumour of any extraordinary occurrence in the Highlands. Reports that some of the Macdonalds had been slain did indeed, in about three weeks, travel through Edinburgh up to London. But these reports were vague and contradictory; and the very worst of them was far from coming up to the horrible truth. The Whig version of the story was that the old robber MacIan had laid an ambuscade for the soldiers, that he had been caught in his own snare, and that he and some of his clan had fallen sword in hand. The Jacobite version, written at Edinburgh on the twenty-third of March, appeared in the Paris Gazette of the seventh of April. Glenlyon, it was said, had been sent with a detachment from Argyll's regiment, under cover of darkness, to surprise the inhabitants of Glencoe, and had killed thirty-six men and boys and four women. In this there was nothing very strange or shocking. A night attack on a gang of freebooters occupying a strong natural fortress may be a perfectly legitimate military operation; and, in the obscurity and confusion of such an attack, the most humane man may be so unfortunate as to shoot a woman or a child. The circumstances which give a peculiar character to the slaughter of Glencoe, the breach of faith, the breach of hospitality, the twelve days of feigned friendship and conviviality, of morning calls, of social meals, of health-drinking, of card-playing, were not mentioned by the Edinburgh correspondent of the Paris Gazette; and we may therefore confidently infer that those circumstances were as yet unknown even to inquisitive and busy malcontents residing in the Scottish capital within a hundred miles of the spot where the deed had been done. In the south of the island the matter produced, as far as can now be judged, scarcely any sensation. To the Londoner of those days Appin was what Caffraria or Borneo is to us. He was not more moved by hearing that some Highland thieves had been surprised and killed than we are by hearing that a band of Amakosah cattle stealers has been cut off, or that a bark full of Malay pirates has been sunk. He took it for granted that nothing had been done in Glencoe beyond what was doing in many other glens. There had been a night brawl, one of a hundred night brawls, between the Macdonalds and the Campbells; and the Campbells had knocked the Macdonalds on the head.

By slow degrees the whole truth came out. From a letter written at Edinburgh about two months after the crime had been committed, it appears that the horrible story was already current among the Jacobites of that city. In the summer Argyll's regiment was quartered in the south of England, and some of the men made strange confessions, over their ale, about what they had been forced to do in the preceding winter. The non-jurors soon got hold of the clue, and followed it resolutely: their secret presses went to work; and at length, near a year after the crime had been committed, it was published to the world. But the world was long incredulous. The habitual mendacity of the Jacobite libellers had brought on them an appropriate punishment. Now, when, for the first time, they told the truth, they were supposed to be romancing. They complained bitterly that the story, though perfectly authentic, was regarded by the public as a factious lie. So late as the year 1695, Hickes, in a tract in which he endeavoured to defend his darling tale of the Theban legion against the unanswerable argument drawn from the silence of historians, remarked that it might well be doubted whether any historian would make mention of the massacre of Glencoe. There were in England, he said, many thousands of well educated men who had never heard of that massacre, or who regarded it as a mere fable.

Nevertheless the punishment of some of the guilty began very early. Hill, who indeed can hardly be called guilty, was much disturbed. Breadalbane, hardened as he was, felt the stings of conscience or the dread of retribution. A few days after the Macdonalds had returned to their old dwelling-place, his steward visited the ruins of the house of Glencoe, and endeavoured to persuade the sons of the murdered chief to sign a paper declaring that they held the Earl guiltless of the blood which had been shed. They were assured that, if they would do this, all His Lordship's great influence should be employed to obtain for them from the Crown a free pardon and a remission of all forfeitures. Glenlyon did his best to assume an air of unconcern. He made his appearance in the most fashionable coffeehouse at Edinburgh, and talked loudly and self-complacently about the important service in which he had been engaged among the mountains. Some of his soldiers, however, who observed him closely, whispered that all this bravery was put on. He was not the man that he had been before that night. The form of his countenance was changed. In all places, at all hours, whether he waked or slept, Glencoe was for ever before him.

But, whatever apprehensions might disturb Breadalbane, whatever spectres might haunt Glenlyon, the Master of Stair had neither fear nor remorse. He was indeed mortified: but he was mortified only by the blunders of Hamilton and by the escape of so many of the damnable breed. 'Do right, and fear nobody'; such is the language of his letters. 'Can there be a more sacred duty than to rid the country of thieving? The only thing that I regret is that any got away.'

On the sixth of March, William, entirely ignorant, in all probability, of the details of the crime which has cast a dark shade over his glory, had set out for the Continent, leaving the Queen his viceregent in England.

17

The Non-jurors

[*With his coronation as King, William automatically became Supreme Governor of the Church of England, and by a new Act of Parliament all the holders of clerical benefices were required to recognize him as such, and swear allegiance to him, on pain of deprivation, by 1 August 1689. This Act caused some difficult problems for the tory clergy. For many years they had preached the doctrine of divine right, and passive obedience. They claimed to have refused obedience to the usurper Cromwell. In the years since the Restoration, they had committed themselves, more deeply than ever, to the Stuart cause. It is true, James II's Catholic policy had put them in a quandary, and most of them, headed by the Seven Bishops, had in fact resisted the King's breach of the implicit treaty between the true Church and the legitimate Crown. But their purpose had been, by temporary pressure, to restore that alliance. They had never intended to make a revolution in the state. Now such a revolution had been made and the clergy found that they were obliged not merely to accept it as a fact but to adjust their theories. By swearing obedience to William, and praying for him, as head of the Church, they must implicitly repudiate the doctrines of passive obedience and royal legitimacy. This was more than many of them could do; and when the day of decision came, these purists (who included five out of the Seven Bishops) preferred to surrender their livings rather than deny their beliefs. They were known as the 'Non-jurors', and survived as schismatics within the Anglican Church for another century.*

The same problem, in another form, arose in Scotland. There, the liberal settlement of 1690 was rejected not only by rigid Episcopalians, comparable with the English non-jurors, who resented the re-establishment of Presbyterianism by a usurping King, but also by the extreme 'Cameronian' Presbyterians who objected to its liberal, 'Erastian', tolerant character.

The Episcopalian non-jurors – both English and Scottish – were, in general, devout and scholarly men. In their retirement, they pro-

duced some notable works of religion and learning. The Cameronian
non-jurors were rustic bigots. Macaulay, who valued political real-
ism above any theoretical consistency, was impatient of both alike, as
the following passages show. The first is from Chapters XIV and
XVII, the second from Chapter XVI.]

A. THE ENGLISH NON-JURORS

THE first of August had been fixed by Act of Parliament as the
day before the close of which all beneficed clergymen and all persons holding academical offices must, on pain of suspension,
swear allegiance to William and Mary. During the earlier part of
the summer, the Jacobites hoped that the number of non-jurors
would be so considerable as seriously to alarm and embarrass the
Government. But this hope was disappointed. Few indeed of the
clergy were Whigs. Few were Tories of that moderate school
which acknowledged, reluctantly and with reserve, that extreme
abuses might sometimes justify a nation in resorting to extreme
remedies. The great majority of the profession still held the doctrine of passive obedience: but that majority was now divided
into two sections. A question, which, before the Revolution, had
been mere matter of speculation, and had therefore, though
sometimes incidentally raised, been, by most persons, very super-
ficially considered, had now become practically most important.
The doctrine of passive obedience being taken for granted, to
whom was that obedience due? While the hereditary right and
the possession were conjoined, there was no room for doubt: but
the hereditary right and the possession were now separated. One
prince, raised by the Revolution, was reigning at Westminster,
passing laws, appointing magistrates and prelates, sending forth
armies and fleets. His Judges decided causes. His Sheriffs arrested debtors and executed criminals. Justice, order, property,
would cease to exist, and society would be resolved into chaos,
but for his Great Seal. Another prince, deposed by the Revolution, was living abroad. He could exercise none of the powers and
perform none of the duties of a ruler, and could, as it seemed, be
restored only by means as violent as those by which he had been

displaced. To which of these two princes did Christian men owe allegiance?

To a large part of the clergy it appeared that the plain letter of Scripture required them to submit to the Sovereign who was in possession, without troubling themselves about his title. The powers which the Apostle, in the text most familiar to the Anglican divines of that age, pronounces to be ordained of God,[1] are not the powers that can be traced back to a legitimate origin, but the powers that be. When Jesus was asked whether the chosen people might lawfully give tribute to Caesar, he replied by asking the questioners, not whether Caesar could make out a pedigree derived from the old royal house of Judah, but whether the coin which they scrupled to pay into Caesar's treasury came from Caesar's mint, in other words, whether Caesar actually possessed the authority and performed the functions of a ruler.

It is generally held, with much appearance of reason, that the most trustworthy comment on the text of the Gospels and Epistles is to be found in the practice of the primitive Christians, when that practice can be satisfactorily ascertained; and it so happened that the times during which the Church is universally acknowledged to have been in the highest state of purity were times of frequent and violent political change. One at least of the Apostles appears to have lived to see four Emperors pulled down in little more than a year.[2] Of the martyrs of the third century a great proportion must have been able to remember ten or twelve revolutions. Those martyrs must have had occasion often to consider what was their duty towards a prince just raised to power by a successful insurrection. That they were, one and all, deterred by the fear of punishment from doing what they thought right, is an imputation which no candid infidel would throw on them. Yet, if there be any proposition which can with perfect confidence be affirmed touching the early Christians, it is this, that they never once refused obedience to any actual ruler on account of the illegitimacy of his title. At one time, indeed, the supreme power was claimed by twenty or thirty competitors. Every province

[1. 'The powers that be are ordained by God' (Romans 13.1).]
[2. In A.D. 69.]

from Britain to Egypt had its own Augustus. All these pretenders could not be rightful Emperors. Yet it does not appear that, in any place, the faithful had any scruple about submitting to the person who, in that place, exercised the imperial functions. While the Christian of Rome obeyed Aurelian, the Christian of Lyons obeyed Tetricus, and the Christian of Palmyra obeyed Zenobia. 'Day and night' – such were the words which the great Cyprian, Bishop of Carthage, addressed to the representative of Valerian and Gallienus – 'day and night do we Christians pray to the one true God for the safety of our Emperors.' Yet those Emperors had a few months before pulled down their predecessor Æmilianus, who had pulled down his predecessor Gallus, who had climbed to power on the ruins of the house of his predecessor Decius, who had slain his predecessor Philip, who had slain his predecessor Gordian. Was it possible to believe that a saint, who had, in the short space of thirteen or fourteen years, borne true allegiance to this series of rebels and regicides, would have made a schism in the Christian body rather than acknowledge King William and Queen Mary? A hundred times those Anglican divines who had taken the oaths challenged their more scrupulous brethren to cite a single instance in which the primitive Church had refused obedience to a successful usurper; and a hundred times the challenge was evaded. The non-jurors had little to say on this head, except that precedents were of no force when opposed to principles, a proposition which came with but a bad grace from a school which had always professed an almost superstitious reverence for the authority of the Fathers.

To precedents drawn from later and more corrupt times little respect was due. But, even in the history of later and more corrupt times, the non-jurors could not easily find any precedent that would serve their purpose. In our own country many Kings, who had not the hereditary right, had filled the throne: but it had never been thought inconsistent with the duty of a Christian to be a true liegeman to such Kings. The usurpation of Henry the Fourth, the more odious usurpation of Richard the Third, had produced no schism in the Church. As soon as the usurper was firm in his seat, Bishops had done homage to him for their domains: Convocations had presented addresses to him, and granted him supplies; nor had any casuist ever pronounced that such submission to a prince in possession was deadly sin.[3]

With the practice of the whole Christian world the authoritative teaching of the Church of England appeared to be in strict harmony. The Homily on Wilful Rebellion, a discourse which inculcates, in unmeasured terms, the duty of obeying rulers, speaks of none but actual rulers. Nay, the people are distinctly told in that Homily that they are bound to obey, not only their legitimate prince, but any usurper whom God shall in anger set over them for their sins. And surely it would be the height of absurdity to say that we must accept submissively such usurpers as God sends in anger, but must pertinaciously withhold our obedience from usurpers whom He sends in mercy. Grant that it was a crime to invite the Prince of Orange over, a crime to join him, a crime to make him King; yet what was the whole history of the Jewish nation and of the Christian Church but a record of cases in which Providence had brought good out of evil? And what theologian would assert that, in such cases, we ought, from abhorrence of the evil, to reject the good?

On these grounds a large body of divines, still asserting the doctrine that to resist the Sovereign must always be sinful, conceived that William was now the Sovereign whom it would be sinful to resist.

To these arguments the non-jurors replied that Saint Paul must have meant by 'the powers that be' the rightful powers that be; and that to put any other interpretation on his words would be to outrage common sense, to dishonour religion, to give scandal to weak believers, to give an occasion of triumph to scoffers. The feelings of all mankind must be shocked by the

3. One of the most adulatory addresses ever voted by a Convocation was to Richard the Third. It will be found in Wilkins's *Concilia*. Dryden, in his fine *rifacimento* of one of the finest passages in the Prologue to the Canterbury Tales, represents the Good Parson as choosing to resign his benefice rather than acknowledge the Duke of Lancaster to be King of England. For this representation no warrant can be found in Chaucer's Poem, or anywhere else. Dryden wished to write something that would gall the clergy who had taken the oaths, and therefore attributed to a Roman Catholic priest of the fourteenth century a superstition which originated among the Anglican priests of the seventeenth century.

proposition that, as soon as a King, however clear his title, however wise and good his administration, is expelled by traitors, all
his servants are bound to abandon him, and to range themselves
on the side of his enemies. In all ages and nations, fidelity to a
good cause in adversity had been regarded as a virtue. In all ages
and nations, the politician whose practice was always to be on the
side which was uppermost had been despised. This new Toryism
was worse than Whiggism. To break through the ties of allegiance because the Sovereign was a tyrant was doubtless a very
great sin: but it was a sin for which specious names and pretexts
might be found, and into which a brave and generous man, not
instructed in divine truth and guarded by divine grace, might
easily fall. But to break through the ties of allegiance, merely because the Sovereign was unfortunate, was not only wicked, but
dirty. Could any unbeliever offer a greater insult to the Scriptures
than by asserting that the Scriptures had enjoined on Christians
as a sacred duty what the light of nature had taught heathens
to regard as the last excess of baseness? In the Scriptures was
to be found the history of a King of Israel, driven from his palace by an unnatural son, and compelled to fly beyond Jordan.
David, like James, had the right: Absalom, like William, had the
possession. Would any student of the sacred writings dare to
affirm that the conduct of Shimei on that occasion was proposed
as a pattern to be imitated, and that Barzillai, who loyally adhered to his fugitive master, was resisting the ordinance of God,
and receiving to himself damnation? Would any true son of the
Church of England seriously affirm that a man who was a strenuous royalist till after the battle of Naseby, who then went over
to the Parliament, who, as soon as the Parliament had been
purged, became an obsequious servant of the Rump, and who, as
soon as the Rump had been ejected, professed himself a faithful
subject of the Protector, was more deserving of the respect of
Christian men than the stout old Cavalier who bore true fealty to
Charles the First in prison and to Charles the Second in exile,
and who was ready to put lands, liberty, life, in peril, rather than
acknowledge, by word or act, the authority of any of the upstart
governments which, during that evil time, obtained possession
of a power not legitimately theirs? And what distinction was

there between that case and the case which had now arisen? That Cromwell had actually enjoyed as much power as William, nay much more power than William, was quite certain. That the power of William, as well as the power of Cromwell, had an illegitimate origin, no divine who held the doctrine of non-resistance would dispute. How then was it possible for such a divine to deny that obedience had been due to Cromwell, and yet to affirm that it was due to William? To suppose that there could be such inconsistency without dishonesty would be not charity but weakness. Those who were determined to comply with the Act of Parliament would do better to speak out, and to say, what everybody knew, that they complied simply to save their benefices. The motive was no doubt strong. That a clergyman who was a husband and a father should look forward with dread to the first of August and the first of February was natural. But he would do well to remember that, however terrible might be the day of suspension and the day of deprivation, there would assuredly come two other days more terrible still, the day of death and the day of judgment.

The swearing clergy, as they were called, were not a little perplexed by this reasoning. Nothing embarrassed them more than the analogy which the non-jurors were never weary of pointing out between the usurpation of Cromwell and the usurpation of William. For there was in that age no High Churchman who would not have thought himself reduced to an absurdity if he had been reduced to the necessity of saying that the Church had commanded her sons to obey Cromwell. And yet it was impossible to prove that William was more fully in possession of supreme power than Cromwell had been. The swearers therefore avoided coming to close quarters with the non-jurors on this point as carefully as the non-jurors avoided touching the practice of the primitive Church.

The truth is that the theory of government which had long been taught by the clergy was so absurd that it could lead to nothing but absurdity. Whether the priest who adhered to that theory swore or refused to swear, he was alike unable to give a rational explanation of his conduct. If he swore, he could vindicate his swearing only by laying down propositions against which every honest heart instinctively revolts, only by proclaiming that Christ had commanded the Church to desert the righteous cause as soon as that cause ceased to prosper, and to strengthen the hands of successful villainy against afflicted virtue. And yet, strong as were the objections to this doctrine, the objections to the doctrine of the non-juror were, if possible, stronger still. According to him, a Christian nation ought always to be in a state of slavery or in a state of anarchy. Something is to be said for the man who sacrifices liberty to preserve order. Something is to be said for the man who sacrifices order to preserve liberty. For liberty and order are two of the greatest blessings which a society can enjoy: and, when unfortunately they appear to be incompatible, much indulgence is due to those who take either side. But the non-juror sacrificed, not liberty to order, not order to liberty, but both liberty and order to a superstition as stupid and degrading as the Egyptian worship of cats and onions. While a particular person, differing from other persons by the mere accident of birth, was on the throne, though he might be a Nero, there was to be no insubordination. When any other person was on the throne, though he might be an Alfred, there was to be no obedience. It mattered not how frantic and wicked might be the administration of the dynasty which had the hereditary title, or how wise and virtuous might be the administration of a government sprung from a revolution. Nor could any time of limitation be pleaded against the claim of the expelled family. The lapse of years, the lapse of ages, made no change. To the end of the world, Christians were to regulate their political conduct simply according to the genealogy of their ruler. The year 1800, the year 1900, might find princes who derived their title from the votes of the Convention reigning in peace and prosperity. No matter: they would still be usurpers; and, if, in the twentieth or twenty-first century, any person who could make out a better right by blood to the crown should call on a late posterity to acknowledge him as King, the call must be obeyed on peril of eternal perdition.

A Whig might well enjoy the thought that the controversies which had arisen among his adversaries had established the soundness of his own political creed. The disputants who had long agreed in accusing him of an impious error had now effectu-

ally vindicated him, and refuted one another. The High Churchman who took the oaths had shown by irrefragable arguments
from the Gospels and the Epistles, from the uniform practice of
the primitive Church, and from the explicit declarations of the
Anglican Church, that Christians were not in all cases bound to
pay obedience to the prince who had the hereditary title. The
High Churchman who would not take the oaths had shown as
satisfactorily that Christians were not in all cases bound to pay
obedience to the prince who was actually reigning. It followed
that, to entitle a government to the allegiance of subjects, something was necessary different from mere legitimacy, and different
also from mere possession. What that something was the Whigs
had no difficulty in pronouncing. In their view, the end for
which all governments had been instituted was the happiness of
society. While the magistrate was, on the whole, notwithstanding
some faults, a minister for good, Reason taught mankind to obey
him; and Religion, giving her solemn sanction to the teaching of
Reason, commanded mankind to revere him as divinely commissioned. But if he proved to be a minister for evil, on what
grounds was he to be considered as divinely commissioned? The
Tories who swore had proved that he ought not to be so considered on account of the origin of his power: the Tories who
would not swear had proved as clearly that he ought not to be so
considered on account of the existence of his power.

Some violent and acrimonious Whigs triumphed ostentatiously
and with merciless insolence over the perplexed and divided
priesthood. The non-juror they generally affected to regard with
contemptuous pity as a dull and perverse, but sincere, bigot,
whose absurd practice was in harmony with his absurd theory,
and who might plead, in excuse for the infatuation which impelled him to ruin his country, that the same infatuation had impelled him to ruin himself. They reserved their sharpest taunts
for those divines who, having, in the days of the Exclusion Bill
and the Rye House Plot, been distinguished by zeal for the divine
and indefeasible right of the hereditary Sovereign, were now
ready to swear fealty to an usurper. Was this then the real sense
of all those sublime phrases which had resounded during twenty-
nine years from innumerable pulpits? Had the thousands of

clergymen, who had so loudly boasted of the unchangeable loyalty of their order, really meant only that their loyalty would remain unchangeable till the next change of fortune? It was idle, it was impudent in them to pretend that their present conduct was consistent with their former language. If any Reverend Doctor had at length been convinced that he had been in the wrong, he surely ought, by an open recantation, to make all the amends now possible to the persecuted, the calumniated, the murdered defenders of liberty. If he was still convinced that his old opinions were sound, he ought manfully to cast in his lot with the non-jurors. Respect, it was said, is due to him who ingenuously confesses an error; respect is due to him who courageously suffers for an error; but it is difficult to respect a minister of religion who, while asserting that he still adheres to the principles of the Tories, saves his benefice by taking an oath which can be honestly taken only on the principles of the Whigs.

These reproaches, though perhaps not altogether unjust, were unseasonable. The wiser and more moderate Whigs, sensible that the throne of William could not stand firm if it had not a wider basis than their own party, abstained at this conjuncture from sneers and invectives, and exerted themselves to remove the scruples and to soothe the irritated feelings of the clergy. The collective power of the rectors and vicars of England was immense: and it was much better that they should swear for the most flimsy reason that could be devised by a sophist than they should not swear at all.

It soon became clear that the arguments for swearing, backed as they were by some of the strongest motives which can influence the human mind, had prevailed. Above twenty-nine thirtieths of the profession submitted to the law. Most of the divines of the capital, who then formed a separate class, and who were as much distinguished from the rural clergy by liberality of sentiment as by eloquence and learning, gave in their adhesion to the government early, and with every sign of cordial attachment. Eighty of them repaired together, in full term, to Westminster Hall, and were there sworn. The ceremony occupied so long a time that little else was done that day in the Courts of Chancery and King's Bench. But in general the compliance was tardy, sad and sullen. Many, no doubt, deliberately sacrificed principle to interest. Conscience told them that they were committing a sin. But they had not fortitude to resign the parsonage, the garden, the glebe, and to go forth without knowing where to find a meal or a roof for themselves and their little ones. Many swore with doubts and misgivings. Some declared, at the moment of taking the oath, that they did not mean to promise that they would not submit to James, if he should ever be in a condition to demand their allegiance. Some clergymen in the north were, on the first of August, going in a company to swear, when they were met on the road by the news of the battle which had been fought, four days before, in the pass of Killiecrankie. They immediately turned back, and did not again leave their homes on the same errand till it was clear that Dundee's victory had made no change in the state of public affairs. Even of those whose understandings were fully convinced that obedience was due to the existing government, very few kissed the book with the heartiness with which they had formerly plighted their faith to Charles and James. Still the thing was done. Ten thousand clergymen had solemnly called heaven to attest their promise that they would be true liegemen to William; and this promise, though it by no means warranted him in expecting that they would strenuously support him, had at least deprived them of a great part of their power to injure him. They could not, without entirely forfeiting that public respect on which their influence depended, attack, except in an indirect and timidly cautious manner, the throne of one whom they had, in the presence of God, vowed to obey as their King. Some of them, it is true, affected to read the prayers for the new Sovereigns in a peculiar tone which could not be misunderstood. Others were guilty of still grosser indecency. Thus, one wretch, just after praying for William and Mary in the most solemn office of religion, took off a glass to their damnation. Another, after performing divine service on a fast day appointed by their authority, dined on a pigeon pie, and while he cut it up, uttered a wish that it was the usurper's heart. But such audacious wickedness was doubtless rare and was rather injurious to the Church than to the government.

Those clergymen and members of the Universities who incurred the penalties of the law were about four hundred in number. Foremost in rank stood the Primate and six of his suffragans: Turner of Ely, Lloyd of Norwich, Frampton of Gloucester, Lake of Chichester, White of Peterborough, and Ken of Bath and Wells. Thomas of Worcester would have made a seventh: but he died three weeks before the day of suspension. On his deathbed he adjured his clergy to be true to the cause of hereditary right, and declared that those divines who tried to make out that the oaths might be taken without any departure from the loyal doctrines of the Church of England seemed to him to reason more Jesuitically than the Jesuits themselves.

Ken, who, both in intellectual and in moral qualities, ranked highest among the non-juring prelates, hesitated long. There were few clergymen who could have submitted to the new government with a better grace. For, in the times when non-resistance and passive obedience were the favourite themes of his brethren, he had scarcely ever alluded to politics in the pulpit. He owned that the arguments in favour of swearing were very strong. He went indeed so far as to say that his scruples would be completely removed if he could be convinced that James had entered into engagements for ceding Ireland to the French King. It is evident therefore that the difference between Ken and the Whigs was not a difference of principle. He thought, with them, that misgovernment, carried to a certain point, justified a transfer of allegiance, and doubted only whether the misgovernment of James had been carried quite to that point. Nay, the good Bishop actually began to prepare a pastoral letter explaining his reasons for taking the oaths. But, before it was finished, he received information which convinced him that Ireland had not been made over to France: doubts came thick upon him: he threw his unfinished letter into the fire, and implored his less scrupulous friends not to urge him further. He was sure, he said, that they had acted uprightly: he was glad that they could do with a clear conscience what he shrank from doing: he felt the force of their reasoning: he was all but persuaded; and he was afraid to listen longer lest he should be quite persuaded: for, if he should comply, and his misgivings should afterwards return, he should be the most miserable of men. Not for wealth, not for a palace, not for a peerage, would he run the smallest risk of ever feeling the torments of remorse. It is a curious fact that, of the seven non-juring prelates, the only one whose name carries with it much weight was on the point of swearing, and was prevented from doing so, as he himself acknowledged, not by the force of reason, but by a morbid scrupulosity which he did not advise others to imitate.

Among the priests who refused the oaths were some men eminent in the learned world, as grammarians, chronologists, canonists, and antiquaries, and a very few who were distinguished by wit and eloquence: but scarcely one can be named who was qualified to discuss any large question of morals or politics, scarcely one whose writings do not indicate either extreme feebleness or extreme flightiness of mind. Those who distrust the judgment of a Whig on this point will probably allow some weight to the opinion which was expressed, many years after the Revolution, by a philosopher of whom the Tories are justly proud. Johnson, after passing in review the celebrated divines who had thought it sinful to swear allegiance to William the Third and George the First, pronounced that, in the whole body of non-jurors, there was one, and one only, who could reason.[4]

*

[*The most prominent of the English non-jurors was of course Sancroft. He was Archbishop of Canterbury and Primate of England; he had done much to create the tory alliance of Church and Crown under Charles II; he had led the resistance of the Church to James II. But now he declined to sanction the Revolution by taking the oaths. He was therefore deprived. Like the other deprived bishops he was left undisturbed in his palace for over a year; for the government was reluctant to force the issue. It even considered dispensing the bishops from the oaths. But ultimately fears of Jacobite intrigue impelled it to act, and new bishops were nominated to fill their sees. The new Archbishop of Canterbury who replaced Sancroft was the latitudinarian John Tillotson.*]

[4. This is an over-simplification of Johnson's statement.]

Tillotson was nominated to the Archbishopric, and was consecrated on Whitsunday, in the church of St Mary Le Bow. Compton, cruelly mortified, refused to bear any part in the ceremony.
His place was supplied by Mews, Bishop of Winchester, who
was assisted by Burnet, Stillingfleet and Hough. The congregation was the most splendid that had been seen in any place of
worship since the coronation. The Queen's drawing-room was,
on that day, deserted. Most of the peers who were in town met
in the morning at Bedford House, and went thence in procession
to Cheapside. Norfolk, Caermarthen and Dorset were conspicuous in the throng. Devonshire, who was impatient to see his
woods at Chatsworth in their summer beauty, had deferred his
departure in order to mark his respect for Tillotson. The crowd
which lined the streets greeted the new Primate warmly. For he
had, during many years, preached in the City; and his eloquence,
his probity and the singular gentleness of his temper and manners, had made him the favourite of the Londoners. But the congratulations and applauses of his friends could not drown the
roar of execration which the Jacobites set up. According to them,
he was a thief who had not entered by the door, but had climbed
over the fences. He was a hireling whose own the sheep were
not, who had usurped the crook of the good shepherd, and who
might well be expected to leave the flock at the mercy of every
wolf. He was an Arian, a Socinian, a Deist, an Atheist. He had
cozened the world by fine phrases, and by a show of moral goodness: but he was in truth a far more dangerous enemy of the
Church than he could have been if he had openly proclaimed
himself a disciple of Hobbes, and had lived as loosely as Wilmot.
He had taught the fine gentlemen and ladies who admired his
style, and who were constantly seen round his pulpit, that they
might be very good Christians, and yet might believe the account
of the Fall in the book of Genesis to be allegorical. Indeed they
might easily be as good Christians as he: for he had never been
christened: his parents were Anabaptists: he had lost their religion when he was a boy; and he had never found another. In ribald lampoons he was nicknamed Undipped John. The parish
register of his baptism was produced in vain. His enemies still
continued to complain that they had lived to see fathers of the

Church who never were her children. They made up a story that the Queen had felt bitter remorse for the great crime by which she had obtained a throne, that in her agony she had applied to Tillotson, and that he had comforted her by assuring her that the punishment of the wicked in a future state would not be eternal.

The Archbishop's mind was naturally of almost feminine delicacy, and had been rather softened than braced by the habits of a long life, during which contending sects and factions had agreed in speaking of his abilities with admiration and of his character with esteem. The storm of obloquy which he had to face for the first time at more than sixty years of age was too much for him. His spirits declined: his health gave way: yet he neither flinched from his duty nor attempted to revenge himself on his persecutors. A few days after his consecration, some persons were seized while dispersing libels in which he was reviled. The law officers of the Crown proposed to institute prosecutions; but he insisted that nobody should be punished on his account. Once, when he had company with him, a sealed packet was put into his hands: he opened it; and out fell a mask. His friends were shocked and incensed by this cowardly insult; but the Archbishop, trying to conceal his anguish by a smile, pointed to the pamphlets which covered his table, and said that the reproach which the emblem of the mask was intended to convey might be called gentle when compared with other reproaches which he daily had to endure. After his death a bundle of the savage lampoons which the nonjurors had circulated against him was found among his papers with this indorsement: 'I pray God forgive them: I do.'

The temper of the deposed primate was very different. He seems to have been under a complete delusion as to his own importance. The immense popularity which he had enjoyed three years before, the prayers and tears of the multitudes who had plunged into the Thames to implore his blessing, the enthusiasm with which the sentinels of the Tower had drunk his health under the windows of his prison, the mighty roar of joy which had risen from Palace Yard on the morning of his acquittal, the triumphant night when every window from Hyde Park to Mile End had exhibited seven candles, the midmost and tallest emblematical of him, were still fresh in his recollection; nor had he the wisdom to perceive that all this homage had been paid, not to his person, but to that religion and to those liberties of which he was, for a moment, the representative. The extreme tenderness with which the new government had long persisted in treating him seems to have confirmed him in his error. That a succession of conciliatory messages was sent to him from Kensington, that he was offered terms so liberal as to be scarcely consistent with the dignity of the Crown and the welfare of the State, that his cold and uncourteous answers could not tire out the royal indulgence, that, in spite of the loud clamours of the Whigs, and of the provocations daily given by the Jacobites, he was residing, fifteen months after deprivation, in the metropolitan palace, these things seemed to him to indicate not the lenity but the timidity of the ruling powers. He appears to have flattered himself that they would not dare to eject him. The news, therefore, that his see had been filled, threw him into a passion which lasted as long as his life, and which hurried him into many foolish and unseemly actions.

Tillotson, as soon as he was appointed, went to Lambeth in the hope that he might be able, by courtesy and kindness, to soothe the irritation of which he was the innocent cause. He stayed long in the antechamber, and sent in his name by several servants: but Sancroft would not even return an answer. Three weeks passed; and still the deprived Archbishop showed no disposition to move. At length he received an order intimating to him the royal pleasure that he should quit the dwelling which had long ceased to be his own, and in which he was only a guest. He resented this order bitterly, and declared that he would not obey it. He would stay till he was pulled out by the Sheriff's officers. He would defend himself at law as long as he could do so without putting in any plea acknowledging the authority of the usurpers. The case was so clear that he could not, by any artifice of chicanery, obtain more than a short delay. When judgment had been given against him, he left the palace, but directed his steward to retain possession. The consequence was that the steward was taken into custody and heavily fined. Tillotson sent a kind message to assure his predecessor that the fine should not be exacted. But Sancroft was determined to have a grievance, and would pay the money.

From that time the great object of the narrow-minded and peevish old man was to tear in pieces the Church of which he had been the chief minister. It was in vain that some of those non-jurors, whose virtue, ability and learning were the glory of their party, remonstrated against his design. 'Our deprivation' – such was the reasoning of Ken – 'is, in the sight of God, a nullity. We are, and shall be, till we die or resign, the true Bishops of our sees. Those who assume our titles and functions will incur the guilt of schism. But with us, if we act as becomes us, the schism will die; and in the next generation the unity of the Church will be restored. On the other hand, if we consecrate Bishops to succeed us, the breach may last through ages, and we shall be justly held accountable, not indeed for its origin, but for its continuance.' These considerations ought, on Sancroft's own principles, to have had decisive weight with him: but his angry passions prevailed. Ken quietly retired from the venerable palace of Wells. He had done, he said, with strife, and should henceforth vent his feelings not in disputes but in hymns. His charities to the unhappy of all persuasions, especially to the followers of Monmouth and to the persecuted Huguenots, had been so large that his whole private fortune consisted of seven hundred pounds, and of a library which he could not bear to sell. But Thomas Thynne, Viscount Weymouth, though not a non-juror, did himself honour by offering to the most virtuous of the non-jurors a tranquil and dignified asylum in the princely mansion of Longleat. There Ken passed a happy and honoured old age, during which he never regretted the sacrifice which he had made to what he thought his duty, and yet constantly became more and more indulgent to those whose views of duty differed from his.

Sancroft was of a very different temper. He had, indeed, as little to complain of as any man whom a revolution has ever hurled down from an exalted station. He had at Fressingfield, in Suffolk, a patrimonial estate, which, together with what he had saved during a primacy of twelve years, enabled him to live, not indeed as he had lived when he was the first peer of Parliament, but in the style of an opulent country gentleman. He retired to his hereditary abode; and there he passed the rest of his life in brooding over his wrongs. Aversion to the Established Church became as strong a feeling in him as it had been in Martin Marprelate.[5] He considered all who remained in communion with her as heathens and publicans. He nicknamed Tillotson the Mufti. In the room which was used as a chapel at Fressingfield no person who had taken the oaths, or who attended the ministry of any divine who had taken the oaths, was suffered to partake of the sacred bread and wine. A distinction, however, was made between two classes of offenders. A layman who remained in communion with the Church was permitted to be present while prayers were read, and was excluded only from the highest of Christian mysteries. But with clergymen who had sworn allegiance to the Sovereigns in possession Sancroft would not even pray. He took care that the rule which he had laid down should be widely known, and, both by precept and by example, taught his followers to look on the most orthodox, the most devout, the most virtuous of those who acknowledged William's authority with a feeling similar to that with which the Jew regarded the Samaritan.

Such intolerance would have been reprehensible, even in a man contending for a great principle. But Sancroft was contending merely for a name. He was the author of the scheme of Regency. He was perfectly willing to transfer the whole kingly power from James to William. The question which, to this smallest and sourest of minds, seemed important enough to justify the excommunicating of ten thousand priests and of five millions of laymen was, whether the magistrate to whom the whole kingly power was transferred should assume the kingly title. Nor could Sancroft bear to think that the animosity which he had excited would die with himself. Having done all that he could to make the feud bitter, he determined to make it eternal. A list of the divines who had been ejected from their benefices was sent by him to Saint Germains with a request that James would nominate two who might keep up the episcopal succession. James, well pleased, doubtless, to see another sect added to that multitude of sects which he had been taught to consider as the reproach of

[5. The pseudonymous author of violent puritan tracts published from 1588 to 1590.]

Protestantism, named two fierce and uncompromising non-jurors, Hickes and Wagstaffe, the former recommended by San-croft, the latter recommended by Lloyd, the ejected Bishop of Norwich. Such was the origin of a schismatical hierarchy, which, having, during a short time, excited alarm, soon sank into ob-scurity and contempt, but which, in obscurity and contempt, continued to drag on a languid existence during several genera-tions. The little Church, without temples, revenues or dignities, was even more distracted by internal disputes than the great Church, which retained possession of cathedrals, tithes and peerages. Some non-jurors leaned towards the ceremonial of Rome: others would not tolerate the slightest departure from the Book of Common Prayer. Altar was set up against altar. One phantom prelate pronounced the consecration of another phan-tom prelate uncanonical. At length the pastors were left abso-lutely without flocks. One of these Lords spiritual very wisely turned surgeon: another left what he had called his see, and settled in Ireland; and at length, in 1805, the last Bishop of that society which had proudly claimed to be the only true Church of England dropped unnoticed into the grave.

*

B. THE SCOTTISH NON-JURORS

There were however two parties which regarded the settlement of 1690 with implacable detestation. Those Scotchmen who were Episcopalians on conviction and with fervour appear to have been few: but among them were some persons superior, not perhaps in natural parts, but in learning, in taste, and in the art of compo-sition, to the theologians of the sect which had now become dominant. It might not have been safe for the ejected curates and professors to give vent in their own country to the anger which they felt. But the English press was open to them; and they were sure of the approbation of a large part of the English people. During several years they continued to torment their enemies and to amuse the public with a succession of ingenious and spirited pamphlets. In some of these works the hardships suffered by the rabbled priests of the western shires are set forth with a skill which irresistibly moves pity and indignation. In others, the cruelty with which the Covenanters had been treated during the reigns of the last two kings of the House of Stuart is extenuated by every artifice of sophistry. There is much joking on the bad Latin which some Presbyterian teachers had uttered while seated in academic chairs lately occupied by great scholars. Much was said about the ignorant contempt which the victorious barbarians professed for science and literature. They were accused of anathematizing the modern systems of natural philosophy as damnable heresies, of condemning geometry as a soul-destroying pursuit, of discouraging even the study of those tongues in which the sacred books were written. Learning, it was said, would soon be extinct in Scotland. The Universities, under their new rulers, were languishing and must soon perish. The booksellers had been half ruined: they found that the whole profit of their business would not pay the rent of their shops, and were preparing to emigrate to some country where letters were held in esteem by those whose office was to instruct the public. Among the ministers of religion no purchaser of books was left. The Episcopalian divine was glad to sell for a morsel of bread whatever part of his library had not been torn to pieces or burned by the Christmas mobs; and the only library of a Presbyterian divine consisted of an explanation of the Apocalypse and a commentary on the Song of Songs. The pulpit oratory of the triumphant party was an inexhaustible subject of mirth. One little volume, entitled *The Scotch Presbyterian Eloquence Displayed*, had an immense success in the South among both High Churchmen and scoffers, and is not yet quite forgotten. It was indeed a book well fitted to lie on the hall table of a Squire whose religion consisted in hating extemporaneous prayer and nasal psalmody. On a rainy day, when it was impossible to hunt or shoot, neither the card table nor the backgammon board would have been, in the intervals of the flagon and the pasty, so agreeable a resource. Nowhere else, perhaps, can be found, in so small a compass, so large a collection of ludicrous quotations and anecdotes. Some grave men, however, who bore no love to the Calvinistic doctrine or discipline, shook their heads over this lively jest book, and hinted their opinion that the writer, while holding up to derision the absurd rhetoric by which coarse-minded and ignorant men tried to illustrate dark questions of theology and to excite devotional feeling among the populace, had sometimes forgotten the reverence due to sacred things. The effect which tracts of this sort produced on the public mind of England could not be fully discerned while England and Scotland were independent of each other, but manifested itself, very soon after the union of the kingdoms, in a way which we still have reason, and which our posterity will probably long have reason, to lament.

The extreme Presbyterians were as much out of humour as the extreme Prelatists, and were as little inclined as the extreme Prelatists to take the oath of allegiance to William and Mary. Indeed, though the Jacobite non-juror and the Cameronian non-juror were diametrically opposed to each other in opinion, though they regarded each other with mortal aversion, though neither of them would have had any scruple about persecuting the other, they had much in common. They were perhaps the two most remarkable specimens that the world could show of perverse absurdity. Each of them considered his darling form of ecclesiastical polity, not as a means but as an end, as the one thing needful, as the quintessence of the Christian religion. Each of them childishly fancied that he had found a theory of civil government in his Bible. Neither shrank from the frightful consequences to which his theory led. To all objections both had one answer – Thus saith the Lord. Both agreed in boasting that the arguments which to atheistical politicians seemed unanswerable presented no difficulty to the Saint. It might be perfectly true that, by relaxing the rigour of his principles, he might save his country from slavery, anarchy, universal ruin. But his business was not to save his country, but to save his soul. He obeyed the commands of God, and left the event to God. One of the two fanatical sects held that, to the end of time, the nation would be bound to obey the heir of the Stuarts: the other held that, to the end of time, the nation would be bound by the Solemn League and Covenant; and thus both agreed in regarding the new Sovereigns as usurpers.

The Presbyterian non-jurors have scarcely been heard of out of Scotland; and perhaps it may not now be generally known, even in Scotland, how long they continued to form a distinct class. They held that their country was under a precontract to the Most High, and could never, while the world lasted, enter into any engagement inconsistent with that precontract. An Erastian, a latitudinarian, a man who knelt to receive the bread and wine from the hands of bishops, and who bore, though not very patiently, to hear anthems chanted by choristers in white vestments, could not be King of a covenanted kingdom. William had moreover forfeited all claim to the crown by committing that sin for which, in the old time, a dynasty preternaturally appointed had been preternaturally deposed. He had connived at the escape of his father-in-law, that idolater, that murderer, that man of Belial, who ought to have been hewn in pieces before the Lord, like Agag. Nay, the crime of William had exceeded that of Saul. Saul had spared only one Amalekite, and had smitten the rest. What Amalekite had William smitten? The pure Church had been twenty-eight years under persecution. Her children had been imprisoned, transported, branded, shot, hanged, drowned, tortured. And yet he who called himself her deliverer had not suffered her to see her desire upon her enemies. The bloody Claverhouse had been graciously received at Saint James's. The bloody Mackenzie[6] had found a secure and luxurious retreat among the malignants of Oxford. The younger Dalrymple who had prosecuted the Saints, the elder Dalrymple who had sat in judgment on the Saints, were great and powerful. It was said, by careless Gallios, that there was no choice but between William and James, and that it was wisdom to choose the less of two evils. Such was indeed the wisdom of this world. But the wisdom which was from above taught us that of two things, both of which were evil in the sight of God, we should choose neither. As soon as James was restored, it would be a duty to disown and withstand him. The present duty was to disown and withstand his son-in-law. Nothing must be said, nothing must be done that could be construed into a recognition of the authority of the man

[6. Sir George Mackenzie of Rosehaugh, Lord Advocate of Scotland from 1674 to 1685, a distinguished scholar and jurist, was regarded as a great persecutor of the saints. He withdrew to the safety of Oxford in 1690 and died next year in London.]

from Holland. The godly must receive no wages from him, must sign no instruments in which he was styled King.

Anne succeeded William; and Anne was designated, by those who called themselves the remnant of the true Church, as the pretended Queen, the wicked woman, the Jezebel. George the First succeeded Anne; and George the First was the pretended King, the German Beast. George the Second succeeded George the First: George the Second too was a pretended King, and was accused of having outdone the wickedness of his wicked predecessors by passing a law in defiance of that divine law which ordains that no witch shall be suffered to live.[7] George the Third succeeded George the Second; and still these men continued, with unabated steadfastness, though in language less ferocious than before, to disclaim all allegiance to an uncovenanted Sovereign. So late as the year 1806, they were still bearing their public testimony against the sin of owning his government by paying taxes, by taking out excise licenses, by joining the volunteers, or by labouring on public works. The number of these zealots went on diminishing till at length they were so thinly scattered over Scotland that they were nowhere numerous enough to have a meeting house, and were known by the name of the Non-hearers. They, however, still assembled and prayed in private dwellings, and still persisted in considering themselves as the chosen generation, the royal priesthood, the holy nation, the peculiar people, which, amidst the common degeneracy, alone preserved the faith of a better age. It is by no means improbable that this superstition, the most irrational and the most unsocial into which Protestant Christianity has ever been corrupted by human prejudices and passions, may still linger in a few obscure farm-houses.

[7. In 1736 an Act of Parliament (9 Geo. II c.5) abolished the crime of witchcraft. The abolition led to an outcry among the extreme Presbyterians in Scotland.]

18

The War with France

A. THE BATTLE OF LA HOGUE, 24 MAY 1692

[*Unable to maintain a party in either Ireland or Scotland, James II could still hope to return to England through a French conquest; and after the naval battle of Beachy Head, and the French landing at Teignmouth, such a conquest seemed possible. In England those events roused great resentment. Immediately after the battle, Torrington was deprived of his command and sent to the Tower, and in December 1690 he was tried by court-martial. Though unanimously acquitted by a board of well-qualified naval officers, he was never restored to his command, which was given to his second-in-command, and rival, Edward Russell. Russell was a whig who had accompanied William to England in 1688; but he was now dissatisfied with William and in touch with James. This encouraged James to hope that a new naval descent on England might still secure his restoration. In March 1692, when William left for the Continent, such a descent was in fact prepared. But it was not successful. In the following passage of his eighteenth chapter (which follows immediately after the account of the Massacre of Glencoe) Macaulay describes the new invasion and its outcome; the English victory of La Hogue.*]

HE would perhaps have postponed his departure if he had been aware that the French Government had, during some time, been making great preparations for a descent on our island. An event had taken place which had changed the policy of the Court of Versailles. Louvois[1] was no more. He had been at the head of the military administration of his country during a quarter of a century: he had borne a chief part in the direction of two wars which had enlarged the French territory, and had filled the world with the renown of the French arms; and he had lived to see the be-

[1. See above, p. 298 fn. 2. Louvois had been the most powerful minister at the French court since 1672.]

ginning of a third war which tasked his great powers to the utmost. Between him and the celebrated captains who carried his plans into execution there was little harmony. His imperious temper and his confidence in himself impelled him to interfere too much with the conduct of troops in the field, even when those troops were commanded by Condé, by Turenne or by Luxemburg. But he was the greatest Adjutant General, the greatest Quartermaster General, the greatest Commissary General, that Europe had seen. He may indeed be said to have made a revolution in the art of disciplining, distributing, equipping and provisioning armies. In spite, however, of his abilities and of his services, he had become odious to Lewis and to her who governed Lewis.[2] On the last occasion on which the King and the minister transacted business together, the ill humour on both sides broke violently forth. The servant, in his vexation, dashed his portfolio on the ground. The master, forgetting, what he seldom forgot, that a King should be a gentleman, lifted his cane. Fortunately his wife was present. She, with her usual prudence, caught his arm. She then got Louvois out of the room, and exhorted him to come back the next day as if nothing had happened. The next day he came; but with death in his face. The King, though full of resentment, was touched with pity, and advised Louvois to go home and take care of himself. That evening the great minister died.

Louvois had constantly opposed all plans for the invasion of England. His death was therefore regarded at Saint Germains as a fortunate event. It was however necessary to look sad, and to send a gentleman to Versailles with some words of condolence. The messenger found the gorgeous circle of courtiers assembled round their master on the terrace above the orangery. 'Sir,' said Lewis, in a tone so easy and cheerful that it filled all the bystanders with amazement, 'present my compliments and thanks to the King and Queen of England, and tell them that neither my affairs nor theirs will go on the worse by what has happened.' These words were doubtless meant to intimate that the influence of Louvois had not been exerted in favour of the House of Stuart.

[2. That is, Madame de Maintenon, to whom Louis XIV was now secretly married.]

One compliment, however, a compliment which cost France dear, Lewis thought it right to pay to the memory of his ablest servant. The Marquess of Barbesieux, son of Louvois, was placed, in his twenty-fifth year, at the head of the war department. The young man was by no means deficient in abilities, and had been, during some years, employed in business of grave importance. But his passions were strong; his judgment was not ripe; and his sudden elevation turned his head. His manners gave general disgust. Old officers complained that he kept them long in his antechamber while he was amusing himself with his spaniels and his flatterers. Those who were admitted to his presence went away disgusted by his rudeness and arrogance. As was natural at his age, he valued power chiefly as the means of procuring pleasure. Millions of crowns were expended on the luxurious villa where he loved to forget the cares of office in gay conversation, delicate cookery and foaming champagne. He often pleaded an attack of fever as an excuse for not making his appearance at the proper hour in the royal closet, when in truth he had been playing truant among his boon companions and mistresses. 'The French King,' said William, 'has an odd taste. He chooses an old woman for his mistress, and a young man for his minister.'

There can be little doubt that Louvois, by pursuing that course which had made him odious to the inmates of Saint Germains, had deserved well of his country. He was not maddened by Jacobite enthusiasm. He well knew that exiles are the worst of all advisers. He had excellent information: he had excellent judgment: he calculated the chances; and he saw that a descent was likely to fail, and to fail disastrously and disgracefully. James might well be impatient to try the experiment, though the odds should be ten to one against him. He might gain; and he could not lose. His folly and obstinacy had left him nothing to risk. His food, his drink, his lodging, his clothes, he owed to charity. Nothing could be more natural than that, for the very smallest chance of recovering the three kingdoms which he had thrown away, he should be willing to stake what was not his own, the honour of the French arms, the grandeur and the safety of the French monarchy. To a French statesman such a wager might well appear in a different light. But Louvois was gone. His master yielded to the importunity of James, and determined to send an expedition against England.

The scheme was, in some respects, well concerted. It was resolved that a camp should be formed on the coast of Normandy, and that in this camp all the Irish regiments which were in the French service should be assembled under their countryman Sarsfield. With them were to be joined about ten thousand French troops. The whole army was to be commanded by Marshal Bellefonds.

A noble fleet of about eighty ships of the line was to convoy this force to the shores of England. In the dockyards both of Brittany and of Provence immense preparations were made. Four and forty men of war, some of which were among the finest that had ever been built, were assembled in the harbour of Brest under Tourville. The Count of Estrees, with thirty-five more, was to sail from Toulon. Ushant was fixed for the place of rendezvous. The very day was named. In order that there might be no want either of seamen or of vessels for the intended expedition, all maritime trade, all privateering was, for a time, interdicted by a royal mandate. Three hundred transports were collected near the spot where the troops were to embark. It was hoped that all would be ready early in the spring, before the English ships were half rigged or half manned, and before a single Dutch man of war was in the Channel.

James had indeed persuaded himself that, even if the English fleet should fall in with him, it would not oppose him. He imagined that he was personally a favourite with the mariners of all ranks. His emissaries had been busy among the naval officers, and had found some who remembered him with kindness, and others who were out of humour with the men now in power. All the wild talk of a class of people not distinguished by taciturnity or discretion was reported to him with exaggeration, till he was deluded into a belief that he had more friends than enemies on board of the vessels which guarded our coasts. Yet he should have known that a rough sailor, who thought himself ill used by the Admiralty, might, after the third bottle, when drawn on by artful companions, express his regret for the good old times, curse the new government, and curse himself for being such a fool as to fight for that government, and yet might be by no means prepared to go over to the French on the day of battle. Of the malcontent officers, who, as James believed, were impatient to desert, the great majority had probably given no pledge of their attachment to him except an idle word hiccoughed out when they were drunk, and forgotten when they were sober. One of those from whom he expected support, Rear Admiral Carter, had indeed heard and perfectly understood what the Jacobite agents had to say, had given them fair words, and had reported the whole to the Queen and her ministers.

But the chief dependence of James was on Russell. That false, arrogant and wayward politician was to command the Channel Fleet. He had never ceased to assure the Jacobite emissaries that he was bent on effecting a Restoration. Those emissaries fully reckoned, if not on his entire cooperation, yet at least on his connivance; and there could be no doubt that, with his connivance, a French fleet might easily convoy an army to our shores. James flattered himself that, as soon as he had landed, he should be master of the island. But in truth, when the voyage had ended, the difficulties of his enterprise would have been only beginning. Two years before he had received a lesson by which he should have profited. He had then deceived himself and others into the belief that the English were regretting him, were pining for him, were eager to rise in arms by tens of thousands to welcome him. William was then, as now, at a distance. Then, as now, the administration was entrusted to a woman. Then, as now, there were few regular troops in England. Torrington had then done as much to injure the government which he served as Russell could now do.[3] The French fleet had then, after riding, during several weeks, victorious and dominant in the Channel, landed some troops on the southern coast. The immediate effect had been that whole counties, without distinction of Tory or Whig,

[3. This is grossly unfair to Torrington. Macaulay misinterpreted the evidence concerning the battle of Beachy Head and, as usual, moralized his interpretation. In fact, Torrington lost the battle of Beachy Head because he obeyed the orders of the Admiralty, who over-ruled his strategy and insisted that he engage a superior force in a disadvantageous position.]

Churchman or Dissenter, had risen up, as one man, to repel the foreigners, and that the Jacobite party, which had, a few days before, seemed to be half the nation, had crouched down in silent terror, and had made itself so small that it had, during some time, been invisible. What reason was there for believing that the multitude who had, in 1690, at the first lighting of the beacons, snatched up firelocks, pikes, scythes, to defend their native soil against the French, would now welcome the French as allies?

And of the army by which James was now to be accompanied the French formed the least odious part. More than half of that army was to consist of Irish Papists; and the feeling, compounded of hatred and scorn, with which the Irish Papists had long been regarded by the English Protestants, had by recent events been stimulated to a vehemence before unknown. The hereditary slaves, it was said, had been for a moment free; and that moment had sufficed to prove that they knew neither how to use nor how to defend their freedom. During their short ascendency they had done nothing but slay, and burn, and pillage, and demolish, and attaint, and confiscate. In three years they had committed such waste on their native land as thirty years of English intelligence and industry would scarcely repair. They would have maintained their independence against the world, if they had been as ready to fight as they were to steal. But they had retreated ignominiously from the walls of Londonderry. They had fled like deer before the yeomanry of Enniskillen. The Prince whom they now presumed to think that they could place, by force of arms, on the English throne, had himself, on the morning after the rout of the Boyne, reproached them with their cowardice, and told them that he would never again trust to their soldiership. On this subject Englishmen were of one mind. Tories, Non-jurors, even Roman Catholics, were as loud as Whigs in reviling the ill fated race. It is, therefore, not difficult to guess what effect would have been produced by the appearance on our soil of enemies whom, on their own soil, we had vanquished and trampled down.

James, however, in spite of the recent and severe teaching of experience, believed whatever his correspondents in England told him; and they told him that the whole nation was impatiently expecting him, that both the West and the North were ready to

rise, that he would proceed from the place of landing to Whitehall with as little opposition as when, in old times, he returned
from a progress. Ferguson[4] distinguished himself by the confidence with which he predicted a complete and bloodless victory.
He and his printer, he was absurd enough to write, would be the
two first men in the realm to take horse for His Majesty. Many
other agents were busy up and down the country, during the
winter and the early part of the spring. It does not appear that
they had much success in the counties south of Trent. But in the
north, particularly in Lancashire, where the Roman Catholics
were more numerous and more powerful than in any other part
of the kingdom, and where there seems to have been, even among
the Protestant gentry, more than the ordinary proportion of
bigoted Jacobites, some preparations for an insurrection were
made. Arms were privately bought; officers were appointed; yeomen, small farmers, grooms, huntsmen, were induced to enlist.
Those who gave in their names were distributed into eight regiments of cavalry and dragoons, and were directed to hold themselves in readiness to mount at the first signal.

   One of the circumstances which filled James, at this time, with
vain hopes, was that his wife was pregnant and near her delivery.
He flattered himself that malice itself would be ashamed to repeat
any longer the story of the warming pan,[5] and that multitudes
whom that story had deceived would instantly return to their
allegiance. He took, on this occasion, all those precautions which,
four years before, he had foolishly and perversely forborne to
take. He contrived to transmit to England letters summoning
many Protestant women of quality to assist at the expected birth;
and he promised, in the name of his dear brother the Most
Christian King, that they should be free to come and go in safety.
Had some of these witnesses been invited to Saint James's on the
morning of the tenth of June 1688, the House of Stuart might,
perhaps, now be reigning in our island. But it is easier to keep a
crown than to regain one. It might be true that a calumnious

[4. Robert Ferguson, the whig 'Plotter', who had conspired for Monmouth and then for William, now considered himself inadequately rewarded
and was conspiring for the Jacobites.]
[5. See above, p. 218 fn. 3.]

fable had done much to bring about the Revolution. But it by no means followed that the most complete refutation of that fable would bring about a Restoration. Not a single lady crossed the sea in obedience to James's call. His Queen was safely delivered of a daughter; but this event produced no perceptible effect on the state of public feeling in England.

Meanwhile the preparations for his expedition were going on fast. He was on the point of setting out for the place of embarkation before the English government was at all aware of the danger which was impending. It had been long known indeed that many thousands of Irish were assembled in Normandy; but it was supposed that they had been assembled merely that they might be mustered and drilled before they were sent to Flanders, Piedmont, and Catalonia. Now, however, intelligence, arriving from many quarters, left no doubt that an invasion would be almost immediately attempted. Vigorous preparations for defence were made. The equipping and manning of the ships was urged forward with vigour. The regular troops were drawn together between London and the sea. A great camp was formed on the down which overlooks Portsmouth. The militia all over the kingdom was called out. Two Westminster regiments and six City regiments, making up a force of thirteen thousand fighting men, were arrayed in Hyde Park, and passed in review before the Queen. The trainbands of Kent, Sussex, and Surrey marched down to the coast. Watchmen were posted by the beacons. Some non-jurors were imprisoned, some disarmed, some held to bail. The house of the Earl of Huntingdon, a noted Jacobite, was searched. He had had time to burn his papers and to hide his arms; but his stables presented a most suspicious appearance. Horses enough to mount a whole troop of cavalry were at the mangers; and this evidence, though not legally sufficient to support a charge of treason, was thought sufficient, at such a conjuncture, to justify the Privy Council in sending him to the Tower.

Meanwhile James had gone down to his army, which was encamped round the basin of La Hogue, on the northern coast of the peninsula known by the name of the Cotentin. Before he quitted Saint Germains, he held a Chapter of the Garter for the purpose of admitting his son into the order. Two noblemen were honoured with the same distinction, Powis, who, among his brother exiles, was now called a Duke, and Melfort, who had returned from Rome, and was again James's Prime Minister. Even at this moment, when it was of the greatest importance to conciliate the members of the Church of England, none but members of the Church of Rome were thought worthy of any mark of royal favour. Powis indeed was an eminent member of the English aristocracy; and his countrymen disliked him as little as they disliked any conspicuous Papist. But Melfort was not even an Englishman: he had never held office in England: he had never sat in the English Parliament; and he had therefore no pretensions to a dignity peculiarly English. He was moreover hated by all the contending factions of all the three kingdoms. Royal letters countersigned by him had been sent both to the Convention at Westminster and to the Convention at Edinburgh; and, both at Westminster and at Edinburgh, the sight of his odious name and handwriting had made the most zealous friends of hereditary right hang down their heads in shame. It seems strange that even James should have chosen, at such a conjuncture, to proclaim to the world that the men whom his people most abhorred were the men whom he most delighted to honour.

Still more injurious to his interests was the Declaration in which he announced his intentions to his subjects. Of all the State papers which were put forth even by him it was the most elaborately and ostentatiously injudicious. When it had disgusted and exasperated all good Englishmen of all parties, the Papists at Saint Germains pretended that it had been drawn up by a staunch Protestant, Edward Herbert, who had been Chief Justice of the Common Pleas before the Revolution, and who now bore the empty title of Chancellor. But it is certain that Herbert was never consulted about any matter of importance, and that the Declaration was the work of Melfort and of Melfort alone. In truth, those qualities of head and heart which had made Melfort the favourite of his master shone forth in every sentence. Not a word was to be found indicating that three years of banishment had made the King wiser, that he had repented of a single error, that he took to himself even the smallest part of the blame of that revolution which had dethroned him, or that he purposed to follow a course in any respect differing from that which had already been fatal to him. All the charges which had been brought against him he pronounced to be utterly unfounded. Wicked men had put forth calumnies. Weak men had believed those calumnies. He alone had been faultless. He held out no hope that he would consent to any restriction of that vast dispensing power to which he had formerly laid claim, that he would not again, in defiance of the plainest statutes, fill the Privy Council, the bench of justice, the public offices, the army, the navy, with Papists, that he would not re-establish the High Commission, that he would not appoint a new set of regulators to remodel all the constituent bodies of the kingdom. He did indeed condescend to say that he would maintain the legal rights of the Church of England: but he had said this before; and all men knew what those words meant in his mouth.

Instead of assuring his people of his forgiveness, he menaced them with a proscription more terrible than any which our island had ever seen. He published a list of persons who had no mercy to expect. Among these were Ormond, Caermarthen, Nottingham, Tillotson and Burnet. After the roll of those who were doomed to death by name, came a series of categories. First stood all the crowd of rustics who had been rude to His Majesty when he was stopped at Sheerness in his flight. These poor ignorant wretches, some hundreds in number, were reserved for another bloody circuit. Then came all persons who had in any manner borne a part in the punishment of any Jacobite conspirator: judges, counsel, witnesses, grand jurymen, petty jurymen, sheriffs and undersheriffs, constables and turnkeys, in short, all the ministers of justice from Holt down to Ketch. Then vengeance was denounced against all spies and all informers who had divulged to the usurpers the designs of the Court of Saint Germains. All justices of the peace who should not declare for their rightful Sovereign the moment that they heard of his landing, all gaolers who should not instantly set political prisoners at liberty, were to be left to the extreme rigour of the law. No exception was made in favour of a justice or of a gaoler who might be within a hundred yards of one of William's regiments, and a hundred miles from the nearest place where there was a single Jacobite in arms.

It might have been expected that James, after thus denouncing vengeance against large classes of his subjects, would at least have offered a general amnesty to the rest. But of general amnesty he said not a word. He did indeed promise that any offender who was not in any of the categories of proscription, and who should by any eminent service merit indulgence, should receive a special pardon.[6] But, with this exception, all the offenders, hundreds of thousands in number, were merely informed that their fate should be decided in Parliament.

The agents of James speedily dispersed his Declaration over every part of the kingdom, and by doing so rendered a great service to William. The general cry was that the banished oppressor had at least given Englishmen fair warning, and that, if, after such a warning, they welcomed him home, they would have no pretence for complaining, though every county town should be polluted by an assize resembling that which Jeffreys had held at Taunton. That some hundreds of people – the Jacobites put the number so low as five hundred – were to be hanged without mercy was certain; and nobody who had concurred in the Revolution, nobody who had fought for the new government by sea or land, no soldier who had borne a part in the conquest of Ireland, no Devonshire ploughman or Cornish miner who had taken arms to defend his wife and children against Tourville, could be certain that he should not be hanged. How abject too, how spiteful, must be the nature of a man who, engaged in the most momentous of all undertakings, and aspiring to the noblest of all prizes, could not refrain from proclaiming that he thirsted for the blood of a multitude of poor fishermen, because, more than three years before, they had pulled him about and called him Hatchetface. If, at the very moment when he had the strongest motives for trying to conciliate his people by the show of clemency, he could not bring himself to hold towards them any language but that of an implacable enemy, what was to be expected from him when he should be again their master? So savage was his nature that, in

[6. Macaulay conveniently omits to note that they were also to receive a special reward.]

a situation in which all other tyrants have resorted to blandishments and fair promises, he could utter nothing but reproaches and threats. The only words in his Declaration which had any show of graciousness were those in which he promised to send away the foreign troops as soon as his authority was re-established; and many said that those words, when examined, would be found full of sinister meaning. He held out no hope that he would send away Popish troops who were his own subjects. His intentions were manifest. The French might go; but the Irish would remain. The people of England were to be kept down by these thrice subjugated barbarians. No doubt a Rapparee who had run away at Newton Butler and the Boyne might find courage enough to guard the scaffolds on which his conquerors were to die, and to lay waste our country as he had laid waste his own.

The Queen and her ministers, instead of attempting to suppress James's manifesto, very wisely reprinted it, and sent it forth licensed by the Secretary of State, and interspersed with remarks by a shrewd and severe commentator. It was refuted in many keen pamphlets: it was turned into doggerel rhymes; and it was left undefended even by the boldest and most acrimonious libellers among the non-jurors.

Indeed, some of the non-jurors were so much alarmed by observing the effect which this manifesto produced, that they affected to treat it as spurious, and published as their master's genuine Declaration a paper full of gracious professions and promises. They made him offer a free pardon to all his people with the exception of four great criminals. They made him hold out hopes of great remissions of taxation. They made him pledge his word that he would entrust the whole ecclesiastical administration to the non-juring bishops. But this forgery imposed on nobody, and was important only as showing that even the Jacobites were ashamed of the prince whom they were labouring to restore.

No man read the Declaration with more surprise and anger than Russell. Bad as he was, he was much under the influence of two feelings, which, though they cannot be called virtuous, have some affinity to virtue, and are respectable when compared with mere selfish cupidity. Professional spirit and party spirit were strong in him. He might be false to his country, but not to his flag; and, even in becoming a Jacobite, he had not ceased to be a Whig. In truth, he was a Jacobite only because he was the most intolerant and acrimonious of Whigs. He thought himself and his faction ungratefully neglected by William, and was for a time too much blinded by resentment to perceive that it would be mere madness in the old Roundheads, the old Exclusionists, to punish William by recalling James. The near prospect of an invasion, and the Declaration in which Englishmen were plainly told what they had to expect if that invasion should be successful, produced, it should seem, a sudden and entire change in Russell's feelings; and that change he distinctly avowed. 'I wish,' he said to Lloyd,[7] 'to serve King James. The thing might be done, if it were not his own fault. But he takes the wrong way with us. Let him forget all the past: let him grant a general pardon; and then I will see what I can do for him.' Lloyd hinted something about the honours and rewards designed for Russell himself. But the Admiral, with a spirit worthy of a better man, cut him short. 'I do not wish to hear anything on that subject. My solicitude is for the public. And do not think that I will let the French triumph over us in our own sea. Understand this, that if I meet them I fight them, ay, though His Majesty himself should be on board.'

This conversation was truly reported to James; but it does not appear to have alarmed him. He was, indeed, possessed with a belief that Russell, even if willing, would not be able to induce the officers and sailors of the English navy to fight against their old King, who was also their old Admiral.

The hopes which James felt, he and his favourite Melfort succeeded in imparting to Lewis and to Lewis's ministers. But for those hopes, indeed, it is probable that all thoughts of invading England in the course of that year would have been laid aside. For the extensive plan which had been formed in the winter had, in the course of the spring, been disconcerted by a succession of accidents such as are beyond the control of human wisdom. The time fixed for the assembling of all the maritime forces of France at Ushant had long elapsed; and not a single sail had appeared at the place of rendezvous. The Atlantic squadron was still de-

[7. David Lloyd, a Jacobite secret agent.]

tained by bad weather in the port of Brest. The Mediterranean squadron, opposed by a strong west wind, was vainly struggling to pass the pillars of Hercules. Two fine vessels had gone to pieces on the rocks of Ceuta. Meanwhile the admiralties of the allied powers had been active. Before the end of April the English fleet was ready to sail. Three noble ships, just launched from our dockyards, appeared for the first time on the water. William had been hastening the maritime preparations of the United Provinces; and his exertions had been successful. On the twenty-ninth of April a fine squadron from the Texel appeared in the Downs. Soon came the North Holland squadron, the Maes squadron, the Zealand squadron. The whole force of the confederate powers was assembled at Saint Helen's in the second week of May, more than ninety sail of the line, manned by between thirty and forty thousand of the finest seamen of the two great maritime nations. Russell had the chief command. He was assisted by Sir Ralph Delaval, Sir John Ashley, Sir Cloudesley Shovel, Rear Admiral Carter, and Rear Admiral Rooke. Of the Dutch officers Van Almonde was highest in rank.

No mightier armament had ever appeared in the British Channel. There was little reason for apprehending that such a force could be defeated in a fair conflict. Nevertheless there was great uneasiness in London. It was known that there was a Jacobite party in the navy. Alarming rumours had worked their way round from France. It was said that the enemy reckoned on the cooperation of some of those officers on whose fidelity, in this crisis, the safety of the State might depend. Russell, as far as can now be discovered, was still unsuspected. But others, who were probably less criminal, had been more indiscreet. At all the coffeehouses admirals and captains were mentioned by name as traitors who ought to be instantly cashiered, if not shot. It was even confidently affirmed that some of the guilty had been put under arrest, and others turned out of the service. The Queen and her counsellors were in a great strait. It was not easy to say whether the danger of trusting the suspected persons or the danger of removing them were the greater. Mary, with many painful misgivings, resolved, and the event proved that she resolved wisely, to treat the evil reports as calumnious, to make a solemn appeal to the honour of the accused gentlemen, and then to trust the safety of her kingdom to their national and professional spirit.

On the fifteenth of May a great assembly of officers was convoked at Saint Helen's on board the *Britannia*, a fine three-decker, from which Russell's flag was flying. The Admiral told them that he had received a despatch which he was charged to read to them. It was from Nottingham.[8] The Queen, the Secretary wrote, had been informed that stories deeply affecting the character of the navy were in circulation. It had even been affirmed that she had found herself under the necessity of dismissing many officers. But Her Majesty was determined to believe nothing against those brave servants of the State. The gentlemen who had been so foully slandered might be assured that she placed entire reliance on them. This letter was admirably calculated to work on those to whom it was addressed. Very few of them probably had been guilty of any worse offence than rash and angry talk over their wine. They were as yet only grumblers. If they had fancied that they were marked men, they might in self-defence have become traitors. They became enthusiastically loyal as soon as they were assured that the Queen reposed entire confidence in their loyalty. They eagerly signed an address in which they entreated her to believe that they would, with the utmost resolution and alacrity, venture their lives in defence of her rights, of English freedom and of the Protestant religion, against all foreign and Popish invaders. 'God,' they added, 'preserve your person, direct your counsels, and prosper your arms; and let all your people say Amen.'

The sincerity of these professions was soon brought to the test. A few hours after the meeting on board of the *Britannia* the masts of Tourville's squadron were seen from the cliffs of Portland. One messenger galloped with the news from Weymouth to London, and roused Whitehall at three in the morning. Another took the coast road, and carried the intelligence to Russell. All was ready; and on the morning of the seventeenth of May the allied fleet stood out to sea.

Tourville had with him only his own squadron, consisting of

[8. Daniel Finch, Earl of Nottingham, Secretary of State and chief confidant of Mary, was also responsible for the fleet.]

forty-four ships of the line. But he had received positive orders to protect the descent on England, and not to decline a battle. Though these orders had been given before it was known at Versailles that the Dutch and English fleets had joined, he was not disposed to take on himself the responsibility of disobedience. He still remembered with bitterness the reprimand which his extreme caution had drawn upon him after the fight of Beachy Head. He would not again be told that he was a timid and unenterprising commander, that he had no courage but the vulgar courage of a common sailor. He was also persuaded that the odds against him were rather apparent than real. He believed, on the authority of James and Melfort, that the English seamen, from the flag officers down to the cabin boys, were Jacobites. Those who fought would fight with half a heart; and there would probably be numerous desertions at the most critical moment. Animated by such hopes he sailed from Brest, steered first towards the north east, came in sight of the coast of Dorsetshire, and then struck across the Channel towards La Hogue, where the army which he was to convoy to England had already begun to embark on board of the transports. He was within a few leagues of Barfleur when, before daybreak, on the morning of the nineteenth of May, he saw the great armament of the allies stretching along the eastern horizon.

He determined to bear down on them. By eight the two lines of battle were formed; but it was eleven before the firing began. It soon became plain that the English, from the Admiral downward, were resolved to do their duty. Russell had visited all his ships, and exhorted all his crews. 'If your commanders play false,' he said, 'overboard with them, and with myself the first.' There was no defection. There was no slackness. Carter was the first who broke the French line. He was struck by a splinter of one of his own yard arms, and fell dying on the deck. He would not be carried below. He would not let go his sword. 'Fight the ship,' were his last words: 'fight the ship as long as she can swim.' The battle lasted till four in the afternoon. The roar of the guns was distinctly heard more than twenty miles off by the army which was encamped on the coast of Normandy. During the earlier part of the day the wind was favourable to the

French: they were opposed to half of the allied fleet; and against that half they maintained the conflict with their usual courage and with more than their usual seamanship. After a hard and doubtful fight of five hours, Tourville thought that enough had been done to maintain the honour of the white flag, and began to draw off.

But by this time the wind had veered, and was with the allies. They were now able to avail themselves of their great superiority of force. They came on fast. The retreat of the French became a flight. Tourville fought his own ship desperately. She was named, in allusion to Lewis's favourite emblem, the *Royal Sun*, and was widely renowned as the finest vessel in the world. It was reported among the English sailors that she was adorned with an image of the Great King, and that he appeared there, as he appeared in the Place of Victories, with vanquished nations in chains beneath his feet. The gallant ship, surrounded by enemies, lay like a great fortress on the sea, scattering death on every side from her hundred and four portholes. She was so formidably manned that all attempts to board her failed. Long after sunset, she got clear of her assailants, and, with all her scuppers spouting blood, made for the coast of Normandy. She had suffered so much that Tourville hastily removed his flag to a ship of ninety guns which was named the *Ambitious*. By this time his fleet was scattered far over the sea. About twenty of his smallest ships made their escape by a road which was too perilous for any courage but the courage of despair. In the double darkness of night and of a thick sea fog, they ran, with all their sails spread, through the boiling waves and treacherous rocks of the Race of Alderney, and, by a strange good fortune, arrived without a single disaster at Saint Malo. The pursuers did not venture to follow the fugitives into that terrible strait, the place of innumerable shipwrecks.

Those French vessels which were too bulky to venture into the Race of Alderney fled to the havens of the Cotentin. The *Royal Sun* and two other three-deckers reached Cherbourg in safety. The *Ambitious*, with twelve other ships, all first rates or second rates, took refuge in the Bay of La Hogue, close to the headquarters of the army of James.

The three ships which had fled to Cherbourg were closely chased by an English squadron under the command of Delaval. He found them hauled up into shoal water where no large man of war could get at them. He therefore determined to attack them with his fireships and boats. The service was gallantly and successfully performed. In a short time the *Royal Sun* and her two consorts were burned to ashes. Part of the crews escaped to the shore; and part fell into the hands of the English.

Meanwhile Russell with the greater part of his victorious fleet had blockaded the Bay of La Hogue. Here, as at Cherbourg, the French men of war had been drawn up into shallow water. They lay close to the camp of the army which was destined for the invasion of England. Six of them were moored under a fort named Lisset. The rest lay under the guns of another fort named Saint Vaast, where James had fixed his headquarters, and where the Union flag, variegated by the crosses of Saint George and Saint Andrew, hung by the side of the white flag of France. Marshal Bellefonds had planted several batteries which, it was thought, would deter the boldest enemy from approaching either Fort Lisset or Fort Saint Vaast. James, however, who knew something of English seamen, was not perfectly at ease, and proposed to send strong bodies of soldiers on board of the ships. But Tourville would not consent to put such a slur on his profession.

Russell meanwhile was preparing for an attack. On the afternoon of the twenty-third of May all was ready. A flotilla consisting of sloops, of fireships, and of two hundred boats, was entrusted to the command of Rooke. The whole armament was in the highest spirits. The rowers, flushed by success, and animated by the thought that they were going to fight under the eyes of the French and Irish troops who had been assembled for the purpose of subjugating England, pulled manfully and with loud huzzas towards the six huge wooden castles which lay close to Fort Lisset. The French, though an eminently brave people, have always been more liable to sudden panics than their phlegmatic neighbours the English and Germans. On this day there was a panic both in the fleet and in the army. Tourville ordered his sailors to man their boats, and would have led them to encounter the enemy in the bay. But his example and his exhortations were vain. His boats turned round and fled in confusion. The ships were abandoned. The cannonade from Fort Lisset was so feeble and ill directed that it did no execution. The regiments on the beach, after wasting a few musket shots, drew off. The English boarded the men of war, set them on fire, and having performed this great service without the loss of a single life, retreated at a late hour with the retreating tide. The bay was in a blaze during the night; and now and then a loud explosion announced that the flames had reached a powder room or a tier of loaded guns.

At eight the next morning the tide came back strong; and with the tide came back Rooke and his two hundred boats. The enemy made a faint attempt to defend the vessels which were near Fort Saint Vaast. During a few minutes the batteries did some execution among the crews of our skiffs: but the struggle was soon over. The French poured fast out of their ships on one side: the English poured in as fast on the other, and, with loud shouts, turned the captured guns against the shore. The batteries were speedily silenced. James and Melfort, Bellefonds and Tourville, looked on in helpless despondency while the second conflagration proceeded. The conquerors, leaving the ships of war in flames, made their way into an inner basin where many transports lay. Eight of these vessels were set on fire. Several were taken in tow. The rest would have been either destroyed or carried off, had not the sea again begun to ebb. It was impossible to do more; and the victorious flotilla slowly retired, insulting the hostile camp with a thundering chant of 'God save the King.'

Thus ended, at noon on the twenty-fourth of May, the great conflict which had raged during five days over a wide extent of sea and shore. One English fireship had perished in its calling. Sixteen French men of war, all noble vessels, and eight of them three-deckers, had been sunk or burned down to the keel. The battle is called, from the place where it terminated, the battle of La Hogue.

The news was received in London with boundless exultation. In the fight on the open sea, indeed, the numerical superiority of the allies had been so great that they had little reason to boast of their success. But the courage and skill with which the crews of the English boats had, in a French harbour, in sight of a French army, and under the fire of French batteries, destroyed a fine French fleet, amply justified the pride with which our fathers pronounced the name of La Hogue. That we may fully enter into their feelings, we must remember that this was the first great check that had ever been given to the arms of Lewis the Fourteenth, and the first great victory that the English had gained over the French since the day of Agincourt. The stain left on our fame by the shameful defeat of Beachy Head was effaced. This time the glory was all our own. The Dutch had indeed done their duty, as they have always done it in maritime war, whether fighting on our side or against us, whether victorious or vanquished. But the English had borne the brunt of the fight. Russell who commanded in chief was an Englishman. Delaval who directed the attack on Cherbourg was an Englishman. Rooke who led the flotilla into the Bay of La Hogue was an Englishman. The only two officers of note who had fallen, Admiral Carter and Captain Hastings of the *Sandwich*, were Englishmen. Yet the pleasure with which the good news was received here must not be ascribed solely or chiefly to national pride. The island was safe. The pleasant pastures, cornfields and commons of Hampshire and Surrey would not be the seat of war. The houses and gardens, the kitchens and dairies, the cellars and plate chests, the wives and daughters of our gentry and clergy would not be at the mercy of Irish Rapparees, who had sacked the dwellings and skinned the cattle of the Englishry of Leinster, or of French dragoons accustomed to live at free quarters on the Protestants of Auvergne. Whigs and Tories joined in thanking God for this great deliverance; and the most respectable non-jurors could not but be glad at heart that the rightful King was not to be brought back by an army of foreigners.

The public joy was therefore all but universal. During several days the bells of London pealed without ceasing. Flags were flying on all the steeples. Rows of candles were in all the windows. Bonfires were at all the corners of the streets. The sense which the government entertained of the services of the navy was promptly, judiciously and gracefully manifested. Sidney and Portland were sent to meet the fleet at Portsmouth, and were accompanied by Rochester, as the representative of the Tories. The three Lords took down with them thirty-seven thousand pounds in coin, which they were to distribute as a donative among the sailors. Gold medals were given to the officers. The remains of Hastings and Carter were brought on shore with every mark of honour. Carter was buried at Portsmouth, with a great display of military pomp. The corpse of Hastings was brought up to London, and laid, with unusual solemnity, under the pavement of Saint James's Church. The footguards with reversed arms escorted the hearse. Four royal state carriages, each drawn by six horses, were in the procession: a crowd of men of quality in mourning cloaks filled the pews; and the Bishop of Lincoln preached the funeral sermon.

While such marks of respect were paid to the slain, the wounded were not neglected. Fifty surgeons, plentifully supplied with instruments, bandages, and drugs, were sent down in all haste from London to Portsmouth. It is not easy for us to form a notion of the difficulty which there then was in providing at short notice commodious shelter and skilful attendance for hundreds of maimed and lacerated men. At present every county, every large town, can boast of some spacious palace in which the poorest labourer who has fractured a limb may find an excellent bed, an able medical attendant, a careful nurse, medicines of the best quality, and nourishment such as an invalid requires. But there was not then, in the whole realm, a single infirmary supported by voluntary contribution. Even in the capital the only edifices open to the wounded were the two ancient hospitals of Saint Thomas and Saint Bartholomew. The Queen gave orders that in both these hospitals arrangements should be made at the public charge for the reception of patients from the fleet. At the same time it was announced that a noble and lasting memorial of the gratitude which England felt for the courage and patriotism of her sailors would soon rise on a site eminently appropriate.

Among the suburban residences of our kings, that which stood at Greenwich had long held a distinguished place. Charles the Second liked the situation, and determined to rebuild the house and to improve the gardens. Soon after his Restoration, he began to erect, on a spot almost washed by the Thames at high tide, a mansion of vast extent and cost. Behind the palace were planted long avenues of trees which, when William reigned, were scarcely more than saplings, but which have now covered with their massy shade the summer rambles of several generations. On the slope which has long been the scene of the holiday sports of the Londoners, were constructed flights of terraces, of which the vestiges may still be discerned. The Queen now publicly declared, in her husband's name, that the building commenced by Charles should be completed, and should be a retreat for seamen disabled in the service of their country.

*

B. THE PEACE OF RYSWICK, 1697

[*The battle of La Hogue guaranteed England against invasion ; but the European war continued. On one side was Louis XIV ; on the other the 'League of Augsburg', of which William was the moving spirit: England, Holland, Spain, the Empire, Sweden, Savoy. From his central position, Louis won brilliant victories ; but the superior resources of his enemies wore him down, and by 1696 he was in extremity. The Allies demanded the renunciation of all French conquests since 1659. Then Louis secured a sudden reprieve. Savoy deserted the Allies. Thanks to this defection Louis found himself in a much stronger position. He was able to divert his army of Italy to other fronts, and from this stronger position he was able to bargain for better terms. After long negotiations peace was signed at Ryswick. Though Louis saved something from the wreck, the peace was an Allied victory. The hero of the peace was William. By it he secured the frontiers of Holland and he established, finally and formally, the Revolution in England. Louis renounced his support of James II, recognized William as King of England and Scotland, and accepted the Protestant Anne, not James or his son, as heir to the throne. In the following passage (from his twenty-second chapter) Macaulay describes the conclusion of the negotiations (the effective part of which was carried out by direct discussion between Bentinck, now Earl of Portland, and Louis's representative, the Marquis de Boufflers) and the reception of the news in England.*]

Before the end of July everything was settled, as far as France and England were concerned. Meanwhile it was known to the ministers assembled at Ryswick that Boufflers and Portland had repeatedly met in Brabant, and that they were negotiating in a most irregular and indecorous manner, without credentials, or mediation, or notes, or protocols, without counting each other's steps, and without calling each other Excellency. So barbarously ignorant were they of the rudiments of the noble science of diplomacy that they had very nearly accomplished the work of restoring peace to Christendom while walking up and down an alley under some apple trees. The English and Dutch loudly applauded William's prudence and decision. He had cut the knot which the Congress had only twisted and tangled. He had done in a month what all the formalists and pedants assembled at the Hague would not have done in ten years. Nor were the French plenipotentiaries ill pleased. 'It is curious,' said Harlay, a man of wit and sense, 'that, while the Ambassadors are making war, the generals should be making peace.' But Spain preserved the same air of arrogant listlessness; and the ministers of the Emperor, forgetting apparently that their master had, a few months before, concluded a treaty of neutrality for Italy without consulting William, seemed to think it most extraordinary that William should presume to negotiate without consulting their master. It became daily more evident that the Court of Vienna was bent on prolonging the war. On the tenth of July the French ministers again proposed fair and honourable terms of peace, but added that, if those terms were not accepted by the twenty-first of August, the Most Christian King would not consider himself bound by his offer.

William in vain exhorted his allies to be reasonable. The senseless pride of one branch of the House of Austria and the selfish policy of the other were proof to all argument. The twenty-first of August came and passed; the treaty had not been signed: France was at liberty to raise her demands; and she did so. For just at this time news arrived of two great blows which had fallen on Spain, one in the Old and one in the New World. A French army, commanded by Vendôme, had taken Barcelona. A French squadron had stolen out of Brest, had eluded the allied fleets, had crossed the Atlantic, had sacked Cartagena, and had returned to France laden with treasure. The Spanish government passed at once from haughty apathy to abject terror, and was ready to accept any conditions which the conqueror might dictate. The French plenipotentiaries announced to the Congress that their master was determined to keep Strasbourg, and that, unless the terms which he had offered, thus modified, were accepted by the tenth of September, he should hold himself at liberty to insist on further modifications.

Never had the temper of William been more severely tried. He was provoked by the perverseness of his allies: he was provoked by the imperious language of the enemy. It was not without a hard struggle and a sharp pang that he made up his mind to consent to what France now proposed. But he felt that it would be utterly impossible, even if it were desirable, to prevail on the House of Commons and on the States General to continue the war for the purpose of wresting from France a single fortress, a fortress in the fate of which neither England nor Holland had any immediate interest, a fortress, too, which had been lost to the Empire solely in consequence of the unreasonable obstinacy of the Imperial Court. He determined to accept the modified terms, and directed his Ambassadors at Ryswick to sign on the prescribed day. The Ambassadors of Spain and Holland received similar instructions. There was no doubt that the Emperor, though he murmured and protested, would soon follow the example of his confederates. That he might have time to make up his mind, it was stipulated that he should be included in the treaty if he notified his adhesion by the first of November.

Meanwhile James was moving the mirth and pity of all Europe by his lamentations and menaces. He had in vain insisted on his right to send, as the only true King of England, a minister to the Congress. He had in vain addressed to all the Roman Catholic princes of the Confederacy a memorial in which he adjured them to join with France in a crusade against England for the purpose of restoring him to his inheritance, and of annulling that impious Bill of Rights which excluded members of the true Church from the throne. When he found that this appeal was disregarded, he put forth a solemn protest against the validity of all treaties to which the existing government of England should be a party. He pronounced all the engagements into which his kingdom had entered since the Revolution null and void. He gave notice that he should not, if he should regain his power, think himself bound by any of those engagements. He admitted that he might, by breaking those engagements, bring great calamities both on his own dominions and on all Christendom. But for those calamities he declared that he should not think himself answerable either before God or before man. It seems almost incredible that even a Stuart, and the worst and dullest of the Stuarts, should have thought that the first duty, not merely of his own subjects, but of all mankind, was to support his rights; that Frenchmen, Germans, Italians, Spaniards, were guilty of a crime if they did not shed their blood and lavish their wealth, year after year, in his cause; that the interests of the sixty millions of human beings to whom peace would be a blessing were of absolutely no account when compared with the interests of one man.

In spite of his protests the day of peace drew nigh. On the tenth of September the Ambassadors of France, England, Spain and the United Provinces, met at Ryswick. Three treaties were to be signed; and there was a long dispute on the momentous question which should be signed first. It was one in the morning before it was settled that the treaty between France and the States General should have precedence; and the day was breaking before all the instruments had been executed. Then the plenipotentiaries, with many bows, congratulated each other on having had the honour of contributing to so great a work.

A sloop was in waiting for Prior.[9] He hastened on board, and on the third day, after weathering an equinoctial gale, landed on the coast of Suffolk.

Very seldom had there been greater excitement in London than during the month which preceded his arrival. When the west wind kept back the Dutch packets, the anxiety of the people became intense. Every morning hundreds of thousands rose up hoping to hear that the treaty was signed; and every mail which came in without bringing the good news caused bitter disappointment. The malcontents, indeed, loudly asserted that there would

[9. Matthew Prior, the poet, was secretary to the English plenipotentiaries.]

be no peace, and that the negotiation would, even at this late hour, be broken off. One of them had seen a person just arrived from Saint Germains: another had had the privilege of reading a letter in the handwriting of Her Majesty; and all were confident that Lewis would never acknowledge the usurper. Many of those who held this language were under so strong a delusion that they backed their opinion by large wagers. When the intelligence of the fall of Barcelona arrived, all the treason taverns were in a ferment with non-juring priests laughing, talking loud, and shaking each other by the hand.

At length, in the afternoon of the thirteenth of September, some speculators in the City received, by a private channel, certain intelligence that the treaty had been signed before dawn on the morning of the eleventh. They kept their own secret, and hastened to make a profitable use of it; but their eagerness to obtain Bank stock, and the high prices which they offered, excited suspicion; and there was a general belief that on the next day something important would be announced. On the next day Prior, with the treaty, presented himself before the Lords Justices at Whitehall. Instantly a flag was hoisted on the Abbey, another on Saint Martin's Church. The Tower guns proclaimed the glad tidings. All the spires and towers from Greenwich to Chelsea made answer. It was not one of the days on which the newspapers ordinarily appeared: but extraordinary numbers, with headings in large capitals, were, for the first time, cried about the streets. The price of Bank stock rose fast from eighty-four to ninety-seven. In a few hours triumphal arches began to rise in some places. Huge bonfires were blazing in others. The Dutch ambassador informed the States General that he should try to show his joy by a bonfire worthy of the commonwealth which he represented; and he kept his word; for no such pyre had ever been seen in London. A hundred and forty barrels of pitch roared and blazed before his house in Saint James's Square, and sent up a flame which made Pall Mall and Piccadilly as bright as at noonday.

Among the Jacobites the dismay was great. Some of those who had betted deep on the constancy of Lewis took flight. One unfortunate zealot of divine right drowned himself. But soon the

party again took heart. The treaty had been signed: but it surely
would never be ratified. In a short time the ratification came: the
peace was solemnly proclaimed by the heralds; and the most
obstinate non-jurors began to despair. Some divines, who had
during eight years continued true to James, now swore allegiance
to William. They were probably men who held, with Sherlock,[10]
that a settled government, though illegitimate in its origin, is entitled to the obedience of Christians, but who had thought that
the government of William could not properly be said to be
settled while the greatest power in Europe not only refused to
recognise him, but strenuously supported his competitor. The
fiercer and more determined adherents of the banished family
were furious against Lewis. He had deceived, he had betrayed
his suppliants. It was idle to talk about the misery of his people.
It was idle to say that he had drained every source of revenue dry,
and that, in all the provinces of his kingdom, the peasantry were
clothed in rags, and were unable to eat their fill even of the coars-
est and blackest bread. His first duty was that which he owed to
the royal family of England. The Jacobites talked against him,
and wrote against him, as absurdly, and almost as scurrilously, as
they had long talked and written against William. One of their
libels was so indecent that the Lords Justices ordered the author
to be arrested and held to bail.

But the rage and mortification were confined to a very small
minority. Never, since the year of the Restoration, had there
been such signs of public gladness. In every part of the kingdom
where the peace was proclaimed, the general sentiment was
manifested by banquets, pageants, loyal healths, salutes, beating
of drums, blowing of trumpets, breaking up of hogsheads. At
some places the whole population, of its own accord, repaired to
the churches to give thanks. At others processions of girls, clad
all in white, and crowned with laurels, carried banners inscribed
with 'God bless King William.' At every county town a long

[10. William Sherlock, Master of the Temple under James II, had been a
prominent non-juror until the moment of decision, when he turned about,
swore allegiance to William and Mary, and was rewarded with the deanery of
St Paul's. Macaulay credits him with philosophical reasons for so rational a
change. Contemporaries did not.]

cavalcade of the principal gentlemen, from a circle of many miles, escorted the mayor to the market cross. Nor was one holiday enough for the expression of so much joy. On the fourth of November, the anniversary of the King's birth, and on the fifth, the anniversary of his landing at Torbay, the bellringing, the shouting, and the illuminations were renewed both in London and all over the country. On the day on which he returned to his capital no work was done, no shop was opened, in the two thousand streets of that immense mart. For that day the chief avenues had, mile after mile, been covered with gravel: all the Companies had provided new banners; all the magistrates new robes. Twelve thousand pounds had been expended in preparing fireworks. Great multitudes of people from all the neighbouring shires had come up to see the show. Never had the City been in a more loyal or more joyous mood. The evil days were past. The guinea had fallen to twenty-one shillings and sixpence. The bank note had risen to par. The new crowns and half-crowns, broad, heavy and sharply milled, were ringing on all the counters.

After some days of impatient expectation it was known, on the fourteenth of November, that His Majesty had landed at Margate. Late on the fifteenth he reached Greenwich, and rested in the stately building which, under his auspices, was turning from a palace into a hospital. On the next morning, a bright and soft morning, eighty coaches and six, filled with nobles, prelates, privy councillors and judges, came to swell his train. In Southwark he was met by the Lord Mayor and the Aldermen in all the pomp of office. The way through the Borough to the bridge was lined by the Surrey militia; the way from the bridge to Walbrook by three regiments of the militia of the City. All along Cheapside, on the right hand and on the left, the livery were marshalled under the standards of their trades. At the east end of Saint Paul's churchyard stood the boys of the school of Edward the Sixth, wearing, as they still wear, the garb of the sixteenth century. Round the Cathedral, down Ludgate Hill and along Fleet Street, were drawn up three more regiments of Londoners. From Temple Bar to Whitehall gate the trainbands of Middlesex and the Foot Guards were under arms. The windows along the whole route were gay with tapestry, ribands and flags. But the finest part of the show was the innumerable crowd of spectators, all in their Sunday clothing, and such clothing as only the upper classes of other countries could afford to wear. 'I never,' William wrote that evening to Heinsius,[11] 'I never saw such a multitude of well-dressed people.' Nor was the King less struck by the indications of joy and affection with which he was greeted from the beginning to the end of his triumph. His coach, from the moment when he entered it at Greenwich till he alighted from it in the court of Whitehall, was accompanied by one long huzza. Scarcely had he reached his palace when addresses of congratulation, from all the great corporations of his kingdom, were presented to him. It was remarked that the very foremost among those corporations was the University of Oxford. The eloquent composition in which that learned body extolled the wisdom, the courage and the virtue of His Majesty, was read with cruel vexation by the non-jurors, and with exultation by the Whigs.

The rejoicings were not yet over. At a council which was held a few hours after the King's public entry, the second of December was appointed to be the day of thanksgiving for the peace. The Chapter of Saint Paul's resolved that, on that day, their noble Cathedral, which had been long slowly rising on the ruins of a succession of pagan and Christian temples, should be opened for public worship. William announced his intention of being one of the congregation. But it was represented to him that, if he persisted in that intention, three hundred thousand people would assemble to see him pass, and all the parish churches of London would be left empty. He therefore attended the service in his own chapel at Whitehall, and heard Burnet preach a sermon, somewhat too eulogistic for the place. At Saint Paul's the magistrates of the City appeared in all their state. Compton ascended, for the first time, a throne rich with the sculpture of Gibbons, and thence exhorted a numerous and splendid assembly. His discourse has not been preserved: but its purport may be easily guessed; for he preached on that noble Psalm: 'I was glad when they said unto me, Let us go into the house of the Lord.' He doubtless reminded his hearers that, in addition to the debt

[11. Antony Heinsius, Pensionary of Holland, was William's intimate friend and confidant.]

which was common to them with all Englishmen, they owed as Londoners a peculiar debt of gratitude to the divine goodness, which had permitted them to efface the last trace of the ravages of the great fire, and to assemble once more, for prayer and praise, after so many years, on that spot consecrated by the devotions of thirty generations. Throughout London, and in every part of the realm, even to the remotest parishes of Cumberland and Cornwall, the churches were filled on the morning of that day; and the evening was an evening of festivity.

There was indeed reason for joy and thankfulness. England had passed through severe trials, and had come forth renewed in health and vigour. Ten years before, it had seemed that both her liberty and her independence were no more. Her liberty she had vindicated by a just and necessary revolution. Her independence she had reconquered by a not less just and necessary war. She had successfully defended the order of things established by the Bill of Rights against the mighty monarchy of France, against the aboriginal population of Ireland, against the avowed hostility of the non-jurors, against the more dangerous hostility of traitors who were ready to take any oath, and whom no oath could bind. Her open enemies had been victorious on many fields of battle. Her secret enemies had commanded her fleets and armies, had been in charge of her arsenals, had ministered at her altars, had taught at her Universities, had swarmed in her public offices, had sat in her Parliament, had bowed and fawned in the bedchamber of her King. More than once it had seemed impossible that anything could avert a restoration which would inevitably have been followed, first by proscriptions and confiscations, by the violation of fundamental laws, and the persecution of the established religion, and then by a third rising up of the nation against that House which two depositions and two banishments had only made more obstinate in evil. To the dangers of war and the dangers of treason had recently been added the dangers of a terrible financial and commercial crisis.

But all those dangers were over. There was peace abroad and at home. The kingdom, after many years of ignominious vassalage, had resumed its ancient place in the first rank of European powers. Many signs justified the hope that the Revolution of

1688 would be our last Revolution. The ancient constitution was adapting itself, by a natural, a gradual, a peaceful development, to the wants of a modern society. Already freedom of conscience and freedom of discussion existed to an extent unknown in any preceding age. The currency had been restored. Public credit had been re-established. Trade had revived. The Exchequer was overflowing. There was a sense of relief everywhere, from the Royal Exchange to the most secluded hamlets among the mountains of Wales and the fens of Lincolnshire. The ploughmen, the shepherds, the miners of the Northumbrian coalpits, the artisans who toiled at the looms of Norwich and the anvils of Birmingham, felt the change, without understanding it; and the cheerful bustle in every seaport and every market town indicated, not obscurely, the commencement of a happier age.

19

Economic Consequences of the Revolution

[*The new regime in England had important economic consequences. For the first time in a century, the Crown was engaged in a great foreign war for which it could rely on parliamentary support. Consequently, Parliament was willing to consider new means of mobilizing, for the purposes of government, the hitherto unexploited financial resources of the country. In the next two passages (from Chapters XIX and XX respectively), Macaulay describes the beginnings of the National Debt in 1693 and the foundation of the Bank of England in 1694: two institutions which, incidentally, created a vested interest in the stability of the revolutionary settlement. The first passage follows an account of the other financial measures of Parliament in 1692, including the land tax, which was to be a standing charge on landowners for over a century.*]

A. THE NATIONAL DEBT, 1693

STILL, however, the estimated revenue was not equal to the estimated expenditure. The year 1692 had bequeathed a large deficit to the year 1693; and it seemed probable that the charge for 1693 would exceed by about five hundred thousand pounds the charge for 1692. More than two millions had been voted for the army and ordnance, near two millions for the navy. Only eight years before fourteen hundred thousand pounds had defrayed the whole annual charge of government. More than four times that sum was now required. Taxation, both direct and indirect, had been carried to an unprecedented point: yet the income of the state still fell short of the outlay by about a million. It was necessary to devise something. Something was devised, something of which the effects are felt to this day in every part of the globe.

There was indeed nothing strange or mysterious in the expedient to which the government had recourse. It was an expedient familiar, during two centuries, to the financiers of the Continent, and could hardly fail to occur to any English states-man who compared the void in the Exchequer with the overflow in the money market.

During the interval between the Restoration and the Revolu-tion the riches of the nation had been rapidly increasing. Thousands of busy men found every Christmas that, after the expenses of the year's housekeeping had been defrayed out of the year's income, a surplus remained; and how that surplus was to be employed was a question of some difficulty. In our time, to invest such a surplus, at something more than three per cent, on the best security that has ever been known in the world, is the work of a few minutes. But in the seventeenth century a lawyer, a physician, a retired merchant who had saved some thousands and who wished to place them safely and profitably, was often greatly embarrassed. Three generations earlier, a man who had accumulated wealth in a profession generally purchased real property or lent his savings on mortgage. But the number of acres in the kingdom had remained the same: and the value of those acres, though it had greatly increased, had by no means increased so fast as the quantity of capital which was seeking for employment. Many too wished to put their money where they could find it at an hour's notice, and looked about for some species of property which could be more readily transferred than a house or a field. A capitalist might lend on bottomry or on personal security: but, if he did so, he ran a great risk of losing interest and principal. There were a few joint stock companies, among which the East India Company held the foremost place: but the demand for the stock of such companies was far greater than the supply. Indeed the cry for a new East India Company was chiefly raised by persons who had found difficulty in placing their savings at interest on good security. So great was that difficulty that the practice of hoarding was common. We are told that the father of Pope the poet, who retired from business in the City about the time of the Revolution, carried to a retreat in the country a strong box containing near twenty thousand pounds, and took out from time to time what was required for household expenses; and it is highly probable that this was not a solitary case. At present the quantity of coin which is hoarded by private persons is so small that it would, if brought forth, make no perceptible addition to the circulation. But, in the earlier part of the reign of William the Third, all the greatest writers on currency were of opinion that a very considerable mass of gold and silver was hidden in secret drawers and behind wainscots.

The natural effect of this state of things was that a crowd of projectors, ingenious and absurd, honest and knavish, employed themselves in devising new schemes for the employment of redundant capital. It was about the year 1688 that the word stockjobber was first heard in London. In the short space of four years a crowd of companies, every one of which confidently held out to subscribers the hope of immense gains, sprang into existence: the Insurance Company, the Paper Company, the Lutestring Company, the Pearl Fishery Company, the Glass Bottle Company, the Alum Company, the Blythe Coal Company, the Swordblade Company. There was a Tapestry Company which would soon furnish pretty hangings for all the parlours of the middle class and for all the bedchambers of the higher. There was a Copper Company which proposed to explore the mines of England, and held out a hope that they would prove not less valuable than those of Potosi. There was a Diving Company which undertook to bring up precious effects from shipwrecked vessels, and which announced that it had laid in a stock of wonderful machines resembling complete suits of armour. In front of the helmet was a huge glass eye like that of a cyclops; and out of the crest went a pipe through which the air was to be admitted. The whole process was exhibited on the Thames. Fine gentlemen and fine ladies were invited to the show, were hospitably regaled, and were delighted by seeing the divers in their panoply descend into the river and return laden with old iron and ship's tackle. There was a Greenland Fishing Company which could not fail to drive the Dutch whalers and herring busses out of the Northern Ocean. There was a Tanning Company which promised to furnish leather superior to the best that was brought from Turkey or Russia. There was a society which undertook the office of giving gentlemen a liberal education on low terms, and which assumed the sounding name of the Royal Academies Company.

In a pompous advertisement it was announced that the directors of the Royal Academies Company had engaged the best masters in every branch of knowledge, and were about to issue twenty thousand tickets at twenty shillings each. There was to be a lottery: two thousand prizes were to be drawn; and the fortunate holders of the prizes were to be taught, at the charge of the Company, Latin, Greek, Hebrew, French, Spanish, conic sections, trigonometry, heraldry, japanning, fortification, book-keeping and the art of playing the theorbo.

Some of these companies took large mansions and printed their advertisements in gilded letters. Others, less ostentatious, were content with ink, and met at coffeehouses in the neighbourhood of the Royal Exchange. Jonathan's and Garraway's were in a constant ferment with brokers, buyers, sellers, meetings of directors, meetings of proprietors. Time bargains soon came into fashion. Extensive combinations were formed, and monstrous fables were circulated, for the purpose of raising or depressing the price of shares. Our country witnessed for the first time those phenomena with which a long experience has made us familiar. A mania of which the symptoms were essentially the same with those of the mania of 1720, of the mania of 1825, of the mania of 1845, seized the public mind. An impatience to be rich, a contempt for those slow but sure gains which are the proper reward of industry, patience and thrift, spread through society. The spirit of the cogging dicers of Whitefriars took possession of the grave Senators of the City, Wardens of Trades, Deputies, Aldermen. It was much easier and much more lucrative to put forth a lying prospectus announcing a new stock, to persuade ignorant people that the dividends could not fall short of twenty per cent, and to part with five thousand pounds of this imaginary wealth for ten thousand solid guineas, than to load a ship with a well-chosen cargo for Virginia or the Levant. Every day some new bubble was puffed into existence, rose buoyant, shone bright, burst, and was forgotten.

The new form which covetousness had taken furnished the comic poets and satirists with an excellent subject; nor was that subject the less welcome to them because some of the most unscrupulous and most successful of the new race of gamesters were men in sad coloured clothes and lank hair, men who called cards the Devil's books, men who thought it a sin and a scandal to win or lose twopence over a backgammon board. It was in the last drama of Shadwell that the hyprocrisy and knavery of these speculators was, for the first time, exposed to public ridicule. He died in November 1692, just before his *Stockjobbers* came on the stage; and the epilogue was spoken by an actor dressed in deep mourning. The best scene is that in which four or five stern Nonconformists, clad in the full Puritan costume, after discussing the prospects of the Mousetrap Company and the Fleakilling Company, examine the question whether the godly may lawfully hold stock in a Company for bringing over Chinese rope-dancers. 'Considerable men have shares,' says one austere person in cropped hair and bands; 'but verily I question whether it be lawful or not.' These doubts are removed by a stout old Roundhead colonel who had fought at Marston Moor, and who reminds his weaker brother that the saints need not themselves see the rope-dancing, and that, in all probability, there will be no rope-dancing to see. 'The thing,' he says, 'is like to take: the shares will sell well; and then we shall not care whether the dancers come over or no.' It is important to observe that this scene was exhibited and applauded before one farthing of the national debt had been contracted. So ill informed were the numerous writers who, at a later period, ascribed to the national debt the existence of stockjobbing and of all the immoralities connected with stockjobbing. The truth is that society had, in the natural course of its growth, reached a point at which it was inevitable that there should be stockjobbing whether there were a national debt or not, and inevitable also that, if there were a long and costly war, there should be a national debt.

How indeed was it possible that a debt should not have been contracted, when one party was impelled by the strongest motives to borrow, and another was impelled by equally strong motives to lend? A moment had arrived at which the government found it impossible, without exciting the most formidable discontents, to raise by taxation the supplies necessary to defend the liberty and independence of the nation; and, at that very moment, numerous capitalists were looking round them in vain for some good mode of investing their savings, and, for want of such a mode, were keeping their wealth locked up, or were lavishing it on absurd projects. Riches sufficient to equip a navy which would sweep the German Ocean and the Atlantic of French privateers, riches sufficient to maintain an army which might retake Namur and avenge the disaster of Steinkirk, were lying idle, or were passing away from the owners into the hands of sharpers. A statesman might well think that some part of the wealth which was daily buried or squandered might, with advantage to the proprietor, to the taxpayer and to the State, be attracted into the Treasury. Why meet the extraordinary charge of a year of war by seizing the chairs, the tables, the beds of hardworking families, by compelling one country gentleman to cut down his trees before they were ready for the axe, another to let the cottages on his land fall to ruin, a third to take away his hopeful son from the University, when Change Alley was swarming with people who did not know what to do with their money and who were pressing everybody to borrow it?

It was often asserted at a later period by Tories, who hated the national debt most of all things, and who hated Burnet most of all men, that Burnet was the person who first advised the government to contract a national debt. But this assertion is proved by no trustworthy evidence, and seems to be disproved by the Bishop's silence. Of all men he was the least likely to conceal the fact that an important fiscal revolution had been his work. Nor was the Board of Treasury at that time one which much needed, or was likely much to regard, the counsels of a divine. At that Board sat Godolphin the most prudent and experienced, and Montagu the most daring and inventive of financiers.[1] Neither of these eminent men could be ignorant that it had long been the practice of the neighbouring states to spread over many years of peace the excessive taxation which was made necessary by one year of war. In Italy this practice had existed through many generations. France had, during the war which began in 1672 and ended in 1679, borrowed not less than thirty millions of our money. Sir

[1. Sidney Godolphin, afterwards Earl of Godolphin, and Charles Montagu, afterwards Earl of Halifax, were the ablest financial ministers of the reigns of William and Anne.]

William Temple, in his interesting work on the Batavian federation, had told his countrymen that, when he was ambassador at the Hague, the single province of Holland, then ruled by the frugal and prudent De Witt, owed about five millions sterling, for which interest at four per cent was always ready to the day, and that when any part of the principal was paid off the public creditor received his money with tears, well knowing that he could find no other investment equally secure. The wonder is not that England should have at length imitated the example both of her enemies and of her allies, but that the fourth year of her arduous and exhausting struggle against Lewis should have been drawing to a close before she resorted to an expedient so obvious.

On the fifteenth of December 1692 the House of Commons resolved itself into a Committee of Ways and Means. Somers took the chair. Montagu proposed to raise a million by way of loan: the proposition was approved; and it was ordered that a bill should be brought in. The details of the scheme were much discussed and modified; but the principle appears to have been popular with all parties. The moneyed men were glad to have a good opportunity of investing what they had hoarded. The landed men, hard pressed by the load of taxation, were ready to consent to anything for the sake of present ease. No member ventured to divide the House. On the twentieth of January the bill was read a third time, carried up to the Lords by Somers, and passed by them without any amendment.

By this memorable law new duties were imposed on beer and other liquors. These duties were to be kept in the Exchequer separate from all other receipts, and were to form a fund on the credit of which a million was to be raised by life annuities. As the annuitants dropped off, their annuities were to be divided among the survivors, till the number of survivors was reduced to seven. After that time, whatever fell in was to go to the public. It was therefore certain that the eighteenth century would be far advanced before the debt would be finally extinguished. The rate of interest was to be ten per cent till the year 1700, and after that year seven per cent. The advantages offered to the public creditor by this scheme may seem great, but were not more than sufficient to compensate him for the risk which he ran. It was not impossible that there might be a counter-revolution; and it was certain that, if there were a counter-revolution, those who had lent money to William would lose both interest and principal.

Such was the origin of that debt which has since become the greatest prodigy that ever perplexed the sagacity and confounded the pride of statesmen and philosophers. At every stage in the growth of that debt the nation has set up the same cry of anguish and despair. At every stage in the growth of that debt it has been seriously asserted by wise men that bankruptcy and ruin were at hand. Yet still the debt went on growing; and still bankruptcy and ruin were as remote as ever. When the great contest with Lewis the Fourteenth was finally terminated by the Peace of Utrecht, the nation owed about fifty millions; and that debt was considered, not merely by the rude multitude, not merely by foxhunting squires and coffeehouse orators, but by acute and profound thinkers, as an incumbrance which would permanently cripple the body politic. Nevertheless trade flourished: wealth increased: the nation became richer and richer. Then came the war of the Austrian Succession; and the debt rose to eighty millions. Pamphleteers, historians and orators pronounced that now, at all events, our case was desperate. Yet the signs of increasing property, signs which could neither be counterfeited nor concealed, ought to have satisfied observant and reflecting men that a debt of eighty millions was less to the England which was governed by Pelham than a debt of fifty millions had been to the England which was governed by Oxford. Soon war again broke forth: and, under the energetic and prodigal administration of the first William Pitt, the debt rapidly swelled to a hundred and forty millions. As soon as the first intoxication of victory was over, men of theory and men of business almost unanimously pronounced that the fatal day had now really arrived. The only statesman, indeed, active or speculative, who did not share in the general delusion was Edmund Burke.

David Hume, undoubtedly one of the most profound political economists of his time, declared that our madness had exceeded the madness of the Crusaders. Richard Coeur de Lion and Saint Lewis had not gone in the face of arithmetical demonstration. It was impossible to prove by figures that the road to Paradise did not lie through the Holy Land: but it was possible to prove by figures that the road to national ruin was through the national debt. It was idle, however, now to talk about the road: we had done with the road: we had reached the goal: all was over: all the revenues of the island north of Trent and west of Reading were mortgaged. Better for us to have been conquered by Prussia or Austria than to be saddled with the interest of a hundred and forty millions. And yet this great philosopher – for such he was – had only to open his eyes, and to see improvement all around him, cities increasing, cultivation extending, marts too small for the crowd of buyers and sellers, harbours insufficient to contain the shipping, artificial rivers joining the chief inland seats of industry to the chief seaports, streets better lighted, houses better furnished, richer wares exposed to sale in statelier shops, swifter carriages rolling along smoother roads. He had, indeed, only to compare the Edinburgh of his boyhood with the Edinburgh of his old age. His prediction remains to posterity, a memorable instance of the weakness from which the strongest minds are not exempt.

Adam Smith saw a little and but a little further. He admitted that, immense as the burden was, the nation did actually sustain it and thrive under it in a way which nobody could have foreseen. But he warned his countrymen not to repeat so hazardous an experiment. The limit had been reached. Even a small increase might be fatal. Not less gloomy was the view which George Grenville, a minister eminently diligent and practical, took of our financial situation. The nation must, he conceived, sink under a debt of a hundred and forty millions, unless a portion of the load were borne by the American colonies. The attempt to lay a portion of the load on the American colonies produced another war. That war left us with an additional hundred millions of debts, and without the colonies whose help had been represented as indispensable.

Again England was given over; and again the strange patient persisted in becoming stronger and more blooming in spite of all the diagnostics and prognostics of State physicians. As she had been visibly more prosperous with a debt of a hundred and forty millions than with a debt of fifty millions, so she was visibly more prosperous with a debt of two hundred and forty millions than with a debt of one hundred and forty millions. Soon however the wars which sprang from the French Revolution, and which far exceeded in cost any that the world had ever seen, tasked the powers of public credit to the utmost. When the world was again at rest the funded debt of England amounted to eight hundred millions. If the most enlightened man had been told, in 1792, that, in 1815, the interest on eight hundred millions would be duly paid to the day at the Bank, he would have been as hard of belief as if he had been told that the government would be in possession of the lamp of Aladdin or of the purse of Fortunatus. It was in truth a gigantic, a fabulous debt, and we can hardly wonder that the cry of despair should have been louder than ever.

But again that cry was found to have been as unreasonable as ever. After a few years of exhaustion, England recovered herself. Yet, like Addison's valetudinarian, who continued to whimper that he was dying of consumption till he became so fat that he was shamed into silence, she went on complaining that she was sunk in poverty till her wealth showed itself by tokens which made her complaints ridiculous. The beggared, the bankrupt society not only proved able to meet all its obligations, but, while meeting those obligations, grew richer and richer so fast that the growth could almost be discerned by the eye. In every county, we saw wastes recently turned into gardens: in every city, we saw new streets, and squares, and markets, more brilliant lamps, more abundant supplies of water: in the suburbs of every great seat of industry, we saw villas multiplying fast, each embosomed in its gay little paradise of lilacs and roses. While shallow politicians were repeating that the energies of the people were borne down by the weight of the public burdens, the first journey was performed by steam on a railway. Soon the island was intersected by railways. A sum exceeding the whole amount of the national debt at the end of the American war was, in a few years, voluntarily expended by this ruined people in viaducts, tunnels, embankments, bridges, stations, engines. Meanwhile taxation was almost constantly becoming lighter and lighter: yet still the Exchequer was full. It may be now affirmed without fear of contradiction that we find it as easy to pay the interest of eight hundred millions as our ancestors found it, a century ago, to pay the interest of eighty millions.

It can hardly be doubted that there must have been some great fallacy in the notions of those who uttered and of those who believed that long succession of confident predictions, so signally falsified by a long succession of indisputable facts. To point out that fallacy is the office rather of the political economist than of the historian. Here it is sufficient to say that the prophets of evil were under a double delusion. They erroneously imagined that there was an exact analogy between the case of an individual who is in debt to another individual and the case of a society which is in debt to a part of itself; and this analogy led them into endless mistakes about the effect of the system of funding. They were under an error not less serious touching the resources of the country. They made no allowance for the effect produced by the incessant progress of every experimental science, and by the incessant efforts of every man to get on in life. They saw that the debt grew; and they forgot that other things grew as well as the debt.

A long experience justifies us in believing that England may, in the twentieth century, be better able to bear a debt of sixteen hundred millions than she is at the present time to bear her present load. But be this as it may, those who so confidently predicted that she must sink, first under a debt of fifty millions, then under a debt of eighty millions, then under a debt of a hundred and forty millions, then under a debt of two hundred and forty millions, and lastly under a debt of eight hundred millions, were beyond all doubt under a twofold mistake. They greatly overrated the pressure of the burden: they greatly underrated the strength by which the burden was to be borne.

It may be desirable to add a few words touching the way in which the system of funding has affected the interests of the great commonwealth of nations. If it be true that whatever gives to intelligence an advantage over brute force and to honesty an advantage over dishonesty has a tendency to promote the happiness and virtue of our race, it can scarcely be denied that, in the largest view, the effect of this system has been salutary. For it is

manifest that all credit depends on two things, on the power of a
debtor to pay debts, and on his inclination to pay them. The
power of a society to pay debts is proportioned to the progress
which that society has made in industry, in commerce, and in all
the arts and sciences which flourish under the benignant influence of freedom and of equal law. The inclination of a society to
pay debts is proportioned to the degree in which that society respects the obligations of plighted faith. Of the strength which
consists in extent of territory and in number of fighting men, a
rude despot who knows no law but his own childish fancies and
headstrong passions, or a convention of socialists which pro-
claims all property to be robbery,[2] may have more than falls to
the lot of the best and wisest government. But the strength which
is derived from the confidence of capitalists such a despot, such a
convention, never can possess. That strength – and it is a strength
which has decided the event of more than one great conflict –
flies, by the law of its nature, from barbarism and fraud, from
tyranny and anarchy, to follow civilisation and virtue, liberty and
order.

*

B. THE BANK OF ENGLAND, 1694

[*After describing other financial measures of 1694, Macaulay goes
on:*]

By the lottery loan, as it was called, one million was obtained.
But another million was wanted to bring the estimated revenue
for the year 1694 up to a level with the estimated expenditure.
The ingenious and enterprising Montagu had a plan ready, a
plan to which, except under the pressure of extreme pecuniary
difficulties, he might not easily have induced the Commons to
assent, but which, to his large and vigorous mind, appeared to
have advantages, both commercial and political, more important
than the immediate relief to the finances. He succeeded, not only

[2. A reference to the French socialist theorists of Macaulay's own time,
and in particular to Joseph Pierre Proudhon, the author of the phrase '*la
propriété, c'est le vol*'.]

in supplying the wants of the State for twelve months, but in creating a great institution, which, after the lapse of more than a century and a half, continues to flourish, and which he lived to see the stronghold, through all vicissitudes, of the Whig party, and the bulwark, in dangerous times, of the Protestant succession.

In the reign of William old men were still living who could remember the days when there was not a single banking house in the city of London. So late as the time of the Restoration every trader had his own strong box in his own house, and, when an acceptance was presented to him, told down the crowns and Caroluses on his own counter. But the increase of wealth had produced its natural effect, the subdivision of labour. Before the end of the reign of Charles the Second, a new mode of paying and receiving money had come into fashion among the merchants of the capital. A class of agents arose, whose office was to keep the cash of the commercial houses. This new branch of business naturally fell into the hands of the goldsmiths, who were accustomed to traffic largely in the precious metals, and who had vaults in which great masses of bullion could lie secure from fire and from robbers. It was at the shops of the goldsmiths of Lombard Street that all the payments in coin were made. Other traders gave and received nothing but paper.

This great change did not take place without much opposition and clamour. Old-fashioned merchants complained bitterly that a class of men who, thirty years before, had confined themselves to their proper functions, and had made a fair profit by embossing silver bowls and chargers, by setting jewels for fine ladies, and by selling pistoles and dollars to gentlemen setting out for the Continent, had become the treasurers, and were fast becoming the masters, of the whole City. These usurers, it was said, played at hazard with what had been earned by the industry and hoarded by the thrift of other men. If the dice turned up well, the knave who kept the cash became an alderman: if they turned up ill, the dupe who furnished the cash became a bankrupt. On the other side the conveniences of the modern practice were set forth in animated language. The new system, it was said, saved both labour and money. Two clerks, seated in one counting house, did what, under the old system, must have been done by twenty clerks in twenty different establishments. A goldsmith's note might be transferred ten times in a morning; and thus a hundred guineas, locked in his safe close to the Exchange, did what would formerly have required a thousand guineas, dispersed through many tills, some on Ludgate Hill, some in Austin Friars, and some in Tower Street.

*

No sooner had banking become a separate and important trade, than men began to discuss with earnestness the question whether it would be expedient to erect a national bank. The general opinion seems to have been decidedly in favour of a national bank: nor can we wonder at this: for few were then aware that trade is in general carried on to much more advantage by individuals than by great societies; and banking really is one of those few trades which can be carried on to as much advantage by a great society as by an individual. Two public banks had long been renowned throughout Europe, the Bank of Saint George at Genoa, and the Bank of Amsterdam. The immense wealth which was in the keeping of those establishments, the confidence which they inspired, the prosperity which they had created, their stability, tried by panics, by wars, by revolutions, and found proof against all, were favourite topics. The Bank of Saint George had nearly completed its third century. It had begun to receive deposits and to make loans before Columbus had crossed the Atlantic, before Gama had turned the Cape, when a Christian Emperor was reigning at Constantinople, when a Mahomedan Sultan was reigning at Granada, when Florence was a Republic, when Holland obeyed a hereditary Prince. All these things had been changed. New continents and new oceans had been discovered. The Turk was at Constantinople: the Castilian was at Granada: Florence had its hereditary Prince: Holland was a Republic: but the Bank of Saint George was still receiving deposits and making loans. The Bank of Amsterdam was little more than eighty years old: but its solvency had stood severe tests. Even in the terrible crisis of 1672, when the whole Delta of the Rhine was overrun by the French armies, when the white flags were seen from the top of the Stadthouse, there was one place where, amidst the general consternation and confusion, tranquillity and order were still to be found; and that place was the Bank. Why should not the Bank of London be as great and as durable as the Banks of Genoa and of Amsterdam?

Before the end of the reign of Charles the Second several plans were proposed, examined, attacked and defended. Some pamphleteers maintained that a national bank ought to be under the direction of the King. Others thought that the management ought to be entrusted to the Lord Mayor, Aldermen and Common Council of the capital. After the Revolution the subject was discussed with an animation before unknown. For, under the influence of liberty, the breed of political projectors multiplied exceedingly. A crowd of plans, some of which resemble the fancies of a child or the dreams of a man in a fever, were pressed on the government. Pre-eminently conspicuous among the political mountebanks, whose busy faces were seen every day in the lobby of the House of Commons, were John Briscoe and Hugh Chamberlayne, two projectors worthy to have been members of that Academy which Gulliver found at Lagado. These men affirmed that the one cure for every distemper of the State was a Land Bank. A Land Bank would work for England miracles such as had never been wrought for Israel, miracles exceeding the heaps of quails and the daily shower of manna. There would be no taxes; and yet the Exchequer would be full to overflowing. There would be no poor rates: for there would be no poor. The income of every landowner would be doubled. The profits of every merchant would be increased. In short, the island would, to use Briscoe's words, be the paradise of the world. The only losers would be the moneyed men, those worst enemies of the nation, who had done more injury to the gentry and yeomanry than an invading army from France would have had the heart to do.

These blessed effects the Land Bank was to produce simply by issuing enormous quantities of notes on landed security. The doctrine of the projectors was that every person who had real property ought to have, besides that property, paper money to the full value of that property. Thus, if his estate was worth two thousand pounds, he ought to have his estate and two thousand pounds in paper money. Both Briscoe and Chamberlayne

treated with the greatest contempt the notion that there could be
an over-issue of paper as long as there was, for every ten pound
note, a piece of land in the country worth ten pounds. Nobody,
they said, would accuse a goldsmith of over-issuing as long as his
vaults contained guineas and crowns to the full value of all the
notes which bore his signature. Indeed no goldsmith had in his
vaults guineas and crowns to the full value of all his paper. And
was not a square mile of rich land in Taunton Dean at least as
well entitled to be called wealth as a bag of gold or silver? The
projectors could not deny that many people had a prejudice in
favour of the precious metals, and that therefore, if the Land
Bank were bound to cash its notes, it would very soon stop payment. This difficulty they got over by proposing that the notes
should be inconvertible, and that everybody should be forced to
take them.

The speculations of Chamberlayne on the subject of the currency may possibly find admirers even in our own time. But to
his other errors he added an error which began and ended with
him. He was fool enough to take it for granted, in all his reasonings, that the value of an estate varied directly as the duration.
He maintained that if the annual income derived from a manor
were a thousand pounds, a grant of that manor for twenty years
must be worth twenty thousand pounds, and a grant for a hundred years worth a hundred thousand pounds. If, therefore, the
lord of such a manor would pledge it for a hundred years to the
Land Bank, the Land Bank might, on that security, instantly
issue notes for a hundred thousand pounds. On this subject
Chamberlayne was proof to ridicule, to argument, even to arithmetical demonstration. He was reminded that the fee simple of
land would not sell for more than twenty years' purchase. To
say, therefore, that a term of a hundred years was worth five
times as much as a term of twenty years, was to say that a term of
a hundred years was worth five times the fee simple; in other
words, that a hundred was five times infinity. Those who reason-
ed thus were refuted by being told that they were usurers; and
it should seem that a large number of country gentlemen thought
the refutation complete.

In December 1693 Chamberlayne laid his plan, in all its naked absurdity, before the Commons, and petitioned to be heard. He confidently undertook to raise eight thousand pounds on every freehold estate of a hundred and fifty pounds a year which should be brought, as he expressed it, into his Land Bank, and this without dispossessing the freeholder. All the squires in the House must have known that the fee simple of such an estate would hardly fetch three thousand pounds in the market. That less than the fee simple of such an estate could, by any device, be made to produce eight thousand pounds, would, it might have been thought, have seemed incredible to the most illiterate foxhunter that could be found on the benches. Distress, however, and animosity had made the landed gentlemen credulous. They insisted on referring Chamberlayne's plan to a committee; and the committee reported that the plan was practicable, and would tend to the benefit of the nation. But by this time the united force of demonstration and derision had begun to produce an effect even on the most ignorant rustics in the House. The report lay unnoticed on the table; and the country was saved from a calamity compared with which the defeat of Landen and the loss of the Smyrna fleet would have been blessings.

All the projectors of this busy time, however, were not so absurd as Chamberlayne. One among them, William Paterson, was an ingenious, though not always a judicious, speculator. Of his early life little is known except that he was a native of Scotland, and that he had been in the West Indies. In what character he had visited the West Indies was a matter about which his contemporaries differed. His friends said that he had been a missionary; his enemies that he had been a buccaneer. He seems to have been gifted by nature with fertile invention, an ardent temperament and great powers of persuasion, and to have acquired somewhere in the course of his vagrant life a perfect knowledge of accounts.

This man submitted to the government, in 1691, a plan of a national bank; and his plan was favourably received both by statesmen and by merchants. But years passed away; and nothing was done, till, in the spring of 1694, it became absolutely necessary to find some new mode of defraying the charges of the war. Then at length the scheme devised by the poor and obscure

Scottish adventurer was taken up in earnest by Montagu. With Montagu was closely allied Michael Godfrey, the brother of that Sir Edmund Berry Godfrey whose sad and mysterious death had, fifteen years before, produced a terrible outbreak of popular feeling.[3] Michael was one of the ablest, most upright and most opulent of the merchant princes of London. He was, as might have been expected from his near connection with the martyr of the Protestant faith, a zealous Whig. Some of his writings are still extant, and prove him to have had a strong and clear mind.

By these two distinguished men Paterson's scheme was fathered. Montagu undertook to manage the House of Commons, Godfrey to manage the City. An approving vote was obtained from the Committee of Ways and Means; and a bill, the title of which gave occasion to many sarcasms, was laid on the table. It was indeed not easy to guess that a bill, which purported only to impose a new duty on tonnage for the benefit of such persons as should advance money towards carrying on the war, was really a bill creating the greatest commercial institution that the world had ever seen.

The plan was that twelve hundred thousand pounds should be borrowed by the government on what was then considered as the moderate interest of eight per cent. In order to induce capitalists to advance the money promptly on terms so favourable to the public, the subscribers were to be incorporated by the name of the Governor and Company of the Bank of England. The corporation was to have no exclusive privilege, and was to be restricted from trading in anything but bills of exchange, bullion and forfeited pledges.

As soon as the plan became generally known, a paper war broke out as furious as that between the swearers and the nonswearers, or as that between the Old East India Company and the New East India Company.[4] The projectors who had failed to

[3. The murder of Sir Edmund Berry Godfrey, a justice of the peace for Westminster, in October 1678, had precipitated the scare of the Popish Plot. This Michael Godfrey was in fact the nephew, not the brother, of the victim.]

[4. The struggle between the established (or 'Old') East India Company, which had become a 'tory' body, and the whig 'New East India Company', which sought to break its monopoly, had been raging since 1680, and was not gain the ear of the government fell like madmen on their more fortunate brother. All the goldsmiths and pawnbrokers set up a howl of rage. Some discontented Tories predicted ruin to the monarchy. It was remarkable, they said, that Banks and Kings had never existed together. Banks were republican institutions. There were flourishing banks at Venice, at Genoa, at Amsterdam and at Hamburg. But who had ever heard of a Bank of France or a Bank of Spain? Some discontented Whigs, on the other hand, predicted ruin to our liberties. Here, they said, is an instrument of tyranny more formidable than the High Commission, than the Star Chamber, than even the fifty thousand soldiers of Oliver. The whole wealth of the nation will be in the hands of the Tonnage Bank – such was the nickname then in use – and the Tonnage Bank will be in the hands of the Sovereign. The power of the purse, the one great security for all the rights of Englishmen, will be transferred from the House of Commons to the Governor and Directors of the new Company. This last consideration was really of some weight, and was allowed to be so by the authors of the bill. A clause was therefore most properly inserted which inhibited the Bank from advancing money to the Crown without authority from Parliament. Every infraction of this salutary rule was to be punished by forfeiture of three times the sum advanced; and it was provided that the King should not have power to remit any part of the penalty.

The plan, thus amended, received the sanction of the Commons more easily than might have been expected from the violence of the adverse clamour. In truth, the Parliament was under duress. Money must be had, and could in no other way be had so easily. What took place when the House had resolved itself into a committee cannot be discovered: but, while the Speaker was in the chair, no division took place.

The bill, however, was not safe when it had reached the Upper House. Some Lords suspected that the plan of a national bank had been devised for the purpose of exalting the moneyed interest at the expense of the landed interest. Others thought

---

settled till the reign of Anne. Macaulay gives a graphic description of it in his eighteenth chapter.]

that this plan, whether good or bad, ought not to have been submitted to them in such a form. Whether it would be safe to call
into existence a body which might one day rule the whole commercial world, and how such a body should be constituted, were
questions which ought not to be decided by one branch of the
Legislature. The Peers ought to be at perfect liberty to examine
all the details of the proposed scheme, to suggest amendments, to
ask for conferences. It was therefore most unfair that the law
establishing the Bank should be sent up as part of a law granting
supplies to the Crown.[5] The Jacobites entertained some hope
that the session would end with a quarrel between the Houses,
that the Tonnage Bill would be lost, and that William would
enter on the campaign without money. It was already May, according to the New Style. The London season was over; and
many noble families had left Covent Garden and Soho Square
for their woods and hayfields.

But summonses were sent out. There was a violent rush back
to town. The benches which had lately been deserted were
crowded. The sittings began at an hour unusually early, and
were prolonged to an hour unusually late. On the day on which
the bill was committed the contest lasted without intermission
from nine in the morning till six in the evening. Godolphin was
in the chair. Nottingham and Rochester proposed to strike out
all the clauses which related to the Bank. Something was said
about the danger of setting up a gigantic corporation which might
soon give law to the King and the three Estates of the Realm.
But the Peers seemed to be most moved by the appeal which was
made to them as landlords. The whole scheme, it was asserted,
was intended to enrich usurers at the expense of the nobility and
gentry. Persons who had laid by money would rather put it into
the Bank than lend it on mortgage at moderate interest. Caermarthen said little or nothing in defence of what was, in truth,
the work of his rivals and enemies. He owned that there were
grave objections to the mode in which the Commons had provided for the public service of the year. But would their Lord-

[5. 'Money bills' – i.e. bills granting money to the Crown – were debated
and decided exclusively by the House of Commons.]

ships amend a money bill? Would they engage in a contest of which the end must be that they must either yield, or incur the grave responsibility of leaving the Channel without a fleet during the summer? This argument prevailed; and, on a division, the amendment was rejected by forty-three votes to thirty-one. A few hours later the bill received the royal assent, and the Parliament was prorogued.

In the City the success of Montagu's plan was complete. It was then at least as difficult to raise a million at eight per cent as it would now be to raise thirty millions at four per cent. It had been supposed that contributions would drop in very slowly; and a considerable time had therefore been allowed by the Act. This indulgence was not needed. So popular was the new investment that on the day on which the books were opened three hundred thousand pounds were subscribed: three hundred thousand more were subscribed during the next forty-eight hours; and, in ten days, to the delight of all the friends of the government, it was announced that the list was full. The whole sum which the Corporation was bound to lend to the state was paid into the Exchequer before the first instalment was due. Somers gladly put the Great Seal to a charter framed in conformity with the terms prescribed by Parliament; and the Bank of England commenced its operations in the house of the Company of Grocers. There, during many years, directors, secretaries and clerks might be seen labouring in different parts of one spacious hall. The persons employed by the Bank were originally only fifty-four. They are now nine hundred. The sum paid yearly in salaries amounted at first to only four thousand three hundred and fifty pounds. It now exceeds two hundred and ten thousand pounds. We may therefore fairly infer that the incomes of commercial clerks are, on an average, about three times as large in the reign of Victoria as they were in the reign of William the Third.

It soon appeared that Montagu had, by skilfully availing himself of the financial difficulties of the country, rendered an inestimable service to his party. During several generations the Bank of England was emphatically a Whig body. It was Whig, not accidentally, but necessarily. It must have instantly stopped

payment if it had ceased to receive the interest on the sum which
it had advanced to the government; and of that interest James
would not have paid one farthing. Seventeen years after the passing of the Tonnage Bill, Addison, in one of his most ingenious
and graceful little allegories, described the situation of the great
Company through which the immense wealth of London was
constantly circulating. He saw Public Credit on her throne in
Grocers' Hall, the Great Charter over her head. the Act of
Settlement full in her view. Her touch turned everything to gold.
Behind her seat, bags filled with coin were piled up to the ceiling.
On her right and on her left the floor was hidden by pyramids of
guineas. On a sudden the door flies open. The Pretender rushes
in, a sponge in one hand, in the other a sword which he shakes at
the Act of Settlement. The beautiful Queen sinks down fainting.
The spell by which she has turned all things around her into
treasure is broken. The money bags shrink like pricked bladders.
The piles of gold pieces are turned into bundles of rags or faggots
of wooden tallies. The truth which this parable was meant to convey was constantly present to the minds of the rulers of the
Bank. So closely was their interest bound up with the interest of
the government that the greater the public danger the more ready
were they to come to the rescue. In old times, when the Treasury
was empty, when the taxes came in slowly, and when the pay of
the soldiers and sailors was in arrear, it had been necessary for
the Chancellor of the Exchequer to go, hat in hand, up and down
Cheapside and Cornhill, attended by the Lord Mayor and by the
Aldermen, and to make up a sum by borrowing a hundred
pounds from this hosier, and two hundred pounds from that iron-
monger. Those times were over. The government, instead of
laboriously scooping up supplies from numerous petty sources,
could now draw whatever it required from an immense reservoir,
which all those petty sources kept constantly replenished. It is
hardly too much to say that, during many years, the weight of
the Bank, which was constantly in the scale of the Whigs, almost
counterbalanced the weight of the Church, which was as constantly in the scale of the Tories.

*

C. THE DARIEN SCHEME, 1695–9

[*In Scotland also new economic projects were proposed. Since 1680 the Scottish economy had been in decline and the years from 1690, 'King William's years' (as the Jacobites called them), had been years of dearth and famine. In an attempt to discover and exploit new markets, the Scottish Parliament, in 1695, passed an act for 'a company trading to Africa and the Indies'. This was to be a joint Anglo-Scottish company, and it was supported by the 'New East India Company' in England, which hoped thus to break the monopoly of the Old Company. But the Old Company was politically more powerful and persuaded the English Parliament to intervene and force the English subscribers to withdraw their subscriptions. The Scots then went ahead with the project alone, and in November 1698 planted a 'colony' in Darien, on the isthmus of Panama. The result was disastrous. The capital subscribed was insufficient, and the loss of English commercial expertise and naval protection exposed the colony to economic failure and Spanish reprisals. It was abandoned in June 1699.*

The Darien scheme is of importance because of its political consequences. It exposed the inconveniences of the 'Union of Crowns' in which England and Scotland had been associated since 1603. Hitherto the Scottish economy had been at the mercy of English foreign policy; now English foreign relations had been jeopardized by Scottish economic policy. The experience was not lost on either side of the Border. Although some Scotchmen were reinforced in their demands for a complete separation of crowns, others deduced that there must be a complete union; and the political dangers of a different dynasty in Scotland led English statesmen to the same conclusion. William himself always recommended a union of the two countries. It was achieved under his successor, Queen Anne, in 1707.

Macaulay's account of the Darien scheme (in his Chapter XXIV) is erroneous in one important respect. He assumes throughout that half the capital had been raised in Scotland before any attempt was made to draw on the London money market and that the English Parliament, by its intervention, left the company committed by the possession of Scottish subscriptions. This is an inversion of the true order of events. In fact the English capital was raised in October

1695 ; the English Parliament intervened in December 1695 ; the Edinburgh subscriptions were raised in February 1696. By that time it was already clear that no English money would be available.

Macaulay introduces his account of the Darien scheme in his twenty-fourth chapter, when dealing with the diplomatic rupture between England and Spain caused by the Second Partition Treaty. By this treaty William and Louis XIV agreed to a division of the Spanish Empire on the death of Charles II, King of Spain, then (rightly) believed to be imminent. The Spanish ambassador in England, the Marqués de Canales, delivered a note so strong that William ordered his expulsion and recalled his own ambassador from Madrid.]

It is probable that Canales would have expressed himself in a less unbecoming manner, had there not already existed a most unfortunate quarrel between Spain and William, a quarrel in which William was perfectly blameless, but in which the unanimous feeling of the English Parliament and of the English nation was on the side of Spain.

It is necessary to go back some years for the purpose of tracing the origin and progress of this quarrel. Few portions of our history are more interesting or instructive: but few have been more obscured and distorted by passion and prejudice. The story is an exciting one; and it has generally been told by writers whose judgment had been perverted by strong national partiality. Their invectives and lamentations have still to be temperately examined; and it may well be doubted whether, even now, after the lapse of more than a century and a half, feelings hardly compatible with temperate examination will not be stirred up in many minds by the name of Darien. In truth that name is associated with calamities so cruel that the recollection of them may not unnaturally disturb the equipoise even of a fair and sedate mind.

The man who brought these calamities on his country was not a mere visionary or a mere swindler. He was that William Paterson whose name is honourably associated with the auspicious commencement of a new era in English commerce and in English finance. His plan of a national bank, having been examined

and approved by the most eminent statesmen who sat in the
Parliament house at Westminster and by the most eminent merchants who walked the Exchange of London, had been carried
into execution with signal success. He thought, and perhaps
thought with reason, that his services had been ill requited. He
was, indeed, one of the original Directors of the great corporation which owed its existence to him; but he was not re-elected.
It may easily be believed that his colleagues, citizens of ample
fortune and of long experience in the practical part of trade, aldermen, wardens of companies, heads of firms well known in
every Burse throughout the civilised world, were not well pleased
to see among them in Grocers' Hall a foreign adventurer whose
whole capital consisted in an inventive brain and a persuasive
tongue. Some of them were probably weak enough to dislike him
for being a Scot: some were probably mean enough to be jealous
of his parts and knowledge: and even persons who were not unfavourably disposed to him might have discovered, before they
had known him long, that, with all his cleverness, he was deficient in common sense; that his mind was full of schemes which,
at the first glance, had a specious aspect, but which, on closer
examination, appeared to be impracticable or pernicious; and
that the benefit which the public had derived from one happy
project formed by him would be very dearly purchased if it were
taken for granted that all his other projects must be equally
happy. Disgusted by what he considered as the ingratitude of the
English, he repaired to the Continent, in the hope that he might
be able to interest the traders of the Hanse Towns and the princes
of the German Empire in his plans. From the Continent he returned unsuccessful to London; and then at length the thought
that he might be more justly appreciated by his countrymen than
by strangers seems to have risen in his mind.

Just at this time he fell in with Fletcher of Saltoun,[6] who
happened to be in England. These eccentric men soon became
intimate. Each of them had his monomania; and the two mono-

[6. Andrew Fletcher of Saltoun, the Scottish 'patriot', was a violent whig
and a Scottish nationalist. He had supported both Monmouth and William.
He opposed the union with England, advocating complete Scottish independence under the rule of a slave-owning oligarchy of landlords.]

manias suited each other perfectly. Fletcher's whole soul was possessed by a sore, jealous, punctilious patriotism. His heart was ulcerated by the thought of the poverty, the feebleness, the political insignificance of Scotland, and of the indignities which she had suffered at the hand of her powerful and opulent neighbour. When he talked of her wrongs his dark meagre face took its sternest expression: his habitual frown grew blacker; and his eyes flashed more than their wonted fire. Paterson, on the other hand, firmly believed himself to have discovered the means of making any state which would follow his counsel great and prosperous in a time which, when compared with the life of an individual, could hardly be called long, and which, in the life of a nation, was but as a moment. There is not the least reason to believe that he was dishonest. Indeed he would have found more difficulty in deceiving others had he not begun by deceiving himself. His faith in his own schemes was strong even to martyrdom; and the eloquence with which he illustrated and defended them had all the charm of sincerity and of enthusiasm. Very seldom has any blunder committed by fools, or any villainy devised by impostors, brought on any society miseries so great as the dreams of these two friends, both of them men of integrity and both of them men of parts, were destined to bring on Scotland.

In 1695 the pair went down together to their native country. The Parliament of that country was then about to meet under the presidency of Tweeddale,[7] an old acquaintance and country neighbour of Fletcher. On Tweeddale the first attack was made. He was a shrewd, cautious, old politician. Yet it should seem that he was not able to hold out against the skill and energy of the assailants. Perhaps, however, he was not altogether a dupe. The public mind was at that moment violently agitated. Men of all parties were clamouring for an inquiry into the slaughter of Glencoe. There was reason to fear that the session which was about to commence would be stormy. In such circumstances the Lord High Commissioner might think that it would be prudent to appease the anger of the Estates by offering an almost irresistible bait to their cupidity. If such was the policy of Tweed-

[7. John Hay, Marquess of Tweeddale, had succeeded the Duke of Hamilton as William's High Commissioner in Scotland.]

dale, it was, for the moment, eminently successful. The Parliament, which met burning with indignation, was soothed into good humour. The blood of the murdered Macdonalds continued to cry for vengeance in vain. The schemes of Paterson, brought forward under the patronage of the ministers of the Crown, were sanctioned by the unanimous voice of the Legislature.

The great projector was the idol of the whole nation. Men spoke to him with more profound respect than to the Lord High Commissioner. His antechamber was crowded with solicitors desirous to catch some drops of that golden shower of which he was supposed to be the dispenser. To be seen walking with him in the High Street, to be honoured by him with a private interview of a quarter of an hour, were enviable distinctions. He, after the fashion of all the false prophets who have deluded themselves and others, drew new faith in his own lie from the credulity of his disciples. His countenance, his voice, his gestures, indicated boundless self-importance. When he appeared in public he looked – such is the language of one who probably had often seen him – like Atlas conscious that a world was on his shoulders. But the airs which he gave himself only heightened the respect and admiration which he inspired. His demeanour was regarded as a model. Scotchmen who wished to be thought wise looked as like Paterson as they could.

His plan, though as yet disclosed to the public only by glimpses, was applauded by all classes, factions and sects, lords, merchants, advocates, divines, Whigs and Jacobites, Cameronians and Episcopalians. In truth, of all the ten thousand bubbles of which history has preserved the memory, none was ever more skilfully puffed into existence; none ever soared higher, or glittered more brilliantly; and none ever burst with a more lamentable explosion. There was, however, a certain mixture of truth in the magnificent day dream which produced such fatal effects.

Scotland was, indeed, not blessed with a mild climate or a fertile soil. But the richest spots that had ever existed on the face of the earth had been spots quite as little favoured by nature. It was on a bare rock, surrounded by deep sea, that the streets of

Tyre were piled up to a dizzy height. On that sterile crag were woven the robes of Persian satraps and Sicilian tyrants: there were fashioned silver bowls and chargers for the banquets of kings: and there Pomeranian amber was set in Lydian gold to adorn the necks of queens. In the warehouses were collected the fine linen of Egypt and the odorous gums of Arabia; the ivory of India, and the tin of Britain. In the port lay fleets of great ships which had weathered the storms of the Euxine and the Atlantic. Powerful and wealthy colonies in distant parts of the world looked up with filial reverence to the little island; and despots, who trampled on the laws and outraged the feelings of all the nations between the Hydaspes and the Ægean, condescended to court the population of that busy hive. At a later period, on a dreary bank formed by the soil which the Alpine streams swept down to the Adriatic, rose the palaces of Venice. Within a space which would not have been thought large enough for one of the parks of a rude northern baron were collected riches far exceeding those of a northern kingdom. In almost every one of the private dwellings which fringed the Great Canal were to be seen plate, mirrors, jewellery, tapestry, paintings, carving, such as might move the envy of the master of Holyrood. In the arsenal were munitions of war sufficient to maintain a contest against the whole power of the Ottoman Empire. And, before the grandeur of Venice had declined, another commonwealth, still less favoured, if possible, by nature, had rapidly risen to a power and opulence which the whole civilised world contemplated with envy and admiration. On a desolate marsh overhung by fogs and exhaling diseases, a marsh where there was neither wood nor stone, neither firm earth nor drinkable water, a marsh from which the ocean on one side and the Rhine on the other were with difficulty kept out by art, was to be found the most prosperous community in Europe. The wealth which was collected within five miles of the Stadthouse of Amsterdam would purchase the fee simple of Scotland. And why should this be? Was there any reason to believe that nature had bestowed on the Phœnician, on the Venetian, or on the Hollander, a larger measure of activity, of ingenuity, of forethought, of self-command, than on the citizen of Edinburgh or Glasgow? The truth was that, in all those qualities which conduce to success in life, and especially in commercial life, the Scot had never been surpassed; perhaps he had never been equalled. All that was necessary was that his energy should take a proper direction; and a proper direction Paterson undertook to give.

His esoteric project was the original project of Christopher Columbus, extended and modified. Columbus had hoped to establish a communication between our quarter of the world and India across the great western ocean. But he was stopped by an unexpected obstacle. The American continent, stretching far north and far south into cold and inhospitable regions, presented what seemed an insurmountable barrier to his progress; and, in the same year in which he first set foot on that continent, Gama reached Malabar by doubling the Cape of Good Hope. The consequence was that during two hundred years the trade of Europe with the remoter parts of Asia had been carried on by rounding the immense peninsula of Africa. Paterson now revived the project of Columbus, and persuaded himself and others that it was possible to carry that project into effect in such a manner as to make his country the greatest emporium that had ever existed on our globe.

For this purpose it was necessary to occupy in America some spot which might be a resting place between Scotland and India. It was true that almost every habitable part of America had already been seized by some European power. Paterson, however, imagined that one province, the most important of all, had been overlooked by the short-sighted cupidity of vulgar politicians and vulgar traders. The isthmus which joined the two great continents of the New World remained, according to him, unappropriated. Great Spanish viceroyalties, he said, lay on the east and on the west; but the mountains and forests of Darien were abandoned to rude tribes which followed their own usages and obeyed their own princes. He had been in that part of the world, in what character was not quite clear. Some said that he had gone thither to convert the Indians, and some that he had gone thither to rob the Spaniards. But, missionary or pirate, he had visited Darien, and had brought away none but delightful recollections. The havens, he averred, were capacious and secure: the sea swarmed

with turtle: the country was so mountainous that, within nine
degrees of the equator, the climate was temperate; and yet the in-
equalities of the ground offered no impediment to the conveyance of goods. Nothing would be easier than to construct roads
along which a string of mules or a wheeled carriage might in the
course of a single day pass from sea to sea. The soil was, to the
depth of several feet, a rich black mould, on which a profusion of
valuable herbs and fruits grew spontaneously, and on which all
the choicest productions of tropical regions might easily be
raised by human industry and art; and yet the exuberant fertility
of the earth had not tainted the purity of the air. Considered
merely as a place of residence, the isthmus was a paradise. A
colony placed there could not fail to prosper, even if it had no
wealth except what was derived from agriculture. But agriculture
was a secondary object in the colonisation of Darien. Let but that
precious neck of land be occupied by an intelligent, an enterprising, a thrifty race; and, in a few years, the whole trade between
India and Europe must be drawn to that point. The tedious
and perilous passage round Africa would soon be abandoned.
The merchant would no longer expose his cargoes to the mountainous billows and capricious gales of the Antarctic seas. The
greater part of the voyage from Europe to Darien, and the whole
voyage from Darien to the richest kingdoms of Asia, would be a
rapid yet easy gliding before the trade winds over blue and
sparkling waters. The voyage back across the Pacific would, in
the latitude of Japan, be almost equally speedy and pleasant.
Time, labour, money, would be saved. The returns would come
in more quickly. Fewer hands would be required to navigate the
ships. The loss of a vessel would be a rare event. The trade
would increase fast. In a short time it would double; and it
would all pass through Darien. Whoever possessed that door of
the sea, that key of the universe – such were the bold figures
which Paterson loved to employ – would give law to both hemi-
spheres; and would, by peaceful arts, without shedding one drop
of blood, establish an empire as splendid as that of Cyrus or
Alexander. Of the kingdoms of Europe, Scotland was, as yet, the
poorest and the least considered. If she would but occupy Darien, if she would but become one great free port, one great ware-

house for the wealth which the soil of Darien might produce, and for the still greater wealth which would be poured into Darien from Canton and Siam, from Ceylon and the Moluccas, from the mouths of the Ganges and the Gulf of Cambay, she would at once take her place in the first rank among nations. No rival would be able to contend with her either in the West Indian or in the East Indian trade. The beggarly country, as it had been insolently called by the inhabitants of warmer and more fruitful regions, would be the great mart for the choicest luxuries, sugar, rum, coffee, chocolate, tobacco, the tea and porcelain of China, the muslin of Dacca, the shawls of Cashmere, the diamonds of Golconda, the pearls of Karrack, the delicious birds' nests of Nicobar, cinnamon and pepper, ivory and sandal wood. From Scotland would come all the finest jewels and brocade worn by duchesses at the balls of St James's and Versailles. From Scotland would come all the saltpetre which would furnish the means of war to the fleets and armies of contending potentates. And on all the vast riches which would be constantly passing through the little kingdom a toll would be paid which would remain behind. There would be a prosperity such as might seem fabulous, a prosperity of which every Scotchman, from the peer to the cadie, would partake. Soon, all along the now desolate shores of the Forth and Clyde, villas and pleasure grounds would be as thick as along the edges of the Dutch canals. Edinburgh would vie with London and Paris; and the baillie of Glasgow or Dundee would have as stately and well furnished a mansion, and as fine a gallery of pictures, as any burgomaster of Amsterdam.

This magnificent plan was at first but partially disclosed to the public. A colony was to be planted: a vast trade was to be opened between both the Indies and Scotland: but the name of Darien was as yet pronounced only in whispers by Paterson and by his most confidential friends. He had however shown enough to excite boundless hopes and desires. How well he succeeded in inspiring others with his own feelings is sufficiently proved by the memorable Act to which the Lord High Commissioner gave the Royal sanction on the 26th of June 1695. By this Act some persons who were named, and such other persons as should join with them, were formed into a corporation, which was to be named the Company of Scotland trading to Africa and the Indies. The amount of the capital to be employed was not fixed by law; but it was provided that one half of the stock at least must be held by Scotchmen resident in Scotland, and that no stock which had been originally held by a Scotchman resident in Scotland should ever be transferred to any but a Scotchman resident in Scotland. An entire monopoly of the trade with Asia, Africa and America, for a term of thirty-one years, was granted to the Company. All goods imported by the Company were during twenty-one years to be duty-free, with the exception of foreign sugar and tobacco. Sugar and tobacco grown on the Company's own plantations were exempted from all taxation. Every member and every servant of the Company was to be privileged against impressment and arrest. If any of these privileged persons was impressed or arrested, the Company was authorised to release him, and to demand the assistance both of the civil and of the military power. The Company was authorised to take possession of unoccupied territories in any part of Asia, Africa or America, and there to plant colonies, to build towns and forts, to impose taxes, and to provide magazines, arms and ammunition, to raise troops, to wage war, to conclude treaties; and the King was made to promise that, if any foreign state should injure the Company, he would interpose, and would, at the public charge, obtain reparation. Lastly it was provided that, in order to give greater security and solemnity to this most exorbitant grant, the whole substance of the Act should be set forth in Letters Patent to which the Chancellor was directed to put the Great Seal without delay.

The letters were drawn: the Great Seal was affixed: the subscription books were opened; the shares were fixed at a hundred pounds sterling each; and from the Pentland Firth to the Solway Firth every man who had a hundred pounds was impatient to put down his name. About two hundred and twenty thousand pounds were actually paid up. This may not, at first sight, appear a large sum to those who remember the bubbles of 1825 and of 1845, and would assuredly not have sufficed to defray the charge of three months of war with Spain. Yet the effort was marvellous when it may be affirmed with confidence that the Scotch people voluntarily contributed for the colonisation of Darien a larger proportion of their substance than any other people ever, in the same space of time, voluntarily contributed to any commercial undertaking. A great part of Scotland was then as poor and rude as Iceland now is. There were five or six shires which did not altogether contain so many guineas and crowns as were tossed about every day by the shovels of a single goldsmith in Lombard Street. Even the nobles had very little ready money. They generally took a large part of their rents in kind, and were thus able, on their own domains, to live plentifully and hospitably. But there were many esquires in Kent and Somersetshire who received from their tenants a greater quantity of gold and silver than a Duke of Gordon or a Marquess of Atholl drew from extensive provinces. The pecuniary remuneration of the clergy was such as would have moved the pity of the most needy curate who thought it a privilege to drink his ale and smoke his pipe in the kitchen of an English manor house. Even in the fertile Merse there were parishes of which the minister received only from four to eight pounds sterling in cash. The official income of the Lord President of the Court of Session was only five hundred a year; that of the Lord Justice Clerk only four hundred a year. The land tax of the whole kingdom was fixed some years later by the Treaty of Union at little more than half the land tax of the single county of Norfolk. Four hundred thousand pounds probably bore as great a ratio to the wealth of Scotland then as forty millions would bear now.

The list of the members of the Darien Company deserves to be examined. The number of shareholders was about fourteen hundred. The largest quantity of stock registered in one name was three thousand pounds. The heads of three noble houses took three thousand pounds each, the Duke of Hamilton, the Duke of Queensbury and Lord Belhaven, a man of ability, spirit and patriotism, who had entered into the design with enthusiasm not inferior to that of Fletcher. Argyll held fifteen hundred pounds. John Dalrymple, but too well known as the Master of Stair, had just succeeded to his father's title and estate, and was now Viscount Stair. He put down his name for a thousand pounds. The number of Scotch peers who subscribed was between thirty and forty. The City of Edinburgh, in its corporate capacity, took three thousand pounds, the City of Glasgow three thousand, the City of Perth two thousand. But the great majority of the subscribers contributed only one hundred or two hundred pounds each. A very few divines who were settled in the capital or in other large towns were able to purchase shares. It is melancholy to see in the roll the name of more than one professional man whose paternal anxiety led him to lay out probably all his hardly earned savings in purchasing a hundred pound share for each of his children. If, indeed, Paterson's predictions had been verified, such a share would, according to the notions of that age and country, have been a handsome portion for the daughter of a writer or a surgeon.

That the Scotch are a people eminently intelligent, wary, resolute and self-possessed, is obvious to the most superficial observation. That they are a people peculiarly liable to dangerous fits of passion and delusions of the imagination is less generally acknowledged, but is not less true. The whole kingdom seemed to have gone mad. Paterson had acquired an influence resembling rather that of the founder of a new religion, that of a Mahomet, that of a Joseph Smith, than that of a commercial projector. Blind faith in a religion, fanatical zeal for a religion, are too common to astonish us. But such faith and zeal seem strangely out of place in the transactions of the money market. It is true that we are judging after the event. But before the event materials sufficient for the forming of a sound judgment were within the reach of all who cared to use them. It seems incredible that men of sense, who had only a vague and general notion of Paterson's scheme, should have staked everything on the success of that scheme. It seems more incredible still that men to whom the details of that scheme had been confided should not have looked into any of the common books of history or geography in which an account of Darien might have been found, and should not have asked themselves the simple question, whether Spain was likely to endure a Scotch colony in the midst of her Transatlantic dominions. It was notorious that she claimed the sovereignty of the isthmus on specious, nay, on solid, grounds. A Spaniard had been the first discoverer of the coast of Darien. A Spaniard had built a town and established a government on that coast. A Spaniard had, with great labour and peril, crossed the mountainous neck of land, had seen rolling beneath him the vast Pacific, never before revealed to European eyes, had descended, sword in hand, into the waves up to his girdle, and had there solemnly taken possession of sea and shore in the name of the Crown of Castile. It was true that the region which Paterson described as a paradise had been found by the first Castilian settlers to be a land of misery and death. The poisonous air, exhaled from rank jungle and stagnant water, had compelled them to remove to the neighbouring haven of Panama; and the Red Indians had been contemptuously permitted to live after their own fashion on the pestilential soil. But that soil was still considered, and might well be considered, by Spain as her own. In many countries there were tracts of morass, of mountain, of forest, in which governments did not think it worthwhile to be at the expense of maintaining order, and in which rude tribes enjoyed by connivance a kind of independence. It was not necessary for the members of the Company of Scotland trading to Africa and the Indies to look very far for an example. In some highland districts, not more than a hundred miles from Edinburgh, dwelt clans which had always regarded the authority of King, Parliament, Privy Council and Court of Session, quite as little as the aboriginal population of Darien regarded the authority of the Spanish Viceroys and Audiences. Yet it would surely have been thought an outrageous violation of public law in the King of Spain to take possession of Appin and Lochaber. And would it be a less outrageous violation of public law in the Scots to seize on a province in the very centre of his possessions, on the plea that this province was in the same state in which Appin and Lochaber had been during centuries?

So grossly unjust was Paterson's scheme; and yet it was less unjust than impolitic. Torpid as Spain had become, there was still one point on which she was exquisitely sensitive. The slightest encroachment of any other European power even on the outskirts of her American dominions sufficed to disturb her repose and to brace her paralysed nerves. To imagine that she would tamely suffer adventurers from one of the most insignificant kingdoms of the Old World to form a settlement in the midst of her empire, within a day's sail of Portobello on one side and of Cartagena on the other, was ludicrously absurd. She would have been just as likely to let them take possession of the Escurial. It was, therefore, evident that, before the new Company could even begin its commercial operations, there must be a war with Spain and a complete triumph over Spain. What means had the Company of waging such a war, and what chance of achieving such a triumph? The ordinary revenue of Scotland in time of peace was between sixty and seventy thousand a year. The extraordinary supplies granted to the Crown during the war with France had amounted perhaps to as much more. Spain, it is true, was no longer the Spain of Pavia and Lepanto. But, even in her decay, she possessed in Europe resources which exceeded thirty fold those of Scotland; and in America, where the struggle must take place, the disproportion was still greater. The Spanish fleets and arsenals were doubtless in wretched condition. But there were Spanish fleets; there were Spanish arsenals. The galleons, which sailed every year from Seville to the neighbourhood of Darien and from the neighbourhood of Darien back to Seville, were in tolerable condition, and formed, by themselves, a considerable armament. Scotland had not a single ship of the line, nor a single dockyard where such a ship could be built. A marine sufficient to overpower that of Spain must be, not merely equipped and manned, but created. An armed force sufficient to defend the isthmus against the whole power of the viceroyalties of Mexico and Peru must be sent over five thousand miles of ocean. What was the charge of such an expedition likely to be? Oliver had, in the preceding generation, wrested a West Indian island from Spain[8]: but, in order to do this, Oliver, a man who thoroughly understood the administration of war, who wasted nothing, and who was excellently served, had been forced to spend, in a single year, on his navy alone, twenty times the ordinary revenue of Scotland; and, since his days, war had been constantly becoming more and more costly.

It was plain that Scotland could not alone support the charge of a contest with the enemy whom Paterson was bent on pro-

[8. Oliver Cromwell, by his war with Spain in 1655, had acquired Jamaica for England.]

voking. And what assistance was she likely to have from abroad? Undoubtedly the vast colonial empire and the narrow colonial policy of Spain were regarded with an evil eye by more than one great maritime power. But there was no great maritime power which would not far rather have seen the isthmus between the Atlantic and the Pacific in the hands of Spain than in the hands of the Darien Company. Lewis could not but dread whatever tended to aggrandise a state governed by William. To Holland the East India trade was as the apple of her eye. She had been the chief gainer by the discoveries of Gama; and it might be expected that she would do all that could be done by craft, and, if need were, by violence, rather than suffer any rival to be to her what she had been to Venice. England remained; and Paterson was sanguine enough to flatter himself that England might be induced to lend her powerful aid to the Company. He and Lord Belhaven repaired to London, opened an office in Clement's Lane, formed a Board of Directors auxiliary to the Central Board at Edinburgh, and invited the capitalists of the Royal Exchange to subscribe for the stock which had not been reserved for Scotchmen resident in Scotland. A few moneyed men were allured by the bait: but the clamour of the City was loud and menacing; and from the City a feeling of indignation spread fast through the country.

In this feeling there was undoubtedly a large mixture of evil. National antipathy operated on some minds, religious antipathy on others. But it is impossible to deny that the anger which Paterson's schemes excited throughout the south of the island was, in the main, just and reasonable. Though it was not yet generally known in what precise spot his colony was to be planted, there could be little doubt that he intended to occupy some part of America; and there could be as little doubt that such occupation would be resisted. There would be a maritime war; and such a war Scotland had no means of carrying on. The state of her finances was such that she must be quite unable to fit out even a single squadron of moderate size. Before the conflict had lasted three months, she would have neither money nor credit left. These things were obvious to every coffeehouse politician; and it was impossible to believe that they had escaped the notice of men

so able and well informed as some who sat in the Privy Council
and Parliament at Edinburgh. In one way only could the conduct
of these schemes be explained. They meant to make a dupe and a
tool of the Southron. The two British kingdoms were so closely
connected, physically and politically, that it was scarcely possible for one of them to be at peace with a power with which the
other was at war. If the Scotch drew King William into a quarrel,
England must, from regard to her own dignity which was bound
up with his, support him in it. She was to be tricked into a bloody
and expensive contest in the event of which she had no interest;
nay, into a contest in which victory would be a greater calamity
to her than defeat. She was to lavish her wealth and the lives of
her seamen, in order that a set of cunning foreigners might enjoy
a monopoly by which she would be the chief sufferer. She was to
conquer and defend provinces for this Scotch Corporation; and
her reward was to be that her merchants were to be undersold,
her customers decoyed away, her exchequer beggared. There
would be an end to the disputes between the old East India Company and the new East India Company; for both Companies
would be ruined alike. The two great springs of revenue would
be dried up together. What would be the receipt of the Customs,
what of the Excise, when vast magazines of sugar, rum, tobacco,
coffee, chocolate, tea, spices, silks, muslins, all duty free, should
be formed along the estuaries of the Forth and of the Clyde, and
along the Border from the mouth of the Esk to the mouth of the
Tweed? What army, what fleet, would be sufficient to protect the
interests of the government and of the fair trader when the whole
kingdom of Scotland should be turned into one great smuggling
establishment? Paterson's plan was simply this, that England
should first spend millions in defence of the trade of his Company, and should then be plundered of twice as many millions by
means of that very trade.

The cry of the city and of the nation was soon echoed by the
legislature. When the Parliament met for the first time after the
general election of 1695, Rochester called the attention of the
Lords to the constitution and designs of the Company. Several
witnesses were summoned to the bar, and gave evidence which
produced a powerful effect on the House. 'If these Scots are to

have their way,' said one peer, 'I shall go and settle in Scotland, and not stay here to be made a beggar.' The Lords resolved to represent strongly to the King the injustice of requiring England to exert her power in support of an enterprise which, if successful, must be fatal to her commerce and to her finances. A representation was drawn up and communicated to the Commons. The Commons eagerly concurred, and complimented the Peers on the promptitude with which their Lordships had, on this occasion, stood forth to protect the public interests. The two Houses went up together to Kensington with the address. William had been under the walls of Namur when the Act for incorporating the Company had been touched with his sceptre at Edinburgh, and had known nothing about that Act till his attention had been called to it by the clamour of his English subjects. He now said, in plain terms, that he had been ill served in Scotland, but that he would try to find a remedy for the evil which had been brought to his notice. The Lord High Commissioner Tweeddale and Secretary Johnstone were immediately dismissed. But the Act which had been passed by their management still continued to be law in Scotland; nor was it in their master's power to undo what they had done.

The Commons were not content with addressing the throne. They instituted an inquiry into the proceedings of the Scotch Company in London. Belhaven made his escape to his own country, and was there beyond the reach of the Serjeant-at-Arms. But Paterson and some of his confederates were severely examined. It soon appeared that the Board which was sitting in Clement's Lane had done things which were certainly imprudent and perhaps illegal. The Act of Incorporation empowered the directors to take and to administer to their servants an oath of fidelity. But that Act was on the south of the Tweed a nullity. Nevertheless the directors had, in the heart of the City of London, taken and administered this oath, and had thus, by implication, asserted that the powers conferred on them by the legislature of Scotland accompanied them to England. It was resolved that they had been guilty of a high crime and misdemeanour, and that they should be impeached. A committee was appointed to frame articles of impeachment; but the task proved a difficult one; and the prosecution was suffered to drop, not however till the few English capitalists who had at first been friendly to Paterson's project had been terrified into renouncing all connection with him.

Now, surely, if not before, Paterson ought to have seen that his project could end in nothing but shame to himself and ruin to his worshippers. From the first it had been clear that England alone could protect his Company against the enmity of Spain; and it was now clear that Spain would be a less formidable enemy than England. It was impossible that his plan could excite greater indignation in the Council of the Indies at Madrid, or in the House of Trade at Seville, than it had excited in London. Unhappily he was given over to a strong delusion; and the blind multitude eagerly followed their blind leader. Indeed his dupes were maddened by that which should have sobered them. The proceedings of the Parliament which sat at Westminster, proceedings just and reasonable in substance, but in manner doubtless harsh and insolent, had roused the angry passions of a nation, feeble indeed in numbers and in material resources, but eminently high spirited. The proverbial pride of the Scotch was too much for their proverbial shrewdness. The votes of the English Lords and Commons were treated with marked contempt. The populace of Edinburgh burned Rochester in effigy. Money was poured faster than ever into the treasury of the Company. A stately house, in Milne Square, then the most modern and fashionable part of Edinburgh, was purchased and fitted up at once as an office and a warehouse. Ships adapted both for war and for trade were required: but the means of building such ships did not exist in Scotland; and no firm in the south of the island was disposed to enter into a contract which might not improbably be considered by the House of Commons as an impeachable offence. It was necessary to have recourse to the dockyards of Amsterdam and Hamburg. At an expense of fifty thousand pounds a few vessels were procured, the largest of which would hardly have ranked as sixtieth in the English navy; and with this force, a force not sufficient to keep the pirates of Sallee in check, the Company threw down the gauntlet to all the maritime powers in the world.

It was not till the summer of 1698 that all was ready for the expedition which was to change the face of the globe. The number of seamen and colonists who embarked at Leith was twelve hundred. Of the colonists many were younger sons of honourable families, or officers who had been disbanded since the peace. It was impossible to find room for all who were desirous of emigrating. It is said that some persons who had vainly applied for a passage hid themselves in dark corners about the ships, and, when discovered, refused to depart, clung to the rigging, and were at last taken on shore by main force. This infatuation is the more extraordinary because few of the adventurers knew to what place they were going. All that was quite certain was that a colony was to be planted somewhere, and to be named Caledonia. The general opinion was that the fleet would steer for some part of the coast of America. But this opinion was not universal. At the Dutch Embassy in Saint James's Square there was an uneasy suspicion that the new Caledonia would be founded among those Eastern spice islands with which Amsterdam had long carried on a lucrative commerce.

The supreme direction of the expedition was entrusted to a Council of Seven. Two Presbyterian chaplains and a precentor were on board. A cargo had been laid in which was afterwards the subject of much mirth to the enemies of the Company: slippers innumerable, four thousand periwigs of all kinds from plain bobs to those magnificent structures which, in that age, towered high above the foreheads and descended to the elbows of men of fashion, bales of Scotch woollen stuffs which nobody within the tropics could wear, and many hundreds of English bibles which neither Spaniard nor Indian could read. Paterson, flushed with pride and hope, not only accompanied the expedition, but took with him his wife, a comely dame, whose heart he had won in London, where she had presided over one of the great coffeehouses in the neighbourhood of the Royal Exchange. At length on the twenty-fifth of July the ships, followed by many tearful eyes, and commended to heaven in many vain prayers, sailed out of the estuary of the Forth.

The voyage was much longer than a voyage to the Antipodes now is; and the adventurers suffered much. The rations were scanty: there were bitter complaints both of the bread and of the meat; and, when the little fleet, after passing round the Orkneys and Ireland, touched at Madeira, those gentlemen who had fine clothes among their baggage were glad to exchange embroidered coats and laced waistcoats for provisions and wine. From Madeira the adventurers ran across the Atlantic, landed on an uninhabited islet lying between Porto Rico and St Thomas, took possession of this desolate spot in the name of the Company, set up a tent, and hoisted the white cross of St Andrew. Soon, however, they were warned off by an officer who was sent from St Thomas to inform them that they were trespassing on the territory of the King of Denmark. They proceeded on their voyage, having obtained the services of an old buccaneer who knew the coast of Central America well. Under his pilotage they anchored on the first of November close to the Isthmus of Darien. One of the greatest princes of the country soon came on board. The courtiers who attended him, ten or twelve in number, were stark naked: but he was distinguished by a red coat, a pair of cotton drawers, and an old hat. He had a Spanish name, spoke Spanish, and affected the grave deportment of a Spanish don. The Scotch propitiated Andreas, as he was called, by a present of a new hat blazing with gold lace, and assured him that, if he would trade with them, they would treat him better than the Castilians had done.

A few hours later the chiefs of the expedition went on shore, took formal possession of the country, and named it Caledonia. They were pleased with the aspect of a small peninsula about three miles in length and a quarter of a mile in breadth, and determined to fix here the city of New Edinburgh, destined, as they hoped, to be the great emporium of both Indies. The peninsula terminated in a low promontory of about thirty acres, which might easily be turned into an island by digging a trench. The trench was dug; and on the ground thus separated from the main land a fort was constructed: fifty guns were placed on the ramparts; and within the enclosures houses were speedily built and thatched with palm leaves.

Negotiations were opened with the chieftains, as they were called, who governed the neighbouring tribes. Among these savage rulers were found as insatiable a cupidity, as watchful a jealousy, and as punctilious a pride, as among the potentates whose disputes had seemed likely to make the Congress of Ryswick eternal. One prince hated the Spaniards because a fine rifle had been taken away from him by the Governor of Portobello on the plea that such a weapon was too good for a red man. Another loved the Spaniards because they had given him a stick tipped with silver. On the whole, the new comers succeeded in making friends of the aboriginal race. One mighty monarch, the Lewis the Great of the isthmus, who wore with pride a cap of white reeds lined with red silk and adorned with an ostrich feather, seemed well inclined to the strangers, received them hospitably in a palace built of canes and covered with palmetto royal, and regaled them with calabashes of a sort of ale brewed from Indian corn and potatoes. Another chief set his mark to a treaty of peace and alliance with the colony. A third consented to become a vassal of the Company, received with great delight a commission embellished with gold thread and flowered riband, and swallowed to the health of his new masters not a few bumpers of their own brandy.

Meanwhile the internal government of the colony was organised according to a plan devised by the directors at Edinburgh. The settlers were divided into bands of fifty or sixty: each band chose a representative; and thus was formed an assembly which took the magnificent name of Parliament. This Parliament speedily framed a curious code. The first article provided that the precepts, instructions, examples, commands and prohibitions expressed and contained in the Holy Scriptures should have the full force and effect of laws in New Caledonia, an enactment which proves that those who drew it up either did not know what the Holy Scriptures contained or did not know what a law meant. There is another provision which shows not less clearly how far these legislators were from understanding the first principles of legislation. 'Benefits received and good services done shall always be generously and thankfully compensated, whether a prior bargain hath been made or not; and, if it shall happen to be otherwise, and the Benefactor obliged justly to complain of the ingratitude, the Ungrateful shall in such case be obliged to give

threefold satisfaction at the least.' An article much more credit-
able to the little Parliament, and much needed in a community
which was likely to be constantly at war, prohibits, on pain of
death, the violation of female captives.

By this time all the Antilles and all the shores of the Gulf of
Mexico were in a ferment. The new colony was the object of
universal hatred. The Spaniards began to fit out armaments. The
chiefs of the French dependencies in the West Indies eagerly
offered assistance to the Spaniards. The governors of the English settlements put forth proclamations interdicting all communication with this nest of buccaneers. Just at this time, the
Dolphin, a vessel of fourteen guns, which was the property of the
Scotch Company, was driven on shore by stress of weather under
the walls of Cartagena. The ship and cargo were confiscated, the
crew imprisoned and put in irons. Some of the sailors were
treated as slaves, and compelled to sweep the streets and to work
on the fortifications. Others, and among them the captain, were
sent to Seville to be tried for piracy. Soon an envoy with a flag of
truce arrived at Cartagena, and, in the name of the Council of
Caledonia, demanded the release of the prisoners. He delivered
to the authorities a letter threatening them with the vengeance of
the King of Great Britain, and a copy of the Act of Parliament by
which the Company had been created. The Castilian governor,
who probably knew that William, as Sovereign of England,
would not, and, as Sovereign of Scotland, could not, protect the
squatters who had occupied Darien, flung away both letter and
Act of Parliament with a gesture of contempt, called for a guard,
and was with difficulty dissuaded from throwing the messenger
into a dungeon. The Council of Caledonia, in great indignation,
issued letters of marque[9] and reprisal against Spanish vessels.
What every man of common sense must have foreseen had taken
place. The Scottish flag had been but a few months planted on
the walls of New Edinburgh; and already a war, which Scotland,
without the help of England, was utterly unable to sustain, had
begun.

By this time it was known in Europe that the mysterious voy-

[9. 'Letters of marque' were documents authorizing the bearer to make
private war, by way of reprisal, on the ships or property of specified enemies.]

age of the adventurers from the Forth had ended at Darien. The ambassador of the Catholic King repaired to Kensington, and complained bitterly to William of this outrageous violation of the law of nations. Preparations were made in the Spanish ports for an expedition against the intruders; and in no Spanish port were there more fervent wishes for the success of that expedition than in the cities of London and Bristol. In Scotland, on the other hand, the exultation was boundless. In the parish churches all over the kingdom the ministers gave public thanks to God for having vouchsafed thus far to protect and bless the infant colony. At some places a day was set apart for religious exercises on this account. In every borough bells were rung; bonfires were lighted; and candles were placed in the windows at night. During some months all the reports which arrived from the other side of the Atlantic were such as to excite hope and joy in the north of the island, and alarm and envy in the south. The colonists, it was asserted, had found rich gold mines, mines in which the precious metal was far more abundant and in a far purer state than on the coast of Guinea. Provisions were plentiful. The rainy season had not proved unhealthy. The settlement was well fortified. Sixty guns were mounted on the ramparts. An immense crop of Indian corn was expected. The aboriginal tribes were friendly. Emigrants from various quarters were coming in. The population of Caledonia had already increased from twelve hundred to ten thousand. The riches of the country – these are the words of a newspaper of that time – were great beyond imagination. The mania in Scotland rose to the highest point. Munitions of war and implements of agriculture were provided in large quantities. Multitudes were impatient to emigrate to the land of promise.

In August 1699 four ships, with thirteen hundred men on board, were despatched by the Company to Caledonia. The spiritual care of these emigrants was entrusted to divines of the Church of Scotland. One of these was that Alexander Shields whose *Hind Let Loose* proves that in his zeal for the Covenant he had forgotten the Gospel. To another, John Borland, we owe the best account of the voyage which is now extant. The General Assembly had charged the chaplains to divide the colonists into congregations, to appoint ruling elders, to constitute a presby-

tery, and to labour for the propagation of divine truth among the
Pagan inhabitants of Darien. The second expedition sailed as the
first had sailed, amidst the acclamations and blessings of all Scotland. During the earlier part of September the whole nation was
dreaming a delightful dream of prosperity and glory; and tri-
umphing, somewhat maliciously, in the vexation of the English.
But, before the close of that month, it began to be rumoured
about Lombard Street and Cheapside that letters had arrived
from Jamaica with strange news. The colony from which so much
had been hoped and dreaded was no more. It had disappeared
from the face of the earth.

The report spread to Edinburgh, but was received there with
scornful incredulity. It was an impudent lie devised by some
Englishmen who could not bear to see that, in spite of the votes
of the English Parliament, in spite of the proclamations of the
governors of the English colonies, Caledonia was waxing great
and opulent. Nay, the inventor of the fable was named. It was declared to be quite certain that Secretary Vernon was the man. On
the fourth of October was put forth a vehement contradiction of
the story. On the fifth the whole truth was known. Letters were
received from New York announcing that a few miserable men,
the remains of the colony which was to have been the garden, the
warehouse, the mart, of the whole world, their bones peeping
through their skin, and hunger and fever written in their faces,
had arrived in the Hudson.

The grief, the dismay and the rage of those who had a few
hours before fancied themselves masters of all the wealth of both
Indies may easily be imagined. The Directors, in their fury, lost
all self-command, and, in their official letters, railed at the be-
trayers of Scotland, the white-livered deserters. The truth is that
those who used these hard words were far more deserving of
blame than the wretches whom they had sent to destruction, and
whom they now reviled for not staying to be utterly destroyed.
Nothing had happened but what might easily have been foreseen.
The Company had, in childish reliance on the word of an enthusiastic projector, and in defiance of facts known to every educated
man in Europe, taken it for granted that emigrants born and bred
within ten degrees of the Arctic Circle would enjoy excellent

health within ten degrees of the Equator. Nay, statesmen and scholars had been deluded into the belief that a country which, as they might have read in books so common as those of Hakluyt and Purchas, was noted even among tropical countries for its insalubrity, and had been abandoned by the Spaniards solely on account of its insalubrity, was a Montpelier. Nor had any of Paterson's dupes considered how colonists from Fife or Lothian, who had never in their lives known what it was to feel the heat of a distressing midsummer day, could endure the labour of breaking clods and carrying burdens under the fierce blaze of a vertical sun.

It ought to have been remembered that such colonists would have to do for themselves what English, French, Dutch, and Spanish colonists employed Negroes or Indians to do for them. It was seldom indeed that a white freeman in Barbadoes or Martinique, in Guiana or at Panama, was employed in severe bodily labour. But the Scotch who settled at Darien must at first be without slaves, and must therefore dig the trench round their town, build their houses, cultivate their fields, hew wood, and draw water, with their own hands. Such toil in such an atmosphere was too much for them. The provisions which they had brought out had been of no good quality, and had not been improved by lapse of time or by change of climate. The yams and plantains did not suit stomachs accustomed to good oatmeal. The flesh of wild animals and the green fat of the turtle, a luxury then unknown in Europe, went but a small way; and supplies were not to be expected from any foreign settlement. During the cool months, however, which immediately followed the occupation of the isthmus there were few deaths. But, before the equinox, disease began to make fearful havoc in the little community. The mortality gradually rose to ten or twelve a day. Both the clergymen who had accompanied the expedition died. Paterson buried his wife in that soil which, as he had assured his too credulous countrymen, exhaled health and vigour. He was himself stretched on his pallet by an intermittent fever. Still he would not admit that the climate of his promised land was bad. There could not be a purer air. This was merely the seasoning which people who passed from one country to another must expect. In November all would be well again. But the rate at which the emigrants died was such that none of them seemed likely to live till November. Those who were not laid on their beds were yellow, lean, feeble, hardly able to move the sick and to bury the dead, and quite unable to repel the expected attack of the Spaniards. The cry of the whole community was that death was all around them, and that they must, while they still had strength to weigh an anchor or spread a sail, fly to some less fatal region. The men and provisions were equally distributed among three ships, the *Caledonia*, the *Unicorn*, and the *Saint Andrew*. Paterson, though still too ill to sit in the Council, begged hard that he might be left behind with twenty or thirty companions to keep up a show of possession, and to await the next arrivals from Scotland. So small a number of people, he said, might easily subsist by catching fish and turtles. But his offer was disregarded: he was carried, utterly helpless, on board of the *Saint Andrew*; and the vessel stood out to sea.

The voyage was horrible. Scarcely any Guinea slave ship has ever had such a middle passage. Of two hundred and fifty persons on board of the *Saint Andrew*, one hundred and fifty fed the sharks of the Atlantic before Sandy Hook was in sight. The *Unicorn* lost almost all its officers, and about a hundred and forty men. The *Caledonia*, the healthiest ship of the three, threw overboard a hundred corpses. The squalid survivors, as if they were not sufficiently miserable, raged fiercely against one another. Charges of incapacity, cruelty, brutal insolence, were hurled backward and forward. The rigid Presbyterians attributed the calamities of the colony to the wickedness of Jacobites, Prelatists, Sabbath-breakers, Atheists, who hated in others that image of God which was wanting in themselves. The accused malignants, on the other hand, complained bitterly of the impertinence of meddling fanatics and hypocrites. Paterson was cruelly reviled, and was unable to defend himself. He had been completely prostrated by bodily and mental suffering. He looked like a skeleton. His heart was broken. His inventive faculties and his plausible eloquence were no more; and he seemed to have sunk into second childhood.

Meanwhile the second expedition had been on the seas. It

reached Darien about four months after the first settlers had
fled. The new comers had fully expected to find a flourishing
young town, secure fortifications, cultivated fields, and a cordial
welcome. They found a wilderness. The castle of New Edinburgh was in ruins. The huts had been burned. The site marked
out for the proud capital which was to have been the Tyre, the
Venice, the Amsterdam of the eighteenth century was overgrown with jungle, and inhabited only by the sloth and the
baboon. The hearts of the adventurers sank within them. For
their fleet had been fitted out, not to plant a colony, but to recruit
a colony already planted and supposed to be prospering. They
were therefore worse provided with every necessary of life than
their predecessors had been. Some feeble attempts, however,
were made to restore what had perished. A new fort was constructed on the old ground; and within the ramparts was built a
hamlet, consisting of eighty or ninety cabins, generally of twelve
feet by ten. But the work went on languidly. The alacrity which
is the effect of hope, the strength which is the effect of union,
were alike wanting to the little community. From the councillors
down to the humblest settlers all was despondency and discontent. The stock of provisions was scanty. The stewards embezzled
great part of it. The rations were small; and soon there was a cry
that they were unfairly distributed. Factions were formed. Plots
were laid. One ringleader of the malcontents was hanged. The
Scotch were generally, as they still are, a religious people; and it
might therefore have been expected that the influence of the
divines to whom the spiritual charge of the colony had been confided would have been employed with advantage for the preserv-
ing of order and the calming of evil passions. Unfortunately
those divines seem to have been at war with almost all the rest of
the society. They described their companions as the most profligate of mankind, and declared that it was impossible to constitute
a presbytery according to the directions of the General Assembly; for that persons fit to be ruling elders of a Christian Church
were not to be found among the twelve or thirteen hundred emigrants. Where the blame lay it is now impossible to decide. All
that can with confidence be said is that either the clergymen

must have been most unreasonably and most uncharitably aus-tere, or the laymen must have been most unfavourable specimens of the nation and class to which they belonged.

It may be added that the provision by the General Assembly for the spiritual wants of the colony was as defective as the pro-vision made for temporal wants by the directors of the Company. Nearly one third of the emigrants who sailed with the second ex-pedition were Highlanders, who did not understand a word of English; and not one of the four chaplains could speak a word of Gaelic. It was only through interpreters that a pastor could com-municate with a large portion of the Christian flock of which he had charge. Even by the help of interpreters he could not impart religious instruction to those heathen tribes which the Church of Scotland had solemnly recommended to his care. In fact, the colonists left behind them no mark that baptized men had set foot on Darien, except a few Anglo-Saxon curses, which, having been uttered more frequently and with greater energy than any other words in our language, had caught the ear and been retained in the memory of the native population of the isthmus.

The months which immediately followed the arrival of the new comers were the coolest and most salubrious of the year. But, even in those months, the pestilential influence of a tropical sun, shining on swamps rank with impenetrable thickets of black mangroves, began to be felt. The mortality was great; and it was but too clear that, before the summer was far advanced, the second colony would, like the first, have to choose between death and flight. But the agony of the inevitable dissolution was shortened by violence. A fleet of eleven vessels under the flag of Castile anchored off New Edinburgh. At the same time an ir-regular army of Spaniards, creoles, negroes, mulattoes and In-dians marched across the isthmus from Panama; and the fort was blockaded at once by sea and land.

A drummer soon came with a message from the besiegers, but a message which was utterly unintelligible to the besieged. Even after all that we have seen of the perverse imbecility of the directors of the Company, it must be thought strange that they should have sent a colony to a remote part of the world, where it was certain that there must be constant intercourse, peaceable or hostile, with Spaniards, and yet should not have taken care that there should be in the whole colony a single person who knew a little Spanish.

With some difficulty a negotiation was carried on in such French and such Latin as the two parties could furnish. Before the end of March a treaty was signed by which the Scotch bound themselves to evacuate Darien in fourteen days; and on the eleventh of April they departed, a much less numerous body than when they arrived. In little more than four months, although the healthiest months of the year, three hundred men out of thirteen hundred had been swept away by disease. Of the survivors very few lived to see their native country again. Two of the ships perished at sea. Many of the adventurers, who had left their homes flushed with hopes of speedy opulence, were glad to hire themselves out to the planters of Jamaica, and laid their bones in that land of exile. Shields died there, worn out and heartbroken. Borland was the only minister who came back. In his curious and interesting narrative, he expresses his feelings, after the fashion of the school in which he had been bred, by grotesque allusions to the Old Testament, and by a profusion of Hebrew words. On his first arrival, he tells us, he found New Edinburgh a Ziklag. He had subsequently been compelled to dwell in the tents of Kedar. Once, indeed, during his sojourn, he had fallen in with a Beer-lahai-roi, and had set up his Ebenezer: but in general Darien was to him a Magor Missabib, a Kibrothhattaavah. The sad story is introduced with the words in which a great man of old, delivered over to the malice of the Evil Power, was informed of the death of his children and of the ruin of his fortunes: 'I alone am escaped to tell thee.'

20

The New Threat: Parliamentary Corruption

[The Revolution had ended the 'tyranny' of the Stuarts. It had made the policy of the Crown dependent on the majority in Parliament, and it had made that Parliament independent of the royal prerogative. But this 'Glorious Revolution' had its inglorious side. As Macaulay observed at the very beginning of his work (see above, p. 52), it 'gave birth to a new class of abuses from which absolute monarchies are exempt'. Ministers of the Crown, dependent on a sufficiency of parliamentary votes, and disposing of the patronage of the Crown, found that if they could no longer coerce or circumvent the legislature, they could often buy it. This parliamentary corruption did not begin with the reign of William III; it had already been practised in the reign of Charles II. But it undoubtedly increased under William. It increased still further under the Hanoverian kings, and it was not effectively checked till the reforms of the nineteenth century. In the early eighteenth century it was violently attacked by the tory Lord Bolingbroke as the peculiar invention of the whigs, and especially Sir Robert Walpole. Macaulay, in his fifteenth chapter, analyses it more profoundly and shows, incidentally (and no doubt with relish), that it was first used on a large scale by 'tory' ministers: first by Lord Clifford, the Lord Treasurer of the 'Cabal'; then by Clifford's successor Thomas Osborne, Earl of Danby, who was Lord Treasurer to Charles II from 1673 to 1678 and who returned to power, as Marquis of Caermarthen and Duke of Leeds, under William III.]

THE history of the rise, progress, and decline of parliamentary corruption in England still remains to be written. No subject has called forth a greater quantity of eloquent vituperation and stinging sarcasm. Three generations of serious and of sportive writers wept and laughed over the venality of the senate. That venality was denounced on the hustings, anathematized from the pulpit, and burlesqued on the stage; was attacked by Pope in brilliant verse, and by Bolingbroke in stately prose, by Swift with savage hatred, and by Gay with festive malice. The voices of Tories and Whigs, of Johnson and Akenside, of Smollett and Fielding, contributed to swell the cry. But none of those who railed or of those who jested took the trouble to verify the phenomena, or to trace them to the real causes.

Sometimes the evil was imputed to the depravity of a particular minister: but, when he had been driven from power, and when those who had most loudly accused him governed in his stead, it was found that the change of men had produced no change of system. Sometimes the evil was imputed to the degeneracy of the national character. Luxury and cupidity, it was said, had produced in our country the same effect which they had produced of old in the Roman republic. The modern Englishman was to the Englishman of the sixteenth century what Verres and Curio were to Dentatus and Fabricius. Those who held this language were as ignorant and shallow as people generally are who extol the past at the expense of the present. A man of sense would have perceived that, if the English of the time of George the Second had really been more sordid and dishonest than their forefathers, the deterioration would not have shown itself in one place alone. The progress of judicial venality and of official venality would have kept pace with the progress of parliamentary venality. But nothing is more certain than that, while the legislature was becoming more and more venal, the courts of law and the public offices were becoming purer and purer. The representatives of the people were undoubtedly more mercenary in the days of Hardwicke and Pelham than in the days of the Tudors. But the Chancellors of the Tudors took plate and jewels from suitors without scruple or shame; and Hardwicke would have committed for contempt any suitor who had dared to bring him a present. The Treasurers of the Tudors raised princely fortunes by the sale of places, titles, and pardons; and Pelham would have ordered his servants to turn out of his house any man who had offered him money for a peerage or a commissionership of customs. It is evident, therefore, that the prevalence of corruption in the Parliament cannot be ascribed to a general depravation of morals. The taint was local: we must look for some local cause; and such a cause will without difficulty be found.

Under our ancient sovereigns the House of Commons rarely interfered with the executive administration. The Speaker was charged not to let the members meddle with matters of State. If any gentleman was very troublesome he was cited before the Privy Council, interrogated, reprimanded, and sent to meditate on his undutiful conduct in the Tower. The Commons did their best to protect themselves by keeping their deliberations secret, by excluding strangers, by making it a crime to repeat out of doors what had passed within doors. But these precautions were of small avail. In so large an assembly there were always tale-bearers ready to carry the evil report of their brethren to the palace. To oppose the Court was therefore a service of serious danger. In those days, of course, there was little or no buying of votes. For an honest man was not to be bought; and it was much cheaper to intimidate or to coerce a knave than to buy him.

For a very different reason there has been no direct buying of votes within the memory of the present generation. The House of Commons is now supreme in the State, but is accountable to the nation. Even those members who are not chosen by large constituent bodies are kept in awe by public opinion. Everything is printed: everything is discussed: every material word uttered in debate is read by a million of people on the morrow. Within a few hours after an important division, the lists of the majority and the minority are scanned and analysed in every town from Plymouth to Inverness. If a name be found where it ought not to be, the apostate is certain to be reminded in sharp language of the promises which he has broken and of the professions which he has belied. At present, therefore, the best way in which a government can secure the support of a majority of the representative body is by gaining the confidence of the nation.

But between the time when our Parliaments ceased to be controlled by royal prerogative and the time when they began to be constantly and effectually controlled by public opinion there was a long interval. After the Restoration, no government ventured

to return to those methods by which, before the civil war, the
freedom of deliberation had been restrained. A member could no
longer be called to account for his harangues or his votes. He
might obstruct the passing of bills of supply: he might arraign
the whole foreign policy of the country: he might lay on the
table articles of impeachment against all the chief ministers; and
he ran not the smallest risk of being treated as Morrice had been
treated by Elizabeth, or Eliot by Charles the First. The senator
now stood in no awe of the Court. Nevertheless all the defences
behind which the feeble Parliaments of the sixteenth century had
entrenched themselves against the attacks of prerogative were
not only still kept up, but were extended and strengthened. No
politician seems to have been aware that these defences were no
longer needed for their original purpose, and had begun to serve
a purpose very different. The rules which had been originally
designed to secure faithful representatives against the displeasure
of the Sovereign, now operated to secure unfaithful representatives against the displeasure of the people, and proved much
more effectual for the latter end than they had ever been for the
former. It was natural, it was inevitable, that, in a legislative body
emancipated from the restraints of the sixteenth century, and not
yet subjected to the restraints of the nineteenth century, in a
legislative body which feared neither the King nor the public,
there should be corruption.

The plague spot began to be visible and palpable in the days of
the Cabal. Clifford, the boldest and fiercest of the wicked Five,
had the merit of discovering that a noisy patriot, whom it was no
longer possible to send to prison, might be turned into a courtier
by a goldsmith's note. Clifford's example was followed by his
successors. It soon became a proverb that a Parliament resembled
a pump. Often, the wits said, when a pump appears to be dry, if a
very small quantity of water is poured in, a great quantity of
water gushes out: and so, when a Parliament appears to be
niggardly, ten thousand pounds judiciously given in bribes will
often produce a million in supplies. The evil was not diminished,
nay, it was aggravated, by that Revolution which freed our
country from so many other evils. The House of Commons was

now more powerful than ever as against the Crown, and yet was not more strictly responsible than formerly to the nation. The government had a new motive for buying the members; and the members had no new motive for refusing to sell themselves. William, indeed, had an aversion to bribery: he resolved to abstain from it; and, during the first year of his reign, he kept his resolution. Unhappily the events of that year did not encourage him to persevere in his good intentions. As soon as Caermarthen was placed at the head of the internal administration of the realm, a complete change took place. He was in truth no novice in the art of purchasing votes. He had, sixteen years before, succeeded Clifford at the Treasury, had inherited Clifford's tactics, had improved upon them, and had employed them to an extent which would have amazed the inventor. From the day on which Caermarthen was called a second time to the chief direction of affairs, parliamentary corruption continued to be practised, with scarcely any intermission, by a long succession of statesmen, till the close of the American war.

Neither of the great English parties can justly charge the other with any peculiar guilt on this account. The Tories were the first who introduced the system and the last who clung to it: but it attained its greatest vigour in the time of Whig ascendency. The extent to which parliamentary support was bartered for money cannot be with any precision ascertained. But it seems probable that the number of hirelings was greatly exaggerated by vulgar report, and was never large, though often sufficient to turn the scale on important divisions. An unprincipled minister eagerly accepted the services of these mercenaries. An honest minister reluctantly submitted, for the sake of the commonwealth, to what he considered as a shameful and odious extortion. But during many years every minister, whatever his personal character might be, consented, willingly or unwillingly, to manage the Parliament in the only way in which the Parliament could then be managed. It at length became as notorious that there was a market for votes at the Treasury as that there was a market for cattle in Smithfield. Numerous demagogues out of power declaimed against this vile traffic: but every one of those demagogues, as soon as he was in power, found himself driven by a kind of fatality to engage in that traffic, or at least to connive at it. Now and then perhaps a man who had romantic notions of public virtue refused to be himself the paymaster of the corrupt crew, and averted his eyes while his less scrupulous colleagues did that which he knew to be indispensable, and yet felt to be degrading. But the instances of this prudery were rare indeed. The doctrine generally received, even among upright and honourable politicians, was that it was shameful to receive bribes, but that it was necessary to distribute them. It is a remarkable fact that the evil reached the greatest height during the administration of Henry Pelham, a statesman of good intentions, of spotless morals in private life, and of exemplary disinterestedness. It is not difficult to guess by what arguments he and other well-meaning men, who, like him, followed the fashion of their age, quieted their consciences. No casuist, however severe, has denied that it may be a duty to give what it is a crime to take. It was infamous in Jeffreys to demand money for the lives of the unhappy prisoners whom he tried at Dorchester and Taunton. But it was not infamous, nay, it was laudable, in the kinsmen and friends of a prisoner to contribute of their substance in order to make up a purse for Jeffreys. The Sallee rover, who threatened to bastinado a Christian captive to death unless a ransom was forthcoming, was an odious ruffian. But to ransom a Christian captive from a Sallee rover was, not merely an innocent, but a highly meritorious act. It would be improper in such cases to use the word corruption. Those who receive the filthy lucre are corrupt already. He who bribes them does not make them wicked: he finds them so; and he merely prevents their evil propensities from producing evil effects. And might not the same plea be urged in defence of a minister who, when no other expedient would avail, paid greedy and low-minded men not to ruin their country?

It was by some such reasoning as this that the scruples of William were overcome. Honest Burnet, with the uncourtly courage which distinguished him, ventured to remonstrate with the King. 'Nobody,' William answered, 'hates bribery more than I. But I have to do with a set of men who must be managed in this vile

way or not at all. I must strain a point; or the country is
lost.'

It was necessary for the Lord President to have in the House of
Commons an agent for the purchase of members; and Lowther[1]
was both too awkward and too scrupulous to be such an agent.
But a man in whom craft and profligacy were united in a high degree was without difficulty found. This was the Master of the
Rolls, Sir John Trevor, who had been Speaker in the single Parliament held by James. High as Trevor had risen in the world,
there were people who could still remember him a strange-
looking lawyer's clerk in the Inner Temple. Indeed, nobody who
had ever seen him was likely to forget him. For his grotesque
features and his hideous squint were far beyond the reach of
caricature. His parts, which were quick and vigorous, had enabled him early to master the science of chicane. Gambling and
betting were his amusements; and out of these amusements he
contrived to extract much business in the way of his profession.
For his opinion on a question arising out of a wager or a game at
chance had as much authority as a judgment of any court in
Westminster Hall. He soon rose to be one of the boon companions whom Jeffreys hugged in fits of maudlin friendship over the
bottle at night, and cursed and reviled in court on the morrow.
Under such a teacher, Trevor rapidly became a proficient in that
peculiar kind of rhetoric which had enlivened the trials of Baxter
and of Alice Lisle. Report indeed spoke of some scolding matches
between the Chancellor and his friend, in which the disciple had
been not less voluble and scurrilous than the master. These contests, however, did not take place till the younger adventurer had
attained riches and dignities such that he no longer stood in need
of the patronage which had raised him. Among High Churchmen Trevor, in spite of his notorious want of principle, had at
this time a certain popularity, which he seems to have owed
chiefly to their conviction that, however insincere he might be in
general, his hatred of the dissenters was genuine and hearty.
There was little doubt that, in a House of Commons in which the
Tories had a majority, he might easily, with the support of the

[1. Sir John Lowther, a respectable tory, had been made first Lord of the
Treasury by Caermarthan's influence.]

Court, be chosen Speaker. He was impatient to be again in his old post, which he well knew how to make one of the most lucrative in the kingdom; and he willingly undertook that secret and shameful office for which Lowther was altogether unqualified.

21

The Summing Up

[*Macaulay never completed his History. He never carried it forward from the English to the French Revolution, or even to the accession of the House of Hanover. He was not able even to sum up the positive achievements of the English Revolution (as distinct from the dangers which it averted). But shortly before beginning work on his History, he had written a long essay reviewing the fragmentary work of his predecessor, Sir James Mackintosh ; and in this essay he gave his summary of the major reforms secured by the Revolution. He also, incidentally, struck a double blow at his two ideological enemies: at the radicals, who regarded the Revolution of 1688 as a mere aristocratic coup d'état, and at the tory historian whose interpretation he was determined to overthrow: David Hume.*]

AND what were the reforms of which we speak? We will shortly recount some which we think the most important; and we will then leave our readers to judge whether those who consider the Revolution as a mere change of dynasty, beneficial to a few aristocrats, but useless to the body of the people, or those who consider it as a happy era in the history of the British nation and of the human species, have judged more correctly of its nature.

Foremost in the list of the benefits which our country owes to the Revolution we place the Toleration Act. It is true that this measure fell short of the wishes of the leading Whigs. It is true also that, where Catholics were concerned, even the most enlightened of the leading Whigs held opinions by no means so liberal as those which are happily common at the present day. Those distinguished statesmen did however make a noble, and, in some respects, a successful struggle for the rights of conscience. Their wish was to bring the great body of the Protestant Dissenters within the pale of the Church by judicious alterations in the liturgy and the articles, and to grant to those who still remained without that pale the most ample toleration. They framed a plan of comprehension which would have satisfied a great majority of the seceders; and they proposed the complete abolition of that absurd and odious test which, after having been, during a century and a half, a scandal to the pious and a laughing-stock to the profane, was at length removed in our own time. The immense power of the Clergy and of the Tory gentry frustrated these excellent designs. The Whigs, however, did much. They succeeded in obtaining a law in the provisions of which a philosopher will doubtless find much to condemn, but which had the practical effect of enabling almost every Protestant Nonconformist to follow the dictates of his own conscience without molestation. Scarcely a law in the statute-book is theoretically more objectionable than the Toleration Act. But we question whether in the whole of that vast mass of legislation, from the Great Charter downwards, there be a single law which has so much diminished the sum of human suffering, which has done so much to allay bad passions, which has put an end to so much petty tyranny and vexation, which has brought gladness, peace, and a sense of security to so many private dwellings.

The second of those great reforms which the Revolution produced was the final establishment of the Presbyterian Kirk in Scotland. We shall not now inquire whether the Episcopal or the Calvinistic form of Church government be more agreeable to primitive practice. Far be it from us to disturb with our doubts the repose of any Oxonian Bachelor of Divinity who conceives that the English prelates, with their baronies and palaces, their purple and their fine linen, their mitred carriages and their sumptuous tables, are the true successors of those ancient bishops who lived by catching fish and mending tents. We say only that the Scotch, doubtless from their own inveterate stupidity and malice, were not Episcopalians; that they could not be made Episcopalians; that the whole power of government had been in vain employed for the purpose of converting them; that the fullest instruction on the mysterious questions of the Apostolical succession and the imposition of hands had been imparted by the very logical process of putting the legs of the students into wooden boots, and driving two or more wedges between their knees; that a course of divinity lectures, of the most edifying kind, had been given in the Grass-market of Edinburgh; yet that, in spite of all the exertions of those great theological professors, Lauderdale and Dundee, the Covenanters were as obstinate as ever. To the contest between the Scotch nation and the Anglican Church are to be ascribed near thirty years of the most frightful misgovernment ever seen in any part of Great Britain. If the Revolution had produced no other effect than that of freeing the Scotch from the yoke of an establishment which they detested, and giving them one to which they were attached, it would have been one of the happiest events in our history.

The third great benefit which the country derived from the Revolution was the alteration in the mode of granting the supplies. It had been the practice to settle on every prince, at the commencement of his reign, the produce of certain taxes which, it was supposed, would yield a sum sufficient to defray the ordinary expenses of government. The distribution of the revenue was left wholly to the sovereign. He might be forced by a war, or by his own profusion, to ask for an extraordinary grant. But, if his policy were economical and pacific, he might reign many years without once being under the necessity of summoning his Parliament, or of taking their advice when he had summoned them. This was not all. The natural tendency of every society in which property enjoys tolerable security is to increase in wealth. With the national wealth, the produce of the customs, of the excise, and of the post-office, would of course increase; and thus it might well happen that taxes which, at the beginning of a long reign, were barely sufficient to support a frugal government in time of peace, might, before the end of that reign, enable the sovereign to imitate the extravagance of Nero or Heliogabalus, to raise great armies, to carry on expensive wars. Something of this sort had actually happened under Charles the Second, though his reign, reckoned from the Restoration, lasted only twenty-five years. His first Parliament settled on him taxes estimated to produce twelve hundred thousand pounds a year. This they thought sufficient, as they allowed nothing for a standing army in time of peace. At the time of Charles's death, the annual produce of these taxes considerably exceeded a million and a half; and the King who, during the years which immediately followed his accession, was perpetually in distress, and perpetually asking his Parliaments for money, was at last able to keep a body of regular troops without any assistance from the House of Commons. If his reign had been as long as that of George the Third, he would probably, before the close of it, have been in the annual receipt of several millions over and above what the ordinary expenses of civil government required; and of those millions he would have been as absolutely master as the King now is of the sum allotted for his privy-purse. He might have spent them in luxury, in corruption, in paying troops to overawe his people, or in carrying into effect wild schemes of foreign conquest.

The authors of the Revolution applied a remedy to this great abuse. They settled on the King, not the fluctuating produce of certain fixed taxes, but a fixed sum sufficient for the support of his own royal state. They established it as a rule that all the expenses of the army, the navy, and the ordnance should be brought annually under the review of the House of Commons, and that every sum voted should be applied to the service specified in the vote. The direct effect of this change was important. The indirect effect has been more important still. From that time the House of Commons has been really the paramount power in the state. It has, in truth, appointed and removed ministers, declared war, and concluded peace. No combination of the King and the Lords has ever been able to effect anything against the Lower House, backed by its constituents. Three or four times, indeed, the sovereign has been able to break the force of an opposition by dissolving the Parliament. But if that experiment should fail, if the people should be of the same mind with their representatives, he would clearly have no course left but to yield, to abdicate, or to fight.

The next great blessing which we owe to the Revolution is the purification of the administration of justice in political cases. Of the importance of this change no person can judge who is not well acquainted with the earlier volumes of the State Trials. Those volumes are, we do not hesitate to say, the most frightful record of baseness and depravity that is extant in the world. Our hatred is altogether turned away from the crimes and the criminals, and directed against the law and its ministers. We see villainies as black as ever were imputed to any prisoner at any bar daily committed on the bench and in the jury-box. The worst of the bad acts which brought discredit on the old parliaments of France, the condemnation of Lally, for example, or even that of Calas,[1] may seem praiseworthy when compared with the atrocities which follow each other in endless succession as we turn over that huge chronicle of the shame of England. The magistrates of Paris and Toulouse were blinded by prejudice, passion, or bigotry. But the abandoned judges of our own country committed murder with their eyes open. The cause of this is plain. In France there was no constitutional opposition. If a man held language offensive to the government, he was at once sent to the Bastile or to Vincennes. But in England, at least after the days of the Long Parliament, the King could not, by a mere act of his prerogative, rid himself of a troublesome politician. He was forced to remove those who thwarted him by means of perjured witnesses, packed juries, and corrupt, hard-hearted, brow-beating judges. The Opposition naturally retaliated whenever they had the upper hand. Every time that the power passed from one party to the other, there was a proscription and a massacre, thinly disguised under the forms of judicial procedure. The tribunals ought to be sacred places of refuge, where, in all the vicissitudes of public affairs, the innocent of all parties may find shelter. They were, before the Revolution, an unclean public shambles, to which each party in its turn dragged its opponents, and where each found the same venal and ferocious butchers waiting for its custom. Papist or Protestant, Tory or Whig, Priest or Alderman, all was one to those greedy and savage natures, provided only there was money to earn, and blood to shed.

Of course, these worthless judges soon created around them, as was natural, a breed of informers more wicked, if possible, than themselves. The trial by jury afforded little or no protection

[1. Thomas Arthur, Comte de Lally-Tollendal, was the French general who surrendered Pondicherry, in India, to the English in 1761; for which, on his return to France, he was imprisoned in the Bastille and finally executed. Jean Calas was a Huguenot who was broken on the wheel in Toulouse in 1762 on a false charge of murdering his son, a Catholic convert. Both cases roused the indignation of Voltaire.]

to the innocent. The juries were nominated by the sheriffs. The sheriffs were in most parts of England nominated by the Crown. In London, the great scene of political contention, those officers were chosen by the people. The fiercest parliamentary election of our time will give but a faint notion of the storm which raged in the city on the day when two infuriated parties, each bearing its badge, met to select the men in whose hands were to be the issues of life and death for the coming year. On that day, nobles of the highest descent did not think it beneath them to canvass and marshal the livery, to head the procession and to watch the poll. On that day, the great chiefs of parties waited in an agony of suspense for the messenger who was to bring from Guildhall the news whether their lives and estates were, for the next twelve months, to be at the mercy of a friend or a foe. In 1681, Whig sheriffs were chosen; and Shaftesbury defied the whole power of the government. In 1682 the sheriffs were Tories. Shaftesbury fled to Holland. The other chiefs of the party broke up their councils, and retired in haste to their country seats. Sidney on the scaffold told those sheriffs that his blood was on their heads. Neither of them could deny the charge; and one of them wept with shame and remorse.

Thus every man who then meddled with public affairs took his life in his hand. The consequence was that men of gentle natures stood aloof from contests in which they could not engage without hazarding their own necks and the fortunes of their children. This was the course adopted by Sir William Temple, by Evelyn, and by many other men who were, in every respect, admirably qualified to serve the State. On the other hand, those resolute and enterprising men who put their heads and lands to hazard in the game of politics naturally acquired, from the habit of playing for so deep a stake, a reckless and desperate turn of mind. It was, we believe, as safe to be a highwayman as to be a distinguished leader of Opposition. This may serve to explain, and in some degree to excuse, the violence with which the factions of that age are justly reproached. They were fighting, not merely for office, but for life. If they reposed for a moment from the work of agitation, if they suffered the public excitement to flag, they were lost men. Hume, in describing this state of things, has employed an image which seems hardly to suit the general simplicity of his style, but which is by no means too strong for the occasion. 'Thus,' says he, 'the two parties actuated by mutual rage, but cooped up within the narrow limits of the law, levelled with poisoned daggers the most deadly blows against each other's breast, and buried in their factious divisions all regard to truth, honour, and humanity.'

From this terrible evil the Revolution set us free. The law which secured to the judges their seats during life or good behaviour did something. The law subsequently passed for regulating trials in cases of treason did much more. The provisions of that law show, indeed, very little legislative skill. It is not framed on the principle of securing the innocent, but on the principle of giving a great chance of escape to the accused, whether innocent or guilty. This, however, is decidedly a fault on the right side. The evil produced by the occasional escape of a bad citizen is not to be compared with the evils of that Reign of Terror, for such it was, which preceded the Revolution. Since the passing of this law scarcely one single person has suffered death in England as a traitor, who had not been convicted on overwhelming evidence, to the satisfaction of all parties, of the highest crime against the State. Attempts have been made in times of great excitement, to bring in persons guilty of high treason for acts which, though sometimes highly blamable, did not necessarily imply a design falling within the legal definition of treason. All those attempts have failed. During a hundred and forty years no statesman, while engaged in constitutional opposition to a government, has had the axe before his eyes. The smallest minorities, struggling against the most powerful majorities, in the most agitated times, have felt themselves perfectly secure. Pulteney and Fox were the two most distinguished leaders of Opposition since the Revolution. Both were personally obnoxious to the Court. But the utmost harm that the utmost anger of the Court could do to them was to strike off the 'Right Honourable' from before their names.

But of all the reforms produced by the Revolution, perhaps the most important was the full establishment of the liberty of unlicensed printing. The Censorship which, under some form or other, had existed, with rare and short intermissions, under every government, monarchical or republican, from the time of Henry the Eighth downwards, expired, and has never since been renewed.

We are aware that the great improvements which we have recapitulated were, in many respects, imperfectly and unskilfully executed. The authors of those improvements sometimes, while they removed or mitigated a great practical evil, continued to recognise the erroneous principle from which that evil had sprung. Sometimes, when they had adopted a sound principle, they shrank from following it to all the conclusions to which it would have led them. Sometimes they failed to perceive that the remedies which they applied to one disease of the State were certain to generate another disease, and to render another remedy necessary. Their knowledge was inferior to ours: nor were they always able to act up to their knowledge. The pressure of circumstances, the necessity of compromising differences of opinion, the power and violence of the party which was altogether hostile to the new settlement, must be taken into the account. When these things are fairly weighed, there will, we think, be little difference of opinion among liberal and right-minded men as to the real value of what the great events of 1688 did for this country.

We have recounted what appear to us the most important of those changes which the Revolution produced in our laws. The changes which it produced in our laws, however, were not more important than the change which it indirectly produced in the public mind. The Whig party had, during seventy years, an almost uninterrupted possession of power. It had always been the fundamental doctrine of that party, that power is a trust for the people; that it is given to magistrates, not for their own, but for the public advantage; that, where it is abused by magistrates, even by the highest of all, it may lawfully be withdrawn. It is perfectly true, that the Whigs were not more exempt than other men from the vices and infirmities of our nature, and that, when they had power, they sometimes abused it. But still they stood firm to their theory. That theory was the badge of their party. It was something more. It was the foundation on which rested the

power of the houses of Nassau and Brunswick. Thus, there was a
government interested in propagating a class of opinions which
most governments are interested in discouraging, a government
which looked with complacency on all speculations favourable to
public liberty, and with extreme aversion on all speculations
favourable to arbitrary power. There was a King who decidedly
preferred a republican to a believer in the divine right of kings;
who considered every attempt to exalt his prerogative as an
attack on his title; and who reserved all his favours for those who
declaimed on the natural equality of men, and the popular origin
of government. This was the state of things from the Revolution
till the death of George the Second. The effect was what might
have been expected. Even in that profession which has generally
been most disposed to magnify the prerogative, a great change
took place. Bishopric after bishopric and deanery after deanery
were bestowed on Whigs and Latitudinarians. The consequence
was that Whiggism and Latitudinarianism were professed by the
ablest and most aspiring churchmen.

Hume complained bitterly of this at the close of his history.
'The Whig party,' says he, 'for a course of near seventy years,
has almost without interruption enjoyed the whole authority of
government, and no honours or offices could be obtained but by
their countenance and protection. But this event, which in some
particulars has been advantageous to the state, has proved des-
tructive to the truth of history, and has established many gross
falsehoods, which it is unaccountable how any civilised nation
could have embraced, with regard to its domestic occurrences.
Compositions the most despicable, both for style and matter' –
in a note he instances the writings of Locke, Sidney, Hoadley,
and Rapin – 'have been extolled and propagated and read as if
they had equalled the most celebrated remains of antiquity. And
forgetting that a regard to liberty, though a laudable passion,
ought commonly to be subservient to a reverence for established
government, the prevailing faction has celebrated only the partisans of the former.' We will not here enter into an argument
about the merit of Rapin's History or Locke's political speculations. We call Hume merely as evidence to a fact well known to
all reading men, that the literature patronised by the English

Court and the English ministry, during the first half of the eighteenth century, was of that kind which courtiers and ministers generally do all in their power to discountenance, and tended to inspire zeal for the liberties of the people rather than respect for the authority of the government.

There was still a very strong Tory party in England. But that party was in opposition. Many of its members still held the doctrine of passive obedience. But they did not admit that the existing dynasty had any claim to such obedience. They condemned resistance. But by resistance they meant the keeping out of James the Third, and not the turning out of George the Second. No Radical of our times could grumble more at the expenses of the royal household, could exert himself more strenuously to reduce the military establishment, could oppose with more earnestness every proposition for arming the executive with extraordinary powers, or could pour more unmitigated abuse on placemen and courtiers. If a writer were now, in a massive Dictionary, to define a Pensioner as a traitor and a slave, the Excise as a hateful tax, the Commissioners of the Excise as wretches, if he were to write a satire full of reflections on men who receive 'the price of boroughs and of souls,' who 'explain their country's dear-bought rights away,' or

> whom pensions can incite
> To vote a patriot black, a courtier white,

we should set him down for something more democratic than a Whig. Yet this was the language which Johnson, the most bigoted of Tories and High Churchmen, held under the administration of Walpole and Pelham.

Thus doctrines favourable to public liberty were inculcated alike by those who were in power and by those who were in opposition. It was by means of these doctrines alone that the former could prove that they had a King *de jure*. The servile theories of the latter did not prevent them from offering every molestation to one whom they considered as merely a King *de facto*. The attachment of one party to the House of Hanover, of the other to that of Stuart, induced both to talk a language much more favourable to popular rights than to monarchical power. What took place at the first representation of *Cato*[2] is no bad illustration of the way in which the two great sections of the community almost invariably acted. A play, the whole merit of which consists in its stately rhetoric, a rhetoric sometimes not unworthy of Lucan, about hating tyrants and dying for freedom, is brought on the stage in a time of great political excitement. Both parties crowd to the theatre. Each affects to consider every line as a compliment to itself, and an attack on its opponents. The curtain falls amidst an unanimous roar of applause. The Whigs of the Kit Cat[3] embrace the author, and assure him that he has rendered an inestimable service to liberty. The Tory secretary of state presents a purse to the chief actor for defending the cause of liberty so well. The history of that night was, in miniature, the history of two generations.

We well know how much sophistry there was in the reasonings, and how much exaggeration in the declamations of both parties. But when we compare the state in which political science was at the close of the reign of George the Second with the state in which it had been when James the Second came to the throne, it is impossible not to admit that a prodigious improvement had taken place. We are no admirers of the political doctrines laid down in Blackstone's *Commentaries*.[4] But if we consider that those *Commentaries* were read with great applause in the very schools where, seventy or eighty years before, books had been publicly burned by order of the University of Oxford for containing the damnable doctrine that the English monarchy is limited and mixed, we cannot deny that a salutary change had taken place. 'The Jesuits,' says Pascal, in the last of his incomparable letters, 'have obtained a Papal decree, condemning Galileo's doctrine about the motion of the earth. It is all in vain. If the world is really turning round, all mankind together will not be able to keep it from turning, or to keep themselves from turning with it.' The decrees of Oxford were as ineffectual to stay the

[2. Addison's *Cato* was first performed in 1713.]

[3. The Kit Cat was the social club of the whigs in the reign of Queen Anne.]

[4. Sir William Blackstone, the jurist, whose *Commentaries* were published in 1765-9, was a tory.]

great moral and political revolution as those of the Vatican to stay the motion of our globe. That learned University found itself not only unable to keep the mass from moving, but unable to keep itself from moving along with the mass. Nor was the effect of the discussions and speculations of that period confined to our own country. While the Jacobite party was in the last dotage and weakness of its paralytic old age, the political philosophy of England began to produce a mighty effect on France, and through France, on Europe.

Index

A selection of books published by Penguin is listed on the following pages.

For a complete list of books available from Penguin in the United States, write to Dept. DG, Penguin Books, 299 Murray Hill Parkway, East Rutherford, New Jersey 07073.

For a complete list of books available from Penguin in Canada, write to Penguin Books Canada Limited, 2801 John Street, Markham, Ontario L3R 1B4.

If you live in the British Isles, write to Dept. EP, Penguin Books Ltd, Harmondsworth, Middlesex.

THE HISTORY OF THE KINGS OF BRITAIN

Geoffrey of Monmouth
Translated with an Introduction by Lewis Thorpe

It is difficult to say whether Geoffrey of Monmouth, in writing his famous *Historia Regum Britanniae*, relied more on the old chroniclers or on a gift for romantic invention. Whatever its merits as history, however, his heroic epic of such half-legendary kings as Cymbeline, Arthur, and Lear enjoyed great popularity and served to inspire Sir Thomas Malory, Edmund Spenser, and William Shakespeare, among other writers. Geoffrey's taste for quaint historical episodes, real or imaginary, and his varied style, which skillfully echoes every mood from quiet description to impassioned oratory, still lend living interest to this twelfth-century chronicle.

A HISTORY OF THE ENGLISH CHURCH AND PEOPLE

Bede
Translated with an Introduction by Leo Sherley-Price
Revised by R. E. Latham

This wonderfully alive tapestry of Saxon England and Celtic Britain written in A.D. 731 still has the power to transport us back to the forests, fens, and mountains and to the problems that men faced during these crucially formative years when Britain had still to be wrought into one entity. Leo Sherley-Price has well succeeded in his aim of producing an accurate and readable version of Bede's work in modern English, and as he remarks in his Introduction, 'We realize even more clearly that the past is not dead and done with, but a force to be reckoned with, silently moulding the present and the future'.

THE PELICAN HISTORY OF ENGLAND

THE ENGLISHNESS OF ENGLISH ART

Nikolaus Pevsner

No one is better qualified than Professor Nikolaus Pevsner to undertake this discussion of the national characteristics of English art. Born and educated on the Continent, he has the unbiased eye of the foreigner, and having lived and worked in England for over thirty years, he possesses an unrivalled knowledge of the subject. To draw the contours of this 'geography of art' it is necessary, says the author, to look at matters in terms of 'polarities', since it is only in examining the seeming contradictions of art that we can hope to discover what is specifically English in each distinctive style. Two such polarities are the decorated and the perpendicular styles in architecture – the one all undulating curves and playful spatial rhythms, the other relying entirely on the straight line for its effect of uninterrupted spatial clarity – and yet, in that both are anticorporeal, denying volume any part in the performance, both are unmistakably English.

ARCHITECTURE IN BRITAIN 1530–1830

John Summerson

In this heavily illustrated volume in The Pelican History of Art Series Sir John Summerson describes the architecture of the period that stretches from the Early Renaissance to the post-Waterloo Greek and Gothic revivals. Among the great names of those centuries were Inigo Jones, Christopher Wren, Robert Adam, and John Nash. During the same period were built Hampton Court, Hatfield, the new St. Paul's, the City churches, the graceful London squares, and the crescents and terraces of Bath. In addition to the main text two long appendices deal with Scottish architecture and the buildings in the thirteen colonies of America. With the numerous plans specially drawn for it, this study, as *The Times Literary Supplement* (London) forecast, 'will certainly remain the standard textbook for many years to come'.

A HISTORY OF MODERN FRANCE

Alfred Cobban

VOLUME 1: OLD REGIME AND REVOLUTION
1715-1799

Professor Alfred Cobban writes: 'The French eighteenth century is not a period of great, dominating political figures. . . . The eighteenth century . . . was, and above all in France, the nursery of the modern world. Ideas and social forces, the seeds of which were sown much earlier, can be seen now pushing above the surface.'

VOLUME 2: FROM THE FIRST EMPIRE
TO THE SECOND EMPIRE 1799-1871

The second volume of Professor Cobban's *History of Modern France* begins with the refashioning of French laws and institutions under Napoleon Bonaparte in 1799 and ends with the Commune of Paris in 1871. Although there is an ample supply of 'facts', Professor Cobban devotes most attention to the great turning points of the period; he does not aim to force agreement with his own interpretation but rather to stimulate the reader to ask his own questions and formulate his own judgements.

VOLUME 3: FRANCE OF THE REPUBLICS 1871-1962

This volume covers the period from the Franco-Prussian war to Charles de Gaulle. Professor Cobban steers the reader skillfully through the political and social problems besetting modern France. His balanced and stimulating account of the three republics is invaluable to anyone interested in the development and present position of a great European nation.